"This collection provides a unique and valuable insight into one of New Zealand's most influential Gospel thinkers and strategic leaders—and is worth reading not only for the insights and wisdom within, but to lay alongside the record of John's many projects, to see a brilliant example of how a renewed mind can inform Gospel strategy in context."

—**ROSHAN ALLPRESS,**
National Principal, Laidlaw College

"People seek to make sense of the Good News within their cultures and their traditions . . . John offers a sound theological reflection based in his inter–transcultural experience grounded in his biblical field of expertise. A must-read for everyone looking to venture into the fascinating world of contextualizing God's word and his message of salvation with the one example par excellence given to us through the missionary journey of Paul as the apostle of the gentiles."

—**GEOVANNE BUSTOS,**
Senior Lecturer, Divine Word University

"A detailed and careful resource for thoughtful Christians wondering why to bother with cultures and mission. I highly recommend this timely book and have already put it on my class reading list!"

—**REBECCA DE JONG,**
Lecturer in Missions, Laidlaw College

"This book captures Hitchen's love for the Pacific peoples and his willingness to question his own missiological and theological upbringing. . . a must read for Pacific theologians, church leaders and those who want to work with Pacific peoples."

—**MAXON MANI,**
Principal, Christian Leaders' Training College, Papua New Guinea

"I am thrilled with this collection of John Hitchen's thinking. This book enables contextually-concerned, theologically-inclined ministry practitioners to navigate their way to a culturally authentic engagement with scripture and society—sorely needed as the world threatens to fragment back into national or ethno-cultural silos. We urgently need to embrace a biblically faithful theology of cultural diversity, outworked in the unity of the Church, for the glory of God in the world. Here, John has laid a foundation for successive generations to build on."

—JAY MĀTENGA,
Executive Director, World Evangelical Alliance Mission Commission

"Hitchen's pinnacle publication of *Reclaiming the Good News* provides a comprehensive basis for grappling with Gospel cultural issues that are vital wherever we serve in our multicultural world. This book is a passionate, wise, mature, challenging, biblically grounded, and clearly illustrated contribution to understanding and serving the Lord Jesus today. Based on a lifetime of biblical studies and research, it offers a practical guide and refreshing approach that will benefit all who aim for excellence in Gospel communication."

—DAVID PRICE,
Leadership Development, Pioneers of Australia

"This book of essays testifies to the lived experience of a life dedicated to mission. John offers us thorough scholarship, attentiveness to both Scripture and context, and pertinent challenges for today with real life examples that help us to see theological ideas fleshed out. This is missiology at its best—figuring out how to live and communicate Gospel truths amidst the messy realities of daily life. This is also scholarship at its best because it emerges from a long life of faithful discipleship to Christ."

—CATHY ROSS,
Head, Pioneer Mission Leadership Training, Church Mission Society

"Contextualization is the realization of biblical content in a particular time and place. For John Hitchens that time and place is his life of ministry from

1965 to the present in Papua New Guinea, New Zealand, and Australia. John's wholistic reflection of biblical truth (good news) mixed with cultural insight for contextual value is the essence of this volume. Thanks, Tim Meadowcroft, for making it possible."

—**R. DANIEL SHAW,**
Senior Professor of Anthropology and Translation,
Fuller Theological Seminary

"This book is the fruit of a lifetime of study of the Scriptures and involvement in mission—and it shows! In this treasure trove of wisdom and insight, John Hitchen engages with the vital issue of the contextualization of the gospel, an issue which is central to knowing and sharing Christ Jesus as Lord in our world today. This is a book that is deeply rooted in Scripture, and which gives us profound and practical discussions about the Gospel, its implications, and its relationship to culture. It will greatly assist us all as we seek to re-present the unchanging message of the Gospel to the multiplicity of different cultural settings of today's world."

—**PAUL TREBILCO,**
Professor of New Testament Studies, University of Otago

Reclaiming the Good News

Australian University of Theology Publications

SERIES EDITOR EDWINA MURPHY

Australian University of Theology Publications offers scholars, church leaders, and the wider community uniquely Australian and New Zealand perspectives on matters of significance for research and practice.

Dr Edwina Murphy
Deputy Vice-Chancellor (Research)

Reclaiming the Good News

Gospel, Culture, and Contextualization
in the South-West Pacific

John M. Hitchen

Edited by Tim Meadowcroft

WIPF & STOCK · Eugene, Oregon

RECLAIMING THE GOOD NEWS
Gospel, Culture, and Contextualization in the South-West Pacific

Australian University of Theology Publications

Wipf & Stock
An Imprint of Wipf and Stock Publishers
199 W. 8th Ave., Suite 3
Eugene, OR 97401

www.wipfandstock.com

PAPERBACK ISBN: 979-8-3852-6123-9
HARDCOVER ISBN: 979-8-3852-6124-6
EBOOK ISBN: 979-8-3852-6125-3

VERSION NUMBER 02/26/26

For Ann

Contents

Section 3: Factors in Contextualization

Section 4: Contextualization in Context

Editor's Preface

For close to sixty years now, John Mason Hitchen has thought about, taught, and lived the mission of the church in several cross-cultural environments, primarily in Papua New Guinea and then in New Zealand. Much of his work has taken place in theological educational settings, and has revolved consistently around the call to critical contextualization of the gospel. John's work features pastoral sensitivity and careful analysis of culture, buttressed by wide reading. Above all, though, everything he writes and thinks is rooted in and drawn from the Scriptures, particularly the New Testament, and even more particularly from his favorite bit, the Pauline writings of the New Testament. And everything he writes is in support of the mission of the church; he longs for the power of the gospel to be "reclaimed" (as the title of this book indicates) for the transformation of both church and society. To that end, there are few missiologists who have based their thinking so deeply in Scripture in the way that John has. That, in my opinion, is the greatest gift his work offers to the church.[1]

Because John's work has been done primarily in response to particular settings, it has so far remained scattered across disparate published and unpublished venues. It seemed good that his thinking should be shaped and drawn together under one monograph. Roughly half of the essays in this volume have been published in earlier forms. Some reflect thought that has so far only appeared in institutional documents and other obscure contexts and are reworked and presented herein for the first time. And others make their debut in this volume.

While these essays are in the nature of a compendium or anthology, there is also a progression of thought. Section one considers the gospel that the church needs to reclaim. Section two then draws primarily on the work

1. In more extensive appreciation of John's work, see Meadowcroft, "Introduction," 17–21.

of the apostle Paul to explore from a range of angles the contextualization inherent in the incarnation of Jesus. Section three builds on the biblical work to offer more theological, educational, historical, and personal reflection on the gospel in society. And, finally, section four lands this thinking in selected examples of the potential impact of this reclaimed gospel for the everyday challenges of Christian vocation: death and loss, pastoral responsibility, politics, and business.

Although these essays have been organized to express a developing theme, they do not necessarily reflect a chronological development of John's thinking. Of course his work has changed and matured and adapted to changing times across these sixty years, as readers will discern, but in working on this collection, I have been struck by the consistency of John's thought. He has never wavered in his love for Christ and the revelation of Christ in the Bible, or in his desire to see the power of the gospel known and lived in whatever cultural and vocational settings Jesus is encountered.

At a personal level, beyond anything he may have written, I have witnessed this consistency of vision in John's life since my first brief encounter with him over fifty years ago, and then across thirty years of working more closely with him. In that time he has mentored me, believed in me, opened new horizons for me, and taught me much. I am honored and deeply grateful for the opportunity to collaborate with him in bringing this collection to fruition.

We are grateful to a number of people for the support of this project. We thank Edwina Murphy and Louise Gosbell at the Australian University of Theology (formerly the Australian College of Theology) for accepting this volume into the Australian University of Theology Publication series, and also Greta Morris for her work on copyediting and indexing. Grace de Jong was instrumental in rescuing one chapter from an otherwise unusable format. Russell Thorp at Beacon Partnerships and Roshan Allpress at Laidlaw College have been generous in their funding—thank you. We are also grateful for permissions given to reuse material; these are acknowledged elsewhere.

James Chalmers, the great nineteenth-century missionary to Papua New Guinea and the subject of John's doctoral research, was fond of signing off communications with reference to the one "whose we are and whom we serve." It became a favorite phrase also of John's. It is our privilege to offer this set of writings in the name of him whose we are and whom we serve.

Tim Meadowcroft
August 2025

Introduction

Why Bother About Cultural Differences?

Serious mention of culture or cultural differences can quickly raise hackles in many of our newly independent nations, and in most of our ethnically diverse older Western nations, stirring resentments and arousing fear. But the issues will not just go away. We urgently need a solid basis for answering the basic question: Why bother about cultural differences? I need to first explain something of the genesis of this chapter.[1]

The First Question

It was 1990, and we had only returned to our homeland, Aotearoa New Zealand, a few years earlier, after fifteen years serving in cross-cultural equipping of Papua New Guineans and other Pacific Islanders for church and community leadership in their fast developing nations. We had also just completed five years postgraduate study in Scotland intended to set us up for a return to Papua New Guinea service. But the doctors put paid to that return. My wife's health demanded we continue in New Zealand. I had struggled with that. That is, until just a few days before the night I want to describe. You see, Muri Thompson, a well-known Māori evangelist was staying in our home. Muri had come to give a public lecture on a Māori perspective on the importance of our nation's founding document, the treaty signed between the original inhabitants of the land, the Māori, and the British Crown in 1840. That Treaty of Waitangi had guaranteed certain rights and responsibilities to both signatories, and was the basis

1. Much of the content of this introduction appeared in an earlier form in the editorial for *Reaper* 72, no. 3 (June–July 1990) 3, 4–7. Used with the permission of Laidlaw College Inc.

upon which Māori had welcomed British settlers into New Zealand. One hundred and fifty years later, by the night I am describing, a national resurgence of Māori self-confidence had led to calls to address some of the many unjust failures to uphold those Treaty agreements. This, in turn, had drawn fresh attention to the treaty itself and a concern to recapture its meaning and intent to help ease the upsurge of interracial tensions caused by long years of political and social injustice and unequal development which had plagued Māori in their own land—a land which we non-Māori, the Pākehā descendants of those original British settlers, had always called "God's Own Country," where we Pākehā had boasted that we had treated our indigenous Māori people well, and we were free from the racial strife prevalent in other nations. But as 1990 dawned the actual social realities showed that such boasting was ill-founded. Far too many of our Māori population were facing serious educational, economic, and social inequities which they were no longer willing to tolerate. Hence, the importance of a Māori view of the treaty.

But Muri had gone further than that while in our home. He stayed on to encourage some of the fast-growing Māori congregations flourishing around my hometown—congregations of which, to my shame as a local evangelical church leader, I knew nothing. Muri also asked me seriously about my University of Aberdeen PhD thesis. Unlike most who had asked that question and whose eyes quickly glazed over with bored disinterest when I began to explain, Muri quickly said, "Tell me more, we Māori church leaders are grappling with these same issues. I need to bring some local Māori leaders together, and you need to explain some of this to them." So that's what had happened. Fourteen Māori, all leaders in Māori congregations around the city, gathered in our home. Muri was in his element and had given me an overly generous introduction.

The evening was going along pleasantly enough. I had shared some of the issues my thesis raised about the need for relating the gospel to local cultures and applying biblical insights to enhance their respect for their own cultural heritage, and, of course, what that meant for relations with the dominant Pākehā culture. They were now discussing between themselves, often in Te Reo, their Māori language. I was an intrigued outsider listening to Māori debating their own attitudes to these issues.

Then one said, "Yes, but it's the same for all the other cultures, too. The Pacific Islanders have the same problems as us Māori." Suddenly the air was electric. That comment had clearly upset many in the room. One of the younger ones could not contain himself: "That's not true. They are guests just like the Pākehā. No other group has it just like us Māori. All the others followed us. The real issue is not multiculturalism, but biculturalism." His depth of feeling radiated through every word. We were no longer merely mouthing the right words. Hearts were bared now, and eyes were ablaze. There were further quick endorsements of this deeply felt conviction, until one of the kaumātua called for a waiata of aroha—the previously quiet elder calmed things by asking for a song of love.

In those few moments I had seen and felt something I had never understood before. I had sensed the injustice felt by many Māori when we Pākehā suggest the real issue is how to relate to the many cultures of Aotearoa, not particularly to the Māori. As that night's discussion went on to show, there is a multicultural issue and we will not answer our nation's current concerns until we enable people of all our diverse cultures to find their place in our nation.

But there is a prior question—prior, for Māori, in importance as well as time. That is the bicultural one. How do we Pākehā—descendants of white European migrants and now the dominant culture in New Zealand—accept and respect the Māori as the tangata whenua, the original "people of the land"? How are we European New Zealanders going to give due honor to those who already inhabited Aotearoa when our first ancestors arrived—the Māori who welcomed our ancestors as guests and have done the same for each of the other cultural groups who later came to these shores? Until we have grasped the importance of this prior question, the bicultural one, we are not likely to be able to bring about the reconciliation we all desire.

This is why the Treaty of Waitangi has gained and deserves such prominence since the Māori renaissance of the 1980s. Claims to have a concern for all the cultural groups now in our country have a hollow ring if there is no justice for the first group with a rightful claim upon such concern. Justice begins at home. Thus the Māori have a right to ask for something to be done about land ownership abuses; about the root causes of unequal opportunity in our school systems; about means for them to express their own way of life without exploitation by the more dominant race; about freedom to express family and tribal loyalties without being disadvantaged in the wider national scene. And they are right to be skeptical about well-intentioned plans for multicultural solutions if they are not built upon adequate attention to the prior bicultural problems.

I could go on, but it is these deeply felt local intercultural realities that highlight the importance of Christians formulating a basic theology of respect for other cultures.[2] The Aotearoa New Zealand situation is distinct, but today virtually every independent nation globally has its own version of bicultural and/or multicultural tensions, unresolved ethnic difficulties, and festering discriminatory hurts crying out for attention. Indeed, intercultural problems are one of the genuinely global commonalities of our time, as the global "Black Lives Matter" movement of 2020 highlighted so clearly.

Cultural Differences Are God's Idea

So, let us outline a biblical approach to cultural diversity.

The Bible traces the source of human cultures, and of the diversity between cultures, right back to God himself. Cultural differences are already evident in the biblical description of the original dispersion of humanity away from their place of beginnings. Take this definition:

> Culture is an integrated system of beliefs (about God or reality or ultimate meaning), of values (about what is true, good, beautiful and normative), of customs (how to behave, relate to others, talk, pray, dress, work . . . etc.), and of institutions which express these beliefs, values and customs (government, law courts, temples or churches, family, schools, hospitals, factories . . . etc.), which binds a society together and gives it a sense of identity, dignity, security, and continuity.[3]

2. But this is not the place to explain how that evening enabled me to move beyond the depression that had dogged my steps since learning I could not return to PNG. I began to see that night that, like Paul coming to grips with having to stay in Athens when he longed to return to Thessalonika (1 Thess 2:17—3:2), I too could accept God's purposes, and be content to remain in New Zealand and its theological education world, while still equipping others to go to partner in the work in PNG. Again, this is not the place to discuss how that evening had highlighted the different ways different peoples have experienced the colonial era; the contrast between the New Zealand Māori and the PNG nationals' experience of colonialism is very real. This was due in no small measure to the way British missionaries to PNG determined and challenged the British Public and Foreign Office to commit not to let the New Zealand mistakes of the 1860s and 1870s be repeated in PNG. But that's another story we have touched on elsewhere. See Hitchen, "Training Tamate," 777; Chalmers, "Past, Present and Future," 103–7; Chalmers and Gill, *Work and Adventure*, 17–19.

3. Lausanne Movement, *Willowbank Report*, 7.

Basic forms of these elements of culture are present in the Genesis 4 account of the primordial family. Abel differs from Cain culturally as well as spiritually. Cain later develops urban culture. Jabal initiates the nomadic herdsman lifestyle. Jubal develops a new musical culture. Tubal-Cain uses bronze and iron for tools, sparking consequent technological innovation. Diversified cultures are inherent in the initial dispersion of human life (Gen 4:2, 17, 20, 21, 22, 26).

The Tower of Babel event did not initiate cultural differences. Rather, at Babel, God intervened against humanity's proud grasping after monolithic power and glory instead of furthering God's original intention for the global spread of culture (Gen 11:1–9).

Certainly, the fall of Adam and Eve radically affected culture. From that point the darker side became rampant. But the first trial in the garden did not originate cultural differences. It simply tested the already existing capacities for cultural diversity. Without the powers of appreciation, thought, and choice, there could have been no temptation.

The Bible traces cultural diversities right back to God's creating humans in his own image. God gives "life and breath and everything" to all. Echoing the original creation record, Acts 17:25 points to the stamp of God's image upon our humanity as the root from which culture and cultural diversity both grow (Gen 1:26–27; 2:7).

Humans bear God's representative likeness on planet earth, with social capacities, intellectual capacities, moral and spiritual capacities. All of these produce culture. We cannot demonstrate our God-likeness, or live as responsible managers of his resources as God intended, unless we do so culturally (Gen 1:28–31; 9:1–11).[4]

The claim of Acts 17:26 that "from one [human] God made all the nations," takes us another step. Every ethnic or cultural group derives its life from this common, original human source, so each people group also shares the same original dignity and value before God. Christianity rejects the lie of some races being inherently superior. Our common source, nature, and need declare all ethnic groups equal before God. This is good news for each of our multiethnic societies around the world today.

God also controls ethnic history. He "determines allotted periods" (Acts 17:26); the rise and fall of nations; seasons of cultural grandeur and of decline; migrations of tribes and movements of races. All these are

4. We explore this more fully in chapter 2.

superintended by the living God, as Scripture regularly declares (e.g., Isa 40:23–24).

Moreover, God allocates living space for every nation (Acts 17:26). The original promise to Abraham focused on God's gift of a particular land. Canaan would "belong" to Abraham's descendants (Gen 17:8). But God also desires and ensures "a place to call our own" for all peoples (Deut 32:8; Jer 12:14–17). The whole earth is his (e.g., Ps 24:1; Lev 25:23). He "lends" habitation rights to us humans. "The land"—and all it means to those entrusted with it—looms large in God's purposes for humanity. Like indigenous peoples globally, Māori in New Zealand have grasped this aspect of biblical teaching, perhaps more clearly than most Pākehā. They appreciate the link between cultural identity and God-entrusted land at a level modern Europeans in the antipodes have lost.

The basic rights of tangata whenua—the people of the land—are well-known rights in the Scriptures, traced right back to God's action as Lord of history. This does not remove land claims from the controls of justice. But it reminds us that rights to land and property are important for human dignity and cultural identity.

God had good reason for this cultural diversity and global dispersion. He gave ethnic identity, and entrusted times, seasons, and lands to each nation, so that people ". . . would seek him and perhaps reach out for him and find him" (Acts 17:27). God designed us so that our quest for him is integral to our cultural identity. No culture can find its fullest expression until it discovers the living God. Only when he is Lord does our culture achieve his intended goal. We must bother about cultures, then, because culture is God's idea.

God's Present Purposes Demand Cultural Sensitivity

The *final goal of God's activity in this present age* involves representatives of every culture sharing his rule as royal attendants in his kingdom (Rev 5:9–10). Every tribe, language, people group, and nation will be present. Their cultural differences will still be apparent. Indeed, that very diversity will enhance the greatness and glory of Christ. The "glory and honor of the nations" will be brought into the heavenly city as an inherent part of its abiding beauty (Rev 21:24–26).

Every ethnic group on the last day will bring praise and harmonious worship to our God. He intends the church today to do the "choir practice."

Only cultural diversity here and now can prepare us adequately for heavenly harmony.

The *way to achieve God's purposes* also demands cultural sensitivity. We are to go and make disciples of all nations (Matt 28:18–20): not just go and pluck individuals out of every cultural group, but go to them *as* cultural groups. We are to respect their cultural identity. As we approach others within their ethnic setting we announce, "Christ in you, the hope of glory" (Col 1:27).[5] Christ's ambassadors, therefore, aim to understand and appreciate what God sees as distinctive and attractive—worth redeeming—in every culture.

Teaching those who respond "to observe all that Christ commands" also involves cultural sensitivity. We cannot obey Christ in a vacuum. We must express his life within our own cultural setting and with that culture's own tools of thought, language, and creativity.

For the evangelist this demands different approaches and applications depending on the cultural background of the converts. "To the Jews, I became like a Jew . . . to those not having the law I became like one not having the law" (1 Cor 9:19–23; 10:31—11:1). This skill of relating the unchanging message of the gospel to the very different cultural settings of those who hear is known as "contextualization." This is the process of fitting our presentations and explanations of the message so they relate closely to the local context of the gospel-listeners. At an earlier stage of mission work this was called "indigenization"—planting the seed of the gospel so that it grows naturally in the local soils and comes to share the qualities and characteristics of that local culture. The words "indigenization" and "indigenous" came to refer only to churches in non-Western countries. But the need to relate the good news to the local setting is just as important in the Western world—particularly in our postmodern setting with so many different subcultures. So, in the 1970s the international theological educator, Shoki Coe, suggested the better word is "contextualization," for all cultural groups need to grapple with the task of ensuring the message is properly understood in their cultural context, right around our globe.[6]

Growing Christians will quickly reach out beyond their own culture; only unhealthy Christians remain bound up within the limits of their own ethnic group. But a person's cultural background is the normal starting

5. Note the "you" is plural.

6. Coe, "Contextualizing Theology," 19–24.

point for responding to Christ. Good evangelists, therefore, are good students of culture.

Our *resources for achieving Christ's present purposes* also demand cultural sensitivity. As we have just hinted, our commission is not to transplant full-grown churches but to plant seed. This living "seed" is the message of the kingdom, the good news of Christ Jesus (Matt 13:1–19).

Paul rejoiced that this gospel was taking root, producing fruit and growing all round the known world (Col 1:6). Our good news "belongs" in every cultural setting. This makes the Christian gospel unique. You do not have to adopt another dominant culture's way of life before you become a follower of Christ.

Paul confronted this issue in his letter to the Galatians.[7] Simple faith opens the door to Christ direct from every culture. We do not have to enter the Jewish hall marked "circumcision," nor the Pākehā hall marked "respectable Western Christianity," before we can find Christ. No, the door to Christ is accessed direct from every culture where the good news is heard and grasped. This highlights another key attribute of those who would share the good news. There is no place for ethnocentrism amongst Christians. No one culture is superior to others. If I assume my own culture is the standard or norm that others must measure up to, then I have misunderstood the way God values every culture. Self-centered pride in our own culture, as if ours is superior to other cultures, fails to see how Christ's death on the cross declares all people of every culture are equally welcome in God's family. Just as Paul had to challenge the ethnic pride of the Jews in his letters—especially to the Galatians—so we need to challenge ethnocentric pride wherever it rears its ugly head in our churches.

Our good news, then, is this inherent power to meet every person in his or her own cultural setting and see them transformed as Christ's people. This was the previously unrealized "secret" of the early church: the promise of the Spirit is for peoples of every tribe, race, and nation (Col 1:26–27; Eph 3:1–6; Gal 3:14). No wonder good evangelists are good students of culture!

The New Commandment Demands Cultural Sensitivity

The hallmark of his followers, according to Jesus, is love. But love is not envious or self-seeking (1 Cor 13:3–5). Both these attributes imply alternative ways of doing things—cultural diversity again. Love specifically

7. As we explore further in chapter 5.

reaches out beyond the familiar. Love bridges cultural gaps with respect and appreciation.

Moreover, love is not rude (1 Cor 13:3–5). Rudeness does not refer to unchanging moral principles. Rudeness has to do with cultural differences. The young person is rude to the older person when he or she does not respect the older person's "way of doing things," their culture. Love, then, obliges us to respect ethnic expectations. When we are invited to the marae we will take off our shoes. We do so, not out of superstitious fear of tapu or taboo, but out of love for our hosts as Christ requires. Not to do so would be rude, unloving.

Christ himself most clearly demonstrated the way love reaches across cultural barriers. Think about the cultural adjustments required as Jesus came into our world, became our servant, and finally died for us (Phil 2:5–8; Gal 4:4–6). Christ walked a pathway of humiliation and unselfish love into an alien culture. And he asks us to follow him.

This love, however, is not naive. Love is alert to the deceitful ways in which humans of every culture devise ways of twisting and perverting the will and purposes of God. So, we work with local Christians to test, discern, and distinguish between good and evil in our own and every society (Phil 2:5–8; Gal 4:4–6). The Lausanne Covenant presents an important balance in this:

> Because humans are God's creature, some of their culture is rich in beauty and goodness. Because they are fallen, all of [their culture] is tainted with sin and some of it is demonic. The Gospel does not presuppose the superiority of any culture to another, but evaluates all cultures according to its own criteria of truth and righteousness, and insists on moral absolutes in every culture.[8]

Christian messengers seek to avoid syncretism in any culture—that is, mixing aspects of the truth of God's word with half-truths or denials of that truth—as often happens in popular religious beliefs. We need to develop our skills in identifying syncretism in our own culture before daring to set ourselves up as judges of another culture's lifestyles and customs. This is precisely what love requires: humility to recognize our own faults; and, before judging others, "not delighting in evil but rejoicing in the truth. Love always protects, always trusts, always hopes, always perseveres" (1 Cor 13:4–7).

8. Stott, *Lausanne Covenant*, 25; adapted for inclusive language.

The Church Is Called to Embrace Cultural Differences

The church, then, is expected to be a transcultural reality. From its Day of Pentecost birth, the new family of God has embraced Jews with their special religious trust and heritage, and those from "the other" ways of the nations, the gentiles. Both belong at home in God's family in the same way: through simple faith in Christ. "For through him we both have access to the Father by one Spirit" (Eph 2:11–18). This made the early church stand out markedly. The authorities did not like it. It was potentially revolutionary.

Take Thessalonica, for instance. When some prominent non-Jewish women and their notably religious friends of various ethnic backgrounds joined the Jews in their new church, they had a recipe for a riot. "Society" and the religious establishment could not take this kind of unity in diversity. To fraternize like this "turned the world upside down" (Acts 18:1–8). The world does not like taking a tumble. But the church does that by its very nature. That is, a true church does.

People of different cultural backgrounds can relate to each other in three basic ways. The way of *apartheid* chooses not to relate. Separation and separate development are enforced by law.

The way of *assimilation* assumes that one culture is superior. The less dominant culture is expected to surrender its own distinctive heritage and conform to the values and expectations of the dominant culture. This approach is doomed to failure for it involves one group losing their God-given identity. Christianity rejects the assimilation model. Christ has given dignity to every ethnic group and desires the demise, or domination, of none.

The Christian option is not apartheid, nor assimilation, but *partnership*. Here each culture respects and makes way for the others to inform, rebuke, and enhance their own lifestyles and behavior. Partnership recognizes that we need each other. No one culture is omnicompetent. Without cultural interchange we are locked into a deprived cultural experience.

In this new millennium, will our churches link hands internationally, across the cultural divides? In New Zealand, will we as Pākehā change our worship patterns to learn to praise from a Māori perspective? Will we as Palagi[9] change our rules for meetings to follow the more biblical Polynesian ways of consensus decision-making (cf. Acts 15:6–21)? Will our

9. This is the word used by Eastern Polynesian peoples to refer to non-Polynesians of European descent, equivalent to the Māori term, Pākehā.

generationally divided churches learn from Asian Christians their cross-generational respect to bring richer unity in our fellowships? In our white, Anglo-Saxon, Protestant congregations at points like these, we could well receive help from Māori, Polynesians, and Asians in bridging these gaps in our churches. Transcultural sharing could quickly enrich our congregational life.

God uses the congregation which grapples with cultural diversity and chooses partnership. He uses such churches to reach out to other nations. Compare the church at Jerusalem and the church at Antioch in Acts 2–16. Antioch became the new outreach center because it learned the cross-cultural lessons, even though that meant public debates between the apostles (Gal 2:11–21).[10] Jerusalem refused to grapple with these issues. God bypassed her as the center for global outreach. Antioch in Syria, with its multicultural leadership, became the sending church for mission outreach (Acts 13–14).

Why bother about cultural differences? We have no choice—God made us this way. His present purposes challenge us to appreciate cultural diversity. Both the Great Commission and the Great Commandment oblige us to respect and understand each other. And as the people of God we are false to our true selves if we continue as a monocultural clique. For the sake of our Lord let us be like him who cares about cultural differences.

How Do We Start?

Let us be willing to unlearn attitudes and prejudices from our past. A fresh, humble reading of our own national history would be a good first step. But that may mean rereading the ethnocentrically biased views of our history that characterized some earlier versions of it. In Aotearoa New Zealand, our Pākehā schooling system, for instance, used to teach that an assimilationist view of intercultural relationships was best for Māori. A better reading suggests we Pākehā need to accept a proper responsibility for the mistakes of our colonial past, without taking on a false sense of guilt, and that we respect the Māori concern to uphold and express their own cultural heritage within the wider unity which is Aotearoa New Zealand. This means we will accept anew the obligations embraced in the founding documents of our nation. A fresh appreciation of our history will give a firm stand for the

10. See, e.g., chapter 4 on the multicultural lessons faced by the early church as recorded in Acts.

forward moves into richer partnership. Accurately relearning history is a vital step towards Christ-honoring present-day patterns.

Let us also check the attitudes and values we inculcate in our homes. How do we speak about other racial groups at our meal table? In our jobs? With our children? How do we train our children to relate to those of other cultures in their school classroom? Discriminatory attitudes and prejudice need to be banned from our family life, by example as well as word.

To start, try contacting one person of another ethnic group and reach out in friendship. Only when "those Māori" become "my friends Hine and Hoani," will we impact our nation for good. Can we make room around our meal table this week for someone from another cultural background? It is well worth a try!

Postscript

In this chapter, we have introduced a number of key concepts in intercultural relationships. These will be constant discussion topics in the following chapters: *biculturalism, multiculturalism, contextualization, ethnocentrism, syncretism, apartheid, assimilation, partnership, culture, essentials of the gospel.*

Section 1

The Gospel and Contextualization

Chapter 1

Why Mission Today?

The Ongoing Challenge of Romans

He had shown himself a real workaholic in his chosen career, had worked himself out of a job, and had now successfully made himself redundant. But instead of retiring, he was into it again. He writes to set out his plans for yet more expansion. What was his driving motivation? Why bother to keep going when he could be taking early retirement?

You know whom I am talking about. Yes, Paul the apostle. The year is about AD 58. He is probably in Ephesus, then in the Roman Province of Asia, modern Turkey, as we read in Acts 19:21. Romans 15:18–19 sums up the situation. Christ has accomplished great things through Paul, proclaiming the gospel fully and establishing churches all the way from Jerusalem to Illyricum on the border of Italy. But Paul was not quitting; he wants Rome to become his new center, and the Roman church a new home base for mission to the West: to Spain and the unreached barbarians beyond (Rom 15:20; 23–24).[1] But Paul had done his overseas stint. Why not settle down? Why bother about more mission?

As Paul sets out his reasons for a new phase of mission from Rome,[2] he explains the reason for mission in every age, including our own. But modern doubts have undermined cross-cultural mission motivation.

1. Miller, "Romans," 22–23: "As Antioch had become the point from which the Church's mission spread throughout the East, so Rome must become the heart of the missionary movement to the West."

2. We acknowledge that the writer may have also had other intentions in writing, but from the text of the letter itself, mission expansion is a, if not the, major concern.

Consider the following objections. Each has a modern ring, but rests on debatable, and not so new, underlying assumptions.

For some in the West mission is simply *outmoded*, and outdated: a hangover from the Victorian heyday of Western expansionism. As early as the 1970s David Howard surveyed committed Christian students from a variety of US faith-based and secular colleges, asking what came to mind when they heard the word "missionary." Their responses included: "spinster, fink, outmoded, cannibal, dowdy, old-fashioned, slides, poor dress, no make-up, jungle . . ."[3]

For others mission is a *form of imperialism*. Mission smacks of a colonial mentality and ignores the reality of healthy nationalism. In this view, the "Great new fact of our times" —as Archbishop William Temple in 1946 called the global reality of national churches—presumably dispenses with any need for more mission. National churches do not need Western Christians telling them what to do. Even in the 1970s African Christians called for a "moratorium" on missions from the West.[4] Today, the majority of Christians live in the non-Western world. The center of gravity of Christianity has moved to the continents of Africa, Asia, Latin America, and Oceania,[5] so many assume that, surely, the mission enterprise is over.

For others, mission is *culturally destructive*. Anthropology and sociology students in the West are often taught that Western missions destroyed cultures and imposed foreign values and lifestyles on peoples of other cultures. Glen Barclay, Pacific historian, in his 1978 university textbook, claimed:

> Christian propagandists . . . relied heavily on techniques of intellectual or emotional persuasion, involving direct repudiation of the traditional values of their prospective converts. The Christian missionary thus tended to appear as the ultimate cultural chauvinist. . . . The Polynesians survived only to the extent that the missionaries failed.[6]

With the recent renaissance of indigenous religions and the efforts of the marginalized, exploited, indigenous peoples to revive their traditions

3. Howard, *Student Power*, 114.

4. Anderson, "Moratorium on Missionaries?" 43–45.

5. See, e.g., Robert, "Shifting Southward," 50–58; Jenkins, *Next Christendom*, 1–14.

6. Barclay, *History*, 61–62. For a slightly more nuanced example of similar assumptions, see Gray, "History of Rarotonga."

and cultures we are told such peoples no longer need those cultural iconoclasts called missionaries.

For still others, mission is *irrelevant* in today's sophisticated world. Voluntary aid, development projects for social or economic advance, and technological assistance, done in the right way, can be helpful. In Australia, for instance, we have cohorts of bright, well-educated, "white, anti-racists" who have left the urban centers to provide benevolent welfare services to outback tribespeople they regard as the victims of colonialism.[7] For this new breed of well-qualified, self-denying idealists, three types of dangerous people still undermine the well-being of such tribal people: "mercenaries, missionaries and misfits."[8] For them, traditional missionary work demands only a strong "No."

Moreover, it is *hypocritical*, we are told, for one culture to force their worldview on others. Churches in Western countries are losing ground. There is so much social injustice, pollution, and moral chaos in our Western countries, we should clean up our own cultures instead of telling other nations how to believe.[9]

Even in theological circles, many Westerners think mission is *theologically naive*. Don't all religions share the truth? David Bosch explains:

> Because of the dechristianization of the West and the multiple migrations of people of many faiths we now live in a religiously pluralist world, in which Christians, Muslims, Buddhists, and adherents of many traditional religions rub shoulders daily. This proximity to others has forced Christians to reexamine their traditional stereotypical views about those faiths. Moreover, the devotees of other faiths often prove to be more actively and aggressively missionary than the members of Christian churches are.[10]

We could go on to note how some say "pietistic" soul-saving is wrong, or that political liberation and justice are the real issues. While others tell us, "Box on regardless," and "Just preach the old-fashioned gospel." We need to listen carefully to such concerns and criticisms—especially heeding

7. See, e.g., Kowal, *Trapped in the Gap*, esp. 6–7, 10, 49, 139–47.

8. Kowal, *Trapped in the Gap*, 141–47.

9. Bosch, *Transforming Mission*, 3. "The advance of science and technology and, with them, the worldwide process of secularization, seem to have made faith in God redundant, why turn to religion [for other peoples] if we ourselves have other ways and means of dealing with the exigencies of modern life?"

10. Bosch, *Transforming Mission*, 3.

the call of national Christians to reappraise methods. Bosch, again, even by 1989, summed up "the crisis" facing mission:

> For centuries, Western theology and Western ecclesial ways and practices were normative and undisputed, also in the "mission fields." Today the situation is fundamentally different. The younger churches refuse to be dictated to and are putting a high premium on their "autonomy." In addition, Western theology is today suspect in many parts of the world. It is often regarded as irrelevant, speculative, and the product of ivory tower institutions. In many parts of the world it is being replaced by Third-World theologies . . . This circumstance has also contributed to profound uncertainties in Western churches, even about the validity of the Christian mission as such.[11]

We need adequate answers to such criticisms. The word of God offers just such a response, with the apostle Paul the most eloquent defender of missions. Paul's Letter to the Romans is our charter explaining the reasons for mission. Romans 1:1–7 shows Paul conceived his whole life and purpose as an apostle, a "sent one," or in our terms, a missionary. So, we can ask, "Why did Paul, the prototype missionary, bother about mission?" Paul's answer is unequivocal. According to Rom 1:14–15 he was involved in mission, *because we have no choice—we are under obligation*: "I am obligated both to Greeks and non-Greeks, both to the wise and the foolish. That is why I am so eager to preach the gospel to you also who are in Rome." For Paul, mission was a personal, present, pressing, global debt he was duty bound and excited to repay. He was "compelled" to preach (1 Cor 9:16–17). What he had experienced and enjoyed of Christ filled him with an eager responsibility he could not ignore. As for Paul, so for us: m*ission is our privileged duty.*

The whole of Romans explains Paul's reasons for this obligation. Each of the letter's next three verses (Rom 1:16–18), as with most of the subsequent sections of the letter, commences with the little Greek connecting word *gar*, meaning "for."[12] Each section adds a further reason why Paul must preach the gospel, or be a missionary. We shall look at Romans with eyes alert for reasons, particularly theological reasons, why Paul's motives

11. Bosch, *Transforming Mission*, 3–4. See also Moreau et al., *Introducing World Missions*, 18–23, in which the opening chapter, "Missions in the Modern World," concludes with ten "Misunderstandings about Missionaries and Mission."

12. For the rest of this chapter, Bible references refer to the Letter to the Romans, unless designated otherwise.

for mission still apply to Christians today, and how they answer the objections mentioned above.

Because of What the Gospel Is and Does for All People, Romans 1:16–17

The apostle turns first to the nature of the gospel itself. Appreciating what the gospel alone does and brings worldwide, obligates us to share it with and beyond our immediate friendship group.

The Global Uniqueness and Relevance of the Gospel

Surrounded as he was on every hand by reminders of the might of the colonizing Roman authorities, Paul speaks immediately of essential features of his good news about Christ Jesus. He declares what the gospel is: *the power of God*, the *dunamis tou theou* in Greek. Paul presents not another rival, merely human power, but God's own transforming, distinctive, new kind of power, entrusted into human hands. A power to be reckoned with, over and above all the other political, social, economic, organizational, and administrative power of the Roman Empire, and of the Greek civilization and lifestyle within which Paul's hearers and readers lived their lives. The message of the death and resurrection of the Lord Jesus Christ, the gospel, makes the power of God available and accessible for all peoples. Unlike other wise words or good advice, the gospel message is itself an enabling, effective power that works within human lives.

The apostle highlights what the gospel brings: *salvation.* In a setting where human power was used regularly, and primarily for destructive or dominating purposes, Paul announces a rescuing, restorative power which brings wholeness or salvation: a power to pick up broken humans, renew those who have been exploited and discarded, and renovate with hope, where despair and fear had prevailed. As a YMCA youth worker, we often entertained lively boys on wet-day holiday programs by screening a sixteen millimetre film showing the careful laying of charges and running of fuses under and around the towering old chimney stack of a disused kiln, before it was blown up in a shower of tiny fragments and massive dust clouds; much to the delight of the boys who whooped and hollered to see such powerful destructive force on film. But, once the dust settled, every time we showed that film, the boys would shout out, "Again, again, backwards this time!" Dutifully, we would replay the film backwards. The clouds of dust would slowly clear, the fragments came back together, and always in awed silence on the part of the watching boys, steadily the towering chimney stack came back together, till it stood there again, perfectly rebuilt. And you could hear the boys exhale in the silence. There was an indescribable something about watching the full and perfect restoration of a totally devastated chimney, that made a rowdy crowd silent. It literally took the boys' breath away. Humans long for a power that can make whole again. That is precisely what only the gospel can do for humans. This is what makes the gospel distinctive: it brings the wholeness of salvation.

Paul goes on to tell what the gospel shows: *the righteousness or justice of God*. No other news explains how to become right with God. The good news about Jesus Christ is all about the one and only way that righteousness comes from God and is shared amongst humans. Only the gospel shows how just and right God is in his actions and nature when he forgives sin and brings men and women back to a warm, personal relationship with himself and each other. The gospel is the one power that consistently works for restoration, wholeness, and ultimate human well-being. In doing so, the gospel achieves and demonstrates the justice and good that always characterize God's work.

This sets the gospel apart from other powers rightly criticized in our postmodern age. Postmodernity as a philosophy stands on a number of unproven assumptions: that all power is oppressive and domineering; that there is no single "grand narrative" that applies to all peoples equally, rather there are only many local narratives, each with its own relevance and validity; that those who impose their views on others are really seeking power for themselves by dominating others; that therefore respect and tolerance of other views are the final values in life; and that there is no ultimate truth, we can only know what is good for us. But the gospel is good news indeed for today's generation, as it offers a positive alternative to each of these negative tenets of postmodernism.

The gospel demonstrates that there is a power that is not oppressive or corrupt. The ethical value of power depends on the character of the person who wields it. When the God who is the source and ultimate expression of love, the Father of our Lord Jesus Christ, wields his power, it is restorative, wholesome, and fulfilling for all who will receive it. Moreover, this is the news that applies equally for all humans as it presents a way for all to flourish and reach their full potential. Only the gospel enhances each personality and satisfies the deepest yearnings of every culture. The gospel liberates and does not oppress others, since it rests on the twin bases of the love of God and the assurance that every human being is created in God's image and likeness. Every person is of such worth to God, that the Son of God gave himself even to die for our restoration and new life. As it works effectively the gospel also highlights the upright justice of God, which is always good, satisfying, and the very best for all his human creatures. To know this for ourselves obligates us to share this message.

Church history shows that organized religion, even sound and thoroughly orthodox Christianity, has very often fallen far short of this gospel pattern. We acknowledge, regret, and repudiate those evil mistakes. But it is our Lord Jesus himself, and his gospel, who and which most clearly highlight, judge, and condemn all such failures. Thus, Christians have no grounds for arrogance, self-righteousness, or proud hypocritical attitudes or behavior. Our gospel requires that we bow always as humble, penitent, servants of others, in awe that the mercy and grace of forgiveness and restoration offered even to us, is accessible for all peoples. This realization spurs us into mission.

The Global Availability of the Gospel

Paul never tires of announcing whom the gospel embraces: *all cultures, Jews, and those of other cultures (gentiles as they were called by the Jews).* Peoples of all cultures are acceptable, and suitable as vehicles through whom the gospel can come, and by whom the gospel can be lived out to the full. Peoples of every culture can turn to—be converted to—Christ from their own cultural context. There is no need to imitate the customs or religious heritage of any other culture to be right with God. Christ broke into this world as the savior of the whole world. No one culture can claim exclusive priority rights over this great news. Christ Jesus himself is good news indeed in our postmodern, pluralist world.

Paul's final point in this early summary of the letter's message declares how the gospel works: *by faith for all.* Other religions require humans to search and contribute in some way to find human fulfillment. Only the gospel is a gift "from first to last," provided in full by God himself, to be received simply by faith—a trust which relies wholly on the actions and goodness of God in Christ. Quoting Hab 2:2 the apostle announces that the Christian life operates wholly by faith.

So, why mission today? We have no choice; it is our bounden duty, our privileged responsibility (1:14). Once we grasp and enjoy the good news for ourselves, we want to do our part in mission because of what the gospel is, what it does, and by whom and how it is accessed.

Because of the Global Reality of God's Holy Anger and Human Need, Romans 1:18—3:20

We are all increasingly concerned about pollution of our physical environment. And rightly so, for God has the same concern. The world we humans are abusing belongs to God and he has entrusted it to our care. But, if we rightly become angry and speak up against misuse of physical resources, then how much more is God also right to respond with indignation and righteous anger when we misuse his entrusted social and spiritual resources. The rest of Rom 1 tells us this is in fact how God responds to our human behavior, and is a further reason for Christian mission today.

God's Revealed Wrath Highlights the Importance of Mission (1:18)

God is opposed to, and in protest shows his holy indignation against, our human moral and spiritual pollution. He shows his anger, pure and upright anger, against human abuse of God-given resources. God reacts specifically against two aspects of human behavior. First, God opposes all godlessness—or mere secularism. Squeezing the living God out of our thinking, planning, explanations of reality, our priorities, and business and leisure pursuits, is an affront to God. That is secularism, and when we exclude him, God responds by revealing his right judgment—what the Scriptures call God's wrath—against such proud, human independence. Secondly, God opposes all the injustice or wickedness of those who suppress available truth. God also reacts when, knowing what God expects, we still choose to go our own way and simply ignore God's desires for our lives. When we disregard his life-instructions, God responds by proper judgment against such self-centered injustice and deliberate opposition to him.

The living, personal God requires upright living, and reciprocal love in human societies. Therefore, all corruption, crooked dealing, selfishness, hatred, proud divisiveness, is wickedness in God's sight. Such godlessness affronts and offends God; it deserves to be punished. But the idea of God responding in anger or upright wrath to godlessness and injustice goes against modern ways of thinking. J. I. Packer, speaking about our reluctance, even as Christians, to give due emphasis to God's wrath, says:

> The root cause of our unhappiness seems to be a disquieting suspicion that ideas of wrath are in one way or another *unworthy of God* . . . God's wrath in the Bible is never the capricious, self-indulgent, irritable, morally ignoble thing that human anger often is. It is, instead, a right and necessary reaction to objective moral evil. God is only angry where anger is called for . . . God's wrath in the Bible is always *judicial*—it is the wrath of the Judge, administering justice . . . [it] is something which [humans] choose for themselves . . . The essence of God's action in wrath is to *give* [humans] *what they choose*, in all its implications: nothing more, and equally nothing less.[13]

Moderns prefer tolerance, compromise, diplomacy, and peace above everything else. But perhaps that is the problem. We have reduced our understanding of God to human categories and expectations. But what if God has a higher set of standards by which he lives, and which he expects of humans, too? What if all self-centeredness is repugnant to God, or if all pride repulses him? Surely God has the right to protest when we keep on doing such things? We have become so used to humans failing to live up to God's standards, that we assume merely human standards are all that matter. But that is precisely what being secular, or ungodly, means. And that is what God reacts against. God's whole nature yearns for his human creatures to honor and obey his higher standards willingly and freely, as only humans can.

Our human difficulty is realizing how awful wrongdoing and disobedience really are to the purity, uprightness, and perfection of God's character. When the judge of all the earth has revealed the highest standards for us all to know (Gen 18:25), God has every right to hold us to account in judgment when we consistently flout his revealed expectations. Mission accepts the need to proclaim this God-centered concern for our human predicament. Romans 1:18–32 explains why judgment is both necessary and just from God's perspective.

13. Packer, *Knowing God*, 166–70; emphasis original.

God's Reasons for Wrath Confirm the Importance of Mission (1:18–32)

God takes our choices seriously and holds us accountable for making those choices. Anything less would be to say God is irresponsible and treats us as less than human.

The roots of sin and the reasons for God's wrath grow from three human behaviors (1:18–21). First, all humans have rejected truth which can be known about God: particularly that God is by nature eternal; that he is awesomely powerful; and that he is greater than merely human, being God. These three fundamentals are plain for all to see in the created universe. But our lifestyles confirm we humans suppress and ignore the reality and implications of these manifest truths about God (1:18–20). Moreover, and secondly, all humans refuse to acknowledge God, by not giving him the honor his nature deserves. Giving our supreme respect to any other person or thing robs the true God of his due worship (1:21). Finally, all humans also show proud ingratitude towards God, when we receive our life from him, and continue to accept the necessities of life from him, but we forget to thank him for these provisions. Such presumptuous self-sufficiency is a form of rebellious opposition towards God, giving further cause for God to show his upright indignation toward us (1:21).

Responding to God's generosity by ignoring his reality, not acknowledging his supremacy, and not thanking him, are the root of what God opposes. Sadly, those roots lead to an inevitable regression, demonstrated in the features of our godless lifestyles, identified in the verses which follow (1:21–32). First, ignoring God produces deluded minds and twisted values (1:21b, 22, 25a). Anyone failing to acknowledge the true God risks devoting their powers of mind and heart to serving lesser powers, as the range of human philosophies, religions, and value systems testify. Scripture judges such wisdom, or insights, even when they contain aspects of truth or bear some societal worth. If the potential wisdom ignores God's active rule over his universe, it is ultimately futile and insufficient, precisely because it disregards the living God (1:21b–22). Whether expressed in fear of spirit powers, or in more sophisticated phobia and neuroses, or when presented in very learned philosophical systems, such thinking is "foolishness," "exchanging the truth about God for a lie" (1:25).

Following on from that, refusing to acknowledge the living God means turning to substitute gods (1:23, 25b). Human beings cannot choose whether we will worship, only who or what to worship. We are so deeply spiritual by nature that we must worship someone or something. But worshipping creatures or creation instead of the Creator is a poor second best. We were created for "I—You" intimacy with the living God, not for an impersonal "I—it" relationship with things or powers. We must choose between a personal friendship with our loving Father God, or continually searching for satisfaction and meaning by serving material things and earthly prestige.

This twisted thinking and worship lead to perversion of desires and bodies (1:24, 26–27). When we restrict our minds to merely human and secular worldviews, and limit our human capacities to worship only created things, human desires quickly turn into lusts, and we exploit our bodies rather than rightly using and caring for them. Since God fully respects our human choices, he "gives us over to," or allows us, what we most want (1:24). But sinful "desires of the heart" turn God's beautiful gifts and powers of sex into something impure, and we degrade and abuse our bodies. Thus, as in vv. 25–27, rejecting right thinking and depersonalizing worship again mean that God allows our shameful human desires, inflamed as lusts, to pervert what God intended for our true joy and fulfillment in our sexuality and gender. Dirtied, these bring more shame.

The outcome of this regression is seen in corrupt conduct pervading our cultures (1:28–31). After concisely summarizing the regression just outlined (v. 28), Paul indicates the final product of these roots: being "filled with every kind of wickedness, evil, greed and depravity" (v. 29). The examples in 1:29b–31 illustrate this pervasive spread of evil, and describe behaviors common in our godless Western societies—so common, sadly, in our entertainments and reading, that we take them for granted, disregarding God's evaluation of them. We rename such lifestyles, hoping thereby to sanitize them. We assume we can imbibe such patterns with impunity, as the apostle's final comment warns. Instead of recognizing that such conduct confirms God has given those who practice such things over to their own perversions (1:28), evil openly accepted leads to flagrant public denial of moral absolutes and standards God condemns. Every person's idea of truth is thought as good as the next person's, and we forget how to blush. Thus, God, in justice, must step in and judge such ingrained wrongdoing (1:32).

God takes our choices so seriously that, if we want to exclude him totally from our priorities, he accepts that; but he insists that we carry the responsibility for rejecting him. He is the source of all that is right, good, upright, pure, lovely, kind, and wholesome; so rejecting him is a very serious choice, with judicial consequences, as Rom 1 has made clear. Moreover, realizing this, we share the responsibility to announce it and take preventative action—hence mission.

The whole of Rom 1:18–32 is stated in universal terms—as true of all humanity, everywhere, at all times. But on hearing this, some people, especially religious people like many of the Jews hearing Paul, have reacted, and still react strongly. They quickly say, "Yes, that's true, very true of those irreligious people of other cultures, like the gentiles around us, *but we are not like that. We are good religious people, so God must surely be pleased with us.*" Sincere people will then list the beauties of their religious heritage, rituals, and achievements: the artistic, geographic, scientific, environmental, or other aspects of their "high culture." They assume that with their history and traditions it should be self-evident that nice, religious people should be excused, at least by God, for their much more "spiritually minded" behavior. The academically inclined among these folk may even say, "Romans 1 evaluation sounds like a proud expatriate, a cultural imperialist, writing off as evil the cultures they haven't understood; little wonder the locals want to be rid of such people." But even very spiritual activities, once stained by performing them in pride, become tawdry and polluted, of no inherent value.

Romans 2 will address such religious people. But before too quickly skipping over Rom 1, let us be clear: it is intended for peoples of all cultures. Paul is declaring God's assessment of all cultures in which people do not give Christ his proper place: the Western technologically dominated culture just as much as any "different" worldview. Moreover, this Rom 1 emphasis on the universal prevalence of human godlessness has stirred up many missionaries, not to have a proudly critical attitude towards other cultures, but to have a deep, burdened concern for those living without access to the good news which answers this bad news of the human predicament plaguing all humanity.

When we recognize the fundamental direction of lifestyles which deny Christ his proper place, then we realize the justice of God's wrath, and the importance of our responsibility for global mission. I have spent my life serving Papua New Guineans, not because I thought them "poor unenlightened heathen." I didn't, and don't. I served because I was concerned lest, like me before I met Christ, they did not have the power of the gospel to release them from the grip of their own self-centered ways of living. Knowing something of the meaning of Rom 1 meant "the love of Christ compelled me into mission (2 Cor 5:14).

God Treats All Peoples and Cultures the Same in Judgment and in the Need for Mission (2:1–29)

If any Westerners, especially missionaries, were nodding in agreement with Rom 1:18–32 as a true analysis of the society and culture they serve, and gloating over it—as some of Paul's original Jewish readers may have been doing, thinking of gentile nations (2:1)—then these next verses quickly cut them down to size.

Romans 2 addresses the religious person with a double challenge: first, to hold the truth humbly (2:1–6). All peoples are equally accountable before God (2:1–2). Pointing accusing fingers at other people is dangerous, for, human nature being what it is, even the deeply religious person fails to achieve God's standards in her or his own strength. Although we may know much more about God, and religion, than another person, even the best of us fails to honor and acknowledge God fully and consistently all the time. We do not always give thanks to God for all his provisions. The way sin characterizes our lifestyles too, means we are all equally guilty and therefore equally needy (2:1–4).

Those who know the right, and fail to live up to it, deserve God's judgment. But God often delays that judgment, giving us opportunity to change our mind: to repent and acknowledge we have proudly disregarded such opportunities to change our ways. Sadly, we have been "storing up wrath . . . for the day of God's wrath when [God's] righteous judgment will be revealed" (2:5). We all are, as 2:4–5 reminds us, also rejecting known truth, in the sense of not living up to it, just as the godless person was doing in 1:18–21. God is not impressed by the self-righteous claims or vain practices of any peoples (2:6). He gives each of us exactly what our heart attitude deserves. Both the blatantly ungodly, and the proudly religious person come under the same assessment criteria and the same judgment.

Secondly, as God holds all people accountable, so all peoples are called to honor God, not self, and to do good consistently and gratefully (2:7–11). God is totally impartial in his approach to all peoples. He sees and respects the good wherever it can be found with sincerity and consistency (2:7–10). He alone fully knows human motives and desires, and how we express them (Heb 4:12; John 2:24–25; 1 Cor 4:4–5). But equally fairly, God also judges evil wherever he finds it, for, as v. 11 sums it up: "God does not show favoritism!"

The general principle of 2:6 is then expanded to show how the same standards apply equally to all peoples (2:12–29). All are judged by how we respond to the light we have received (2:12–16). What we do with what we know about God is always the test. We are never judged for failing to do something we did not know about. For some, like the Jews who rejoiced that they had the Old Testament law, the judgment question is: What have you done with what you know about God and his requirements in the law? (2:12–13). For those of other cultures the question becomes: What have you done with what you know about God and his requirements from the knowledge of God available in creation, and from your own conscience (2:14–15)? And, for those who have heard the gospel, the question is: What have you done with what you know about God and his requirements in Christ (2:16)? For all peoples the question is: What have you done with the light or truth you have received and that was available to you about God? This is why proclaiming the gospel—mission—is so vital. All peoples need to hear and understand the gospel well enough to make their own choice about Christ's free, gracious offer of forgiveness. We only know this offer through the gospel.

All are judged by how we behave, not by our religious claims or rituals (2:17–24). Religious people too, can deceive themselves, and pride often distorts our self-assessment. Religious persons who do not live righteous lives also become an obstacle to others and are judged accordingly. Paul is perhaps referring here to the Jewish missionaries of his day, who went all round the Mediterranean, making proselytes to their religion (cf. Matt 23:13–15). They declared what the Old Testament Law required, but never lived up to it in their own lives, with the result that, "God's name is blasphemed among the peoples of other cultures because of you" (2:24). Paul roundly condemns that kind of hypocrisy.

Our performance counts in God's judgment, not our privileges (2:25–29). God's standard is not, how much do you know about God, but how much have you obeyed of what you know about him? Religious rituals are only valuable when our behavior is consistent with what the ritual symbolizes. The sheer grace of God shown in Christ Jesus makes this clear. God's work for us in Christ, not any religious act or ritual, is the way to right standing before God. Thus, Paul can even say that uncircumcised people who trust in what Christ has done for them are the true people of God, not just those who claim to have received the religious symbol of circumcision, or those who claim to be physical descendants of Abraham.

The message of Rom 2 is summed up in the key words of 2:8–11: *God treats all equally*. I have found that the things which blight and curse my own culture—the basic rejection of a living friendship with God, with its consequent mistrust and loss of purpose—can undermine any culture. And the wholesale export of our false Western values scares me. More than that, I have found that education, economic development, redistributed wealth, in themselves are only of limited value. They do not correct the basic problems of any culture. The need for an answer to our human bias towards sin is more fundamental and more basic than all of those other important needs. Likewise, a misplaced longing for Western ways can be a major disrupting force in third world countries. Only sharing the gospel speaks to the basic needs of our human lives.

None of Us Lives Up to the Knowledge We Have (3:1–20)

Our gospel faces the fact that we all know better than we live. *And this is our problem as humans*. As I said, I knew I had not lived up to the light I had about God before I met Jesus. My need was not for better knowledge of what I should do, but for the power to do what I already knew was right. And I humbly fear that is the problem for other people, too. Romans 3:1–20 says it plainly, and 3:9, and 23 summarize this truth.

All have sinned and fall short of the glory of God (3:23). Realizing this problem of guilt is worldwide, and that we all share the common need for an answer from outside ourselves has motivated me as a missionary. As D. T. Niles, the Indian missiologist put it, we go into mission "as one beggar telling other beggars where to find food."[14] By clarifying the importance of this problem of human sin, we have also answered many of the objections we considered about mission. Too many of those criticisms disregard our most basic human problem. Only mission ensures we keep our focus on this fundamental issue of our sinful nature as humans.

14. Niles, *That They May Have Life*, 96, referring to 2 Kgs 7:1–9.

Because of the Answer to Human Sin, Now Globally Available in Christ, Romans 3:21—8:39

To this point we have concentrated on many negatives about sin and wrath. We have done so because they are often confused, ignored, or unwisely explained away. But the motivation for mission grows even more importantly from the positive provisions God has made in Christ to meet our need. When we know what Christ gives to deal with human sin, our duty to share the news about these provisions is so much greater.

Pardon and Forgiveness through the Death and Resurrection of Christ (3:21—5:21)

Paul now explains the new way humans are made right, or receive righteousness, from God. Paul introduces several key words explaining the meaning of Christ's death at Calvary: faith, the gift of grace, justification (or righteousness), redemption, expiation (or propitiation, or a sacrifice of atonement), the demonstration of God's love, and reconciliation. This section explains the heart of the gospel by setting out the positive steps by which any people can come into a living relationship with God.

To start with, faith in Christ and his gift of grace is set out as the new way to become right with God (3:21–24). We become right with God only by trusting Jesus Christ to deal with our sin and to change our love of wrongdoing to a desire for what is true and right. Faith combines both this turning from what is wrong (repentance), and turning to Jesus and depending on him to change us at the center of our thoughts and our desires. Struggling to keep the law of God is not the way to become right with him; God has opened up a new way to living in friendship with him which rests on a different foundation from law-keeping.

Rom 3:22–24 reminds us there is no difference or distinction between different peoples. All of us, rich or poor, brown or white, educated or uneducated, Jew or gentile, have sinned and missed the mark or standard of behavior God requires. Therefore, we all have the same need. The good news is that God offers the answer to our need as a free gift—a gift of his "grace." Grace gives freely. A grace gift is not a reward for good behavior, nor a payment we have earned; it is a kindness or blessing we did not deserve which God gives on the basis of the work Jesus has fulfilled on our behalf by dying for us at Calvary. Since all people have the same need for

God to act to make us right with himself, the free gift comes to all people in the same way. It is always by grace, through faith, as Eph 2:8 confirms.

Paul then explains the heart of the gospel in concise statements explaining key words describing Christ's death.

Justification or Righteousness

"All are justified freely by [God's] grace . . ." (3:24), and God did this "to demonstrate his justice at the present time, so as to be just and the one who justifies those who have faith in Jesus" (3:26). Everyone who receives God's grace/gift is justified by God. "Justify" is a legal term used in a law court. When the judge has heard the evidence and witnesses for and against the accused wrongdoer, he gives his decision. If the judge declares, "This man is not guilty," then the accused is set free, he has been justified.

Since Christ Jesus paid the penalty for our sins by dying in our place on the cross, God can forgive our sins. To justify us is to declare us no longer guilty before God. It does not mean that God has suddenly made us perfect so that we never sin again. No, it means that God declares, or announces plainly, that he has pardoned and forgiven us. Jesus Christ has done all that was necessary to remove our sin and bring us back to God. We are free by putting our trust or faith in Jesus Christ and accepting his forgiveness to deal with the penalty of our sin. Jesus has taken our place and removed the debt of our sin. Now God accepts us as right, or righteous, before him. In the Greek language of the New Testament justification and righteousness are translations of the same word.

Redemption By Paying a Ransom

"All are justified freely by his grace through the redemption that came by Christ Jesus" (3:24). Redemption and redeemed were common words used in the marketplace to speak about buying something by paying a price. Likewise, when one tribe took a prisoner in battle they would sometimes allow the prisoner to go free if the other tribe paid a ransom (something of great value) to free the prisoner. When the ransom was paid the prisoner was redeemed, or "bought back."

Jesus Christ has paid the ransom or price to set us free from the power of sin (Mark 10:45). We are free from the power of sin and curse of the law because we are redeemed by Christ's death for us (Gal 3:13–14). The precious blood of Christ was the price paid for our ransom (1 Pet 1:18–19). When we realize Christ died to set us free from the penalty and shame of sin, we want to tell others about this great redemption. So the least we can do is share the gospel of Jesus with others.

An Atoning Death, Expiation, Propitiation

"God presented Christ as a sacrifice of atonement through the shedding of his blood—to be received by faith" (3:25). "An atoning death" was translated in older Bible versions as "expiation" or "propitiation." This word was used in the Jewish temple for a sacrifice made to atone for, or cover a person's sin, so they could continue to worship God acceptably. Sin creates a barrier between the sinner and God. In Old Testament times, only the prescribed sin offerings were sufficient to restore a person's relationship with God after they had sinned. Disregarding God's purity and holiness could not be lightly forgiven. A sacrifice was needed to restore a broken relationship with God. In Old Testament times this was the sacrifice of an animal.

So, too, Christ had to die as the sin offering to cover our human sin, and for God to restore us to a right relationship with him. His death as the sacrifice for our sin makes us right with God. Jesus died as the one and only sufficient atoning sacrifice for the sins of the whole world (1 John 2:1).

God's Love Demonstrated in the Death of Christ

Only the amazing love of God for us humans is enough to explain the way the Father sent and allowed his Son, Jesus, to die for us (5:5–8). This love of God is experienced and made real to us as the Father pours his Holy Spirit into our lives to live within us as God's gift. These verses remind us how seldom humans will lay down their lives for another person. But the measure of God's love is seen in the way he gave his dearly loved Son to die for us while we were still rebelliously opposed to him (5:8). Before we had even begun to listen to God the Father, or seek his help, he had already reached out and made the greatest possible sacrifice by sending his Son to die to rescue and renew us (1 John 4:7–14). To know and appreciate such love calls for a willingness to tell his love to others, and this motivates Christians into mission today.

Reconciliation and Peace with God

The next explanation of the death of Christ is developed in two ways in this paragraph, listing benefits of the death of our Savior (5:1, 10–11). In 5:1 Paul announces victoriously, "We have peace with God." He refers to the same reality again three times in 5:10–11, using the related words "reconcile" and "reconciliation." Both in the minds of God's individual creatures, and in the forces at work in our fallen world, a battle continues between the good forces of God, and the powers of evil opposing God, the Lord of the universe. Humans become involved in these power plays, either willingly or unintentionally, by the way we relate to our Lord Jesus Christ. For Paul, as for us, peace with God is a valued possession in such a world: "while we were God's enemies, we were reconciled to [God] through the death of his Son" (5:10). To know the conflict has been decided, the enmity overcome, and God's harmony restored, are spiritual riches to value and enjoy (Col 1:19–23). But again, realizing how freely God gives us his peace, and how undeserving we are to receive it, also means we share the responsibility to invite others to receive this peace.

Paul has used illustrative terms from common human experience to explain the meaning of the death of Christ: justification, a legal term; redemption, a commercial term; atoning sacrifice, a temple term; God's love, a strongly emotive, warm personal term; and reconciliation, another strongly relational term. These key word picture terms, or metaphors explaining Christ's death, are relevant and apply in all cultures globally. Some, like "an atoning sacrifice or propitiation," had very specific meanings within Jewish culture in Jesus's day, but the concept of animal sacrifice to cover human wrongs is widely understood around the world. Even in a post-Christian, secular Western culture, the idea of a just compensation, and usually a costly payment, to put the wrong right, is readily understood as necessary to appease those affected by wrongdoing. These metaphors explaining Christ's death on the cross are well understood globally, making the gospel readily understood in mission today.

United with Christ to Live a New Life Serving Him (6:1—7:25)

These positive explanations of what Christ did on the cross *for* humanity, while central and vital, do not exhaust the depth of the significance of his death. The gospel also invites us to share *with* Christ Jesus in his Calvary experience. Romans 6–7 explain the believer's relationship with Christ by explaining the meaning of baptism, before coming back to the old problem of the believer's continuing struggle with sin.

The problem of ongoing sin in a Christian's life, and how Christ provides an answer for us, is central to the meaning of baptism. We have already seen how grace abounds and fully overcomes sin through Christ Jesus (5:21). So, someone might ask, "Why not, then, keep sinning so we can know more of this grace?" (6:1). But Paul quickly rejects that suggestion: "God forbid—Christians have died to sin, so how can we live in it any longer?" (6:2). There is no place for sin in a Christian's life because we have been united with Christ and share in all he did in his death, burial, and resurrection. When we go into the water of baptism we are declaring that we have decisively put an end to the sinful way of life we previously lived; we have been joined with Christ in his burial; and like Jesus, we have risen from the baptismal water to live a new, resurrected life (6:3–4; cf. Gal 2:20).

Paul confirms this truth in the next paragraphs. Still explaining the meaning of baptism, he tells us two things we can know for sure (6:5–10), and two things we can count, or reckon, as true, along with their outcome (6:11–14). Since baptism unites us with Jesus in a death like his, it also unites us in a resurrection like his. So we now *know* that our old self-centered life has been crucified together with Christ in his death. By declaring in our baptism that we are dying with Christ, we are set free from the control of our old life with its desires and habits, and we are no longer enslaved to it (6:5–7).

Not only so, but we also *know* that "since Christ was raised from the dead, he cannot die again . . . The death he died he died to sin once for all, but the life he lives he lives to God" (6:9–10). "In the same way," we read, "count (or reckon) yourselves dead to sin but alive to God in Christ Jesus" (6:11). This Scripture challenges us to live out the meaning of our baptism. Don't let sin rule in our bodies, rather, offer all our abilities to God as tools for his service (6:13–15).

Baptism and its meaning answer the question in 6:1: "Shall we go on sinning so that grace may increase?" A proper understanding of grace and baptism are the reason we turn decisively from sin, not an excuse to yield to its temptations.

At the same time, as humans we are all servants by nature. We are not independent. We all need someone, or some thing, to serve and live for. Because of the way we are made we cannot choose whether or not to serve;

we can only choose whom or what we will serve. God has given us all a free will to decide whom we shall serve and obey (6:16). When a person makes Christ their Lord and Master they are turning from one service to another. Sin once controlled us; we followed the sinful desires and habits of our old self. But, praise God, there came a day when we were redeemed from slavery to sin, and wholeheartedly trusted and obeyed the true teaching we had received. We became servants of Christ (6:17, 19). We now serve what is upright and true (6:18).

In the rest of this chapter (6:19–23) Paul contrasts the outcomes and results, or "wages," of sin with the gift of God's righteousness and the harvest that brings when we are united with Christ as servants of God: "The wages of sin is death, but the gift of God is eternal life in Christ Jesus our Lord" (6:23). Romans 6, then, has explained the reality of our union with the resurrected Christ and the living relationship that brings us into, and which we declare is ours in baptism. As Christians this is all part of the gospel entrusted to us to share with those who have not yet heard the message.

The next chapter then returns to concerns Christians face relating to the law of God, and to dealing with sin and our sinful human nature, as we yield our bodies to serve the Holy Spirit.[15] Paul introduces each section with a question.

15. Note the key terms Paul uses from 7:1 to 8:17: (a) he speaks about our "sinful nature" or "the flesh" in 7:5, 7, 18, and 25; and then again in 8:3, 4, 5, 8, 9, 12 and 13; (b) he refers to "sin" repeatedly, not so much to occasional wrong actions, but to the regular habit of wrongdoing, and to sin as a force or power at work in us (7:7, 8 [2x], 9, 11, 13 [3x], 14, 17, 20; 8:3, 10; (c) the law of God, given through Moses, is referred to in every verse from 7:1–9, as well as 7:12, 14, 16, 22, and 25, using the general term "law." From 7:8–12, God's law is spoken about in the singular ("commandment" referring to the law not to covet). In each of these verses law is referred to as the standard God expects for all his children. But in chapter 7 "law" is also sometimes used in a wider sense to refer to the law in a negative sense, as something that condemns us for not achieving what it demands: "although I want to do good, evil is at work there too" (7:21); called in 7:23 "another law at work in me" (7:23), and further described as "the law of sin" or "the law of sin and death" (7:25; 8:2). The principle which that rule fights against is called "the law of my mind" (7:25; 8:5b; 6b). The themes of death and resurrection also recur throughout Rom 7–8; see 7:2, 3, 4, 5, 6, 8, 9, 10, 11, 13 (2x), 24; 8:2, 6, 10, 11, 13. And finally, the Holy Spirit is introduced in 7:6, and then becomes central later; see 8:2, 4 (2x), 5, 6, 9 (2x), 10, 11 (2x), 13, 14, 15 (2x), 16.

Don't You Know Law Is Only in Force Until Death (7:1–6)?

We have just seen that when we give ourselves as slaves of God, it leads to holiness and eternal life (6:22). It is fair to ask, then, "Does that mean the relationships created by God's law also continue after death?" The marriage law of the time illustrates the response. When a woman marries, she is joined by law to her husband. Does that relationship continue after one of the marriage partners dies? The answer is clearly "no"; if one partner dies, the surviving partner is free to remarry another person (7:1–3).

Paul applies the illustration, still with the meaning of baptism in mind. Like a married woman whose partner has died, since Christ died on the cross, Christians have died to the law by being joined into the body of the resurrected Christ, who is alive again from death. The resurrected Christ is like our new marriage partner, and we now bear fruit for God (7:4). Or, as the next section explains, we have died to the old sinful nature with its desires which were stirred up by the law, so that we are released from the law and are free to serve God in the new relationships created by the Holy Spirit (7:5–6; 8:1–9). The old way of the law as a written code has been replaced by our new faith-union with the resurrected Christ through the Holy Spirit.

Is the Law Sinful (7:7–12)?

What Paul has just explained raises a further question about the law (7:7). Is the law sinful? In a strong exclamation which Paul uses ten times in this letter, he replies, "certainly not."[16] The thought was repulsive to Paul; he uses the personal pronoun "I" in his response: "I wouldn't have known what sin was had it not been for the law." The law of God makes sin known, but is never sinful in itself. Paul illustrates by referring to the law against coveting. Paul testifies he had not been troubled by coveting until he became aware of the commandment against it (7:7–8). Then he found sin was stirred up and he began coveting in a variety of ways. Sin in him used the commandment to stimulate longings which dragged him into desiring the very things the commandment forbade (7:8–11). But in all this the law itself is holy, righteous, and good; it is not wrong or evil in any way (7:12). This raises a third question.

16. See Rom 3:4, 6, 31; 6:2, 15; 7:7, 13; 9:14; 11:1, 11. Literally translated, "let it never be."

Did the Law, Then, Which Is Good, Become Death to Me (7:13–25)?

Following what v. 12 has said, someone might ask, "Well, did the good law lead me into death before God?" Paul responds, again with a strong, "forbid the thought," before answering that sin used the law to show just how powerful, and sinful, sin is when we allow it to work in us; and it is sin, not the law, that leads to spiritual death (7:13). Then, in a strongly autobiographical section, Paul describes the struggles he has with sin, even as a Christian.

In doing so, Paul follows the Hebrew poetic pattern of a "chiasm" (7:14–20).[17] Hebrew writers used chiasms to clarify key issues, to emphasize major points, and to help with memorization. In this culturally significant way, Paul shows that indwelling sin, or what he calls his "sinful nature" (or "flesh") is the root of the Christian's problem, and we are helpless to overcome this root without help from beyond ourselves (7:17–18). Paul sums this up in his three clear statements in 7:21–23: "Although I want to do good, evil is right there with me"; "In my inner being I delight in God's law"; and "Another law (is) at work in me, waging war against the law of my mind and making me a prisoner of the law of sin at work in me."

This calls forth his double cry—of anguish, and of thanks—in 7:24–25: "What a wretched man I am! Who will rescue me from this body of death? Thanks be to God, who delivers me through Jesus Christ our Lord." Paul will show more fully how Christ rescues us in chapter 8, but he rounds off this section by summarizing what he has shown so far: "I myself in my mind am a slave to God's law, but in my sinful nature a slave to the law of sin" (7:25b). Again, the Christian gospel is not a list of impossible demands; it is a call to humbly and realistically face our weaknesses and come to the Lord Jesus for his free gift of salvation.

17. A chiasm builds up through a series of items to a central point, then repeats the ideas as it works back to the first point:

v. 14: We know the law is spiritual, but I am unspiritual, sold under sin (the problem introduced).

v. 15: I don't understand what I do.

v. 15b: What I want to do, I don't do.

v. 15c: But what I hate, I do.

v. 16: If I do what I don't want to do, I agree the law is good (the main idea).

v. 17: It's no longer I myself doing it; it's sin living in me.

v. 18: Good itself doesn't dwell in me, in my sinful nature.

v. 18b: For I have the desire to do what is good, but can't carry it out.

v. 19: I don't do the good I want to do, but keep on doing the evil I don't want to.

v. 20: If I keep on doing what I don't want to do, it's no longer I who do it.

v. 20b: But it is sin living in me that does it (the main idea repeated).

God Gives the Holy Spirit (Romans 8:1–39)

Romans 8 explains how God deals with the problem just described in chapter 7, how to overcome the power of sin at work in our "flesh," or human nature. The letter reaches the high point it has been working towards since 1:16: being empowered by the Holy Spirit to live as children of God. Notice how each person of the Trinity has their own part to play to win this victory.

The Triune God Frees Us from the Power of Our Sinful Nature (8:1–4)

Our sinful nature weakened the upright law of God (8:3), so that we were enslaved to sin and faced sin's consequences, as Rom 6:7 and 8:2–3 have shown. But God the Father has done what the law was unable to do: he sent his Son, Christ Jesus, to become a human being, just like us, but free from sin; to die for us as a sin offering; and through the Holy Spirit, break sin's power over us (8:3). So we are no longer ruled by our sinful nature, but by the Holy Spirit living in us (8:4). Therefore, we join Paul in the victory shout of v. 1: "There is now no condemnation for those who are in Christ Jesus."

Christians Live Controlled by the Holy Spirit, Not by Their Sinful Nature (8:5–13)

Paul clarifies the tension he discussed in 7:4–25 between living controlled by our human nature or by the Holy Spirit. He contrasts these two lifestyles. The life controlled by our human nature thinks constantly about merely human desires; it leads ultimately to death, is hostile to God, does not submit to him, cannot please him, does not have the Holy Spirit, and does not belong to Christ (8:5–9).

But the life controlled by the Spirit desires what the Spirit desires; it focuses its thoughts on life and peace, enjoys the fruit of righteousness, participates in Christ's life through the Holy Spirit, and even though the Christians' bodies are mortal, they anticipate resurrection to eternal life through the Spirit, who already lives in them (8:5–7, 9–11). The contrast between living under the control of the sinful, flesh-dominated, nature, and life in the Spirit, could not be greater.

This, then, is the answer we seek; allowing the Holy Spirit to rule our desires and minds sets us free from the power of the sinful nature, and enables us to enjoy victory over sin. We are faced with a choice, as seen in

8:12–13—we are obliged no longer to live according to our sinful nature, for it leads only to death, but to put to death the misdeeds and desires of that old nature and live by and with the Holy Spirit. This is the only true option for a Christian, as the next paragraph explains.

Believers Live by the Spirit as Full Members of God's Family (8:14–17)

Paul brings his whole argument together by confirming how the Holy Spirit works in the Christian's life. The Spirit leads us as true children within the Father's family (8:14). As our companion and guide, the Holy Spirit shows us the path to follow and guides and guards us over the rough parts of that way. Moreover, to yield ourselves to the Holy Spirit's control is never a return to slavery, fear, and harsh treatment by a cruel master. No, the Holy Spirit welcomes believers into the full rights and privileges of sons and daughters within God's own family (8:15). Paul uses the word for adoption into a free Roman family, and explains the honor and dignity of this adoption as empowering us to call God, *Abba* (or "Father" in Christ's own vernacular language of Aramaic). As we receive this adoption, our human spirit resonates with the Holy Spirit as he testifies that we are now children of God (8:16). God's family business, standards, interests, name, and honor now become ours, to pursue, uphold and enjoy. The purpose and will of our Father become our chief concern, wherever he may "place" or "appoint" us to bear fruit in his vineyard (John 15:16).

More than that, the Father makes us his heirs. Christ Jesus is the unique Son with the responsibilities and honor of the "firstborn" in the family of God (Mark 12:1–11; Col 1:15, 18; Heb 1:2). So the Father and the Son invite, and the Holy Spirit empowers, every adopted child to share in the Father's inheritance, as coheirs together with Christ Jesus (8:17).

There is, however, one condition that goes with this honor of sharing Christ's inheritance: we must "share in Christ's sufferings so that we may also share in his glory" (8:17). These central teaching chapters of the letter conclude with sections contrasting the reality of suffering in our Christian lives, as well as three witnesses to our Christian hope (8:18–27), the great certainty guiding our relationship with God (8:28–30), and a final hymn of praise for our victory made certain in Christ (8:31–39).

Suffering and the Threefold Witness to Christian Hope (8:18–27)

Any present suffering for a Christian is as nothing compared with the greatness of the glory to be made known in us in a coming day. The depths of a Christian's suffering and the counterbalancing greatness of the glory God shares with his adopted children stimulate hope, and give further reason why we must share this message with others. Three witnesses contribute to our Christian hope, beginning with the whole of creation. Until now, creation has been characterized by frustration, decay, and natural disasters, like a woman's labor pains in childbirth. But creation eagerly awaits the freedom it will enjoy at Christ's return, when "the glory will be revealed" in us Christians (8:18). Scripture only gives this glimpse of what it calls "the revelation" and "the freedom and glory of the children of God" (8:19, 21; cf. Isa 65:17–25; Acts 3:19–21; 2 Pet 3:8–13).

Christians add their own witness to take this expectation a step further (8:23–25). Since we have already received the initial evidence, or "firstfruits," of the Holy Spirit at work in our lives, we also yearn deeply for the full completion of salvation. We are already assured of our adoption as children of God (8:15–16). But we still long for this new relationship to be worked out more deeply within us; we groan inwardly as we wait eagerly for our adoption to be more complete and for our bodies to be fully redeemed (8:23). We understand our salvation as a "now—but not yet" reality. Salvation is rooted in hope already received and motivating our present lives. But that hope will only be fully consummated and finalized in our future resurrection life in Christ Jesus (8:24–25).

A third witness, the Holy Spirit, is with us to strengthen and support us at just these points of present need. When our human weakness means we don't even know what we ought to pray for, the Holy Spirit steps in and prays for us with wordless groans, which the Father hears and responds to, because the Holy Spirit prays in line with the will of God (8:26–27).

So this section, which began by reminding us we are called to suffer for Christ (8:17–18), ends with three references to groaning: the groaning of creation (8:22), the groaning of believers (8:23), and the groaning of the Holy Spirit (8:26)—each witnessing to the twin realities of the hope and costliness of God's ongoing work in us until we are welcomed into his glorious presence.

The Certainty Guiding Our Relationship with God (8:28–30)

The next three verses summarize the certainty with which Christians walk through life, and the basis of that certainty in all that God has done for each of us.

Our certainty is that in everything—from suffering to rejoicing, groaning to thanksgiving—God works for the good of all who love him, and do his will in our lives. Of all the relationships God longs and looks for in his followers, love comes first. And this love between the Christian and their Lord sets the gospel and Christian faith apart from all other religions.

The basis for this certainty is in God and all he has done for us, which Paul spells out with five great words describing God's work for us, from eternity past right on to eternity future. First God *foreknew* every believer, seeing, hearing, and understanding every desire and yearning, every weakness and failure, every victory, success, and honest attempt; knowing the reasons, the situation, the background, and the difficulties which would come with each achievement or disappointment. In eternity past, God knew and saw all that would happen in our lives, both before they happened and as they developed, and he still loves us and brings good from those very things.

Knowing all of that, God *predestined* each of us. He marked out a life pathway for us. Not, as some teachers of predestination imply, with a harsh, legal set of restrictions to hem us in, but with a warmth of love, support, and encouragement so we are made increasingly like his Son, being conformed to Christ's image. At each step, we are joined more closely into his family where Christ receives the honor like the "firstborn," eldest child supporting each other family member as they mature and grasp opportunities for growth.

Turning from God's work in eternity past to the actual lifetime of each believer, those God predestined, he *called* into his family. God himself, through his Son and Spirit, sought us out, and wooed us back to himself, with intimate care and personal concern, as the Gospels show so clearly (Matt 4:18–20; 9:9; 10:1–8; Mark 3:13–19; 6:6–12; 10:46–52; Luke 5:27–32; 6:12–16; 9:1–6; 19:1–10; John 1:35–51).

Those Jesus called, he also *justified* as we each responded to the gospel. All the terms used to describe Christ's earthly work in 3:21–26—justification, redemption, and atoning sacrifice—are gathered under the one term "justified," to include all that Christ accomplished by his death at Calvary, together with all that was explained in 5:1—8:28: being reconciled and united with Christ in his death and resurrection through baptism; and enjoying our new life led by the Holy Spirit. Being justified, or made righteous, touches on each of these more detailed descriptors of Christ's ongoing work, both for us at Calvary, and in us as we become more like him every day during our earthly pilgrimage of faith and grace.

Not only so, the process takes a final step: "those God justified, he also *glorified*." Boldly stating a future reality as an already accomplished fact, what will only be fulfilled in eternity future is ours already.

So, Rom 8:28–30 has set out our assurance and confidence as Christians, and answers the heart longings of our whole human species. Through the historical work of God in Christ, God has atoned for our sin, united us with Christ Jesus himself in his resurrection life, and thus identified with us and filled us by his Spirit, thereby pouring the love of God freely into our lives.

Praise for the Victory That Is Ours in Christ Jesus (8:31–39)

The apostle cannot move on without pausing to give thanks and reflect on these wonders of our salvation. The Holy Spirit has revealed something of the great goal of glory which is ahead for each Christian. Now a hymn of praise tells us God wants us to enjoy victory over every power that seeks to turn us aside in this life. Three sets of questions frame the concluding argument of the chapter.

Who Is Against Us (8:31–32)?

When God is on our side, working for good in whatever is happening around us, then no power or person can overcome us. If God did not hold Christ back from death for us, then he will give whatever else may be necessary to ensure our final salvation (8:32).

Who Can Condemn Us (8:33–34)?

Two further questions both ask if anyone can bring us into further condemnation. No-one can read a charge against us listing the wrongs we have done, for God himself has already declared us free from guilt; Christ Jesus has not only died in our place, but has also risen from the dead, and is in God's presence continually interceding for us (8:34).

Who Shall Separate Us from the Love of God (8:35–39)?

The victorious conclusion to the first part of Paul's letter asks whether anything, material or spiritual, is able to cut us off from the love of God available in Christ Jesus. Verses 35–37 list a number of material powers humans fear: tribulations (or difficulties and trials); distress (sudden upsets); persecutions, or suffering for Christ; famine (lack of food); nakedness (lack of adequate clothing); perils (threatening dangers); and the sword (physical attack for supporting Christ). But Christians need not fear any of these, as the love of God makes us more than conquerors through all such attacks, even though they may come against us repeatedly as we follow Christ (8:36).

Moreover, a number of spiritual realities or powers seek to dominate us, but again the Holy Spirit assures us that none of these forces can cut us off from God's love in Christ Jesus: neither death, nor life; nor angels nor principalities (spiritual powers); nor things present, nor things to come, nor powers of any kind; nor deep places, nor high places; nor anything else in all creation (8:38–39).

To experience these saving realities is to be under obligation for mission. Each aspect of the gospel of Christ set out so carefully from 1:16 to 8:39 has added further reasons why all who have experienced this gospel are also responsible to make it known.

Because of the One Way to Access Christ's Answer to Our Need, Romans 9:1—11:36

Romans 9–11 explain the way God works in history—for both the Jews and gentiles, that is, peoples of other cultures. These three chapters address difficult questions about God's work in history, such as: Why didn't God's own people, the Jews, respond gladly to Christ Jesus, since he is their Messiah? Where do the Jews fit into God's ongoing plans? And, has God turned from the Jews forever? In these chapters Paul addresses three major issues:

- God chose Israel in mercy, according to his sovereign plan (9:1–29).

- Because of Israel's present unbelief, other cultures have their opportunity for a friendship relationship with God (9:30—10:21).
- One day, God will restore Israel through Christ, in line with his purposes in history for all cultures (11:1–36).

These chapters speak repeatedly about God's election of Israel as his chosen people. As Lesslie Newbigin points out in his various writings on "the logic of election,"[18] God chose, or "elected," Israel to reinforce two great truths about the way he works in our world. First, election is not for privilege, but for responsibility. Israel was no better than other nations around them (Deut 7:7–9); they were chosen as God's people simply because of the love and mercy of God. But, since God did choose them, they were responsible to pass on the light of God's message to other nations. They were chosen to serve the nations, as God's representatives.

Moreover, election teaches us that each nation must be humble enough to receive God's word through those who have already received it—often those we despise and think inferior to us. But unless we are prepared to receive God's message through them, we exclude ourselves from access to God's love and grace. We cannot receive God's life and blessings in isolation. We must come to those who already know him to learn of him. So, in their future restoration Jews will have to receive the salvation message through those whom they called "the non-Jews," the gentiles.

At the heart of Paul's explanation of the way God chooses those who will come to him, he addresses directly our questions about why mission is necessary today (10:6–17). He begins by affirming that the only way to receive Christ is to call on, believe in, and confess Christ Jesus (10:6–13). To come to faith in Christ requires a wholehearted commitment to him, as 10:9–10 says clearly: "If you declare with your mouth, 'Jesus is Lord,' and believe in your heart that God raised him from the dead, you will be saved. For it is with your heart that you believe and are justified, and it is with your mouth that you confess your faith and are saved." This follows from what the previous sections of the letter have explained and it is so for all peoples, Jews and gentiles, regardless of religious or ethnic background or cultural setting.

But that public confession presupposes a series of steps (10:14–15): calling depends on believing (v. 14a); believing depends on hearing (v.

18. E.g., Newbigin, *Pluralist Society*, 80–88, a chapter titled "The Logic of Election"; *Open Secret*, 68–90.

14b); hearing depends on preaching (v. 14c); and preaching depends on being sent (v. 15). This process is the only way anyone can receive the saving message of Jesus Christ. Following that sequence in Paul's teaching, we need the following factors for effective mission.

We begin with a partnership in mission between a church sending, and messengers going with the gospel message. Local churches are God's means for recruiting, ensuring training, and equipping, selecting, and commissioning the people of God's choice to go as their mission partners on God's mission. This involves all that we mean by "commending" or commissioning, sending, and supporting a person for mission service.

Then, as the mission partner goes, those who do not yet know Christ learn of God's truth through the personality of his chosen messengers. People need to see the good news lived out in the life of a real Christian to give credibility to the message.

But just being present is not enough. Preaching the life-giving and life-changing gospel is vital. This involves all the effort of knowing the Scriptures, language and culture learning, doing the translation, contextualizing the message, and presenting it in culturally relevant, and equivalent, ways. Only then can a person, with real faith, call on Jesus as their own Savior and Lord. The amazing thing is that this response of faith, in whatever language, carries the same life-changing efficacy in the sight of God.

So, in his wisdom God uses these steps, or this "logic of election," as Newbigin calls it, and the apparent "foolishness" of working through the preaching of human messengers (1 Cor 1:21), as the channel by which the gift of transforming salvation comes to every people group around the world. But once we have received this transforming experience, we, in turn, must become the next link in the chain passing the message on to those only we can reach with the good news. This only global way of access to this answer in Christ gives us the privileged responsibility of becoming involved in mission.

Because of the Global Interdependence of the Church, Romans 12:1—15:24

The early verses of Rom 12 are the practical hinge of the whole letter, reminding us that gratitude is the only appropriate response to all the grace God offers us in Christ. When we have known the "mercies of God"—as set out in the central sections of Romans—we have an obligation to live out and share the book's missional message. But as soon as mission crosses a cultural boundary the workers face new kinds of problems, addressed in Rom 12–15.

Three Essential Responses (Romans 12:1–8)

Every Christian must address three basic responses of faith for fruitful life and service. Together, these responses entail the "what," "how," and "why" of service in mission.

To begin with the "what": Paul pleads with his readers to offer their whole personality to God as devoted sacrifices (12:1), not just our money or some "thing"—no matter how valuable it may be. God is a personal being and desires our friendship, companionship, love, devotion, and fellowship. Primarily, God longs for us to be his people. This has always been his yearning (Exod 19:3–6). But how are we to present ourselves to God? He asks us not just to *bring*, but to *be* a living sacrifice, an apparent contradiction in terms. Normally a sacrifice has been given to God by being put to death. But God desires us to be fully alive, presenting our life and all our abilities, potential, and desires, given over for him to use or dispose of as he chooses. Our whole self is to be set apart, or "holy," and kept for his service—for him to use however he desires. This is the only kind of offering that is acceptable and pleasing to him. But why such a step? This is the only sensible response to all God has done for us in Christ. When we grasp the extent and depth of his mercies shown to us, the logical response is to give God all that are and can ever be. This relationship with God comes first.

Secondly, God desires that each of his children find and prove in action his will for each of us, towards the transforming of our minds (12:2). This is always the good, clean and upright option; it is always pleasing both to God and ultimately to us, and it is the very best we can know in practical terms. God's will is not always the easiest, but it is always the best (v. 2b). The "how" of finding and following God's will for us involves both choosing to turn from just copying the fashions and values of the culture around us, and being radically changed in our thinking and understanding: not being conformed to the world's lifestyles, but being transformed by the renewal of our minds. Our relationship with the world and its values is the stumbling block on which many Christians are held back in living a Christlike life.

Finally, we are called to accept ourselves and our place in the global body of Christ by accepting and fully utilizing the gifts entrusted to us

(12:3–8). Many of us are serious Christians, we genuinely desire to offer our body and life to Christ, and we seek to live a pure and upright life, but we struggle with this third key relationship. We have too high, or too low, an opinion of ourselves. The challenge is to find the balance of a humble but sensible—or sober—view of our own part within the global body of Christ. This is true, both personally, and culturally. Too often we Westerners read these verses as if they are written to isolated individuals, when Paul is actually addressing the groups of believers in the church at Rome. The gospel gives new dignity to, and new respect for, every culture within the one mission of the worldwide church. Each Christian person, and each people group, is entrusted with particular gifts and contributions for the sake of the whole church globally. We have a multinational and multicultural task. God is trusting the whole church to take the whole gospel to the whole world.

Global Church Partnerships of Love and Loyalty to Christ (Romans 12:9–21)

The patterns of lifestyle behavior set out in these verses demonstrate the gospel at work amongst believers, and ensure a clear testimony to endorse their gospel preaching. Our whole lifestyle contributes to our presentation of the gospel, so we are to make love the hallmark of our lives together.

This is the case in church and community (12:9–21). Practical love is key to intercultural relationships: loving without hypocrisy, for love hates evil, and clings to the good (v. 9); loving each other as family, honoring others above ourselves (v. 10); maintaining spiritual fervor; in difficulties being joyful in hope, patient under pressure, and persistent in prayer (vv. 11–12); and sharing hospitably with those in need, wherever they may be (v. 13). We also uphold love's relational commitments (12:14–16): responding to others kindly not critically (v. 14); feeling with others whatever their situation, sad or glad (v. 15); and being thoughtful of others by dealing with proud conceit and being available to help (v. 16). Finally, such practical love includes handling conflict in love (12:17–21): never repaying evil with evil, but doing right before all (v. 17); doing our part to live at peace with all (v. 18); always letting God handle revenge (v. 19); and overcoming evil by returning good (vv. 20–21).

Interpersonal relationships are the key to any effective Christian service—especially mission! And it is the worldwide, single body of Christ this passage tells us to care for, relate to, and love. All these commands are to be worked out with all true believers across cultural barriers internationally. We are, in short, to become "glocal" citizens—global and local—partnering with our brothers and sisters in the church worldwide, but also active in our own neighborhood.

Practical Loyalty to Christ as the New Public Behavioral Standard (Romans 13:1–14)

Expanding on 12:19, the text now turns to civil society as the context for working out love, for civil authority derives from God (13:1–7). Governments are God's servants to uphold the right and good for the sake of their citizens (vv. 3–4); to uphold justice and administer punishment, as God's delegated agents (vv. 4–5); and to administer taxes for citizens' welfare—as "temple servants" or "benefactors" (v. 6).

Our Christian duties to government, then, are to submit to their authority (vv. 1, 5); accept and obey their proper requirements; and aim for integrity of conscience before God in filling our responsibilities. This means paying our dues—taxes and revenue—and showing respect and honor (v. 7). Love and loyalty to Christ is to extend across every aspect of social relationships, so that by respect and obedience we foster good government and keep doors open for effective witness.

In the matter of wider public lifestyles, love is the key to a regulated society (13:8–14). Owe only one thing—to love (v. 8)—for love fulfills the law: by upholding the basic sanctities of humanity, namely the sanctity of sex and marriage; of life itself; of work and ownership; and of other people's rights and relationships (v. 9). Love never harms the other but always cares for neighbors as for oneself. Therefore love fulfills all good law, and is the cement of a healthy society (v. 10). Love lives and breathes the teachings of the Sermon on the Mount (Matt 5–7), and understands John 13:34–35. Moreover, love grasps opportunities by "putting on Christ Jesus" (vv. 11–14).

Love is alert to the significance of the hour (v. 11), wearing the "armor of light" with a lifestyle that is open and honest, fit for the "day" when Christ returns to judge our actions. Love rejects deeds of darkness, which indulge our base appetites, perverting desires and destroying relationships. We clothe ourselves with Christ, no longer pandering to selfishness or dirty desires. Only a Christ-filled life grasps today's global opportunities. Love and integrity are the way: choosing Christ's new standards, not living by the old pre-Christian patterns of self-centeredness (vv. 13–14).

So, we need each other, globally, to fulfill the task! Multicultural, international, Christ-centered partnerships are the norm for effective mission.

Accepting Other Christians with Differing Views on Practical Matters (Romans 14:1—15:13)

The differences Paul mentions here between "weaker" and "stronger" brothers and sisters refer to Christians who disagree and argue over practical applications of their faith, such as food rules and holy days and how to observe them (14:1). Such distinctions can refer to problems between people of the same culture as well as between different cultures. The same disciples can be "weaker" Christians on some issues and "stronger" believers on others, and can also change their positions over time. These particular instructions about food and holy days are examples of arguments over disputable matters common in churches today. Clothing styles, views about sports or entertainments, and various cultural practices, can become similar issues. We must consider whether, and in what ways, such issues apply to each of us personally, and also how they apply to our own culture's accepted rules and customs.

Such issues often become major concerns and points of disagreement when the gospel crosses into another culture. Should the Christians in the new culture observe the rules and practices of the culture that brought the gospel to them? Or are the Christians in the new culture free to make their own decisions about how they do or don't eat their food, or observe special days? In Paul's day the issues focused around Jewish and gentile practices. Today it is often likely to be a question of whether the new believers should copy the practices of the missionary's culture, or be free to make their own decisions about secondary matters.

Paul encourages believers to accept those who differ without quarrelling over disputable matters; God is our judge—and theirs (14:1–12). Some Christians regard some food as unclean and will not eat it. But others eat anything, including foods banned by the first group. Judging each other over such things is wrong because God accepts people on the basis of their faith, not their food. Moreover, each person is accountable to our Lord and Master, not to other Christians, for what we eat or refrain from eating. Similarly, for the way we regard the sacredness of particular days.

Some Christians regard every day as equally sacred for Christ; others set some days apart as specially holy for the Lord. What we eat and how we respect a day are things we do for the Lord, and every believer should be fully convinced of their personal views about such things. Whether or not we treat one day as more holy than another, we do so for the Lord (vv. 5b–9). Each of us will stand before God's judgment seat, and will give an account to God of our attitudes and practices in such things (vv. 10, 12), so we should leave all judging of others to God.

The next section (14:13—15:2) has a series of negative warnings for those of us who think we are strong Christians: "Let us stop passing judgment on one another" (14:13); "make up your mind not to put any stumbling block or obstacle in the way of a brother or sister" (14:13); "do not by your eating destroy your brother or sister for whom Christ died" (14:15); "do not destroy the work of God for the sake of food" (14:20); "we who are strong ought to bear with the failings of the weak and not to please ourselves" (15:1).

Between those warnings are a series of equally strong statements about things we can know or do: "I am convinced . . . that nothing is unclean in itself. But if anyone regards something as unclean, then for that person it is unclean" (14:14); "If your brother or sister is distressed because of what you eat, you are no longer acting in love" (14:15); "the kingdom of God is not a matter of eating or drinking, but of righteousness, peace and joy in the Holy Spirit" (14:17); "make every effort to do what leads to mutually building each other up" (14:19); "all food is clean, but it is wrong for a person to eat anything that causes someone else to stumble" (14:20); "so whatever you believe about these things keep between yourself and God" (14:22); "we should all please our neighbors for their good, to build them up" (15:2).

Christians are free from rules and regulations about what we can eat or drink. But that does not mean we can just please ourselves about such things. We are responsible for the way our eating and drinking influences others. While we have the right to eat or drink what we like, we also have a higher right to never harm another person's faith by the way we use our liberty in Christ. In all these doubtful matters, we are to please our neighbors for their good, to build them up in their love and trust in Christ, and sometimes that will mean refraining from eating or drinking something a fellow Christian thinks is wrong.

Jesus himself is our example for putting others before ourselves, and pleasing others, rather than insisting on our own way. In our relationships in the church, we are to imitate Christ's pattern taught in Mark 10:42–45 and Phil 2:3–5. In fact, the Scriptures were written to teach us endurance and encouragement so we might have hope. Only by cultivating that same endurance and encouragement, will we develop the same attitude as Christ and thereby bring glory to God (15:4–6). The principle of love rather than knowledge is the basis for partnership between all believers, of all cultures. Mature Christlike love transcends both cultural differences, and personal preferences on matters which do not affect the essentials of our Christian faith. When we are busy sharing the good news across a cultural divide, the rule is: "accept one another, then, just as Christ accepted you, in order to bring praise to God" (15:7). Only thus can we fulfill God's great central purpose for humanity: to reach all cultures in mission.

Each New Frontier Becomes the Next Mission Sending Base, Romans 15:8–33

The whole argument in the letter now comes to its climax, although many surveys of Romans miss out these sections entirely.

Two phases of Christ's mission to our world are highlighted. First, that Christ was incarnated in one particular culture—that of the "circumcision," or Jews (15:8a)—so as to demonstrate the truth of God's word and to confirm the promises made to and through the "patriarchs," or Jewish chief leaders (15:8b). Only in this way could Jesus the Messiah fulfill the hopes and expectations of the Jewish nation. Moreover, by faithfully fulfilling all the Jewish expectations, Christ Jesus also made the mercy of God available to peoples of all other cultures, expressed here as the gentiles (15:9).

Each part of the Old Testament (the Law, the Prophets, and the Writings), shows that God has always had both phases in mind, as confirmed by the Old Testament passages quoted in 15:9–12 (see 2 Sam 22:50; Ps 18:49; Deut 32:43; Ps 117:1; Isa 11:10, LXX). The calling of the Jewish patriarchs was always intended for the good of the gentile nations.

Paul then bursts into prayer for his readers (15:13). He is overwhelmed by the wonder of what he has just explained. Prayer for the God of hope to fill us with joy, peace, trust, and overflowing hope through the Holy Spirit is the only appropriate way to respond to such an amazing and unexpected plan and purpose of God.

God limits himself to reveal himself in a particular culture as the fulfillment of the hopes and dreams of that culture, so that he may equip people in that culture to break out of their cultural self-centeredness and reach out in mission to the next culture with the gospel. Initially, Christ worked in this way with the Jews for the peoples of other cultures. Since then, he has worked with various cultures successively, until today we have a global church comprised of multiple cultures. This is God's one and only plan for global mission.

Then the practical intent of the Letter to the Romans is made explicit (15:14–24). As he draws the letter to a close, Paul summarizes how he understands his service, and how he has gone about it, before making his final point. He has been wanting all along to convince the Romans of their part in his plans: "I hope to see you as I travel through (Rome), and *to be sent there (to Spain) with your support* after having enjoyed your company for a while" (15:24, NEB; cf. 1 Cor 16:6, 11; 2 Cor 1:16).

For Paul, gospel proclamation is priestly service (15:14–16). Throughout Old Testament times, and indeed, at many points in the history of the church, service for God has been focused on holy places or church buildings and their upkeep. But here Paul shows that the true priestly work is preaching the gospel to nonbelievers. The only "sacrifices" God desires, now that Christ has given the one, all-sufficient, sacrifice for sin, is to reach out with the good news to those who have not yet responded to it. This is the "acceptable offering" God asks for in our day and age. And the "sanctified" service the Holy Spirit brings to God today is new believers of every culture coming to Christ by faith (15:14–16). This is still the "priestly duty" we are under obligation to fulfill for Christ, as we have seen in each section of the letter.

Paul's mission principles of operating in this priestly service have remained the same since his conversion (15:17–24):

- by word and deed, to lead peoples of other cultures to Christ, with the power of the Spirit confirming his message with signs and wonders
- to fully proclaim the gospel
- from Jerusalem, and right round the north-eastern Mediterranean as far as Illyricum, pushing the frontiers all the way
- now to Rome—as the new center for outreach—with Spain as the next frontier for new mission, after a necessary trip to Jerusalem, for which Paul asks special prayer (see Acts 21:17–28, 31).

Paul has achieved his purpose; he has shown his Roman readers why they, like him, should bother about mission. He has set out his carefully reasoned explanations why Roman Christians, and indeed, the whole church in Rome, should partner with him to make Rome the new mission base for his next outreach to Spain and the islands beyond (like Britain so recently incorporated into the Roman Empire [44 BC]). Roman Christians have the privileged duty of becoming part of God's mission, for they have themselves entered into and are enjoying the transforming reality of the good news of our Lord Jesus Christ.

Conclusion

In the light of Paul's work in his Letter to the Romans, let's pause and recap further on some of the implications of his response to objections to mission. First, *syncretism is out*: All religions do not have saving truth. No doubt all have good insights, some valuable customs, things we ought to learn about interpersonal relationships, perhaps helpful lessons about religious discipline. But only the gospel is God's power bringing salvation. Only the good news of the death and resurrection of Jesus Christ has accomplished the work necessary to make us right with God. He alone brings us into living fellowship with the Lord of the universe (Acts 4:12; John 14:6).

The good news is universal, or global, in its scope and availability, but that does not mean everyone is already saved by their religious sincerity; nor that everyone will eventually be saved. Only those who believe, and receive Christ will be. Humans must make a responsible choice to enjoy salvation. Only when we enter a living relationship with Christ by faith does the potential in the gospel become a reality. Sadly, many people resist or ignore the invitation to receive Jesus and therefore fail to find the life he offers.

Furthermore, *we cannot share the good news only in our own culture and ignore others*. Paul has explained throughout this letter that our obligation is to mission both across the street and around the world. Acts 1:8 describes it as a "both . . . and" responsibility. This is especially important in the present-day "glocalized" world, where global concerns influence every local setting. Our gospel is available equally to both Jews and peoples of other cultures, to "Greeks" and "barbarians." Every cultural group is equally eligible, and equally acceptable to receive God's good news.

In the great central section of Romans, chapters 3–8, which explain Christ's wonderful provision to meet our human needs before God, we find other important answers to more of those original objections. Technological assistance, and voluntary aid and development programs are vital for international relations, but *they are no substitute for the new life only the gospel provides.* To offer the various forms of material assistance without also offering the message of wholeness in Christ is to sell people short and to withhold the one essential reality that can be found in no other way.

Moreover, *only this good news brings fulfillment and purpose to every culture, and satisfies and perfects the deepest longings of every culture* (15:1–11). If missionaries have contributed to the destruction of traditional cultures, they have been contradicting important aspects of their own good news which declares that God welcomes and values peoples of all cultures, and he wants to renew and transform every culture with his life-giving presence and Word.

Now these later chapters, 12–15, have also answered other criticisms. We cannot leave it all to the newer or younger churches, or leave local congregations to evangelize their own people; we must share with them, for the task is given to the church in all cultures. The true nature of the church is never adequately expressed by members of a single culture. *The church is international and intercultural in its very essence.*

And we *should not leave overseas responsibilities until all the needs at home are satisfied.* The global character of our duty must be demonstrated in all mission outreach by the international character of mission teams. The Acts 1:8 "both . . . and" principle gives all Christians both a local and global responsibility.

Indeed, the whole Letter to the Romans drives us back to the key verses at the beginning, 1:14–16. We have no choice; we have the privileged duty; we must make the good news known—for Paul's five major reasons:

- because of what the gospel is and does (1:16–17)
- because of the global reality of God's wrath and our human need (1:18—3:20)
- because of the global answer available only in Christ Jesus (3:21—8:39)
- because of the global way of access to this answer (10:9–17)
- because of the global interdependence of the church in mission (12:1—15:24).

In explaining his obligation and motivation Paul has defined the worldwide purpose of God in mission. What is our response?

Chapter 2

What Do You Mean, Contextualize the Gospel?

LIKE MANY ASPECTS OF Christian experience, we cannot choose whether or not we shall contextualize. We can only choose whether we shall do so well or poorly. We are so much a part of our culture and our world, and contextualization is so much a part of living as Christians in our culture for the sake of our world that we are constantly involved in the contextualization process. The word contextualization may have been newly added to theological jargon, but the activity is dear to the heart of every Christian, whether we realize it or not.[1]

What is Contextualization, and Why Bother about It?

What is it? In essence, contextualization is all that is involved in faithfully applying the word of God in a modern setting. In contextualization we go, with all our culturally acquired assumptions, experience, and agenda, to the Scriptures, with their different cultural background, presuppositions, and priorities. We hear for ourselves the same living message God intended for the first readers, so that we can then go to people in our own or another cultural setting who hold yet another list of expectations and action priorities, and explain the biblical message so that they receive it with the same

1. This chapter develops ideas first published in Hitchen, "Our Approach," 211–21; expanded in presentation form, then reprinted as Hitchen, "Culture and the Bible." Used with the permission of the Melanesian Association of Theological Schools (see bibliography for further details).

impact as it held for the first readers. The task is often described as moving from within our cultural horizon to hear with authenticity the message God spoke within the cultural horizon of the biblical world, so we may in turn present the message with equal authenticity within the cultural horizon of another group of people.[2]

Contextualization, then, is the task of re-presenting in a new cultural context the message of God so that it speaks the same message as originally given in the biblical context. It impinges on, and at least partially embraces, the tasks of biblical understanding (exegesis), interpretation (hermeneutics), translation and explanation (communication), and application (indigenization and inculturation).[3]

This chapter presents an explicitly evangelical approach to contextualization. We see the task as primarily relating the authoritative message of the Christian gospel in the Christian Scriptures into the thought-forms and lifestyles of people within their own cultural settings, taking their culture seriously in the process. We take the authority of Scripture as God's revelation to all humanity as the essential starting point for the contextualization process. Other approaches, notably Catholic and some mainline Protestant, start with the cultural realities as more, or equally, important as sources of truth. They give the Scriptures only relative authority alongside culture, church tradition, human reason, experience, and the social sciences and other disciplines. For some, these may potentially carry equal authority as sources for the contextualization process.[4] But evangelicals start from the conviction that the Scriptures are the primary source of God's revelation and therefore play a central role in all adequate contextualization. We are not presenting a "model" to be followed, but rather are highlighting key principles which should inform whatever approach we may take to the contextualization process.[5]

2. For standard evangelical discussions of the topic, see Thiselton, *Two Horizons*; Carson, *Biblical Interpretation*; Hesselgrave and Rommen, *Contextualization*. For concise introductions, see Padilla, "Interpreted Word," 18–23; Goldsmith, "Contextualization," 18–23; Hesselgrave, "Contextualization of Theology," 294–95; Hiebert, *Anthropological Reflections*, 75–92; Flemming, *Contextualization*; Kraft, *Appropriate Christianity*; Van Rheenen, ed., *Contextualization and Syncretism*; Vanhoozer, "One Rule," 85–126. For an overview of developments to 2010, see Moreau, *Contextualization*.

3. For discussion of initial evangelical fear of the term "contextualization," and its relationship to developing local theologies, see Jacobs, "Contextualisation," 235–44, and Tienou, "Indigenous Theologies," 245–52.

4. See Bevans, *Models*, for the major alternative approaches.

5. Moreau, "Evangelical Models." Moreau identifies various categories, models,

Culture, as we are using the term, is "An integrated system of beliefs . . . of values . . . of customs . . . and of institutions which express these beliefs, values, and customs . . . which binds a society together and gives it a sense of identity, dignity, security, and continuity."[6]

Why bother about contextualization? Our introductory answer is simple: the nature of God's way of salvation demands it.

First-century believers were startled to hear that the gospel was available equally for women and men of all cultures. We have lost this sense of surprise. Paul declares this is the unexpected "mystery" the Holy Spirit had forced upon the reluctant minds of the apostles (Eph 3:1–12). God had, of course, planned it all along. But, despite the many Old Testament allusions, hints, and forthright statements about it, this was a secret Jewish national aspirations were reluctant to acknowledge. For Paul, the "apostle to the peoples of other cultures," however, this was the most radical treasure of the new covenant (Col 1:20–29; Eph 2:11–22). Paul wondered deeply that he should be entrusted to declare this new reality openly. This news powerfully motivated his whole ministry (Eph 3:7–11; 1 Tim 2:3–7; 1 Thess 2:4–13; Rom 1:1–5). Central to the gospel age, then, is this unexpected news that God's word can be received fully by peoples of every different ethnic background (1 Thess 2:13). To grapple with that reality means contextualizing.

As Paul concludes his great mission manifesto in Romans, this theme forms his climax (Rom 15:7–17). God's Christ came to serve one distinct cultural group: "the circumcision" or Jews. To serve God's truth this was essential. God's truth always operates in the real world of particular cultures, not in some virtual or Platonic "ideal" realm. Only thus could God's longstanding purposes and promises be fulfilled. These promises, likewise, were firmly earthed in the cultural history of the "Fathers" of this same ethnic group (15:8). Yet the whole purpose of this specific inculturation amongst the Hebrew/Jewish people was so that this good news could impact the whole world. This was the only way "the peoples of other cultures," the gentiles, could discover and respond to God's mercy (15:9). This cultural particularity focusing on the needs and heritage of the Jews became God's means for blessing all other cultures. Every strand of Hebrew culture's literature—law, history, poetry, and prophecy—testified that God had

and approaches to contextualization by evangelicals. In this chapter, Moreau more helpfully introduces the varieties of contextualization, than in his more methodologically restricted 2012 volume cited above.

6. Lausanne Movement, *Willowbank Report*, 7.

always intended to bless all nations by this means of choosing one of them (15:9–12). These are the classic foundations for contextualization. God chose to work out our salvation within the time-space realm of planet earth; therefore, commencing from the Jewish nation, we must exegete, interpret, translate, communicate, and apply his word in all the diverse languages and cultures of our globe.[7]

God's purposes for our age culminate in penetrating hearts and minds globally, in all the world's diverse cultures. The biblical message, the gospel, belongs to every culture. This gospel is eminently translatable into every culture. In fact, as we shall see, this great news is incompletely grasped and lived without this intercultural dimension. Contextualization is an essential response to these realities of our faith.

This chapter considers *key principles or factors in evangelical contextualization* under three headings: grasping the cultural factors in contextualization; upholding the biblical truth factors in contextualization; and working for an appropriate interface between culture and biblical truth for contextualized church life, evangelism, and discipleship.

Grasping the Cultural Factors in Contextualization

Human cultures, from their trivial outer forms to the attitudes underlying each worldview, are the first part of our contextualization formula. The Christian message takes cultural settings seriously. We need a *Christian theology of culture* to become effective in contextualization. The following assumptions about culture should inform us as we contextualize:

i. *Christians accept and respect cultures as part of God's original intention for humanity because the Scriptures trace the source of human cultures back to God himself.*

Genesis 1–2 lay two firm foundations for developing human cultures. First, our distinctive capacities as creatures made in the image of God are the basic source of human culture (Gen 1:26–27). Created like the living God as his representatives within the created order, our distinctly human intellectual, communication, social, spiritual, and moral competencies are all culture-producing abilities. Second, God's original commands to the first humans, Gen 1:28–31 and 2:15–20, are culture-producing commands,

7. We have made this point using Rom 15:7–17. We could have equally well used the only slightly different language of Gal 3:7–14, 22–29, as we do in chapter 5.

rightly referred to as our "cultural mandate." Encapsulated in these commands we find humans are responsible for family and societal life (be fruitful and multiply); responsible for exploring, understanding, and mastering, developing, utilizing, and conserving the resources of our universe as a trust from God for the good of our fellow humans; and responsible for accountable evaluation and choice in both the moral and spiritual realms. These responsibilities are fulfilled in and through our culture-producing behaviors. These cultural capacities and God's original intention for them antedate the first human sin, the fall, as we call it in theology (Gen 2:15–25). These cultural capacities are at the heart of what God pronounced "very good" as he surveyed his original creation (Gen 1:31). We respect cultures as the expression of God's good intentions for humanity from the first.

ii. *God oversees the historical development of the cultures of the nations.*

Not only as Creator, but also as Lord of history, God himself supervises the destinies and affairs of every ethnic group (Acts 17:24–28; 1 Sam 2:2–10; Jer 12:14–17). Though not always in the foreground of the biblical story, God's intentions of blessing all the families of humanity are always at the foundation of the biblical narrative. The "God blessed them . . ." of Gen 1:28, becomes, "all peoples on earth will be blessed through you," in Gen 12:3 as the focus turns to the specific story of the descendants of Abraham.[8] The New Testament age bursts into life with a spectacular celebration of praise from all the accessible cultures of the day (Acts 2:1–12). This gospel interest in the diverse settings of ethnic groups sets Christianity apart from other world religions.[9]

iii. *God honors human cultures by the incarnation of his Son.*

When God chose to reveal himself in history, he confirmed the importance of human cultures for eternity. God did not shout his message from the distance by some intergalactic sonic "Boom!" He came in person into an ordinary human setting—born of woman, born under the law. Thereby he gave dignity and value to our human scene—to human cultures. Moreover, Jesus Christ tied proper understanding of his salvation to the particular culture into which he was born—that of a Jewish woman, living under Jewish law. This one culture is set apart from others, "for salvation

8. Cf. the "so that" of Ps 67:1–2.

9. Sanneh, *Translating the Message*, 7–8, 211–34, makes this point in contrast to Islam.

is of the Jews." Hebrew salvation-history is made normative and authoritative for defining all valid salvation experience (John 4:22; Acts 4:12). The incarnation made Jewish biblical culture of distinctive importance for all time. But, as we have seen from Rom 15, that was not the end of the story.

iv. *God's purpose is to transform all cultures and enable each to flourish in Christ.*

God cares about every people group, and longs to bring each one to fulfillment. As noted in our introduction, when Christ came into this world, he was born within "the circumcision"—the Hebrew people—a specific historical people group (Gal 4:4). This historical particularity was for a dual purpose: to serve the Jews and to fulfill the promises made to them as a particular people (Rom 15:8); but also to set a pattern for all other cultures. As Rom 15:9 declares: Christ came "in order that the peoples of other cultures may glorify God for his mercy" (Rom 15: 9). Through this "mystery of the gospel," offered first to Jews, God exalts cultural plurality by way of historical particularity. Following the Old Testament preparation, by showing clearly in Jesus's Jewish home in Nazareth that one culture matters to him, God demonstrated, beyond the cross and Pentecost, that every culture matters to him. Our task in contextualization is to give similar honor to all cultures.

v. *In Christ each gospel-receiving culture's life and heritage is purified and fulfilled.*

"Christ among you"—you peoples of other cultures—is the hope of glory for Christians of every culture (Col 1:27). Jesus alone is the "Messiah"—or answer to the deepest cultural longings—not just for the Jews, but for every people group (John 4:42; 12:32; 1 John 4:13–15). As "Son of Man," Christ Jesus offers fulfillment for all human aspirations. Renewed members of every tribe, linguistic group, people, and culture will not only be present in the final glorious kingdom, they will each contribute something distinctive to its splendor (Rev 5:9–10; 7:9; 21:24).

Here and now, too, Christ transforms each culture he invades. He reproduces the pattern of the incarnation:

> When God became man, Christ took flesh in a particular family, members of a particular nation, with the tradition of customs associated with that nation. All that was not evil he sanctified. Wherever he is taken by men in any time and place he takes that

> nationality, that society, that "culture," and sanctifies all that is capable of sanctification by his presence . . .[10]

Not that this process takes place easily:

> . . . that society never existed, in East or West, ancient time or modern, which could absorb the word of Christ painlessly into its system. Jesus within Jewish culture, Paul within Hellenistic culture, take it for granted that there will be rubs and frictions—not from the adoption of a new culture, but from the transformation of the mind towards that of Christ.[11]

Developing this refined cultural "mind" is the focus of much of Paul's instruction. We suggest it is also the real testing ground of effective contextualization today (Rom 12:2–8; Phil 2:5–11; Eph 4:17–24).

vi. *In Christ, we receive and participate in a new "adoptive" cultural heritage.*

Here is a distinctly new aspect to the impact of the gospel upon a Christian's culture. God makes believers of all nations heirs of Hebrew salvation-history through Christ. Again, Andrew Walls puts it lucidly:

> . . . The Christian is given an adoptive past. He is linked to the people of God in all generations (like him [or her], members of the faith family), and most strangely of all, to the whole history of Israel, the curious continuity of the race of the faithful from Abraham . . . all Christians of whatever nationality, are landed by adoption with several millennia of someone else's history, with a whole set of ideas, concepts and assumptions which do not necessarily square with the rest of their cultural inheritance; and the Church in every land, of whatever race and type of society, has this same adoptive past by which it needs to interpret the fundamentals of the faith.[12]

When contextualizing the gospel, then, every cultural group has in this biblical heritage, an abiding standard and "reference point" to continually inform and enrich the process of cultural transformation. But that does not make the Christian community merely backward looking or conservative.

vii. *In Christ, each culture is liberated for global impact and destiny.*

10. Walls, "Gospel as Prisoner," 44; republished in Walls, *Missionary Movement*, 3–15. The paragraph cited is omitted in the republished version.

11. Walls, "Gospel as Prisoner," 45.

12. Walls, "Gospel as Prisoner," 45.

The process Rom 15 described for the Jews is repeated in every culture invaded by the gospel. Christ breaks in to fulfill the deepest longings of that particular culture, so that, in its turn, that culture can make its contribution to the "blessing" of all nations. Nothing less can satisfy the implications of Jesus's parting words: "As the Father has sent me, so I send you . . ." (John 20:21). Every nation receives a share in the global responsibility. Even spirit powers look on to learn from this expression of the unconfined wisdom of God (Eph 3:10). It is expressed in each successive culture as its people make Christ their Lord, and he renews their own cultural customs and practices, and then they reach out through their own culture to enrich others also.

The New Testament, then, building on the universal expectations embedded in the Old Testament, and confirming thereby the importance of the Old Testament for Christian maturity, calls us to grasp the high value God gives to the diverse cultures of our globe.

Culture Is an Ever-Present Limiting Factor in Adequate Contextualization

i. *All cultures have been spoiled by human sin.*

God's original intention has been damaged and spoiled. The apostle Paul trenchantly analyzes contemporary cultures in Rom 1:18–32. All human cultures are characterized by godlessness or secularity. All lack uprightness. This distortion in their cultural habits and customs suppresses God's truth (Rom 1:18). Paul traces this tragic reality to a threefold root which produces an inevitable regression in cultural lifestyles. The root causes of cultural degradation are, first, we humans reject or ignore the truth about God accessible within the world around us. Second, in consequence we refuse to acknowledge God or give him his due place in our human thought and value systems. Third, in our proud ingratitude we do not thank God for his abundant provisions for us as his creatures (Rom 1:19–21a). These roots necessarily invite God's judgment (1:18). This threefold turning away from God at the same time leads all cultures into a pattern of increasing steps into secularism. These interrelated and inevitable stages involve becoming deluded in our minds and values because we exclude the Godward dimensions and leave human thought earthbound—reductionist and lightweight (vv. 21b, 22, 25a). This leaves us with only *substitute gods*. We favor nonpersonal quests for material creatures or things, rather than mature personal relationships with the living Lord of the universe (vv. 23, 25b). Such alternative worship leads on to perverted desires and improper use of our bodies. As a result, we exploit women and develop sexually distorted societies (vv. 24, 26–27). This in turn, opens the floodgates to pervasive corrupt conduct permeating our lifestyles, entertainments, and leisure pursuits (vv. 28–30). Finally, the pattern results in open rebellion against right behavior, with flagrant denial of moral absolutes and public acceptance of standards God condemns (v. 32). When cultures no longer know when to blush, they are in serious trouble indeed.

Romans 2 gives a similarly devastating analysis of the way even deeply religious cultures, like the Jews, pursued a parallel regression. They allowed growing space for the same roots as they too rejected available further knowledge of God, refused to give proper place to the fuller revelation in Christ, and allowed gratitude to give way to presumption (2:1–29). In the analyses of Rom 1 and 2, all human cultures fall short of God's requirements. All humans need a transforming salvation.

Thus, in the Christian view, cultures receive both the highest, and the lowest possible assessment. Cultures are inherently capable of expressing the goodness of godlike capacities—for we are all made in God's likeness. But inevitably we reflect the awful tragedy of entrenched sinfulness. Good contextualization attempts to be true both to the potentially great, but only partially realized good, and to be alert to the distorted and twisted characteristics present in every human culture.[13]

ii. *Our cultural presuppositions are so all-pervasive they influence all we do when contextualizing.*

It usually takes an extended cross-cultural exposure to reveal our own cultural biases. Christian anthropologists helpfully describe how our own culture shapes our perceptions of other cultures and even influences the way we read the Scriptures. Alan Tippett describes how culture distorts our perceptions by his "theory of parallaxis."[14] Our attitudes towards our own and the other culture; our historical perspective; our part in promoting a cause; the role or function of our missional activities; our professional

13. We could continue to explore how this ambiguity about culture is evident in the terms used to refer to human cultures in the Scriptures, such as "the world." God loved the world so much he sent his Son for its salvation; but we are not to love the world, since its secularized ways so easily corrupt our motivation and values (John 3:16; 1 John 4:9, 14; 2:15–17; and elsewhere).

14. Tippett, "Parallaxis," 91–151.

standing; and our own perceptions of ourselves, all skew the way we perceive and respond to other cultures. Tippett shows factors like these carry either negative or positive influences. As we seek to pass on biblical truth across the cultural horizon of our own society, then, we are liable to distort both the original intention of the Scriptures and the responses of those we serve, because these usually unconscious, culturally determined attitudes govern our actions.[15]

This domineering influence of our own culture comes to its most sensitive expression in the universally present tendency to be ethnocentric as we approach other cultures. We all have a tendency to assume that our own ways of thinking, acting, and doing things are not only right, but also the best for others, too. This is not only true for people from a Western European background. In several Papua New Guinean languages their local tribal name is simply their vernacular word for saying "we are the people." By implication, all other tribes are not truly people in the way their tribe is! Hence, ethnocentrism is an occupational hazard in the contextualization process for all of us. Particularly when we are bringing a life-giving message to people of another culture, we readily assume the way our culture has responded to the gospel, and the way we apply biblical teachings are the right and preferred ways for all people to respond to the teachings of Scripture. Some aspects of human experience are genuinely universal and there are some biblical absolutes that need to be obeyed in directly comparable ways in all cultures. But there are many more aspects of Scripture which can be, and need to be, expressed and applied differently, if they are to carry the same importance and relevance in another culture. Patterns of decision-making, how we express the fruit of the Spirit, how to work out the commands to love and to lead as servants, to mention just a few areas of biblical teaching, can all be expressed in a wide variety of culturally authentic, but different, ways in different cultures. So, we must recognize this tendency

15. David Hesselgrave and Edward Rommen broaden the list of cultural factors affecting contextualization in their "seven-dimension paradigm" which includes: worldviews—ways of viewing the world; cognitive processes—ways of thinking; linguistic forms—ways of expressing ideas; behavioral patterns—ways of acting; communication media—ways of channelling the message; social structures—ways of interacting; and motivational sources—ways of deciding. Hesselgrave and Rommen, *Contextualization*, 203–11. See my further exploration of how cultural presuppositions influence our missionary thinking in Hitchen, "Cross-Cultural Communication," 25–37.

to expect others to express their faith and values in our own, ethnocentric ways, and guard against it, whenever we cross cultural boundaries.[16]

Given such all-pervasive cultural influences, it is little wonder that when contextualizing the biblical message, *culture tends to narrow selectively where Scripture broadens and diversifies.* For example, our culture predisposes Westerners to prefer particular modes of thought where scriptural revelation comes through many such modes. As Westerners we are assured about the vital importance of propositional teaching for a clear grasp of biblical truth. As heirs of Greek thought, it could hardly be otherwise. But we Westerners are much less sure about the authoritative importance of allegory or parable. Historical narrative is acceptable to us, but with caution; we are not too happy about the way Paul or the writer to Hebrews used it in passages like Gal 4:21–31, or Heb 4:1–11. Biography is permissible as revelation, for we quickly identify with David or Joseph and his brothers. But Qoheleth's wisdom, the singer's love song, and some poetry—especially the imprecatory kind—leave us Westerners rather unhappy about the imprecision—to our minds—of their teachings.

But then, I had no answer when our Melanesian students asked why we did not teach the Proverbs as initial tools for pre-evangelism in their proverb-rich, oral society. I remember well being the only one in a congregation of sixty who needed an explanation of the neo-Melanesian parable following the communion in a Sepik (Northwest PNG) service. Only a dumb European would not realize that the dramatic exhortation to prune the coffee trees that week was a reminder that the special offering was due next Sunday. There had been no reference to an offering, but the imagery of tending the trees for the sake of a good harvest had been enough to make the point for their image-rich oral thought patterns.

Only an international breadth of theological input will keep our contextualization from the ever-present tendency for our own culture to limit our perspective.[17]

16. Charles Kraft has a helpful discussion of the way ethnocentrism and monocultural attitudes influence us in Christian service in *Anthropology*, 70–72, 81–84.

17. For just two African examples of pleas for such non-Western input to theology, see Bediako, "Holy Spirit," 45; and Tienou, "Christian Theology," 37–51.

Cultures Are Always Integral to Experiencing and Understanding Truth

God's way of honoring cultures makes them indispensable for our understanding of his message, despite their weaknesses and distortions.

i. *We can never express truth in a purely "supracultural" form.*

It is fruitless to attempt to state the "supracultural" aspects of the gospel by isolating the divine kernel from the cultural husk. As soon as we express any aspect of God's truth, we do so by cultural means—our thought patterns and language. As Martin Goldsmith puts it:

> . . . all theology is contextual. It must be, for all of us interpret the Bible through the spectacles of our philosophical background. And we then express our beliefs within the framework of those terms . . . All theology throughout history has been expressed within the context of current religious and philosophical movements. This contextualization inevitably adds to or subtracts from the biblical revelation.[18]

We Westerners need to accept that our theology is as much a "local theology," shaped and limited by our Western cultural background and context, as any theology coming from any other part of the world. The idea that any one cultural group writes *the* universal theology is simply wrong. God's message always comes to us in the wrappings of a particular cultural form and language. There is no such thing as "the biblical culture" which we simply announce in another culture. We have unchanging, abiding seeds of the gospel message and the abiding revelation of God in Christ in the written Scriptures. But these always have to be planted and nurtured in and through the processes of translation and contextualization using the languages, thought-forms, habits, ideas, and lifestyles of each local culture.

ii. *Cross-cultural awareness and experience confirm and clarify truth.*

Moving across a cultural boundary to live for a period, often opens our minds to fresh aspects of biblical meaning previously unrealized. Take this list of some of the "non-Western" cultural understandings and related aspects of Scripture we discovered in Melanesia, of which we had been only dimly aware previously, in our own culture:

18. Goldsmith, "Contextualization," 20–21.

- Unseen forces are involved in everyday life, and Christ's role includes being cosmic ruler and upholder of both nature and spirit powers (Col 1:16–18).
- Ancestors are involved continually in ongoing tribal life, and previous generations of believers interact with us and we depend on them (Heb 11:39–40; 12:22–24).
- Time and the future are understood quite differently from Western ideas of history and lineal progress.
- Religion is the integrating factor for the whole of life, not a one-day-a-week ritual.
- Personal value and righteousness are understood in terms of our value to the tribe and in maintaining tribal obligations, and virtually every ethical command in Paul's writings is communal in its nature and intent.
- Spirit forces intervene directly in the natural world, so we need take no interest in secondary causes.
- Preliterate societies expect both the word and the Spirit always to interrelate with each other.

The cross-cultural journey also threw fresh light on various teachings we thought we knew well, and highlighted aspects of Scripture which had seemed of little importance in Western society.[19] Thus, in Papua New Guinea aspects of biblical truths came alive in ways we had never grasped in our previous Bible college training in New Zealand. We need cross-cultural insights to more fully, and more adequately, grasp God's word. As René Padilla puts it:

> Every culture possesses positive elements, favourable to the understanding of the Gospel . . . every culture makes possible a certain approach to the Gospel that brings to light certain salient aspects that in other cultures may have remained less visible or even hidden. Seen from this perspective . . . cultural differences . . . serve as channels of expression of aspects of the truth of the

19. For instance: the present implications of our future hope; the importance of a doctrine of work and manual labor for human dignity; the creation ordinances governing economic development and ecological concerns; the implications of all humans being made in the image of God for racial and "payback" (retaliation) issues; and the importance of land and inheritance for God's people.

> Gospel, aspects that a theology tied down to one particular culture can easily overlook.[20]

iii. *Contextualizing the gospel across cultural boundaries brings a "boomerang effect" back to the missionary-sending community.*

Missionaries almost inevitably return to their sending church with uncomfortable questions about how adequately their home church grasps truth. When Paul returned to Antioch with his "lessons from the frontier" of mission in Galatia he had a newly focused perception of the essence of the gospel. It brings a new relationship both with our living God and with people of other cultures who trust in him. This caused a public confrontation with the monocultural teachers dominating the Antioch church (Acts 14–15; Gal 2). The different roles of Antioch and Jerusalem from this point in Acts confirm that diverse cultural awareness is crucial for us to adequately transmit, or contextualize, the biblical message. Today, the churches of the West stand at a similar point. The focal center of global Christianity has moved from its previous Western homelands to Africa, Asia, South America, and the Pacific.[21] If we Western Christians fail to heed the questions asked and criticisms made of us by those on the new frontiers—questions about such things as our affluence, our individualism, our rationalism, the skepticism with which we approach the Bible, the unbiblical confidence we place in nuclear families—then our candle may be removed from its lampstand as happened to the Jerusalem church as it drew back from cross-cultural openness in the first century.

Cultural diversity enriches contextualization because it is only "with all the saints" that we discover the "length, breadth, height and depth" of truth (Eph 3:17–19). Power to grasp the depths of biblical meaning is limited for isolated believers. We need each other in order to adequately understand Scripture. And if we need the ministry of others for our spiritual perception in the local arena, it is equally true globally. As the Lausanne Covenant puts it, the Spirit ". . . illumines the minds of God's people in every culture to perceive [the Scripture's] truth fresh through their own

20. Padilla, *Contextualization*, 4–5.

21. Andrew F. Walls has most consistently explained and developed the implications of this in his various articles published since the 1970s, e.g., "Culture and Coherence," 214–25, now collected in Walls, *Missionary Movement*, 16–25.

eyes and thus discloses to the whole church ever more of the many coloured wisdom of God."[22]

We need both the "teaching and admonishing of one another" within our own cultural group, and the challenge, warning, and correction of insights into truth from other cultural backgrounds. Only thus can we grasp the fullness of God's word. Thankfully, we need not despair:

> . . . since none of us can read the Scriptures without cultural blinkers of some sort, the great advantage, the crowning excitement which our own era of Church history has over all others is the possibility that we may be able to read them together. Never before has the Church looked so much like the great multitude whom no man can number out of every nation and tribe and people and tongue. Never before, therefore, has there been so much potentiality for mutual enrichment and self-criticism, as God causes yet more light and truth to break forth from His word.[23]

Culture, then, looms large in "making fully known" God's word (Col 1:25–29). We must rightly appreciate culture to rightly contextualize biblical truth. We are entitled to utilize culture with enthusiasm, with humility, and with discernment as we approach the contextualization task. But there are other factors to keep in balance too.

Upholding the Biblical Truth Factor in Contextualizing

If a Christian theology of culture is essential for proper contextualizing, so too is a proper way of understanding and reading the truth of God's word. We need to read the Scriptures missionally. Our understanding of the nature of God's truth—as authoritative revelation through the Scriptures by the Spirit for the sake of others as well as ourselves—provides the other regulative and dynamic factor in adequate contextualization.

God's Truth Is Always Greater than Our Best Grasp of It

God himself, his purposes in creation, the human predicament, and Christ's work for our redemption are all too great to convey adequately in any one

22. Lausanne Covenant, para. 2, in Douglas, *Let the Earth*, 3.

23. Walls, "Gospel as Prisoner," 51, reprinted in Walls, *Missionary Movement*, 15.

formulation. Our human minds cannot hold together at one time any more than a very small part of the whole truth.

i. *Since God is one and infinite, this is inevitable.*

By definition, God is beyond human grasp. He is the sum of all his attributes, and more, yet we are obliged to consider only one aspect of his wholeness at a time. Human language, human experience, our restriction within the time/space continuum, let alone the impairment of our faculties by sin, all force us to take a piecemeal approach to knowing God. When contextualizing, the danger is that we forget we are only human and assume greater competence than we can attain. Henry Robert Reynolds, principal of the Congregationalist Cheshunt College, in Hertfordshire, England, through the latter part of the nineteenth century, highlighted the inherent danger:

> We must admit that every element of the glory of Christ is so absolute, so perfect in itself, so absorbing, so engrossing, so beneficent, that if it beams or glances on the soul, it conveys the impression—which may turn out to be no other than an illusion—that it is the *whole* revelation, the fullness of Him that filleth all in all . . . [thus we need to ask ourselves] whether the one colour of the million-hued bow of promise in which [we] find so much is the whole of the one living Christ, and whether [we] have not much to learn . . . from those who are analogously led to believe that they too have, alas! the entire glory of God beaming through another chink of the curtain which conceals the Holiest of all.[24]

ii. *When contextualizing, then, we must recognise God's truth is always many-sided.*

We too quickly grasp one aspect of truth which has impressed us as if it is the sum total of truth. The Scriptures present every central doctrine in a range of ways.

At first glance, "Christ died for our sins according to the Scriptures," may seem self-evidently clear in its meaning. But the reality is so vast that the Scriptures give a wide range of explanations of the inherent meaning of both Christ's death and our sin. Scriptures draw on a wide range of common human experience for terms to explain the *work of Christ* in his death at Calvary:

24. Reynolds, "Heno-Christianity," 325, 341.

- The language and rituals of temple worship and the common human experience of animal sacrifice provide the conceptual background explaining Christ's death as his work as high priest and as our expiatory and propitiatory sacrifice.
- Human familial, emotional, and social yearnings for understanding, acceptance, belonging, and for trustworthy friends, provide the ideas explaining Christ's death as the ultimate expression of the love of God.
- The commercial language and transactional experience of the marketplace inform the metaphor of Christ's death "redeeming" us.
- Interpersonal relationships, international political relationships, battles and conflict, and our sense of shame and lapses in loyalty lie behind the reconciliation terms explaining Christ's work at the cross as mediator.
- We go to the law courts to appreciate the legal terminology explaining Christ's death as justifying the believer.
- Binding international treaties, human contracts and wills, and upholding formally enacted political commitments lie behind our descriptions of Christ's death initiating the new covenant or inaugurating the new age.
- Our ubiquitous human awareness of sickness, danger, and captivity comprise the conceptual background when we announce that Christ died as our Savior to restore us to the wholeness of salvation.

No one of these explanations is adequate in itself, but each is true according to the Scriptures. And this list is certainly not exhaustive! The reality is so deep, wide, and extensive, a range of explanatory metaphors are essential to make clear what Christ Jesus achieved through his death and resurrection.[25]

Likewise, in the Scriptures the following nine metaphors (amongst others) describe the nature of sin: missing the mark; iniquity or wrongdoing; lawlessness or rebellion; transgression; evil or wickedness; desire, lust, or passion; disobedience; ungodliness; and trespass. Moreover, each of the Ten Commandments gives further specific illustrations of the nature of sin.

So we could go on with each central doctrine of the faith. At least twenty different names or titles describe Satan's nature in the pictorial

25. For further discussion of the terminology and metaphors used in Scripture to convey the gospel message, see chapter 3.

language of metaphors, or consider the wide-ranging terminology used for other aspects of the doctrine of evil.[26] Or, again, consider the various New Testament pictures of the church as: the body, the bride, the branches of the vine, the army of God, the pilgrim people, the household or family of God, the living temple of God, the kingdom of priests, and so on.[27]

The "many-sided wisdom of God" (Eph 3:10) keeps the contextualizer humble when offering each necessarily partial explanation of such huge themes. Appreciating and utilizing this diversity of metaphors explaining all the key truths of the gospel becomes crucial in contextualizing, as we shall illustrate.

iii. *The nature of truth as "seed" requires diverse "soils" in which to display its fullness.*

Building on Christ's common use of the seed-sowing/plant-producing metaphor (e.g., Matt 13:1–23, 31–32), Paul highlights the way the message of grace had been contextualized amongst the Colossians of Asia just as amongst other peoples around the then-known world (Col 1:5–6; 2:6). He enlarges on the same theme as he further develops the "fruit-bearing" imagery of Gal 5–6 and Eph 5.

iv. *This nature of truth also means the Spirit always has more light to break forth from the word of God.*

The living presence of the author of Scripture in the person of the Spirit of God gives biblical truth a dynamic quality. The prophets, even in their heights of conscious inspiration, were aware of their own only partial grasp of the depths of the divine message birthed through their own frail experience (1 Pet 1:10–12). The Reformers, and, when they faltered in their consistency, their stepchildren the Anabaptists, were ready to give their lives for this insight about God's truth. Contextualization challenges us to apply these insights again at the cultural frontier. For evangelicals this confidence in the Scriptures as Spirit-breathed, plus our conviction of the

26. Note the range of terms for spirit beings: e.g., angels, demons, evil spirits, elemental spirits of the universe, spiritual hosts of wickedness; for the wide range of other powers which dominate humans—e.g., principalities and powers, authorities, thrones, rules, world rulers of this present darkness, death; for the teachings which enslave—e.g., doctrines of demons, the course of this world, philosophy and empty deceit; and for evil people who become the tools of the evil one—e.g., sorcerers, magicians, diviners, soothsayers, mediums, false prophets.

27. Cf. Hitchen, *Work of the Church*.

abiding presence of the same active Spirit, brings a creativity to our humility as we cross cultural divides holding forth the word of life. We can never know what the Spirit may yet choose to bring out from this treasure store of his word.

God's Truth Is Universally Applicable and Can Be Known in Truth in Every Culture

The wonder for the New Testament writers is that Christ belongs in every culture.

Lamin Sanneh highlighted one aspect of this truth by stressing Christianity's "translatability":

> Christianity is remarkable for the relative ease with which it enters living cultures. In becoming translatable it renders itself compatible with all cultures. It may be welcomed or resisted in its Western garb, but it is not uncongenial in other garb. Christianity broke free from its absolutized Judaic frame and, through a radical pluralism, adopted the Hellenic culture . . .[28]

That pattern has continued as the story of the Christian mission. Our Christian message rejoices in "a radical pluralism"[29] in that every culture is equally acceptable to God as a setting in which his truth can be received and obeyed.

i. *The Bible uses what we can call "transcultural metaphors" or "word pictures" to define almost all the central ideas of the faith.*

This feature ensures the universal relevance of Scripture in diverse cultures. We have touched on this in highlighting the many-sided nature of God's truth. But it stands out yet more clearly in cross-cultural settings. For example, each word picture Jesus uses in John's Gospel to describe himself is part of the ordinary experience of peoples worldwide.[30] This is

28. Sanneh, *Translating the Gospel*, 50. Andrew Walls develops this insight in *Missionary Movement*, 26–42.

29. The terms "pluralism," "pluralist," and other words from the same root are used in a range of different and sometimes conflicting ways. Lesslie Newbigin has a helpful paragraph suggesting better ways to distinguish and use the word group in *Pluralist Society*, 14.

30. Think, e.g., of "bread," "door," "way," "light," "resurrection," "vine," "living water," and even "shepherd." These are either universal experiences or refer to particulars which

also true of the key theological terms of the New Testament letters. As we have shown, "redemption" is a common marketplace or commerce term; "justify" belongs to the worldwide experience of law courts; and "expiation and sacrifice" may not be universal, but the need for appeasement to which they speak is a universal human need.

Some specific theological words or concepts may not be found in each culture. But the background of ideas, or life experiences, of the great majority of these theological metaphors are found universally. By using a range of transculturally meaningful metaphors to explain the many-sided truth of the facts of our salvation in the Scriptures, God the Holy Spirit has opened ways for us to contextualize these truths into local cultures by using the common human experiences to which the metaphors refer.

Every culture, then, offers a valid context for authentic experience of truth. The constrictions of our humanity—particularly our sinful humanity—mean our understanding is at best partial. But it is nonetheless valid. By his gift of speech and language, and by our creation in his own likeness, God has made humans capable of personal, intimate, and real experience of him, whatever our culture.

By God's gift of his self-revealing word in forms and language we can understand, we can also distinguish truth from counterfeit and error. Ensuring local terms and illustrations correspond with the meaning and semantic range of the biblical metaphors is another safeguard against syncretistic dilution of the gospel message in any particular cultural setting.

God's Truth Has Been Definitively "Incarnated" in Culture

God exalts cultures by linking his truth inseparably to human settings. We are not left to grope in the dark or merely make "guesses about God."[31]

i. *The distinctive and authoritatively definitive features of human salvation and how to receive it have been set out in the Scriptures.*

In the prophets, in the apostles, and supremely in Jesus Christ, God's abiding truth has been distilled and spelled out in human terms for sinful, faltering women and men to see, read, and receive in language and

---

have cultural equivalents around the world.

31. William Barclay's *Daily Study Bible* term for the confused ideas circulating at Colossae.

thought-forms which are too clear for us ever to claim ignorance again (Heb 1:1; 2:1–4).

The ultimate expression of truth capable of comprehension by culture-bound humans comes in Jesus Christ. The very glory of God shines from the face of Jesus for those whose reason has been sufficiently healed by faith to recognize him (2 Cor 4:4–6). This uniqueness of Christ is set forth in his relationship to every aspect of culture and reality in central New Testament christological passages. He alone is Lord over the physical universe, the revelatory process, the needy realm of morally corrupt creatures, the new order of salvaged rejects in the church, the universal control center of God, the ultimate Majesty, and even the spirit world of angelic beings, according to Heb 1:1–4 and Col 1:16–18. These declarations are nonnegotiable. Jesus Christ alone is Lord in this culturally and religiously pluralistic world (1 Cor 8:5–7). His uniqueness as a person leads necessarily into the uniqueness of his gospel. Paul's clearest discourse on the issues at stake in contextualization—the Galatian letter—begins defiantly and unashamedly with the declaration that there is one and only one gospel: the gospel preached and recorded definitively by the apostles.

If that was the emphasis in one of Paul's earliest letters, the same conviction rings equally clearly in the last recorded writings of the apostles. Peter's authoritative provision for true understanding after his death is his, and his fellow apostle's, letters, not some human lineage (2 Pet 1:15; 3:1–2, 14–18). For John, likewise, truth enlivened by the anointing of the Spirit is recognizable as we hear and heed the apostles' testimony (1 John 2:18–27; 4:1–6). For Paul, too, the standard of truth is still "the preaching entrusted to me," and now entrusted to the next generation as a "good deposit" to be guarded and "continued in" (Titus 1:1–3; 2 Tim 1:13–14). In fact, Paul has at least the next three generations in mind as he hands on this abiding reservoir of Spirit-protected teaching (2 Tim 1:14; 2:2).[32] Here, then, in the Scriptures is normative teaching for global contextualization.

ii. *Our task is to discern both the authoritative and the exemplary aspects of apostolic teaching.*

Since truth has been deposited and experienced in this way, we are responsible to distinguish between the abiding principle of God-given Scripture, and its cultural form of expression as we relate it to modern contexts. There are no simple rules for such discernment. We can only, in our final

32. See chapter 9, on transition planning and generational change.

section, lay some basic foundations and illustrate their application for such contextualization. But, in doing so, we take seriously our duty to read the Scriptures as they were intended: as the Word breathed out by God himself to equip us for every good work as we serve one another in our global community (2 Tim 3:16–17).

Appropriate Interface between Culture and Biblical Truth for Contextualized Evangelism and Discipleship

Contextualization, then, involves bringing together these two factors: culture and biblical truth. We integrate a respectful Christian theology of culture and the written word of God read and understood missionally as we contextualize. We apply these contextualization principles both in our initial evangelistic contacts and in leading believers on to maturity in fruitful discipleship. The following interrelationships make for faithful contextualization.

i. *Culture identifies the most relevant starting points for contextualizing biblical truth.*

As we saw when noting the many-sidedness of God's truth, God has not limited himself to one "biblical analogy," or "redemptive analogy."[33] Rather, by employing a range of "transcultural metaphors" (our term) God declares the holistic, rich truth of our salvation.[34]

Therefore, different aspects of truth suit different people groups and worldviews as relevant starting points for an encounter with Christ and understanding truth. The life values and basic assumptions of different peoples mean that different terminology explaining the gospel will have varying appeal and challenge. Some biblical terms will have immediate relevance to the values and attitudes of one culture, while others, at first, may appear strangely foreign.

The metaphors or word pictures explaining the cross as victory over spirit forces (the redemption word group) will provide an important point for initial evangelism and a focal point for growth amongst people who live

33. Dye, *Bible Translation Strategy*, 125–29; Richardson, *Peace Child*, 329.

34. C. H. Kraft deals in part with the same kind of idea in his threefold division of Bible teachings into the three levels of "Basic Ideals," "General Principles," and "Specific Cultural Forms." What I am calling transcultural metaphors fit into the first two of Kraft's categories. Kraft, *Christianity and Culture*, 139–43.

in fear of spirit powers. Amongst a society such as our New Zealand Māori, who emphasize the extended family and its mutual obligations, the church as the family of God will provide a good starting point in discussing the people of God.

Wayne Dye shows the importance of this insight for focusing on relevant sins.[35] Don Richardson's *Peace Child* is a good example of how the transcultural word pictures of reconciliation and mediator were already a traditional religious focal point amongst the Sawi people of West Papua.[36]

This aspect of contextualization is not new. On Saturday June 18, 1910, at the World Missionary Conference in Edinburgh, as Johannes Warneck, the great German mission administrator and theorist, concluded his comments during the discussion of the *Report of Commission IV* on "The Missionary Message in Relation to Non-Christian Religions," he stated:

> It is of great importance for all missionaries among the different animistic nations to observe carefully which part of the gospel is the most needed there, and that should be emphasized first in our preaching. Therefore, we require a careful study of the heathen mind and of the effect of the gospel on that mind. It is my conviction that Christ is not only the Saviour for all mankind, but that He has a special gift or blessing too for each nation according to its special wants and needs. And so, if we consider the effects of the gospel on the different heathen peoples, we see with astonishment and joy that Christ grows greater and greater, and all kinds of men find in Him what they need and seek.[37]

ii. *Culture determines the communication means and modes, the conceptual frameworks to utilize, and teaching/learning styles to adopt when contextualizing.*

Effective contextualization, as we have indicated, involves planting seed in well-prepared soil, not transplanting full-grown samples grown in a foreign setting. Culture shapes the way the gospel is grasped and lived. The thought-forms, worldview, and appropriate linguistic forms will determine how the Christian message is presented, heard, received, and learned. The "news" of the gospel can only be grasped as the hearers relate it to their existing, culturally determined, religious ideas and concepts. This is why

35. To use Wayne Dye's term in *Translation Strategy*.

36. To use Don Richardson's term in *Peace Child*.

37. World Missionary Conference, *Report of Commission IV*, 300–301.

the skills of culturally relevant communication are so important for good contextualization.

Careful attention to the traditional beliefs, religious rituals, and explanatory "myths" of the community will indicate how the local "elemental spiritual forces" have acted as "guardians" and "schoolmasters" to control and prepare the community for the coming of Christ as the only one who fulfills their culturally shaped desires and longings (cf. Gal 3:19—4:9).[38] A good grasp of these religious customs will also indicate the deep-seated wrongs, injustices, fears, and "webs of lies" which so often ensnare and hamper the community from finding the fullness of life the gospel offers.[39] Not only so, those beliefs and customs will also provide the terms, values, and longings, often expressed in local proverbs, parables, "redemptive analogies," or "universally relevant metaphors," through which the gospel can be appropriated and applied in the local culture.

Local culture will also guide in choosing the appropriate communication language and media: which dialect, language level, idioms, figures of speech, and illustrations to use; whether to use oral, literary, or digital forms; which genre is more appropriate for each message—narrative storytelling, biography, proverbial sayings, parable, dialogical or lineal logical argument; likewise, whether the culture prefers the message in prose, poetry, song, drama, or audiovisual styles and forms. Combinations of these usually also enshrine and convey the cultural values, cherished ambitions, and sense of identity, and also hurt or shame which the culture carries within its wider context.

Communication and educational technologies, learning processes and preferences, decision-making choices, and speed of progress will all be guided by the desires and needs of the community, not by the preferences of the person bringing the message. Equally important, the patterns of response, means of confession and commitment, and particularly how to express contrition, repentance, and faith, should all be culturally appropriate, guided, and determined by local cultural priorities, not those of the message bringer.[40] Understanding such cultural patterns and preferences is vital for contextualization.

38. We explore these ideas more fully in chapter 5 on the Letter to the Galatians.

39. For the concept of "web of lies," see Myers, *Walking with the Poor*, 75–79. Myers is summarizing ideas developed by Christian, *God of the Empty-Handed*, 157–61.

40. Paul Hiebert's insightful "critical contextualization" process, although originally written to guide Western missionaries, is still helpful if due allowance is made for the fact that local Christian leaders are more likely to be initiating the contextualization process

iii. *From the culturally relevant starting point we reach up to embrace the full range of biblical metaphors in contextualizing truth for Christian maturity.*

Choosing the most relevant explanations of each aspect of truth is the essential starting point in contextualization. But for Christian maturity the contextualizing must continue filling out the initial response so as to grasp and apply a full range of biblical teaching for mature discipleship and Christian living. To illustrate, in Western churches the neglect of the atonement as victory over spirit powers has left churches open to the current inroads of occult teachings. A lack of emphasis on the church as the pilgrim people of God encourages the complacent materialism of nominal Christianity in the West. So too, Papua New Guineans need to understand sin as rebellion and disobedience, not just broken relationships, if they are to have a firm faith in Christ, and to address some of the issues of corruption in high places in their nation.

This broadening of understanding is essential to avoid unhealthy syncretism. When one aspect of biblical teaching is overused, or treated as if it is all the Bible teaches on that topic, we can easily distort truth. The various metaphors given in Scripture to fill out the meaning of central theological concepts all need to be considered and applied in order for believers to develop mature Christian lifestyles. A limited grasp of the fullness of Scripture leads to immaturity of faith and life. Covering the biblical range of explanation for each central doctrine is necessary to correct possible misunderstandings or distortions of our new life in Christ. Every culture favors their own ethnocentric readings of the Scriptures. Good contextualization guards against such syncretizing readings by striving to make the word of God fully known in the diversity of the full range of explanatory metaphors describing each aspect of truth.

At different stages of growth in the church, different aspects of the one truth will need emphasis to ensure ongoing growth. Common problems such as legalism, having only a nominal grasp of church ritual instead of a living relationship with Jesus Christ, seeking shortcuts to holiness, or unwillingness to face the cost of discipleship, continue to challenge groups of

today. Thus, local believers will be taking the role Hiebert assumed expatriate missionaries would fill, and these local leaders will need to enlist other local believers to participate in guiding and controlling the process. Hiebert, "Critical Contextualization," 104–12; republished in Hiebert, *Anthropological Reflections*, 75–92. These two versions update his earlier chapter with the same title in *Anthropological Insights*, 171–92.

Christians in every culture at different times. Different aspects of biblical insight bring answers to each of these problems. Thus, all parts of Scripture are needed. Maturity in Christian behavior and social involvement require an in-depth grasp of a full range of biblical teachings towards such matters as: a grasp of ethical issues; competence in discerning true and false spirit powers; judging between justice and injustice in social and political life; responsible management of human and environmental resources for the glory of God and the good of future generations; fostering leadership patterns suited to the culture but free from the human lust for ambition, power, position, and prestige; and motivating and mobilizing communities of believers for effective missional outreach. Too often our biblical teaching just repeats the few original evangelistic emphases which first brought our people to faith, and we wonder why they do not grow to maturity. We need to grasp this link between filling out the whole range of biblical explanations of each of our key teachings and the growth of believers to spiritual maturity. If the first part of the Great Commission in Matt 28:18–20 requires cultural sensitivity to choose the culturally appropriate metaphors and cultural insights to bring people to initial faith and baptism, then the second part of the commission—to teach disciples to live out all that Jesus has commanded—requires ongoing contextualization.

There is a balance, then, between choosing culturally relevant initial steps into truth and insisting that all God's word is relevant for long-term growth and maturity. In both cases, cultural sensitivity will guide in where to start and how to continue.

iv. *In-depth cultural transformation is the goal of adequate contextualization.*

We must contextualize to the point of transforming not only lifestyles, but also worldviews. Harold W. Turner, building on Lesslie Newbigin's work, suggested that the Christian mission has seldom gone deep enough. Mission to the person—seeking personal conversion and transformation as disciples of Christ—has long been the subject of study and practice. Recent decades have seen a resurgence of attention to mission at a second level—mission to society. This level of mission as social service, or as social reform, has also been the focus of much study and praxis. But the third level, mission to the cultural base, the worldview level, remains largely untouched.[41] The challenge in contextualizing is to transform worldviews in

41. Turner, "Three Levels," 61–68.

depth. To use the jargon, we aim to bring the limiting factors of the cultural horizon into conformity to the biblical horizon.

Harvie Conn, quoting Orlando Costas, sums it up well:

> The ultimate test of any theological discourse, after all, is not only erudite precision but also transformative power. "It is a question of whether or not theology can articulate the faith in a way that is not only intellectually sound but spiritually energizing, and therefore, capable of leading the people of God to be transformed in their way of life and to commit themselves to God's mission in the world."[42]

While contextualization begins with transforming people as they receive Christ and make him Lord of their social group and whole society, it should never stop there. The gospel of Christ transforms people so they in turn can share that transformation with others. We are transformed to transform the deepest depths of our own worldview and cultural longings, so that we can reach beyond ourselves in the mission of Christ to the whole world.

v. *Biblical loyalty is the measure of contextual validity and truth within every culture.*

We have simply been recommending the Bible's own standard. New Testament wisdom is a lifestyle (Jas 3:13–17). The goal is such a release from inadequate values, thought-forms, and goals that the people of God work out in their own setting whatever the Scriptures require of them. John Stott encapsulates it clearly in his definition of an evangelical: "The real hallmark of the evangelical is not only a present submission to what he or she believes the Scripture teaches, it is a prior commitment to be submissive to what we may subsequently learn to be the teaching of Scripture, whatever Scripture may be found to teach."[43]

With progressive personal and cultural transformation as its goal, it follows that contextualization is an ongoing process. It involves at least three generations of Christian leadership as the gospel penetrates a new cultural group. The first generation of converts and Christian messengers, whether missionaries or local evangelists, face one set of issues and questions. They grapple with the initial confrontation between the gospel and the traditional cultural values and beliefs. The children of those first converts face different

42. Conn, "Contextual Theologies," 63, citing Costas, "Evangelical Theology," 7–13.

43. Stott, in *EFAC Bulletin* 40 (1990) 3.

issues and questions, usually focusing on matters concerning their identity as Christians within the still resistant surrounding culture. They often do not need to make a drastic break with a non-Christian past, since they have grown up under the "nurture and admonition" of the church community. But they need to express their cultural heritage in fresh, distinctively Christian ways. This demands a second stage of contextualization of the Scriptures. The third generation faces further new issues and questions, often struggling with ways to impact the social structures and worldview philosophies of their society. This demands a third level of contextualization. As a result, contextualization is never a one-off, quickly completed task.[44] Each Christian generation must identify and address the new questions with which the surrounding culture is challenging the gospel.

Contextualization is ongoing in another sense as well. This process of relating the good news of Christ to the cultural presuppositions of its hearers began on the day of Pentecost, and has continued as a primary church concern ever since. We did not call it contextualization, though, until quite recently. Adaptation, assimilation to local beliefs, indigenizing the gospel, or, particularly in Catholic circles, inculturation, were the common terms. But in 1972, when Shoki Coe, the head of the World Council of Churches' Theological Education Fund, suggested contextualization as a better word, he noted one specific advantage.[45] The previous terms were connected with people of European backgrounds making the gospel relevant in, to them, overseas cultures. Coe preferred "context" as the root of the new term, as it stressed this is something the church must take seriously in every culture at all times. European culture needs contextual application of the gospel just as much as any other culture. Coe was right, although his association with the WCC as well as the new term's initial links with certain kinds of political involvement, meant that at first many evangelicals were cautious about its use.[46] Some of the best evangelical advocates of contextualization, in their concern to stress the importance of the new term, claimed the periods of Christian mission before the 1950s were the "era of noncontextualization,"[47] as if the process itself, not just the term, was new. This is quite wrong. We

44. For development of these ideas, see Walls, "Old Athens," 148–50.

45. Coe, "Contextualizing Theology," 20–21.

46. See, e.g., Hesselgrave and Rommen, *Contextualization*, 149–50; Nicholls, "Theology of Gospel," 49–62.

47. As Paul Hiebert does in his otherwise very helpful and influential article, "Critical Contextualization."

learn vital lessons about contextualizing from earlier, and every, generation of Christian missionaries. Contextualization not only takes three generations to become deeply embedded in a particular culture, it also spans wider time and geographical boundaries.

Conclusion

These, then, are essential foundations for contextualization. Our illustrations have emphasized the cross-cultural aspect of the task. But wherever we cross the divide to another cultural subgroup the same principles apply. Often today the divides are as deep and wide between generations in the same ethnic group, or between the socioeconomic extremes in the same city, as between any two racial groups. The same issues challenge the increasingly larger number of non-Western Christians moving across linguistic and cultural boundaries to spearhead new Christian witness in what, to them, are foreign nations, or at least significantly different cultures within their own nation. Moreover, the patterns of "reverse" migration into Western nations from previous colonial dependencies of Western countries, make these cross-cultural contextualization principles essential tools for most Christian ministries in post-Christendom Western nations today. The increasingly cosmopolitan, religiously pluralist, and multicultural constituencies of our urban populations globally reinforce the need for contextualization competency.

Thus, to effectively bring the living message to those on the other side of any of these cultural divides we must: discover the heartbeat of their cultural values so as to identify the most relevant aspects, metaphors, and forms of scriptural instruction to commence the transformation; adopt culturally appropriate communication processes, conceptual frameworks, and learning styles to ensure the content and methods of contextualization confirm and ensure the message is being applied into the heart of the culture; continue empathizing with the culture so as to identify and present an ever-widening range of biblical truth for mature Christian living; and work towards the goal of bringing each cultural worldview and experience into conformity with the biblical experience of wholeness of life in Christ with all its ramifications of a transformed worldview and daily life in our global village.

We have called for a Christian theology or understanding of culture, for an effective missional reading and understanding of Scripture, and attentiveness to the Holy Spirit as we bring those factors together for effective contextualization. These principles also highlight the point of this chapter: contextualization is at the heart of knowing and sharing Christ Jesus as Lord. We cannot avoid it. We can only choose whether to do it faithfully or poorly.

Chapter 3

What Is Our Gospel?

WHAT IS THE GOSPEL?[1] This is, perhaps, the crucial question lying behind each topic in this book. Certainly, it is the most significant question for Christian mission today. Without a clear grasp of our gospel, we can have no driving vision for our purpose as Christians in the world. Strangely, we Christians are slow to define it. We often act and speak as if our good news is self-evident. Our evangelism often assumes the good news itself is already understood in our society. If that were ever a fair assumption it is sadly misplaced today. General awareness of biblical concepts, teachings, or even personalities is so shallow that we are fools to think something as radical and unpredictable as the gospel is commonly understood. We must not ignore the task of defining our message.

The good news is power, announcement, and summons.

God's Power in Action

Our Christian gospel is fundamentally *God's power in action*. We lust after power in our modern world. This lust drives political ambition. Its energy is blatantly exploited in the business world. Our best brains pursue the lure of power in every field of human enquiry. Many of our most emotive words focus on this theme. Just think of the images conjured up by the words: "the powerless," "abuse of power," "empowering the exploited," or "corridors

1. A version of this chapter was originally published in Patrick, *New Vision*, 147–57. Used here with the permission of Vision Network, now the New Zealand Christian Network (see bibliography for further details).

of power." Vast financial resources are poured into achieving power across the spectrum of human achievement. But most pointedly, we are all too conscious of our lack of power over ourselves. We are haunted by the helplessness of not being able to cleanse our own sense of inner failure and guilt. We know all too well the sheer frustration of having great hopes and good intentions but lacking the moral fiber to achieve them. We feel our own powerlessness as we watch families disintegrate and personal lives crumble under the pressure of our modern lifestyles. And where we do see power at work, so often it destroys or further undermines the fabric of our society.

Into this context the gospel comes as a radically different power. "I am not ashamed of the gospel, for it is the power of God," wrote the apostle Paul (Rom 1:16). Unlike other modern forms, this power alone picks up broken bits and pieces and makes them whole again. The gospel reintegrates personalities torn apart from drug abuse. The gospel cleanses the sense of failure and self-condemnation left in the train of incest and teenage promiscuity. The gospel releases the middle-aged man frustrated with no higher purpose for living than accumulating possessions and gadgets, and involves him in strategic community service and building bridges across the ethnic divisions in our nation. The gospel turns the street kid brought up with no contact with her own parents into a generous and thoughtful mother, wife, and homemaker. The gospel changes introspective, inhibited, shame-ridden young men and women into quietly confident, courageous innovators grappling with ethical standards in the business world; offering serious assistance to members of the gay community; developing aid, community leadership, and spiritual welfare services in third world countries globally; and crossing socioeconomic barriers in our own country to provide fresh opportunities to those still reeling from the latest economic downturn. The gospel takes ordinary, decent Kiwis—whether Pākehā, Māori, Islander, or Asian—and loosens the grip of endemic selfishness, complacency, and preoccupation with material things. This gospel gives a new ability to face up to our own inner needs, to begin to let go of crippling pride and prejudice, and become honest citizens with a worthwhile value system and sense of direction in today's world.

I know it is easy to write like that. But I am thinking of particular people in each of these categories. People with names who have crossed my path in my daily church work.

Yes, the good news of Jesus Christ is all about life changing. It is a dynamic working to restore and renew dysfunctional persons and to set them on the path to wholeness. That's the point of Paul's ". . . the gospel is the power of God for salvation . . ." (Rom 1:16). Salvation is wholeness of life—becoming integrated, wholesome people again. Through this gospel the living God shares his own life amongst us. He demonstrates he is here and available with his own reconstructive touch to renew our lives today. The gospel is the igniting power which releases love, faith, and hope to penetrate our needy society in person—through renewed women and men discovering the way to full-orbed living. News of a good power in our day is good news indeed.

Announcing Answers to Our Need

But the gospel is announcement as well as power. The gospel announces and explains God's action in Christ for us. The good news declares what God has done. This good news interprets certain crucial events in a particular way.

The announcement is that in Jesus of Nazareth God *came* into our human scene. God has broken into history in person. The originator and controller of all that is has made a live appearance on planet earth. That is news. God cares about his creatures. So, he came to us in person (e.g., John 14:10–11; 17:21–24; 2 Cor 5:19; Phil 2:5–9).

He even *lived* a human life. And what a life it proved to be. A life lived totally for others. Clean, kind, and wholesome in every way. Ignoring the expectations of his stratified society Jesus related to commoners and leaders alike, even disregarding their national and religious backgrounds. Despite his efforts to conceal his true origins, his uniqueness shone through. His mastery over the powers of nature, his penetrating knowledge of human hearts, his awesome control over raw spirit powers, and his intense hatred of hypocrisy showed he was no mere human. Yet Jesus demonstrated his divine origins only to serve the needy. Displaying love as the hallmark of his true humanity he accepted equally all he encountered across the full spectrum of society, so much so that he proved a popular hero, for a time. And an embarrassment to the religious establishment till he was disposed of, it seemed, by their plots (John 11:47–53; Acts 10:36–40).

The way Jesus *died* became the focal point of the news. He taught his followers to understand his death as God's answer to the basic needs and yearnings of the human heart. Conscience itself, as an inner reflection of the standards of our unchanging God, demands satisfaction, punishment, and restitution for wrongs done. The law of God declares this indelibly. The Jewish sacrificial system reflected the universal human need for forgiveness through an atonement—an adequate way of making us humans right before God. God presented Jesus as that sacrifice of atonement. Christ died to deal with the global sin problem. As both perfect sacrifice and high priest—strange though that combination may seem—Jesus personally dealt with the human defilement which banished us from our Maker's presence. His death reopened direct access to the upright, holy God. Reflecting fully and perfectly the love and concern of the Father, Jesus's perfect life offered up in willing death, he taught, is a pardoning ransom. He died on behalf of self-opinionated, sinful humans. He thereby satisfied totally the legal condemnation rightly barring proud rebels like us from enjoying the presence of God. This death, therefore, frees, cleanses, and renews all who will admit their broken relationships with God. By humbly accepting Jesus Christ's death as God's judgment on our own disobedience, we find the only adequate basis for readmission into family fellowship with God. Moreover, this death portrays vividly the depths to which the yearning heart of our heavenly Father would go to reclaim us for his intended purposes. In this death, true love has been displayed and redefined once and for all (e.g., Mark 10:33–34, 45; Luke 24:44–47; Rom 3:21–26; 1 John 4:9–10).

Powerful though Jesus's death would have been on its own, it did not stand alone. As the life and character of the person who died would lead us to expect, the news is that Jesus the Christ *rose* from the dead (Acts 2:23–24; 1 Cor 15:3–7). The unembellished historical facts have withstood the critical scrutiny of two thousand years. The apostles' recorded testimony, the fact and endurance of the church, and the personal experience of the risen Christ by successive generations of Christians, are best accounted for by the fact of the resurrection. This rewrites our understanding even of death. Good news indeed.

But the good news is no antiquated message. This same Jesus of Nazareth, by the express action of God, now *rules* the universe as Lord. The gospel is described as the good news of the kingdom—the kingly rule of God. The forces released through Jesus's death and resurrection have impacted not merely our globe, but the whole universe. A person, this Lord Jesus Christ, now sits in control of the affairs of the universe. This is good news. The ultimate authority in the cosmos is not some impersonal force, not blind fate, and certainly not inexorable law. Rather, the living, loving, accessible person, our Lord Jesus Christ, the friend of sinners, holds final control. The gospel announces and presents Jesus Christ as our king waiting in sovereign majesty for us, his subjects, to acknowledge his rule (Eph 1:20–22; Col 1:15–17; Heb 1:2–3).

This announcement goes one step further. Jesus Christ, the active Lord of creation, will *return* personally to our globe. History is heading to God's predetermined goal. The details are not spelled out. Jesus himself warned of our continuing ignorance about such details. But he spoke often and clearly about the fact. Jesus will return in person to wrap up God's present purposes for planet earth. His return will confirm the seriousness of human accountability. If God never holds us accountable for our actions, he is treating us as less than free, responsible beings. At Christ's return our dignity as humans will be finally validated. We shall each account for the way we have lived our lives. For all the accumulated human evil in our world never to be brought to justice is unthinkable. Christ will return as judge. Only thus will patience and hope be shown in their true colours: as essential to human life. Only thus will God be finally vindicated. The role of his grace and forbearance underpinning the very structures of human existence will finally be made clear. On the basis of the work of Christ thus far in human history, his return is eminently rational. It is integral to the apostolic gospel (John 5:25–29; Rom 14:9–12; 2 Cor 5:10; 1 Thess 1:9–10; Titus 2:11–14; Heb 9:26–28).

These, then, are the constituent ingredients of the announcement we call the gospel. God in Christ—came—lived—died—rose—rules, and is returning as our Savior, Lord, prophet, priest, judge, advocate, and King.

A Summons to Respond

But this gospel is more than power and announcement. It also summons us to enjoy the benefits of this action. The gospel is God's active power announced—an invitation—calling for response. Once we have heard and understood this news, we become freshly accountable to God. He summons us to enter his kingdom. He calls for ongoing commitments as his loyal subjects. Good news brings great responsibility (John 3:3–5; 12:47–50; Rom 1:18—2:16).

The gospel summons us to change in every aspect of life. It invites us first to a radically *new understanding of God himself.* We now know God as Jesus Christ explained him. We can enjoy him as our loving Father. He yearns for intimate personal relationships with peoples of every cultural background. God can no longer be conceived of as the exclusive property of one specially religious nation. He is equally accessible to all peoples. This gospel revelation of God reclaims and reinstates the categories of love and family life which are so abused in our human experience. The gospel demonstrates their intended fullness as Jesus Christ sets forth through his life and death the essence of God as love (John 1:18; Gal 4:4–7; 1 John 4:7–16).

The gospel also summons us to embrace the *news about human purpose.* We who had lost our way, who had become alienated from our intended goals and purpose, have now been found. The gospel opens for us a renewed sense of direction. We can rediscover our true identity as God's pilgrim people en route to an eternal appointment with him. This involves a new worldview. Time takes on new significance in the light of the eternal. Values are determined from an other-worldly, not merely this-worldly, perspective. Possessions lose their depth of attraction in the light of their only transient significance. Relationships, and people as persons, take on a new sense of ultimate permanence and priority. Too often our evangelism never summonses us to this renewal at the worldview level. But such ultimate meaningfulness is newsworthy indeed (Luke 19:10; Eph 2:1–13; Heb 11:13–16).

At its heart the gospel invites us to discover the *good news about human sin.* Christians hardly need to highlight that we humans have "blown it" in our modern world. Our newspapers give daily coverage of that reality. Our gospel, however, offers a radical reinterpretation of our dilemma by tracing its roots back to our disrupted relationships with God. Any adequate analysis of human need must take into account humanity's basic rejection of God—what the Bible calls sin.

But God now offers cleansing from sin's pollution. Christ's in-depth forgiveness deals with our fundamental human bias towards evil. The distorting, corrupting effects of habitually choosing our own selfish way can at last be corrected. Christ's inner clean-up and moral restoration renews us as whole persons. But it goes further than that. Christ has bridged permanently the awful chasm our sin created between ourselves and our holy God. We have peace with God. Our rebellion and enmity have been dealt with. We are reconciled through trust in Christ (Rom 3:21—5:21; Col 1:19–23; 1 John 1:5—2:2).

The gospel also summons us to demonstrate the *news about human society.* The Christian gospel creates new social relationships. Jesus's love in us immediately reinstates a healthy social concern. Love becomes the distinctive hallmark of believers. The gospel constantly reconciles enemies. Its very nature challenges social divisions. This open secret had never dawned on God's people in previous ages. But now the gospel makes the hope of Christ available to every cultural group worldwide. Any "gospel" which does not involve its adherents in cross-cultural friendship was publicly condemned by the apostles (Gal 2:11–16).

The gospel's inherent concern for people also releases *power for social action*. Christ's zeal for justice and social righteousness now infuses his followers. For all their apparent conservatism in regard to moral values, those who drink the new wine of Christ's gospel create a ferment for social structures which restore sanctity and dignity to human life. History warns of the shortsightedness of political powers which underestimate the social impact of the death and resurrection of Christ (John 13:34–35; Eph 2:11–22; Col 1:3–8; Jas 2:1–12; 1 John 4:11, 19–21).

The biblical gospel contains other components often overlooked in the West. Christ's gospel includes unexpected *news about spirit powers*. During his earthly life Christ Jesus demonstrated his authority over demonic powers. He proved his right to establish the kingdom of God by freeing those dominated by the powers of darkness. Even more, Christ's death and resurrection have permanently affected the cosmic good and evil forces. Angelic powers now serve the interests of believers. Christ's peace accomplished at calvary means that evil powers have been finally subjugated. Through the cross all the powers of wickedness have been disarmed and publicly displayed in their true weakness. Christ has dealt the decisive blow to all the powers of evil, even if rearguard actions still abound on their part. This is good news indeed for men and women living in the fear of spirit powers, including increasing numbers in the Western world. Those who open their lives to the living Christ through his Spirit are rescued from the dominion of darkness and receive a transfer into the kingdom of God's Son. Our gospel summons needs to reinstate these cosmic aspects of Christ's great redemptive victory (Col 1:16–20; 2:9, 15; Eph 1:20–22; 3:10; 6:11–13; Heb 1:14; 1 John 4:1–4).

The gospel also includes *news about our global environment*. Our understanding of the universe is reinterpreted in the gospel. Creation is a household inheritance gifted by God to his "firstborn," Jesus Christ. This transforms our attitude to the world around us. Not only is it the inheritance of an ever-living person, but the true intent and proper use of the whole cosmos is to glorify Christ. Creation awaits and participates significantly in God's eternal purposes, sharing somehow in our redemption as children of God. Thus, serious environmental concern becomes a gospel honor and duty (Rom 8:22–25; Col 1:15–17; Heb 1:1–3, 10–12).

The gospel also includes radical *news about human suffering*. Christ's suffering at calvary transforms our understanding of suffering. God brings love, faith, and hope into human suffering. Christ's shouldering of human suffering in person means God is available—in *love*—to relieve human suffering. Moreover, God transforms suffering—through *faith*—to make it productive. Perseverance, character, and *hope* are generated specifically in the furnace of suffering. So, far from expecting every hurt to be immediately relieved, gospel resources enable us even to rejoice in suffering as one way God prepares us for the ultimate consummation of the kingdom (Rom 5:1–5; 8:18–39; 1 Pet 1:6–7; 4:12–19).

Yet the gospel is not merely "pie in the sky when you die." We Christians certainly have plenty to look forward to. But our good news is that *God comes right into our present daily experience* too. The kingdom which will be completed at Christ's return is accessible already. Our faith link with Christ the King is a living reality now. We experience his presence bringing us courage and peace to face the pressures of modern life. He delights to do the unexpected to demonstrate his power and gracious concern for his wayward creatures. He does heal. He does demonstrate his victory over evil forces. He miraculously works to confirm his role as Lord in his own universe. Most amazing of all, he condescends to share with us humans on a daily basis. His followers each experience the Holy Spirit of God living within their own life and personality. He renews our lives and equips us with previously unrealized gifts to serve him. His kingdom is already available, but not yet here in its fullness. There is no contradiction in the gospel between our present experience of both suffering and the indwelling Spirit. After all, our miracle-working Savior willingly submitted to the awful suffering of the cross (John 1:12–13; 14:17–27; 16:33; Acts 1:8; 1 Cor 6:19–20; 12:4–13; 2 Cor 5:17).

The Whole Gospel

Initially different aspects of such a comprehensive gospel appeal to different peoples. We all run the risk of trying to domesticate and reduce both its scope and impact. We are prone to latch onto the personal aspects of the gospel and ignore its social and worldview implications. Or, once alerted to the broader social implications we overlook the depths of personal integrity upon which they are based and work for a bland social betterment without calling for its essential cutting edge of personal transformation and commitment through repentance and conversion. Or, in our personal zeal, we are blind to the way our own worldviews (be they Western materialistic ones, or of a more eclectic nature) remain largely unchanged and we hold back from the costly process of working to transform our societal values and thought patterns until they too, come into line with the demands of the gospel.

The real challenge is to grasp, demonstrate, and proclaim this good news ever more fully, more adequately, and, therefore, more humbly. This is the vision-imparting news our nations need as we move on in this twenty-first century, becoming transformed people, transforming our societies. Thanks be to God for his indescribable gift (2 Cor 9:15)!

Section 2

New Testament Examples

Chapter 4

The Early Church Discovers Its Identity

Mission and Contextualization in Acts

The church's growth to self-awareness seems to mirror that of an individual. Our human potential, though present from birth, demands time, nurture, experience, and training, if not testing, to flourish and reach maturity. The early church as described in the book of Acts tracks a similar pathway. Key aspects of its essential nature, though present and partially realized from the beginning, were only fully appropriated over time. This chapter explores the way the early church came to terms with its own missional and multicultural dimensions. Both dimensions are essential aspects of the nature of Christ's church, and both are central for the interrelationship of gospel, culture, mission, and theological education.[1]

A clear grasp of the nature of the church, ecclesiology, is vital as the church moves into the twenty-first century.[2] If, as we have claimed, one crucial question facing evangelical Christians worldwide is, "What is the gospel?" then equally crucial follow-up questions would have to be: "Who

1. The senses in which we are using the terms "missional" and "multicultural" will become evident as we proceed. Suffice to say "missional" refers to the local church's responsibility to reach out beyond itself in witnessing to the Lord Jesus Christ; and "multicultural" speaks of incorporating peoples of other cultures and ethnicities into the life of the local congregation. We shall use it interchangeably with "multiethnic."

2. An earlier version of this chapter was previously published as Hitchen, "Missional," 63–78. Used here with the permission of Vision Network, now the New Zealand Christian Network (see bibliography for further details).

is our God?" and "What is the church?"[3] In this chapter we will reflect on, "What is the church?" in following the story of the early believers through the book of Acts. We structure our reflections around three phases: foundational steps; transitional steps; and taking and defending the final steps.

Foundational Steps: Towards a Missional, Multiethnic Church in Jerusalem, Acts 1–7

In Acts, Luke lays important foundations for understanding the nature, mission, and growth of the church. The opening chapters explain the way believers slowly discovered, "the pilgrim Church is missionary by its very nature."[4]

The Triune God Calls the Church to Mission, 1:1–11

This carefully constructed introductory passage presents a Trinitarian foundation for understanding the nature and purpose of the church. The Father's kingly rule continues at the heart of Jesus's teaching after the resurrection (1:3); the Father's promised self-giving, his gift of the Spirit, is the essential prerequisite for mission (1:4–5); and the Father retains purpose and timetabling authority over this age (1:6–7).

The Son continues his teaching and work, revealing himself alive and active in our age (1:1, 3). His completed suffering, proven resurrection, living presence, current exaltation, and promised return provide the parameters within which the church exists (1:3, 9–11). The Son chooses, instructs, and commissions partners for his task in the world, requiring the church to break all ethnic, national, and geographic boundaries as it shares its vital experience of the Christ. Indeed, he is the focus and content of the church's missional witness (1:2, 8). This Jesus is exalted to heaven to assume joint cosmic control with the Father until his assured return (1:9–11).

The Holy Spirit provides essential teaching, enabling, and guiding to equip believers to share in Christ's missional task (1:2, 4–5, 8).

3. See chapter 3, "What Is Our Gospel?"

4. From the Vatican II Document, *Ad Gentes* (Decree on the Mission Activity of the Church), cited by Bosch, *Transforming Mission*, 372.

These basic truths become building blocks supporting the biblical claim that God is essentially a sending or missionary God. The church's mission, therefore, is to participate in the "mission of God," or *missio Dei.*[5]

The church is trusted with a radically redefined missional message: the kingdom of God. In this present age the kingdom is not about restoring international supremacy to Israel (1:6). Instead, it centers on witnessing to the kingly reign of Jesus Christ, and calling people of every culture to trust in him (1:8). The apostles were not ready for mission until they grasped this fundamental reorientation of expectation.[6] As David Bosch succinctly puts it: "the good news of the reign of God is Jesus Christ, incarnated, crucified and risen, and what he accomplished."[7] We too often separate what these verses combine, the message of the kingdom and witness to the living Jesus here and now. In so doing we rob the message of its primary, Christ-centered focus. We also rob mission of its fundamental link with the central message of Jesus's earthly ministry, the kingly rule of God, and thereby miss the relevance of much of Jesus's teaching for mission today.[8]

Acts 1:8 also clarifies the nature and priority of mission for the church. Mission is being sent as witnesses to Jesus, declaring by life, word, and actions what we personally know and have experienced of him. In theologian Emil Brunner's words, "The church exists by mission, just as fire exists by burning."[9] Or to quote Karl Barth, "[The church's] mission (its being sent) is not secondary to its being; the church exists in being sent and in building up itself for the sake of its mission," or again, apart from mission "the church ceases to be the church."[10]

Such mission involves both local and global responsibility and impact. The Bible knows nothing of two different tasks, one called "evangelism"

5. On God's missionary nature, see Holmes, "Trinitarian Missiology," 72–90; Flett, *Witness of God*. For mission as *missio Dei*, see Bosch, *Transforming Mission*, 389–92; Kirk, *What Is Mission?*, 23–55. For the changing understanding of mission, see Van Engen, *Mission on the Way*, 145–56, and throughout.

6. For the meaning of the "kingdom of God" for mission, see Hitchen, "Church's Role"; and Guder, "God's Mission," 28–48.

7. Bosch, *Transforming Mission*, 116.

8. On the relation between the kingdom and mission, see Kirk, *What Is Mission?*, 29–37; the chapters by Johannes Verkuyl, Paul Hiebert, and J. Robertson McQuilkin in Van Engen et al., *Good News*, 71–81, 162–80.

9. Brunner, *Word and the World*, 108. Michael Green explains the centrality of "witnessing" in mission in *Evangelism*.

10. Barth, *Church Dogmatics*, 725; and "Living Congregation," 72.

for reaching people of our own culture, and the other called "mission," for peoples of other cultures. Acts 1:8 speaks of a single, unified task of witnessing to Jesus beginning in the disciples' immediate context, "Jerusalem"; reaching out to every dimension of their own nation, "in all Judea"; embracing their nearest neighbors of another culture, "Samaria"; and going right on to include all people, everywhere, "to the ends of the earth." Every local church is to have both a local and a global perspective as its mission. Both the church's nature and the scope of its task transcend the geographic and ethnic boundaries implied in these places listed.[11] Thus, influencing every aspect of our own culture, and crossing boundaries to reach beyond the restrictions of our own culture, are essential aspects of what it means to be the church.

Local churches are not free to choose whether or not to be "missionary minded." Acts 1:1–11 declares the church is "missionary by its very nature." The early believers took some time to grasp and appropriate these realities as vital features of their common life. It takes time to become what we are.

The Church Is Birthed and Grows through Mission, 2:1–47

The implicit teachings of Acts 1:1–11 became explicit on the day of Pentecost. After his resurrection, Jesus stressed that his disciples were dependent on the Holy Spirit's empowering for all he expected them to be and do (1:4–5, 8). The baptism in the Spirit at Pentecost was essential for inaugurating the new age and fresh way of relating to God promised by the Father long ago. Hence, Jesus's command to await that decisive event before launching into mission, (1:8).[12]

At Pentecost, the impact of God's mission began. Its universal relevance and global program were demonstrated miraculously as the message was announced to representatives from all over the Mediterranean world (2:5–12). The Holy Spirit enabled the disciples to speak in the languages of each ethnic group gathered in Jerusalem for the feast (2:6). The gift at Pentecost answers the quest of all nations and thus points to the global, multiethnic nature and mission of the church.

11. For further on the missional significance of Acts 1:1–11, see Hitchen, "Church's Role."

12. For the Holy Spirit in mission, see Murray, *Missionary Problem*, 116–34; Paton, *Ministry of the Spirit*, 1–61, and elsewhere; Boer, *Pentecost and Missions*; Green, *I Believe*, 68–89.

Mission historian Andrew Walls describes "the translation principle" which lies at the heart of mission and was so clearly demonstrated at Pentecost. The good news of Jesus Christ belongs in the vernacular languages of every people group around the world. The Holy Spirit is poured out so the church can complete this task of translating the news. This translation principle ". . . is given Gospel authentication as the Pentecost crowd of Dispersion Jews hears the wonderful works of God, not in the sacred language of the Temple liturgy (the object of their pilgrimage), but in the languages of the various nations that were their real mother tongues."[13]

The experience of receiving a globally relevant message continued to shape the church in every aspect of its development throughout the story in Acts.

The Church Impacts Its Own Community in Mission, 2–5

The church's first preaching on the day of Pentecost was a missionary message which the apostles understood fulfilled the deepest hopes of their people (2:14–41). Peter focused on the incarnate, crucified, risen Jesus as Lord and Christ. He offered forgiveness, salvation, and a living relationship with God through the Spirit, to "everyone who calls on the name of the Lord . . ." (2:21), for "the promise is for you and your children and for all who are far off, for all whom the Lord our God will call" (2:39).

The church was immediately involved in full-orbed mission. The community acted in kindness and mercy, declared the word, demonstrated God's miraculous power, and showed courageous faith. They responded to individuals, challenged the crowds, and confronted their civic leaders. They met in the privacy of their homes and in the temple grounds. They were summoned to formal council meetings and witnessed generally in public. Their holistic church life supported and fostered mission involvement. Worship, teaching, prayer, social concern and support, communion, and fellowship all featured in their spontaneous life as the community of believers. In that context, not surprisingly, they saw steady numerical growth (2:42–47; 4:32–37; 5:12–16; 6:1–6).

They gladly accepted the cost as public vilification followed their witness. Official scrutiny, opposition, imprisonment, questioning, and threats soon became their lot (4:2–3, 7, 21). Formally forbidden to continue preaching in Jesus's name in the city, they faced the governing council's

13. Walls, "Translation Principle," 32.

wrath when they ignored its orders (4:18; 5:27–28, 41–42). Despite their popularity with the people at large, they faced increasing calumny and false accusation from the authorities (6:8–14).

The region felt the impact of their centralized ministry as concern for both material and spiritual needs attracted crowds from the surrounding towns. Geographically, the "all Judea" obligation of their witnessing task was soon satisfied (5:12–16).

The Church Took Cultural Factors Seriously, 2:42—6:6

From the beginning, the Jerusalem believers paid heed to the cultural dimension inherent in being the church of Jesus Christ. The ethnic variety of their audience on the day of Pentecost set the scene for the way they addressed their teaching, fellowship, and leadership.

Relating Their Teaching to Jewish Audiences

The apostles carefully guarded their teaching as a vital priority for the expansion of the church.[14] The records highlight how they "contextualized" their message to the cultural background of their hearers. Events like the crucifixion and the resurrection took on new relevance to Jewish experience and understanding. Peter's messages in Acts 2–5 show him steadily developing new explanations of Christ and his work, relating each to the deep cultural yearnings of Jewish people. Jesus is the "God-accredited man" (2:22); he is "Lord" and "Christ" (2:36; 3:18); he is the Spirit-giver (2:17–21, 33); to him belong Isaiah's favorite titles, "Holy and Righteous Servant" (3:14; 4:27, 30); Jesus bears the powerful name (3:6, 16; 4:10, 12, 17–18, 30); and he is the new pioneer or author of life (3:15; 5:31). Apart from "Lord" and "Christ" few of those terms had been used commonly during Jesus's earthly ministry. Peter skillfully enriched the use of concepts common in the Gospels when he spoke of Jesus as fulfiller of prophecy, a prophet like Moses, fulfiller of the covenant, and seed of Abraham in 3:21–26; or rejected stone, now capstone in 4:11. Perhaps most important was the way

14. In the following verses Luke puts references to teaching in close proximity to references to the growth of the church in the bracketed verses. For Luke the connection seems important: 2:42 (47); 4:2 (4); 5:21 (28); 6:4 (7). Throughout Acts, teaching is central in the church's mission, and the connection with wider expansion is often made: eg., 11:24–25; 17:2–4, 10–12; 18:10–11; 19:8–10.

Peter filled the ancient concept of "only Savior" with fresh meaning in these early messages (2:40; 4:12; 5:31).

Missional teaching relates biblical concepts to the specific context of the hearers, always striving for a balance of local cultural relevance and biblical faithfulness in the way terms are used and understood. Contextualizing the message is one implication of the "translatability" of the message. Each new generation or subculture within a healthy society develops its own thought-forms, expressions, and jargon, so the church needs to understand this heart language and present its message with dynamic relevance. At this early stage the church was not crossing ethnic or cultural boundaries to "contextualize" the message. As Jews they were preaching to Jews. But they were crossing boundaries of traditional religious meaning and experience. They were developing old terms in new ways, even coining new terms, like "Pioneer" or "Author of Life," to explain Christ's relevance. Contextualization is not just something done in other peoples' cultures. With every new generation, and each group of people with different religious experiences, or the lack of them, Christ's witnesses have to find the best terms, concepts, and metaphors to bring the living gospel to life for each group of listeners. Contextualization is an ever-present need and reality for the church.

Fellowship

It took no time at all for seeds of dissension to start blossoming along cultural lines in the early church. Meeting the social needs of the poor provided a devilish opportunity for grumbling. One ethnic group, whose native language was Greek, not the local Semitic dialect, Aramaic, claimed they were being treated unfairly in the food distribution (6:1–6). The apostles involved the whole church to address these interethnic differences. Fellowship across cultural boundaries is an inherent requirement of being the body of Christ, then as now. Cultural and language tensions need to be overcome promptly to maintain harmony and avoid any feeling of exclusion.

At this stage the Jerusalem church was not prepared to say that the Greek speakers might be happier going off to commence their own congregation. That would be an easy cop-out. To be in Christ meant Greek and Aramaic speakers had to work together to overcome language and cultural differences. They had to demonstrate publicly their fundamental unity in Christ by developing an inclusive fellowship in which both groups were welcome to participate. This pattern challenges our ethnically divided, multicultural societies in so many nations today.

Leadership

The Jerusalem church, with the apostles' endorsement, ensured ethnic representation and a new level of cross-cultural participation in their leadership (6:5–6). The names of each of the new team of leaders suggest they came from the disaffected group of Greek speakers. The apostles initially appointed these new leaders for routine food distribution, but the Holy Spirit showed he is no respecter of ethnic background in his allocation of gifts. Very soon the Greek-speaking leaders were thrust out into teaching and preaching ministries (6:8–10; 8:5–13). This new level of cross-cultural sharing led to further growth amongst another distinct group in the community, the priests (6:7). Before this, we had only heard of Nicodemus and Barnabas as converts from priest and Levite circles. Priests had good reason to consider the claims of Jesus as the Messiah. As each different group's needs were properly addressed, other groups realized they also were welcome in a truly multiethnic church.

Cultural issues are still inherent in any proclamation of Christ. In the 1980s, as in Western nations around the world, New Zealand urban churches often served in largely monocultural contexts. This is no longer the case. We now live in both bicultural and multicultural settings. How to handle this cultural diversity in our teaching, fellowship, and leadership is a significant challenge for us as the church in Aotearoa New Zealand. These aspects of congregational life serve as a thermometer indicating how well we have appropriated the multiethnic nature of the church.

Penetrating Jerusalem Society: Stephen's Mission and Martyrdom, 6:7—8:1

Stephen's ministry was in a context of strategic groups responding to the gospel within "all Judea." As well as the priestly group, Stephen was soon in dialogue with the Hellenist, or Greek-speaking Jewish synagogue members. These "appear to be a Jewish subculture within Jerusalem who had adopted at least some elements of Greek culture . . ."[15] We can assume that

15. Flemming, *Contextualization*, 32.

the apostles, who themselves were Aramaic-speaking Jews, welcomed and respected Stephen's ministry to this different, and resistant, language group in their city (6:8–10). Stephen himself, like Saul of Tarsus, may well have come from this Hellenist background.[16] Certainly, the way Stephen presented Christ and drew such a strong reaction from members of this synagogue suggests he applied his proclamation forcefully to their particular thought-world (6:10–14). From the way he was falsely accused we conclude his contextualizing of the message was just too pointed for these zealous Jewish thinkers to bear.

When the missionary's presentation of Christ is unanswerably clear, he or she becomes a threat, particularly to the religious teachers in the community, and is best disposed of quickly. Effective contextualization never removes the inherent stumbling block of the cross of Christ, which proves objectionable to human pride in any culture.

These opening chapters of Acts present a clear understanding of the new people of God, the followers of Jesus Christ, as his commissioned representatives on earth. Their essence as a community was inherently linked to the ongoing mission of the Triune God in the world. Though fully occupied to this point with relating their gospel to the differing religious and cultural subgroups within the Jewish capital itself, the early church had already caught a glimpse of the way different cultures belong together as equals before God. They began to sense that mission and multiethnicity were part of their essential being.

Transitional Steps: Towards a Global, Missional, Multicultural Church, Acts 8–11

Luke next follows particular church leaders as, step by step, they move across cultural barriers to discover a larger view of God's people. Their monoethnic experience and ethnocentric assumptions were challenged in the process.

Philip's Mission: To Samaria, an Ethiopian, and Beyond, 8:4–40

Philip was another of the Greek-speaking leaders appointed to administer the daily food distribution to the needy. Caught up in the persecutions

16. See Bruce, *New Testament History*, 206–21.

following Stephen's death, he was the first of many scattered in this way who grasped the opportunity for more evangelism (8:4).

Philip began working out the wider implications of the Lord's commission of 1:8 by proclaiming Christ in an urban setting in Samaria. In Philip's day, "Jews had no dealings with Samaritans" (John 4:9).[17] Now that he and his Greek-speaking friends had been welcomed fully into the life and fellowship of the Jerusalem church, Philip knew there was something inconsistent about a Christian continuing an ancient animosity towards other cultures. Expelled from Jerusalem by persecution, he was compelled by the Spirit to share the good news with Samaritans. The Holy Spirit confirmed his spoken message with miraculous healings and release from oppression, which in turn led to more careful attention to the word preached (8:5–8). Soon Jerusalem was talking about the way Samaritans were responding (8:14). Jesus's own spiritual harvest in Samaria and the way he had broken down prejudices against these "strangers and foreigners" living on the Jewish doorstep (John 4:1– 42) had laid the foundation for Philip to make this significant move beyond acceptable Judaism.

God then directed Philip to a roadside appointment with an Ethiopian government official, an African, returning home after a spiritual pilgrimage to Jerusalem. This foreign courtier, however powerful and influential in his homeland, may well have only found partial acceptance as a eunuch in Jerusalem.[18] But his interest in the ancient Jewish writings gave Philip the ideal basis for presenting Christ Jesus, with immediate results. The first gentile baptism of the New Testament era took place in the obscurity of a rural roadside pool. Another significant step was thereby taken in what proved to be a centuries-long saga of the introduction of the gospel to Africa. Now Ethiopia could be listed alongside Egypt, Libya, and Cyrene for whom Pentecost was the beginning.

The First "Boomerang Challenge": Peter and John Consolidate Cross-Cultural Mission, 8:14–25

Meanwhile the apostles, largely unaffected by the persecutions and still able to live in Jerusalem, heard that Samaria had accepted the word of God. This

17. See 2 Kgs 17:1–41 and Ezra 4:2–4, for the historic background to the antipathy between Jews and Samaritans in New Testament times.

18. See Marshall, *Acts*, 162, for discussion of the term eunuch and its ritual implications in Judaism.

news sparked a key dynamic in the history of the expansion of Christianity through the centuries. God repeatedly called the original sending churches to sustain their cutting-edge vitality through challenges coming back to them from the new frontiers of mission. We call them "mission boomerang challenges"; they played a crucial role in developing the church's self-understanding from this point.

These challenges require the sending church to apply to their own worldview, lifestyles, and practice the implications of the gospel taking root in and transforming other cultures. This can mean difficult choices for the "sending" church, as we shall see.

The first such boomerang challenge, news of Samaritans putting their faith in Christ, landed relatively softly in Jerusalem, but it demanded an active response. Would the Jerusalem believers embrace the Samaritans as fellow members of the new people of God? Would they lay aside their traditional prejudices and welcome Samaritans into the expanding fellowship of the church? They had to check out what was happening, at least. Peter and John went to evaluate Philip's work (8:14–24), and found themselves significantly extending their own mission involvement. Peter and John led the new Samaritan converts into a full-orbed experience of the Holy Spirit (8:14–17). They challenged and corrected a counterfeit religious practitioner (8:18–24), and then reached out in Samaritan village evangelism as they returned to Jerusalem (8:25).

The Jerusalem believers thus shared as partners, supporters, and direct contributors to new mission initiatives across ethnic and religious boundaries into traditionally no-go areas. The boomerang challenge from Samaria was graciously accepted and the apostles' concept of the church thereby expanded to embrace this new cultural center.

The Second "Boomerang Challenge": Accepting the Ministry of a Convert from the Mission Periphery, 9:1–30

Saul, the bigoted Pharisee, religiously fastidious, impeccably self-righteous, determined to wipe out followers of the Way wherever he could find them, was, like the Ethiopian, dramatically turned around through a personal encounter with the risen Christ (9:1–25).

The Jerusalem church's mission now reached a significant point. Its influence had spread far enough for its impact to launch further boomerang repercussions back to Jerusalem. Saul, widely feared as the arch-persecutor of Christians, claimed conversion through a fellowship of scattered Christians in Damascus, a distant mission frontier in foreign territory. On his return to Jerusalem after a number of years away he wanted to share in ministry and mission with the Jerusalem elders (9:26). This was a tricky new situation.

The Jerusalem elders did not want a bar of it; they were comfortable with existing arrangements, thank you. But one of their members had experienced the grace of God some time back (4:32–33), and his Levitical background had been greatly enriched to make him a people-encourager. Luke tells how Barnabas interceded with the apostles and opened the door into the Jerusalem church for Saul. Initially reluctant to welcome a converted troublemaker into their midst, they were soon grateful as Paul tackled mission amongst the still-resistant Hellenist ethnic enclave in their city (9:28–29). But they sent him home to the provinces when he stirred up too much reaction (9:30).

So, this boomerang challenge was only partially accepted. How do we handle similar challenges in our churches today? Are converts from overseas gladly welcomed into our ministry teams? Can those who were a problem to us in their youth, having met the Lord while away from us, expect a warm welcome back in our midst? Is international ministry experience respected and integrated into our church's ministry team? By only partially accepting what Saul had to offer, the Jerusalem church elders shut off some of the insights they soon needed more fully.

Two Crucial Transformations: Peter's Preparation and Cornelius's Conversion, Acts 10:1—11:18

Peter turned to the remaining coastal Mediterranean strip of "all Judea," consolidating growth, meeting needs, and stimulating response in Lydda, Sharon, and Joppa (9:31–43). There he had a vision that transformed his most fundamental cultural assumptions, forcing him to reassess his whole approach to mission and to people of other ethnicities. As a loyal Jew, he shunned gentiles as inherently unclean and ceremonially unacceptable before God. In the vision, however, the Lord commanded Peter to eat food he had traditionally regarded as unclean. This was quickly followed by a real-life request for him to go to the home of an "unclean" Roman army officer, Cornelius (10:9–23).

As he obeyed the Spirit's specific instructions, Peter realized two things about his vision. He was taken aback by the way Cornelius and his household responded to their own vision from God, eagerly welcoming Peter as God's mouthpiece (10:23–33). Peter confessed, "I now realize how true it is that God does not show favoritism, but accepts those from every nation who fear him and do what is right" (10:34–35). As Dean Flemming puts it,

> The notion of divine impartiality had Old Testament precedence (Deuteronomy 10:17; 2 Chronicles 19:7), but here the emphasis falls on the fresh realization that God's love and favor is independent of a person's nationality, culture or ethnic identity . . . Peter discovers that God accepts people as they are, within their concrete national and cultural homes, yet on a basis that transcends any single ethnic identity or practice.[19]

But even more surprising for Peter was Cornelius's ready acceptance of the gospel message. When the Holy Spirit came upon this household just as clearly as on the first disciples at Pentecost, Peter had no choice but to receive these non-Jews as fully equal brothers and sisters in Christ and baptize them immediately (10:23–48).

Peter took one giant step towards fulfilling the "and to the ends of the earth" part of the master plan of Acts 1:8. He had gone cross-cultural, but although he could never be the same again, it would take him time to assimilate the implications of this shock to his prejudices. Harold Dollar makes the point well: "Luke shows that the theological challenge of the Gentile mission is not the reluctance of the Gentiles to respond to the gospel but the reluctance of the Jews to preach to them." Flemming adds, "Consequently, 'the "conversion" of the messenger' must come before the conversion of those who need the message."[20] But was the Jerusalem church also ready for such a change of attitudes?

The conversion of Cornelius presented another major boomerang challenge for the Jerusalem church. First, they learnt that their mission delegate, none other than the apostle Peter, had broken their Jewish customs, entered the home of a gentile, and actually eaten at his table, a serious lapse in culturally appropriate behavior. They expected to discipline their apostle as soon as Peter returned to Jerusalem (11:1–3).

19. Flemming, *Contextualization*, 37.

20. Flemming, *Contextualization*, 37, citing Dollar, *Biblical-Missiological Exploration*, 184–85.

Far from being apologetic, however, Peter made matters worse by claiming that such mission to people of other cultures was what God now required (11:4–17)! The church was challenged to change their minds about gentile foreigners. This is the fundamental challenge mission always brings back to sending churches. Can they accept peoples of other cultures as acceptable to God, and therefore their spiritual equals, simply because they have put their faith in Christ Jesus?

With characteristic understatement, Luke records their response. When the church heard the details from Peter, "they had no more objections, and praised God" (11:18). This was the high point of Peter's mission involvement. The Jerusalem church embraced cross-cultural mission in response to his testimony.

Acts 11:18 culminates the story of the steps necessary to prepare the way for multiethnic congregations. God's mission is to embrace all peoples as his sons and daughters through the gospel of grace. He chooses to do it by transforming the attitudes of his previously narrow-minded and culturally-blinkered people so that they genuinely praise him when peoples of other cultures find their fulfillment in him.

The Lord prepared Peter through expanding his cross-cultural experiences: first, the need to contextualize the message for his own people; then to resolve ethnic tensions in the bilingual Jerusalem church community; deeper interaction with the Greek-speaking migrant community; excursions into Samaria and the outer Judean rural communities; and, finally, the transforming vision that prepared him for the conversion of Cornelius and the embrace of a gentile family as fellow believers.

How far have the churches of our own culture progressed along their pathway towards becoming missional, multicultural churches? Too many of our long-established churches have either not noticed, or resisted, the urging of the Holy Spirit towards such transitional experiences. Short-term mission trips and excursions across cultural boundaries are fine for the youth group and enthusiasts, but few of our mature church leaders allow the Spirit of God to take them along Peter's inner transformative pathway. Too many key Christians have seldom, if ever, spent even a night in the home or meeting place of Christians of another culture, to learn firsthand about a different cultural perspective.[21] This lack of church leaders' expo-

21 In his study of New Zealand multiethnic churches, Phillip Donnell found "previous cross-cultural experience in New Zealand or overseas to be the key factor" in preparation for leaders. Donnell also found, "It is evident that leaders currently interpret from experience rather than from exegesis, and from pragmatism rather than from

sure to cross-cultural experience is worrying if we want to see more openness to cross-cultural mission and multiethnic congregations.

The Final Steps: A Multiethnic Church Becomes the New Global Mission Base, Acts 11:19—21:16

We see the roles of the major players developing significantly in the final phase of Luke's story.

Breakthrough at Antioch: Reciprocal Partnership for a New Global Mission Base, 11:19–30; 12:25; 13:1–3

This new phase of mission was still, in one sense, a follow-up of the initial scattering of unnamed Jerusalem-based disciples by the Holy Spirit at the time of Stephen's persecution (8:1, 4; 11:19).

Crossing the Cultural Boundary, a Language Breakthrough, 11:19–21

The continuity was simple and developed quite naturally. Christians traveling away from Jerusalem up the Phoenician coast moved to the island of Cyprus in the west, and Antioch inland to the east, evangelizing Jewish communities as they went. In another sense, this new phase was radically different. As the exiled Jewish converts dispersed, they gossiped the gospel to all they met, including gentile Syrians. They "began to speak to Greeks also, telling them the good news about the Lord Jesus" (11:20). Andrew Walls explains the significance of words we too readily take for granted:

> In all previous proclamations, Jesus had been presented as the Messiah, the Savior of Israel. In this new, Hellenistic-pagan context, he is given the title of *Kyrios* [Lord], the title Hellenistic pagans gave to their cult divinities. . . . But in the first encounter, the loading of *Kyrios* with the cult divinity idea was vital. It is doubtful whether unacculturated pagans in the Antiochene world could have understood the significance of Jesus in any other way. None of us can take in a new idea except in terms of the ideas we already have. Once implanted however, this understanding of the word received a new set of controls from its new biblical frame

philosophy." Donnell, "Where the World," 1:44.

> of reference. In time much of the original [pagan] loading of the word disappeared altogether.[22]

By this fresh application of the "translation principle," the church initiated a new evangelistic methodology consistent with its nature as a multicultural, missional body. Christ was presented as the answer to the hopes and yearnings of non-Jewish communities in terms that spoke to their hearts. This is a fundamental aspect of being the church of Jesus Christ as it moves explicitly towards "the ends of the earth" (11:19–20). Such translation skill is now essential for evangelism in the multicultural cities of our worldwide "global village."

A Mission Partnership Role for Barnabas, Acts 11:19–26

The Jerusalem church soon learnt of a cultural breakthrough in Antioch (11:22). What would they do with this boomerang challenge? Should Jerusalem react violently and go and straighten out this irregular behavior? Or should they just ignore it?

They decided to become involved, authorizing Barnabas to check up on this major move into the cultural region of Syrian Antioch, the third largest city in the Roman Empire at this time.[23] Barnabas now became the Jerusalem church's mission partner-delegate to Antioch in Syria (11:19–26), the first of a new generation of church leaders in mission. Given the qualities we have already noted in Barnabas, plus his filling with the Spirit and faith, we are not surprised to find him rejoicing at what he found. He encouraged this new work immediately, consolidating and extending it substantially. An effective Jerusalem–Antioch partnership developed (11:23–24).

Mutual Partnership for Quality Growth and Holistic Mission, 11:25–30

Developments in Antioch led to a series of new relationships between the Jerusalem and Antioch churches, and another mission boomerang challenge. Barnabas recognized the potential of these new opportunities, and typically unselfishly, rather than grapple with them on his own, he recruited as assistant the one who had shown such disturbing promise at least eleven years earlier, Saul of Tarsus (11:25). Having once opened the door into the

22. Walls, *Missionary Movement*, 34–35.

23. Bruce, *New Testament History*, 220.

church for Saul, Barnabas now opened the door for him into mission. Together they laid a solid base for a new mission outreach through consecutive teaching in the Antioch church for a full year. This Bible teaching had such an effect that the city saw the distinctive, transformed lifestyles of the disciples and gave them a particular nickname for the first time (11:26). We gladly accept the nickname, but do we also display the lifestyles that gave it birth?

A group of itinerant prophets from Jerusalem challenged the young church in Antioch to embrace yet another dimension of what it means to be the church of Jesus Christ. Their message, true to the Old Testament prophetic heritage and in line with God's missional heart, was a strong call to social action. They advised the Antioch church of impending famine across the Roman world, particularly in Judea (11:27–28). The Antioch Christians responded with holistic depth in their commitment, taking it for granted that there should be mutuality between sending and receiving churches in mission. Since they had received spiritual enrichment from Jerusalem's outreach, the least they could do was return some of their material blessing in responsive gratitude. Barnabas and Saul were sent as Antioch delegates with aid to Jerusalem (11:29–30). A New Testament understanding of the nature of the church has a deep commitment both to reciprocity and to missional social action like this.

Luke is quiet about how the Jerusalem elders received the gifts. Certainly they encouraged Saul and Barnabas to maintain such concern for the poor (Gal 2:1–10). In response, the Jerusalem church also released one of their promising young men, John Mark, back to Antioch as a new mission partner (12:25).

Thus, a mutual interchange of spiritual and material ministries was established between two culturally distant churches. One of their leaders later described this "sharing in giving and receiving" as a spiritual sacrifice that greatly pleases the heart of God and as the practical basis upon which God intends his mission to extend (Phil 4:14–19).

The church in Antioch was characterized by serious Bible teaching, transformed lifestyles, and commitment to social action. Acts 13:1–2 adds another two distinctive factors. Antioch developed an effective cross-cultural, multiple-member leadership team. To Barnabas's background of Cypriot birth and Jerusalem workplace, and Saul's Cilician birthplace and Jerusalem education, were added Simeon's African heritage. Lucius was another North African from Cyrene, and Manaen brought his courtier's upbringing from Galilee. When a local church develops multicultural leadership it is well placed to reach out to other cultures with the gospel. A church which cannot grapple with cultural diversity at the leadership level in its local situation is restricted in its ability to express the fullness of the New Testament model for an effective church. It will be hampered in equipping cross-cultural workers, and less able to adequately understand and support its mission partners.

With these defining qualities blossoming, one last factor became the spark through which the Spirit of God made the Antioch church the new center for mission around the Mediterranean world. God entrusted his purposes and concerns to those who gave priority to seeking his face and listening for his voice (13:2). As it was then, the call to mission today comes most clearly through acts of worship.

Each of the three missionary journeys that fill the rest of the story of Acts had Antioch in Syria as its base: the first, 13:3—14:28; the second, 15:36—18:22; and the third, 18:23—21:16. The Jerusalem church fades into the background from this point in the story. Perhaps her failure to cultivate the qualities we have identified at Antioch explains why the missional leadership moved to a new center.[24]

Facing a Major Mission Boomerang Challenge: The Place of the Dominant Church's Culture, 15:1–35

The steps taken to discover the full missional and multiethnic nature of the early church were not gained or retained easily. The "Jerusalem Conference," as it is often called, proved crucial in the life of the early churches. The issues addressed and the way they were handled set the direction for the subsequent development of God's mission in our world.

The Issue Comes to a Head in Syrian Antioch, 15:1–3 (Gal 2:11–17)

A group of Jerusalem Christians, claiming the Jerusalem church's authority, came to Antioch in Syria teaching that there could be no salvation without the Jewish cultural-religious sign of circumcision. The Antioch church was thrown into confusion (15:1–2a). The problem was quite specific. Jewish

24. It is beyond the scope of this chapter to explore the ways in which the Antioch church contributed to those missionary journeys. For an overview, see Hitchen, "Church's Role."

Christians were the ethnically dominant group, and Jerusalem the "senior" church of the day. With their heritage and links back to the birthplace of the good news they assumed, or were accorded, the authoritative voice on how Christianity should develop. They dispensed the heritage of the "fathers" of the faith like Abraham and Moses. The Law, prophetic preparation, and the gospel itself, had come through them. Their God-given distinctive cultural practices like circumcision showed their special relationship with God, setting them apart from all other cultures.

From this perspective it seemed right that Christians of other cultures, like any convert to Judaism, should be baptized, pay the temple tax, and, if male, be circumcised. Jewish Christians probably never thought of themselves as the dominant religious culture; dominant cultures seldom do! As God's covenant people, Jews believed they must not lose their distinctiveness. Fraternizing with those who were not circumcised would compromise the purity of their relationship with God. So Jewish Christians should, they thought, keep themselves separate from converts of other cultures and not celebrate communion together, nor eat in each other's homes. Perhaps uncircumcised gentiles could fellowship with each other, but Christian Jews would be wrong to join them.

This teaching undermined the whole concept of a unified, multiethnic church. The Jewish attitude was leading toward a form of Christian apartheid with separate, ethnically-based congregations. Peter and Barnabas appeared willing at first to go along with this compromise while the Jerusalem personnel were in Antioch, perhaps thinking that to keep the peace was the wiser strategy.

But, as we shall find more fully in a later chapter, Paul was not happy at all.[25] For him it was pure hypocrisy not to continue their open multiethnic fellowship. To insist on anything more than faith in Christ as a necessary condition for fellowship denied the essence of the gospel, and he told Peter so publicly (Gal 2:11–17). For Paul, it boiled down to the fundamental question, "Is the cross of Christ or Jewish cultural tradition the basis for right standing before God and fellowship between believers?" As Luke comments, there was, "no little dissension and debate" (15:2).

The Antioch church leaders decided the only way forward was to confer with the Jerusalem elders. This was not the supposedly "older" or "mother" church in Jerusalem calling the "younger" or "daughter" church

25. See chapter 5, "Cultural Boundaries and the True Gospel: Contextualizing in Galatia."

to account, far from it. The younger Antioch church chose to confer for the sake of the gospel. Paul and Barnabas went as delegates to Jerusalem to thrash out the issues.

The Process and Progress of the Debate

The process is informative.[26] In a public forum the issues were aired fully with firsthand reports and reaction (15:4–5). The elders then called a formal meeting in which debate, reminders of precedents, factual evidence, and a summary using relevant Scriptures led to a consensus (15:6–21). They decided there was no need for circumcision. No extra burden should be added to faith in Christ as the basis for right standing before God and fellowship in the church.

Having established this central issue, the meeting called on people of other cultures to uphold ethical requirements and to facilitate social contacts by showing sensitivity towards Jews regarding food and its preparation. The whole church endorsed and reported this Spirit-directed outcome (15:22–35). With Paul and Barnabas, Judas Barsabbas and Silas delivered the letter from Jerusalem disclaiming responsibility for the previous false teachings, commending Paul and Barnabas, indicating the Holy Spirit's consensus, and formally repeating the conference decision. The church at Antioch gladly welcomed the report (15:30–35), and accepted its decisions. How fully both churches grasped their implications is open to question.

The Importance of the Conference Decision

It is hard to overestimate the importance of this outcome. The joint church conference clarified the crucial issues for all time. There is only one gospel for all peoples. "By grace through faith" is the way to God for people of every culture. The Christian faith is the way of conversion, not proselytism.[27] Every culture is equal before Christ and accepted as an adequate setting for discipleship. Christ expects to be Lord of every culture, bringing his transforming touch to every ethnic group. Moreover, every church is obligated to continue the task of cross-cultural mission to other cultures. Mission is

26. Flemming, *Contextualization*, 43–55, expounds it as a model for cross-cultural contextualization.

27. For the significance of this distinction, see Walls, "Converts or Proselytes," 1–6.

not any one culture's sole responsibility. The tasks of Bible translation and contextualization are necessary for and in every culture.

In addition, the decision shows that intercultural fellowship flows from and is rooted in the unity of all believers in the one body of Christ. No addition to faith is necessary for full fellowship across cultural boundaries.

This issue is still central for cross-cultural fellowship in our churches today. The tendency for one cultural group to dominate and expect others to assimilate and conform to their norms is never far below the surface in discussions between Māori and Pākehā (people of European descent) discussions in my homeland, New Zealand. Similar questions lie behind the number of separate congregations based on ethnicity springing up in our cities. Andrew Walls encapsulates the issues helpfully:

> There are two dangers. One lies in an instinctive desire to protect our own version of Christian faith, or even seek to establish it as the standard, normative one. The other, and perhaps the more seductive in the present condition of Western Christianity, is the postmodern option: to decide each of the expressions and versions is equally valid and authentic, and that we are therefore each at liberty to enjoy our own in isolation from all the others. Neither of these approaches is the [Christian] way. . . . Only in Christ does completion, fullness, dwell. And Christ's completion . . . comes from all humanity, from the translation of the life of Jesus into the lifeways of all the world's cultures and subcultures through history. None of us can reach Christ's completeness on our own. We need each other's vision to correct, enlarge and focus our own; only together are we complete in Christ.[28]

The Multiethnic Principle Applied in the Church's Mission, Acts 20:1–6

Our final episode sees the two essential features of the church brought together. We skip to the apostle Paul on his third missionary journey. Paul had enlisted a thoroughly multicultural team to accompany him on itinerant mission: three Macedonians—Sopater, Aristarchus, and Secundus; two Galatians—Gaius and Timothy; and two from the Roman province of Asia—Tychicus and Trophimus (20:4).

The composition of this team also suggests the young churches of Derbe and Lystra in Galatia, Berea and Thessalonica in Macedonia, and

28. Walls, *Cross-Cultural Process*, 78–79.

at least Ephesus (and perhaps Colossae) in Asia were all actively involved in Paul's missionary outreach through the release of key workers as Paul's partners. On his part, Paul realized the importance of multicultural contributions in mission and for adequate preparation for the next generation of church leaders. Thus, the multiethnic principle at the heart of congregational life was applied to mission methodology. By the end of the mission journeys in Acts we have a pattern of churches cooperating internationally across cultural and linguistic boundaries to supply multiethnic ministry teams for missional effectiveness.

Conclusion

The nature of the church as a multiethnic and missional community was fully grasped, defended, and creatively implemented. The church was such from its inception. But it took time, trials, experience, debate, and misunderstandings, plus repeated divine intervention, for the church to first understand and then become what it was: missional and multiethnic in its essential nature.

Perhaps our pathway also shows a third feature of the church's essence. As well as being essentially missional and multicultural, the church of Jesus Christ is always growing, learning, failing, and growing again to become who we are. As church we are a dynamically developing, growing, and maturing body, and maybe God ordained it this way!

Chapter 5

Cultural Boundaries and the True Gospel

Contextualizing in Galatia

Galatians is one letter in the New Testament specifically dealing with the issue of contextualization where the gospel had crossed a cultural frontier, a situation that has occurred often in later Christian mission history.[1] Representatives of a culture with its own strong religious heritage—in this original case, a Jewish heritage—had introduced the gospel to Galatia. The good news came into a setting where some of the first Christian converts had previously been Jews, or Jewish proselytes and "God-fearers," who were already learning of the Jewish way of life. Before becoming Christians they had grown up with, or had already adopted, much of the strong Jewish religious heritage and its practices. And, of course, the missionaries who brought them the gospel, Paul and Barnabas, also had a Jewish cultural and religious background before their conversions. But many others of the first Galatian converts, the "gentiles," had not shared that Jewish cultural heritage. They had either followed one of the many Greek or Roman philosophies, or primal religious beliefs about spirit or ancestral powers and magical forces controlling daily life. Paul's letter to these Galatian Christians

1. This paper is an adaptation of Hitchen, "Primal Religious Groups," 139–71. Used here with the permission of Regnum Books from *Mission and Postmodernities*, 2011, ISBN 978-1-870345-972 (see bibliography for further details). An earlier version of the outline of this paper formed the concluding section of Hitchen, "Culture and the Bible," a paper presented at the South Pacific Association of Bible Colleges Biennial Conference in Sydney on July 1–5, 1991.

of different religious backgrounds addresses the basic issue raised by the effective mission outreach of the early church.

The unexpected influx of believers in Christ Jesus from other, non-Jewish cultures—"gentiles," or "the uncircumcision," as the Jews called them—posed a fundamental dilemma. As these new believers from other cultures repented of their sin and rebellion towards God and turned to Christ, how were they to express their new loyalty to Christ in their own cultural setting? They faced a choice, the classic choice at the heart of contextualization. Should they follow the well-established pathway of proselytism and adopt the lifestyle expectations of the dominant religious culture from which the good news came to them? In this case, must they accept the Jewish cultural and religious sign of circumcision and conform to Jewish religious and cultural customs to show they now belonged to the covenant people of God? Must they observe the food laws, the clothing styles, the music, and language forms of the Jewish customs to be true people of God?

Some Jewish Christian teachers who had gone from Jerusalem to supplement Paul's teaching in the new churches in Galatia took for granted that this way of proselytism was the only right way for people of any culture to show they now belonged to Christ, the Messiah. So they were telling the new Christian converts they needed to adopt the Jewish custom of circumcision and follow the Jewish food laws as well as put their faith in Jesus Christ. But was that really the Christian way?

Or was the response for these gentile converts different? The gospel of faith in Christ Jesus converts believers, and makes Christ Lord of the new believers' own culture and context. Christ wanted to transform their Galatian languages, their music, their dress styles, and food habits so that taking on the customs of another cultural tradition—like Jewish circumcision—was not only unnecessary for gentile believers, but also a contradiction of the heart of the gospel itself.[2]

Restating the issue, no particular cultural expression of the gospel, as distinct from the truths of the gospel itself, is to be absolutized as the universal norm for all believers, regardless of their cultural setting. Paul wrote the Letter to the Galatians to address this issue. His response was unequivocal: each culture has direct access to salvation on the same basis of faith alone, without having to adopt any other culture's set of practices and forms to enjoy and fully express their new life in Christ Jesus.

2. On the contrast between becoming proselytes or converts, see Walls, "Converts or Proselytes," 1–7.

Many, if not most, present-day fast-growing churches around the world face parallel situations. They are often indebted to representatives of Western forms of Christianity for introducing them to the gospel. Moreover, their own cultures have often already absorbed key aspects of the globalized patterns of Western culture. The question is: Must these churches in many varied different local cultures adhere to the outward forms and patterns of Christianity which are expected and taken for granted in the West? Or are believers in these diverse cultures free to apply the gospel message in different ways in their own cultures and can they expect the gospel to be at home in, to enrich, and to transform the sociocultural forms of their own locality and heritage?

The contextualized answer to these questions, for the Galatians, is given in the combined message of all the themes covered in the whole Letter to the Galatians, not just in a few proof texts taken from the letter. Paul outlines the issues at stake in all similar contextualization situations. As we work through the letter's carefully developed argument, the apostolic answer offers us a series of principles we need to grasp and reapply as evaluative standards for all our contextualizing.

Keeping Loyal to the Apostolic Gospel, Galatians 1:1—2:10

The first section of the letter holds up the original apostolic teaching of the gospel as the unique and unchanging standard for every cultural setting. Adequate contextualization needs to address the issues relating to authority in matters of faith. Right at the outset the Letter to the Galatians declares that apostolic authority is the foundation for contextualization in all cultures. Apostolic authority must be upheld and expressed in the contextualization task. The New Testament statement of the good news gives our faith a definite shape and content—a "given-ness"—which we cannot just adapt, alter, or change as we please for every new context, or as every missionary advises. This section of Galatians warns against turning to "a different gospel—which is really no gospel at all" (1:6–7).

The danger the apostle addresses is that heeding a distortion of the gospel too quickly becomes turning away from God's free grace given to us in Christ. To put some other religious formality, such as circumcision, above gratitude for the love and forgiveness offered in Christ is to betray Christ's love shown on the cross. It turns a vital personal relationship into a merely formal ritual. Such confusion easily becomes a distortion of the Christian message and is not the good news Christ offers.

Paul warned that the danger can come from various sources (1:8–9). Those who once taught faithfully may change the message and thereby deny its essence. Paul is not reacting against alternative teachings out of envy or fear of losing his influence. He warns that if even he himself (v. 8), or "anyone" (v. 9), distorts the message as originally preached and received in the apostolic churches, then that person comes under the judgment of God against such false teachers. Another potential source of distortion claims angelic origins for its distinctive features. Many people claim their visions, dreams, séances, or special spiritual experiences are the authority for their teachings, which turn out to be distortions of the simple gospel of faith in Christ. Any such perversion of the gospel as authoritatively stated in the apostolic writings of the New Testament is so serious that Paul pronounces a ban on such false teachers, handing them over to the judgment of God. Nothing could be more serious.

This comes as a real challenge to our age when Western postmodern and post-Christian societies exalt tolerance of religious diversity as if it is the most important religious value. As Paul defended his own apostolic loyalty against those who were challenging his authority, he stressed the integrity of his motives as a gospel preacher, the divine provenance of his message, God's initiative in revealing it to him, and the confirmation of the Jerusalem apostles of the universal truth of the message he preached (1:10—2:10).

This biographical reflection in the first section of Galatians reminds us that in any contextualization of the Christian message, faithfulness to the apostolic gospel as set out in the New Testament Scriptures is essential. Distortion of the Christian message can arise through willfully or unconsciously adding requirements to the message that was first received, often on the basis of apparently significant new spiritual experiences. Distortion also easily develops from either neglect or overemphasis of aspects of the message. Upholding the apostolic gospel as the one and only standard for teaching in every culture directly challenges postmodern assumptions that metanarratives are necessarily exploitative. The apostle insisted that imposing a single culture's religious rituals is what is hegemonic and exploits people, not the gospel metanarrative. By insisting the one and only gospel message is applicable globally, Paul claimed that this particular gospel metanarrative, far from dominating or repressing people, is actually liberating and enriching for every culture, as the themes of the letter will explain progressively.[3]

These dangers are occupational hazards in all serious contextualization. We usually call failures in these areas syncretism: mixing incompatible aspects of another religious system with the true teachings or practices of the gospel message. We must recognise syncretism that distorts the truth of the gospel as a threat, and guard against mixing contradictory religious ideas with the gospel in all our contextualization. The tendency towards syncretism is common to all cultures. As we relate the good news meaningfully and relevantly to the worldview assumptions, value systems, and beliefs of any cultural context we are forced to make decisions about the extent to which aspects of the local cultural heritage can faithfully express or incorporate the gospel.[4] This is never straightforward, since cultures are dynamic, developing realities. Appropriate contextualization in one setting at one time may be seen as serious syncretism from another perspective at another time. Western theology regularly syncretizes the gospel with the West's individualistic, materialistic, and rationalistic rereadings of biblical texts. We should not be surprised, then, to find other cultural traits favored in other cultural contexts. Moreover, human nature proves us all more able and ready to see syncretistic tendencies in other peoples' adaptations of Scripture to their cultural values than we see in our own. Kevin Vanhoozer suggests there are good and bad ways to approach the issues around syncretism, and calls for a "critical syncretism" which discerns between them, and which always upholds the "final primacy" of Scripture in contextualizing the gospel.[5]

Local believers themselves need to be taught and trusted to make the judgments about what is, and what is not, faithful adherence to the once-for-all gospel in their cultural setting. Expatriate missionaries or fraternal partners can ask questions about customs and proposed interpretations and practices, but the local believers alone can decide whether or not the truth of the Scriptures is being appropriately upheld in a local situation. Expatriates can also model a self-critical awareness and willingness to learn

3. See Bauckham, *Bible and Mission*, 88–90.

4. See para. 10, "Evangelism and Culture," in Lausanne Movement, "Lausanne Covenant."

5. Vanhoozer, "One Rule," 102–4, 110. See also Roxborogh, "Loyalty to Christ," 345–58.

from peoples of other cultures about their own ethnocentric, syncretistic tendencies.[6]

Expressing this first principle as a question—Is the contextualizing loyal to the one and only apostolic message?—highlights the importance of teaching Christians to study and understand the apostolic Scriptures in active dependence upon the Holy Spirit as their teacher and guide in the task of relating the gospel to their cultural context.

Welcoming the Justified of All Cultures in Cross-Cultural Hospitality, Galatians 2:11–21

The Judaizing delegation from Jerusalem polarized the Syrian Antioch church ethnically. Even Peter and Barnabas had opted to keep the peace with the Jewish Christians who had come from Jerusalem, saying Antioch Christians must be circumcised. So, Peter and Barnabas withdrew from fellowshipping with the non-Jews, even though they had previously gladly shared hospitality with them (2:11–13). By their actions they sided with the views of the dominant religious culture. No Christian likes a fight over issues like this; and it is not difficult to rationalize doing so with chapter and verse.

Andrew Walls sets out the issue succinctly:

> One of the features of life in the Jesus community in Jerusalem had been that the followers of Jesus took every opportunity to eat together . . . What was to happen when there were also Gentile followers of Jesus, uncircumcised, following Hellenistic eating patterns? Would it still be the mark of the followers of Jesus that they ate together? The test was the meal table, and clearly many old believers found it difficult to break the tradition of centuries and sit at table with fellow servants of the Messiah who still bore all the marks of their alien background. What could be defended on grounds of theological principle sometimes demanded great resolution in the face of peer pressure. Thus, Peter can argue from traditional premises for the liberty of Gentile believers (Acts 15:7–11), but find it more convenient not to share a table with them when there was a chance of being observed by his home

6. See Van Rheenen, "Syncretism and Contextualization"; and Hiebert's development of his previous articles in Hiebert, "Syncretism and Social Paradigms," 1–46.

> constituency (Gal 2:11–14). The shared table was the acid test. It stood for diverse humanity redeemed by Christ and sharing in him.[7]

For the apostle Paul gospel truth was at stake here. His verdict on Peter and Barnabas separating from non-Jewish Christians was devastating: "... they were not acting in line with the truth of the gospel" (2:14). Refusing to sit at table with another believer because of culturally-based religious rules totally contradicts the message and work of Christ.

Our shared life in Christ makes us one. Not to express that unity around our meal tables is to deny the death which has made us new creatures. Our social behavior is a clear test of the adequacy of the way we have both understood and contextualized the gospel. As long as peoples of other cultures are not welcome in our homes and at our meals, we have failed to properly apply what the cross of Christ has done in and for believers. None of us won our own acceptance before God on the basis of our religious rule-keeping. Each of us needed Christ's death to deal with our failure before God. Only faith in Christ Jesus justifies us before God (2:15–16). Religious (or any other kind of) rule-keeping is irrelevant for being accepted by God. Therefore, it must be the same for accepting each other. We will welcome anyone Christ welcomes. Whom we invite to our homes as guests indicates whether or not we have contextualized the essence of the gospel. Adequate contextualizing does not just agree with the dominant culture's religious rules. The gospel takes up the cause of those who are pushed to the side. The well-contextualized gospel respects and upholds the perspective of the minority culture when it comes to sharing in social fellowship in the church. In this way the gospel also provides a unique basis for respecting cultural diversity without hegemonic domination. This is good news indeed for both the global resurgences of "first nation" or indigenous identity, and for the longings of postmodernity for integrity in communal relationships.

So, valid contextualizing leads to lifestyle consistency across cultural barriers. Contextualization's aim is that our hearers will "act in line with the gospel" (2:14). This practical goal offers an important test for all suggested contextualization. Do the suggested meanings or principles of Scripture apply biculturally and multiculturally, particularly in the area of social relations and hospitality? If not, the contextualization is not yet adequate. In the very process of particularizing the message we must always reflect its universal scope.

7. Walls, *Cross-Cultural Process*, 77–78.

Dependence on the Spirit and an "Adoptive" Heritage of Faith, Galatians 3:1–18

Having clarified the way justification works through faith and results in the believers' dynamic union with the living Christ (2:20), Paul goes straight into a strong rebuke lest the Galatians forget or underestimate the role of the Holy Spirit in bringing them to faith and equipping them in every aspect of life and service as Christ's followers (3:1–5). Moreover, one purpose of justification through Christ's redemptive work is that we enjoy the reality of the Holy Spirit sharing in our daily lives (3:10–14). The Galatians, from a primal religious background, had previously depended on capricious and unpredictable spirit powers. But now, in Christ, that old way had been transformed so they no longer relied on a ritualistic or legalistic self-competence. Rather, they now had an ongoing relationship with the Holy Spirit of God actively working in response to vital faith in the message of the gospel (3:1–5). This rich spirituality also answers the postmodern yearning for something more than rational self-competence. Christian spirituality focused on personal experience of the indwelling Holy Spirit is also deeply rooted in human history.

The gospel not only opens us to new present-day cultural richness; it also gives us a rich new cultural inheritance. Every believer in Christ becomes a "descendant" of Abraham. He becomes our "father" when we join the family of believers. In Christ we receive roots and rights which make us heirs of a large part of the Hebrew-Jewish past. Faith alone brings us to Christ. Faith alone keeps us going on with Christ. But this principle of faith does not cut us off from all the preparatory history of the times before Christ. Realizing that no one else's culture is necessary as a prerequisite for life in Christ does not mean our own culture is all we need as we grow in him. Rather, our experience of Christ's rescue through faith unites us with all those who have lived by faith in previous ages. Those who have faith are sharing in the blessing given to the great progenitor of faith—Abraham. By following the same principle by which Abraham lived, namely, trusting the word of God, we, too, have come to enjoy the rescue operation of Christ. That same experience has freely given us a share in the heritage and the promises God gave to Abraham—regardless of our human lineage or traditional culture (3:6–9).[8]

8. See Walls, *Missionary Movement*, 8–15, on this concept of the "adoptive heritage" of Christians.

This can be a bit of an embarrassment. We now have to integrate our own history, with its culture heroes, and even its mythology, with the biblical history and the biblical heroes. Our Western heritage has found this biblical heritage difficult to reconcile with the Enlightenment and scientific ideas permeating our schooling. New Zealand Māori have an equally challenging task to reconsider their traditional stories and teachings in the light of this "adoptive" heritage from the Scriptures. But adequate contextualization of the gospel means becoming bicultural in the new sense of being people both with a biological cultural heritage, and also this biblical cultural heritage. One aspect of the Holy Spirit's ministry is to initiate us into this continuing participation in the heritage of faith (3:14).

This biblical adoptive heritage changes the stance from which we approach different cultural perspectives as we work at contextualization. Instead of having a conflict between the dominant and the minority cultures, we have a common ground together as believers in our shared adoptive past. This means we can listen to each other as we both struggle to relate the demands of our biblical faith into our own culture. Both cultures sit under biblical scrutiny in the contextualization process. As Andrew Walls sums it up: "[S]ince none of us can read the Scriptures without cultural blinkers of some sort, the great advantage, the crowning excitement which our own era of Church history has over all others, is the possibility that we may be able to read them together . . ."[9]

We should test the adequacy of our proposed contextualization, then, by asking: Is the meaning or application we are suggesting true to the already received truth in our Abraham-Moses-Christ-Pentecost deposit of faith? Contextualization takes place within the family of the faithful, guided by the Holy Spirit. It must therefore reflect the family heritage even as it embraces the new family members and all the disruption any addition brings to the family.

The Role of Local Cultural and Religious Heritage, Galatians 3:19—4:7

The next item on the Galatian contextualization agenda raises another basic question: What about the local cultural heritage and particularly its religious aspects? How should we handle these in the contextualization process?

9. Walls, *Missionary Movement*, 15.

For Paul's Jewish readers the gospel created a major problem by offering a way to be true children of Abraham that was not based on the Mosaic law which they were observing meticulously. Little wonder, then, they asked: "What, then, was the purpose of the law?" (3:19). How should they regard this central aspect of their cultural heritage? Paul's response to this question offers a paradigm for the way Christians should regard the pre-Christian religious aspects of their cultural heritage.

The law was given, Paul explains, "because of transgressions, until the promised seed had come." Human nature needs to be shown what is right and wrong. Without rules and warnings, we go off track, we transgress. But the law was for a specified time and limited in what it could do. Like a Roman slave appointed to guard and ensure the owner's children turned up for instruction, the law constantly watched over the Jews, defining the depth and seriousness of their sin problem. The law also prepared God's people for their Messiah. A promised descendant of Abraham would come who could give the new life the law could not provide, but showed humans' need. The law's continuing reminders of their shortcomings, and of God's good purposes for them, kept alive the yearning for a better way. The law acted as a protection from the excesses of sin until the full solution became available in the Christ (3:19–23). These instructing and protecting roles of the law were vital, though limited. We respect guardians and policemen and appreciate their work, giving it due honor, but never expecting too much of them. Likewise with the law. Its corrective and formative roles were to be highly valued, but the law could not, in itself, give new life (3:21). The Messiah was desperately needed for that, as the law confirms.

In this way, Paul answered the Jewish question about the place of the law and their whole Hebrew-Mosaic religious heritage. But what about those of other cultures in the Galatian churches? Their heritage focused on elemental spirit beliefs about unseen forces active in every realm of daily life. Their traditional religions feared these "powers." What about these elemental spirits or basic religious principles as they were called? In 4:1–3 Paul takes his argument further. As F. F. Bruce summarizes it, "The Law has been compared [3:20–25] to a prison-warden, 3:23, and a slave attendant, 3:24; now [4:1–3] its role is compared to that of guardians and trustees appointed to take care of a minor and his property," until the minor became an adult.[10] Paul likened the pre-Christian experience to an heir, destined one day to be lord of the estate, being treated as a slave (4:1). He summed

10. Bruce, *Galatians*, 192.

it up, "So also when we were children, we were in slavery under the basic principles of the world" (4:3). The law not only prepared and protected, it also enslaved its adherents. To make his point, Paul the converted Jew, makes quite remarkable claims. To describe the extent and nature of this Jewish bondage to the law, Paul seems deliberately to choose a phrase, "elements, or basic principles, of the world" (*stoicheia tou kosmou* in the Greek), which was understood in different ways in different cultures.

The "basic principles" for a Jew would mean the ABC of the Mosaic law.[11] But the apostle well knew, and (whether or not he intended the "we" of v. 3 to include Jews and gentiles, which is debated) in 4:8–9 he will make explicit that for most of his non-Jewish readers the same phrase referred to those elemental spirits they believed controlled the forces of wind, fire, earth, and water which regulate the whole universe. Putting together 4:1–3 and 4:8–9, then, Paul says these traditional religious beliefs in spirit powers filled for non-Jews the same kind of protecting, preparatory, but restricting role as the law had done for the Jews. Factually, that is almost self-evident. For their followers, primal religions restrain evil, confirm human sinfulness, and show how much a divine initiative is needed for ultimate human welfare. These functions directly parallel the policing and instructing/protecting functions of the Hebrew Law. F. F. Bruce summarizes the teaching of this passage:

> [Stoicheia], it is now made plain, not only regulated the Jewish way of life under the law; they also regulated the pagan way of life in the service of the gods that were no gods . . . For all the basic differences between Judaism and paganism, both involved subjection to the same elemental forces. This is an amazing statement for a former Pharisee to make; yet Paul makes it—not as an exaggeration in the heat of argument but as the deliberate expression of a carefully thought out position.[12]

Paul has defined limits to the value of Jewish traditional religion. But in doing so, he has retained a proper respect for its role in regulating society and in preparing for the gospel (3:19–25). He has then attributed the same roles to the traditional belief systems of other, non-Jewish cultures (4:1–3). In these respects, at least, the apostle recognizes a positive role for pre-Christian cultural values. This suggests that in the contextualization

11. For the Jew, being "under the basic principles of the world" (4:3) is the same as being "under the law" (4:4). See Bruce, *Galatians*, 193–94.

12. Bruce, *Galatians*, 202–3.

process we should have a healthy respect for the way local or traditional religions can reveal to their adherents their need as humans, and thus point towards Christ. We can expect to gain real insight into the thought-world of others, and into the diverse ways in which human sin and human hopes operate in different cultures, by a proper study of their religious ideas. This is vital for effective contextualization. This aspect of the teaching of Galatians offers a way for us to move beyond misjudging another culture's religions. It challenges us to listen and learn rather than criticize and blame.

All contextualization should do the same, as we present Christ as the fulfiller of the "desires of the nations" (Hag 2:7). There is an important sense in which new converts in every culture need to "redeem" their religious history as they respond to Christ. Their cultural heritage is not replaced by some other religion, not even another ethnic version of Christianity. Rather the whole heritage is renewed as aspects that are incompatible with Christ are discarded, and compatible aspects find a new center and significance as members of the culture themselves reorient their cultural traditions to serve the living Christ. Their values, art forms, architecture, communication processes and spiritual insights find new integrating and creative development potential with Christ as their Lord.[13]

Appropriate contextualization, then, will address this key issue: "How should we understand and relate to the local cultural traditions and religious heritage?" This section of Galatians has offered constructive guidelines for grappling with these global concerns (and the next section of the letter will say more to keep this emphasis in balance).

But the time of protection and preparation would, and has, come to an end, for both the Jews and those from primal religious backgrounds. "At the right time," or "In the fullness of time," in one of the most clearly Trinitarian passages of the Bible, Paul describes the roles of all three persons of the Godhead in bringing God's great salvation purposes to their climax.

13. See Walls, "Old Athens," 146–53, with his conclusion: "The Christian consciousness of Africa and Asia is likely to reflect the pre-Christian cultural processes, including the pre-Christian religious processes, of these continents. On all past showing, these processes are not replaced—that would be the way of the proselyte. They are redirected, for that is the way of the convert. Christian Theology—active, *working* Christian theology—is constructed under the Spirit's guidance from pre-Christian materials. The vessels and hangings of the tabernacle, while divinely directed in the making, consist of Egyptian gold and Egyptian cloth. The most urgent reason for the study of the religious traditions of Africa and Asia, of the Amerindian and the Pacific peoples, is their significance for Christian theology; they are the substratum of the Christian faith and life of the greater number of the Christians of the world" (153).

God's Mission Initiative (4:4)

When God the Father's purposes had properly matured, "At the right time," he took decisive action in two "sendings," two acts of mission.

God's Mission Purpose (4:5)

The timely sending of the Son: the one who shared fully the life, being, and nature of God was commissioned to be "born of woman," to share fully the reality and nature of humans; to be "born under law" to know the depths of the human problem of restriction and control by law and lore Paul had just described in v. 3; to win release for them by his redemptive death; to provide the only way for humans to enjoy full freedom and the intimacy the love of God desires with the ex-prisoners being fully adopted into the family of God. The Son was sent to rescue those enslaved under their old religion, to enter a new relationship as sons and daughters in God's own family circle. It was only possible through his death as the redemptive sacrifice to break the bondage and release the humble believers from their previous slavery to those basic religious principles and powers. It cost the fully human and truly divine God-man his life to buy our release and freedom. But there is more.

God's Mission Follow-Up (4:6)

The Father confirmed the mission with his second, equally appropriate "sending" of the Holy Spirit, not just to a humble stable this time, but to the most humble of all locations: to dwell in those who became his adopted children.

God's Mission Outcome (4:7)

Men and women who believe are freed for our part in God's family and an assured future. Those now released enjoy the closest of all relationships with this three-in-one God: fully at home in a present, open relationship, sharing as children, and with the additional assurance of an ultimate share in God's own inheritance.

"God sent his Son . . ." (4:4), and "God sent his Spirit . . ." (4:6). In this way the law-dominated waiting was over, and the full and complete way of redemption was opened. At last, those of both Jewish and other cultures, who had known the bondage and frustration of being restricted under their old religions, can in the one same way, by faith, find a welcome as fully adopted children in the family life and inheritance of God himself (4:4–7). This is the gospel of the living God.

Living Up to Our Dignity as Christ's Family, Galatians 3:25—4:31

Paul stresses next what Christ offers which no other religion can achieve. Christ puts us right with God as we trust in him. He frees us from a fearful, slavelike condition before God's law, or other religious powers, and adopts us as full members of his intimate family circle. Christ does all that the protective and preparatory law and elemental spirits could not do; he rescues us from our own estrangement and condemnation before God and comes to share God's life with us through the indwelling of the Spirit. Through Christ, God redeems believers from the just judgment of the law and welcomes us, through adoption into his intimate family circle. He showers upon us the privileges of mature children. This includes direct access to the Father through prayer and a guaranteed share in the family inheritance (4:4–7). And as Christ offers all this, he transcends all the social and cultural barriers which normally keep us apart. On the basis of the Father's double mission (sending) of the Son (4:4) and the Spirit (4:6), every Christian has equal access to these family entitlements regardless of race, socioeconomic standing, and gender. Clothed in Christ and his own life-qualities we become joint-heirs in his new, united, multiethnic family. We are, in the deepest sense, "All one in Christ" (3:26–29).

These faith realities provide the Galatian believers with a new identity as the family of God. As the gospel challenges each people group to make Christ Lord of their culture, questions of identity always come to the fore. In sacral, holistic societies, personal and communal identity are closely related to the shared religious beliefs of the community. To convert to Christ calls the convert's identity into question. Adequate contextualization reinforces the believers' new identity established in Christ—we have become the children, or family of God. With all the joy of newborn babes we learn our new identity, calling to God as "Abba, Father" (4:6).

Valid contextualization also means the global family of God will discover more and more of Christ's greatness as those of diverse cultural backgrounds express how Christ Jesus fulfills their cultural expectations. As fellow family members we will gladly make allowances as some of our brothers and sisters show they are more noisy, more exuberant, more demonstrative, or more contemplative about Christ than our own culture expects us to be. We will rejoice to find in the way other brothers and sisters use our common biblical language about the cross (and most other areas of theology), new depths of insight our own culture had not yet discovered.

Through contextualization each other's cultural insights will also challenge and keep us from forgetting our family dignity and slipping back under the oppression of the pressures and assumptions of our old cultural ways. In every culture we run the risk that contextualization may lead back into the bondage or religious legalism of either the gospel-sending or the receiving culture. So, Paul pleads with Christians not to revert to a merely traditional religious level of interaction with God. The old cultural customs and fears can easily ensnare us again. Our rights and privileges as Christ's family make us responsible not to slip back into a slavelike relationship again with either the law or spirit powers. Rather, we are to live up to our position as children of God (4:8–11). Or, with Paul, to change the metaphor, we let Christ be formed in us, with all that means for a process of ongoing growth into him (4:12–20).

Respect for the proper role of traditional religion does not mean we encourage reversion to it. But effective contextualization discerns this difference and builds believers up to grasp and enjoy their new dignity and identity as the children of God. Here is the balance to the last section. Proper relationships across cultural boundaries will foster both a proper respect for cultural traditions, and an exclusive loyalty to Christ.

Sustaining Encounter with Christ, Galatians 1:4; 2:15—3:5; 3:10–14, 26–29; 4:4–7, 9, 19

Running through Galatians 1–4 is a series of Trinitarian, christological, theological statements which we have only mentioned in passing. These form both the substance and heart of the theological and experiential thrust of the contextual message. They refer to a dynamic life-transforming encounter and ongoing relationship between the believer and God in Christ through the Holy Spirit. Adequate contextualization will ensure this personal relational encounter grows and develops for every believer.

In Galatians, the believers' relationship with Christ is redemptive. From the announcement in the opening greeting of Christ's self-giving to rescue us from the present corrupt age to fulfill God's will (1:4), Paul uses both forensic "justification" and commercial "redemption" explanatory metaphors to unpack the impact of Christ's death for us. Both the objective, historical realities of pardon, restored relationship with God, and release from servitude, on the one hand, and, on the other, the richly subjective, personal, and communal union with and incorporation into Christ Jesus, the risen living Lord, receive due emphasis (2:15–16, 20–21; 3:10–13, 26–29; 4:4–7). The vital reality of this encounter and continuing faith relationship forms the evangelical heart of the message to be contextualized.

For the Galatian letter both the objective and subjective aspects of this redemptive experience also relate directly to the work of the Holy Spirit. After carefully clarifying the way justification works through faith and results in the believers' dynamic union with the living Christ (2:20–21), as we have shown above, Paul in the next verses (3:1–5), reminds them of their experience of the Holy Spirit working amongst them to confirm the reality of their faith. The Galatians were not to forget or underestimate the role of the Holy Spirit in giving and sustaining their new life of faith and in equipping them for service as Christ's followers. In 3:10–14, Paul shows the close interrelationship of Christ's justifying and redemptive work for the believer, and the Holy Spirit's work enabling us to enjoy what the Father intends we shall know in a richly experiential way.

These same verses use the language of promises fulfilled and long-awaited expectations purposefully accomplished, to describe this encounter between believers and Christ. Christ Jesus not only fulfills the Jewish national hopes and desires for their long-promised Messiah. He also deeply and fully satisfies the yearnings of peoples of every culture who "know" God, or who discover God has found and known them. This awareness that in finding Christ we find fulfillment for personal and communal yearnings—and at the same time discover our place within those ongoing purposes—is one aspect of the "goodness" of the gospel (3:8, 14, 18–29; 4:1–7). Knowing who we are and where we fit in the ongoing mission of God is a strong motivating foundation for daily living. Good contextualization brings these empowering forces into the reach of ordinary believers.

Galatians particularly stresses being crucified with Christ to share a cruciform (cross-shaped) self-denial of the patterns and values of self and the world (2:20–21; 5:13–18, 24; 6:14, 17). The vital reality of this encounter and continuing faith relationship forms the evangelical heart of the message for people whose previous lives have been dominated by other spirit powers, and who, in a postmodern context, seek wholeness of life.

Contextualization, then, needs to sustain this evangelical, redemptive, purposeful encounter with Christ through the Holy Spirit for each new generation of believers.

Finding and Expressing Our Freedom in Christ, Galatians 5:1–15

Kevin Vanhoozer pointedly notes: "Thanks to their new appreciation for context, theologians now see their task in terms of not only theoretical deliberation but also practical liberation."[14] We are tempted to ask how theologians could ever have not seen this if they used New Testament letters as their model for theologizing. For, having laid and applied such a well-balanced theoretical and practical foundation in chapters 1–4, the apostle now turns to address Christian freedom in the rest of the letter. But Paul does so in a way that the postmodern mindset rejects a priori: Paul claims that the metanarrative he proclaims can be universally applicable and at the same time genuinely liberating. Galatians declares the one universal gospel frees people of every culture in the fullest possible sense. Believers find release from bondage to other hegemonic cultural expectations (5:1–6). In fact, Christ frees us particularly from the bondage of inappropriate cultural expectations.

No matter how important they may appear from within their own cultural tradition, there is no single universal cultural requirement or experience which other cultures must adopt to live as true Christians. Circumcision, or any other such cultural particular, is no longer necessary. In Christ, all we need to enjoy God's acceptance and pleasure is freely available through faith alone. And effective contextualization shows it is available directly from each of our own cultural backgrounds. No matter what the pressures to conform to another dominant religious culture's customs or expectations, in Christ we can be ourselves and know Christ accepts us just as we are. Paul put it plainly, "in Christ Jesus neither circumcision nor uncircumcision has any value. The only thing that counts is faith expressing itself in love" (5:6).

14. Vanhoozer, "One Rule," 93.

Today, as at Galatia, some are still adept at tripping up their fellow runners by wrongly imposing their cherished cultural religious expectations on believers of other cultures. The call of the Galatian letter is to pick each other up, enable each one to stand tall in their own cultural integrity, and get back into the race (5:7).

Gospel freedom is also distinctive in explaining freedom, not as license to indulge self-centered desires, but being freed from them to serve others. Knowing who we are culturally and how fully we are accepted in Christ sets us free to live beyond the petty confines of cultural bigotry. We are free to serve each other instead of backbiting and destroying each other. This is God's intention for each of us and for us all in our multicultural church communities. It is easy to serve our own tribal or ethnic group. We have no trouble noticing the way we can help those who share our educational background and work or business goals. But God looks for Christlike love. This kind of love breaks out beyond our cultural norms to serve those who don't think or act like us. Once we know who we are ethnically in Christ, he frees us for this kind of service (5:13–15).

Careful contextualization guards against anyone else's culture, even the dominant culture of the bringer of the gospel, being imposed on top of the new Christians' own faith in Christ. They are to be free to express their faith in their own responsive love and service.

Allowing the Spirit to Transform Lifestyles, Galatians 5:16—6:10

Gospel freedom and intercultural relationships in the church develop within a wider spiritual context of conflict between the ways of the Holy Spirit of God and the ways of selfish humanity (5:19–26). The church is called in each culture to live by the Spirit, not by the attitudes, values, and lifestyles of the "flesh": our personal, ingrained, self-centered choices and habits. Here is a worldview-transforming understanding, enabling us to admit the awful depths of evil and depravity in our societies, without attributing them to the work of external spirit powers or nonpersonal beings. Instead, we can honestly face the evil and acknowledge that along with any real external factors, accountable human agency is at the root of our social and personal dysfunction. These evils are properly named "works of the flesh." In a primal society, as well as in the postmodern intellectual climate, this is a radically new analysis and prescription. Our desires, thoughts, and choices are the root cause of sexual indiscipline which dehumanizes. Human jealousies and actions distort worship. Our human attitudes and actions, not spirits of ancestors or place, continue and renew subservience to sorcery and idolatry, even where the gospel has done away with them at earlier stages of Christian growth in those same societies. The ethnocentric and narrow, proud attitudes which divide and disrupt attempts at intercultural partnership arise in the hearts of humans. To blame other spirit powers, or neuroses, or peer pressure, or other societally imposed deprivations for these "works of the flesh," contradicts this biblical description of their nature.

Only the overflow of the fruit of the Holy Spirit in our lives is sufficient to transform these basically self-centered attitudes ingrained within each of us personally from our own ethnic backgrounds. Christ's love, his joy, and his self-control are unnatural to the basic bias of every human society and culture. The productive activity of the Holy Spirit, sourced through dynamic dependence on him through faith, is essential for this depth of lifestyle liberation. This choice between "works of the flesh" and bearing "fruit of the Spirit" places moral responsibility firmly on us as human beings. The gospel calls us to freedom in the Spirit, whereby we "keep in step with the Spirit" within our own cultural context. God's own life released through our redeemed personalities as we unite across our ethnic divisions is the pattern (5:22–25).

As he concludes the main teaching of the letter, Paul emphasizes further particulars he knows are essential, both negatively, for a community threatened by cultural conflict, and positively, for healthy multiethnic cooperation in a congregation. Conceit, provocation, and grasping after what rightly belongs to others are excluded. There is no place for a naive romanticism about each other. We have to face squarely the reality of each other's sin and faults, but starting with nonjudgmental humility. We are also responsible to become involved in lightening the other person's burden, while not shirking our own load. Here is a real call to depth in contextualization that will ensure such a balanced approach to relational and intercultural issues in church or community. And proper pride in our personal and cultural achievements need not be marred by empty comparisons with others (5:26—6:5). Recognizing and providing for Bible teachers who are skilled in making these contextual applications in each Christian community is a vital ingredient in dealing with tensions between cultures (6:6). Transforming personal and cultural values and attitudes is long-term work. Seeds sown inevitably bear fruit (6:7–10).

These practical evidences of spiritual maturity remind us that the real proof of contextualization is the depth of its transforming effect within the new culture. Life in the Spirit seen in its social outworking, not in imposed shibboleth or external ritual, is the test.

Summary, Galatians 6:11–18

As Paul takes up the pen from his secretary to sign the letter, he can't resist a summary paragraph. He pointedly labels the colonizing intention of the circumcision party as cowardice. They attempt to impose their own cultural norms upon others because they cannot face the costly demands of making Christ's crucifixion the pattern for their own lifestyles. To really grasp what Christ did for us in his death means dying to our own pride of person, of possessions, and of culture, and laying down all our boasting at the foot of the cross. Then, as the undeserved grace of God overwhelms and recreates us, we rise as full members of our own culture, to take our place alongside every other new creature within the true "Israel of God," a title no longer restricted to one ethnic or cultural group, but now rightly attributed to the "one new humanity" God is creating from both Jews and peoples of other cultures (6:16).[15] The climax of the letter comes in Paul's two-sentence summary of the overall message: "Neither circumcision nor uncircumcision means anything: what counts is a new creation. Peace and mercy on all who follow this rule—the Israel of God" (6:15–16).

To glorify Christ crucified and to share with others as the multiethnic people of God, these are the true goals of appropriate contextualization in our multiethnic and multicultural societies of today. Galatians, I suggest, as a unified whole offers an integrated set of principles for contextualization. Paul's presentation of them also offers a set of vital tests. Effective contextualization will

- foster apostolic loyalty;
- promote justification that brings equity in social relationships and hospitality;
- uphold a living relationship with the Holy Spirit and continuity with the adoptive heritage of faith;
- respect cultural and religious heritage;
- ensure daily life in Christ's family, not reversion to old bondages;

15. As explained most fully in Eph 2:14–18, and expounded eloquently by Walls, "Ephesian Moment," 72–81.

- sustain the evangelical, redemptive, purposeful encounter with Christ through the Holy Spirit;
- facilitate freedom to serve others with love within diverse cultures;
- guide towards transformational response to the Holy Spirit within each culture;
- enable new life in Christ as God's unified people.

This is no simplistic formula for answering every difficulty in the contextualizing task. But it offers guiding principles and an overall framework of assessment for the process. In these Galatian themes the Holy Spirit directs our attention to aspects of the contextualization task we may not have included on our own agenda. We could restate these nine areas as a list of issues or areas of concern contextualization must address:

- biblical authority and orthodoxy-syncretism issues
- social and communal implications of salvation in Christ
- historical, interethnic, and intergenerational continuity of the people of God
- continuity and discontinuity with local cultural and religious worldviews
- Christian and cultural identity and the dangers of reversion and nominalism
- personal integrity and vitality of evangelical faith-relationships and experience with the indwelling Holy Spirit, in contrast to formalism in religious adherence
- personal, social, and cultural dimensions of spiritual liberation
- Holy-Spirit directed lifestyle choices and character and value formation
- Christocentric motives and priorities in Christian leadership and ministry.

By thus tabulating the tests and concerns that the letter to the Galatians suggests for contextualization, we have also confirmed the centrality of contextualization for Christian discipleship and involvement in God's mission today.

Chapter 6

People, Principles, and Patterns in Mission

Paul at Ephesus

MISSION IS A MUCH misunderstood term today. In this study we want to look at what mission meant for Paul as he came to the previously unreached city of Ephesus and its surrounding region. In the Acts account this Ephesian ministry is held up as the high point of Paul's mission. We agree with Witherington that, ". . . here Luke is intending to present a lasting model of what a universalistic Christian mission ought to look like."[1] The apostle's ministry at Ephesus offers a practical example of mission as originally initiated and directed by the Holy Spirit. It stands as a paradigm for mission throughout the church age.

The book of Acts, of course, does not contain all, or the only, legitimate models for mission. But it does present early and Holy Spirit-blessed ones we ignore at our peril. These examples clarify principles and patterns and offer authoritative, foundational models for mission in every age. We can, and must, reapply these models appropriately. By carefully studying the originals, we develop strong foundations for effective present-day mission (1 Cor 10:6, 11; Rom 15:4). We shall focus particularly on the record in Acts 18–20 with some reference to the Letter to the Ephesians.

1. Witherington, *Acts of the Apostles*, 572–73.

Mission Involves Mobile People and Communities, Acts 18:18—19:10

God's methods are people—people relating and interacting in communities. Mission involves sending and being sent, and demands we become skilled students of people and their relational networks. Acts introduces us to key people. The Ephesus story begins, like all mission, with a person being available, released, and sent, with Paul's transition from Corinth.

Paul had tried moving to Ephesus earlier, but had been "kept by the Holy Spirit from preaching the word in the province of Asia" (16:6). Paul continued for an extended period at his previous assignment in Corinth through the Lord's explicit direction in a vision (18:6–11, 18a). But the time had now come for a new move and a new location. Paul had learned well that the Lord controls and directs all missionary effort by his Spirit.

Missionaries are not necessarily intended to settle in one location forever. Despite Paul's unmistakable divine guidance to stay in Corinth till then (18:9–11), the time came when it was right "to farewell the believers" (18:18b). For personal reasons of gifting, and ministry strengths and weaknesses, this is right. Especially for the growth of the local churches, missionaries, at the right time, need to move on or return to their commissioning churches.

Mission involves releasing, proper transfer, and closure. The word "farewelled" implies not merely leaving, but also putting things in order. Effective mission means transferring responsibility from the missionary to local leaders who accept the accountability and pressures involved.

This process of transition at the personal and family levels is a bereavement. Paul left those who had become the focus of his love and commitment for the two years in Corinth. Paul faced such bereavements often in his Christian service (cf. 1 Thess 2:17—3:10). We are still learning the importance of closure and debriefing between locations in mission today. Too often the mission partner feels he or she must continue in the place or work to which the Lord originally called them. But to stay indefinitely can hinder the development of local leaders and prevent new initiatives. God's purposes move on. He often redeploys his workers. He knows the best places for their accumulated experience and insights to be made available to others. As we shall see, there are good reasons to "keep moving" in mission.

On their part, missionaries must recognize when a church is ready to release experienced workers and take up new responsibilities (18:18b). Paul even took with him from Corinth another couple as his colleagues, Priscilla and Aquila. Paul already knew the principles of taking the best workers from the older work to establish a new work, and the importance of teamwork in new outreach (cf. 13:1–4). Churches grow by giving—giving their best for new work and allowing new people to assume the leadership within the already established work. The Corinthian church was ready to release Paul, Priscilla, and Aquila because of the stage of maturity they had already achieved, despite their ongoing problems. First Corinthians 1:4–9 explains how these Corinthians were not lacking any gifts, and were living expectantly in the light of Jesus's coming. Seeing this breadth of equipping, Paul was confident they would be continually strengthened by Christ and be blameless on the day. So Paul set sail for Syria, but called at Ephesus en route (18:18–21).

Arriving at Ephesus (18:19–20), Paul went first, as usual, to the Jewish synagogue—to the established traditional religion and place of Paul's own ethnic contacts. He dialogued with the Jews, so they invited him to stay longer. But it is sometimes right to say "No" to appeals from local leaders. Every need does not constitute a call, nor a personal responsibility. One of the hardest decisions for a missionary to make is to refuse a call from local leaders to stay and develop a vital new work. But Paul had good reason to move on. He delegated the opportunity at Ephesus to his less experienced colleagues, Priscilla and Aquila. We can imagine an emergency meeting of his team, and Priscilla and Aquila's apprehensive acceptance of this unexpected responsibility. But all three were learning it is right, sometimes, to leave younger, well-gifted, but less experienced colleagues in charge of a new work. We often find it hard to realize that no particular worker is indispensable in God's ongoing purposes—not even us!

Luke notes four reasons Paul did not stay on for a longer period at Corinth, nor initially at Ephesus. First, Paul had made an earlier vow (18:18c)—probably a kind of Nazarite vow—perhaps following some special experience of God's help in Corinth (e.g., Acts 18:9–11). Now he must fulfill that earlier vow and move on from Corinth. Missionaries today often have to fulfill the implications of family, or marriage vows made earlier, even when it means leaving their present spheres of service. In our case, doctors advised we were not to return to service in Papua New Guinea because of my wife's health situation. My marriage commitment made many years earlier meant there was no question what we should do. It was right for us to remain in New Zealand and not return to the field, despite the personal trauma involved of letting go of the work and place of service that had become our first love.

Secondly, Paul "took leave of the believers" for reporting and accountability at "the church" (18:22–23). Paul was right to leave Corinth and not stay on in Ephesus because he needed to report back to the mother church in Jerusalem (18:22), and to spend extended time with his "sending church" at Antioch in Syria (18:22–23), as he had done after his first missionary journey (14:26–28). God especially sends mission partners back to their sending churches with "mission boomerang challenges" for the ongoing health and growth of the sending churches.[2]

Thirdly, Paul needed to consolidate his earlier work (18:23). After that "home assignment" in Antioch, when the way did open up for a return to Ephesus, Paul took the inland route to revisit, and no doubt follow up, the young churches he had established in the Roman province of Galatia on earlier mission trips. Consolidating existing work sometimes takes precedent over starting new projects.

But primarily, and fourthly, in all these decisions about whether to go on or stay in particular places, Paul was committed to the will of God more than to any particular location or work (18:21). So, as he left the Ephesian leaders on his first visit, he could confidently say he expected to return—so long as it was in fact God's will for him to do so. Commitment to the will of God as our first and basic desire frees the mission partner from needing to cling to a particular work or role as the key to their sense of personal worth or for satisfaction in service.

Being mobile, available for redeployment, and grappling with the interpersonal changes and separations or bereavements inherent in following Christ's will, is still vital in effective service today. Such attitudes may require a fundamental mindset change or mental transformation for many of us as Christian workers today.

2. For a development of this concept of "mission boomerang challenges," in which the ongoing development of the older churches depends upon the extent to which they accept and apply the insights and lessons coming back to them from the new mission frontiers, see Hitchen, "Church's Role."

Developing Mission at Ephesus, Acts 18:24—19:10

On their arrival in Ephesus, Priscilla and Aquila looked first for local people potential (18:24–28). We know comparatively little about this couple. They were mobile, having come from Rome (18:2–3), and would later return there (Rom 16:3–4). They were always referred to as a couple, with Priscilla mentioned first, perhaps reflecting her greater gifting and role as initiator. Otherwise, they are unremarkable—but they know who they are in Christ so that they are not intimidated, even when with hugely gifted persons like Apollos.

Apollos was a spiritual enthusiast from Alexandria in Egypt. He is described as "a learned man," with a thorough knowledge of the Scriptures, and the "way of the Lord." He spoke accurately of Jesus "with great fervor" (literally, "in the Spirit"), even though he had only been a disciple of John the Baptist, until Priscilla and Aquila took him home to more fully instruct, equip, encourage, and commission him to strengthen and build up the Corinthian church. This he did very capably, particularly in convincing local Jews that Jesus was the Messiah (18:28). Fruitful mission is alert to opportunities for further discipleship growth, and builds from what keen learners like Apollos already know, leading them on to an increasingly bold, vigorous, and public confirmation of their faith (18:25–28).

Establishing Disciples

For his part, the heart of Paul's mission was the establishment and teaching of true disciples (19:1–10). On his return to Ephesus, Paul located a spiritually hungry group and led them towards a mature Christian experience, accepting their restricted starting point (19:1–9). Luke notes the stages of this new religious group's progress. First, Paul *discovered* a dozen disciples of John the Baptist, probably centered around migrant Jews who had begun to follow John's teachings before they left Palestine for the capital of the Roman province of Asia. He then *evaluated* their religious experience, finding they knew only the baptism of John. Luke had earlier summarized John's teaching (in Luke 3:7–17) as focusing on repentance: with a negative assessment of the moral trends of their society, and calling for a turn from the secular (godless) lifestyle of the day to a fresh commitment to high moral standards and a stand for justice in the community. Paul probably recognized such belief as sub-Christian, but he does not despise it as a starting point for Christian mission! This was John the Baptist's teaching, but it is not full-orbed Christianity. So Paul *discipled* these seekers, by challenging them to an active faith in Christ expressed in baptism into the name of the Lord Jesus Christ, putting on Christ, and making him the focus of hope, love, and values. Finally, Paul *enabled* them to receive the gift of new life through the Spirit of God, as evidenced in the expression of fresh spiritual gifts. Paul found and accepted these seekers as they were in their religious quest, then led them to mature faith in Christ.

This process of discovering, evaluating, discipling, and enabling is worth pondering as a modern model. New Age groups in the West have much in common with the "disciples" Paul found in Ephesus. Likewise, the adherents of "new religious movements" from other cultures coming to the West. Many Islamic and Buddhist refugees also have similar attitudes to this group of seeking, but "not-yet" Christians in Ephesus. There is an ever-growing range of religious groups like this—all seeking the truth, but seldom thinking it will be found in the church. They represent a new frontier for mission here in Australia and Aotearoa New Zealand.

The Migrant Jewish Community

Next Paul returned to the migrant Jews who had already established a Jewish synagogue (19:8–9). Migration has always been a significant factor in mission and the movements of the gospel.[3] Migrants of the Jewish "diaspora" were known to have been in Ephesus from as early as the Seleucid period, three hundred years before Christ. The Jewish community was well established in the city and many Jews had attained citizenship status.[4] Like migrant peoples of all ages, the Jews maintained their national identity through their religion and no doubt still thought of themselves as "the people of God." Paul had ethnic roots linking him to them, had been accepted warmly on his brief earlier contact (18:19), and knew he would be accepted as a travelling rabbi. Throughout his first and second missionary journeys, Paul had developed a consistent pattern of using the migrant Jewish communities as the initial point of contact in a new town or city. We are living in the midst of major new migrations that offer us important contact points with nominal Christians and traditional religionists whose migration experience often makes them particularly open to the gospel.

3. See Walls, "Mission and Migration," 3–11.

4. Josephus, *Ant.*, 13.3.2 §125.

Paul's approach is noteworthy. He began with persuasive dialogue for three months on their home ground, speaking boldly and arguing persuasively about the kingdom of God. Some responded positively and became disciples of the Way, but others responded negatively, with obstinacy, refusing to believe. They "maligned the Way" abusively, causing a division. Paul withdrew, taking with him those who had become disciples.

Paul knew that to impact a city with the gospel those who claim loyalty to Christ Jesus must live out the wholeness of life he offers. Therefore, Paul had *looked* for those with a religious desire, *perfected* the partial, *built* on the existing foundations of Old Testament or pre-Christian knowledge, and *cultivated* the seed already sown until they grew to *fullness in Christ.*

The "disciples" of John the Baptist and the Jews meeting at the synagogue probably already thought of themselves as the "people of God." Paul did not merely lament their immaturity, nor criticize the superficiality of their biblical understanding, nor complain of their shallow experience. Rather, he saw their presence in this foreign city as a special opportunity for mission. He respected and built on their evident sincere desires and background knowledge. Paul led them on until John's disciples and many of the Jews came to mature Christian experience.

Our challenge is to reach out both to adherents of the New Age, new religious movements, and traditional religions around us, and to the sincere but superficial nominal Christians in our churches. These are open doors for mission. Many are fed up with the moral decay in our societies, seeking spiritual options in a materialistic world. Sensitively, ever alert to the dangers of syncretism or cultural captivity of the gospel, and always upholding the uniqueness of salvation in Christ, we can take a positive approach to the preparatory role of these imperfect spiritual desires (Gal 3:19—4:7), and lead these seekers on to a clear understanding of the way of Christ.

Equipping the Disciples

Paul's missional "follow-up" or "discipling" methods are spelt out in 19:9–10. When confrontation divided the Jewish synagogue, Paul withdrew with the Christians to teach steadily and consistently in a well organized "Bible school." The text gives a comprehensive outline of the program located in the "hall" of Tyrannus. Probably a learning center used for philosophy classes during the normal daily study times, we assume the name denoted the owner, rather than his teaching methods! The program ran for two years, allowing good time for the regular, systematic, progressive teaching which is vital for growing maturity. The timetable was arranged daily from the fifth to tenth hour (as in the Western Text of Acts, as given in the NRSV footnote), that is, about 11 am to 4 pm, while the rest of the city took siesta. Paul was able to use the hall in the hours when the Ephesian businesses were normally closed because of the midday heat. It takes a dynamic teacher to sustain student interest through those hours for two years!

Paul's curriculum and methods are described as "dialogue" or "debate" (19:9), suggesting participatory interaction with plenty of questions and answers. Paul gave a likely expansion of this in his testimony in chapter 20: "proclaiming the message and teaching you" (20:20–21); "proclaiming the kingdom" (20:25–26); and "declaring the whole counsel of God" (20:27). He suggests the school's ethos and outcomes in 19:10, 20, 26b and in 20:17–32. The students effectively impacted the city of Ephesus, and region of the Roman province of Asia, creating awareness of the word of God cross-culturally, amongst both Jews and Greeks. Moreover, Ephesus is the one church for which we have a clear record of Paul transferring full responsibility to local elders (20:17–38), presumably because they had been well taught in Paul's Bible school.

Theological education has a bad press these days, but was seen as essential in apostolic times. The "apprenticeship" model so often held up as Christ's pattern for discipling is here balanced by the "schooling" approach; both are "biblical," and are mutually complementary. So, congregationally-based, denominationally-based, and special ministry-based Bible teaching programs are essential for an adequate twenty-first-century impact on our communities and regions. There is no substitute for well-taught, systematic biblical/theological foundations and practical application. Devoted time, as in a full-time study program, is a vital ingredient of the lifestyle of any Christian serious about their commitment to Christ's service.

As a result of Paul's teaching in Ephesus, the whole region, and each of the main cultures within it, came to understand the message of Christ, with the ethnic groupings each receiving valid instruction (19:10). And Paul was able to delegate the ongoing work of church leadership into the hands of local elders (19:10; 20:17–38). They were ready and equipped through the in-depth biblical study for full leadership responsibility. These same two outcomes are still vital today. Regional impact and readiness for local mission are the heart of mission and both depend upon the quality of biblical teaching received by the local churches.

Mission Impact on City and Church, Acts 19:11–20

The record of mission in Ephesus stands out for its depth of influence on the city. Here the gospel touches not only individual lives of believers, but the marginalized outcasts of society; the nominal, half-hearted Christians; the business community and its leaders; and even the city's civic authorities. We need to explore these dimensions with some care.

Serving the Marginalized in the Power of the Spirit

The systematic teaching of 19:9–10 was balanced by social service, and interaction with the miraculous and supernatural (19:11–17), bringing relief for the honor of Christ. This breadth of interaction was itself an evidence of the depth of the teaching received.

God also added miracles to their practical service (19:11–12). When Christians are involved in meeting physical need and offering release from demonic oppression through Christ, then God adds the miracles. When handkerchiefs (the same word is translated "cloths" in John 11:44 and 20:7) and aprons that had touched Paul's skin were taken to the sick and demonized, they were healed. This may have been the result of people specially coming and asking for a blessing upon their articles of clothing. Something comparable to that is seen in the attitude of the woman who touched the hem of Jesus's cloak in the crowd (Luke 8:42–48). But the other, more likely possibility, we suggest, was that when Paul was involved in common, routine, thankless service needing sweat rags, handkerchiefs, and aprons to serve the sick, the unwanted, and those in deep physical need, God acted. Some found that when their cloths and aprons had touched Paul's skin and then touched other needy people, healing followed as the result.

When God's family express God's heart of care for the marginalized, the oppressed, and those rejected by society, his miraculous touch accompanies them. God blesses handkerchiefs and aprons, not toys and handouts! He still cares about sick bodies and captive spirits. Mission today requires us to address humans holistically, meeting the practical, physical, social, and material needs of those we serve.

In the process, we may expect power encounters for the exposure of counterfeit spirituality (19:13–16). Spiritual warfare is a reality in the area of demonic possession. "Power encounters," where adherents of one set of religious loyalties are confronted with a choice between their own ideas of spiritual power and the reality of the power of God, are still appropriate today to demonstrate the lordship of Christ in the realm of spirit powers.

The seven sons of Sceva, and their confused syncretism of Jewish, pagan, and Christian ideas, were no match for the expression of raw power from the evil one. Luke's account is masterly in its conciseness, simplicity, and drama. Given the trauma and excitement that must have accompanied the event, Luke's brevity of language is amazing. The danger of intruding into the realm of the demonic is manifest. But Christ's mission expects to confront the enemy in whatever way he insinuates his purposes and malicious intentions amongst God's creatures, whether by the lusts of the flesh, the enticements of the world, or, as on this occasion in Ephesus, by direct demonic attack.

The outcome of this encounter is that Christ is given the honor (19:17). This is the point. Let us avoid arguments over methods and whether or not certain manifestations of the Spirit are for today. We need to regain a desire to see Christ recognized and revered amongst all the ethnic groups in our society. Openness to the miraculous may be an important key to this, still.

This section leaves us with a call to serve the marginalized, physically suffering, and spiritually oppressed. There is an increasing need for Christian initiatives in the fields of health, unemployment, poverty, and relief from material and spiritual exploitation both in our own land as well as in majority world countries. Demonstrating a holistic concern for needy people reflects the heart of the gospel of Christ. We must move beyond a belief system that keeps a dichotomy between the spiritual and physical needs of our fellow humans. In Christ's name, we must embrace and serve both, like Christ and for his glory.

Renewing Half-Hearted Christians

In the light of the new level of honor coming to Christ, the church members themselves experienced renewal (19:18–20).

As the Holy Spirit works through the church in the world, those within the church are convicted of their double lives. Christians had been holding on to alternative value systems. There had been a lack of integrity in their Christian testimony. Plain idolatry had not been dealt with as they turned to Christ. These are still the all-too-normal features of nominal Christianity. They had been Christians in name only, not in reality. This kind of compromise needs to be dealt with as part of our mission task if we are to have Christian impact in our society or in the societies of the churches we help establish in other parts of the world.

Under the Spirit's conviction the Ephesian Christians publicly brought out and burned their books of magic (19:19). In their society sorcery was the normal cultural way to find and exercise power over others. Knowing how to control and manipulate unseen spiritual powers was seen as a fundamental pathway to influence and success in society. The hoarding and use of books on the occult was clear evidence that their conversion had not yet transformed their worldview assumptions.

The value of the things publicly renounced is worth pondering. A drachma was the equivalent of a day's wage of laborers in Ephesus at that time. To convert the 50,000 drachma into a rough modern equivalent, if we take $200 as a conservative figure for a daily working wage today, this equals $10,000,000 in our coinage. It would be interesting to know the monetary value of the material possessions that may well be our modern "false gods" or "idols." Think, for instance, of the possessions that are devoted to selfish leisure pursuits, that nominal Christians in our city have stored away at home. Imagine what kind of citywide impact the public surrender of these to the total lordship of Christ could mean in our own community if it were accompanied by a renewal of wholehearted devotion to Christ!

This kind of nominality, false values, and expenditure on idolatrous habits, needs to be addressed if we want our evangelism to ring true in our wider communities. We need to beware of New Age occultism creeping, or seeping, into the church. Again, this needs to be challenged with a call to wholehearted renewal of faith in Christ. Do we hold on to old magic beliefs? Do we have a load of old "books," or things related to our old religious past or selfish idolatries which we have not brought out and handed over to God?

We cannot serve two masters. We must make a clean break with the superstition and false beliefs of the old ways. We cannot expect any lasting urban impact without such renewal of consecration and commitment.

Equipping, Refreshing, and Empowering Workers

Before looking at the even deeper impact of the gospel on Ephesian society demonstrated in the riot, notice three other references that tell more about the roots of this urban influence. During his Ephesian ministry, or as a result of it, Paul focused on three further matters (19:29; 20:4–6, 17–18; 2 Tim 1:16–18).

Building Multicultural Ministry Teams

During this Ephesian ministry Paul involved multicultural partners, like Gaius and Aristarchus, who even took the blame in the riot (19:29). Acts 20:4 explains their cultural backgrounds. Paul also recruited and involved the multicultural team we read of in 20:4–6. The nationality and ethnic background of each of his fellow workers shows that Paul had gathered around him a multicultural band of fellow workers. He knew, as he taught clearly in Eph 2:13—3:13, that the full impact, and indeed the heart of the gospel is not fully demonstrated in monocultural lifestyles. In a world divided by ethnic and cultural discrimination, Paul knew the message of Christ was all about reconciliation between those of different cultures. To ensure this central dimension of the good news was not clouded, he included a cross-cultural mix of workers in his ministry team. This is another significant reason for the depth of impact God brought through Paul's ministry.

So for us, we need to put off our monocultural blinkers in our understanding of the gospel and in our approach to mission and ministry. We need each other—Aboriginal, Asian, Māori, Polynesian, and European—for insight into our own shortcomings and to bring out the wide-ranging meaning and significance of Christ's work on our behalf. Only thus will the radical nature of Christian unity be demonstrated and believed in our skeptical cities today. Our whole Australasian society is surely waiting to see effective models in this area of modern living.

Refreshing and Pastoring Leaders

Second Timothy 1:16–18 also refers in part to Paul's time in Ephesus. Paul had a "household" who particularly cared for his physical, emotional, and refreshment needs. Any healthy, holistic church ministry will express proper concern for worn-out and potentially burnt-out Christian workers. The refreshment and diversity of help Onesiphorus provided for Paul reminds us of the importance of the practical support any effective ministry team needs. Caring like Onesiphorus's household did is still vital for deep impact in the city. The resilience and "freshness" of spiritual leaders is crucial for the health and impact of any church or Christian ministry.

Empowering Local Leaders and Transferring Responsibility

As we noted above, it is only at Ephesus that we read of this fundamental apostolic/missionary goal and duty being put into practice. Here Paul localized the leadership. He handed over full responsibility for the continuance of the work to the local Ephesian elders. Perhaps a brief outline of Paul's "commissioning" message for these elders (20:17–35) will give a feel for the significance of what took place when Paul called the Ephesian elders to farewell them at Miletus, the seaport of Ephesus:

- Warning for potential church leaders (20:28): Watch yourself—self-care and self-discipline are vital in church leading.
- Pastoral work (20:28–30): The leader will watch, guard, and feed all the "flock" you are leading.
- Motivating reason (20:28–30): The Spirit appoints leaders to their task; the church, every member, is precious to God; and the enemy is active and must be resisted.
- The way to fulfill any leadership responsibility (20:31–35): Be alert (20:31); remember Paul's apostolic example (20:31); trust God (20:32); take his word (20:32); and choose whom you will imitate as your lifestyle models (20:33–35).

It is quite possible that Paul had another later visit to Ephesus after his first trial, as the most likely reading of parts of 2 Timothy would suggest. But by this early point in Paul's ministry he hands over to the local Ephesian elders full responsibility for the ongoing life of the church. That is a central goal of every true missionary. To see those who have followed you towards Christ go on following him without your guidance is sheer joy for the true servant of Christ.

Mission Impacts Worldviews, Acts 19:24–41

Soon after Paul hands over to local elders, as Luke comments with characteristic understatement, "no little disturbance broke out concerning the

Way" (19:23). Luke blends various viewpoints in his account of the riot that follows.

Concerns of the Business Community: Economic, Social, Religious

Demetrius, a silversmith who made silver shrines of "Artemis" or "Diana," the goddess of love whose temple dominated the life of Ephesus, spoke out with his assessment of the impact of the Christian gospel upon his trade. Demetrius appears to have had an influential position within the silversmith "guild." He brought "no little business" to the artisans. Presumably, he was active in the entrepreneurial, marketing, or wholesale aspects of the trade. He convened a stopwork meeting of what we would call "the Silversmiths and Allied Workers' Union" and made allegations against Paul and his ministry.

Demetrius addressed the "known" assumptions undergirding their trade: "You know . . ." (19:25). There are always "public facts," or worldview presuppositions accepted as true by people at each level of society. For these silversmiths, their vested interest in the religion of the goddess Diana was the source of their economic security. Demetrius could take for granted that all his union "knew" this. To confirm such assumptions publicly at times of stress guaranteed the emotional support of the hearers. Demetrius also appealed to the popular perceptions and assumptions about the "foreign religion" of Paul: "You also see and hear . . ." (19:26). The things they had witnessed of the apostle's work were "seen" through the grid of their own cultural assumptions, reinterpreting the intention and meaning of the apostle's actions. These perceptions were then fed by the rumors they "heard" around the city. Societies integrated around a common religion, like any "in-group," usually endorse the public consensus of generally accepted values, views, and attitudes—especially towards outsiders. The silversmith's guild were ready to react strongly to the impact of the Christian message.

The Gospel Threatened the Economic Viability of Their Trade

The message of the gospel was undermining the theological foundations of their business, on a wide scale geographically, so that the source of their economic security was under threat. Demetrius reminded them of their dependence on the stability of their religion for their business security: "We get our wealth from this business" (19:26). This is the common approach of a "sacral" society, where every aspect of personal and public life is undergirded by an unquestioned, single religion. This sacred belief system gave meaning and significance to their business employment, just as it did to every other part of life. Business and religion were closely interrelated in their worldview, as is still the case in sacral societies—such as many primal societies as well as fundamentalist expressions of historic religions—today.

Paul was understood as saying "that gods made with hands are not gods," both in the city and region. It is unclear whether Paul directly preached against the idols or whether the astute businessman just saw the obvious implications of Paul preaching that Christ is Lord. Demetrius's clear grasp of the interrelation between theology and economics in his worldview would certainly lead to these conclusions. Luke would have learned about this interpretation from Paul, so Paul had reflected upon it and interpreted it this way. Either way, effective mission requires us to make the connections between the nature of God and the false assumptions of the worldview dominant in the area we are evangelizing. Paul's role model, Stephen, had grasped and made these connections between the temple and Jewish beliefs. The implications were so radical that Stephen lost his life for publicly declaring the gospel truths (Acts 7:48—8:1). Stephen's testimony was so formative for Paul that it would be surprising if Paul did not make similar connections when he saw the place given to the shrine of Diana in Ephesus. To proclaim that the true God does not live in human shrines—that because of his essential nature he is not able to be domesticated by religious, business or political powers—proved highly dangerous for both Stephen and Paul.

The Gospel Called Into Question the Respectability and Social Status of Their Trade

"Our trade will be brought into disrepute," said Demetrius (19:27). Respectability of trade is vital for status, as well as for wealth. For Ephesus, again, their worldview as a sacral society meant the integration of profession, trade, business life, economic position, and social status. If the popular religion they promoted was denigrated by the truth of the gospel, then their social standing also became vulnerable. No one accepts social demotion, with its attendant loss of respect, influence, and civic power without a fight.

The Gospel Challenged the Role of the Public Religious Center of the City

"The Temple of the Great Goddess Artemis will be scorned," Demetrius continued (19:27). The public religious shrine, and its icons, served as focal points upholding and giving plausibility to the economic and social structures of the region. Worldview assumptions always do this. But the preaching of Paul called the validity of these plausibility structures into question. If, however, the deity did not dwell in temples made by human hands, then Diana's shrine would be seen to be a sham. What this would mean for their economy, their tourist trade, and their regional and international status was serious indeed, from Demetrius's perspective.

The Gospel Challenged the Honor Due to Diana

If Paul continued to teach unchecked, the goddess Diana would lose her efficacy and influence in the region and beyond (19:27). Demetrius's evident concern for the popular religion may well derive from questionable motives—given his particular line of business—but he touched a raw nerve of his society. He knew there would be strong and deep resentment against any teaching or person causing the goddess to lose her "majesty." Diana's perceived respect, dignity, and honor amongst the populace were sacrosanct. Her international attraction for her adherents, with all the associated influence, acclaim, and popularity, was recognized as vital to the stability of the economic and social structures of the city and its regional and international standing.

The gospel had clearly moved well beyond a merely personal and private set of opinions. Its worldview level impact was evident: touching economic, social, and communal beliefs, attitudes, and vested interests.

Popular Response and Phases of the Riot

Demetrius's appeal to the religious and political loyalties of the crowd evoked the response he desired (19:28). They began the chant, "Great is Artemis (Diana) of the Ephesians," in response to his emotive presentation using the popular media of the day. With their religion integral to their citizenship, they could not tolerate any new religion. Hence the fervor of the opposition.A populist crowd reaction took over (19:29). The city was filled with confusion. The instinct for action spurred a rush to the city's public rallying center, the theater. Paul's companions, members of his multicultural ministry team, were accosted as potential scapegoats.

Attempts were made to control the reaction (19:30–31). Paul had to be restrained from personally rushing to the theater to address the crowd. The leading advocates of a cause, like Paul, are not always the best judges of how to react to unexpected public responses to the gospel. The local Christians sensed more accurately than Paul the psychological impact and likely serious implications if he took any further public action. The local government officials, described accurately by Luke as "Asiarchs," "who were friendly" to Paul, likewise sent an urgent message to restrain Paul. Here (as in Cyprus on the first missionary journey, Acts 13:4–12), Paul appears to have taken some earlier steps to befriend the civic leaders, and to have won their respect. His policy may well have been to openly advise such leaders of his mission and message. The apostle saw his gospel as of urban, communal, and societal importance. He appears to have been aware of the possible civic, political, and economic fallout of his preaching and to have prepared for it in advance. Local leaders must be heeded in such situations, so Paul kept away from the action.

As the confusion, ignorance, and differing opinions began to surface, the "Jews," being effective opportunists, instructed a spokesperson, Alexander, to step in and use the moment to foment further anti-Christian feeling (19:32–34). But they underestimated the ethnic sensitivities and only created a louder chant. The process of rabble-rousing and the characteristic procedures for stirring up and manipulating riots do not seem to have changed much over the years.

Official Action and Resolution

The town clerk finally quietened the mob. He appealed to their dignity as citizens (19:35). He confirmed the civic importance or plausibility and/or validity of the central concern of their chant, reinforcing their own worldview (19:35–36). But he also defended the Christians against the implied charges. He apparently had sufficient firsthand knowledge of the gospel to enable him to discern between the populist fears Demetrius had ignited and the actual truth of Christian teachings (19:37). Again, we can only surmise that Paul or one of his band had previously conveyed a reasonably clear explanation to him. The town clerk rebuked Demetrius for not following due civic process (19:38), appealing to his followers to use the proper civic structures for any valid complaint (19:39). Finally, the town clerk gently rebuked them for failing in their civic responsibilities and being "in danger of being charged with rioting without justification" (19:40–41). Local officials like this town clerk exercised wide powers under their Roman overlords—so long as they maintained social harmony. This was an exceptional display of political leadership and understanding of how to effect public calm. By inference he also demonstrated a considerable display of respect for the gospel and for Paul.

Concluding Reflections on the Public Nature of the Gospel

This incident highlights several key lessons about the open, public nature of the good news.

The riot as reported in Acts challenges perceptions and practices that see the gospel as merely a private set of "opinions" or "values" to guide our personal spirituality and morality, or as just one choice amongst many options in the pluralistic world of today. The gospel is not just a personal preference that some may choose and others ignore. It is public truth—true for all people, of all time in every place. The good news is not just for believers. Here is a metanarrative that cannot be reduced to a local discourse, to use postmodern jargon. God, in the gospel, sets out his understanding of what is good for the whole human race.

Paul's proclamation of the gospel publicly confronted the ruling worldview in Ephesus. It was seen as effectively attacking the religious presuppositions undergirding the economic, business, and sociopolitical structures of the city. The integrated, sacral approach to life saw their own popular religion as holding together all these other aspects of daily living. A rival religion was perceived as attacking the civil obligations and social cohesion of loyal members of Ephesian society.

We need to recognize the fundamental difference inherent in our "tolerant," "pluralistic" Western worldview. Ours is fundamentally secular, and has relegated religion to the sphere of the private and optional, for enthusiasts, somewhat like various hobbies—some quaint and some weird, but all to be tolerated. But for large sections of our global society the Ephesian pattern is much nearer their experience of reality, be they adherents of Islamic, primal, or other Eastern religious worldviews. Religion still regulates and unifies all of life for many communities around our world.

The gospel, too, makes absolute claims involving the whole of life. To relegate it to the periphery is to undermine its essence. Good news about the kingly rule of Christ, the kingdom of God, cannot be pigeonholed and ignored as a merely private matter. The gospel is a public declaration of God's intention for all people. He is Lord. Our God rules in sovereign majesty.

Moreover, theological, philosophical, or worldview precepts do undergird the economy, the social structures, and the value and virtue systems of every community. If we do not see the relevance of the gospel at this level of our society, then we have likely already absorbed and uncritically accepted the reigning dogmas of our secular society. Materialistic values; personal, self-centered advancement; worship of wealth, status and power; exploiting the world's resources for the sake of private profit (also known as greed); gambling and risk-taking to improve the bank balance—of the business or of our private account: these are some of the reigning presuppositions which guide our modern-day Western societies. They are diametrically opposed to the Christian gospel and need to be exposed in their opposition.

What is more, through information technology, entertainment, leisure and sporting pursuits, global economic and financial systems, and our mass media and communication networks, we have exported our worldview presuppositions to every other culture worldwide in recent decades. Western presuppositions are in active conflict with traditional worldviews globally.

But do we understand the significance of the good news well enough to be able to identify the way it challenges and confronts alternative worldview assumptions? Can we articulate the distinctive Christian understandings, principles, and values that offer a viable alternative to the ruling viewpoints of the day? Can we express those gospel tenets relevantly for a Western, an Islamic, or a primal worldview setting?

Which of the twenty-first-century Western idols do we need to confront to allow the gospel to be seen once more as the global "story" for all peoples of all places? Paul was reported as proclaiming that things made with human hands do not deserve, and cannot claim, our total allegiance; and the marketers of silver shrines trembled economically. What teachings would create a similar result in our marketplace today? Should the makers of expensive cars, or jet skis, or clothing, or leisure wear fear the Christian church members' buying power? Paul's message was seen as challenging the great religious center of the city, the sacred shrine which confirmed their civic identity and their place in the region and internationally. What sacred shrines are under threat from the gospel in our society? Paul's preaching threatened a key status indicator of his society. Worshipping Artemis showed your civic loyalty and confirmed your position in the social pecking order. What icons, persons, or practices fill the same function in our society, and how does the gospel challenge them? What concerted action of Christians would bring out the picket lines of our city?

More significantly, how do you identify the aspects of the gospel that challenge the ruling worldview of the West as well as the worldviews of the societies to which we send missionaries?

- communal responsibility rather than individual satisfaction
- work as service to God and fellow humans, not as a means of individual power or status building
- unreserved dedication to the Lord God alone, not to lesser, non-personal "gods" of materialism ("things"), power, authority, and popular acclaim, or even sexual gratification
- respect for every human being, so that we reject murder, anger, or abuse as acceptable foci for entertainment.

Paul's evangelistic or mission strategy made the ruling authorities aware of the focus and basic emphases of his message. Paul was known personally in the political scene in Ephesus.

- Local civic leaders could, and did, discriminate between charges arising from popular emotive attacks and the realities of the content and practices of the Christian faith.
- Local leaders knew Paul well enough to influence his decisions when he contemplated inappropriate public action.
- Local civic leaders had personal friendship links with the Christian leaders, sufficient to elicit their warnings and support publicly.

What strategies, relationships, and priorities for mission do we need to cultivate, change, and rethink for similar outcomes? How do we need to adjust our approach to mission to ensure comparable recognition and acceptance of the Christian message and its messengers in the public, sociopolitical worlds we live in today?

Paul's service at Ephesus calls us to reexamine our understanding of people, principles, and patterns of mission in and from our Christian communities today.

Chapter 7

The Uniqueness of Christ

Contextualizing in Colossae

PAUL'S LETTER TO THE Colossians responds to teachings challenging the message the true gospel evangelists like Epaphras had presented earlier as they established the church in that city (Col 1:7). Paul's letter provides insights for dealing contextually with similar error wherever or whenever it may arise at later times in the church. Colossians offers a hermeneutic shield: protecting hearts and minds globally by confirming the one, apostolic message of the gospel of our Lord Jesus Christ. In this chapter we explore another New Testament letter giving an explicit example of contextualization in action.

The letter is a positive, constructive response to teachings which were threatening the Colossian church. To grasp the message of the letter we need a grip on the emphases of these threatening teachings. But Paul does not directly explain the teachings to which he is responding.[1] As with most of the New Testament letters, as we read them we are hearing only one perspective on the issues, namely, Paul's encouragement telling the church how to respond to the new and different teaching. We have to attempt to reconstruct the ideas Paul was seeking to correct by reflecting on his proposed answers.

1. This paper assumes the apostle Paul was the author of the letter, on grounds such as those laid out in Bruce, *Epistles*, 28–33; and in Mombi, "Christ, Salvation and Eschatology," 30–36. The authorship does not substantially affect the emphases of the paper, so it is not necessary to defend my confidence in the authenticity of the letter as from the pen of the apostle.

Aware of the difficulties in that approach, we suggest the challenges to the Colossian church appear to have been coming from four possible sources.

Pressure from the Dominant Foreign Religion, Judaism

We assume that, as in other places in Asia Minor, a proportion of the Colossian church had converted from a Jewish background, being either converted migrant Jews, or local people who had previously turned to Judaism as proselytes, or had been attending the Jewish synagogue with a desire to know of the God of Israel.[2] Now they had turned to Christ they were still under pressure to heed the previous Jewish ways and teachings. The local Jewish synagogue would have claimed to be the true people of God, to be the guardians of the Abrahamic and Mosaic traditions, to uphold the clear, definite law of God, and to follow the true moral code and superior monotheism of the one living God. These claims needed to be answered. How Christ Jesus fitted into these teachings needed to be explained. Such teachings would have been powerful pressures, probably backed up with family connections and business advantages, challenging the Christians to go back to the Jewish teachings. To give in and return to the secure prescriptions of Judaism was a constant pressure for newly converted Christian believers.

Continuing Syncretistic Influences from Traditional Religious Backgrounds, both Jewish and Primal

Why not just combine the old and the new? This was another ever-present option for the new Christian converts. Just be circumcised, keep the Mosaic purity code with its food preferences, ritual cleansings, and avoidance of contaminated places, things, or persons. Why not just add these further restrictions onto the new Christian emphases and keep a foot in both camps?[3]

This challenge also came from the local religious background of the Colossian Christians. They, too, were used to religious festivals, ritual

2. For a concise summary of the evidence of Jewish migrants in the Lycus Valley neighbourhood of the first century AD, see Bruce, *Epistles*, 8–14.

3. For the dual Jewish and pagan backgrounds of the Colossian church, and the various views on the "threat to faith" or "Colossians Heresy" challenging the church, see Bruce, *Epistles*, 17–26.

ceremonies, and offerings, and a calendar regulated with duties to perform for local deities and spirit powers. Surely it was alright for a Christian to keep on with the traditional customs, laws, and religious performances. Why does Christianity have to be so exclusive and separate from all the past values and rules?

These are the thoughts of new converts in a multicultural religious world like Colosse—or Ibadan, or Nairobi, or Istanbul, or Seoul, or Kuala Lumpur, or Sydney, or Auckland—then and now.

The Pervasive Religious and Political Ideology of the Surrounding Imperial Culture

Or there was the third option. Political and social power, status, and influence in Colosse at the time were all in the hands of those who played it safe with their Roman overlords.[4] Those who pleased Rome found options for leading vocational positions, widespread recognition from others, and a secure, comfortable, peaceful future. The cult of the emperor was gaining a foothold wherever Roman political power was imposed on local populations—and Roman authority was ubiquitous. Emperor worship seemed so sophisticated:

- The Roman way had integrated all aspects of life, social, economic, and political, and achieved freedom from strife and uncertainty through the *Pax Romana*, the Peace of Rome. Its benefits were evident on every hand, with ease of movement through safe roads and seas. New relationships with previous enemies could be explored through the now widespread use of international languages of trade and learning. These in turn brought new values and new confidence that international harmony could be achieved in a realizable future. And all this without all the complications of the local or imported religions.
- Why not pay homage to the emperor, offer the necessary dues to his cult, and secure the promise of a safe, politically popular, fullness and knowledge for humanity? There was an attractiveness about the new ways of the colonial power, so why not embrace its cult as well?
- And who wants to be old-fashioned when all the authority and influence seemed to be with the new empire and its ways of life: its breadth

4 For a recent recovery and expansion of earlier emphases on the influence of the imperial presence on the themes of the letter, see Maier, "Sly Civility," 323–49.

of liberty extending across social and political boundaries, its depth of learning, its excitement and freshness?

The Call to Return to and Refresh Local Traditional Religious Views

A fourth option has often arisen when Christians have faced a combination of challenges like this from a dominant introduced religion, from pragmatic voices suggesting a mixture of all the options, and a widespread political ideology accepted by the majority. This fourth call is to reject all the newer options and rejuvenate the older, original, or primal, religious beliefs of the local people. This tendency is seen in the return to witchcraft and sorcery occurring in Melanesia, in the "Māori Rennaissance" in New Zealand, and in the fresh emphases on "First Nation" cultures in Australia. Revitalizations of traditional beliefs have followed the preaching of the gospel in many parts of the world.[5] Challenges to turn back to a revised, and often purified, form of the traditional local religion are a common challenge confronting Christian believers, particularly second- or third-generation believers.[6]

Alluring options like these were pressing in on the new believers in Colosse. There may have been a strong heretical teacher offering one or the other of these alternatives to the new Christian way. Or, perhaps more likely, it was just that these subtle alternative, less demanding, and apparently more materially rewarding philosophies of life were right there in the everyday experience of the Colossians. Similar alternative lifestyles deceptively beckon Christians in so many parts of our globalized, Western-dominated economies, and urbanized social and religious values of the twenty-first century.

Paul did not at any point spell out these threats or attack them head on. But the positive advice he gave the Colossians implied that concerns such as those outlined were present in their context. His purpose in the letter was to strengthen the believers to withstand such pressures. As he pursued that purpose Paul also provided in the message of Colossians, a pattern for discipling believers facing comparable pressures in any of our modern-day, multireligious contexts.

5. See, e.g., Walls, "History," 18–26; Turner, *Roots of Science*, 7–8, 132–60. Turner takes many of these issues further in his elaboration of the relations between religion and culture in Turner, *Frames of Mind*.

6. Walls, "Old Athens," 148–49; "In Quest," 98–105.

We suggest Paul's major steps in approaching this contextualization challenge were to

- confirm the importance of ongoing growth (1:1–14);
- declare Christ's cosmic role and all-sufficient redemption (1:15–24);
- reaffirm the theological educator's role (1:25—2:3);
- develop a constructive, Christ-centered, cruciform approach (2:4–3:4);
- address essential moral and social transformations (3:5–17);
- apply particular behavioral patterns (3:18—4:18).

We shall follow these six steps in the contextualization process in order.

The Importance of Ongoing Growth, Colossians 1:1–14

Appreciating what we have already achieved, and what we already possess in Christ is fundamental. Paul then confirms the importance of continuing to grow in the Christian walk.

Reiterating the Pattern of Their Previous Growth into Christ

To help prevent them defecting or turning from their relationship with Christ, Paul reminds the Colossian believers of the way they had commenced their Christian pathway. They had responded, and were continuing in *faith* (1:4), the upward dimension of their response to encountering Christ. Amidst the uncertainty in Colosse they had met Christ and committed themselves to an ongoing relationship with him. As hinted in 1:2 they were in a living, trusting relationship with Christ: their life orientation depended upon Christ as their source of life, meaning, and purpose; they believed Christ and his teachings as their ongoing truth; they were trusting Christ and his desires for them as the scale for their values; and they were committed to Christ as the focal point for their lives. His plans were now their plans; he participated in their homes and work. They depended actively upon him as their guide, provider, and friend. Faith is a central theme of the letter (1:23; 2:5–7; 2:12), because right response towards God in an active, ongoing faith was the foundation for growth in Christ, and the basis for protection against the subtle appeals of alternative religions (Eph 6:16).

They also responded in *love* (1:4), the outgoing dimension of an encounter with Christ. Their response showed in "the love [they had] for all the saints." Meeting Christ had transformed the way they related to others. The unselfish, practical thoughtfulness, and kindness of Christ was now being shown for all God's family: not just to those they related to easily, but to those of different ethnic or cultural groups in Colosse—Phrygians, Greeks, Jews, and Romans, at least. They had begun to welcome, accept, and live for those of different social, educational, economic, and religious backgrounds. Philemon and Onesimus, the master and his returned slave, were now in the same congregation together. This had meant crossing the expected boundaries in their social concern and relationships. As Herbert Carson puts it: "The communion of saints means, not a series of loosely related cliques, but an all embracing and self-abnegating fellowship."[7] Again, love is a continuing theme of the letter: 1:8, love comes from Spirit; 2:2, love knits believers together and is the prerequisite for understanding Christ in depth; 3:14, love unites them in a real harmony; and 3:19, love is the oil and driving strength of homelife. Right relationships to each other—love in their internal social relationships in the fellowship—was another strength protecting against the threats they faced from outside.

Their response grew from *hope* (1:5), the forward moving dimension of encounter with Christ. Grounds for faith and freedom to love others arise from a right response to time and to the challenge of the future. Being certain through hope about their future destiny in Christ had freed them to concentrate on the right way to get there. Hope is all about purpose and goals. The Colossians had a "hope stored up for [them] in heaven," and that hope: transformed their attitude to time, turning them around from dependence on the past to anticipating ongoing purpose in the future; transformed their attitude to death—to see it as a doorway, not an end; transformed their values—only what contributes to and lasts into eternity is of priority value; gave meaning to history and destiny to humanity; and focused in the person of Jesus Christ, who is returning personally. He is the friend with whom they would share eternity.

Hope, too, is a theme repeated through the letter: 1:12, their hope was a share in the inheritance of God's family; 1:23, this hope gave stability to their faith; 1:27, Christ present personally among them as a people, even

7. Carson, *Epistles of Paul*, 31.

though a non-Jewish culture, was their assurance of glory; 3:4, Christ who sustained their lives will appear and they will share in his appearing; 3:24, the certainty of the inheritance gave meaning to hard work here and now. Their growth, then, stemmed from the kind of hope which fostered trust and love.

First Thessalonians 5:8 calls this triad of faith-love-hope the believers' "armour." The Colossians had responded with these three aspects of a transformed lifestyle, and their response gave grounds for confidence about their ability to withstand the pressures of being "in Colossae."

In responding thus to the gospel, the Colossian believers' depth of appreciation of its nature was vital for withstanding the alternative religious pressures. Paul noted three ways in which they had understood the gospel. First, the gospel is *universal-personal truth* amidst religious confusion. Christ's good news relates at the personal level to peoples of every culture, globally. Just as it was becoming "theirs," so Paul assured them it was doing the same in other cultural settings elsewhere. This "infinite translatability" of the Christian message makes it unique amongst world religions.[8] No other message is so richly personal as well as being universally applicable.

The gospel is also *globally productive seed*. In Christ the Colossians had much more substantial news and an even wider scope for application than the rival aspirations, even imperial ones.[9] Paul picked up on the Lord's description of the word of God as potentially effective seed, planted in various kinds of soil (Matt 13:18–22), to highlight both its productive capacity and its challenge to the emperor's claim to bring "good news" to the whole empire. When a dominant political, economic, and social system claims the total allegiance of its citizens, it is vital to grasp the deeper news value of another kind of all-pervasive, transformative power, not based on military might and secular ambition. This alternative, love-based power is found in the gospel.

Thirdly, the Colossians had understood that the gospel is *centered in grace* (1:5–6). Herein lies the difference; the gospel of Christ Jesus flowed from the freely offered, undeserved, generosity and kindness of their loving Savior. Appreciating this distinctiveness and matchless reality of the news the Colossian Christians had discovered in Christ was a solid basis for resisting the subtle enticements of the alternatives.

8. Sanneh, *Translating the Message*, 50. Walls develops this insight in *Missionary Movement*, particularly 22–23, 26.

9. Maier, "Sly Civility," 325–26.

Paul also acknowledges their messenger, Epaphras, as a model missionary (1:7–8). The attraction of different teachings too often focuses around the personality of the new teacher. As an antidote Paul rehearsed the strengths of the one who had brought them the good news. Epaphras stood out for having demonstrated the real qualities of a leader: he was a good teacher (1:7a), for they had learned from him;[10] a teamworker, both as a cooperative hard worker, and as one appreciated and loved by those he served; a dependable, trusty toiler, or faithful deacon; and one who spoke well of those he served, rather than criticizing them. He evidently rejoiced in reporting the Holy Spirit at work in the Colossian Christians' lives, knowing the true evidence was in their character formation, expressed in relationships with others.

These features of their previous growth into Christ had laid a firm foundation for going on to maturity. Paul's reminding them of these facts built a solid foundation for helping them recommit to the gospel. But reminders are insufficient on their own.

Call for Further Growth in Christ

Paul also confirmed the need to keep going by calling for further growth in Christ (1:9–14). Prayer is the necessary companion of reminders. Paul's prayer challenged the Colossians, rather than defecting to another religious system, to enter more fully into the faith in Christ they have already begun. He knew complacency about one's relationship with God leaves a person vulnerable to the wooing of other religious ideas. He asked God continually that they might grow in four areas.

In Knowing God's Will (1:9)

That the living God has plans and purposes for frail human beings is the most surprising of spiritual revelations inherent in the incarnation and atoning work of Christ. That we are able, and expected, to discover and enjoy fulfilling that purpose, is the ultimate in human destiny. Thus, Paul's

10. Epaphras appears to have been one of those who, as recorded in Acts 19:9–10, had attended Paul's Bible teaching in the Hall of Tyrannus which ran daily for two years. He is one of those who had helped make true the claim of Acts 19:10 that because of this Bible teaching program, "all the Jews and Greeks of Asia heard the word of the Lord." Thus, Paul is showing his appreciation in Col 1:8 for the work of one of his graduates.

yearning was that they continue in pursuing God's will for his people, fully and wisely, through the Spirit. There are depths of insight, comprehension, and understanding of God's purposes that are only accessible to the judicious, discerning wisdom which comes through the Spirit of God. The temptation facing the Colossians was to seek after a pseudo-fullness of knowledge when they could be plumbing the reality in Christ.

In Living Lives Fit for God (1:10)

Moreover, God's will leads to a different kind of lifestyle and behavior, not to mere head knowledge or transitory spiritual experience. The life—or "walk" as Paul called it—they needed was to be worthy of the Lord they professed to follow. He explained what this means in three concise, pervasive ("every way," "every good work," and "increasing") descriptions: their behavior was to please their Lord Jesus in every way; it was to be productive, not merely of good times, but of good done to benefit others; and it was to foster increasing intimacy in their relationship with God himself. If the emperor worship claimed token loyalty from every citizen, the Lord's will went further: to claim allegiance in every aspect of daily lifestyle. Paul was well aware that this demanded more than human resources. Hence his next petition.

In Experiencing God's Power (1:11)

The Colossians would need the full range of God's resources—"strengthening," "all power," and "glorious might"—to persist patiently with joy against the options being presented before them. They were not restricted to the power or resources of the Roman military and political might. They, through prayer, had access to power which, like the wisdom they needed, came through the Spirit of God himself. Moreover, they had a strong experiential and objective basis on which to develop their endurance in their quest to live the will of God fully amidst the challenges of their context, as the final section of Paul's prayer reminds them.

In Thanking the Father (1:12–14)

Disgruntled believers are easily sidetracked into false paths. But thanksgiving for the range of actions God had already achieved in Christ on their behalf, would keep the focus on the right way to make progress.

So, Paul asked that the Colossians might have God's resources to express their gratitude for the specific benefits they had already received from Christ in the three areas in which the surrounding pressures were telling them to look for something else:

- They were already qualified for a share in the inheritance of God's holy people in the light, so there was nothing more Jewish customs could add for them.
- They were already delivered or rescued from the dominion of darkness, so the spirit powers which once controlled them no longer had any jurisdiction over them.
- They had already been transferred into the realm or kingly reign of the Son of God's love, in whom they had full redemption and their sin had been forgiven, so the much vaunted rule of the emperor had nothing to offer them.

Paul's prayer, then, has set the agenda to be developed through the rest of the letter, and has given strong reasons to go further in and with Christ, not succumbing to the surrounding inferior offers. A firm grasp of what had been achieved already, and actively continuing in the will of God were essential, and more than enough, to protect from their current pressures.

The Extent of Christ's Cosmic Role and Redemption, Colossians 1:15–24

Paul, the master-teacher, now picks up on key aspects of the threatening teachings and weaves a positive, wholly constructive picture of Christ and the way he transcends and uniquely fulfills anything the alternative teachings had to offer. He presents this section in a hymn, either using and adapting an existing hymn, or, more likely, composing one of his own, to encapsulate his instruction.[11] Paul knew engaging the whole personality was essential for in-depth learning, so the combined mental and emotive

11. See Wright, "Poetry and Theology."

form of a hymn best suited the rich theology of the passage, and, no doubt assured good memorization and use in ongoing worship—essential aspects of Christian formation and discipleship.[12]

Christ's Cosmic Supremacy and Sufficiency

Behind each of the rival teachings seeking the Colossians' allegiance lay the fundamental human quest to know and experience at the deepest, worldview level, answers to concerns about human meaning and purpose and a resolution to our manifest failures in achieving depth of satisfaction in living. Paul believed fervently that this quest had been fully answered in Christ. Therefore, to ensure Christians were not drawn away to lesser perceptions, he presented Christ in his many-sided superiority over all other claimants in the crucial epistemological, cosmological, and soteriological aspects of the human search.

Christ Reveals the Father (1:15)

Christ revealed the true nature of the unseen ultimate reality. All people long to know what the unseen realm is really like, and the teachings bombarding the Colossians, presumably, each had its answer to this quest. Paul announced crisply and clearly that Christ is the exact image of God in personal, accessible human form. He alone fully satisfies humanity's epistemological search. As Christ Jesus broke into this human scene he boldly declared: "No one knows the Father except the Son and anyone to whom the Son chooses to reveal him" (Matt 11:27); "I and my Father are One" (John 10:30); and "Whoever has seen Me has seen the Father" (John 14:9). Thus, God has revealed himself in Christ, so his people can have true knowledge of ultimate realities. Since humans also share something of that image of God, though a pale reflection, they are capable of receiving knowledge about God. Christ has become the personal guarantor of such truth about God. He claimed: "I am the truth . . . no person comes to the Father, but by me" (John 14:6).

12. As explored in Smith, *Desiring the Kingdom*.

Christ Controls the Universe (1:15–19)

A second area of human yearning asks, "How does God relate to the material universe?" This cosmological question also finds its answer in Christ, who is Lord over the whole seen and unseen universe. Paul spelt out three key relationships Christ Jesus fills towards the created universe.

Christ Has the Position of "Firstborn" (1:15)

This is not, "the first one created" (see vv. 16–17), but the one who has all the rights, privileges, position, and duties of the firstborn son of a family. As Heb 1:2 says, "God appointed him heir of all things." All creation belongs to him and is responsible to him. The good news is that God himself owns the universe, and he has entrusted it to his unique Son as his inheritance. Only these personal, household categories can explain the essence of the material world. By implication, then, spirit powers do not control the material realms, for they are themselves created beings. Concepts which portray the universe as controlled by impersonal, inexorable, principles or laws also rest on a false analysis of the nature of reality. The universe is not itself sacred, nor does it partake of divinity in itself, but it is to be respected as Christ's possession and inheritance.

As the source and agent of all creation, Christ's position of priority includes priority over the "powers" (1:16–17a): "For in him all things were created: things in heaven and on earth, visible and invisible, whether thrones or powers or rulers or authorities; all things have been created through him and for him." Whatever names different cultures give the unseen forces, the gospel announces that, in so far as they have reality, they are all part of the handiwork of the Savior. "All things were made through him and without him was not anything made that was made" (John 1:3–4). He, therefore, is the maker and ultimate ruler of all political and social powers, including those claimed by the emperor. Christ Jesus is the designer and ultimate guarantor of all scientific principles; the owner and ultimate dispenser of all economic powers; and the head and ultimate ruler of all spirit powers. The implications of these truths are profound. Christ is not part of creation, but superior to it. The universe is a contingent, not a necessary universe. God in Christ chose to bring it into being, and he retains his autonomy and independence from it. These fundamental cosmological truths derive from these facts about Christ's person and role.

At the same time, Christ is also the goal and sustainer of the whole created reality (1:16c, 17b), ensuring a meaningful cosmology. Each component part of the universe, including human activity and every activity of spirit powers, only has meaning and fulfills its intended purpose in so far as it glorifies Christ. Christ, moreover, is the upholder, the integrator, the sustainer of all material life, for "in him all things consist." These sweeping claims set Christ far above the options on offer through the deceptive teachings in Colosse.

The apostle here describes various realms or aspects of reality that have been interpreted and contextualized differently in different cultures. Westerners, since the Enlightenment of the seventeenth century, have increasingly depersonalized these powers and thought of them reductively, not as spiritual powers or rulers, nor as sources of religious power and authority, but as natural physical realities to be included for study by science. What Paul calls by more personal names as rulers and authorities exercising dominion, sovereign influence, and control (thrones and powers), Westerners speak of in terms of environmental forces, economic pressures, climate change, the power of mass media, social control of peers, psychological influences, mental aberrations, and the like. This has been the Western way of contextualizing these realms or areas of cosmology: depersonalize and reclassify them to fit into the greatly reduced areas of reality which fit with Western rationalism, the scientific method, and the belief that human reason is sufficient to explain and control everything.

But many other cultures have retained a fuller understanding of reality, and, like the apostle Paul here, recognized an important aspect of reality operating between the living God and the natural world: the spiritual realm of these principalities, powers, and authorities. Māori here in Aotearoa New Zealand, as well as their belief in Io, the supreme being exalted high above other realms, have traditionally understood another category of beings: their primeval parents (Rangi and Papatūānuku); other supernormal beings, or "originating powers," like Tāne, Tangaroa, Rongo, Tūmatauenga, and Whiro, each with their own areas of operating (whom Pākehā Europeans named "departmental gods"); along with other active forces like Mauri, Mana, Tapu, and Noa; and even some categories of humans, like ancestor Tipune, Ariki, and Rangitira (chiefs and rulers), all able to operate in this higher realm of reality, as well as being active in the realm of the human. Māori have always been conscious of this reality area Paul called principalities and powers, and in which other parts of Scripture also include angelic beings (e.g., Heb 1:4–14).

And, of course, Melanesian friends and colleagues know well their many tribal terms for describing the range of beings able to operate in this realm: whether a supreme being; or lesser local divinities and spirits of that territory; or local traditional culture heroes with superhuman powers; or, sometimes at another level, ancestors and persons with supernormal powers; and again, forces like magic, sorcery, or witchcraft.[13] These Melanesian categories closely parallel the many African cultures with their living awareness of similar powers at work in our world, as Andrew Walls shows in his important chapter on "Worldviews and Christian Conversion" in *Crossing Cultural Frontiers: Studies in the History of World Christianity*.[14]

The point is that whichever culture determines how we contextualize and understand these verses, Paul is announcing the good news that Christ created all such realms of reality, and he rules over them all. This is basic to New Testament understanding. We can sum all these crucial aspects of Christ's relationship with the physical universe in one word: LORD. Christ is Lord of his creation. Christ's superiority over all rival claimants is seen in the way he reveals the Father, and is Lord of the physical universe.

But Christ also has a unique relation to the new creation, in that Christ directs the church (1:18). The church is God's new creation, his new people and family. Christ is head of the body, the church. Christians are totally dependent upon Christ for spiritual life. He is the only true ruler and controller of the church. He fulfills for the church the same functions as the head does for the body; he is the life, strength, brain, and center of authority for the church. He is the decision-maker who chooses the values, sets the standards, determines the priorities, and establishes the goals. He is the church's life source: giving new birth, encouraging, sustaining, and correcting. Christ is also the church's source. The church was Christ's idea. His life, death, and resurrection were the essential foundation for the distinctly new age of the church that Christ inaugurated at Pentecost. And all the church's life continues to flow from him. He also fills the position of the "firstborn from the dead." The church is conceived as a family, God's new family, and through resurrection Jesus has taken up the position of honor

13. For descriptions of Melanesian understanding of these realms, see, Daimoi, "Exploratory Missiological Study"; Mani, "Marital Violence"; and Mombi, "Christ, Salvation and Eschatology."

14. Walls, *Crossing Cultural Frontiers*, 35–48.

as elder brother over this new family. He has conquered death and the fear of death. He broke through the death barrier and has left the road open for his body to follow. He now holds the keys of death and hell; they are safe in the hands of our elder brother. Finally, Christ is preeminent, exalted above all others in the church.

As Lord over the whole seen and unseen universe, Paul goes on to remind his readers, Christ embodies the fullness of God (1:19); he needs no supplement or successor—he is the *plērōma* or ultimate "fullness," available in person for all who approach him in simple faith. Summarizing these verses, and consummating them:

- This Lord of the cosmos and head of the church is in fact God of very God.
- In him God's full deity gladly dwells.
- All true fullness is brought down to us in person, live, in him.
- There is no further need for vain human quests trying to find a way to the heaven of heavens.
- Mortal, mere human rivals, even emperors, pale into insignificance beside him.
- The glory has been made accessible to all: not just some spiritual elite who have the secret, but to all who will look on the face of Christ Jesus (cf. 2:9, "For in Him the whole fullness of deity dwells bodily").

Christ Jesus is, in the words of Charles Wesley, "our God contracted to a span, incomprehensibly made man." He is the *image*, he is *Lord*, he is *head*, he is *God*. Each of these declarations sets Christ over and above the claims of the Jewish law, the pretensions of the Roman Empire and its Caesar, and the traditional powers of every other local spirit or deity clamoring for obeisance in Colossae.

But, even then, there is more.

Christ Reconciles the World, and Us (1:20–22)

His supremacy and sufficiency are seen not only in who he is—his cosmological significance—but also in what he has accomplished. Christ is the center of God's redemptive—or soteriological—purposes.

What has he done? He reconciled humans to God, making peace for alienated enemies. For some this was a reconciliation they willingly received. For other people and parts of creation it was a pacification achieved by Christ, with or without any acceptance by the other parties. In a setting where the much-admired Pax Romana was celebrated, Christ achieved a whole new kind and level of peacemaking—providing the true alternative to that offered by the imperial powers.

For whom has he done it? For "all things" in the cosmos, the whole spiritual unseen realm and all created reality. And for "you"—personally for the Colossians. This is not teaching universalism, but that Christ's reconciling and pacifying work has implications and effects for every part of the created universe. It assumes a previous, willful breakdown and enmity between the creatures and their creator, which has now been dealt with fully, in all its dimensions and implications. Again, this reconciliation needs to be worked out, or contextualized, for whatever cultural understanding we bring to the "all things" of this verse.

How has he done it? By Christ Jesus's death in his physical body on the cross. This was no merely apparent or spiritual death on Christ's part. Paul used the most explicit terms to portray the raw horror involved in death by crucifixion. The power of such selfless surrender and costly death in love for others contrasted radically to the self-centered aggrandizement of the alternative imperial military might. If Roman crosses outside a town or city announced Roman dominance within the town, then the blood of Christ's cross proclaimed another kind of peace and liberty far higher and richer than the merely political rule of Rome.

And why has he done it? To present you fully acceptable to God. His death has completed all that was necessary to make the transformation from enmity in heart and mind towards God, to full acceptance in a face-to-face relationship before God himself.

Fulfilling the Implications

Paul was not, however, offering cheap grace. There were serious conditions the Colossians must fulfill to confirm their grasp on all that Christ had achieved for them (1:23–24). They were to persist in faith and not move from the universally accessible, apostolic gospel. This is the first of several references Paul made to the role of stability and loyal steadfastness in faith (cf. 1:29; 2:5, 6).

No brief survey like ours can do justice to the height and depth of this declaration in Col 1:15–24 of the superiority of Christ and his gospel over all other offers that claim to take a person further or higher in their spiritual experience. To grasp the significance and uniqueness of the realities Paul has set out here about Jesus Christ provides the strongest possible basis for understanding and enjoying the sufficiency and completeness of Christ's salvation. For all who have come to acknowledge their previous enmity towards God in our attitudes and actions, God himself has made us fit through Christ's death to be presented before God, set apart or holy, without any remaining blemish, and free from any accusation (1:22). There is no more need to search for some secret knowledge, or to have a new visionary dream experience, or to strive by efforts of asceticism and self-control, to find the way to a spiritual experience of God's presence.

Reaffirming Theological Education for the Church, Colossians 1:24—2:3

Paul had learned that when false teachings threaten a church a key part of the response must be better theological education for all the members. He had also learned that to meet such a demand, the teachers themselves must know and fulfill their task with a better grasp than their opponents of the nature, methods, and content of sound theological instruction. Thus, it is not surprising that Paul turns from the heights of his christological hymn to a warmly personal, biographical section setting out his understanding of the theological education task. In making this move, Paul is echoing his Lord Jesus, who had concluded his tirade against the hypocritical theologians of his day with a promise of a new kind and quality of scholar-teacher-sage (Matt 23:1–34, esp. v. 34). For both Christ and Paul, the answer to bad theology was better theological educators and better theological education.[15] Paul's pattern is our model and this passage gives a clear standard against which to test the quality of a theological educator's performance.

Theological Educator's Task

The theological educator has a word-centered commission to fulfill through the church, by discharging management responsibility for God's

15. See Hitchen, "Christian Scholar," 276–87; "Theological Scholars," 9–25.

word (1:24–25). Theological educators serve both the church and the good news. The essence of our task is to make the word fully known: in its global relevance and availability geographically as in Rom 15:19; in its comprehensiveness and diversity, as in Acts 20:20–27; and in its transforming efficacy, to ensure it is received in its fullness, hence Paul's explanation in Rom 15:19, "by the power of signs, wonders, and power of Holy Spirit . . . I have fully proclaimed the gospel of Christ" (cf. 1 Thess 1:5–6; 2:13; 1 Cor 2:4–5). This demands all the theological educator's creativity, concentration, compassion, and relational and communication skills. Without such commitment theological educators must share part of the blame when false teachings overwhelm believers.

Theological Educator's Message

The theological educator has riches to make known to the nations (1:26–27). The gospel is God's open mystery or secret—previously hidden but now made known, disclosing God's global salvation plans to believers (1:26). It is also a rich secret with a wealth of treasure for peoples of all cultures. Specifically, it brings the hope-filled secret of Christ coming to abide or dwell in every culture, even in "You," the gathered Christians in Colossae. His coming fulfills each culture's yearnings and gives a future orientation with inherent character-transforming power for that culture. As Bible teachers we hold this open secret in our hands. We need to allow this global perspective of the good news to permeate all our teaching and our curricula. We need to become seriously oriented towards other cultural groups, no longer holding the good news as if our people, our culture, and our church traditions have priority rights over it. In our teaching and training we have the privilege and responsibility of breaking out of our cultural ghettos and our ethnocentrism, and of challenging our students to do the same. Paul saw his task as a globally oriented, future-focused, hope-imparting commission. For the Colossian Christians to grasp both the wonder of Christ's indwelling amongst them, and their part in the global mission of God, would be another defence against defection.

Theological Educator's Purpose

The essence of the theological educator's task is to bring believers to maturity in Christ (1:28–29). God's mission is always to people, for people. Men and women are the heart of his concern, interest, and love. Just as, in 1:22, Christ's purpose in reconciliation was "to present believers holy in God's sight," now Paul's purpose is "so that we may present everyone fully mature in Christ."

Method and Cost of Theological Education

This purpose entails proclaiming Christ and coaching people with wholehearted commitment (1:28—2:1). Paul combines the preaching and personal formation by wise mentoring or pastoral encouragement in his methodology for developing people. But he frankly admits that this is demanding physically and emotionally and needs the renewing of his inner springs by the Holy Spirit. True pastoral concern in theological education requires both perspiration and inspiration. But there is no other way of protecting and maturing believers in a spiritually hostile context.

The Goal and Environment for Effective Theological Education

Paul's goal is for each believer to enjoy a rich, fulfilling, intimate knowledge of Christ (2:2–3). Paul knows certain conditions are prerequisites for deepening personal encounters with Christ. A learning environment characterized by encouragement and unity is vital for digging more richly into the wealth of deeper knowledge and of a growing relationship with Christ (2:2a–b). In him the supplies and depths of lived knowledge and wisdom are unfathomable (2:2c–3). To think of there being a different source of deep, true, and satisfying intimacy apart from Christ is misguided indeed (2:3–4).

When theological educators rightly fulfill their theological education commission there is no immaturity and no need to supplement or seek any alternative to the fullness in Christ (2:4–5). That is what Paul longed to hear was the case in Colossae.

Developing a Constructive, Christ-Centered Approach, Colossians 2:4—3:4

Having laid his careful foundations to this point, Paul from here commences a series of three further contextualization steps through which the contextualization process continues in an ongoing spiral movement as a church matures. Before identifying essential areas of transformation and distinctively Christian behavioral patterns, Paul first elaborates on key worldview level approaches to answering the threatening challenges.

Identify the Crucial Choices

In the bridging verses (2:4–5) between the previous section and the next, the danger is seen as "deception by fine-sounding arguments." Advocates of the challenging options at Colossae were putting together intellectually alluring alternatives to the gospel. Paul sets them aside as choices to be resisted, contradicting any suggestion they might be valid additions to real faith. Identifying and naming seductive teachings correctly is important to help Christians grow appropriately in faith. Paul distinguishes clever-sounding arguments from teachings which strengthen and put backbone into faith.

He then mixes his metaphors (2:6–7), employing pilgrimage, horticultural, and construction terms to set out the Christian response clearly: "Go on walking, rooted and built up in Christ." Upholding initial practices, strengthening faith, consistent faithfulness, and abundant gratitude are the aims and attitudes Paul adds to the formula for progress, hinting that their opposites leave a Christian vulnerable to other views.

Paul's warning command against being snared by counterfeits was very serious: "See to it that no one takes you captive through philosophy and empty deceit" (2:8). As we have seen, every culture has its basic ruling ideas, philosophies, or worldviews. Paul warns that the foundations of many are inadequate, resulting in their followers being ensnared or trapped. They are based on only *human traditions*, so are earthbound, marred by the bias of fallen human nature, exalting human reason to the position of final authority. Or they are based on *elemental spirit powers*. Paul uses a term (*stoicheia tou kosmou*) he knew Jews would understand as a reference to the "ABC" of the law, but non-Jews would understand as cosmological forces—like the Greek ideas that the elements of earth, air or wind, fire, and water, controlled life and the cosmos; or the common pagan beliefs that elemental forces or spirits regulated the whole natural and spiritual realm.

But in all these cases the real problem was that they were *not based on Christ*. This was the fundamental weakness. It is not that serious thinking or all philosophy is wrong; it is that so much serious thought gives no place to Christ. When any system of thought leaves no room for the presence of Christ as Lord and logos of creation (as in 1:15–18)—and here is where Māori, Melanesian, and African cosmologies must be judged—or is basically secular, and ungodly—as is true of so much Western understanding of the universe, not recognizing Christ's upholding, integrating role in and through the whole created universe—then it is necessarily reductionist and empty: "hollow and deceptive," is Paul's description.[16]

There is a battle going on for the minds of men and women. This is the basic reality of spiritual warfare. So, Paul calls the Colossians to be alert and not to be fooled by clever sounding teachings, or by plausible captivating teachers. Effective contextualization analyzes options and helps believers face the real choices, with good reasons given for making the right choice.

Reiterate the Subjective and Objective Realities of the Gospel

At the heart of Christian experience there are both warmly personal subjective aspects and solidly objective historical facts through which Christians enjoy a personal union with Christ (2:9–15). In 2:9–13a the personal subjective aspects are listed, and in vv. 13b–15 the objective grounds of the personal experience are set out. Everything starts from the solid platform of v. 9: for in him God's fullness dwells, bodily, and this foundational truth answers all rival claims.

Thus, *subjectively*, Christians have been personally united with Christ:

- In him, believers are complete, and the cosmos is reordered (2:10).
- In him, believers have experienced the reality circumcision pointed to; the old human nature has been cut off and removed through being

16. In chapter 13, I reflect on some of the changes in the way Pacific history and anthropology have been written about during my years in Christian service. There I discuss a number of "schools of thought" which I think Paul would include if he were giving a list of viewpoints or philosophies which are "not based on Christ." They are present-day examples of the kind of teaching this Colossian text is warning us about.

united by faith into Christ and sharing in the results of his death (2:11–12).

- With him, believers have been buried and raised, by faith in God's working, symbolized in baptism (2:12).
- With him, believers have been made alive by God (2:13a).

And *objectively*, Paul clarifies the realities Christ's ultimate cross-work achieved for believers:

- He has forgiven our sins (2:13).
- He has wiped out our condemnation (2:14).
- He has disarmed the powers, displaying their defeat in his triumph over them in the cross (2:15).

Here Paul goes another step in his teaching about the powers he had introduced in 1:16–17, and referred to again in 2:9. These powers, in so far as they were ungodly, rejected their place as creatures made by Christ, were based only on human teachings, or left no room for Christ within the system they taught and upheld in opposition to Christ Jesus. They were a crucial part of the spiritual battle against Christ. As Paul explains in 1 Cor 2:8 they did not understand God's wisdom at work in the cross. This demands careful thought, as Paul is not referring to angelic powers which were serving God and his people, described in Heb 1:4–14 as angels. Paul is referring here at Col 2:15 to powers which were set against and opposing Christ and his salvation. In his death Christ defeated all such opposition. He broke the power of their powers, just as if he had taken their weapons from them and left them helpless and harmless at the foot of his cross. From the moment of Christ's death, all such powers working against Christ have been disarmed. They may shout and scare, but their ultimate end has been decided. They are already defeated by the death and resurrection of Christ Jesus. That is good news indeed for people who have lived in fear of spirit powers and their supposed control over death. As Heb 2:14 confirms, "Christ by his death broke the power of him who holds the power of death—that is, the devil." It was a privilege, working in Papua New Guinea, to see the release and freedom which PNG Christians found when they realized this aspect of the meaning of Christ's death. He disarmed the powers, triumphing over them in the cross!!

The Colossians were being enticed to move on to new spiritual experiences. Paul reminded them of their unique and wholly sufficient basis:

ongoing personal experience of union with Christ, and unalterable historic benefits which Christ has given the believer already. To grasp the strength of this foundation throws into relief the hollowness of the alternatives on offer.

Call for the Choice of Fullness in Christ

In response to the cancerous alternatives in the pluralist religious and globalizing political context, Paul now makes his most explicit challenge to the threatening teachings which had the potential to eat the heart out of the Christians' relationships with Christ (2:16—3:4). At each point in his argument, he contrasts the true and false ways.

Paul begins with three warnings not to turn to false alternatives:

- Don't be condemned by shadow-like rituals, rather, enjoy reality in Christ (2:16–17).
- Don't be disqualified by spiritual speculation, rather, keep growing secure in a real relationship with Christ the head (2:18–19).
- Don't be dominated by religious rules, for with Christ believers have died to the elemental powers (2:20–23); their power has been broken through believers being united with Christ in his death, sharing his victory over all those powers.

Instead, continues Paul, believers are to enjoy the reality of new life united with the risen, reigning Lord (3:1–4). He calls them to focus on our resurrection life, united with the living, exalted, enthroned, returning Lord, with whom by faith believers are already tasting the new life of his resurrection.

Paul's challenge to the Colossian Christians is to prove in their own experience Christ's supremacy and superiority over the shallow claims of the rival syncretistic religious systems and the dominant sociopolitical culture.

Essential Areas of Moral and Social Transformation, Colossians 3:5–17

Paul now applies the approach he has just developed at two practical levels. He first addresses the social and moral lifestyle issues necessary to face and overcome the threatening teachings challenging the Colossian believers. In 3:5–17 he addresses the general areas and principles involved. Then in the rest of the letter he will look at more specific practical applications of these principles. In 3:5–17 he has also outlined the moral basis for a contextualized, radically countercultural, missional lifestyle in Colossae. These may be summarized around three key themes.

Deal Decisively with the Old Self

Facing the reality of the roots of evil in our human hearts is vital for the warmth of daily faith experience to handle the pressures from other religious views (3:5–9). Paul used crisp commands, probably reflecting their baptismal instruction.

The Colossian believers are to put to death the earthly thought-patterns of the old life (3:5–6), and to deal drastically with identified dangers: misusing sex; the danger of a dirty mind; and uncontrolled desires and yearnings indicating substitute gods. The awe-filled reason for doing so is that God's holy character cannot tolerate consistent rebellion, so he gives what disobedience desires, and his pure wrath is sure.

And they are to get rid of the old ways (3:7–9), remembering that, because of their death and resurrection with Christ, they have moved from the "then" to the "now" lifestyle. So, they throw out inappropriate attitudes, relations, and speech. They do this for the good reason that they have already stripped off the old self in their baptism, so now they throw out any remaining prebaptism habits.

Put On the Christ-Life

Paul then calls on the believers to acknowledge their faith dependence on a living relationship with Christ. This entails both being renewed continually in their minds into Christlikeness (3:10), and finding themselves and others in Christ (3:11–12). Embracing this new global, multiethnic, and Christ-centered alternative "imperial" reality of the Christian church under their new "Lord" entails several fundamental attitudinal changes. With Christ as the center of a new relational identity and focus, there are to be no more tribal or sociopolitical social boundaries. The resulting new multicultural unity in Christ crosses the old social, economic, religious, ethnic, cultural, and language barriers. This becomes possible as the believers give

Christ his ultimate lordship in everything, embracing their new defining identity: as God's chosen, set apart, and dearly loved family.

Clothe Themselves in Christ

The expression of this new identity in Christ is expressed by Paul in the metaphor of "wearing" a new wardrobe (3:12–14). There are five basic garments involved: compassion, kindness, humility, gentleness, and patience, which "clothe" all their actions (3:12). To extend the metaphor, we might speak of a pair of gloves—forbearance and forgiveness—for handling social relationship (3:13). Over all of this is Christlike love, which integrates every aspect of their daily lives (3:14).

Grow Their Lifestyle Distinctives

Paul concludes this section by enumerating a series of distinctives that will characterize the transformed life (3:15–17). First, peace is to be the social umpire (3:15). Whenever a proposed action could disrupt harmony, let the awareness of the threat be like a "whistle" calling back to a more unifying way. For the body is called to the new, alternative harmony or unity which is in Christ. The church is not to be ruled by one dominant globalizing culture or ethnic group.

Christ's word is the church's resident treasure (3:16). The word must constantly be available through study and memorization so there is always enough for personal needs and ample also available to build up others. And using the word for wise, applied teaching, leads to revitalized praise. Christ's name is the believers' lifestyle quality control (3:17). Seeking to uphold the dignity and honor of Christ's name is itself a practical test for ethical decision-making. Finally, the overall hallmark of the transformed life is thankfulness (3:15, 16, 17). Proper appreciation and gratitude for all Christ has done for believers ensures a consistency, moderation, and integrity in their lifestyles and behavior.

Paul knew that without this progressive transformation from the old moral and social patterns to new Christ-centered lives, the Colossians would remain easy targets for the opponents. There are few people as disgruntled and dissatisfied as compromising, half-hearted Christians, and such are readily captivated by new philosophies.

Applying Particular Behavioral Patterns, Colossians 3:18—4:18

The final contextualization step is to apply the distinctively Christian patterns of behavior for a missional lifestyle to answer the challenges believers face in their daily lives surrounded by the kind of pressures we have noted in their cultural context. Each party is presented with mutual responsibilities to live out, "in the Lord."

With Christ living in them at home, spouses are called to be mutually responsible to each other (3:18–21). In practice, in the Colossian context, this means wives yielding to their spouses as best pleases Christ, and husbands doubly responsible, to love their spouse as Christ loves and not being harsh with them. Likewise, children are to obey in order to please the Lord, and parents to encourage, not provoking their children.

When mutual duties and motives are applied in a Christian approach, Christ living in their work means both workers and employers accept their own responsibilities and become respectfully accountable to each other (3:22—4:1).

With Christ living in them at prayer and in public, Christians are called first to be devoted to missional prayer (4:2–4). How? By being diligent, vigilant, and thankful as they pray. And Paul asks them to pray for "us also," for friends serving Christ. In praying for them, believers are enjoined to pray: asking for opportunities for sharing the Word; for lucid presentation of Christ; for strength to accept the costs of service; for clear communication of the message; and for "cruciform" boldness and power in manifest weakness.

Christians are at the same time called to be involved missionally in public: walking wisely, embracing time as an opportune gift (4:5); and speaking sensibly and relating responsively in public affairs (4:6).

The apostle rounds his behavioral instructions off with a series of greetings and farewell (4:7–18). He commends a networker, Tychicus, and a transformed fugitive, Onesimus (4:7–9). And sends greetings from the team who are supporting him, as well as from Epaphras, a model graduate, now coworker, commending his pattern for prayer, and his steady hard work on their behalf (4:10–13). Finally, there are further specific greetings and parting instructions for fellowship and fulfillment (4:14–18).

Conclusion

We have traced Paul's major steps in approaching this contextualization challenge:

i. Preparing the foundations

- confirming the importance of ongoing growth (1:1–14)
- declaring Christ's cosmic role and all-sufficient redemption (1:15–24)
- reaffirming the theological educator's role (1:25—2:3).

ii. Commencing the contextualization spiral

- developing a constructive, Christ-centered, cruciform approach (2:4—3:4)
- addressing essential social and moral transformations (3:5–17)
- applying particular behavioral patterns (3:18—4:18).

Paul, guided by the Spirit of God, saw these six integrated steps as a whole as his response to the threatening teachings eating away at the Colossian church. His careful positive laying of strong foundations, and constructive and progressive development of a case for renewed commitment to Christ, rather than directly attacking the opposition or surrendering to more defection, offers a pattern for approaching the many subtle ways in which the uniqueness and sufficiency of Christ Jesus come under attack today. Here is a biblical, theological, Christ-centered strategy for strengthening Christian lifestyles and theological awareness of believers as a protective shield in a multireligious, pluralistic society. At its heart, Paul has set out the superiority of Christ over all other contenders for allegiance or devotion, and the complete adequacy of Christ's unique work to satisfy the deepest yearnings of humanity, while also fully satisfying the honor and glory of the Triune God. The relevance for us today of this contextualization process is manifest. Ours is the task of freshly applying this wide-ranging good news to cultivate strong church life and to equip believers for responding to challenges from other faiths in our multireligious, pluralistic societies today.

Chapter 8

Responding to Divisive Teaching

With Timothy at Ephesus

Being at home in the family is great—until arguments between brothers and sisters divide the home. Sadly our Jesus family in Melanesia, indeed around the Pacific, is facing internal family arguments in devastating new ways.[1] In villages where one church truly integrated daily life for generations, we now find two or even more different congregations. City congregations which once served believers from many different locations are being divided according to language, tribe, denomination, culture, or ways of understanding the Bible. Increasing fragmentation and mutual mistrust have undermined once cooperative communities. The rival groups require members to choose one group to which they will belong, splitting family loyalties in the process. In many cases new teachings challenge or contradict the settled views of the past.

What should we do when different teachings disrupt the life and unity of a fellowship of Christians? How would God the Holy Spirit guide us to address such situations? Is the only way to reject the views of anyone who does not agree with us, and take sides in an ongoing debate? Or is there a better way forward? At the same time, different teachings may not be the only, or even the most important, reason for a church division. Accusations about different teachings may be covering over other equally important relational or attitude problems.

1. This chapter appeared originally as Hitchen, "Different Teachings Divide," 173–93. Used here with the permission of Archer Press (see bibliography for further details).

These are not new issues. The New Testament speaks often about divisions in the early churches.[2] First Timothy gives insight into handling church divisions caused by different teachings. The apostle Paul had sent Timothy to Ephesus to correct problems arising from such divisive teachings. But the letter addresses a range of issues, suggesting Paul was aware of other contributing factors as well as the different teaching. The First Epistle to Timothy encourages Timothy in his corrective task. After exploring Paul's motivation for writing to Timothy, our study first identifies the issues facing Timothy and then explores the strategies proposed to counter the divisions.

Motivated by Personal Concern

But first, we turn to the letter writer's motivation. First Timothy expresses the author's deep concern about the church at Ephesus. Accepting that Paul the apostle was responsible for the content of the letter,[3] we can explain a number of his reasons for writing.

Paul cared deeply about Timothy, his own "true son in the faith" (1:2, 18; 1 Cor 4:17; Phil 2:22). Paul had contributed personally to Timothy's discipleship and knew well his bicultural Christian family (2 Tim 1:5; 3:14–15; Acts 16:1–3). Paul had mentored Timothy as an associate on his missionary journeys, as Timothy shared in Paul's teaching and letter-writing ministries over many years. Paul respected Timothy both as a "man of God" (6:11), and as an upcoming "good servant or minister of Christ Jesus" (4:6). Paul felt deeply for Timothy in this difficult Ephesian assignment (cf. 2 Tim 1:3–4).

Paul had shared intimately in the birth and early growth of the church at Ephesus.[4] He had played a key role in bringing the Ephesian church to birth. His discussions had aroused the initial interest in the Jewish synagogue. He commissioned Priscilla and Aquila to develop the nucleus of a church (Acts 18:24–28). When Paul returned, he evaluated a "new religious

2. Of a number of examples, note 1 Cor 1–4; Galatians; Phil 3; Rom 14–15; Eph 4; Jas 4; and 1 John 4.

3. Scholars debate whether Paul was the author of 1 Timothy, or whether it came from a later group of Paul's followers in a writing style using Paul's name to add authority to their message. See, for example, the summary of the debate in Towner, *Letters*, 83–89. We accept the arguments for Pauline authorship.

4. This and the next four paragraphs summarize what we have explored more fully in chapter 6.

movement" amongst a dozen followers of John the Baptist and guided them to a new relationship with Christ through the Holy Spirit (Acts 19:1–7). Paul spent at least another three months with his *wantoks* in the Jewish synagogue, debating about the kingdom of God and receiving a mixed reception (Acts 19:8–9a).[5] When Jewish opposition came to a head, Paul withdrew his disciples and began a two-year Bible school, teaching daily for five hours during the city's siesta period. This teaching resulted in effective cross-cultural evangelism of the major ethnic groups of the whole province (Acts19:9b–10). Timothy was almost certainly with Paul for this Bible teaching which firmly established the Ephesian church and equipped their leaders (Acts 19:22; cf. 20:17–21).

Paul had also shared in the spiritual and socioeconomic impact of the gospel in Ephesus. The Ephesians were familiar with magic, sorcery, and spirit powers; so God's power manifested in healing miracles and power encounters releasing people from spirit-domination brought citywide respect and honor to the name of Christ (Acts 19:11–17). This also convicted the Christians of their own nominal half-heartedness, so they openly renounced their continuing use of magic and sorcery by publicly burning their expensive guide books to such witchcraft. Thus, early in its journey the Ephesian church had faced up to its own hypocrisy, and learned the importance of clear consciences, unreserved commitment, and loyalty to Christ alone.

The gospel had also challenged the city's civic structures when the silversmith Demetrius linked the downturn in sales of silver shrines of the goddess Artemis (Diana) to Paul teaching that the true God does not live in man-made temples. Driven by his economic fears, but appealing to their religious loyalties and communal identity, Demetrius mobilized his fellow tradesmen to riot. Ephesus was a "sacral" society; the Artemis belief system gave meaning and popularity to their business, and to the very foundations of the city's social, economic, and religious structures, as religion still does in "sacral" Islamic states or primal societies today (Acts 19:23–41). Awareness of the gospel's civic influence provided background to Timothy's task.[6]

5. In Melanesian Tok Pisin, one of Papua New Guinea's official languages, a *wantok* is one who shares the same language and cultural heritage as you, and with whom you share reciprocal obligations of welcome, support, and care.

6. For detail on this background to the church at Ephesus, see Arnold, "Ephesus," 251–52.

But Paul's part in the Ephesian church story went even deeper. He had written earlier of "the troubles . . . great pressure, far beyond our ability to endure, we despaired of life itself" (2 Cor 1:8). He could claim, whether literally or figuratively is unclear, "I fought wild beasts in Ephesus" (1 Cor 15:32). Or, more simply, he once decided "to stay on in Ephesus . . . because a great door for effective work has opened to me, and there are many who oppose me" (1 Cor 16:8–9). Paul's concern for Timothy's service at Ephesus reflected his own costly contribution there (cf. Acts 20:19).

Key Reasons for Writing

Paul's main reasons for writing to Timothy had both a negative and positive aspect. On the one hand, the church was being torn apart by "certain persons" (not named for Timothy was well aware of them) who were spreading "different teachings." Timothy was charged to tell them not to go on with their strange teachings (1:3). Despite Paul's earlier warnings that some would arise from among their leaders to attack and disrupt the believers (Acts 20:29–30), it had happened. Some had already "shipwrecked" their faith. Paul had put two, Hymenaus and Alexander, out of church fellowship, hoping to teach them to turn from their wrong teachings (1:19–20). Decisive discipline had already been necessary.

On the other hand, Paul aimed to restore true harmony in the church (1:5); correcting error was just the necessary step to the greater goal of restoring wholehearted love amongst believers and a vital trust in Christ Jesus. Paul saw love, faith, and hope as the reason for thanksgiving and proof of maturity in a church (e.g., Col 1:3–5; 1 Thess 1:3). So in Ephesus, Timothy was to work for love springing from undivided hearts, faith free from hypocrisy, and integrity of conscience to mark the church's life and witness. Timothy was not just to win arguments but to renew the harmony the new teachings had destroyed. Paul emphasized this goal repeatedly (1:14, 19; 2:15; 3:9; 4:2, 12; 6:11).

Paul had contributed richly to shaping this diverse Ephesian church. He had suffered and struggled to bring it to maturity, with only partial success. Little wonder that he cared deeply for his associate trying again to correct the different teachings threatening the church. Relating Scriptures effectively into another culture still demands similar personal involvement, relationships, and commitment.

Problem People and Their Teaching

As in other letters to churches facing different teachings, Paul did not describe those teachings fully. Timothy was familiar already with the opponents' ways of working. But three times Paul made insightful comments (1:3–11; 4:1–5, 7; 6:2b–5). The issues become evident by combining these three glimpses.

The first glimpse is into the basic nature of the "different" teachings. Some teachers in the Ephesian church were giving what Paul simply calls "other teachings" (1:3; 6:3). By Timothy's time the true gospel message was well known. The early Christian churches accepted the teachings of the Lord Jesus himself and of the first apostles as the standard and true test of right teaching. To agree with that apostolic teaching was "orthodox" or "right belief." To teach differently was to be in error. But these teachers liked to be "different." For Paul this was serious. They were "abandoning the faith" (1:6; 4:1; 6:21). Paul never called them "false" teachers, just "different." Their teachings had an "unhealthy" tone because they contradicted the proven, wholesome message of Christ (1:10; 6:3). "Malicious talk" and "evil suspicions" accompanied the new teachings (6:4). Still today, what is "different," can easily become "unhealthy," soon becoming "error," and then turning "evil." So it is best stopped early.

These teachers were "devoting themselves" to wrong priorities. "Myths" and "endless genealogies" (1:4) had become their chief interest and concern. Myths are human, or culture-based stories about a people group's origins, or explanations why an ethnic group considers itself superior to others. Myths often relate key events of formative times in a cultural history. Myths can arise from a tribal leader's significant dreams, or visions, or may explain obscure, or mysterious tribal or even biblical tradition. By giving such myths too much attention the Ephesian teachers had gone astray. For Paul the myths in question in the context of the Ephesian church were merely man-made, and "godless"; he likened them to "old wives' tales" (4:7; 6:4–5).

We do well to consider these warnings. Myths are not necessarily wrong in themselves; they preserve cultural traditions and values, helping to form cultural identity. Garry Trompf claims, "Myths . . . are absolutely necessary for human society, offering security fundamental for social health. . . . Melanesia's mythologies, moreover . . . reflect its people's remarkable affinity with the environment, which was rarely over-exploited for its natural resources." He noted the close link between myths and spirit powers, and added that they ". . . usually squared with experiences and common sense."[7] But, as Paul warned, when myths become central in our interests and a major passion they are too easily given more respect than the Scriptures.

The Ephesian teachers were combining their myth stories with "endless genealogies," tracing links through ancestors back to tribal origins or perhaps to biblical stories. Paul did not give details. But throughout church history people have misused Bible genealogies. For instance, some have seen a similarity between a tribal name and one in an Old Testament genealogy as proof that a tribe was one of the "Lost Tribes of Israel," deserving special status before God.[8] When used properly, biblical genealogies show God's faithfulness in guiding his people from one generation to the next. Bible genealogies pointed forward to their culmination in the genealogy of Jesus and his coming to earth at Bethlehem as our Savior.

In Melanesian and Pacific cultures where names are not just labels, genealogies give dignity, standing, "roots," and identity, and provide a basis for preserving and passing on a group's heritage and culture. They can be used in helpful, God-honoring ways. But when genealogies receive too much priority, and unusual, or secret, magical meanings are found in the names, or in the number of generations in the genealogy, or when parts of the biblical genealogies are mixed with those from a cultural heritage, they are being misused, and, as happened at Ephesus, soon drift away from healthy teachings.

Their different teachings meant the teachers were not doing what they should have been doing, "advancing God's work" (1:4b). Their omission is translated differently in the English versions of the Bible: they were not "furthering the administration of God" (NASB); or they were not "advancing God's work" (TNIV). Paul literally spoke of not promoting God's "household management plan of faith" (*oikonomia tou pistou* in Greek). This figurative language saw the whole universe as God's household, or *oikos*. This overarching plan, God's most essential "work," was to bring all peoples under the lordship and family rule of Christ Jesus. Paul used this "household management plan" concept to describe God's primary purpose for the whole world in Eph 1:9–10. He used the term, also, to explain his own God-given responsibility to preach the gospel to non-Jewish peoples

7. Trompf, *Melanesian Religion*, 18–19.

8. For a recent example from Gogodala, Western Province of PNG, see Dundon, "DNA," 29–43.

(the gentiles), and to bring them to faith (Eph 3:2–6; Col 1:25–27). Now, in this letter, Paul reminded Timothy that the primary task of God's people was to administer, or faithfully discharge this "master plan of mission and evangelism based on faith" in their generation.[9]

In contrast these teachers' motives were wrong. Implicit in the phrase "teachers of the law" (1:6) is a seeking after reputation. Wrong motives can lead into wrong teaching patterns, especially when it is accompanied by ignorance of what is being taught. The Ephesian teachers apparently thought Bible teaching would win them recognition and influence over their followers. But true servants of the word of God know Bible teaching is not for gratifying personal ambition.

In the process, the teachers were applying the Old Testament wrongly (1:8–10). The word of God is always good in itself, but it only does good when taught in line with its proper purpose. The divisive teachers were using Old Testament genealogies, stories, and people, to impose new sets of rules and rituals on others. But the Law was not a new rule book for believers who were already right with God through Christ (1:9). Rather, those who needed the law were disobedient rebels, whose lifestyle was totally secular, who found sin satisfying and entertaining, and who treated sacred things and values as commonplace, with no respect for spiritual realities. Examples of such people were those who cared nothing for the value of human life, abusing and killing their own parents or the innocent; those who misused the gift of sex; those who kidnapped or trafficked in human lives; and those who lived by lying, even lying publicly under oath. Paul added one more category; the law was also for anything else which contradicted healthy, life-supporting teaching (1:10). In other words, used properly, the law showed the nature and seriousness of sin and upheld God's standards for morals and ethics in personal, home, and communal living. Instead of this, the Ephesian teachers were using the law to support their speculations and fuel arguments over their special ideas. Correctly handling the Old Testament was essential to build up, and not divide, the church (cf. 4:6–7, 13–16; 2 Tim 2:15, 23–26).

Further, by applying the law wrongly, the teachers were not using the Old Testament in line with the apostolic gospel (1:11). Christians must read Old Testament teaching in the light of the gospel, not just jump straight

9. Marshall, *Pastoral Epistles*, 367, explains *oikonomia* here as: "the outworking, administration or stewardship of God's plan of salvation through the gospel and its communication." Citing Knight, *Faithful Sayings*, 78–79.

from the "before Christ" setting of the Old Testament to the new settings of present-day believers. The birth, death, and resurrection of Jesus have completed and reoriented all the promises and expectations of the Old Testament. We must filter the law through the realities of grace and love as revealed finally and fully at Calvary, not just apply Old Testament verses straight into our own situation. This rule for interpretation (hermeneutics) of Old Testament Scriptures is essential for Christians of all ages, because the gospel reveals all the fullness, wonder, and beauty of the glory of God himself (1:11; cf. John 1:14). Christ, as known in the gospel, is the glory of God; there is no new glory or greater message to be revealed later. By not keeping the gospel as the heart and test of their teaching the "law-teachers" in Ephesus had lost their way and were dividing the Jesus family in the city.

These different ways of wrongly using the Old Testament have often recurred when the gospel has come to primal societies like those in Melanesia and the Pacific. Some people have responded gladly to the good news, welcoming the Old Testament as preparation for Christ Jesus, and seeing parallels in some of their own cultural traditions which were also preparing them for Christ Jesus. But others have twisted the Old Testament, to fit its message into the traditional beliefs of their area.[10]

Roots and Progress of the Problem

The apostle did not give a detailed description of the particular disruptive teachings undermining the harmony of the church at Ephesus. But he did give important insights into their roots and how they developed and influenced those who accepted and passed them on. Paul explained the signs to look for in several parts of this letter.

For Paul, the different teachings were examples of known warnings the Spirit of God had given about the last days (4:1–5, 7; 6:3–5). Although other powers were clearly at work, God's Spirit was still sovereign even over false teachings. The enemy used three-sided tactics, in Paul's analysis. First, the teaching came through the activity of satanic, demonic spirit powers in deceiving, tempting, and beguiling others (4:1; 5:14b–15). Forces of evil were to be taken seriously, and their work recognized in the struggles within

10. See, e.g., Harold Turner's explanation of "new religious movements" and his special category of "Hebraist" movements which have arisen on every continent, combining local and Old Testament ideas, as a partial response to the gospel. Turner, "New Religious Movements," 581–93.

the church. When Westerners try to explain false teachings in churches today we often neglect the importance of the spirit powers at work in the divisive teachings. But at the same time the enemy worked through human agents. The hypocrisy and hardened consciences of people claiming to do God's work became channels through which error and deception infected the church (4:2). These teachers destroyed themselves and their relationship with God through their human desires and choices (5:11–14; 6:3–4, 9–10, 20–21). Thirdly, Paul also warned of the way wrong ideas became a deceptive force, like ascetism (or its opposite, greed), which rejected (or hoarded and squandered) the good creation provided by God to be enjoyed and shared (4:3–5; 6:17–18).

The way these Ephesian teachers used myths and genealogies only led to further "speculations"—man-made suggestions, ideas, or opinions offered as new truths for others to follow. But without any agreed basis for testing the suggestions, others produced alternative opinions and arguments (1:4a). Soon the "different teachings" had created "an unhealthy interest in controversies and quarrels about words" (6:3–4). Thus, true to human nature, people became "conceited" about their own suggestions; upholding their view became more important than seeking truth, so they and their hearers "understood nothing" (6:4a). It did not stop there, but led to a downward spiral (6:4–5).

When a devout person who is seeking to live a holy life claims God gave them a new explanation of some biblical promise, or a previously uncertain Bible verse, it is very hard to challenge that person's "speculation" about what the passage means. To question their interpretation seems unspiritual or appears to be resisting God's new message. When someone says, "I had a dream and the dream means this or that . . ." there is no easy way to convince them their teaching does not agree with the written Scriptures. The strong reality of the dream is their authority. This sad progression from "different teachings" to "speculations," to "controversies," to "divisions" happens in the Jesus family too often today.

Paul was concerned that the Ephesian teachers had become "conceited" about the new ideas, but in reality were "understanding nothing," "devoid of truth," with "corrupted minds" (6:4–5). Teachers can become so strongly committed to their own wrong views they can no longer see how far they have departed from clear biblical instruction. They do not realize they have embraced contradictory opinions or "hypocrisy" in their teaching and behavior. In fact, the link between theology and ethics is so strong that bad teaching fostered bad behavior to the point the teachers' "consciences were seared" (4:2). Paul gave three examples of this searing: instead of embracing the fullness of Christ-centered family and home life, they now followed rules forbidding marriage; new food restrictions had replaced their earlier thankful enjoyment of God's wide-ranging provisions; and they had even endorsed a "prosperity doctrine" thinking that rules about "godliness" were the way to financial gain (4:2–5; 6:5).

The letter has analyzed the problem Paul had sent Timothy to put right. It involved the teachers' own motives and desires; the nature and influence of teaching which moved away from biblical norms; the priority teachers gave to scriptural and cultural perspectives; the interrelationship between teachers' views and their conduct; and, particularly, the way they handled the Scriptures. Paul's previous involvement in Timothy's life, and in shaping the Ephesian church, meant he cared deeply about meeting the needs of this new situation. Contextualization of the gospel always impacts on all these aspects of life and faith in a new cultural setting.

Foundations for Addressing the Problem

The rest of 1 Timothy responds to the different teachings dividing the Ephesian church. Our question is: What does the letter show about how to address such problems? After explaining his authority, Paul presented a series of strategies for correcting the work of the disruptive teachers.

The apostle was humbled and surprised that the true gospel had been entrusted to him (1:11). In response, Paul gave thanks, told his testimony, and praised God before encouraging Timothy to accept his task. In this, Paul set out the only valid basis on which to challenge those who twisted God's word in the church.

Paul reflected on the wonder of Christ enabling, valuing, appointing, accepting, forgiving, saving, and using him (1:12–17). Christ had shown undeserved love and kindness, mercy, grace, self-sacrifice, and patience in meeting and transforming him. Paul was living proof of the saying, "Christ Jesus came into the world to save sinners." He had become an ongoing example to all believers, since his "murderous, blasphemous threats" and refusal to believe had made him the "chief of sinners." Paul confessed his praise and worship to such an amazing, eternal, sovereign, exalted God (1:17).

Paul then reminded Timothy of his previous spiritual resourcing and motivation for the task before him (1:18–20). He reminded Timothy of earlier prophetic encouragements to strengthen him for his task (1:18; cf. 2 Tim 1:6), before warning of the ever-present danger of making "shipwreck" of the faith (1:18–20). From vv. 11–19 Paul referred eight times to words from the same root: "faith," "entrusted," "trustworthy," "believe," "faithfulness"—highlighting that a vital living faith relationship with Christ was essential to uphold the gospel amidst divisive teachings.

Strategies to Counter Divisive Teaching

The rest of the letter offers ways for Timothy to counter the divisive teachings and to address the related issues which had allowed the teachings to thrive.

Strategy One: Prayer and Lifestyle in Global and Local Context

First Paul addressed the goals of Christian living which the Ephesian teachers were severely restricting. At the same time, he illustrated how the gospel transformed central Old Testament themes. In that respect, Timothy's challenge was to enable the Ephesians to do what "is good and pleases God" (2:3). That required a certain kind of commitment to prayer.

God desires that we pray for all peoples and cultures (2:1–4), particularly the rulers and opinion-formers of the nations, so they will enjoy harmony and freedom from strife and warfare. Settled, well-ordered, "peaceful and quiet" sociopolitical settings promote lifestyles which please God. Paul describes such lifestyles using a key word he will emphasize throughout the letter: "godliness" (*eusebeia* in Greek).

Moreover, since God is at heart the savior, he "wants all people to be saved and come to a knowledge of the truth" (2:4). So, God expected his people to pray with this global perspective and concern for the twin missional goals of leaders working for well-ordered societies in which godliness and human dignity can flourish, and where people can hear and respond to the gospel. But such prayer should not be restricted to one's own family or even one's own tribe; a global perspective embraces "everyone." Traditional Ephesian religion gave a special significance to their city, region, and racial heritage, worshipping the local deity, Artemis, whose famous shrine overlooked their city (cf. Acts 19:26–27). Others insisted they were God's chosen race and their Jewish customs must be upheld alongside the good news about Christ.

In Melanesia, many movements disrupting our churches today give one tribe, or one island group, or the whole Pacific region, a special place in God's purposes, often linked with the modern state of Israel. Starting from a right desire to build up the identity and value of their own people, they exaggerate their people's place in God's plans so they become a new kind of "God's chosen people," more important than others.[11] But, since God "wants all people to be saved," prayer should be for all people, not just our own group. Favoring one race, one culture, or one denomination in worship life brings strife, disunity, and separation.

Such global prayer depends on Christ's redemption (2:5–6a). This missional dimension is rooted in the very nature of God and of Christ Jesus and his work. God is the one and only savior of all humans. Christ Jesus is the one, and only one, mediator between God and humans (2:3–5a). Thus salvation has been achieved once, for all time, for all nations. So, the repeated "all people" in vv. 4 and 6 emphasises a global missional focus in prayer because of the essential saving nature of God, and the equally essential self-giving, human death of Jesus Christ.

Global prayer is also based on the apostolic witness and service (2:6b–7). This global salvation was declared and witnessed to at the right "opportune time" (2:6c); God's actions in history were not self-explanatory. They needed the proper explanation given in the witness of the prophets and apostles written in the Old and New Testaments (cf. Eph 2:20). No new prophet is needed, whether from Medina or Melanesia, to add to or redefine this gospel message, or to proclaim new phases of salvation in the "heavenlies."

Without this global, missional focus on the saving work of Christ and loyalty to Scripture at the heart of its worship, a church is open to disruption from other teachings. But this global perspective in prayer needs to be matched by the right lifestyle in the immediate locality.

To that end, Paul addressed both men and women, and the relationships between them, as he turned from the global perspective to expressing prayer and godliness in the local culture.[12] For men, Paul encourages

11. See, e.g., Timmer, "Straightening the Path," 201–14.

12. This "glocal"—global and local—relevance is one special feature of the Christian gospel. Walls, "Gospel as Prisoner," 3–15.

culturally acceptable outward lifestyles with inward integrity in worship (2:8). Paul expected men to actively participate in public prayer. But those known in their local culture as spiritual leaders in the church needed to ensure their character and attitudes in public matched their roles as men of prayer. For their part, Paul expected women to evidence culturally appropriate public presence and service consistent with their faith profession (2:9–10). Modesty, decency, and "appropriateness"—self-control or "propriety"—were to characterize the women of the church. These attitudes would be most evident publicly, in a woman's three lifestyle aspects of dress, hairstyles, and accessories worn.

Every local culture had its own expected standards for these public indicators of inward character. So two basic tests were suggested: become better known for doing good for the welfare of others; and ensure the clothing styles were fitting for someone who professed to worship God.[13] What this meant would vary from one society to another, since every culture gave its own significance to different dress styles. In the way she dressed the Christian woman was to remember God's desire for well-ordered communities which promote godliness and purity of life. They would ensure that their public appearance, like their service to meet the needs of others, added credibility to their worship and confession of faith in Christ.[14]

In interpersonal roles, Paul called for culturally appropriate learning and teaching relationships consistent with these God-pleasing goals (2:11–15). Twice in vv. 11–12, Paul referred again to the "quietness" quality introduced in v. 2, even though the same word-roots have been translated differently. Encouraging orderliness and not grasping for personal power or influence were at the heart of the warnings of vv. 11–15, with Paul appealing to what the local culture expected of women in teaching and learning settings. Again, in v. 15, he returned to the already mentioned holiness and appropriateness or self-control referred to in vv. 2 and 10, adding faith and love as also necessary.

This first strategy for addressing the different teachings confronting the gospel in Ephesus challenged the Christians to embrace global missional perspectives in prayer. Church members also needed to focus on hypocrisy-free integrity of character, respecting local cultural norms as

13. The Greek word in 2:10 for "God-worshipper," *theosebeia*, has the same root as Paul's often used word "godliness," *eusebeia*.

14. For discussions on the place of women in the local cultural context in Ephesus in Timothy's day, see the commentaries, and Winter, *Roman Wives*.

they cared for others and modelled godliness in well-ordered missional living within the community.

Strategy Two: Character Integrity amongst Church Leaders

The apostle's second strategy was not to attack the troublemakers, but intentionally to strengthen the church leaders and clarify the nature of the church itself. When different teachings disrupt the church, a warning sounds that the leadership patterns and standards may need reevaluating.

Strength of character and exemplary living win spiritual battles better than clever attacks on different teachings (3:1–13). Paul saw leadership as the responsibility of three groups: those with pastoral and teaching roles in the church, the "overseers" (3:1–7); those coordinating the practical welfare of the church community, the "servers" or "deacons" (3:8–10, 12–13); and the deacon's "wives," or the women appointed to share these tasks (3:11). The quality of Christlike living of these leaders, not just their formal teaching, was vital to correct the disruptive teachings. Divisions often arose between those with pastoral duties and those responsible for the practical arrangements, or through tensions between the leading men and women. So Paul focused on the character, lifestyle habits, and leadership competency of these three leadership groups.

Church leadership was worth pursuing, but was not for inexperienced believers. The church lived for the society around them, so church leaders' reputations in that society indicated whether they were fit to lead the church. Lives "worthy of respect" or "above reproach" were to mark all three groups (3:2, 8, 11), exemplifying the quiet, respectful, and godly lifestyles they had been encouraged to pray for and God looked for in every society (2:2). Likewise the sensible, "wise-minded" behavior, required of both men and women in 2:9 and 15, was essential for the church elder (3:2).

In New Testament times a household included the extended family, their servants, and the workers in the trade or business based in the home. Both family and business life centered on the "household." How well leaders managed their families and households indicated their suitability as church leaders. In this passage, Paul described each family "household" as an illustration of a local church. Each of the detailed qualities the leader needed to shun or uphold were seen best in their lives in the community and in their own households. Paul was also conscious of the ever-present activity and temptations of demonic forces seeking to trap or undermine the church leaders' integrity (3:6–7; cf. 4:1–2). Addressing the character and behavior of its own leaders is a vital part of addressing disruptive teachings.

The apostle now made explicit what he had just implied in 2:4–5, 12b: church members formed the "household of God" (3:14–16). God had welcomed believers into his family as his children. As their heavenly Father, he guided, watched over, and regulated his worldwide family like the head of a well-managed household. So, the lifestyle of his household members would show family trust, commitment to the Father's mission, and loyal obedience to the Father's standards. God's household could also be described as "the church of the living God" (3:15). This literally meant believers had been called out or gathered together to know and enjoy God actively living with them. God now dwells among his people as his home and temple (cf. Eph 2:19–22).

The church was also the "pillar and foundation of the truth." The true knowledge which produced the right behavior desired by the living God was not found by controversial speculations, myths, or endless genealogies, but through the "gospel entrusted" to the church by the apostle (1:11). Paul was "a true and faithful teacher" of this gospel (2:7), which the leaders were also "able to teach" (3:2, 9). Thus, as his church, believers were to uphold, guard, and express this truth in their godly lifestyles (3:15). What the church is determined how its members were to live.

For Paul, Christian living and knowing the truth all stemmed from a faith relationship with this risen, exalted Lord who rules all the earthly and heavenly, physical and spiritual, and human and spirit realities (3:16). Western Christians often grasp only the physical and earthly aspects of his person and work; Melanesian and Pacific peoples sometimes focus too much on some aspects of the spiritual. This glorious mystery centered in Christ himself challenges and corrects all our merely partial human views and speculations.

Strategy Three: Enriching the Pastor/Teacher

Paul's final strategy focused on Timothy and his teaching. The repeated "command and teach these things," "instruct," "teach and insist on," (4:6, 11, 16; 5:7, 21; 6:2b), reminded Timothy of Paul's own two-year theological education program in Ephesus (Acts 19:9–10). In effect, Paul offered a vocational enrichment curriculum for one of his Bible college graduates in ministry to combat the divisive teachings in the church.

Paul began by encouraging Timothy to cultivate godliness and teaching competence (4:6–16; 5:21–25). What his letter had already encouraged the whole church to pray for, and set as a primary requirement for church leaders, now became a specific goal for Timothy to pursue: "train yourself in godliness" (4:7). As we have seen, "godliness" was Paul's catch-all word to sum up the distinctly Christian lifestyle which integrated knowledge of gospel truth with daily choices and behavior, and which flowed from the life and ministry of Christ.

To ensure sound corrective teaching the apostle also outlined the skills he recommended for Timothy in his "training in godliness" (4:12–16). He needed to set a full-orbed example, for that was the best way to answer objections that he was too young to lead (v. 12). He must develop skill in public reading of Scripture, since in the semi-literate culture of Ephesus most believers grew by hearing, not reading, the word of God. Likewise, skills of encouragement in preaching, and of regular systematic teaching were the key communication skills to combat the deceptive teachings. Greater levels of literacy or information technology competence in our cultures may helpfully supplement these three basic communication skills, but they will never replace them (v. 13).

Following Paul as a teacher at Ephesus was an intimidating task, but God had given Timothy specific abilities the church needed through him at that time, as Paul often reminded him (4:14; 6:12, 20; 2 Tim 1:6–7). But this demanded constant diligence and commitment, so Timothy's progress would be evident to others (v. 15). Skills in critical self-evaluation, honestly assessing his own conduct and teaching, were also essential for the wholesome growth of others, as well as his own, in the salvation that is in Christ (v. 16).

Strategy Four: Teaching and Reordering in the Church

The final strategic step was for the apostle to advise on specific areas Timothy needed to address to correct the disrupting teachings. The relationships between various groups in the church were particularly significant, since false ideas more easily gained a foothold if relationships were not harmonious. In that respect, several things were seen by Paul as important. In the "household of God," family relationships offered a better pattern for intergenerational relationships than traditional cultural expectations. The family of Christ gave a proper place for each gender and generation to contribute and receive mutually from the others (5:1–2). Providing fair practical support for needy widows challenged the early church as it clarified a new Christian approach to personal, extended family, and the church community's responsibilities for the social welfare of church members (5:3–16).[15] Another new, and, in one sense, healthy, tension in the Ephesian church arose because slaves and their masters were members of the same "household of faith." Paul appealed to the reciprocal responsibilities of both groups, knowing, again, that mutual respect and care were needed to ensure neither group became disgruntled and turned to the disruptive teachings (6:1–2).

When church leaders were managing their responsibilities well, especially when devoting time and energy to teaching, but were not being properly paid and supported, this also could produce the grumbling and complaining through which disruptive teachings could fester (5:17–18; cf. Gal 6:6). And church members needed to become aware of the danger of siding with their favored group against others (5:19–21). When allegations of wrong teaching were being made each person must be treated justly.

With a final reminder, "these are the things you are to teach and insist on" (6:2b), the apostle further clarified what he has implied throughout the letter, especially from 4:1—the divisive teachers contradicted the Christ-centered teachings and godly lifestyle that Timothy was charged to hold to and pursue (cf. 6:3–5, 11–16). Attitudes to wealth highlighted the contrast. The disruptive teachers thought Christian practices and spiritual behavior were a way to make money. Paul warned Timothy the fruit of that root was multiplied evils, snares, ruin, loss of faith, and much grief. True gain, however, came through sincere godliness with acceptance and contentment, knowing that material things last only for this life (6:5–10).

The culmination of this strategy came as Paul charged Timothy to recommit to genuine Christ-centered godliness with its fruit of an upright life before God the life-giver, and of love, faith, and steady gentleness towards others. He reminded Timothy of the motivating example of Jesus holding true to his confession before Pilate, and of Christ's certain return at God's appointed time (6:11–15). All this confirmed the glorious sovereignty,

15 There appear to have been links between disruptive teachings, cultural practices in Ephesus, and the role of some of these widows (cf. 2 Tim 3:6). Compare the role of young women in the Artemis cult in New Testament times in, e.g., Abrahamsen, *Women and Worship*; Cameron and Kuhrt, *Images of Women*.

transcendence, honor, and exaltation of God, which Paul expressed in an outpouring of praise in this last section, just as he had done in his first (6:15–16; cf. 1:17).

Conclusion

Addressing divisive teaching has proved to be an intensely personal matter. The apostle's love for Timothy and deep involvement in the growth of the Ephesian church burdened, and therefore qualified, Paul to address the issues. Paul grasped the nature and influence of the different teachings both on the teachers and on the Ephesian church, and recognized the evil one's agency in the divisions. Paul dared to challenge the disruptive teachers only because of his experience of the grace, mercy, and call of Christ in his own life. The strategies he urged on Timothy were open and straightforward: call the church to prayer for global and local missional lifestyles that please God; cultivate character integrity amongst church leaders, to ensure conduct fit for God's church; and enrich the pastor/teacher's personal godliness, teaching competence, and sound teaching. With these as his approach, Timothy was to tell the divisive teachers to stop their different teaching, and for Timothy to turn from them and guard the true proclamation of the gospel.

We cannot know with certainty how Timothy followed this advice, nor what happened with the other teachers. But we do have one final message to the same church at Ephesus, given this time directly by the risen Christ through John. The Lord Jesus commended this church for the way they had dealt with false teachers (Rev 2:1–3). So presumably, Timothy had acted effectively on Paul's advice. But our Lord Jesus had one continuing concern about the Ephesian church: "You have forsaken the love you had at first." Jesus made a very clear-cut plea: "Consider how far you have fallen, repent and do the things you did at first" (Rev 2:4–7). As we face and grapple with different teachings dividing our churches across Melanesia, Paul's pattern of concern for the Ephesian church, his clear identifying of the issues, and his carefully set out strategies to address these teachings, provide us with a pattern to reapply today. As we challenge those who would divide the Jesus family by their different teachings, we can only echo the words of our risen Lord: "Brothers, Sisters, remember . . . return . . . and renew your first love."

Chapter 9

Leadership Transitioning and Succession Planning

Barnabas, Paul, and 2 Timothy

TRANSITIONING LEADERSHIP TO THE next generation, "succession planning," is a globally relevant issue for the section of the Christian church with whom I have served with for over sixty years: the Christian Brethren churches. We have a history of respecting our past, perhaps to the detriment of necessary forward planning. I find myself asking whether the 1960s comment on Acts 13:36, made by G. C. D. Howley, one of the then widely influential leaders of our movement, is still valid today: "We all know that when David had served God's purpose in his own generation, he died, he was buried with his ancestors, and his body decayed. Our problem in the Brethren movement is that when our leaders die, we don't bury them."[1] Howley's point was that too often we Brethren have assumed that the ideas and influence of an earlier generation should still control and regulate the church life of the present generation, instead of welcoming the fresh vision and leadership of the new generation. Certainly, in our fellowship of churches, preparing for transition to a younger generation, or "succession planning," is controversial, or even considered presumptuous: Will not God himself provide? So there is room for fresh consideration of questions such as: Is succession planning even biblical? Is there any biblical authority and

1. As editor of the British Christian Brethren magazine, *The Witness*, G. C. D. Howley was speaking at a luncheon meeting of Brethren leaders in Christchurch, New Zealand, during his visit in the early 1960s.

guidance for it? How can church leaders "pass on the baton" in the twenty-first century? And when? And to whom?

This chapter turns to this personnel issue in contemporary church life and mission outreach. We focus first on one sequence of leadership transition or succession planning in the New Testament, specifically the Barnabas, Paul, Timothy succession. We then explore Paul's encouragement for Timothy to start transition planning in 2 Tim 1–2, seeking relevant biblical principles, and noting the depth and breadth of concepts the apostle brings to bear when addressing such a practical subject. We identify principles for considering the importance of, and our approach to succession planning and transition in our church and training networks today.

Leadership Transitioning to Paul by Barnabas

The Basis of Barnabas's Concern

A Jew, born in Cyprus and named Joseph, Barnabas shared a Levite's family heritage committed to give God proper priority in their lives, and the blend of privilege and responsibility such a heritage brought. Better known by his nickname, Barnabas, or "son of encouragement," to reflect the character he portrayed in each reference to him in the Scriptures, he was probably brought up in Cyprus as a Jew of the "diaspora." Though living as an expatriate in Jerusalem, and perhaps taking his turn of Levitical duties in the temple, Barnabas maintained links with his home area. He stood out in the early church as an exemplary and reasonably well-off landowner (Acts 4:36–37).

His relatives included the younger John Mark, probably a cousin, for whom he took a particular responsibility, and an aunt (or sister) Mary who owned a substantial home in the religious and business capital of Jerusalem. Again, Mary appears to have been fairly well-off, with household servants in a home large enough for gatherings of Christians (Col 4:10; Acts 12:12–14). Barnabas was also mobile internationally, available for tasks in various places, like Jerusalem, Cyprus, and Antioch in Syria (Acts 11:22–24).

He had already come to faith in Jesus at a time when "great power" and "great grace" were being manifested within the Christian community. He was actively involved in the life of the church, and his nickname hints that he demonstrated the fruit of the Spirit, particularly as an encourager (Acts 4:32–36). Barnabas had also demonstrated his unreserved consecration to

Christ Jesus by selling a field and laying the total income at the feet of the apostles for distribution to meet the needs of the poor, in stark contrast to Ananias and Sapphira's deceptive plot to win status in the church by a show of apparent generosity. As an earlier generation would have put it, Barnabas was wholehearted and unashamed in his "Christian Devotedness,"[2] confirmed, as always, by gladly giving significantly of his accumulated wealth for the service of Christ and his people, and to demonstrate his living trust in Christ for his material needs. The Scriptures highlight these aspects of his relationship with Christ from which, we suggest, his concerns for longer term personnel planning developed.

Barnabas had faith in God's power to change people, and so opened doors into the church (Acts 8:1b–4; 9:1–2, 26–29). He would have been aware of the way the leading young Pharisee, Saul, was "ravaging the church," imprisoning both men and women and scattering most of the common believers. Then, still "breathing threats and murders," Saul had been away from Jerusalem, having gained authorization to bring Syrian Christians back to Jerusalem for trial. Strangely, Barnabas heard no more of Saul for at least three years. Then Saul the persecutor is back, claiming to be converted (Acts 9:26–30)!

The apostles were not convinced, and would not have a bar of this claimed conversion! They simply could not believe it (9:26). But Barnabas (9:27) sat and listened to Saul's story. He dared to believe God could change rebels. Barnabas's faith in God's power to transform people enabled him to expect the impossible. He took the time to hear Saul's story firsthand, and Barnabas became convinced of its integrity. He became the converted persecutor's mediator and advocate. Barnabas pleaded Saul's cause with the apostles, and opened the door into the church for the converted troublemaker.

Barnabas also had faith that the Lord's grace could work in new ways, even to crossing cultural barriers. He was available to be sent to encourage such new developments (Acts 11:19–30). He appeared next in the Acts narrative when, for the first time, some ordinary Christians from Barnabas's home area of Cyprus and from North Africa contextualized the gospel for

2. This was the title of widely influential 1825 tract written by the first Christian Brethren missionary, and significant contributor to the early development of the Brethren movement, Anthony Norris Groves. The booklet played a significant part in establishing the pattern of missionary support known as "Living by Faith." It is available in print and electronic form on a range of internet venues. See, for example, Project Gutenberg, "Christian Devotedness."

their non-Jewish Greek neighbours in the urban sprawl of multicultural Antioch in Syria. They dared to "gossip the gospel," preaching Jesus Christ by means of the new title "the Lord Jesus."[3] The "hand of the Lord" was with them, and "a great number" of these "peoples of other cultures"—gentiles, as the Jews called them—believed and were converted. When this strange news came to "the ears of the church" in Jerusalem, they sent Barnabas, as a trustworthy evaluator, to check it out (11:22).

Showing his special skill and values, Barnabas "saw the grace of God," and rejoiced in it. His faith discerned the hand of God at work in this unprecedented work amongst a non-Jewish community. He recognized that the undeserved goodness and gracious forgiveness of God was touching their lives, just as it had those of his own people. True to his nickname, Barnabas urged the new believers "to remain true to the Lord, and to do so with steadfast devotion" (11:23). This was real pastoral encouragement. His faith bore fruit as "a great many were brought to the Lord"(11:24b). Barnabas could grasp this cross-cultural opportunity because: "He was a good man, full of the Holy Spirit, and full of faith" (11:24a). His goodness and his fullness of the Spirit both focused on faith in God's ability to change the lives of other people. Too often our understanding of true goodness and our expectations concerning the fullness of the Spirit are not characterized by this focus on people and their potential for renewal and for changed lifestyles.

For Barnabas, this discernment led him to give priority to equipping new leaders, and opening doors into service for others (Acts 11:25–26; 13:1). His service in Antioch continued with notable outcomes; he sought, found, and brought into ministry one who had been nearly forgotten. Barnabas "found" Paul buried in his hometown of Tarsus—forgotten by those in the wider Christian world.

Eleven years at least had passed since Barnabas had welcomed Paul into the Jerusalem church (Acts 9:29; cf. Gal 2:1). Together they served as guests of the Antioch church, systematically teaching the word for a year. The transformed lives of the new disciples were noticed by their community and the disciples were given a new nickname, "Christians." The new believers immediately became involved in social action; the first Christian relief offering was taken up to aid the poor in Judea (Acts 11:26–30). Thus,

3. On the significance of this new pattern of evangelism, and the new terminology employed in Syrian Antioch, see Walls, *Missionary Movement*, 17–18; and chapters 4 and 5.

Barnabas helped multiply those available for leadership. When one gifted encourager opened the way for another gifted Bible teacher to teach consistently in one congregation for a year the outcome was a group of now-competent Bible teachers from many different cultural backgrounds (Acts 13:1).

Then Barnabas recognized and obeyed God's call to a new work (Acts 13:1–5). While devotedly fulfilling his current duty, he was called by the Spirit to a fresh work. God called the Antioch church to set Barnabas and Saul apart for a mission to a new geographical area. Barnabas let go of his then current fruitful, influential, leading position, and obeyed, as the young church in Antioch became the new mission-sending center for the next phase of Christian expansion. He was willing to hand over his responsibilities to the new, less-experienced, and only partially proven leaders in Antioch and trust them to continue what he, under God, had built up. Again, Barnabas's faith in God was expressed in trust and confidence in other people. Barnabas went first to his homeland, Cyprus, taking or enlisting his cousin, John Mark, to help in his partnership with Saul, the other commissioned mission delegate.

These references to Barnabas in Luke's early church narrative show the qualities forming the foundations for Barnabas's concerns about planning for the deployment of people in God's work. He had devoted his heritage and upbringing to Christ as his Lord; he had welcomed God's life-transforming work in the life of a key rebel; and he had crossed the cultural boundaries to prove God's love for all peoples and to recognize the Spirit's ability to transform those he had not expected. And, accepting his own limitations, he had sought the help of others and had learned to delegate responsibilities while he responded to new challenges.

Transitioning to a New Leader

Early in this new outreach Barnabas recognized the evident gifts of his colleague, Saul, and he reallocated leadership responsibilities. Notice the change in the order of names in the references in Acts 13:9, 13, 42, and 50. But, Barnabas worked on with the newly named Paul, despite the reaction of Barnabas's relative, John Mark (v. 13). Throughout this mission trip, Barnabas kept encouraging and trusting people as the key strategy at the heart of follow-up for new believers (14:21–23).

Back in Antioch, reporting on their mission, Barnabas struggled to apply the boomerang lessons from the new mission frontiers into the life of the sending church. He and Paul had discovered the big issue, namely that as the gospel crossed into a new cultural setting, the gospel called for converts, not proselytes. But the Jewish Christians had always expected people of other cultures to become proselytes to Judaism in order to become true members of the people of God. Influential Jewish Christians required circumcision as the badge of membership, in addition to faith in Christ. Barnabas had already found that was not necessary, both when he first came to Antioch, and certainly in his experience on the Galatian mission trip. But when Jewish Christians from Jerusalem started demanding the proselyte route as the only acceptable one in Antioch, even Barnabas, the "encourager," preferred non-confrontational harmony, rather than challenging these teachers about the inadequacy of their emphases. So Barnabas had withdrawn from those gentiles with whom he had been enjoying fellowship around their tables—both in the church and socially. Paul, his younger, recently graduated apprentice colleague, rebuked Barnabas and publicly pointed out he was being led astray by going with the separatists (Gal 2:11–14).

Yet when the "encourager" faltered, Barnabas proved such failure was not final. He evidently accepted the rebuke from his former understudy, for when the Antioch church chose delegates to represent them in debating these issues in Jerusalem (Acts 15:2b), Barnabas served supportively with Paul again. Such humbling, even humiliating, lessons, once learned, equip us better to continue our ministry on behalf of others, as Barnabas did as a trustworthy representative at the Jerusalem conference.[4] Willingness to accept rebuke from those who have trained under us, and to work alongside, and under them, are essential if we are serious about transitioning to younger leaders. Such attitudes, however, are not as common as could be expected amongst people committed to the one who, "humbled himself, and became obedient to death, even death on a cross" (Phil 2:8).

4. This sequencing of the events assumes the "South Galatia" explanation of the destination of the Galatian letter, and that it was sent just prior to the Acts 15 recorded "Jerusalem conference." I am aware that a "North Galatia" destination, and, therefore, dating the letter after the mission to that region, possibly referred to in Acts 16:6, would invalidate the timing of these lessons but not the substance of them. I adduce F. F. Bruce's support of the "South Galatia" theory and dating of the letter as an example of the scholarship on which I base my assumptions, as in Bruce, *Galatians*, 10–18.

Reapplying Transitioning Priorities

For Barnabas the costly priority of restoring John Mark as a potential future leader involved the trauma of another public argument with Paul—this time the intensity earned the description, "paroxysm" (Acts 15:39). The point of conflict appeared to be that, for Barnabas, developing potential in people took higher priority than proven competence in "the work." Barnabas wanted to recruit John Mark again for the next missionary trip. He saw more ability in his young cousin than did Paul, and possibly understood more fully the circumstances around Mark's previous "desertion" than Paul did. But Paul, certainly up to this point, always put "the work" first, so he would not accept in his team anyone who "did not go to the work" (Acts 15:38). Quitters, for Paul, have disqualified themselves from further active, frontline service.

The irony is that Barnabas just wanted to do for Mark what Barnabas had already done for the young rebel, Paul; he wanted to open doors into service for his nephew. But it appears that, as now, so then, once a Christian worker had displeased key church leaders, it could be very difficult to bring them back into favor and a return to fruitful ministry.

Moreover, when Paul did not agree with Barnabas's judgment, the church backed Paul. Not only was the first step of Barnabas's long-term transition plan refused, Barnabas himself was dropped from, or chose to drop out of, the mission team and the work. Sadly, we hear nothing more of his ministry from this point in the Acts account. The priority Barnabas gave to developing a still immature person over adhering to the commonly expected work competency criteria, cost Barnabas his own position and acceptance in the church mission program. Personnel issues, particularly when they involve long-term trust, recovery from faltering first steps, and relationships with extended family members, continue to prove difficult areas in Christ's service. Too often key people are lost over such issues.

But the Barnabas story does not end there. Barnabas fades from the picture, but his principles continue to bear fruit. Barnabas, presumably, took Mark and kept on encouraging him. For, although we hear nothing more directly of Barnabas, we can credit him with a major contribution to later outcomes in the New Testament story. Beyond this point, John Mark becomes "useful," as Paul himself finally testifies (Col 4:10; 2 Tim 4:11). Mark goes on to write another gospel. It is hard to imagine what our New Testament would look like without Mark's writing. But it is hard to imagine him doing such work if someone had not worked with him to restore him after he had been labelled by the leading missionary of the day as a failure, and had been rejected by the church most active in recruiting the new generation of Christian workers. The one person in a position to help Mark through such a discouraging rejection was, surely, "the son of encouragement."

Perhaps equally significant, we notice that from this point on in his ministry, Paul mimics Barnabas by recruiting and equipping understudies of his own (Acts 16:3, cf. 21:1–5). Church leaders are often reluctant to publicly admit they may have been wrong, or that they may have wronged one whose ministry they have rejected. But, when they immediately adopt the policies and priorities of those they shamed and wronged, perhaps that is their way of admitting their error. Imitation is ever the sincerest form of flattery. From this point in Paul's ministry he began to do for an increasing number of younger colleagues just what Barnabas had done, humanly speaking, to prepare him for the transition which put him into his leading role. Paul gathered round him Timothy, Titus, Epaphroditus, Silas, Priscilla and Aquila, and those listed in Acts 20:4. Barnabas's priority became Paul's regular policy and practice.

Moreover, Paul used Barnabas's denial of personal rights as an example for the Corinthian church (1 Cor 9:6), suggesting the rift may have been mended, and ensuring Barnabas was not altogether forgotten or unknown in Paul's new churches. Beyond that we can only speculate about Barnabas's later ministry.

Barnabas's example and influence ensured the healthy transition from the first generation of believers to the next in the early church. He was the link person between Jesus's twelve disciples and the ministry of Paul and his team. Barnabas faced and paid the price of ensuring the next generation received and transmitted the gospel faithfully. That is the model for transition and succession planning. We can thank God for the Holy Spirit's comment on his role in the verse to which we have already referred (Acts 11:24): "He was a good man, full of the Holy Spirit and faith." We can further judge Barnabas's effectiveness, by turning now to hear the counsel of his first understudy, Paul, as he drew to the close of his own most effective service.

Paul's Transitioning Instructions to Timothy

We could continue the narrative in the biographical style of the previous section and keep working through Acts and the letters of Paul to show the wide range of ways in which, from his argument with Barnabas over Mark, Paul himself prioritized people development. But we choose, rather, to turn to Paul's last extant letter in which he gathered together his mature reflections on the transitioning process and set out his views in his challenge to Timothy.[5] In the first two chapters of his warmly personal Second Letter to Timothy, Paul is focused on equipping Timothy to transition effectively to a new level of leadership responsibility, and to inculcate principles enabling him to repeat the same process with new developing leaders in the future.

Paul, now an older man, acutely aware he is nearing the end of his life's journey, in the early verses of 2 Tim 1 refers to a number of facts and truths of faith on which he builds his policy and plans for leadership transition in the church. These underlying realities deserve careful attention.

Purpose and Promise

This opening chapter of 2 Timothy reveals a pervading awareness of the importance of time for Christians. Not in the modern sense of a rapid succession of precious moments to grasp productively for material goals, rather, time as a steadily moving, intentional arena in which destinies are forged with long-term significance. Paul's attention will stretch right back to time's very beginnings (1:9b), and on to "the day" of its future fulfillment (1:12). Little wonder, therefore, the apostle Paul weaves into his normal letter greeting awareness that his own missionary role and authority were rooted in the dual foundations of "the will of God" and the "promise of life that is in Christ Jesus" (1:1).

The "will of God" reminds us of purpose—God's purpose—spanning the generations of the life of our galaxy and the whole human story. Writing consciously within that unfolding plan of God gives stability, direction, and certainty. But, since that purpose centers on the "promise of life in Christ Jesus," it is never staid or outdated. Rather, this purpose abounds with vitality, satisfaction, and future-oriented assurance—what we call "hope"—because of the person in whom it culminates: Jesus the Christ. This Christ Jesus answers the hopes and yearnings of all peoples and every generation. In Old Testament times this cross-generational purpose was celebrated in the name of God as the "God of Abraham, Isaac, and Jacob." But in the New Testament the same future hope bursts all bounds in the reality of the generation-transcending life guaranteed in Jesus the Christ,

5. On the Pauline authorship of 2 Timothy see n3 in chapter 8.

who is the same yesterday, today, and forever. God's purpose, deeply rooted in eternity, and Jesus Christ's life-infusing promise, set the parameters for Paul's instructions on succession planning.

Leadership Transition Driven by Gratitude

Significantly Paul draws attention, first, to the heritage both he and Timothy have received from previous generations. Planning forward begins with appreciation of the past (1:3). In doing so, he expressed his gratitude for the succession of conscientious "temple service," or exemplary benevolence (*latreuō* in the Greek) which had extended from his Hebrew ancestors down to Paul himself. Although Paul's parents had not been Christians before him, Paul still appreciated the value of his pre-conversion religious heritage (1:3a). As we have seen from Gal 3:19—4:7, this kind of respect for the function and role of our inherited religion was a continuing gift of the gospel to all new believers in Christ. Too many fail to recognize the way the Spirit of God guided and led in the days before their coming to Christ. Lack of appreciation of our religious heritage makes it so much harder to see the importance of succession planning for the future.

But Paul did not live in the past. His prayer life evidenced an empathetic concern for the rising generation—Timothy, in particular. This balance of appreciating the past and investing prayer in the people of the future, signalled Paul's, and our, level of spiritual maturity. Paul's use of "remembering" and "recalling" (1:3b–4) sets the tone for what follows.

Paul reminded Timothy of the succession of "hypocrisy-free," sincere faith, or faithfulness (*pistis*) in trusting Christ, which had continued from his grandmother, Lois, to mother, Eunice, and, Paul affirmed, was now (alive) in Timothy (1:4–5). The one quality of faith necessary to ensure its transmission across generations without becoming merely formal or nominal, Paul suggested, was integrity or genuineness. Nothing turns children away from their parents' faith more quickly than a lack of consistency in the parents' profession and lifestyles. And none can detect hypocrisy more sharply than one's own teenagers. Equally certainly, the child's faith needs to be genuine, not a mere mimicking of the outward forms of an inherited religion, for the transition to the next generation to be life-giving. Paul knew the importance of remembering and celebrating this dynamic of a personally experienced integrity of faith-life transmitted across three generations.

In an age when Western society is steadily losing its appreciation for its faith heritage, perhaps one gift world Christianity can extend back to the West is this continuing appreciation of the role of an ongoing generational transmission of living faith. This is a vital driver for planning forward.

Keeping Faith Alive

Paul ensures vital faith in the present generation by memory, recall, and reminders (1:3–5). Paul's "remembering" focused intentionally on freshly stimulating present faith, and stepping forward properly prepared for the future. When the Melanesian peoples of Papua New Guinea come to faith, their whole orientation to time is "converted." The traditional Tok Pisin term for the times of the ancestors is *taim bipo*, meaning the time you faced, or the time before your gaze. The customs and *lo* (law) of the ancestors regulated their previous lives. You had to watch your *tumbuna* (ancestors) for guidance. Traditionally, therefore, the time still to come was called *taim bihain*, meaning the time still behind your back which you did not face because you dared not turn your back on the ancestors. The gospel literally turned believers around—converted them. In Christ, the sense of time progressing towards a God-appointed future was radical good news indeed. Likewise, in 2 Timothy, Paul was not merely celebrating the past, but he rejoiced in the onward transmission from previous generations to the present, in order to encourage the process to continue on to future generations. He stressed the importance of each generation discovering the vitality and integrity of the faith. Hence, his further direct encouragements to Timothy.

As Paul called on Timothy to do his part to ensure vitality of faith in his generation (1:6–8), he drew attention to three aspects essential for warmth and growth in Timothy's faith.

First, Paul had been instrumental in Timothy receiving a gift of God's Spirit enabling and equipping him for his part in the service of Christ and the gospel. But Timothy must rekindle the fire and develop and express that gift. Any loss of first-love fervor, or cooling off of ardor when responsibilities became routine, were sure to dampen concern to plan forward and equip others with the grace gifts necessary for fruitful ministry. Stimulating the present-day glow of enthusiastic faith, therefore, was a first step to ensuring the pathway for faith into the next generation is secure.

Secondly, addressing personal weaknesses was also essential if Timothy was to transmit faith to the next generation (1:7). Illustrating his normal approach to pastoral encouragement (see Col 1:28), and building on his regular prayer for Timothy and relationship with his family, Paul warned Timothy and challenged him to take hold of the Spirit of God's offered power, love for others, and "sound-thinking" to address his natural timidity and lack of disciplined initiative-taking. Paul's reference to Timothy's tears, presumably on Paul's most recent departure (1:4), and Paul's repeated references to people being, or not being ashamed (1:8, 12, 16), suggest Timothy had been overly dependent on Paul, and overanxious in the face of difficulties. For Paul, the Spirit's empowering, giving oneself to others in outgoing love, and a well-ordered thought life were the three sufficient ingredients for dealing with such deficits, and for moving forward in service.

And thirdly, Paul encouraged in Timothy courageous, even if costly, witness and partnership in the gospel, empowered by the Spirit (1:8). Fresh commitment and involvement in cooperative service, drawing on the Holy Spirit's power, prepared each generation for serving those who would follow. The old soldier, Paul, expanded his antidote to timidity with this personal call for Timothy to move from a sense of shame about witnessing or identifying with Christians already undergoing trials for the faith, to embrace an active partnership in living and sharing the gospel.

Paul also stressed the Holy Spirit's role in sustaining each generation's vitality of faith (1:6–8). In calling Timothy to move beyond his own frailties, Paul kept reminding him of his proven experience of the Holy Spirit's enabling gift and the availability of the Spirit's power. Paul's concern is with faith's vital, relational connection with the living God in the Spirit, as he prepares for leadership transition, not just with maintaining rituals, forms, or structures of the church.

The apostolic word of encouragement and the equipping of the Spirit of God were the abiding sources of strength for believers facing the pressures and costly self-sacrifice of effective following in the way of the Savior. These two resources are still the necessary grounds for confidence in a succession of life-giving faith to the next generation.

God's Purpose and Grace

Transition planning rests firmly on God's generation-transcending purpose and saving grace (1:9–10). Lest, after these challenges to timid followers to do their part to ensure good succession, we might still have doubts, Paul again reconsidered the time factor in our faith journey. His time perspective reaches well beyond any normal boundaries.

Saving grace was gifted to us in Christ before time began (1:9). Paul was quick to remind Timothy that his salvation experience and call to a set-apart life owed nothing to anything Paul had done. It was all the outworking of God's purpose and free grace. But this was no suddenly devised emergency or contingency plan. God's purposeful grace was "given to us in Christ Jesus before the beginning of time." Here was the true perspective on the timing of how we fit in God's saving plans, what has been called the "kairological schema" for salvation.[6] God's purpose to bring human wholeness and flourishing—his plan of salvation—was set in place, "given" is Paul's word, within the mysterious being of the second person of the Trinity, yes, in Christ Jesus. And this all took place, literally, "before the times of the ages." Before time as we know it came into being, in the preexistent being of God, the grace purpose for our total wellbeing was established. The plan of salvation did not begin with Adam's sin in the garden. God was not caught off guard. Grace expressed and imparted God's original intentions. This should lift us well above restricted concepts of God's desires and plans. Especially, it ought to give us a time consciousness which embraces generations to come, and is never content to simply live for the moment.

This grace purpose has been displayed publicly through the appearance of our Savior Christ Jesus (1:10). The reality and intention was from eternity. But it finally broke into view in the manifestation of our Savior through his incarnation as the Messiah of every nation, Jesus the carpenter's lad. You can sense the awe with which Paul pronounced each word in this extraordinary claim. The one who first imagined time and brought it into being, then, "at the right time" broke into time in person, for "it matters to him about you."[7] But, if the saving purposes of God's grace were formulated before time began, and revealed in the breakthrough appearance of the incarnation of the deity in Christ, that is just the beginning.

If, from God's time perspective, the salvation plan was already given before creation, then from this same perspective the heart of the good news, the death of Christ, has already done away with humanity's last fear and enemy, death, and brought to light a new kind of life beyond the restrictions of death: immortal life (1:10). This vision of life abounding on into eternity future did away with any lingering uncertainties, and gave substance to the

6. Wieland, *Significance of Salvation*, 133, and elsewhere.

7. This is a literal rendering of the final clause of 1 Pet 5:7.

promise of life announced in 1:1. Here were the theological reasons Paul expected Timothy to move beyond: timidity, inappropriate shame, and inaction. Grasping this perspective on time, and the great gracious purpose God was fulfilling in and beyond it, provided the clinching reason for the kind of assurance, confidence, and courage that embraces forward-looking succession planning.

By reminding Timothy of these truths, Paul established a firm basis on which to call Timothy to move ahead with forward planning for leadership transitions and succession planning.

Leadership Transition

With these firm foundations in place, Paul now outlines the specific steps in his transition plan, and what he expects Timothy to do to ensure the purposes of God continue in the next generation. He does so by outlining three principles for leadership transition and succession planning in dependence on the Holy Spirit (1:11—2:3): commissioning, entrusting, and long-term planning.

First Transition Principle: Commissioning

As we have already noted in the earlier verses, effective future transmission depends on the certainty and vitality of the present generation's grasp of the gospel, and their place in its service (1:11–12).

Future needs cannot be met unless we ensure the present generation fulfils its trust properly. Paul reminds Timothy of what the Lord has charged, and entrusted him, Paul, to do. As *herald*, or preacher, he was responsible to announce or declare publicly the message he received: not to invent, add to, or alter, but to proclaim the already-given message of the Savior and his salvation, which he had just been explaining. Paul's role description highlighted his commission as a *missionary*, or "apostle": Christ's authoritative messenger, sent on a delegated mission. As *teacher* he instructed systematically, explaining, clarifying, correcting, and progressively leading his learners into a deeper, richer knowledge of Christ. Paul himself linked this role closely with pastoring concerns in Eph 4:12. The earlier verses of that chapter have exemplified this task in action. Colossians 1:25—2:3 was Paul's classic unpacking of his own understanding of the way he must work out the combined responsibilities of the three roles to which the eternal

God had called and set him apart. Future transitions and plans all depend on effective present-day faithfulness.

The threefold task was inherently costly (1:12a). The message Paul was commissioned to announce publicly confronted the ruling authorities, both religious and political, undercut their imperial claims, and called for exclusive commitment to its tenets. This was more than enough to stir up opposition, as Paul's story to this date had shown. But, knowing who had commissioned him, and the significance of the outcomes of his message, were enough to embolden, encourage, and dispel any need for shame, on either his part or Timothy's. Receiving this gift of such a strategic commission brought with it the obligation and privilege to prove faithful and trustworthy. Such gifts also brought responsibility to transmit the same tasks and responsibilities to suitable persons for the next generation.

Paul's personal friendship with his commissioner, and active trust in him, formed the platform on which he fulfilled his task (1:12b). To be able to say, "I know whom I have believed," gave firm ground on which to stand. This had also convinced Paul of the strength, trustworthiness, and competence of his Lord Jesus Christ to guard, protect, and keep safe what he had entrusted to Paul. And Paul was confident Christ would do so until the day on which all reports are in and the final assessments made of tasks undertaken. Paul had learned to give back to Christ what he had received from Christ in his commission. He then asked and expected Christ to take proper care of what he had put back into his master's hands for safe keeping. Receiving this trust, or "good deposit" (as Paul called it in the next verse), meant Paul now had to manage responsibly the work Christ had delegated to him. This idea of having a deposit or trust to fulfill for Christ formed the essence of the New Testament concept of commissioning. Once we receive a trust or deposit from him, we must quickly ask Christ to care for that deposit or trust, and to protect it as long as it is in our hands (1:12). As we have said, Col 1:25—2:3 explains the substance of this task, and 1 Cor 4:1–7 further explains how to handle it.

The current generation of leaders fulfilling the trust they have received in the strength Christ supplied was the practical first principle of the transition process.

Second Transition Principle: Entrusting

Paul had explained the terms and nature of an entrusted deposit, and had told how he sought to administer it. The next step was to ensure this same deposit was passed on to the next generation.

Paul handed on the "deposit" as a trust for Timothy to keep and guard (1:13–14), and now detailed Timothy's responsibilities. These built on the challenge Paul had already given Timothy to ensure the vitality and integrity of an active faith in Christ, and to enjoy the empowering of the Holy Spirit which more than compensated for Timothy's natural frailties. This entailed three further challenges presented by Paul.

Timothy was to grasp "what you heard from me (Paul)," and set it as his pattern for life and ministry (1:13). Setting the pattern for later generations was inherent in Paul's apostolic role. The pattern was given in what he taught—or "what you, Timothy, heard from me." Here the apostolic teaching was set up as the source for later generations to grasp and adhere to as their authority. Paul constantly repeated this theme to the churches he established (1 Tim 1:18–19; 3:14–15; 1 Cor 11:1–2; Gal 1:6–9; Phil 4:9). Peter, likewise, insisted that the apostolic writings, nothing else, would be their continuing standard after the death of the first generation of apostles (2 Pet 1:12–15; 3:1–2).[8]

Timothy had "heard from Paul" this authoritative teaching on several occasions—including the brief summary later in this same letter. Preeminently in Paul's mind may well have been the two-year Bible school program Timothy had shared in at Ephesus on Paul's "third" missionary journey. Acts 19:9–10 explained the daily, two-year duration of the school, and even (if we respect the added detail of the Western manuscripts) the five-hour time slot they met each day while the rest of the city observed siesta. Paul and Timothy both knew the importance of properly structured, in-depth biblical study for equipping the next generation of leaders, as well as for effective regional, cross-cultural evangelistic and discipleship impact, such as Luke records in Acts 19:10.

Paul added one necessary directive for Timothy to "keep" or "guard" this deposit of faith in the apostolic teachings (1:13). Timothy, and each one who follows him, was to guard the sound teachings, "with faith and love in Christ Jesus." A receptive mindset of attentive, humble trust and

8. The authorship of 2 Peter is contested. In support of my assumption that this epistle comes from the hand of Peter, see Green, *Second Epistle*, 129.

faith was essential for rightly receiving these teachings. Too often we approach the healthy teaching of Scripture with different, other frames of mind, without trust or confidence in their message, then wonder why they seem irrelevant.

If faith was the way to receive the teachings, then love was the way to respond to them. We respond with love and devotion for the word itself, but we also respond to these words with love and compassion for those before whom we live out these words. Cultivating Christlike character of faith and love as we read and apply the Scriptures is still the distinctive way to heed the challenge of this second principle. For the sixth time in the thirteen verses so far in the chapter the title "Christ Jesus" is used of our Lord. He is the partner in all our hearing, reading, and applying of Scripture. The teaching brings us into a living union with him, and the faith and love necessary to rightly appreciate and express these living words are the overflow of that relationship with him. Without experience of regularly living by the standards and patterns of the New Testament teachings, we have nothing of eternal value to offer the next generation. A proven lifestyle demonstrating this word in action makes us fit to engage in the transition process.

What Paul had explained was his own experience in v. 12, he now required of Timothy also: "Guard the deposit entrusted to you—by the help of the indwelling Spirit" (1:14). What he had just described as the received teachings, together with the spiritual gift, the call and commission Timothy already had on his life and ministry, were now reconceived as a "deposit," "entrusted" to him. His duty was to guard what he has received, and to do so through the enabling of the Holy Spirit. The duties of Christian leadership can be explored through many metaphors. Prominent here was the idea of receiving a gift of great value, with the accompanying duty of care to keep it safe.

Another facet of the idea suggested receiving the gift because you have been counted trustworthy. But trustworthiness assumes dependability, faithfulness, and integrity of character and behavior. Both the expectation of responsible care for the gift and of trustworthiness also imply being held accountable, with responsibilities in the way you discharge the trust shown. All these ideas were present in the thought world of "entrusting with a deposit."[9] While the "good deposit" could be seen primarily as the

9. The same ideas were also present in Paul's description and elaboration of the Christian leader as a "resource custodian" (*hupēretes* in Greek) and "responsible manager" (*oikonomos*) in 1 Cor 3:18—4:5. See Hitchen, "Christian Scholar," 276–87.

"healthy pattern of sound teaching," Paul seemed to include here all that Timothy has received to equip and enable him for the leadership task, including the commission to that task. The responsibility to keep the trust safely so as to ensure it was transmitted in its integrity to those who followed him was at the center of the ideas in these verses.

Once more, though, Paul did not impose a duty without at the same time assuring of the resource already on hand to carry the duty well. In this case, "guard it with the help of the Holy Spirit who lives in us" (1:14). Holy Spirit-given gifts are such that they come accompanied by the giver—or to be more theologically correct, they come courtesy of the already resident, indwelling Spirit of God. The one who literally knows each of us "inside-out," also knows exactly the level and kinds of support we each need to properly fulfill the responsible trust we have received.

This, then, is the center of the transitioning process. Those whose commission was near to honorable completion, committed the "deposited trust" they had received to the next generation of leaders, confident that the same Father, Son, and Holy Spirit who commissioned, enabled, and resourced them, would do it again for their successors.

Third Transition Principle: Long-Term Planning

The present generation is obviously responsible to pass on the baton to the next cohort of rising leaders. But the apostolic principles go deeper than that. Paul charged Timothy with transition planning for the next two generations at least (2:2). He looked beyond his own era of leadership, and gave Timothy responsibility to prepare for those who would follow him. We can see three generations in view in 2:2: first, Timothy, with other witnesses who also heard Paul's teaching; second, the "reliable people" chosen to teach "others also"; and third, the "others also." Paul gave Timothy specific instructions to plan for the following two generations. Assuming a "generation" lasts for twenty-five years, Paul was planning ahead for at least seventy-five years. This is the biblical intention for succession planning. Each current generation of leaders needs to equip the next generation in such a way that they are able to equip their following generation as well. When each generation owns responsibility for the next two there is no excuse for any gaps occurring in the transition to the next leaders, or the continuity of faithful transmission of the gospel message.

This third transition principle is given in-between two verses reminding Timothy of the strength available in Christ (2:1), and inviting him to endure the suffering inherent in the task (2:3). Paul had already reminded Timothy of his need of God's power in chapter 1 (vv. 7 and 8). Now the call was to appropriate that power and be strong in the grace which he had also already explained in 1:9 as centered "in Christ Jesus." Timothy's frailties had never been far from Paul's mind since his mention of his tears in 1:4. But rather than focusing on them, Paul encouraged Timothy to draw on his resources in Christ. Paul uses the examples of soldiers (2:3–4), athletes (2:5), and farmers (2:6) to ensure that Timothy reflects and remembers the centrality of cost in serving the gospel (2:7–8). Paul warned against romantic delusions about leadership. He had known more of the costs, pressures, and disciplines, and wanted Timothy to be prepared for them too. Grace and strength, stability, faithfulness, endurance, and steadfastness in face of hardship and trials were the hallmarks of the leadership necessary for effective ongoing succession transition to future generations.

Each section of the rest of the letter progresses the challenge of working out this transition principle another stage. Second Timothy 2:14—3:9 dealt with confronting false teachers and Timothy's character formation for the task. From 3:10—4:6 Paul referred again to his own example and experience as further encouragement, and summoned Timothy to steadily continue in his faith and wise use of the word of God, before a clear and concise charge to keep true to his commissioned service. In 4:6–8, Paul gave his testimony as he faced his own death, before he warmly shared his hopes, warnings, final testimony, and greetings. As he testified, "I have fought the good fight, I have finished the race, I have kept [the trust of] the faith." We can sense the yearning with which he pleaded with Timothy to do the same, and thereby left each succeeding generation in no doubt about the importance of planning well, and discharging properly the transition to the next generations of leadership as an inherent part of our responsibility as present leaders who follow the great apostle's Spirit-given pattern.

Conclusion

The examples of Paul and Barnabas examined in this chapter enable us to check how we are doing in this biblical task of transitioning to new leaders, and accepting that until "The Day," it is right and proper for our successors to bury us when we die, knowing that the succession for which we planned will continue. This succession planning,

- begins with "devotedness" and commitment of the present generation in fulfilling their commission;
- continues with early recognition and empowering of the gifts of the younger generation;
- is cultivated by awareness of the importance of a time perspective which recognizes God's eternal purposes at work in the present;
- is fuelled by faith—in people and in the Holy Spirit—at the local church level;
- is fostered by the "Barnabas policy" which seeks, finds, and grows people of the younger generations—even when misunderstood and rejected for such a concern;
- implements the transition principles of commissioning, entrusting, and long-term planning—in dependence on the Holy Spirit—and prioritizes them in our local churches and in every area of ministry;
- demonstrates willingness to hand over responsibilities, and to continue in subordinate supporting roles, accepting reproof and advice from previous understudies;
- keeps encouraging the younger generation to start succession planning early;
- knows and prays for the names and aspirations of the potential leaders each current leader is mentoring along the transition and succession planning pathway.

Section 3

Factors in Contextualization

Chapter 10

Biblical Factors in Contextualization and Theological Education

This chapter expands on our work in chapter 2 on contextualization. Looking at the missionary task through the portal of contextualization, that chapter in its later sections considered "the biblical truth factor" and an "appropriate interface between culture and biblical truth." This chapter draws on our experience in Papua New Guinea, first, to consider the place of the Bible in curriculum design in a Bible college. We turn, secondly, to suggest pointers for "making the word of God fully known," again drawing on experience at the Christian Leaders' Training College (CLTC) in PNG, before, finally, considering briefly the importance of the Bible teacher's own lifestyle in a Bible teaching ministry.

The Place of the Bible in Curriculum Design

During our time teaching at the Christian Leaders' Training College in Papua New Guinea, 1965–1979, we regularly discussed and debated where and how to incorporate the study of the Scriptures into our curriculum design. Those years coincided with more general debate about how to "do theology" in global theological education circles. It was common at that time to contrast the "old" approach and the "new," with recommendations to make a radical break with the "old." The "old" approach was described as "content-centered" or "teacher centered," with the teacher deciding what he or she thinks is best for the student and then imposing their teaching on the student. In a missionary situation this tends towards cultural imperialism, with the missionary teacher, either consciously or unconsciously, conveying the message that they know what is best for the students, and that the students should passively receive what is best for them. Such attitudes can undermine real sharing between teacher and student, destroy the students' self-respect and respect for their own resources and the value of their own cultural heritage.

Such a "content-centered" approach is also often accused of working against truly Christian learning and growth. The idea that learning means studying a body of academic information and passing tests of intellectual grasp of that information creates an attitude which divorces knowing from doing and thus denies a central thrust of Christ's and the apostles' emphases (e.g., John 13:17; Jas 1:22–25). A "content-centered" approach also exalts mental or intellectual thinking ability to an unbiblical place of priority when spiritual growth and maturity are really based on being and doing rather than primarily just knowing. Imposing information on others also militates against self-discovery by the students and fails to develop the students' own insights and gifts which are the Holy Spirit's ways of stimulating growth. These are serious, and often well-deserved criticisms. We must give due attention to them.

But the popular alternative approach may not be the only one. The "new" approach was described as "people- or student-centered." This means all thinking about course content and curriculum planning commenced by determining the needs, concerns, interests, and abilities of the students and these become the foundation for the teaching experience. There are no general or absolute truths which can be taught to all people; we should rather define the particular "target group," discover their needs, and "enable" or "motivate" them through "self-discovery" to find their own answers. The teacher and the content of the older approach will become important "resources" in the learning process, but they will be supplemented by the students and the community sharing which comes through participation in the learning experience. There will also be a strong emphasis on nonformal "doing" of the things being discussed, rather than a classroom-oriented "ivory-tower" discussion of the matter. Students themselves should be involved in setting their own learning goals on the basis of their felt needs and in determining the methods by which they will use the resources available to achieve those goals.

Again, the importance and value of these emphases are self-evident. But the way they have been worked out in theological education has caused some concern. In the wake of the "new" approach came an emphasis on studying themes of biblical teaching, as themes appeared more relevant than book studies. Likewise, surveys of books studied in their historical settings seemed too much like a "content-centered" approach.

In this chapter, I want to ask whether this setting of the "teacher- or content-centered" approach over against the "student- or person-centered" approach leads to a valid Christian analysis? Or are there other biblical and theological considerations demanding more careful attention before simply accepting the above analysis as the best way to go about planning a theological education curriculum for a residential or extension theological program.

I am suggesting we test the following thesis as an alternative approach to both the "old "and "new" approaches already discussed: that the nature of God, the way he has chosen to reveal himself to humans, the nature of humans, the place of the written word of God in the way God shares his salvation with humanity, and the distinctive form of the biblical writings, all demand that we give special attention to the flow of salvation history throughout the Scriptures; and to the study of complete historical or prophetic books, gospels, or letters within the context of that flow, in order to truly meet the needs of our students and to equip them as men and women of God. In other words, an evangelical theological education curriculum will give central priority to the study of particular biblical books in their historical context, to a grasp of the overall biblical teaching, and to the interrelationship of that teaching within the Bible.

If we must use labels—and I wish there were an alternative—I seek to defend a "Bible-centered" approach to curriculum planning as the best way to conserve the strengths of the "old" approach, and at the same time to achieve the desired improvements proposed by the "new." I will work through each part of the argument for such a Bible-centered approach.

The Nature of God

The living God is an objective reality who both thinks and acts. This God to whom we seek to lead people through our theological education is not simply an influence or motivating force, but a rational being who speaks and acts in rational, objective ways. Thus, to know him we must study and attend to his speaking and his acting. It is only because he has spoken and acted in history that we can know him at all.

God's nature as one who speaks and acts rationally gives priority to mental, and especially verbal, activity for those who would know him. Ritual, movement, art, drama, music, and dance can all become vehicles for some aspects of sharing with him. But none of these can bring anything like the relationship with God which he has chosen to share through verbal speech and intelligible action. Our present-day world emphasizes feelings and experiences of excitement, but God's own nature gives special emphasis to mental and verbal communication as the key to personal knowledge, both of God and our fellow humans. The recent tendency to downgrade the value of speech and thought may well be a tendency towards dehumanization of interpersonal relationships, which those made in God's image should resist for their health's sake!

Since the living God is a being who speaks and acts rationally and intelligently, those who know him must approach him through the media of his thought, his speech, and his intelligent actions. This means we must approach him through the careful, diligent study of the Bible, which is the record of that thought, speech, and action. This gives high priority to the skills of reading, comprehension, thought, and intellectual understanding, since these are essential for knowing this kind of God.

The Nature of God's Self-Revelation

Our second point arises directly from the first. God is eternal and unchanging in his purposes and character. But he has chosen to reveal himself at particular times in human history through human events and people acting at particular places on our planet. He has limited himself to use particular geographical, historical, cultural, and linguistic settings to make himself known.

Moreover, he has chosen to make himself known progressively and in various ways throughout the period covered by the biblical record. Thus, an adequate knowledge of God depends on knowing and understanding the relationship between these various parts of his self-disclosure. In fact, he chose to reveal certain aspects of his purposes, mind, and nature quite definitively at specific points in the history of salvation (e.g., at Sinai and Calvary). Thus, we are not free to tell him what we want to know about him, nor when we are ready to receive it. We must humbly study what he has shown once for all at those God-ordained, historical moments, if we are to grasp and appropriate those aspects of his person and purposes.

God has, furthermore, authorized and inspired a written record and explanation of himself and his work in such a way that he now uses this writing as the authoritative way of revealing himself to us. The written revelation of the Bible is foundational and normative for illumination and knowledge of God today. Hence, there is a "given-ness" about God's way of revealing himself through the Bible. This demands we sit humbly beneath his word and learn from him. We are neither free, nor competent in ourselves to know and understand him, without giving proper priority to the way he has chosen to show himself.

This means, then, that there is a "content" about revelation which must be central in theological education. The word of God in the Bible is not just another resource we can choose, if we like to use it, to help us in our search for spiritual understanding. The Bible must be the very foundation of our search. We can certainly use inductive and other lively approaches to ensure students are interacting personally with the Scriptures to discover for themselves what they are saying. We should beware of any dead approach which makes the living word appear dull, dry, or irrelevant. Likewise, we shall seek to ensure that students interact with the Author of the Scriptures, not just with the lecturer. But the way God has chosen to continue to reveal himself in the Scriptures requires that the Bible itself determines the theological education curriculum in large measure.

Human Nature

This point also is implied and grows out of the last one that human nature demands a Bible-centered approach to curriculum design. Humans are fallen creatures. Our thinking powers, feelings, and wills have all been distorted by sin. Thus, we are unable in ourselves to properly understand either the nature of God or of humans, or the nature and purpose of God's universe.

Much modern educational theory fails to take this fact seriously enough. As human beings we do not always know our own needs accurately, nor in full. What we want to know, do, and be regarding ourselves is not always what we need to know, do, and be. Thus, to adopt a strictly "person-centered" approach to curriculum design, where students themselves determine content and methods of approach, may simply shut us into the restrictions of our human ignorance about ourselves. The God who truly knows and understands us (Jer 17:9–10; John 2:25) has to be allowed to confront us with his demands and explanations of our human predicament, if we are to grow in him.

This does not mean that the teacher alone should decide what is good for the student. The teacher also shares in this distortion of their nature and abilities. Most often they have also absorbed both the benefits and limitations of having trained in one particular culture, thereby almost inevitably having restricted their own views in the process. This emphasizes the value and importance of having an objective authority to which both teacher and student bow for guidance and instruction. The Bible is just such an authority if we take it in its totality and present form. The more we divide it up and treat it selectively, the more prone we are to distort its message. The more we approach it in its self-contained units (as testaments, historical and prophetic books, gospels, letters, and so forth) the more likely we are to hear the undistorted word from God.

Our human nature also has a positive side to it. Humans have not completely lost the image of God within them. Through Christ's redemption our thinking processes can be and are being renewed. Further, the Holy Spirit indwells believers as our teacher and stimulator of thought processes, as well as our desires and wills. Thus, Christian students have fantastic resources as gifts from God which the theological education curriculum must recognize and encourage towards their full development. But, again, the word of God is the regulative means by which the Holy Spirit brings about the renewal and stimulation we need. So again, by keeping the Scriptures central, we will both avoid the danger of wrongly exalting our fallen human nature, and at the same time, stir up the proper self-respect and gifts brought by the indwelling Holy Spirit.

The Bible's Place

As we have just hinted, the Bible is not just a dead textbook of an outdated culture. The Scriptures themselves claim to be the light, the food, the corrective, the teachings, necessary both to bring people to Christ, and "that the servant of God may be complete, equipped for every good work" (Ps 119:105; 2 Pet 2:2; Matt 4:4; 2 Tim 3:16–17, and others). Thus, whether in the regular preaching program of our churches, in our personal sharing of the good news with friends and neighbours, or in a full theological education program, there must always be the hearing, receiving, and doing of this word of God. We do not just use the Bible for theological education; the Bible is theological education, and therefore central to curriculum design. God has not only limited himself to the Bible as the way to reveal himself to humans; he has also chosen to make the Bible his chief means, together with the indwelling of the Spirit of God, by which we experience him, grow into his likeness, and serve him effectively.

But this does not happen mechanically or magically. Through the reading, hearing, meditating on, and working out of this living message in practice, we know and grow in God. Thus, again, we cannot bypass the disciplines of comprehension, analysis, exposition, and relevant application of the Bible for spiritual growth and service. Our theological education curriculum therefore must give priority to serious grappling with this book—the Bible.

Relating Our Teaching to Our Situation

The Bible speaks to, challenges, and transforms the basic life values and attitudes of every culture. It is only through progressive application of the teaching of the word of God to central cultural concerns that our people can "do the truth." Our constant concern as missionaries or indigenous Bible teachers must be to bring this in-depth and progressive biblical challenge to traditional assumptions and habits. This is the "putting off" of the old and "putting on of the new," or "renewal of the spirit of your minds" which the New Testament emphasizes so strongly (Eph 4:22–24). Or as Paul expressed it in Col 1:25, "I have become [the church's] servant by the commission God gave me to present to you the word of God in its fullness."

Without a regular and consistent input of Bible teaching, attitudes of nominalism, reversion, or syncretism are sure to develop in local churches. Christian truth is not a "simple gospel" which is quickly passed on; it is a growing experience of conformity to the mind and likeness of Christ. This requires progressive Bible teaching.

Fullness of Teaching and Correction

To achieve this progressive growth we must be constantly filling out the convert's understanding of central biblical truth. Our aim is for all the biblical metaphors about each particular aspect of truth to take hold of the local converts' hearts and minds and produce appropriately changed living. In other words, the range and depth of biblical truth is the test of faithfulness, not the question of meeting felt needs of the moment. Meeting the felt needs of people is a helpful and necessary starting point. But it can never guarantee maturity. Our fallen human nature means that for all of us some basic needs seldom become felt needs. Our bias of pride and sinfulness often steers us away from our central spiritual needs.

Thus, just ministering to felt needs, or just waiting for spontaneous "good news encounters"[1] will not necessarily ensure healthy church growth. We must, both at the initial stage and at each point of progress, allow the word of God itself to convict us, and all its hearers, of our more basic needs, which have not yet become felt. Bible teachers need to be so involved in the life of their people that central areas of truth which do not appear relevant at first, can become living, prophetic challenges through well-applied teaching. There is a danger in overstressing the need to meet felt needs and making "relevance" our prime concern. The word of God itself can and must stir up, in the new community of the church, hungers and thirsts which have never been thought of or considered before.

We need to be concerned about needs which are not only "felt" but "declared" in Scripture. We do need "relevance," but not simply in the sense of the teaching being readily grasped in the culture. We need relevance in the sense of meeting basic human needs. This highlights the need for regular, planned Bible teaching at the grassroots church level of discipleship, which ensures step-by-step coverage and repetition with increasing depth of the "whole counsel of God." In other words, the Bible itself must determine the range of biblical teaching needed. As long as aspects of biblical teaching have not become living and relevant in this sense, then we need further teaching.

Each biblical word picture explaining any one aspect of truth complements and balances the others. Between the different aspects of the gospel there is a delicate balance which is destroyed if we do not seek the fullness of truth constantly. Allan Tippett develops a helpful description of the stages of growth to maturity in conversion.[2] The convert moves from awareness of Christianity as an alternative lifestyle, often in another culture, through a point of realization (R), to a period of decision-making. This leads to a point of encounter (E), followed by incorporation into the church. But that

1. To use Dye's term, in *Bible Translation Strategy*, 45–61, esp. 45–48.

2. Tippett, "Conversion," 203–21. See therein his helpful diagram.

is not the end. This then leads to a point (or better, a series of points) of confirmation or consummation (C), which leads to growing maturity. Tippett, and the "church growth" writings generally, tend to emphasize the points R, E, and C as the keys to growth. Thus, power encounters (or better, "power choices," as Dye calls them) are essential for growth, as are the spontaneous and often sudden confrontations, choices, and commitments which lead on to the next stage of growth.

We agree with these emphases but want to stress equally the other side of the coin: the regular, step-by-step hearing, thinking through, and contemplating, or reflecting on, consistent teaching of the word of God, which brings a person from one growth point to the next. People only progress through the different periods when there is ongoing Bible teaching. For example, Joseph's sudden confrontation and test with Potiphar's wife (Gen 39:3–21) doubtless led him on to a new stage of maturity. But it was not only the point of confrontation, but also his previous step-by-step assimilation of foundational attitudes to immorality, which gave the growth. We need at village, and all local congregational levels, ongoing, regular teaching which relates Scripture to basic attitudes, beliefs, and assumptions, and stirs up the ingredients out of which faith encounters and choices lead to growth.

Thus, to make the word of God fully known requires growth into truth, not only as felt and desired within the culture, but also as declared and revealed as necessary in the Scriptures. This requires ongoing regular teaching of Scripture using all the variety of patterns described in the book of Acts and the letters of the New Testament.

Attention to the Situation and Form of the Word

As we seek to give this relevant, faithful Bible teaching with a view to strong growing churches we need to take note, not only to the teachings of the text, but also to the form in which they came to us. Or putting this another way: *the biblical form is normative for interpreting God's truth.* As evangelical Christians we are sure that the historical, linguistic, and cultural setting in which the word of God in Scripture was revealed, contributes to its definitive or normative meaning.

As the Willowbank Report puts it:

> The essential meaning of the Biblical message must at all costs be retained. Though some of the original forms in which this meaning was expressed may be changed for the sake of cross-cultural

> communication, we believe that [the forms] too have a certain normative quality. For God himself chose them as wholly appropriate vehicles of his revelation. So each fresh formulation and explanation in every generation and culture must be checked for faithfulness by referring back to the original.[3]

Thus, exegesis to find the original meaning of the biblical text must be the foundation of all our present and ongoing teaching. This is fundamental. Moreover, when God chose to work through a written word for our salvation, he was also choosing a number of specific forms by which to share his message and self-revelation. Thus, to receive that revelation clearly, we must take due notice of the way it has come to us. The biblical form is significant for developing a teaching curriculum in cross-cultural situations.

By the "form" of the biblical message, we mean giving attention to: the historical progression of the message of salvation in the biblical record from Genesis to Revelation; the fact that the historical and narrative sections of the Bible reveal God acting in concrete encounters with his people; the fact that the gospels are a special category of writing, each with their own unity and emphases; the fact that the bulk of the New Testament is a series of letters each written as an entity in itself to meet specific needs; the fact that carefully selected incidents in the life of the church are recorded in Acts, and others are not; and so on. As we plan and develop our Bible teaching programs, we should take note of these distinctive forms through which the message was given and recorded. In a cross-cultural situation they provide an approach which can avoid many of the problems arising from "cultural overhang" when we as missionaries simply reproduce the teaching curricula we learned from our homelands.

In our first year in Papua New Guinea I was tasked with teaching a course on the doctrine of God for twenty mature church leaders with a secondary school level of English competence. They had come from all over PNG and the Solomon Islands to better equip themselves for ongoing church leadership. That first year I simply took the outline of the first-year theology course I had completed at the Bible Training Institute in Auckland, New Zealand, and simplified it, but followed the course structure fairly closely. This meant I began with the communicable attributes of God, moved quite quickly to the Trinity, the deity of the three persons of the

3. Lausanne Movement, "Willowbank Report," 9. Cf. Marshall, "Culture."

Trinity, and the incommunicable attributes, and so on, as we had done in our Auckland course.

I had not gone very far before I realized that I was dealing mainly with abstract ideas and thought-forms which were quite difficult for the students to grasp, because I was dealing with thought-forms beyond their experience. It was not that they could not think abstractly. They could, and did, about things they were familiar with and which they had encountered and discussed first with reference to concrete examples. But the deity, eternity, and aseity of God were not such terms for them. At the same time I was teaching an introductory Old Testament course to the same students. I noticed they quite quickly picked up on the concrete ideas as we discussed the creation, the events and people of the patriarchal period, and the lessons objectified in the structure and furnishings of the tabernacle, the lessons of Judges and the Kings, and the dramatic events played out by the prophets. Teaching this course on one occasion, we had hardly started into the book of Proverbs, when one student shot up his hand, and asked, "Mr Hitchen, why didn't you start this course with these proverbs? Our people have many sayings like this—it would have made the course much easier if we had started here."

Slowly it dawned on me that for the course on the doctrine of God it would be much more sensible in this only partially literate society to follow the concrete and biographical form, content, and order of the biblical books, and only on that foundation start to summarize and synthesize in abstract terminology about God. So, from the second year of teaching the Theology of God course, I began to rearrange and reorder the content. For students in a comparable ethnic and educational context today, I would now recommend incorporating concepts such as the following for a basic theology course:

i. *A basic grasp of the historic development of teaching within the Bible is an essential anchor for grasping and integrating truth.*

Thus surveys and overviews of the expanse of Scripture are necessary, even though demanding in terms of teaching skill. There is an important canonical progression from the Law, to Judges and Kings, to Prophets, to the Messiah and the Gospels, which can be likened to laying successive building blocks for biblical understanding.

ii. *God's revelation of himself in history through concrete situations has continuing significance.*

In teaching the theology of God, the Western approach of starting with abstract philosophical ideas about the Trinity and nature of God as Spirit is unhelpful in Melanesia. I started the revised theology of God course with the creation account of the beginning of the universe, since this is not only where Genesis itself begins, but each New Testament account of God or Christ Jesus encountering a pagan audience starts with creation (Acts 14:15–17; 17:22–31; Rom 1:18–23; Col 1:15–20, for example). Starting from the creation accounts it is possible to draw out the implications of God as owner and ruler of all he has made, moving from the concrete to the more abstract concepts. In Melanesian thought the concepts of the *Papa bilong graun* or *Papa bilong diwai* (the owner of the ground or tree) are readily understood. It is a relatively easy step to move from such locally known ideas to the more abstract ideas of God's relationships with his creation and creatures, or God's sovereignty and omnipotence.

Likewise, studying the occasions on which God revealed a new name for himself to the patriarchs or judges, or introduced a new name later in the biblical record, can be a helpful way to steadily build up a grasp of God's attributes. Although the attributes themselves involve more abstract thought, the situations through which God's name was first revealed were usually concrete events.

iii. *Attention to specific historic incidents and narratives gives a natural sequence and teaching pattern.*

Historic occasions such as the encounters of Noah and Abraham with God, God's progressive work in Moses's life, the events of the exodus and occupation of the promised land, and so forth, give patterns which fit Melanesian thought-forms. The biblical accounts emphasize or exemplify different characteristics of God's nature, such as: God's choice, provision, and promise to Abraham at Mt. Moriah (Gen 22); Jacob's lesson at Peniel (Gen 32); Moses's birth, protection, and learning of the meaning of the name Yahweh in the early chapters of Exodus; and the further insights from Exod 33:12—34:9. Again, the links between the historic events and their revelatory value are significant.

This is particularly so in the biographical passages of Scripture. Gideon shows the power of God and his righteousness in the sense of protecting the oppressed; David's life experiences, together with many of the Psalms he authored, show God's love, faithfulness, mercy, and forgiveness at work; likewise, Isaiah confronting Uzziah in the temple reveals God's holiness;

and Jeremiah and the captivity of Judea in Babylon show other aspects of God's righteousness.

iv. *The form of complete Gospels brings a balance of theory and practice, or doctrine and ethics.*

This is something that is still needed in churches worldwide. When studying the Gospels, less time spent on the Western "synoptic problem" would allow more time for concrete evaluation of the form and interrelationships between events as recorded in particular Gospels, probably leading to a better grasp of Christ's depth of sympathy with a variety of people and the relevance of his responses to their needs. We note how the whole content, order, and pattern of development within the Gospel of John is vital for those who would "believe that Jesus is the Christ, the Son of God," and who by "believing may have life in his name" (John 20:31). Knowing isolated verses or key stories from one of the Gospels is not sufficient. Each "form" developed in the four Gospels makes a vital contribution towards grasping the whole gospel message. Similarly, the book of Acts provides concrete descriptive and problem-solving situations for each generation and people group to reapply within their own culture.

v. *From the New Testament Letters, it is significant that when Paul spoke of Christ's deity and condescension, he did so in the context of humble service to fellow Christians (Phil 2).*

The biblical forms of writing, such as the New Testament letters wonderfully avoid the polarization of theory and practice about which curriculum designers rightly warn us. Giving more attention to systemic exposition and application in practice of the content of biblical units like the New Testament letters, might help us rediscover the balance we seek of knowing and doing the lessons exemplified in the letters.

Thus, I am suggesting that regular, expository study of Scriptures geared to the level of understanding of the congregation is essential for constructing syllabi for Christian growth in our young and struggling churches today, just as much as the strong meat of Paul's writings was necessary for the first generation of young, struggling congregations in his day. There is a continuity and universality of human need and of God's answer to that need which has been met once and for all in the Bible as we now have it. For example, the problem of ethnocentrism and misunderstanding of grace dealt with in the Letter to the Galatians is a recurring issue in church life in every culture. God's method of dealing with that problem is to encourage us to set forth that part of his word clearly, in all its power and relevance. Similarly, the questions dealt with in the Corinthian letters set forth universal principles which are sufficient for church guidance today. All of us long for shortcuts to holiness and new visions, so we need to hear afresh the Colossian emphases on the finality of Christ. God's selection of particular forms for dealing with those issues is still significant today. There is a worldwide temptation to lapse into traditional religion or formalism which makes the book of Hebrews very up-to-date. Our curriculum design needs to bring students to a place where they not only know the content of such parts of Scripture, but where they also know the range of situations and needs to which the various parts of Scripture speak God's message for our churches today.

For such a grasp of the overall relevance of the different units of Scripture, the Christian worker also needs a broad general perspective on the word of God and the interrelationships of its parts. For this, survey studies do not always shine with immediate relevance for the student, but they are essential building blocks for "rightly handling the word of truth" (2 Tim 2:15), and are not to be lightly put aside. The same must also be said of a number of "content-centered" studies which were often included in the "old" types of curriculum.

Underlying this concern to ensure the biblical teaching given is understood and comes alive in another culture are two basic facts. First, the Hebrew and Greek cultures through which God's revelation came were "middle" cultures in the sense that they had rich links with a variety of cultures and were influenced by thought-forms and lifestyles which have in turn influenced many other cultures. In Papua New Guinea, we soon find that biblical culture is closer to Melanesian patterns of thinking than our Western culture at many important points. Second, as we have shown, there is a universal similarity of human nature and religious experience which make the form as well as the content of the biblical writings significant for gospel communications today.

To make the word of God fully known, then, will involve enlarging our understanding of the range of teaching within the word and realizing that the cultural context in which we work offers opportunities for new insights into that large truth. Then, we must seek a pattern of ongoing teaching which will ensure continuing growth into truth, not just superficial experiences. And the word of God itself gives a pattern for effective cross-cultural communication which we would do well to imitate. But we shall find this is a demanding task and like Paul we will need to learn to say, "For this I toil, striving with all the energy he mightily inspires within me" (Col 1:29).

The Attitudes of the Bible Teacher

Our years of service in Bible teaching in Papua New Guinea (1965–1979), of further study in Scotland (1979–1984), and then back to Bible teaching in New Zealand (1985–2017) have confirmed another vital lesson about Bible teaching service: the lifestyle of the teacher impacts every aspect of their teaching ministry. Or, putting it another way, *people are always God's method* of training and equipping others for his service. Who we are in Christ is an integral part of our teaching. First Thessalonians 2 focuses on the apostle Paul's teaching ministry. It appears that Paul had been criticized for leaving the Thessalonian converts so soon after arriving in their city. So, he writes to explain and defend his motives and methods as a pioneer evangelist. He does not address the criticisms directly, but his explanations answer the misunderstandings the criticism had caused. Criticism is not uncommon in Christ's service; Bible teachers are always under scrutiny, with many critics ready to judge their work. Paul knew his share of such critical judgment. He does not refer directly to the criticism, but his personal testimony suggests these were the issues in the background:

- that he had run away from persecution in Thessalonica, leaving the new Christians to endure the cost of his work (2:2)—opting out of responsibilities
- that he taught a quacky perversion of "true" Judaism (2:3)—being culturally and intellectually inferior
- that he used his ministry and religious talk to cover a base desire for sexual gratification (2:3)—charged with immorality
- that he was a con man and trickster, deliberately manipulating others for his own advantage (2:3)—using others for self-gratification
- that he was a *gris-man tru*, as our Papua New Guinean friends call it (2:5)—insincere and a hypocrite
- that he was trying to "rip-off" the money-rich women and big business people of Thessalonica (2:5)—greed and ambition

- that he was power hungry, using religion to try to win a popular following (2:6)—grasping for power and seeking a name for himself.

These are common criticisms of servants of God still. And once made, such accusations are hard to overcome. But Paul's positive motives show he sought to guard against each of them. Paul dealt with criticism by openly reminding the Thessalonians of his lifestyle amongst them (1 Thess 1:9; 2:1, 2, 5, 11). In responding to these implied criticisms in 1 Thess 2, Paul presents a pattern for serving effectively as a Bible teacher of Christ, particularly as a leader amongst a cohort of Bible teachers.

The Bible Teacher's Persistence (2:1–2)

From insults and suffering at Philippi, Paul moved on to courageously tell the good news in Thessalonica. He had not turned from the challenges as he came to Thessalonica, and he did not move on because difficulties arose while he was there; he went on quickly to Berea because he would have made it harder for the Thessalonian believers had he remained in their city.

The Bible Teacher's Integrity and Motives (2:3–4)

Paul was not people-pleasing; he was careful to avoid error, impurity, or deceit in either his teaching or behavior. He did so because his deeper level motivation was always to please God. What he really valued were the humbling, responsible assurances that he was approved, entrusted, and attested by God himself. With transparent humility he could appeal to the Thessalonians' own memory to endorse these claims. Such open and mutual trust and integrity are fundamental for the Bible teacher's task—and for any effective spiritual ministry.

The Bible Teacher's Nurturing Methods (2:5–8)

Paul was not image-making, he did not rely on flattery, and could not be accused of greed. He was no mere popularity-seeker, and as became his regular missionary approach, he did not demand even his basic rights from those he served (2:6; cf. 1 Cor 9). Rather, Paul was sensitive and careful in his service. Putting it positively, Paul reminded the Thessalonians that he did not just objectively pass on a message, but was selflessly committed to them personally, caring, loving, and sharing as a nursing mother with her children. In pastoral relationships, which he accepted as an inherent aspect of his missionary task, Paul adopted a pattern of parenting believers to equip them for a worthy lifestyle, fitting for the new kingdom in which they had been granted citizenship. This reveals an understanding of the task of spiritual nurturing as primarily a people-forming exercise.

For Paul, effectiveness in the battle for the gospel is measured by the maturity and integrity of the lifestyle of the believers being served, and how well the Bible teacher shows parental qualities in his or her methods. This is very different from the strong texts and emails—or demands and commands—we often assume are the way to be "forceful leaders." Such an attitude shows we are not yet in line with the biblical understanding which is all about a gospel of peace and gentle, familial relationships.

The Bible Teacher's Example (2:9–12)

In his work patterns, Paul was never merely clock-watching and made it a point of honor not to be a burden to those he served. Steady, hard work are the pattern for any true Bible teacher. In his relationships as a leader, he could conscientiously claim, and expect both God and the Thessalonians to confirm, he had been pure, upright or fair, just, and blameless. These are essential qualities for handling the tests of loyalty to Christ amid *wantok* pressures, and nepotism. Deceit and favoritism undermine team morale quicker than anything else. To be above reproach or blameless in such matters is the regular New Testament requirement for leadership in spiritual matters.

In the matter of personal relationships (2:11–12), parenting for a worthy walk was the style Paul adopted towards his fellow Christians. Getting to know and relate to fellow Bible teachers and those we serve as a parent, caring for and training his children, is the biblical pattern. But this does not mean adopting paternalistic or authoritarian attitudes. Rather, it means being willing to do the thankless task; seeing the dirty jobs needing to be done, and doing them without having to be asked; taking the responsibility of a parent, but realizing parents give up their personal rights for the sake of the family. And keeping on steadily until the marks, characteristics, and lifestyle of the family "kingdom and glory" are seen in the children's behavior too.

The Bible Teacher's Impact

The outcome of Paul's application of these methods and exhibiting of these attitudes towards the Thessalonian believers provides a clear example of the right way for people to let the word work amongst them; they were hearing, receiving, embracing, and respecting this word from God. Paul, the preacher, was a herald transmitting an entrusted message. The Thessalonians were hearers and heeders, receiving the word. And the Thessalonians accepted the biblical message not merely as a human message, but as it actually is—God's own word. The Bible is God's active power, giving life through the Spirit, at work among those who are believing, doing its ongoing convicting and transforming, producing Christlike behavior and effective witness in and through both the Bible teacher and Bible student.

At the same time, the Thessalonians were copying the patterns in hardship, suffering, and persecution that are essential in spiritual service. They were imitating the Judean churches who had suffered persecution from Jews who continually opposed God's messengers, whether the Old Testament Prophets, or Christ Jesus himself, or Paul (Acts 8:1–4; 11:19). Effective witness for Christ has always been accompanied by persecution, hardship, testings, and trials, down through the ages. The Thessalonian believers embraced that pattern and thereby showed the way for successive generations.

Conclusion

We have explored three aspects of curriculum development and concluded that a "Bible-centered" approach is most suitable, particularly for a cross-cultural approach to Bible teaching We have explored suggestive clues for "making the word of God fully known," drawn from our Papua New Guinean experience; and considered the importance of the life and walk of the Bible teacher for effectiveness in their role. As we have worked through each section, we have hinted at its relevance in a cross-cultural Bible teaching situation. I would also plead for consideration of the same points in Western Bible college settings, particularly with so many international students enrolling in our Western colleges today. At the very least, I would plead for the curriculum issues that I have raised to be taken up and considered seriously. In today's world, contextualization and its implications can no longer simply be regarded as an aspect of mission studies.

Chapter 11

More Cultural Factors in Contextualization

How do we apply biblical teachings with integrity in new cultural settings today, when they were originally addressed to different situations in biblical times?[1] Determining an appropriate methodology to address issues facing their local churches, is a significant issue for theological educators in majority world colleges. The problem is widely recognized in the West as an example of Lessing's philosophical "ditch" problem: there are no natural or historical bridges to cross the gap between the particular occasions for which the teachings were first given, in such a way that those teachings can have binding force in a different situation today. The historical, geographical, cultural, and language differences make the "ditch" between the original and present-day settings too wide to leap over. Our concern in this chapter is with what weight to give cultural factors when grappling with this problem. What components for a theological methodology for contextualizing the gospel can help bridge the cultural gaps between the biblical and present-day contexts?[2]

The question raises different implications in majority world theological education situations where non-Western theologians find something about the issues in their settings locally, that is strangely similar to the biblical setting. The biblical text seems alive with fresh relevance for precisely

1. An earlier version of this chapter was first published as Hitchen, "Clarifying the Contribution," 91–120. Used with the permission of SAIACS Press (see bibliography for further details).

2. Chapters 4 to 9 have largely illustrated the contextualization process in some early churches in the New Testament. Chapter 10 has looked at biblical factors in this process, and the attention of this chapter swivels to further cultural matters.

these kinds of modern situations when looked at through local cultural eyes. But the apparent solution of a culturally oriented reading of the text may be significantly different from the accepted and expected solutions in Western biblical scholarship. And would a fresh, culturally straightforward application of the Scripture, with manifestly different implications in the local context, satisfy questions the majority world executives have to answer regarding their theological college's international recognition, accreditation, and financial support from Western partners? If it became known the college was offering distinctly different, even if culturally relevant, solutions to such issues, would those solutions be labelled syncretistic and threatening to overseas partnerships? The possibility of giving cultural factors more weight in theological contextualizing raises so many questions, that there is a temptation not to question the status quo.

But question we must. This chapter does not address some aspects of these issues, such as the implications of the Western hegemony over theological education standards in the majority world. Rather, our chapter focuses on how cultural factors should contribute to the methodologies local theologians and theological educators adopt as they develop theology, or theological education curricula, to address the local cultural issues challenging their churches today. We suggest three culture-related principles to help shape our methodologies for this contextualization task.

Principle 1: Gospel and Culture Mutual Enhancement

Under this principle we expect the gospel to fulfill local cultural aspirations and local cultural perspectives to enhance our understanding of the gospel. This principle follows from the apostle Paul's conclusion to his missional letter to the Christians at Rome, and is confirmed by the way the gospel has impacted different cultural regions since the day of Pentecost.

Romans 15:7–13

Paul concluded his letter to Rome with a strong appeal to the members of the house churches there, some of whom were from a Jewish background, while others had lived previously in Greek, Roman, or other local cultures. Paul pleaded with them all to leave their culturally exclusive lifestyles and welcome and receive each other. He called them to work together across their cultural boundaries to express the new Christ-centered life and unity they held in common. The all-sufficient reason for heeding Paul's appeal was that Jesus Christ had welcomed believers of each culture in the same way (Rom 15:7), and had united them all in the one, multi-talented and empowered body of Christ (Rom 12:3–8). The apostle then, in 15:8, immediately summarized how this acceptance of all cultures had come about. Christ Jesus broke into one specific culture, that of the Jews, to serve them and fulfill their cultural hopes and aspirations which had grown from the promises made to their cultural forefathers, the patriarchs. The unique person, Jesus of Nazareth, in his life of humble service and redeeming death and resurrection, had gathered up the beliefs and expectations of this one specific culture and fulfilled them, proving himself to be the long-awaited Son of God, their true Messiah or Christ (15:8).

This is how the gospel works. Jesus Christ consummated one people's cultural and religious heritage, satisfying their deepest needs and longings by his atoning death. Enhancing that culture's hopes and desires so unexpectedly required them to rewrite their traditional story to show their new grasp of God's true historic and ongoing purposes for them as people God loved.

Moreover, even more surprising, as the passage further explains, this pattern carried an internal dynamic impelling the first group to reach out to repeat the pattern for people of other cultures too. Those now transformed people of the first cultural group become messengers of this same gospel to peoples of another culture, so people of the second culture might also discover God's mercy and find that the same Jesus of Nazareth fulfills their culture's hopes and yearnings. Thus, they too, within their culture, are transformed and give glory to God. This is God's previously unappreciated pattern of historical, missional action. He chooses and blesses one cultural group so that they share his message with the next culture, who in their turn will find the gospel penetrates their society to its very roots. Thus, they find such a depth of fulfillment and purpose in Christ, that they, in their turn, also reach out to share the gospel, and so on.

Paul explained the process more fully in letters to churches at Ephesus and Colossae, using the idea of a "hidden mystery now disclosed" (Eph 3:1–10; Col 1:5–6, 25–27). But here in Romans, he rounds off his explanation as any Jew would expect, with proof texts from each section of the Jewish Scriptures showing that this pattern had, in fact, been promised all along (Rom 15:9–12).

We are taking this biblical explanation of God's missional purposes for humanity a step further. This pattern also offers a methodological paradigm for contextualizing the gospel message in different cultural settings today. God's way of selecting a particular culture, fulfilling their cultural longings, so they share the transforming message with the next culture, alerts us to look for ways the gospel message speaks to aspects of the cultural heritage, lore, and customs of each new culture. We engage new converts and mature believers in thinking, discussing, and explaining how the central theological concepts of the gospel relate to their culture's traditional narratives, experiences, and cherished hopes.

As we have seen in earlier chapters, virtually all the central truths of the gospel are explained in the Scriptures in metaphors: redemption, justification, reconciliation, atonement; or, Jesus as light, bread, door, shepherd, lamb of God, Savior, and so forth. So, local Bible teachers will encourage people of their local culture to identify how they understand and use the same or parallel metaphors to express their cultural fears, problems, desires, or hopes. By making such comparisons and connections the local theologian will expect to discover ways in which the gospel speaks with new relevance in their setting. This contextualization process encourages local Christians to take the light of the gospel into these recesses of their cultural questions and yearnings, expecting the Spirit of God to reveal how Christ Jesus satisfies their culture's concerns and values. In each new cultural setting, the biblical message will resonate with deeply rooted cultural beliefs. Believers in this local culture will identify longings or hopes long cherished in their society which Christ specifically satisfies, even though those who first brought the gospel had not previously understood that new emphasis as part of the gospel's influence, and were not expecting the gospel to speak in that way. Following this methodological clue, then, can help facilitate the gospel reaching into every aspect of a culture to enrich and fulfill it.

The flip side of applying this methodology is that, as the gospel does this culture-penetrating work, more aspects of the many-sided, but previously unrealized, greatness and grandeur of Christ and his good news will also be displayed (see Eph 3:10). As the gospel becomes deeply rooted in a new culture, different or new insights about the gospel become evident.

This pattern in Rom 15:7–13, offers a methodology principle to guide us in moving from the text of Scripture to building up a local theology.[3]

3. This principle, may then, also meet I. Howard Marshall's desired criterion when he writes: "What we need, then, is some kind of *scriptural* approach to the problem of

The Principle Confirmed in Christian History

We turn to Andrew Walls, missiologist and mission historian, for confirmation of this principle through Christian mission history. In two widely used essays, "The Gospel as Prisoner and Liberator of Culture" and "Culture and Coherence in Christian History,"[4] Walls analyzed the phases of Christian mission history by which the gospel successively penetrated and eventually permeated different cultural regions. In the New Testament, we see the first transition from the initial fully Jewish context to the point where, before the New Testament concludes, Greco-Roman believers were fast becoming the majority. Already, new concepts and explanatory terms for non-Jewish hearers to understand Christ and his work were being set forth to address the concerns of believers from the new majority cultural background.[5]

At the close of the second, Greco-Roman, phase of historical expansion, the church leaders' concern to find exact Greek philosophical terms for the interrelationships of the persons within the Trinity was very different from the priorities of the Jewish phase. These new concerns of the Greek phase also differed from the concerns about the centrality of communal custom and about the territorial nature of national churches throughout the next, or barbarian, phase of Christian history. Walls highlights both the continuities and radically new aspects of Christian expression and cultural concern in each of the six phases he identifies up to the end of the twentieth century.

For each phase, Walls found that as the gospel entered and impacted a new cultural area, believers were grasped by different aspects of the central gospel message as they heard it with their own culturally attuned ears. Or, in his alternative metaphor:

> the Scriptures are read with different eyes by people in different times and places; and in practice, each age and community makes its own selection of the Scriptures, giving prominence to those which seem to speak most clearly to the community's time and

---

[theological] development and interpretation. Can we establish principles that are rooted in the statements and practices of Scripture that will enable us to make progress in framing interpretative procedures and guard us against invalid interpretations and false conclusions?" Marshall, *Beyond the Bible*, 48.

4. After first appearing in 1981 and 1984, respectively, both essays were republished several times before being brought together as the first two chapters of Walls, *Missionary Movement*.

5. Walls, *Missionary Movement*, 4, 17–18. See also chapter 4 above.

> place and leaving aside others which do not appear to yield up their gold so readily.[6]

As the gospel penetrated new cultural regions in each phase, as Walls later differentiated clearly, believers became not "proselytes," but "converts," confirming the biblical principle we have just explained.[7] Converting, or turning, within a culture, with all its heritage, assumptions, and baggage, to Christ and making him Lord within that culture, means that certain aspects of the gospel stand out as more culturally dynamic and transformative than other aspects. Hence, the need for local theologies using local cultural concepts and thought-forms to explain how the gospel soothes where cultural issues leave salvation-seeking itches.

Moreover, in each new cultural heartland of the gospel, new themes are discovered within the gospel message itself which have not been grasped or emphasized in the same way in previous cultural encounters:

> Each phase of Christian history has seen a transformation of Christianity as it has penetrated another culture. There is no such thing as "Christian culture" or "Christian civilization" . . . The reason for this lies in the infinite translatability of the Christian faith . . . And this [translation] principle brings Christ to the heart of each culture where he finds acceptance; to the burning questions within that culture, to the points of reference within it by which people know themselves. That is why each phase of Christian history has produced new [theological] themes: themes which the points of reference of that culture have made inescapable for those who share that framework.[8]

Walls gives examples of this effect at the transition to each new phase of Christian history. He illustrates it for the transition from the Jewish to the Greco-Roman phase by showing how the term so precious and laden with cultural significance for Jews, "Messiah" or "Christ," not long into the Greco-Roman phase became almost only a surname for Jesus. Instead, the term "Lord" (*kurios*), attributed to so many rival persons or powers at the beginning of the transition, in this phase was soon filled with new

6. Walls, *Missionary Movement*, 11–12. Or again: "we all approach the Scriptures wearing cultural blinkers, with assumptions determined by our own time and place . . . Perhaps it is not only that different ages and nations see different things in Scripture—it is that they *need* to see different things" (12).

7. Walls, "Converts or Proselytes?," 1–4.

8. Walls, *Missionary Movement*, 22–23.

significance as Jesus was seen to be the ultimate ruler, no longer merely the promised one of local Jewish expectations, but sovereign even over Caesar the ruler of the mighty Roman Empire.[9] This expanding of the claims of Christ to embrace international and political as well as local cultural realms of authority was significantly beyond Jewish hopes as the earlier phase had conceived them. The latent, but comparatively undeveloped scope of the kurios theme increased in significance as the gospel crossed the cultural divide and found its place within the Roman realms of power.

Walls's studies confirm that repeatedly "the Lord has [had] more truth and light yet to break forth out of his holy Word" as the gospel moved across one cultural boundary to become at home in another cultural domain.[10] Cross-cultural transmission of the gospel has given birth to new applications of old truths, and opened up new, previously unexpected dimensions of insight into the meaning and extent of the gospel message itself.

So, our first principle—of gospel and culture mutual enhancement—suggests that, as local theologians and theological educators develop contextual theologies or theological education curricula for their cultural settings, they should *expect both the gospel to fulfill local cultural aspirations, and local cultural perspectives to enhance our understanding of the gospel.* This implies a theological method which is culturally informed and sensitive, expecting to find points of contact for the biblical message in the local cultural hopes, narratives, and traditions. The theologian will expect these points of contact to lead to dynamic translation of the biblical terms and in-depth experience of the spiritual realities those terms signify, enabling local believers to recognize the gospel as God's good news for them as a cultural group.[11] Moreover, local theologians, with the Scriptures open before them, and confident in the Lord's own promise that the Holy Spirit "will lead into all truth" (John 16:13), can expect to find potentially but latent in those Scriptures, fresh insights, themes, and emphases. As the local theologian's

9. Walls, *Missionary Movement*, 17–18. For further examples of the development of terms opening up fresh insights about the person and work of Christ even in the Jewish phase, see Hitchen, "Missional, Multi-Ethnic Nature," 63–78, esp. 66.

10. In 1620, as those who would soon become the Pilgrim Fathers on the *Mayflower* departed from their place of refuge in Leiden, Netherlands, heading to establish a new colony on the American frontier, their pastor and Puritan divine, John Robinson, encouraged them in his farewell sermon. As they faced the unknown future, he declared, "I am confident the Lord has more truth and light yet to break forth out of his holy Word." See Encyclopaedia Brittanica, "John Robinson."

11. See Walls, *Missionary Movement*, 26–42.

culturally sensitive hands nourish these new insights the new themes will blossom to a new fullness and maturity of meaning as the gospel interacts with the local cultural traditions, cherished themes, and hopes.

Principle 2: Cultural Affinity

Under this principle we understand that the structures, values, and epistemologies of some cultures are aligned to those of biblical times in ways that enable peoples of those cultures to more readily recognize, absorb, and apply biblical teaching than people of cultures that do not share this foundational cultural affinity.

Some ethnic groups share with other cultural groups similar assumptions, values, thought-patterns, and ways of interacting socially, that allow members of those groups to resonate with and feel a sense of shared perspectives with each other. Those same cultural groups may not recognize any comparable affinity with the basically different values, viewpoints, and life goals of some other cultural groups. For example, the cultures in Melanesia—the southwest Pacific nations of Fiji, Vanuatu, Papua New Guinea (PNG), Solomon Islands, and New Caledonia, as well as Timor-Leste and the Indonesian province of West Papua—not only share close similarities with each other, but they have more in common at the worldview level with many African cultures than they do with their Australian neighbors of European descent.

Some cultures also recognize this kind of affinity with the cultural background found in the biblical writings, despite the obvious historical and geographical distances between their world and the biblical cultures. This affinity does not mean identity, but shared basic concepts and values that allow members of some present-day cultures to feel culturally at home with the concerns, styles of approach to issues, and social relations operating in the biblical texts. In such present-day cultures, this affinity can, with due caution, contribute to the theological method they use to develop an appropriate local theology. I will explain this principle by referencing the work of Bruce Malina,[12] with illustrations from Melanesia, particularly Papua New Guinea, where I have been involved in theological education for five decades.[13]

12. Malina, *New Testament World.*

13. My wife and I lived in Papua New Guinea from 1965 to 1979, helping establish an interdenominational theological church and community leadership training college

Three strands contribute to this principle of cultural affinity. First, *all cultures share the same basic human nature and human capacities* which enable humans to relate and communicate beyond their own social network. Sharing a common human nature is essential for any understanding of peoples of other cultures, or time periods. Shared natural human desires, feelings, and longings are essential for any cross-cultural relationships. In his basic text, *The New Testament World: Insights from Cultural Anthropology*, Bruce Malina explores the characteristics of northeastern Mediterranean cultures of the twentieth century, which, he argues, throw light on, and demonstrate continuity with, the background cultures of the biblical texts, particularly the New Testament. Malina's analysis provides a basis for comparison with other cultures today which also sense this kind of affinity with the biblical cultures. Malina draws on the reality of a shared human nature when he explains his basic presupposition that: "All human beings are entirely the same, entirely different, and somewhat the same and somewhat different at the same time."[14] He also assumes our shared human nature when he cites Francis Hsu to confirm continuity between the Mediterranean cultures of the first and twentieth centuries:

> Cultures borrow much from each other in role matters such as foods, artifacts, etiquette, theories of nature, and tools for control of human beings and things. But there is little evidence that people change in any fundamental way, and as a whole, their patterns of feeling about themselves, about each other, and about the rest of the world [continue unchanged].[15]

Or again, "[Hsu] note[s] that while similar values exist in various environments, 'the basic pattern of affect of each society is likely to persist, in some cases, over thousands of years.'"[16] Assuming a basically unchanging human nature is fundamental for any learning from history, and is

---

serving the evangelical churches of the Melanesian region, called the Christian Leaders' Training College (CLTC). After doctoral studies at the University of Aberdeen, Scotland, we returned to our homeland, New Zealand, and have been involved since 1985 in theological education for New Zealand's bicultural and multicultural population, including significant numbers of Māori and Pacific Islanders. We have maintained our links with CLTC, returning each year in the decade 2007–2018, developing graduate level theological education programs.

14. Malina, *New Testament World*, 7–9.

15. Malina, *New Testament World*, xii, citing Hsu, *Rugged Individualism*, 174.

16. Malina, *New Testament World*, 52, citing Hsu, "Passage to Understanding," 142–73.

therefore also essential for any theological method which accepts that the Christian Scriptures have abiding relevance and authority today. But, the principle of affinity we are describing means much more than just being of common human stock.

The second constituent strand of this affinity between some cultures is the *worldview level commitments of the cultures*. The affinity grows from the similarity of their social structures, motivating value systems, thought patterns, and relationships, which build up culturally preferred attitudes and patterns of behavior over generations. There is only affinity between two cultures when they both share at worldview level at least some of the same structures and patterns. We shall select from the worldview level features Malina identifies in Mediterranean cultures to discuss parallels shared with Melanesian cultures.

For Malina, kinship, or family membership, is the basic organizing principle of Mediterranean life. The sense of family "belongingness" is vital, and a person's identity depends on this family acceptance.[17] The family concept in Mediterranean societies is not the Western nuclear, "Mum, Dad, and the kids" concept, but the wider relational and intergenerational concept of the "extended family." Malina devotes a whole chapter to the details of the kinship, family, and marriage arrangements at different periods of biblical history.[18] He shows that family acceptance and family loyalty remained central as the organizing principle of the society, embedded at the worldview level of motivation and behavior-shaping influence.

This familial acceptance depends, in turn, on adhering to the traditional rules of order of the society, and these rules are rooted in the "Pivotal Values of the First-Century Mediterranean World: Honor and Shame."[19] Honor is "basically a claim to worth which is socially acknowledged. It surfaces especially where the three defining features of authority, gender status, and respect come together."[20] These three features set the value framework for the society: who controls behavior; the "oughts" linked with a society's expectations about gender roles; and attitudes and behavior towards those who control you (often expressed as religion or piety). Where the three come together for a person, you find issues of honor or shame. Honor can be *ascribed* through birth into a family with existing recognized status,

17. Malina, *New Testament World*, 29.

18. Malina, *New Testament World*, 134–60.

19. Malina, *New Testament World*, 27–57.

20. Malina, *New Testament World*, 29.

or by having the honor bestowed gratuitously by someone abounding in such honor. Or honor may be *acquired* by achieving some feat of publicly recognized worth, or by accepting and winning a challenge to your status laid down by another person of a similar status. The loser in the challenge is shamed, and the victor acquires increased status. Such status challenges deeply shaped Mediterranean social structures and values in biblical times, as they still do today.

Malina describes a third worldview level feature as "The First-Century Personality: The Individual and the Group."[21] Malina contrasts the introspectively analytical, individualistic understanding of personality, typical of present-day Western North Americans, with the "collectivist" understanding of personality and the concretely described "zones" he identifies in the biblical literature, which peoples with a collectivist perspective use to describe human functioning. Malina links this collectivist personality closely with the quest for honor through affirmation by one's own group. He claims people holding this understanding,

> are persons of careful calculation and discretion, normally disavowing any dependence on others. They are adept at keeping their innermost self concealed with a veil of conventionality and formality. Ever alert to anything that might lead to their making an exhibition of themselves, to anything that would not tally with the socially expected and defined forms of behaviour that have entitled them and their family to respect.[22]

Malina is giving an etic, outsider's individualistic interpretation of this communally focused and motivated understanding of a person's identity. He may not have grasped adequately the very different understanding that people within such societies have of themselves. People with this communal orientation start from the reality that "I belong, therefore I am," and judge all personal actions by how well they serve and uphold the honor of the group. Participation in honor challenges is not merely to avoid personal shame, nor an introverted fear of the disapproval of others, but is for the welfare of the reputation, rank, and status of the extended family; to maintain the equilibrium in material and social capital available to your group; and to retrieve any losses from incursions by other groups. Whatever our assessment of his interpretation, Malina has identified a significant

21. Malina, *New Testament World*, 58–80.

22. Malina, *New Testament World*, 59.

worldview level feature which distinguished biblical cultures, and to which many present-day cultures relate deeply.[23]

Another worldview characteristic Malina sees as the clue to "maintaining one's social status" is "the perception of limited good." [24] Malina carefully categorizes the socioeconomic structures of Mediterranean societies of biblical times as ruralized, agricultural or fishing villages in a symbiotic, dependent, relationship with a regional, preindustrial city, which by Roman times was, in turn, symbiotically related to Rome, the ultimate imperial power holder.[25] Thus,

> such a socially limited and determined existence . . . lead to the perception that all goods available to a person are, in fact, limited. . . . that in society as well as in nature—the total environment—all the desired things in life, such as land, wealth, prestige, blood, health, semen, friendship and love, manliness, honour, respect and status, power and influence, security and safety—literally all the goods in life—exist in finite, limited quantity and are always in short supply.[26]

From this it follows "that individuals, alone or with families, can improve their social positions only at the expense of others. Hence any apparent relative improvement in someone's position with respect to any good in life is viewed as a threat to the entire community."[27] Malina then works out in detail how this limited good, closed socioeconomic system influences virtually every aspect of the society.[28]

23. But Malina's individualistic descriptions and analysis are tinged with ethnocentric condescension and lack appreciation of an emic interpretation of communal self-understandings and their outworking. This is perhaps inevitable when his method was to impose a Western psychological anthropology model onto the concrete ways in which the biblical writings describe the various kinds of human internal thoughts and consequent behaviors. Using a typically Western categorization and explanatory paradigm often runs this risk. In the process of doing this, Malina provides a description surprisingly close to popular Western theological themes of the time Malina was writing, such as Stendahl's conclusions in his, "Apostle Paul," 78–96.

24. Malina, *New Testament World*, chapter heading, 81–107.

25. Malina, *New Testament World*, 81–88.

26. Malina, *New Testament World*, 89.

27. Malina, *New Testament World*, 89.

28. The limited good concept is involved in patron-client relationships; honor-ranking entitlements and obligations; protective measures and indebtedness which maintain positions on the society's status ladder; and in keeping your lifestyle open to the community to avoid suspicion of seeking "good" at the expense of others. Limited good

Malina also explored how envy functioned as "the most grievous of all evils";[29] how kinship fused families together;[30] and how rules of purity permeated the regular rituals and customs of these societies.[31] But we have done enough to show we need to understand the key worldview features of Mediterranean life in biblical times if we are to apply validly any lessons from that world into our worlds of today. More importantly, by exploring these four worldview features—of family membership as the organizing principle of society; honor and shame as the pivotal values; a collectivist perspective as essential for understanding personal identity; and the importance of the concept of limited good—we have found good grounds for establishing that many cultures today share a real affinity with these features of Mediterranean society of biblical times.

We can confirm this claim by illustrating this affinity in Melanesian societies today. Since there are so many distinct cultures within Melanesia—Papua New Guinea alone has over eight hundred distinct language groups each with distinctive aspects to their culture—we need to take care when generalizing about "Melanesian cultures." But, even in this diversity, it is precisely their sharing of these four worldview perspectives we have just discussed that makes Melanesia a distinct cultural region. Melanesian cultures still regard the extended family as their fundamental societal organizing principle and this is closely linked with their communal understanding of personality. The *wantok* system in PNG illustrates the central place of these worldview features in PNG social structures. Maxon Mani notes that

regulates expectations of reciprocal relationships and obligations for gift exchange. It lies behind valuing of maintaining social status above accumulating wealth. In fact, storing up capital is regarded as dishonorable and suspicious, as it can only happen at someone else's expense. Limited good presuppositions also mean someone—not some thing—was always seen as the cause of any hardship or loss. The technologies available in the New Testament world could not guarantee social advancement or freedom from status obligations (Malina, *New Testament World*, 102), and were of only limited use dealing with issues of health or well-being. Help to deal with difficult or inexplicable situations, if not available through a patron of higher rank, had to be sought from a non-human power able to intervene in the human world. This means that in societies adhering to a limited good religion is often expected to supply aspects of what members of other cultures expect to gain from science and technology. Thus, religious influence operated across every realm of life within the limited good, closed system of Mediterranean daily life, as was true also in traditional Melanesian societies.

29. Malina, *New Testament World*, 108–32.

30. Malina, *New Testament World*, 134–59.

31. Malina, *New Testament World*, 161–96.

while *wantok* derives from the trade language, Tok Pisin term for "one talk," meaning, "one who speaks your language," it means much more than that:

> the *wantok* system is a family or community-based system that seeks to provide social networks that provide care and concern, and to build social relationships that extend beyond language, tribe, region and nationality. . . . [it] could be pictured as a mother to Melanesian people groups. It gathers the unwanted, the vulnerable, and the homeless, and it looks beyond borders to embrace others to promote peace and harmony so that life is enjoyable each day.[32]

Little wonder, then, that more recently Mani presents the *wantok* system, refreshed and enhanced in the light of the gospel, as a necessary strand for church and community-based response to social issues, such as the endemic family violence which currently plagues the nation of PNG. Mani shows how closely the *wantok* system is intertwined with the culturally embedded status challenges between males seeking *nem na namba* (name and number-elevated rank and honor), which lie behind the marital violence, and are fundamental features in Melanesian societies, both traditionally and still today.[33]

Thus, Mani links three of Malina's features of biblical Mediterranean worldviews as central, also, to Melanesian societies.[34] While the details of Melanesian socioeconomic and sociopolitical structures may vary considerably from the details of the Mediterranean biblical societies, they are linked at the worldview level by very similar presuppositions and culture-shaping beliefs. The fourth of Malina's features, the concept of "limited good," is similarly confirmed by Garry Trompf's classic account of the reciprocal *pebak* (payback) system of retribution at the core of Melanesian

32. Mani, "Theological and Missiological," 62. Mani explains in more detail, citing Shaw, "Wantok System," 2: ". . . it is much more than a linguistic term . . . it functions as a social security system which offers a safety net in which the poor are rescued, the unwanted are nursed, the homeless are set up in families, the fatherless are fathered, the orphans and disabled are protected. . . . [it] should be pictured as a lifeline, without which life is impaired" (60).

33. Mani, "Marital Violence," 62–65 and 248–49. Mani argues convincingly that a central reason proposed solutions to such violence, including Western feminist and social science-based solutions, have failed to date is because they have not grappled adequately with these more basic male honor and shame contests.

34. These worldview features Mani highlights are confirmed regularly in Melanesian studies. See, e.g., standard descriptions of culture such as the trilogy: Whiteman, *Introduction*; Schwarz, *Melanesian Religions*; and Schwarz, *Ministry in Melanesia*.

traditional justice and social control systems, and which, therefore, shapes large segments of Melanesian custom, ritual, and social structures.[35]

Both Mani's summaries of a wealth of recent scholarship around these themes, and Trompf's well-known religious studies texts, confirm there are clear grounds for claiming affinity at the worldview level between biblical and Melanesian cultures. In doing so, they support our contention that a principle of cultural affinity can form part of an appropriate methodology for moving from the biblical teachings to a Melanesian applied contextual theology.

If *basic human nature* and *shared worldview level assumptions* are the first two strands of a basis for this principle of affinity, the third, not addressed by Malina, is the way *local cultural myth narratives can also relate to biblical narratives.* As I have said elsewhere:

> Myths . . . preserve cultural traditions and values, helping to form cultural identity. Garry Trompf claims, "Myths . . . are absolutely necessary for human society, offering security fundamental for social health. . . . Melanesia's mythologies, moreover . . . reflect its peoples' remarkable affinity with the environment, which was rarely overexploited for its natural resources . . ." He noted the close link between myths and spirit powers, and added, they ". . . usually squared with experiences and common sense."[36]

Myths often gave the initial point of contact by which people from other religious backgrounds first took note of the gospel as a message for them. Religious studies authority, Harold W. Turner, writes of the:

> striking fact [which] has not been examined by historians . . . that there may be some deep-rooted affinity between tribal or primal religions and the Judaeo-Christian tradition. . . . This helps explain the massive response of the Maori and other similar tribal peoples to the early missionaries—a response at their points of strength, in their leadership, rather than of weakness in their marginalised segments of society. So often, when Christian missions have engaged with tribal peoples, these have said: "This is what we have been waiting for."[37]

35. Trompf, *Payback*. For comment related to "limited good" implications in the Melanesian socioeconomic area, see Hitchen, "Theology of Business," 74–104.

36. Hitchen, "Different Teachings," 178, citing Trompf, *Melanesian Religion*, 18–19.

37. Turner, *Roots of Science*, 142.

To confirm this in the case of Melanesia, come with me to the southern mainland coast of Papua New Guinea on October 14, 1883. Aruardaera, a deacon of the nascent church among the Motu, near Port Moresby, is on an evangelistic trip with his London Missionary Society missionary, James Chalmers, at Orokolo in the Papuan Gulf. Aruardaera is speaking with the local people and Chalmers records their dialogue in an article in the *Brisbane Courier*:

> The deacon began at Adam, and I wonder where he intends ending. We have got to the end of the Noachian story and the three ancestors, and of how the white men belong to the youngest. An old man sitting in front of the deacon says, "That is all true indeed, and just what we knew from of old. Your [the deacon's] Motu ancestor and ours soon left their father's presence and began roaming about, but theirs [foreigners] stayed, a beloved child, nursed and cared for by the father, listening to his word and teaching, and when well grown up left with all his knowledge to use in other lands, hence, although the youngest, yet the most superior."[38]

Various versions of the myth of the two sons and their loss of the key to knowledge are known over widely separated parts of PNG,[39] and responses similar to the Papuan Gulf elder's on hearing the biblical story for the first time, and recognizing the affinity between the two accounts, are well documented in Melanesian mission history. But not only in Christianity's initial contact period. If space permitted, we could confirm the affinities between traditional myths and the biblical story in the more recent studies of PNG theologians.[40]

We have said enough, however, to indicate that between primal religious cultures and the original context of the biblical writings, there is a three-stranded affinity, based in a commonly shared human nature, shared worldview level assumptions, and links established through cultural myths. We are proposing that this affinity offers a valid methodological principle for a local theologian moving from the biblical text to applied theological insights in a contextualized local theology. The principle does not establish a direct equivalence of thought or practice to be adopted in the local culture,

38. Chalmers, "New Guinea," 5b. See Hitchen, "Training Tamate," 399.

39. See, e.g., Lawrence, *Road Bilong Cargo*, 21–24, 70, 71, 75–78, 93, 94, 99–103, on the Manup-Kilibob myth; Strelan, *Search for Salvation*, 17, and elsewhere.

40. See in the postscript below my summary of work by Papua New Guinean scholars, Joshua Daimoi and George Mombi, as examples of these affinities. Both in different ways explore christological responses to aspects of their respective cultures.

nor does this principle form an adequate contextual methodology on its own. But this affinity principle encourages the local theologian to look for and expect points at which our common human nature, the characteristic features of the local worldview, and reflection on local myths, will bring to light insights that will make the living message of the gospel come freshly alive, and, with perhaps previously unnoticed emphasis, speak directly to aspirations and values already cherished in the local culture—always with the proviso that those insights pass the test of honoring Christ Jesus and more fully proclaiming the gospel of Christ Jesus within the local culture.

Principle 3: Cultural Traditions Fill a Preparatory Role

God has not left himself without a witness in any part of the world at any time, and local cultures contain features which prepare that culture to receive and respond to the gospel as good news for them. We establish and clarify this principle on the basis of biblical teaching, and the basic principle of learning (or epistemology), that humans can only build new knowledge on the basis of existing knowledge or presuppositions.

Biblical Teaching

We commence at the presuppositional level with the biblical teaching that humans are all created in the image of God, with culture-generating capabilities as part of God's stamp upon our lives. The foundational statement of Gen 1:26–27 makes this clear, with its follow-up expansion in the cultural mandate of Gen 1:28–30 and 2:15–24. These verses declare God's expectations regarding a range of basic human behavior. Humans are responsible before God for human reproduction, family life, multiplication, and dispersion; for agricultural, horticultural, and animal husbandry ventures and their responsible management; for geographical and historical learning and discovery; for social, communal, and political relationships, development, and organization; for economic development and interdependence; for ecological and environmental responsibility, care, and sustenance; for technological and scientific discovery, utilization, and stewardship; for artistic and aesthetic creativity and expression; and more.

These areas of behavior also require human moral responsibility, accountability, and freedom of choice. Moreover, they are all motivated and guided ideally both by spiritual capability and a purposeful relationship of intimacy and worship with our creator. All these activities are components of, and indeed constitute, culture. But this original purpose for human cultural behavior has been disrupted by the willful, disobedient rejection of that available intimacy of relationship with our creator God. The intended relationships and purpose have been distorted by the pervasive influence of evil across all of these areas of cultural potential. Nevertheless, the now sin-stained image of God constituting every human was never removed nor the cultural capacities rescinded, as Gen 3–9 confirm. Thus, along with the culturally disrupting, yet enriching, warning judgment of language diversification in Gen 11, the history of humanity down through the ages has been the history of cultural development, flourishing, and failure. Culture's proper role of preparing for theological insights today derives from these roots.

God has continued to ensure that all cultures are aware of him and can know him at least in part. Again, we need only list these fundamental theological truths. The Logos, or word of God, has always been the source of life-giving moral and spiritual light for all peoples of every culture (John 1:4). This light has continued to shine, through at least the accountable awareness of "eternal power and deity" manifest in nature, and the moral awareness of human conscience (Rom 1:20–21; 2:14–16). Despite the deceitfulness and intentional rebellion of human desires, minds, and lifestyles, "the darkness has not overcome" this light or the enlightening process radiating from the ever-present Logos of God. Ever since the fall of humanity, the God-given human talents and cultural capacities of women and men continue to receive this "light that enlightens every human," regardless of their culture, race, creed, or even moral standing. Thus, down through history, humans have shown both wonderful expressions of that light in some beautiful arts and discoveries, and abysmal failures to understand, plus serious attempts to extinguish the remaining glimmers of light shining around people of diverse cultures, in every part of the globe.

The apostle Paul, as part of the gospel he preached to the non-Jewish Lycaonian-speaking crowd at Lystra, declared: "God has not left himself without testimony" (Acts 14:14–18). Since Pentecost, the Holy Spirit has effectively continued his work in all the world, which Jesus promised would include, "When he comes, he will convince the world of sin and righteousness and judgment" (John 16:8). In contextualizing the gospel, we look for signs and evidence in the local culture of these aspects of God's ongoing ministry, what Western theologians call "general revelation," or "prevenient grace," or "the providence of God." [41]

Galatians 3:19—4:12 explains explicitly, in two parts, this principle that cultural traditions fill a preparatory role for receiving and appropriating the gospel.[42] Verses 19–29 set out this principle as it unfolded in the history of God's chosen people, the Jews. In chapter 5, we have already explained how Paul showed that the Jewish religious heritage, summed up in the law of Moses, prepared Jews to know their need of new life and to be ready for their Messiah to bring this new righteous life as the gift offered in the gospel of Christ Jesus.

Our explanation of Gal 4:1–7, in chapter 5, goes on to show how Paul both confirmed that the law restrictively guarded the Jews, and in doing so gives Christians converted in other cultures a way to understand their cultural heritage too. Both Jews and people of other cultures were all under the domination of the "elements, or basic principles, of the world" (in Greek, *stoicheia tou kosmou*). Thus, Paul demonstrated that the religious heritage of non-Jewish peoples did for them the same protecting, custodial, and preparatory work as the Mosaic law did for Jews. For their followers, primal religions restrain evil, confirm human sinfulness, and show how much a divine intervening, yes, redeeming, initiative was needed to release us from slavery and give us God's intended full position as adopted children (4:4–7). We quoted F. F. Bruce's summary:

> [*Stoicheia*], it is now made plain, not only regulated the Jewish way of life under the law; they also regulated the pagan way of life in the service of the gods that were no gods . . . For all the basic

41. Aspects of this contextualization principle were well understood in earlier generations in the West, especially in missionary education circles. In 1890, Henry Robert Reynolds, Principal of Cheshunt College (where the London Missionary Society sent candidates for training), commissioned five of his graduating students for missionary service, including Charles Abel, William Walker, and Harry Dauncey going to Papua. Reynolds, reminded them that the one who sent them to their respective fields was already there before them: "He is there in the magnificence and prodigality of his handwork. He is there in the torpid and morbid conscience and the disfigured image of Deity. He is there in the struggles of humanity with fate and death. He is there in the judgement of his providence and in the special revelations he has made by his messengers; and, above all, in the power of his Spirit, which not only energises in you, but strives with men." Reynolds, "Charge," 362; and reprinted in Reynolds, *Lamps of the Temple*, 97–98. See also Hitchen, "Training Tamate," 514–15.

42. This section is an adaptation of part of Hitchen, "Mission," 139–71, which had itself grown from earlier published versions.

> differences between Judaism and paganism, both involved subjection to the same elemental forces. This is an amazing statement for a former Pharisee to make; yet Paul makes it—not as an exaggeration in the heat of argument but as the deliberate expression of a carefully thought out position.[43]

Paul defined limits to the value for Christians of Jewish traditional religion and the traditional belief systems of other, non-Jewish cultures. In doing so, he retained a proper respect for their role in regulating society and in preparing people to receive the gospel.[44]

Here we go a step further. We suggest that the biblical evidence, rooted in the creation narrative, sustained by the repeated emphasis on the humanity-wide witness and enlightenment of the word and Spirit, and made explicit in Galatians, provides a sound basis for a methodological principle for contextual theology that expects to find cultural traditions preparing peoples within their own cultures to receive and apply the Christian message as the fulfillment of their deepest cultural yearnings.

Epistemological Confirmation

In the process, new knowledge is built onto existing knowledge. Andrew Walls expresses it like this:

> The Christian consciousness of Africa and Asia is likely to reflect the pre-Christian cultural processes, including the pre-Christian religious processes, of these continents. On all past showing, these processes are not replaced—that would be the way of the proselyte. They are redirected, for that is the way of the convert. Christian theology—active, *working* Christian theology—is constructed under the Spirit's guidance from pre-Christian materials. The vessels and hangings of the tabernacle, while divinely directed in the making, consist of Egyptian gold and Egyptian cloth. The most urgent reason for the study of the religious traditions of Africa and Asia, of the Amerindian and the Pacific peoples, is their significance for Christian theology; they are the substratum of the Christian faith and life of the greater number of the Christians of the world."[45]

43. Bruce, *Galatians*, 202–3.

44. Chapter 5, above, on Galatians adds further explanation of the fulfillment of this preparatory work of religious heritage in the sections commenting on 4:4–7, and 4:4–12.

45. Walls, "Old Athens," 153.

The gospel does not call people to adopt the lifestyle and "Christian" customs of another culture. Evangelism is not about proselytizing, but conversion.[46] The gospel calls people, not to the easy task of accepting another culture's answers to all the issues of living in a local situation, but to turn their whole life, with all those issues, to Christ, and to allow him to renew and transform them as and where they are, until he becomes Lord of every aspect of their lives: culture, religious heritage, and all.

That is why Walls's second comment is important: "... active, *working* Christian theology—is constructed under the Spirit's guidance from pre-Christian materials." No local context is an empty slate—a *tabula rasa*—just waiting to be filled with a newly imported foreign culture. Conversion requires the testing and discerning of the traditional culture, evaluating it at the foot of the cross of Christ, gladly accepting all that can blossom and flourish in service to Christ, rejecting aspects that are wholly incompatible and inconsistent when judged by Christ's life and purposes, and steadily transforming all that remains until its potential is more fully realized by honoring Christ and serving others in love.

But to build on the previous traditional culture in this way requires deep understanding of it. This is where recent studies in how we gain knowledge and interpret literature (epistemology and hermeneutics), and particularly their discussions of "reader-response," can clarify the preparatory role of culture for contextualization. "Reader-response" theories in literary studies stress that whenever a person reads a text, they do so from a particular viewpoint, which influences the way the text is read, and gives meaning to any subsequent action. To understand a particular text requires not only a grasp of the text itself and of the persons and situation behind its composition, but also understanding of the viewpoint the reader brings to the process. As Richard Beach puts it: "As part of . . . socialization, readers acquire certain 'reading formations' or 'subject positions.' Reading formations are those acquired ideological stances that constitute certain subject positions or desired ways of responding."[47] We learn these formations, positions, or orientations, "as members of certain cultural groups or communities."[48] For a person or culture to be transformed, therefore, the new message must interact with this "position-shaping" that controls how they gain knowledge, and is embedded in their traditional beliefs. This may

46. For more on this distinction, see Walls, "Converts or Proselytes?," 1–6.

47. Beach, *Reader-Response Theories*, 129.

48. Beach, *Reader-Response Theories*, 164.

take time—even generations[49]—but it must start by the gospel interacting with the existing fund of cultural knowledge and working a change at this "orientation" or "stance-shaping" level. That is the goal of contextualization.

Knowing how deeply the gaining of new knowledge depends on these culturally ingrained viewpoints confirms the value and significance of the principle that cultural traditions fill a preparatory role for receiving and appropriating the gospel.

Conclusion

We have recommended three principles to shape a methodology for developing local contextualized theology in the interculturally complex world of the twenty-first century, particularly in culturally pluralistic majority world nations. Not that our suggestions are irrelevant in the increasingly interculturally complex post-Christendom Western nations grappling with culturally complicated migration patterns and multiplicity of religions.

Each principle has a distinct contribution to make, and each could be used in combination with one or both of the others. None on its own would solve adequately all the contextualization issues of a particular setting. They will need to be used together with exegetical, literary, or other appropriate methodology components. But these three we have discussed have particular contributions to make in new or bicultural or multicultural situations. The principle of the gospel and local culture mutually enhancing each other can potentially create an expectation of finding points of connection, and unexpected biblical relevance, in the local culture, and unexpected new aspects of the gospel itself which shine afresh in the light of cultural traditions. But this principle, as it makes the theology a "place to feel at home" for their own culture, will be careful to test proposed new insights against the variety of orthodox understandings in the church universal, lest they propose theologies so locally focused that no one else can feel at home with them.[50]

The cultural affinity principle calls local theologians to be alert to the way their own worldview-level characteristics, or local cultural myths, highlight particularly meaningful perspectives, values, or aspirations in their own society. Then, by careful reflection and exegesis, they will explore whether affinities with the biblical themes and context sharpen or extend

49. See Walls, "Old Athens," 148–49.

50. As Walls warned in "Culture and Coherence," 25.

new interpretations of culturally significant texts. They will welcome such affinities and foster increasing local ownership and enjoyment of truths clarified by the identified affinity. But again, the affinity needs to be carefully explored historically and exegetically to ensure they are building on an affinity of substance, not an anachronistic invention, or on a merely superficial similarity. The extent to which fresh theological insight challenges other cultures to broaden their understanding of the text will be an important test of its veracity.

The principle of the preparatory role of the previous cultural heritage will be applied in line with the temporary, anticipatory, custodial, protective, and instructional purposes articulated paradigmatically in the biblical text. It is not an invitation to make the cultural heritage the judge of the relevance or meaning of the biblical text itself. So, again, this principle will be used with other methodology components such as sound exegesis.

We could go on to explore how the three confirm and balance each other. Or how the genre, literary or rhetorical forms of Scripture, when considered from a different cultural perspective, could freshly influence methodologies for shaping contextual theology. And we could emphasize further how these principles call for increasing respect for the dignity of each culture before God. But hopefully, we have highlighted the way both the cultural dimension and loyalty to the authoritative Scriptures, need to be continually respected and plumbed more deeply as the gospel reaches across yet more cultural boundaries for the ongoing glory of our Lord Jesus Christ.

Postscript: Further Examples of the Affinity of Cultural Myths with Biblical Teaching

Joshua Daimoi on Clan Myths of Sentani

Joshua Daimoi describes in detail how the clan myths of his people of Sentani, Papua Province, Indonesia, provide the rationale for leadership, which at the clan level is focused in the *ondoporo*, who is superior over all other authoritative household level leaders, the *kosero*.[51] The myths give the *ondoporo*, together with his "firstborn," the ultimate authority over the full range of functional communal leadership roles, whether in guiding gardening, fishing, housebuilding, or warfare, or for controlling the priestly leaders

51. Daimoi, "Melanesian Ancestral Heritage," 105–75.

in their mediation with the spirit powers, or the like.[52] From this careful analysis of the myths and the communal relations and social structures which are explained by them, Daimoi explores the way Christ is presented in the New Testament book of Hebrews as Son of God, firstborn elder brother, heir and the *archēgos* (chief leader, forerunner), who is superior to the Hebrew high priests and has fulfilled and transformed the whole system of law, sacrificial ritual, and religious practice the Hebrew Scriptures present as flowing from the priestly system.[53] Daimoi compares the Melanesian priestly system with the way the Letter to the Hebrews presents Jesus Christ as fulfilling the Jewish priestly system through his death as the ultimate sacrifice. Daimoi shows how Christ can readily be seen as not only fulfilling the Melanesian priestly and ritual system, but as also offering a superior consummating fulfillment of the role Melanesians have traditionally given to ancestors generally. He shows how Jesus fulfills the specific expectations of his own Sentani peoples regarding the "firstborn" of the *ondoporo* as the true high priestly mediator with the spirit world and as the foundation and head of the community.[54] He concludes, "Jesus could be typically conceived as the greatest conqueror, the supreme warrior, the epitome of the Sentanian community; He is the culmination of all the *kosero* and *ondoporo*. Jesus is the apex of all Sentanian ancestors."[55] Whether or not we endorse his theology, as I do,[56] Daimoi has shown clearly the affinity a Melanesian can feel between their own culture-defining traditional narratives, the myths, and the thrust of the biblical narrative as it builds to its climax in the work of Christ as interpreted in the New Testament.

George Mombi on the Abelam People

George Mombi gives a further example of this myth-based aspect of affinity being worked out in a local Melanesian theology.[57] The Abelam peoples of the East Sepik Province on the northern mainland of Papua New Guinea are famed both for the length of the yams (*dioscorea alata)* they value as a

52. Daimoi, "Melanesian Ancestral Heritage," 123–29.

53. Daimoi, "Melanesian Ancestral Heritage," 136–47.

54. For his application of this last point to Melanesia generally, see Daimoi's more recent chapter, "Melanesian Theology," 117–26.

55. Daimoi, "Melanesian Ancestral Heritage," 173–74.

56. Joshua has been a colleague and friend for fifty years.

57. Mombi, "Jesus Our Wapiken," 79–99.

central part of their food economy and for the religiously observed procedures they follow to grow them. Mombi shows how these elaborate rituals arise from the "Yam myth" about a barren couple, Kumbindi and Kumbediau, whose unusually born son, Wapiken, "had special innate abilities to make crops grow in his parents' garden without any labour." Although he died sadly by suicide when his parents failed to adhere to the strict sexual restrictions Wapiken had imposed as necessary to ensure a good yam crop, his instructions, and the harvest-ensuring regulations which developed around them, form an ongoing part of Abelam custom to this day.[58]

While being careful not to equate the stories of Wapiken and the Christian gospel, Mombi shows how readily a Melanesian can move from the ritual expectations deriving from this myth, to a range of comparable or contrasting aspects of the biblical story, because of the evident affinity between the two. He comments on matters such as: "holiness" requirements in the Old Testament; the readiness of Abelam people to welcome the stress on holiness in certain denominational presentations of the gospel; how the myth predisposed people to grasp the divine-human nature of Christ, his miraculous powers, the importance of his death and resurrection, and his final instructions to his followers; links between Abelam initiation and Christian conversion; yam-growing purity rituals and ongoing devotional commitment in Christian discipleship; the relation between ritual observances and moral purity and success and prosperity in life; and whether, or in what ways, culture heroes like Wapiken may be considered as precursors of Christ Jesus. Again, we may evaluate Mombi's specific suggestions in various ways, but we cannot ignore how taking the Melanesian myth seriously highlights the affinity with biblical concepts and teachings.

58. Mombi, "Jesus Our Wapiken," 82, and elsewhere.

Chapter 12

Preparing People—Then and Now

Biblical Patterns for Equipping Leaders in Melanesia

In the mid-1960s, when the Christian Leaders' Training College (CLTC) was being established in Papua New Guinea (PNG), evangelical Christians did not talk much about relationships with other church groups.[1] Those of us formed in interdenominational Bible schools and colleges would boast that we practiced the ecumenism which the "ecumenical" movement talked about in their numerous conferences and consultations. Certainly, Christians from across the Protestant denominational spectrum shared, studied, and witnessed together in practical Christian union in interdenominational theological colleges and other organizations.

But when we came from that 1960s background to PNG the mission and church setting was rather different. Sure, in 1965 we actively set up the Evangelical Alliance of the South Pacific Islands (EASPI, also shortened to EA) as a forum, to bring evangelical missions and churches to work together on joint social, educational, medical, and youth programs, and other cultural issues. And we established the EASPI[2] partly in reaction to the World Council of Churches (WCC) networks of the mainline

1. The original of this chapter was a paper presented at the Melanesian Association of Theological Schools Study Institute, Banz, Papua New Guinea, January 1976; and published as Hitchen, "Some Biblical Patterns," 85–121. Used with the permission of the Melanesian Institute, from *Point* 1 (see bibliography for further details).

2. See sections on the founding of the Evangelical Alliance in Price, *Live in Tents*, 156–60; Yandit, "Ownership and Support," 49–59; Fergie, "Study of Church/Government"; Liddle, *Into the Heart*, 365–72.

denominations at work in PNG at that time.[3] This reticence to be too closely allied with the international ecumenical movement of the time was widely shared in the evangelical missionary community.[4]

But our experience of interchurch cooperation in PNG was different. We were in contact with other churches from CLTC's beginning, and we found we not only had much in common, but also much to learn from each other, as the nation moved rapidly towards independence (achieved in September 1975). All the churches had been working together for some time in education and medical work as the major players in national partnerships with the government. This soon spread to include more specific projects like a joint church approach to a religious education syllabus for all government-funded schools, and a joint Church-Government Council for Media Coordination, overseeing moral and censorship issues in broadcasting.

It was no surprise, then, that as Bible and theological schools we were soon challenged to work together at educational standards and Melanesian-oriented curricular emphases. The WCC sent mission guru, Charles W. Forman, to encourage the mainline churches of the eastern Pacific to upgrade their training programs by establishing a South Pacific Association of

3. The "mainline" denominations in PNG at the time (and which associated together in the Melanesian Council of Churches) were the United Church of PNG and the Solomon Islands (which united the Papua Ekalesia [formed by the churches of the London Missionary Society] and the Methodist Church [formed by the Methodist Overseas Mission]); the Evangelical Lutheran Church of PNG (formed by the Lutheran Missions of Germany, the United States of America [including the Missouri Synod], and Australia); the Anglican Church of PNG; the Roman Catholic Church; the Salvation Army; and the Baptist Union of PNG (which also belonged to the EASPI). The churches (and the missions from which they had grown) which formed the EASPI, and which sent students to train at CLTC were: the Baptist Union of PNG (Australian Baptist Missionary Society); Evangelical Church of PNG (Unevangelised Fields Mission—later, Asia Pacific Christian Missions, now Pioneers Australia); South Seas Evangelical Church, in both Sepik Province of PNG, and Solomon Islands (South Seas Evangelical Mission); Melanesian Evangelical Churches of Christ (Australian Churches of Christ Mission); Christian Brethren Churches (Christian Missions in Many Lands); and Manus Evangelical Church (Manus Evangelical Mission). Within a few years a group of smaller evangelical missions joined EA and also sent students to CLTC, including the Evangelical Bible Church, Christian Union Mission, and the Kwato Extension Association. Also, within a few years the Wesleyan Churches and the Church of the Nazarene, as well as the major Pentecostal churches, belonged to EA: the Apostolic Church (Apostolic Christian Mission), and Assemblies of God. The Southern Highlands Region of the United Church of PNG and the Solomon Islands (Methodist Overseas Mission—Southern Highlands Region) also joined the EA while also part of the Melanesian Council of Churches.

4. For a sample of this cautious attitude, see Smith and Hitchen, "Papua New Guinea," 501–21.

Theological Schools (SPATS), affiliated with the WCC as a regional schools association. Forman came to PNG and invited all the existing higher level theological training schools to gather to discuss a similar arrangement for PNG. But we at CLTC, along with the Roman Catholics and the Seventh Day Adventists, faced a dilemma. At CLTC we knew the range of churches we served would not countenance us becoming a part of any WCC-affiliated body, yet we had already sensed the help we could gain from such an association, and we already had some experience of the other churches welcoming our distinctive emphases as part of the full church scene in PNG.

So, from CLTC we offered to join the constitution development group, and were charged with drafting the constitution for a new regional schools association. We were able to propose articles safeguarding each school's autonomy and control over their curriculum, plus an article that meant there was no automatic membership of the Melanesian body in any wider international body. Not surprisingly, each denominational school—including the Roman Catholics and Seventh Day Adventists—endorsed these safeguards, for they too were committed to truly Melanesian approaches to theological education. Thus, what was at that time globally the most ecumenical Melanesian Association of Theological Schools (MATS) came into being in 1968. My involvement with MATS and the broad range of its membership was a significant aspect in developing what I have described and called elsewhere an "inclusive rather than exclusive evangelicalism" espoused and fostered at CLTC,[5] and a resultant concern to develop theological training in broader interchurch contexts. This chapter, based on an early paper I presented to a MATS conference, encapsulates my thinking in that direction.

In an age marked by change and uncertainty the Christian church has a continuing source of guidance for its task of training men and women for the service of Christ: "All Scripture is inspired by God . . . So that the person who serves God may be complete, equipped for every good work" (2 Tim 3:16–17). This chapter assumes that guiding principles for training Christian workers in Melanesia today can be learned from the historical events and circumstances through which the Spirit of God prepared God's people in biblical times. We take seriously the apostle Paul's claim that these historical events "were written down for our instruction, upon whom the end of the ages has come" (1 Cor 10:11). We shall also be using the words

5. See Hitchen, "Evangelicals Equipping," particularly 128–32.

"ministerial training" in their widest sense to refer to training for the service of God generally.

Our plan is to look first at some Old Testament examples of the ways in which people were trained for God's service. Then we shall draw some lessons from the way Jesus prepared his disciples for their work of establishing churches. Finally, we summarize the principles learned and apply them to ministerial training in Melanesia today. We by no means cover all the biblical patterns of training, rather, we select some of these patterns which seem to be of special importance for the Melanesian situation today.[6]

Some Old Testament Patterns of Training for Ministry

We turn first to some Old Testament examples. The political and social situations in which God called and equipped these examples were similar in many points to the situations we face in Melanesia today. The one test we focus on from Joseph's life is still a pervasive problem. Moses was called to establish an independent nation and build a healthy national identity amongst a group of slaves with a great heritage, but who had been under foreign domination for many generations. Joshua had the task of taking over leadership from a more widely experienced administrator and bringing his new nation through the physical and spiritual hindrances to national development. Gideon was chosen to recall his people to a pure worship of the true God and at the same time deliver them from foreign oppression. David had the task of building a united nation from the fragmented tribal groups who were struggling for a realistic place in their world of nations. Let us consider the "course of training" the living Lord set out for each of these leaders.

Joseph and the Test of Moral Integrity (Genesis 39:1–21)

Joseph's whole life was a series of training experiences: from discovering God in family difficulties (Gen 37:2–36 and 39:1–2); to coping with sudden changes in status and discovering himself in a foreign land (39:1–6); to the morality challenge and test of sexual integrity (Gen 39:6–21); to a return

6. The original paper did not include the excerpt on Joseph's life, which first appeared as an editorial in the then Bible College of New Zealand magazine, *Reality*: "Sex and National Leadership," 3, 55. The section on Paul's life in the original paper is not included in this chapter, as the material therein is covered in other chapters of this book.

to obscurity and test of patience and perplexity (Gen 40:1–41); through to responsible national leadership (Gen 41:1, 9–16, 25, 32–33, 35–40); to the final relationship changes within his family, with his character proven as the outcome of the tests (Gen 42:1–3; 45:4–8; 50:15–21). Joseph grew and developed into his major international leadership role through these formative and transformative periods of life. We choose just one of these central episodes to look more deeply at God's ways of preparing leaders: the sexual purity test (Gen 39:6–21).

Joseph made moral choices on the basis of his commitment to convictions. The temptation to seek personal gratification, influence, and power at the cost of moral integrity was not a viable option in Joseph's value system. When Potiphar's wife confronted Joseph with her proposition for sex, Joseph already knew what he believed about sexual immorality and moral integrity. It is too late to sort out our views on sexual promiscuity when we first encounter the temptation. We need to make clear choices before we face the peer pressures or sudden attractions, so that we are ready to respond when the pressure is on. Joseph knew what he believed about this basic part of his life and values.

Sexual Immorality Destroys Personal Trustworthiness and Integrity (vv. 8–9a)

But Joseph refused. "With me in charge," he told her, "my master does not concern himself with anything in the house; everything he owns he has entrusted to my care. No one is greater in this house than I am. My master has withheld nothing from me except you . . ."

Joseph's personal integrity was at stake. He was trusted with responsibility. He valued this trust relationship with Potiphar. Adultery blows away trust and trustworthiness. Third parties, in this case the boss, are hurt. Future relationships between them and the guilty parties are permanently scarred. Joseph had thought this through beforehand. He knew what counted most in interpersonal relationships. No fleeting gratification, nor the exhilarating sense of power sometimes accompanying it, can substitute for an ongoing, unsullied trust. Joseph knew this. It was nonnegotiable for him. The answer to Potiphar's wife is, "No."

Sexual Immorality Destroys Personal Identity and Relational Belonging (v. 9b)

Joseph respected Potiphar's wife's identity. She was the wife of his boss; they belonged to each other by marriage. Her identity, and sense of belonging, was permanently intertwined with Potiphar through marriage. Joseph knew better than to tamper with such a fundamental aspect of human identity. He has trained his eyes and mind to look at, and think of her, not as a commodity to be grabbed and used at will, but as a person identified by her marriage relationship with Potiphar.

We abuse this God-given identity indicator only at great personal and societal cost. The human heart is made for undivided commitment. We discover our deepest selves only in relationship with others. Sex is more than a merely physical relationship. It involves two personalities yielding to each other in frank intimacy. It is therefore a richly self-revealing, and self-discovering human action. Adultery cuts across this most intimate of relationships. In adultery a third party intrudes into the heart of the sacred self-revelation inherent in marriage. Trying to discover oneself through loose sex actually threatens the core of our own identity. Joseph knew to whom Potiphar's wife belonged. So, again, the answer is, "No."

Sexual Immorality Destroys Personal Purity (v. 9c)

"How then could I do such a wicked thing?" Misuse of sex defiles. It leaves the inner self unclean. Joseph valued his purity. The supposed gain of the momentary pleasure is a poor exchange for the real stain of the lasting guilt. Moral integrity and a clean conscience may not rate high amongst "accepted community standards" today. There's no substitute, however, for their currency in terms of personal worth and self-respect. Joseph knew God's assessment of immorality differed markedly from popular opinions. No seductive pleasure warrants him throwing away his inner purity. So, again, the answer is, "No."

Sexual Immorality Destroys Relationship with God (v. 9d)

"How then could I do such a wicked thing and sin against God?" When we throw aside God's standards for sex, we are claiming greater moral insight than God has. Our breaking of his standards is an attempt to establish new standards of our own. However, God's integrity cannot be attacked with impunity. If he changed the ultimate standards and realities to suit the whims of his creatures there could be no adequate moral basis for human behavior at all. Human moral values always depend finally upon the moral dependability of God. What he declares wrong is always wrong; sexual promiscuity is sin. It severs open relationships with God. Joseph knew it would spoil his friendship with God. So once again, the answer is, "No."

Moral Integrity Is of Greater Value than Power and Influence Without It (vv. 10–21)

The sequel, as recorded in the rest of Joseph's story, confirms that manipulating people through sexual exploitation or favors is not Yahweh's pathway to responsible leadership. The leadership demands of Egypt's forthcoming international food crisis could only be trusted to a person who has passed this moral integrity test. Joseph had qualified to carry greater leadership responsibility. Taking a stand against promiscuity may mean we lose some popularity for a season. We may even face jibes and put-downs and lose some potential friends. But we retain our integrity, our honor, and our trustworthiness. In the long run these win a much deeper respect than the fleeting acceptance of the crowd for a night.

This powerful personal example comes hard on the heels of the tragic record of lust and incest with its consequent jealousy and dysfunctional family life in ch. 38. Joseph's answer when tempted stands as an abiding challenge for us to internalize our own moral convictions before we face the subtle, sudden, and persistent pleadings and deceit of modern-day mimics of Potiphar's wife and her ilk, and the pervasive insinuations of the many variations on Potiphar's wife's lifestyle today.

Let us not underestimate the value and influence in character formation of models such as a culture-hero like Joseph. In the West we have been through a time of despising hero stories and their influence upon morality—to the point of parading those who live in promiscuity as today's "heroes." Given the awful impact of such modern moral reversals, we would do well to reinstate the Joseph story, and redefine the real heroes!

Moses

The baby Moses was saved from the Pharaoh's death sentence and adopted into the royal household. The unusual way in which this happened and in which he was then entrusted to his own parents for a Hebrew upbringing were signs to his believing parents that the Lord had marked Moses for an important work (Exod 2:1–9; Acts 7:17–21; and Heb 11:23). He received the best formal education available in his day, in a cross-cultural learning situation where his instruction and schooling were given in a "second language" (Exod 2:10; Acts 7:22).

At the end of this formal education Moses faced a personal choice which would determine the future course of his life and service. Hebrews 11:24–25 explains and interprets the decision Moses made. He began to feel the concerns and "burden" of his own people (Exod 2:11). But to identify himself with his own people meant a clear turning away from the advantages and opportunities which his Egyptian schooling had opened to him. Moses made this choice and by faith committed himself to serve his people even though this meant costly personal self-denial for him just as it does for trainees for the ministry today.

Following this formal training Moses immediately began his work full of self-confidence and expecting to be quickly accepted as a leader amongst his people. In his first attempts to bring justice he killed an Egyptian and found his leadership wasn't accepted by his fellow countrymen (Exod 2:11–15; Acts 7:23–29). This initial failure and rejection proved another important preparatory lesson for the task before him. Moses had to become "very meek, more than all men that were on the face of the earth" (Num 12:3). Rejection and learning that his education and abilities did not necessarily bring authority and respect were important steps towards this kind of meekness.

Forty "hidden" years as a shepherd in the wilderness of Midian followed. This provided the training the proud young Egyptian courtier had missed in the royal household. Humbling and hard though such a discipline may have seemed, it was giving firsthand knowledge of the country through which Moses would lead his nation. During this time he also made contact with people whose advice he would greatly appreciate in a coming day. In the divine training program, years of humbling discipline play an important part.

But as this period ends Moses has a personal confrontation with God. In a deeply moving experience, he meets Yahweh as his God and receives both a commission and the spiritual equipment to answer each of his fears and to equip him to deliver his people (Exod 3–4). This personal meeting with the Lord and accepting of his call becomes the foundation for the rest of his life's work.

Thus, with his brother Aaron appointed as a personal assistant (Exod 4:14–16), Moses commences his leadership task. His personal training in faith and in leadership skills continues. In the "school of hard knocks" each problem faced on the way from Egypt in Sinai teaches further lessons (Exod 14–18). The visit of his Midianite father-in-law brings important lessons in organization and administration (Exod 18:13–27; cf. Num 11:16–25). The awe-inspiring depths of fellowship with the Lord God as he received God's self-revelation on Mount Sinai not only transformed Moses's character, but even his appearance was changed (Exod 34:29–35).

But Moses's growth in leadership continued through further rejection and criticism from those he led, as well as personal failure and humbling (e.g., Num 11, 12, 14, 16, and 20). This "in-service training" continued throughout his ministry.

These, then, were the steps which prepared Moses for his work of national leadership: administering social justice; meeting the economic and material needs of his people; teaching and instructing in belief and behavior; disciplining and correcting both nation and family; proclaiming, writing, and singing the truth of God; and praying and standing before God on behalf of his people.

Joshua

In contrast to Moses, we know nothing of Joshua's birth, homelife, or basic education. However, each of the references to Joshua before he takes over from Moses mentions an important part of his preparation as a leader.

Step One: Leadership Potential Tested and Proven

When first mentioned in Exod 17:8–16, Joshua is thrust straight into a position of leadership as captain of the army. Certain leadership skills were already evident. He wholeheartedly obeyed the instructions of his superiors. He was able to judge people and select the best fellow soldiers. He knew how to work in partnership with those who do a "spiritual" work of prayer on the mountain while he does the "practical" hard work on the battlefield.

He knew how to fight on to victory although at times he wasn't doing well. And he especially learned how to give the glory to God for the victory won. Joshua is first shown in action in practical fieldwork. This is perhaps the best place to look for the right kind of recruits for the ministry.

Step Two: Apprenticeship

Next, Joshua enters a personal apprenticeship under Moses. Exodus 24:13 shows that Joshua shared in his tutor's deepest spiritual experiences while serving as his assistant. Exodus 32:17 shows the overenthusiastic assistant misjudging the reactions of the crowd and accepting the more mature discernment of his tutor. The next reference (Exod 33:11) shows the young assistant involved in routine "behind-the-scenes" work in the tabernacle. In Num 11:26–30, Joshua struggled with small-mindedness and jealousy, and was learning to accept the work of others outside his "in-group." These in-service lessons about fellowship with God, discernment, faithfulness, and large-heartedness were vital in his preparation.

Step Three: Representing, Reporting, and Their Results

We next see Joshua selected as a representative acting on behalf of his tribe (Num 13). Through this responsibility he not only learns to evaluate accurately the situation facing the nation, but also fearlessly to give a public report which differed from the consensus, and declared his personal faith. He challenged the nation to faith and commitment to Yahweh (Num 14:4–9). This public stand was rejected by the majority, but upheld by his God (Num 14:10, 30, 36–38). So Joshua, like Moses before him, learned that leadership demands lonely and costly faithfulness to truth.

Step Four: "Hidden Years"

Joshua then goes through a period in which we hear nothing of him—an experience out of the leadership attention—as the plan of God matures. For the whole time of the nation's wilderness wanderings there is no further mention of Joshua until the end of the period (Num 26:65).

Step Five: Public Leadership

But now the time was right for Joshua's public setting apart and commissioning to take over the leadership from Moses. There is a clear transfer of responsibility to the younger man, and the Lord himself gave a fresh assurance of his enabling and continuing presence for the new task ahead (Num 27:12–23; Deut 31:1–29).

Thus, in Josh 1:1–9, the now equipped Joshua takes up his new position.

Gideon

When we first meet Gideon, he is feeling the burden of the oppression of the foreign power of Midian (Judg 6:1–10). His reply to the unexpected message from the Lord suggests he was rebelling against the present situation, against the traditional but unsatisfying explanations of the situation, and against the Lord who allowed nation to exploit and oppress nation. He stands out as an angry young man tired of international injustice (Judg 6:11–13).

For such a young man preparation for service commences with a direct confrontation by the Lord himself, and a challenge to go and provide the answers to the problem (Judg 6:12–14). The suddenness and surprise of this challenge brings a humbling confession of his personal insignificance and a request for some clear evidence that this call is truly from God. Thus, Gideon brings an offering and the angry young man finds peace with God (Judg 6:15–24).

Like Moses and Joshua, Gideon is called to take a public stand to demonstrate his faith before his own family. For Gideon, however, the Lord demanded that he publicly do away with the outward forms of the false worship which his family were following. So Gideon too has to learn the cost of complete obedience to God and the unpopularity which results from it. In a day of syncretism and confusion about truth and error in worship, Yahweh's servant must make a clear commitment to the only true God (Judg 6:25–32).

With this preparation within his own tribe complete, the Spirit of the Lord is now able to take possession of Gideon and use him to attack the injustices of the foreign oppression (Judg 6:33–35). As the purpose and plan of God for this deliverance become clearer to Gideon, he starts to have serious doubts as to whether it will work. But as honest doubts are turned into earnest prayers, God gives the needed assurance through special signs to further encourage Gideon's faith (Judg 6:36–40).

Gideon now selects the army to attack the foreign power. But when the living God corrects the injustices of oppression, he does so in his own way. He does his work, "not by might, nor by power, but by his Spirit" (cf. Zech 4:6 and 2 Cor 10:3–4). God had given Gideon a plan that would leave no room for the Israelites to boast that they had defeated Midian by their strength of numbers. The method used in the battle must clearly show that the victory, and therefore the honor and glory, belong to the Lord alone. Therefore, when thirty-two thousand volunteers gathered to fight, Gideon is commanded to send home those who were fearful. But even the ten thousand remaining were too many for the plan which had formed in Gideon's mind. He must now choose those who will keep alert even when they have opportunity to satisfy their own physical needs. So the God-given test of taking a drink in full view of the enemy army reduces Gideon's "fighting force" to a small group of three hundred men. Before sending back the remaining nine thousand seven hundred men, Gideon borrows their trumpets and jars as his weapons.

But in face of the great enemy army Gideon still has fears as to whether this silly plan of faith will work or not. So the Lord again respects Gideon's uncertainty and gives an opportunity for him to find out for himself about the attitudes and morale of the enemy. A bold spying trip into the enemy camp brought Gideon to his knees in worship. The fears of the Midianite soldiers gave Gideon the final assurance he needed that the way of faith was more powerful than the way of might.

Gideon returned to his small group of men and gave them their final instructions. Then in a masterly example of faith, courage, and insight into the reactions of self-satisfied, overconfident, and godless oppressors, Gideon went out for his surprise attack. His training course had equipped him to bring a decisive victory in a way which clearly showed the power of the God of justice who defends the underprivileged and downtrodden.

For Gideon that training had involved:

- an anger about the injustices facing his people;
- a personal meeting with Yahweh which radically changed his values and attitudes;

- a testing of the depths of this change in a public stand for truth against the false worship of his family;
- a special enabling from the Spirit of God;
- a growing assurance of God's way of working through clear answers to prayer and obedience to the principles of Scripture;
- a willingness to be counted a fool for the sake of working out the purpose of God amongst his people;
- and a deep conviction that faith and right are more powerful weapons against injustice then mere might.

These requirements for spiritual leadership training bring some searching tests to many of our present-day patterns of training.

David

The incidental comments in 1 Sam 16–30 indicate the various stages of David's upbringing and training for his eventual role as King of Judea and then over all Israel.

David's Basic Schooling (1 Sam 16–18)

David grew up as the eighth, and youngest, rather insignificant son of a large family (16:11–12a; 17:28–29). As a shepherd boy he became known for his bravery and personal faith in the living God—not through a crisis experience, it seems, but rather as he discovered that God helps shepherds as they protect their sheep against the problems of weather and wild beasts. His rather lonely life kept him fit, healthy, and handsome, and gave opportunity to become skillful not only as a shepherd, but with sling, harp, and apparently also with words, both in song and speech (1 Sam 16:12, 18).

David's Sudden Anointing to Become King (1 Sam 16:1, 7, 12–13)

Quite unexpectedly this unknown shepherd lad was anointed in front of his family as one specially chosen by God. The spiritual power shown in his life from that time could only be explained as the Spirit of the Lord coming upon him.

David's Practical Experience Broadens (1 Sam 16:19–22; 17:15)

His rural training was now widened as David moved back and forth between the king's court, the battlefield, and his sheepfold. As the king's musician, David learned the ways of the court, and the moods of the national leader. As an occasional armour-bearer for the king, he became familiar with the battle strategies of his day. And when back with his sheep, where his family certainly thought he belonged, he continued to think, work, sing, pray, and compose (1 Sam 16:18–23; 17:14–15).

David's Public Stand in a Crisis, and Great Acclaim (1 Sam 17:1—18:9)

This faithfulness in small duties changed and bore fruit dramatically when concern for the honor of the name of Israel's God made David dare to stand against the Philistine giant. In a public stand he made full use of all the faith, courage, and physical skill developed in his previous training. Even against the opposition of his family, and the king's experience and wisdom, David demonstrated clearly that confidence in Yahweh together with simple, well-honed, personal skill are a far greater force than military might and armor (1 Sam 17:32–50). David had left home that day as the youthful, unknown, family message-boy (17:33, 56), and returned as the heartthrob of the housewives and the subject of the popular songs of the time, but also subject to the king's jealousy (18:6–9). As Goliath fell, David the great singer became a great soldier and a great hero. And with the Lord's help he has continuing success in each of these three positions, and is the favorite of the rest of the royal household (1 Sam 18:1–20, 30).

But since only cabbages mature quickly, the Lord sent his chosen servant back to "school." Few youngsters can carry sudden popularity for long. So David must go through a "hidden years" experience before he will be ready for the leadership for which he has been chosen. King Saul's jealousy and unreasonable desire to kill David was at the back of the various events recorded in the rest of 1 Samuel. Through this hatred and opposition, the Lord develops the training curriculum David needs to be fit to become king. The courses in the curriculum are worth noting.

Step One: Attacks, Both Sudden and Subtle (1 Sam 18:8–11; 18:17—19:17)

The first sudden attack only encouraged faith and faithfulness (1 Sam 18:8–11). But the opposition takes a more deceitful approach as Saul seeks his assassination by sending him to gain an unreasonable bride-price for Michal (18:17–21). Saul, however, had underestimated the reality of the Lord's presence and a woman's love (18:28). As Saul seeks to sour David's friendship with his son, Jonathan, and when Saul's depression returns again, David has to learn to accept the help and encouragement of a loving wife, a godly prophet, and a faithful friend in the persons of Michal, Samuel, and Jonathan. Unreasonable opposition has a way of teaching the value of homelife, "church" life, and loyal friendship (1 Sam 19 and 20).

Step Two: David Fails through Fear, Lies, and Deceit (1 Sam 21)

Continuing opposition breeds fear and 1 Sam 21 shows David failing through deceit and fear. His lies bring death to those who have helped him, and he only saves his own life by acting insanity. When successful men fail, many of them despair and give up. But David had learned to turn his successes into songs of praise and he now does the same with his failures, as Ps 34:4–14 shows. David turned back to the Lord in repentance, found forgiveness, and learned the foolishness of lies and deceit.

David learns failure is not final when he repents and returns to his life as a fugitive. He forms his rough followers into an effective fighting force, he fulfills his family responsibility, and protects his people against foreign oppressors, even though Saul was still trying to kill him (1 Sam 22–23).

Step Three: David Passes the Test of Trust (1 Sam 24 and 26)

On two important occasions David's character is tested at the point where most strong men are weakest. Both in the cave of Engedi and on the hill of Hachilah, David has God-given opportunities to pay back Saul, and in his own way take hold of the position God had so clearly promised him. But David passes the payback test with high honors. His words, "the Lord forbid that I should put forth my hand against the Lord's anointed" (1 Sam 26:11), show how deeply he had learned the value of human life and the seriousness of trying to take for oneself authority which belongs only to the Lord (see v. 10). David has learned that patience and trust in the Lord himself, not payback, is the answer to repeated hate and plotting. The importance of these lessons for present-day Melanesian society can hardly be overstressed.

The last events in this training through testing show David failing again as he joins the Philistines and even tries to fight for them in the battle in which Saul and Jonathan are killed. But he is shown his foolishness once again and as he turns back to his Lord he learns again that failure is not final in the service of God (1 Sam 27; 29; 30).

Thus at the age of thirty, David takes up the position of leadership he had been anointed for probably twelve to fifteen years earlier. These were the steps by which a person "after God's own heart" came to a position of leadership.

From these four Old Testament examples of God's servants-in-training, we can note the following training principles:

- God chooses and prepares his workers, sometimes commissioning them publicly for their work.
- A personal meeting with the Lord, which leads to a wholehearted commitment to him, is the essential foundation for serving God. For some it is a sudden confrontation (like Gideon), for others a steady growth to commitment (like Joshua and David). Sometimes it involves an earlier and later commitment (like Moses before and after the years in Midian).
- This commitment leads to a public stand for Yahweh, often involving family opposition and/or rejection for a time by those the person is to serve.
- Personal knowledge of the burdens and hardships of the people are essential for future leaders.
- The Spirit of God equips and "clothes" his workers with necessary gifts, authority, and ability to do God's work.
- The Lord uses both formal and practical pre-service training and continuing in-service training once a leader is in position.
- A "hidden years" experience of disciplining and waiting is often an important part of the training process.
- Overcoming failure and hardship is necessary for the person who will lead others.

- A willingness to stand for the right against popular wrong views is essential.
- In addition, the following can be noted in the training of these Old Testament leaders: being called on to take important leadership work at a young age; a cross-cultural formal education; a personal apprenticeship under a proven leader; and directly challenging false powers.

Some Patterns Jesus Used in Training for Ministry

As we turn to the Gospels we find that Jesus both followed many of the principles we have noted from the Old Testament and also added his own new emphases.

How Jesus Selected Candidates for Training

Men and women came to Jesus in various ways: sometimes on the recommendation of a preacher (John 1:36–37); sometimes through the witness of a friend (John 1:41, 45); sometimes as an official delegation (John 1:19); sometimes Jesus himself went and found the individual (John 1:43); sometimes it was their personal need or curiosity which brought them to meet Jesus (John 3:1–2; Mark 1:32–33); and sometimes it was for less worthy motives (John 6:26; Matt 23:34–35). But all those who stayed with Jesus and continued in his service were carefully chosen by the Lord himself.

Luke 6:12–13 shows that the Lord chose his special workers only after a whole night in prayer. It is not surprising, then, that we should pray when seeking or selecting needed candidates for his work (Matt 9:37–38).

When Christ called a person to serve him, he demanded a turning away from other interests and a full commitment to him (Matt 4:18–22; Luke 9:23; 14:25–33). This call for commitment was not always given at the first meeting. The meetings of John 1:35–42 almost certainly took place before the calls of Matt 4:18–22. And these same men were to have further, more demanding calls later (e.g., Matt 10:1–2). But those who would not accept this costly self-denial could not enter his service (Mark 10:21–22; Luke 9:57–62). Christ did not count highly a person's family relationships or desire for position and prestige in the community as indicators of readiness for his service. Those he chose were often untried and unproven men and women. Historically this was, of course, unavoidable, but Jesus was prepared to take the risks of selecting raw recruits for pre-service training. Prayerful, challenging selection of potential workers was the pattern Christ used for finding the people for his service.

Three Features of Christ's Training Program

Three features were common to all Christ's methods of selecting coworkers.

Personal Fellowship with Christ Is at the Center

In the Old Testament examples we noted that a personal meeting with God was at the center of the workers' preparation. So in the Gospels, when Jesus trains someone he first calls that person to be with him. The disciples Jesus trained as his apostles lived with him, ate with him, talked with him, and shared all that Jesus did for nearly three years.

In Mark 3:13–14 we read, "He went up into the hills and called to him those whom he desired; and they came to him. And he appointed twelve to be with him and to be sent out to preach. . . ." The first part of his purpose for his special servants was that they may have fellowship with him (cf. Matt 10:1; Luke 9:10). Our Lord longs for personal fellowship with his servants even more than he longs for their service. We see this special feature of Christ's way for ministry most clearly in the teaching on the vine and the branches in John 15. In this passage, which uses fruitfulness as a picture of effective Christian service, the key teaching is that the branch must abide in the vine. The effective Christian worker must be in a living union with his Lord for any useful fruit to come from his service. The first Lord's Supper also showed the Lord's desire to be with and to share with his servants (Luke 22:14). The sacrament when rightly received is still a rich and sweet communing with the Lord himself.

Christ's training program continually taught his workers to want to enjoy his presence and sharing with him. In a very real sense, all true ministry is his ministry. As G. W. Bromiley puts it:

> "All power is given unto me" were his words to his disciples when He commissioned them finally for his continuing ministry. And as though to emphasise the fact that this was a derivative ministry, that they were his servants, privileged to participate in his service, and therefore to draw their strength and humility from him, he added: "Lo, I am with you always, even to the end of the world."

Others are caught up into the ministry of Jesus Christ. But first and last it is his ministry, to be received from him, learned from him, discharged for him, empowered by him.[7]

Instruction Is Central

"Rabbi," or Teacher, was the most common term people used when speaking to Jesus. "Disciples"—or students/learners— was the most common name given to his followers. In an age when we are uncertain about truth and afraid of authority we easily forget the central place Jesus Christ gave to careful, regular teaching for those who would be his workers.

Teaching comes first in the Gospel summaries of Jesus's work, and often special instruction for his disciples is mentioned (e.g., Matt 4:23; 5:1–2; 7:28–29; 9:35; 11:1, 29; 13:53). Christ took his apostles aside for special teaching (Matt 20:17–19). He gave further in-depth explanation of his public teaching for the benefit of the disciples (e.g., Mark 4:33–34). He followed up the things they talked about as they walked, with clear teaching in the house (Mark 9:33–37; 10:32). Even when disciples were slow to learn he took them away on their own repeatedly to teach them (e.g., Mark 9:30–32; Luke 18:31–34).

Jesus marked continuing in his word as the way to become a true disciple as well as the way to know both truth and freedom (John 8:31). The final hours before his death were filled with careful teaching as we find it in the Upper Room Discourses of John 13–16. As Jesus summarizes his work on earth in his prayer before his death, he makes special mention of the way he has taught the disciples (John 17:6, 8, 14, 17). The words spoken about what he did with the crowd were even more true of what Jesus did with his disciples: ". . . again, as his custom was, he taught them" (Mark 10:1).

Jesus Is Careful to Make the Nature of Christian Ministry Clear

Jesus was training his disciples for a distinctive work. He was concerned to make the nature of this work clear. Those who will work for him must become servants. Both in his teaching and example Jesus showed that his kind of work and leadership is different from the usual kinds of leadership in the world. Mark 10:42–45 shows the difference between those who "lord

7. Bromiley, *Christian Ministry*, 18.

it" over others and "exercise authority over" others and those who become their servants. The whole purpose of Jesus coming to earth was not so that other people could serve him, but that he might serve and work for them. His death as a ransom for us humans was the greatest example of this kind of work.

Jesus spoke clearly about this work of being slaves or servants of God and of others more and more at the end of his time on earth. He summed up the importance of it when on the night before his death he himself took the slave's towel and washed his disciples' feet (John 13:1–17). Jesus not only gave this great example, he also commanded the disciples to follow this pattern in their own service: "If I then, your Lord and Teacher, have washed your feet you also ought to wash one another's feet. For I have given you an example that you also should do as I have done to you" (John 13:14–15; cf. Luke 22:24–27).

Yet, as Michael Green points out, the followers of Christ have not always taken note of this command. The Christian church has found this a very hard lesson to learn. Almost all consideration of different types of Christian ministries begins with a discussion of the validity of the orders in question, of their regularity, their authentication, their apostolicity. That is very natural. It is the way of the world. But it is not the way of Jesus Christ. He saw ministry not in terms of status, but rather in terms of function. The pattern for Christian ministry which he set was one of service. Of course, the very word "ministry" means service. But for Jesus this was no idle euphemism. It is no accident that the "ministry" is used to describe the whole of his public life and work. This was his glory; he looked for no other. And so it must be with any ministry which claims to be truly Christian.[8]

So we see fellowship with Christ, teaching, and clarity around the nature of their ministry as key features in the training received by Jesus's disciples.

Some Practical Methods Jesus Used to Train His Disciples

We can also discern particular methods Jesus used to take men and women from the point of commitment to readiness for responsible service.

8. Green, *Called to Service*, 11.

Christ Encouraged Immediate Witnessing and Sharing of What He Had Done

Levi (Luke 5:27–31), Andrew (John 1:40–41), Philip (John 1:43–46), Zaccheus (Luke 19:6–10), and the man who was set free from an unclean spirit (Mark 5:18–19) are some whom Jesus encouraged to become involved in working for him as soon as they had met him personally. This initial practical work for Christ was an important test of their sincerity and their suitability for further training.

Christ Called His Trainees Into a Full-Time Apprenticeship

For the twelve apostles, preparing to serve Christ meant leaving their family and their previous work, and entering a full-time training program (e.g., Matt 4:21–22). This training included several key elements.

First, they learnt by partnership with Christ in the work. Luke summarizes this when he says, "Jesus went on through cities and villages preaching and bringing the good news of the kingdom. And the twelve were with him and also some women . . ." (Luke 8:1). We read about his disciples sharing out the food he had miraculously provided (Matt 14:19); doing the baptizing for Jesus (John 4:2); bringing—or sometimes hindering—enquirers who wanted to meet Jesus (e.g., Matt 19:13–15; John 12:20–22; 6:8–9); making physical preparations for a meeting place (Matt 26:17–19), and so on.

Secondly, practical examples were given for the disciples to follow. We see Jesus giving teaching by example, particularly in regard to prayer (e.g., Luke 11:1–4; Matt 26:36–46), and in forming right attitudes to their work. The apostle Paul used the same method as a central part of his training work (e.g., 1 Cor 4:16; 11:1; Phil 3:17; 4:9; 1 Thess 1:6–7).

And thirdly, personal encouragement and counselling were features. Jesus was always concerned for the individuals in his training classes. He warns, corrects, encourages, and prays for his disciples personally. Jesus rebukes Peter in front of the other disciples (Mark 8:32–33); he encourages John to have a more cooperative attitude (Mark 9:38–41); he particularly warns Peter that he will turn away, and tells him he has prayed for him (Luke 22:31–34). We also see Jesus seeking to lead some of the disciples on to an even deeper level of understanding. He spends special time with Peter, James, and John for this purpose, for example, on the Mount of Transfiguration (Matt 17:1) and in the Garden of Gethsemane (Matt 26:37–38).

Christ's Training Included Times of Practical Experience and Testing

Jesus sent out his disciples in training for limited periods and with limited goals to help them practice the lessons he was teaching. The mission to the "lost sheep of the house of Israel" and the mission of the "seventy" are examples (Matt 10 and Luke 10). In this way the disciples learnt the necessary practical skills and also learnt to report back and evaluate their own work (Luke 10:17–24).

Jesus was careful to help his followers learn from their mistakes. We have referred to the way they hindered the children from coming to him, the narrow-mindedness of John, and the proud boasting of Peter. Mark 9:14–29 shows the disciples failing in their attempt to heal a boy, and Jesus using this failure to teach deeper spiritual lessons. Peter's failure and the gentle restoration explained in John 21 is another example of the way Christ showed that failure is not final in him.

Christ's Training Method Emphasized the Work of the Holy Spirit

Especially towards the end of his training course for the disciples, Jesus gave careful instruction about the need for and work of the Holy Spirit in and through them (John 14–16). His final words before Jesus ascended back to heaven emphasized that without the Holy Spirit to fill and empower them there could be no service (Luke 24:49; Acts 1:8).

Christ Commissioned and Transferred the Responsibility into the Hands of His Trainees

The teaching, prayer, and communion meal on the night before his death, and the appearances after his resurrection, were times when Christ clearly put his work into the disciples' hands. The Great Commission of Matt 28:16–20 is the climax of Christ's training program. The goals, extent, nature of, and power for their work are stated simply but plainly. And Jesus's final words emphasize that, while the pre-service course was finished the teacher himself would continue to give in-service training as the disciples took up this work. The fact that today we are continuing in this same work is silent testimony to the wisdom and effectiveness of the Lord's training methods.

The Relevance of These Biblical Principles for Theological Education in Melanesia

These biblical case studies provide some healthy tests for theological education in Melanesia today. We shall not try to make a point by point application of the various principles and patterns. Rather we shall make a few suggestions under five main headings.

Recruiting and Training

Our case studies have highlighted some abiding patterns. We need to see clear evidence of God's call in the lives of those accepted for training. The recommendation of their own local churches must evaluate this more accurately. Older pastors need help to become "Barnabases" in judging evidence of leadership potential. Present pastors need help in encouraging an interest in church service.

We need to contact and challenge and train those who have already proven themselves capable of leadership responsibility. Traditional patterns whereby the elders gave positive direction to younger men as they took up their life's work could be better used in encouraging the Joshuas, Davids, and Gideons of today. But again, this requires older Christians to understand the need to recruit for the ministry and their responsibility in this.

Those now working in high schools, tertiary institutions, and urban pastoral ministries need special help to see the opportunities for challenging potential church leaders. We need a course for chaplains, counsellors, and town pastors in what to look for and how to develop leadership potential, perhaps in the manner that CLTC has used Theological Education by Extension (TEE) courses and Vacation Bible Courses as recruitment and preliminary training programs for potential staff members.

Recruitment and selection must also confront those interested in ministry with a call to wholehearted commitment and an understanding of the costly nature of their vocation.

Training as a Continuing Process

We need to see training for ministry as a continuing process, not as a once in a lifetime experience. There needs to be a good balance of instruction and practical experience in programs which give church workers continuing training throughout their ministry: "continuing in his words" (John 8:32).

Both pre-service and in-service training programs are needed for effective ministry. Perhaps we have in the South Pacific an opportunity to show that residential and extension courses are not alternative or opposite kinds of training. Residential training can be interrelated with continuing on-the-job learning in an overall program of training for the many different needs facing the church's ministry today. Flexible options, with tailor-made "preliminary" years, or postgraduate courses, could identify and serve some of the special needs churches face as new opportunities arise. The place of internship, fieldwork, vacation ministries, and regular outreach during residential training need continuing evaluation and development.

Seminaries and colleges in Melanesia, and the South Pacific more generally, need to become increasingly involved in ongoing training programs for their graduates. While some aspects of in-service training undoubtedly must be run by other church departments, we must continue to look at the theological college's own responsibilities in this. Where once this was achieved by means of TEE courses and literature and cassette tape distribution, methods and media need constantly to be developed to keep pace with rapidly changing circumstances and information and media technology.

Trainer-Trainee Relationships

In our biblical case studies, we saw a group of methods and patterns which emphasize the right trainer-trainee relationships. These patterns also demonstrate the importance of cross-cultural understanding and sensitivity when expatriates, or even national teachers whose education outstrips that of their trainees, also share in regular practical Christian service alongside their trainees. Facility in vernacular or "trade" languages takes on new significance. And a genuine servant heart which encourages leadership skills in others and does not dominate the practice, along with skill in contextualizing biblical concepts, are important stepping stones for relevant partnership with students in practical learning, just as much as in the formal classroom work.

Similarly, in "shame" cultures, such as those in Melanesia, the principle of using failure as a step in growth and development for ministry is potentially life-changing when students discover real forgiveness at the foot of the cross, and are guided into positive growth from false starts or sincere mistakes. But, again, cross-cultural insight and practical love are vital for positive outcomes, as shame can be devastatingly hurtful when not understood or wrongly exploited.

A pastorally sensitive community life within the college or seminary and follow-up visitation of graduates are two important means for building the kind of relationships which can turn mistakes and failure into growth experiences. Confession and repentance, leading through forgiveness to new levels of respect and trust, have to be multicultural experiences. A range of activities within the common life of a training institution need to be maintained to allow for the development of the healthy relationship patterns needed to foster these dynamics.

Understanding the Nature of Ministry

Developing the right ideas about the nature of ministry is essential. Charles Forman writes, "in the Pacific generally, there was a strong tendency for men to enter the pastorate for the sake of prestige, and to look upon it as a rank rather than as a calling or task."[9] If he is right, then we have a major task to change the accepted idea of church leadership to a more biblical one. But how do we develop and ensure trainees have taken hold of the "service" image of ministry?

For the Bible characters we studied it was often the "hidden years" experience which humbled and disciplined them until they saw service as their chief honor. Carefully guided internships, and vacation ministries during training, have potential to serve a similar function. The graduate's first appointment and early years after graduation are of special importance if he or she is to overcome the "failure through pride" problems which many a modern Moses faces.

Being an example was the method Christ used above all to teach the serving nature of his work. This is particularly challenging for an expatriate teacher, or highly educated national teachers who are so much better off materially and have so much more prestige than the seminary student. Facing rejection from family or friends because you are taking a strong public

9. Forman, "South Pacific Style," 426.

stand for Christ was another experience which showed the true nature of godly service for Gideon (and later for Paul). This is hard to "arrange" but still very necessary today.

Expecting to see and to encourage the spiritual gifts of every Christian is an attitude which quickly emphasizes service more than lording it over others. This would suggest we need greater attention to training students as trainers, working with and through other people as they train. Such skills in training others to do the work are more easily accepted after some field experience, so need fresh emphasis after internship opportunities. Moreover, since service is the overflow of love and humility, we suggest that the example and death of Christ need to be kept vividly in the minds of our students. Love is learnt better at the foot of the cross for that is the ultimate demonstration of true love. It is also the best incentive for encouraging trainees to take a clear public stand for Christ on the costly issues in present-day Melanesian life.

Ministry must increasingly become fellowship with Christ. We need to give the same emphasis to personal fellowship with the living Christ as we find in the Gospels. Thus, the devotional life, chapel services, and special times of challenge to commitment must be seen as potentially the most important experiences in training. Crisis experiences of an emotional spiritual nature, in themselves, are not sufficient to sustain any ongoing ministry. But it is also true that without them a ministry can lack life and spiritual power.

Personal ambitions, desire for "proper" pay, natural desire for recognition, unwillingness to identify with less privileged people—these are just a few of the attitudes which need to be regularly brought under the searching demands of Christ in the trainee's own experience. Our Lord used prayer, direct warning, and clear teaching to help his disciples face these issues in the right way. So must we.

Above all, our task is to prepare men and women with a warm love for the Lord Jesus Christ. Love grows from sharing with, and knowing the loved one more and more. Oh that our training programs might be such experiences for the glory of God and the sake of our needy world. We trust that continuing study of these biblical patterns may stir up further study and experimentation so that in each vital aspect of our training programs, we may more effectively "proclaim Christ, warning every person and teaching everyone in all wisdom, that we may present every person mature in Christ" (Col 1:28).

Chapter 13

Recent Trends in Pacific Historiography and Anthropology

STUDENTS OF CHRISTIAN MISSION—MISSIOLOGISTS—AND theological educators in contexts with primal religions in their community's heritage, have broad boundaries to our task. We necessarily interact with concerns usually addressed within Western theology and social sciences. We walk the same academic corridors as biblical scholars, historians, and cultural anthropologists particularly. This can be both liberating and restricting, as I found when choosing a thesis topic for my doctoral thesis. I had gone in 1979 from fifteen years mission involvement developing an interdenominational Bible college in Papua New Guinea,[1] for doctoral study at the University of Aberdeen, Scotland. In Papua New Guinea (PNG) I had taught across the whole theological curriculum, revelling in the freedom the missional setting gave to bring together a wide gamut of biblical studies, and theological, church historical, and mission growth insights. I intended to develop a thesis on aspects of New Testament theology contextualized for PNG. Aberdeen University's Religious Studies Department, under Andrew Walls, a leading British authority on Christian mission amongst primal peoples, was the ideal place for such study, especially with the resources Andrew and his faculty had built up from around the world.[2]

1. The Christian Leaders' Training College of Papua New Guinea, Inc. (CLTC).

2. Particularly, Harold W. Turner's collections on new religious movements globally. Lamin Sanneh, Adrian Hastings, and James Thrower were other Religious Studies Department faculty at the time (1979–1984). I also audited courses by I. Howard Marshall in the Divinity Faculty.

But the hoped for missional freedom was not open to someone with my Western background and education seeking a first-world doctoral degree. Qualifying for PhD level study was no problem; a research essay on an acceptable topic dealt with that hurdle.[3] The problem was where to locate the thesis acceptably within the recognized fields of 1980 academic study in Britain—and missiology was not yet such a "recognized field." Furthermore, any aspect of theology or biblical studies would have to "belong" in one of the "silos" delineating the suitability of my thesis topic for doctoral study. For in the early 1980s, academic theology and biblical studies meant Western theology and Western biblical studies. Unless you were born a Melanesian, in which case you could contribute an explanatory, descriptive Melanesian perspective on your local theology, as long as you kept within your restricted area. Local theologies were interesting, and therefore acceptable, though uncertainties remained as to whether they were real theology.

I eventually settled on a Christian history orientation researching the formation and motivation of nineteenth-century missionaries to the Pacific, and the emphases of their work. For the thesis I developed a "biographical" methodology which allowed me to evaluate, inter alia, ways both historians and cultural anthropologists have regarded Pacific missionaries. Starting from my approach in the thesis, in this chapter I trace some ways historians and anthropologists have written about missionaries and Christianity up to the present.[4] These two academic disciplines still strongly influence serious study of Pacific missiology and Christianity.

The "Biographical Methodology" in Its Early 1980s Context

At that time in the early 1980s sociological, largely Marxist, socioeconomic orientations dominated Pacific history writing. As early as 1942, the new Victoria University (Wellington) History Department head, J. C. Beaglehole, had "disposed of the alternatives and pronounced 'historical materialism' the appropriate philosophy of history for the antipodes."[5] I surveyed

3. My descriptive and analytical essay was published as Hitchen, "Dreams in Traditional Thought," 5–53.

4. The main substance of this chapter was presented at a Conference of the New Zealand Institute of Christian Studies in Auckland, August 28–29, 2015, during a visit by historian Dr. David Bebbington. The paper has been adapted and supplemented for this chapter.

5. Hitchen, "Training Tamate," 171, citing Beaglehole, "Philosophies of History." Throughout this chapter, and particularly in these opening sections I am drawing heavily

the approaches to missionary motivation of various European, British, and Australasian academics,[6] focusing particularly on Niel Gunson's Pacific application of Beaglehole's desired approach,[7] before proposing an alternative "biographical" historical methodology for my thesis, as a necessary corrective to the sociological approaches of the day. To situate this chapter, I begin with reasons why I chose this biographical approach to study James Chalmers, including the influences upon him as a child, his religious experiences as a youth, and the development of the theological and missiological views he applied in mission service for ten years in the Cook Islands, 1866–77, and for his remaining twenty-four years in what is now Papua New Guinea.

This personal biographical approach arose from dissatisfaction with the methods followed by van den Berg, Gunson, Warren, and their successors. Their approach of extracting common features from large numbers of missionaries' files had the weakness of all "identikit" pictures: it is hard to find an actual missionary who exactly fits the picture. We suspected that the distinctions between missionaries may have been as influential as the carefully documented similarities, even allowing for variations noted. Reading generalizations about what "the missionaries" of each period were or did left us asking, "Which missionary?" The identikit approach also reflected the special interests and presuppositions of the researcher just as much as it depicted the missionaries' views. The source material allowed each scholar to demonstrate immaculate research techniques while highlighting their desired emphases, whether religious for van den Berg, political for Koskinen, sociohistorical for Gunson (on whose methodology I expand below), or socioeconomic for Potter, and so forth. Moreover, the identikit approach largely disregarded the intellectual content of the theological beliefs of the nineteenth-century missionary. When Pacific historians like Hilliard, Wetherell, and Langmore did refer to theological aspects, their vagueness left readers dependent on their own preconceptions to interpret the missionary's beliefs.[8] By focusing as an alternative on a particular person we sought to elucidate the person's religious development and the

from my 1984 doctoral thesis, often using the same terms and phraseology as in the thesis (144–76).

6. Consult Hitchen, "Training Tamate," 146–70 for details. The survey included, among others, Berg, *Constrained by Jesus' Love*; Warren, *Missionary Movement*; *Social History*; Piggin, "Social Background"; Potter, "Social Origins.

7. Gunson, *Messengers of Grace*; Hitchen, "Training Tamate," 161–65.

8. Hilliard, *God's Gentlemen*; Wetherell, *Reluctant Mission*; Langmore, *Tamate*.

theological influences upon them, to clarify the content of their beliefs and presuppositions. A biographical approach presented a real person, against whom we could evaluate the identikit and pigeonholed images of mid-twentieth-century scholarship.

By the completion of my thesis, Beaglehole had been championing "historical materialism" for forty years as the preferred philosophy of history for the antipodes.[9] By 1984, criticisms of Beaglehole's philosophy and its products vindicated the personal biographical approach as an alternative.[10] J. W. Davidson warned against overstressing the imperial political factor which had become prominent through his mentor's approach:

> Even the ablest of [imperial historians] impose a spurious unity on their subject matter . . . The humble participants in trade and navigation, in settlement and missionary work become, in the lofty flights of the imperial historian's imaginations, the exponents of a theory of empire rather than what they actually were, men who went about their various tasks unconcerned, in the main, with any grandiose political conceptions. Imperial history, when it insists on studying the history of European expansion by orienting all its material around the imperial factor, becomes, indeed, the negation of true historical scholarship.[11]

The lesson, evidently, was to avoid "spurious unities" and focus afresh on the "humble participants." But one reason for not embracing a biographical approach, and particularly the "hero" variety of it, Langmore explained, was the then deeper awareness of the "complexity of human motivation."[12]

Herbert Butterfield had suggested that insight should more appropriately lead us back to biographical studies:

> Perhaps the Marxists have never sufficiently appropriated the first fundamental principle of Marx and of all true historiography—namely, that it is men who in reality make history. . . . It is not a disembodied idea, as some . . . have thought, and not an economic factor, as Marxists assert, but the incalculability of a

9. Beaglehole, "Philosophies of History."

10. Beaglehole himself acknowledged that his approach probably had "errors and omissions" which might need "excepting." Beaglehole, "Philosophies of History," 95n1. He may have also bequeathed the way to a better alternative in what one of his most influential protégés noted was "his last message to the members of his profession," namely, his quotation of Micah 6:8. Davidson, "New Zealand Scholar," 154.

11. Davidson, "Problems," 8; Hitchen, "Training Tamate," 172.

12. Langmore, *Tamate*, vi–vii.

> human personality that is "the starting-point of historical change." The idea of process in history is a dangerous clue in the hands of people who do not possess also a high doctrine of personality. The whole texture of historical writing is in question here.[13]

The then prevalent approach of abstracting themes and factors from many missionary candidates' testimonies, failed to give sufficient emphasis to their integrity as persons. As a successor of Butterfield's at Cambridge explained in his 1980 inaugural lecture: "What I have tried to show is that biography has been too much disparaged. When a great historian can mistake a person for a trend, when it is thought more important to analyse social background than opinions, then the time has come for a reaction."[14]

A biographical approach also suited trends in Pacific scholarship. As early as 1966, Davidson had pointed out that, "At the research level, the problem is that of devising methods for the study of multi-cultural situations."[15] Sione Latukefu articulated the concern thus: "The impact of missionary activity on Oceania . . . should be viewed primarily as part of the story of Oceania and not merely as part of the history of European expansion in the Pacific."[16] Whiteman illustrated one way of trying to achieve this.[17] Reworking areas covered by Hilliard, Whiteman combined anthropological and mission history approaches, noting also the Melanesian initiatives in culture contact situations: "In an anthropological study of missionaries as agents of culture change it is necessary to have a thorough understanding of the important personalities that shaped the structure and nature of the cross-cultural relationship in this dynamic arena of Melanesian and missionary interaction."[18] Whiteman gave particular attention in the period from 1850 to 1900 to George Augustus Selwyn and John Coleridge Patteson. But, like Hilliard, he gave little attention to the pre-Pacific experience of these missionaries, assuming either that their earlier formative period was well known, or unimportant.

Pursuing methods suitable for multicultural study also emphasizes the role of Pacific Islander scholars. A European scholar has suggested,

13. Butterfield, *Human Relations*, 88, 94.
14. Beales, *History and Biography*, 24.
15. Davidson, "Problems," 10.
16. Latukefu, "Conclusion," 457.
17. Whiteman, *Melanesians and Missionaries*.
18. Whiteman, *Melanesians and Missionaries*, 170–71.

"probably the best future work will be done by Pacific Islander historians,"[19] and older Pacific Islander scholars like Latukefu preferred a qualified partnership: "I believe it is possible for an outsider with ability, inclination and time to gain a very full understanding of how islanders think and feel. It does, however, require a very real effort to rid oneself of preconceptions and prejudice."[20] In this situation a biographical approach to the missionary's worldview has special importance. The European scholar needs to understand the Pacific cultures, including precontact cultures, to contribute acceptably to discussions of Pacific history. Likewise, Pacific Islander scholars must understand the precontact worldview of the European missionary to enhance our understanding of missional aspects of Pacific history. But if dominant academic trends enclose the nineteenth-century missionary within socioeconomic or sociological frameworks of historical study, Pacific Islander scholars face a double task. Before they can contribute, they must master the Western socioeconomic or anthropological frameworks before joining the historical discussions of their own area.

A biographical approach uses universally recognizable categories, which do not delay such academic participation. Butterfield indicated one area where Pacific scholars may have an advantage, if there is any truth in his observation on trends amongst Western historians:

> One of the great weaknesses of young historical students at the present day is that they know so little of what goes on inside human beings. In times when religion was fashionable and men knew their Bibles by heart, they had one advantage in that by intensive self-examination they learned about the profundities that lie within a human personality; they learned about the intricacies of human motive, and the fund of spiritual forces which enable a man in many things, though not in everything, to conquer his environment and rise above circumstances.[21]

Many Pacific cultures still retain these benefits of corporate religious sensitivity. When we add to these the respect for persons and related social skills fostered by communal living, we can look for fresh historical insights from Pacific scholars. We chose to study Chalmers's religious experiences and beliefs biographically with a view to inviting Melanesian church leaders

19. Garrett, review of *Island Churches*, 78.

20. Latukefu, "Conclusion," 462–63. For comment on this point in the African situation, see Turner, "Way Forward," 3–4.

21. Butterfield, *Human Relations*, 91.

and academics to reassess his significance from their perspective. John Garrett included such biographical "micro-histories" as one kind of study still needed to achieve "thorough interpretation for each island group."[22]

We welcome the renewed interest in Carlyle's dictum, "The History of the World is but the Biography of great men."[23] But we do not desire a return to the romanticism by which Carlyle upheld that view. We also eschew the mere individualism which can characterize biographical studies. We endorse the modern awareness that we are only fully human in community, and that humans are influenced at every point by social, economic, and political powers and power structures. These modern insights ought never to have been forgotten in the study of Christian missions. Christian theology teaches that humans play a decisive role in God's historical purposes. Since men and women share the divine image we are accountable to use our times and opportunities responsibly before God. This high view of personal significance makes biographical study essential in a Christian view of history. In mission history we must take seriously the concept of persons "sent by God" with a "call" and "commission" from God to motivate and direct their work. A historian may claim it is not his work to discuss the objective reality of such a "call." But historians cannot ignore the historic reality of the missionary's consciousness of that call. Our biographical approach meant the intellectual content of Chalmers's beliefs and presuppositions supporting this "call" consciousness were emphasized in the thesis at various stages of his life.

But Christian theology also stresses the communal nature of humanity's role and accountability in history. If our biographies of Christian heroes and particularly missionary heroes have fostered individualism and patterns of missionary service which have not upheld the dignity of communal life, then they have fallen short of their own proper standards and biblical heritage. Mission advocates' neglect of this communal aspect may have hindered historians from understanding the missionary "call," and contributed also to historians' difficulties addressing claims that providence and the Holy Spirit superintend the missionary's work.[24] The communal influ-

22. Garrett, review of *Island Churches*, 78.

23. Carlyle, *On Heroes*, 45, and 21; cf. also Ferguson, *Carlyle as Historian*, 4–7; Campbell, *Thomas Carlyle*.

24. See Bebbington, *Patterns in History*, wherein he refers to historiographical factors which are problematic for a doctrine of providence (66–67), where he discusses justification for historians using providential explanations (177–80), with reference to Butterfield, *Christianity and History*, 94; and Butterfield, "God in History," 7–8.

ences of family; school and its teacher; the church fellowship and its minister; the intense moral and social expectations of theological college and its key leader; and the distinctive partnership of directors, foreign secretaries, and missionary colleagues past and present within the London Missionary Society, loom large in our biography of Chalmers's formation and service.

The Christian Scriptures also emphasize the influence of the "powers" in the Christian world mission. They claim that all the powers—including by inference what we call economic, social, and political forces—are subject to the divine person, Jesus Christ (e.g., Rom 13:1–7; Col 1:15–23; 2:8–15). The New Testament also accords a higher dignity to humans living in community than to any of the "powers." The Christ of God partook of human nature to subjugate the dominating forces of the universe; he did not manipulate them by nonpersonal means (e.g., Heb 2:5–18). In our age when so much dehumanizes humans, we should respect, but guard against an overemphasis on, the role of impersonal powers in historical studies. Men and women are not the pawns of such powers. A biographical approach may not resolve the tensions in the "idealist" versus "positivist" controversy in Western historiography.[25] But by studying the influences contributing to Chalmers's development as a person we sought to do justice to these theological insights regarding the dignity of personality and community, and human relationships with nonpersonal powers.[26]

David Bebbington's now classic analysis in *Patterns in History* was published in 1979, just as my research began.[27] I had settled on an "idealist" methodology to respond to what I considered still a "reductionist" "positivist" approach, emanating from the Australian National University's School of Pacific Studies, led by Niel Gunson.[28] My thesis would have been more persuasive if I had more explicitly justified my biographical approach

25. See Bebbington, *Patterns in History*, 140.

26. This ends the summary of the section of my thesis on its "biographical" methodology.

27. As a student, I had enjoyed David Bebbington's input into a postgraduate seminar for our diverse group of international University of Aberdeen doctoral students studying under Andrew Walls. Although I then read *Patterns in History* and referred to it a number of times in the thesis, I did not assimilate Bebbington's analyses sufficiently at that time.

28. I understand why some pro-mission writers, like Forman, applaud Gunson's recognition of the theological factors as "a counterweight to the reductionist tendency" of other historians, but I still find Gunson's overall influence reductionist since his research methodology sets even his consideration of theological factors within an overarching positivist materialist paradigm. See Forman, "Pacific Islands Christianity," 103.

by referring to Bebbington's thesis that a Christian anthropology, with its biblical balance emphasizing both the depravity of humanity and humanity's potential for transformation, provides the needed foundation for integrating the constructive aspects of both the "positivist" and "idealist" approaches to historiography. I came close to this when stressing the importance of understanding human personality and with my quotes from Butterfield on that subject. In a sense I was trying to illustrate Bebbington's thesis, but was probably too reactionary (or young and immature—in my early 40s?) in my emphases at the time.

But much has changed in Pacific Christian historical study since the early 1980s. Forman has documented one key change: the flourishing of writings from Pacific Islanders themselves.[29] We return to some historiographic implications of this development below. But first, some consideration of postmodernity and the postcolonial framework is in order.

Postmodernity's Ambiguous Gift to Pacific Historical Perspectives

Since the 1980s, Western historical studies have been conducted in a new intellectual context. Of key significance for Pacific historiography have been the twin philosophical moves: from modernity to postmodernity, and from a dominant Marxist socioeconomic interpretive framework to a preference for a postcolonial, sociopolitical framework.[30]

The Western academic move from "modernity" to "postmodernity"[31] has been a mixed intellectual blessing for Pacific cultures with their underlying traditional primal religious backgrounds. Postmodern thought has brought a welcoming but denigrating influence for the primal religious consciousness of Pacific thinkers, as it has amongst indigenous peoples globally. This double-sided influence of postmodernity has been closely intertwined with two further, and not unrelated, recent developments in Pacific study. By confronting modernity's presuppositions and priorities, postmodernity has contributed significantly to the context within which a

29. Forman, "Finding Our Own Voice," 115–22.

30. This section is based on a section of my chapter, Hitchen, "Primal Religious Groups," particularly 140–47.

31. This chapter does not attempt to give a definitive description of the nature and features of postmodernity or postmodernism. As a working basis we are assuming definitions such as those of Grenz, *Primer*, 12.

resurgence of indigenous consciousness has been possible in the final quarter of the twentieth century. In this sense, postmodernity has been a gift to primal societies facilitating their voice on the global stage. A resurgence of awareness of traditional customs, values, and beliefs amongst primal societies is incontestably evident across the African continent, amongst First Nation peoples of North America, and amongst tribal peoples in South America, Polynesia, Melanesia, Micronesia, and Australasia, as well as among those Andrew Walls calls the "Himalayan-Arakan" peoples, spanning the Southeast Asian boundaries of Nepal, India, China, Myanmar, Thailand, and the Malay Peninsula.[32] Comparable primal societies also predominate amongst the migrant and tribal peoples of Europe and mainland Asia.[33] How to explain this resurgence is hotly debated, but its reality as a postmodern phenomenon cannot be ignored. A subset of this development has been the rise of indigenous theology amongst Christians in primal religious cultures.

At the same time, contextualization, or Christian theological interest in indigenous expression or adaptation of the Christian message into the thought-forms and concepts of local cultures, which has characterized Christian mission at every stage of Christian history, has taken a new turn giving it new prominence in mission and theological studies since 1972.[34] Contextualization has burgeoned alongside the primal consciousness renaissance within the wider transition to postmodernity. In the Pacific, contextual theology is proliferating from both Pacific and Pākehā/Palangi theologians.[35] This renewed primal consciousness, contextual theology movements, and postmodernity itself raise issues about Christian history writing in our region.

32. Walls, "Commission One," 34.

33. Descriptions of such resurgences abound. From Australasia, Erich Kolig describes in 2004 the New Zealand Māori movement, including the comment: "While perhaps no more than twenty years ago it seemed as if Māori 'traditional' culture, or any resembling form of it, was inexorably sliding towards its ultimate, inevitable disappearance, it has bounced back thanks to concerted efforts by leading Māori, and perhaps also by some Pākehā [whites of European extraction]." Kolig, "Māori Cultural Renaissance," 146–47.

34. See chapter 2 above.

35. Both these terms refer to people of European or Caucasian extraction resident in New Zealand or the Pacific. Pākehā is the Māori, and Palangi the wider Polynesian term.

Postmodernity's Contribution to the Resurgence of Primal Consciousness, Indigenous Theology, and Contextualization

At least the following features of postmodernity have contributed to this new awareness of primal beliefs and values, and their importance in Christian theological thought. Postmodernity rejects the hegemony of any particular "metanarrative" applying to all peoples, and welcomes instead plurality and diversity of perspective and viewpoint.[36] Insofar as modernity's commitment to the metanarratives of rationalism and the "Enlightenment project" muted the expression of alternative explanatory myths from a primal perspective, and contributed to the dominance of Western expressions of theology as "orthodox," postmodernity has broken those previous hegemonies and opened the arena for fresh input on primal consciousness and local cultural beliefs. As a consequence of this, "Postmodernism has been particularly important in acknowledging 'the multiple forms of otherness as they emerge from differences in subjectivity, gender and sexuality, race and class, temporal . . . and spatial geographic locations and dislocations.'"[37] This welcome for diversity in the postmodern intellectual climate invites those marginalized by modernity's criteria to now step forward, speak up, and expect to be afforded the same dignity as others in public discussion.

Postmodernity's reevaluation invites fresh consideration of concepts and ideas previously relegated to the periphery, downplayed, or devalued by modernity's priorities. Even beliefs and values contradicted or apparently disposed of by modernity's ruling narratives may now be reconsidered. In each of these cases the characteristics of a primal consciousness, and distinctive cultural insights into Christian theology, have something fresh to bring to the discussions, with spinoff consequences for history writing about any region with a primal religious background—as in Melanesia, the Pacific, and Australasia. Postmodernity's focus, the concerns around the primal consciousness resurgence, the desire for indigenous theology, and the quest for contextual theologies, all coalesce around the

36. As Stanley Grenz summarizes it: "The postmodern outlook entails the end of the appeal to any central legitimating myth whatsoever. Not only have all the reigning master narratives lost their credibility, but the idea of a grand narrative is itself no longer credible. We have not only become aware of a plurality of conflicting legitimating stories but have moved into the age of the demise of metanarrative. . . . Consequently the postmodern outlook demands an attack on any claim to universality—it demands, in fact, a 'war on totality.'" Grenz, *Primer*, 45, citing Lyotard, *Postmodern Condition*, 82.

37. Harvey, *Condition of Postmodernity*, 112, citing Huyssens, "Mapping the Postmodern," 50.

issue of cultural identity. As anthropologists like Simon Harrison point out, "increasing trans-national flows of culture seem to be producing, not global homogenization, but growing assertions of heterogeneity and local distinctiveness."[38] This in turn means that "communities may often mobilize themselves by representing themselves as having clear boundaries which are *endangered*—as having essential qualities . . . or distinctive ways of life, which are under threat from the outside."[39] Representations of such perceived threats, according to Harrison, can either see cultural boundaries being "polluted" by the intrusion of foreign cultural forms, or by foreign misappropriation—"piracy"—of their local cultural forms.[40] The common assumption is that cultural identity can only be retained if the assumed cultural boundary is protected from erosion.

Cultural identity has long been an issue in primal religions' response to the Christian gospel. Harold Turner classified new religious movements in primal societies according to their response to the gospel by grouping them along a continuum from "neo-primal" to "synthetist" to "hebraist" to "independent church."[41] Concerns over cultural identity "pollution" or "piracy" are important motifs in movements at the "neo-primal" end of the continuum, whereas claims to a renewed, transformed, or fulfilled cultural identity predominate at the "independent church" end, and we can add, in contextualized local theologies.[42] The way postmodernity has significantly opened up this intellectual context for articulating the identity issues, and thereby drawn fresh attention to primal and localized cultural perceptions, has created a new dimension within which Pacific historical writing now takes place.

Postmodernity has brought the gift of a welcome at the academic discussion table as equal participants, an invitation to present authentic Pacific perspectives, methodologies, and evaluative criteria for the discussion, and a forum in which Pacific identity and "difference" can be unembarrassedly acknowledged amongst respectful others. This is a timely gift.

38. Harrison, "Cultural Boundaries," 10.

39. Harrison, "Cultural Boundaries," 10, citing Cohen, *Symbolic Construction*, 109; emphasis original.

40. Harrison, "Cultural Boundaries," 10–11.

41. Turner, "Religious Movements," 581–93.

42. Missiological discussion of "bounded" and "open" sets provides a further framework for considering these identity questions. See, e.g., Hiebert, "Category *Christian*," 107–36; and Payne, "Mission," 206–16.

Postmodernity's Challenge to a Primal Consciousness, Indigenous Perspectives, and Contextualization

Postmodernity's positive contribution, however, is counterbalanced by challenges postmodern emphases bring to these new intellectual developments. Postmodernity's discourse on primal societies can easily become an idealized discussion of a romantic view divorced from the tensions many primal societies face. Using the Māori in New Zealand society as an example, social anthropologist Steven Webster suggests a "contradictory and ideological relationship between prevailing definitions of Māori culture and the realities of Māori society has developed historically . . . it has been brought to a head by postmodernist interests in Māori culture." Commenting from a socialist perspective, Webster warns, "Māori culture must not be seen abstractly in the Romantic tradition as a 'whole way of life' somehow unique, integral, harmonious and Other than that supposedly led by European societies [in New Zealand]." Rather, "it must be grasped concretely as *a whole way of struggle* inextricably bound up with a particular colonial history."[43] Likewise, Erich Kolig speaks of the "ideal as well as imaginary and highly fictitious scenario," that credits New Zealand with "an international reputation of tranquil, even peaceful, race relations, exemplary protection of indigenous rights, complete religious freedom, and social and legal egalitarianism."[44]

Despite their socialist preferences, Webster and Kolig both warn against the danger in postmodern idealizing of the indigenous reality on ideological grounds or for the sake of "political correctness." Many, if not most such Pacific societies and ethnic groups seeking to make their mark in a globalized postmodern world, grapple with serious contradictions both in applying their traditional cultural values in their very different Westernized settings, and in the ongoing "way of struggle" resulting from pressures and long-standing inequities in relationships with the dominant culture, as Webster highlighted. Bebbington's plea for a Christian understanding of the strengths and weaknesses of human nature leads to similarly balanced analyses.[45] If postmodern theorizing is unable to account for and address

43. Webster, "Postmodernist Theory," 222–26; emphasis original.

44. Kolig, "Māori Cultural Renaissance," 135.

45. Bebbington, *Patterns in History*, 168: "History on the Christian view is about human beings who are like God yet habitual wrongdoers, who have immense creative potential yet are enmeshed in a web of circumstance and who are the shapers and yet also the victims of history. Through the tensions of human life, however, God works out

these conflicting realities then it is inappropriate. But with no recourse to explanatory metanarratives to account for both evil and good in the same humans and their societies, postmodern theory can easily damn with faint praise the cultures they want to idealize, or at least treat as equals. Postmodernity's inability to offer solid hope to answer the darker side of the primal or Pacific societies' daily realities, invites an alternative missional evaluation and prognosis from those with a gospel grounded in a biblical realism about the human predicament.

Postmodern thought presents a further threat by treating primal or distinct cultural voices as just one more view in a diverse range, all of equal significance. Rex Ahdar illustrates this problem when he deals with ways the New Zealand legal system has handled the renewed interest in Māori spirituality.[46] For Ahdar, "New Zealanders' [i.e., Pākehā, or White New Zealanders'] reactions to Māori spirituality and its official fostering and recognition, have been mixed, ranging from hostility and ridicule, at one end of the spectrum, to warm acceptance at the other." He identifies "at least five distinctive views, three of which are critical and two that are sympathetic and supportive . . ."[47] Ahdar's classifications are: "secular rationalists," "egalitarian liberals," "conservative theists," "liberal theists," and "affirmative action liberals." Ahdar points out that this renewed, albeit varied, focus on Māori culture and spirituality only came to fruition in a wider context of "such diverse ideological streams as postmodernism, anti-colonialism, post-colonial guilt feelings and fascination with New Age values."[48]

Such a climate is inherently contradictory; while supporting respect for resurgent Māori spirituality, the postmodern commitment to equal validity for all viewpoints provides no adequate basis for judging between them, or resolving their contradictions. Ahdar tersely sums up from the legal perspective the inherent clashes of belief systems, worldviews, and practical administrative difficulties encountered when a secular state attempts to publicly recognize such a primal religious consciousness: "It is the sort of messy, ad hoc, postmodern situation that has something in it to

the purposes that he will bring to a triumphant conclusion." See also Wright, "Christian," 4–5: "The fallen duplicity of man is that he simultaneously seeks after God his Maker and flees from God his Judge. Man's religions, therefore, simultaneously manifest both these human tendencies. This is what makes a simplistic verdict on other religions—whether blandly positive or wholly negative—so unsatisfactory and, indeed, unbiblical."

46. Ahdar, "Indigenous Spiritual Concerns."

47. Ahdar, "Indigenous Spiritual Concerns," 623.

48. Ahdar, "Indigenous Spiritual Concerns," 631.

offend almost everyone."[49] This is hardly the level of public support committed adherents of Māori spirituality desire, but postmodernism's presuppositions require just such a downplaying of any holistic integration of life around a spiritual center, despite claiming to respect and honor those views.

Probably the most serious challenge to a primal consciousness comes from postmodernism's emphasis on constructivism and the way it can be, and has been, used to explain, or explain away, the whole primal religious "renaissance." We shall again refer to Māori as our example. The fact of Māori cultural "reinvigoration" is undeniable; how to understand it is controversial. In late 1989, Pacific anthropologist Allan Hanson published "The Making of the Māori: Culture Invention and Its Logic."[50] His abstract begins, "'Traditional culture' is increasingly recognized to be more an invention constructed for contemporary purposes than a stable heritage handed on from the past. Anthropologists often participate in the creative process . . ." Hanson's fellow American social anthropologist, Steve Webster, analyses and explains the furore this article occasioned amongst New Zealand academics.[51] Webster sees Hanson's position as the natural flowering of modernist symbolic, meanings-based (semiological) anthropology into a fully-fledged postmodern understanding: "Hanson argues that the construction of cultures is not essentially different from the development of linguistic meanings, a process of (in Derrida's terms) 'sign-substitution in a play of signification.'"[52] Again, Webster explains: "Hanson addresses the dilemma of how anthropologists can be taken seriously if there are no clear criteria by which an account of culture can be assessed as more or less authentic, and if, furthermore, anthropologists are active participants in the 'invention' of culture." Hanson suggested that focusing on cultural authenticity in terms of a "primordial culture" or "historically fixed tradition," in Derrida's postmodern categories, was a form of "metaphysics of presence," "logocentrism," or "nostalgia." "Cultural authenticity," from this postmodern perspective, can mean no more than that bearers of the culture claim it as their heritage.[53] Webster goes on to contrast positions taken by other New Zealand academics in response to Hanson's article, distinguishing between those retaining a concrete historical and political approach

49. Ahdar, "Indigenous Spiritual Concerns," 636.

50. Hanson, "Making of the Māori," 890–902.

51. Webster, "Postmodernist Theory," 222–39.

52. Webster, "Postmodernist Theory," 229.

53. Webster, "Postmodernist Theory," 230.

and those espousing modern "meanings-based" or semiological views. For Webster the latter face the same philosophical problems as Hanson's more consistently postmodern approach.[54]

If, as a postmodern position suggests, there are no criteria for evaluating the validity of claims to have "revived" or "reinvigorated" a "traditional culture," and if pragmatic present-day political, socioeconomic, or prestige concerns motivate cultural renewal or "invention," then the so-called "renaissance" is on shaky ground indeed. Nor is this simply a Māori cultural issue. In 2003, Erich Kolig carefully documented arguments regarding the "traditional validity" of testimonial evidence used in the "construction of indigeneity" in the "women's business" aspects of the Hindmarsh Island Case involving First Nation Australians.[55] Similar Zulu cases from Southern Africa are available.[56]

Postmodernity, then, proves an ambivalent friend of the primal religious consciousness, and renewed interest in indigenous, or contextualized theologies. Postmodernity allows an attitude that recognizes the presence of other contextualized theologies, but provides no requirement to take them seriously. Feminist theologians complain of similar treatment at postmodern fora.[57] The reality of the move beyond modernity's hegemony over intellectual discussions to a more open, respectful, and welcoming public space with room for primal or alternative Pacific perspectives is a real gift for diverse societies. But the "often unacknowledged"[58] alternative metanarrative of postmodernism which threatens to become a new hegemony, leaves any primal or alternative viewpoint vulnerable in these new discussions.

54. Webster, "Postmodernist Theory," 231–34. Webster's discussion raises the probability that Christians confronting some postmodern philosophical positions may find in continuing Marxist theorists, like Webster, if not allies, then at least cobelligerents!

55. Kolig, "Legitimising Belief," 209–28. See also, Maddock, "Modern Constructions," 25–46.

56. David Chidester, "Credo Mutwa," 69–88.

57. Cf. Sprague and Zimmerman, "Overcoming Dualisms," 48–50.

58. Webster, "Postmodernist Theory," 223.

From Socioeconomic to Sociopolitical: Marxist to Postcolonial Transitions

Just five years after submitting my thesis the Berlin Wall fell—in 1989—and with it the reign of Marxist socioeconomic historiographic dominance. That accounts for my not having published my thesis in other than digital format. It needs reworking to focus on more recent postcolonial concerns rather than assuming that socioeconomic preferences would continue to shape the context into which I was speaking. We shall expand further on the kind of research methodology and inherent historiography I was addressing in the 1984 thesis, using Niel Gunson as an example, before exploring a little of what the transition to postcolonialism means for Pacific history writing.

Gunson's Socioeconomic Research Methodology

My thesis highlighted and challenged the research methodology Niel Gunson used in his socioeconomic explanation of the nineteenth-century missionary contribution to Pacific history.[59] Gunson's methodology started from his assumed socioeconomic explanatory theory, went to the mission archives, and with immaculate, precise scholarship, extracted suitable evidence supporting his thesis. By drawing widely from missionary candidate papers, reports, minutes of field meetings, and correspondence with their London headquarters, Gunson developed what I called an identikit picture of "the nineteenth-century missionary" to the Pacific. My thesis summarized Gunson's approach.

Gunson analyzed the "godly mechanic" grouping in the lower middle class, from which most nineteenth-century Pacific missionaries came.[60] He found they characteristically sought to "better oneself," achieve "respectability," and were zealous for social and religious "improvement."[61] They commonly referred to an experience of both conversion and previous frustration or trials which Gunson read as a sense of vocational failure linked with a "highly developed sense of sin and guilt."[62] Gunson explained this

59. Gunson, *Messengers of Grace*.

60. Gunson, *Messengers of Grace*, 31–32. My comments on Gunson's methodology are at Hitchen, "Training Tamate," 161–65.

61. Gunson, *Messengers of Grace*, 33–63.

62. Gunson, *Messengers of Grace*, 33–63, esp. 49, 51–52.

common experience in terms of what he called, "the doctrine of reparation, the attempt by the Calvinist missionary to atone for the past, for the period of 'hopelessness' before his conversion."[63] Missionary candidates saw their conversion experience closely linked to their sense of "call" which was "doubled" when they became convinced they were to serve overseas.[64] Gunson also linked this reparation doctrine closely to other evangelical teachings on the corrupt natural state of humans, the fear of hell, and salvation by revelation alone.[65] Gunson then went on in later chapters to show how he believed this call and the view of the sanctity of manual labor characteristic of the missionary candidate's social class were reinforced by their education, theological training, and church work before they left for overseas.[66] He also drew on his understanding of this formative background to explain the missionaries' work at their places of service.[67]

After summarizing the way Gunson extended his thesis to include later nineteenth-century missionaries in another journal article,[68] and discussing his attempts to account for the way many of these ill-prepared candidates made excellent contributions to the ethnographical understanding of those they served,[69] I summarized my evaluation of his methodology thus:

> In his writings Gunson has helpfully highlighted the importance of "the interaction of social and doctrinal forces" in missionary motivation and worldview. But his use of theological terminology does not make up for his lack of attention to the intellectual content of that theology as the missionaries understood it. His stress on the role of social class and his "doctrine of reparation" also need to be reappraised with closer attention to the ontological realities undergirding the missionary's religious experience and theology. What an historian has suggested recently as true when considering qualifications for history Professors, is perhaps also true for missionaries: "Intellectual formation is far more powerful than social or geographical origin or physical location."[70]

63. Gunson, *Messengers of Grace*, 33, 49.
64. Gunson, *Messengers of Grace*, chapter 2, "Doubly Called," 47–63.
65. Gunson, *Messengers of Grace*, 49–50.
66. Gunson, *Messengers of Grace*, chapter 3, 64–87; and chapter 4, 88–104.
67. Gunson, *Messengers of Grace*, 214.
68. Gunson, "Victorian Christianity," 183–97; Hitchen, "Training Tamate," 162.
69. Hitchen, "Training Tamate," 163–64.
70. Hitchen, "Training Tamate," 165, citing Gunson, *Messengers of Grace*, 3; and

My concern with Gunson's methodology was the way his overarching socioeconomic explanation was assumed at the beginning and confirmed by careful, selective use of the archival data. This meant reinterpreting in sociological terms the theological emphases of the missionaries' writings and preferencing the economic context of the missionary candidate to account for their missionary motivation, rather than considering any existential or ontological reality inherent in their religious experiences (like their conversion or call to mission). This reduction of theological realities to see them as merely socioeconomic motivators, suggested the need for another methodology. The identikit manufactured "missionary" was hard to find amongst actual missionaries, unless, of course, you disregarded potential contradictory evidence. My thesis examined one apparently obvious example of Gunson's thesis, James Chalmers. Son of a lower middle-class stonemason, Chalmers, through his missionary service, won acceptance in upper class circles in Britain—being lionized by them on furlough. He also influenced British Foreign Office policy to some extent. He appeared to be the perfect example of Gunson's thesis. But examination of the actual formative influences on his life indicated that his personal and communal religious experiences were considerably more significant in his formation and service than Gunson's theory, or others based on similar socioeconomic presuppositions, countenanced.[71]

A more humanly holistic methodology or historiography was necessary to uncover more than the socioeconomic factors. My thesis found that in other aspects, too, nineteenth-century missionaries' views on Pacific peoples and cultures were quite different from the conclusions the socioeconomic theories have led students of Pacific history to believe. For instance: on the use of terms like "heathen" and "savage"; on the missionaries' actual relationships with Pacific Islanders; on missionaries' interest and participation in cultural anthropological and ethnographic study; and their roles in the evangelization of the Pacific.[72] But I also have residual doubts that the move to a postcolonial historiography will go very far in correcting those inherited history-telling mythologies.

Beales, *History and Biography*, 12.

71. Another example of a thesis based on similar presuppositions to those of Gunson, and which has been similarly influential in the area about which he wrote, is the thesis by Gray, "History of Rarotonga." See my critique of Gray in Hitchen, "Understanding the Church," 2–3, 148–85, and elsewhere in text and footnotes.

72. See, e.g., Hitchen, "Training Tamate," 603–45, 664–740, 741–813; "Missiology and Anthropology," 455–78.

Issues in Postcolonial Historiography in the Pacific

The swing to a postcolonial perspective in history writing has broadened and sharpened critique of the missionary period in the Pacific, and changed the terminology, but only slightly reoriented the kinds of historiography and research methodologies Pacific history writers employ. This is not the place to compare the intellectual content or philosophical stances of postcolonial theory over against Marxist historical materialism. Suffice to say that it would appear few postcolonial writers heeded Davidson's 1966 warning in the first volume of the *Journal of Pacific History*, which we noted in our thesis methodology section: "Imperial history, when it insists on studying the history of European expansion by orienting all its material around the imperial factor, becomes, indeed, the negation of true historical scholarship."[73]

It is not yet clear just what postcolonialism means for Pacific historiography. At present it appears to mean various different things. This is not surprising when we consider the diverse kinds of colonialism experienced by different island nations. On the one hand, Tonga can boast it was never a colony of any foreign power, but it is one of the most widely Christianized nations in the world. At the other extreme, American Samoa, and French territories like French Polynesia and New Caledonia, have never gained independence from colonial control. If those are the two extremes, the nations between them are still diverse. Australian First Nation Aboriginals and New Zealand Māori, while both minorities in their own now settler-dominated countries, and both with continuing waves of new migrants, especially from other Pacific Islands, have each had different experiences of, and responses to, colonialism. Papua New Guinea, thanks in significant measure to early missionary intervention, has never had colonial settlers in significant numbers, but has a legacy from three different colonial overlords, as well as the continuing uncertainty of half of its land mass being a province of Indonesia, despite the arbitrary nature of the boundary between the two nations. Fiji's continuing struggle over how to integrate the now numerically superior descendants of migrant laborers from India, introduced to serve goals of previous colonial rulers, gives it a unique postcolonial situation. And we could go on. It is little wonder in the light of such diversity of colonial experience that postcolonial history writing takes various forms.

73. Davidson, "Problems," 8. See the fuller quote and references at n11 above.

In her introduction to *The Cambridge History of the Pacific Islands* (1997), Jocelyn Linnekin identifies two major groups deserving the label "postcolonial historians." The mainly expatriate Australian and New Zealand "'Island-oriented' revisionists" from the 1960s "offered an 'island-oriented' historiography which differentiated itself from Eurocentric imperial discourse by attempting to view events from the Islanders' point of view."[74] We should note, however, that many of these "revisionists" employed a Marxist-oriented socioeconomic historiography in their "postcolonial" writing, making uncertain just when the transition to postcolonial history began for the Pacific.

Linnekin's second group are the "Indigenous Post-colonial Historians."[75] Linnekin summarizes key issues in discussing postcolonial Pacific historiography when she notes concerning writers from Samoa (like Albert Wendt and Malama Meleisea) and Tonga (like Epeli Hau'ofa) who came to prominence from the 1960s:

> Their writings illustrate the complex relationships between different genres of historiography and the dilemmas of producing "decolonised" historical accounts. As might be expected, university-trained Island historians use the narrative format, adopt the objective authoritative voice of academic writing, and publish in English. Post-colonial indigenous historians meet all the formal criteria of Western scholarship but attempt to assert a native cultural and political point of view, particularly by critically evaluating the actions of Westerners.[76]

These issues of status in their communities, Western-imposed media and styles of writing, and subject matter deserve at least brief comment. As long as Pacific history writing comes from elitist, university-trained writers it is likely, as in all cultures, to be prone to losing touch with grassroots cultural concerns, or, as Forman notes, to tend to address urban and cosmopolitan rather than village-oriented issues. Given the increasing gap between those worlds this may become an increasing concern. Since that gap also often coincides with a generation gap, the Pacific perhaps needs something like the late Kwame Bediako's Ghanaian project at his Akrofi-Kristaller Institute, which combined with a fully accredited tertiary theological education program, another program which gathered older, often

74. Linnekin, "Contending Approaches," 24–25.

75. Linnekin, "Contending Approaches, 26–28.

76. Linnekin, "Contending Approaches," 27.

only oral-fluent men and women, and recorded their memories, insights, and wisdom as ongoing resources for history writing and theological reflection. Wendt took a step in this direction in the Pacific by using "folk history" narrative sources from his elders in his doctoral work. To assume established Western educational requirements and writing protocols are the only appropriate pathway to readiness as Pacific history writers is neocolonialist indeed.[77]

Moreover, the Pacific scene has already highlighted that the formal Western academic writing genres are restrictive for Pacific historians. Following the lead and encouragement of Wendt and Epeli Hau-ofa, several better-known Pacific writers have either turned to or combined writing of novels to address historical themes. Michelle Keown focuses on several in this category in her *Postcolonial Pacific Writing: Representations of the Body*;[78] the treatment of historic colonially related themes by novelists Witi Ihimaera[79] and Alan Duff[80] have also gone the further step and been reproduced as internationally acclaimed films.

When our Laidlaw College Māori Rūnanga/Council designed our indigenous theology track within a Diploma for Graduates program the first distinctly new course was one on mōteatea, the Māori language sayings, chants, proverbs, waiata/songs, and karakia/prayers, or even haka, which arose from specific historical incidents or events and have been used traditionally at life cycle occasions to convey insight and guidance across the generations. As distinctly Māori media for historical communication, these were seen by the rūnanga as essential aspects of indigenous learning which were not being covered in our Pākehā curriculum. The second new course was on Māori wairuatanga/spirituality which specifically addressed the need for a holistic worldview approach to all learning, including theology and history, and which embraces the spiritual and material in an integrated

77. Hence my plea at the WCC sponsored Edinburgh 2010 Conference for better international standards to recognize these cultural differences. See Hitchen, "Theological Education," 240–48, esp. 247.

78. Keown, *Postcolonial Pacific Writing*. Keown discusses this issue in her introduction, before devoting a chapter to each of the following: Albert Wendt and Sia Figiel from Samoa; Epeli Hau'ofa from Tonga; Alistair Te Ariki Campbell from the Cook Islands; and each of the four Māori, Keri Hulme, Witi Ihimaera, Patricia Grace, and Alan Duff.

79. Ihimaera, *Whale Rider*, was adapted for film by screenwriter and producer, Nicki Caro, in 2003.

80. Duff, *Once Were Warriors*, was produced in a film version in 1994, directed by Lee Tamahori.

cosmological framework. In this course whakapapa/genealogy was seen as one of the integrative tools for such a cosmology. From Melanesia, Bernard Narakobi used what Papua New Guineans call *Tok Bokis* or allegorical, parable-like language in his richly emotive contribution, "Christianity and Melanesian Cosmos: The Broken Pearls and a Newborn Shell," for the essay collection, *The Gospel is Not Western: Black Theologies from the Southwest Pacific*.[81] Narokobi's layers of meaning and rich allusions to his cultural heritage carry a depth objective narrative could not attain. But it needed a Melanesian mind to utilize such genre.

That leaves us with Linniken's third issue: the content or topics for indigenous postcolonial history writing. The concentration on anti-colonial critique, and the quest for regional (in Hau'ofa's case) or national identity, have been understandably something of a preoccupation to this point. Linnekin noted Meleisea's acknowledgment that "indigenous scholars face the difficulty of defining a point of view that is distinct not only from Eurocentric colonial scholarship but also from sympathetic liberal revisionism."[82] Perhaps our Kiwi pragmatism partially explains the valuable methodological work of Linda Tuhiwai Smith, *Decolonizing Methodologies: Research and Indigenous Peoples*, in which she pleads for, and explains how to achieve cross-cultural sensitivity and respect when nonindigenous writers address indigenous topics.[83] There is a host of historic Pacific topics awaiting fresh attention from Pacific writers and there do not yet appear to be strong centers, movements, or personalities directing the choices of subjects to address.

The diverse colonial experience we have referred to may account for comparatively less evidence of approaches to date which adopt the deconstructive hermeneutics of Foucault or the Comaroffs or Said and this school of ideological or doctrinaire "postcolonialist" writing. But as one example of such works currently circulating in Melanesia, we should refer to Wayne Fife, "Creating the Moral Body: Missionaries and the Technology of Power in Early Papua New Guinea."[84] Comparing his historiographical approach with that of Gunson clarifies the direction the transition from socioeconomic to postcolonial writing is taking. Fife explains his thesis in his preamble:

81. Narakobi, "Melanesian Cosmos," 32–37.

82. Linnekin, "Contending Approaches," 29.

83. Smith, *Decolonizing Methodologies*.

84. Fife, "Creating the Moral Body," 251–69.

> Education by missionaries became, in an interpretation paralleling the theories of Michel Foucault, technologies of power for imposing particular forms of social discipline upon individuals so they might want to become part of the institutional relationships that favoured Christianity and colonialism at the expense of local forms of life. These technologies of power were established during the early stages of missionary education.[85]

After a one-sentence summary of the coming to New Guinea of the first London Missionary Society party of two European and nine "native teachers from the Loyalty Islands in 1871," Fife quotes one of the Europeans, A. W. Murray, to give the goal of this mission as the "overthrow of the reign of darkness throughout New Guinea and the almost numberless islands that skirt its shores, and the establishment in its room of the kingdom of light and life." Without any discussion of what Murray may have meant by such a theological statement, laden as it is with biblical allusions, Fife claims in the next paragraph, that the LMS coming to Papua New Guinea is "an excellent example of the beginning of what Foucault refers to as a 'disciplinary society': i.e., the imposition of discipline over individuals soon becomes part of the continual recreation of institutionalizing social bodies or 'technologies of power.'" Fife locates his essay firmly in the international postcolonial hermeneutical school referencing key leaders in the movement. He then reiterates his intention to "examine the kinds of discipline that were brought to bear" by the LMS on those they worked amongst in the first fifty years to find "what they reveal about the give and take of colonizing that shaped the personhood of those who lived in [Papua's] various villages."[86]

So, methodologically Fife has chosen a postcolonial theory as his framework, identified one key concept—discipline as a "technology of power"—which sustains the framework, and declared his intention to use the LMS in a quite ahistorical manner to demonstrate the validity of the theory. He is fully assured his theory is a better interpretation of the situation than whatever the missionaries may have thought they were doing. He has already assumed the LMS was basically a colonizing agency, and has introduced key concepts to support the theory, such as "that colonization tends to bring with it pressures for a new kind of person; one that will be amenable to the modernizing forms of discipline required for life within a

85. Fife, "Creating the Moral Body," 251.

86. Fife, "Creating the Moral Body, 251–52.

very different social milieu than the kind that previously existed." Fife next takes up a comment from anthropologist and theologian, Anthony Giddens, that to form Foucault's "political anatomy" of the new social bodies colonization creates, often requires places of "enclosure" or "confinement."[87]

Having prepared his theoretical tools, all borrowed from Western philosophers with no reference to the PNG setting, Fife then begins to fit aspects of the LMS historical developments into that framework. The development of a basic lesson sheet for the Polynesian teachers to use as a tool for literacy teaching is the first key step, for it confirms the hierarchy of control from the Western missionary at the top and ensures the Polynesian teachers' methods are standardized, making such control easier. That was a first "Pioneering the Form" step towards schools which would play "a dominating role in the evangelization of the villages."[88] Although the contacts with local people were unstructured at first, the second stage of "Developing the Form" involved building separate school and church buildings on each station, and pressuring the young to attend school regularly, to shape their moral formation, and insist on regular church attendance. The schools and churches were, like the missionaries' residences, enclosed in fences which became in Fife's schema, sites for the "enclosure" Giddens spoke of as a "technology of power" to shape the younger generation into the new person the colonial pattern expected.[89] The fact that untethered pigs worked devastation on unfenced gardens and buildings made from edible palm materials, and that the fencing of mission properties usually followed the local village custom of fencing gardens to protect them from marauding pigs, had either escaped Fife's consideration or such practical actions were transposed into symbols of a deeper social engineering intention, as the theory suggested. Each new development—parental resistance to school attendance; incidents of Polynesian teachers' strict enforcement of rules; training and appointing Papuans as teachers to take over from Polynesian teachers; the balance of subjects in the school curriculum; school examinations; missionary reports of teachers' wives taking leadership initiatives in their villages; development of money-earning plantations to support mission stations; the more commercially oriented introduction of "industrial mission" program and training in trades; the filling in of malaria-proliferating swamps; and even expressions of concern about the

87. Fife, "Creating the Moral Body, 251–52.

88. Fife, "Creating the Moral Body," 253.

89. Fife, "Creating the Moral Body," 255.

personal hygiene of school children or villagers; as well as whatever the missionaries had in mind when they referred to evangelism or teaching the gospel—was explained or interpreted by Fife as further evidence of "technologies of power" enclosing Papua New Guineans with a view to shaping them into the new moral "colonial bodies" Fife's theory demanded.[90]

Fife is either unaware of, or chooses not to consider, major source material on the missionaries' expressed views against colonial settlement, with pleas in the Brisbane Press to use the open spaces of the Queensland outback for settlements rather than seek to colonize Papua New Guinea;[91] or papers like James Chalmers's before the Colonial Institute, presented while on furlough in England, warning against "Anglicizing" Papuans, and calling on the British Government, after annexation had already happened, to ensure they kept "New Guinea for the New Guineans, and New Guineans for New Guinea"; [92] or the missionaries' pleas not to repeat the mistakes made in New Zealand, but, "for once in [Britain's] history," to rule New Guinea "for right and righteousness, in justice and mercy, and not for self and pelf in unrighteousness, blood and falsehood";[93] or their letters, jointly with explorers, to British parliamentarians seeking to ensure that "the rights of the natives to their soil, as well as their right to various reefs on the coast, which have belonged to them from all past time down to the present, will be fully respected and that they may not be alienated from them."[94]

Our concern with Fife's approach is that he assumes throughout that Westerners have the right to impose their philosophical structures and systems onto Papuans and Papuan history with no regard for the way the Papua New Guineans and those working directly with them explained what they were doing. Fife's assumption appears to be that Western philosophy is not only superior, but that it has no need to interact with Papua New Guineans and their history in any other way than as an object of Western analysis in the cause of Western hypothesizing. If Fife's postcolonialism is the kind of historiography we should expect as the preferred pattern for the future, then one wonders whether history has become a new form of

90. Fife, "Creating the Moral Body," 254–67.

91. E.g., Chalmers, "Our Own Correspondent"; "Pretended Land Sale." See also Langmore, *Tamate*; Hitchen, "Training Tamate," 76, 775–91.

92. Chalmers, "Past, Present, and Future," 105–6; Hitchen, "Training Tamate," 776.

93. Chalmers, *Adventures*, 16–17.

94. *British Parliamentary Papers* 1884, 5–6; Hitchen, "Training Tamate," 779–80.

imaginative speculation or "academic neo-colonialism" with no basis for evaluation or critique, since there appears to be no basis on which one can challenge its hermeneutical and deconstructive freedoms.

Looking Forward: Signs of the New, More of the Old

As we conclude the first quarter of the twenty-first century, the historiography and anthropology scenes for the Pacific hold promise of new possibilities, but also signs that even in the new directions, old assumptions may yet hold sway. There are indications of change amongst Pacific history, anthropology, and mission writers, particularly if New Zealand and Australian contributions are good indicators.

The Role of Women in Mission History

Cathy Ross has significantly forwarded the as yet largely untouched task of presenting the Pacific mission story as seen through a woman's eyes, with her *Women with a Mission: Rediscovering Missionary Wives in Early New Zealand*.[95] Ross tells the stories of Charlotte Brown, Elizabeth Colenso, Kate Hadfield, and Anne Wilson, all Anglican CMS missionary wives who worked amongst nineteenth-century Māori.[96] The mainstream publisher, Penguin, was quick to publish such material—at least when focused on establishment Anglican subjects. But we still await progress on the more difficult task of presenting the voice of the wives of the Pacific Island missionaries. Mary and Kevin Salisbury have taken an important step in this by documenting for the first time in one place, the names of Mere Banaba, Napoua, Tungāne, Batesepa, Mikaranui, and Maki, the wives of the first six Cook Islands missionaries to PNG in 1872.[97]

Another aspect of women contributing to global mission will come into focus when someone documents the stories of such nineteenth-century British families and their descendants as the Hitchcocks. Three Hitchcock daughters became wives of LMS missionaries: Sara married Aaron Buzacott of Rarotonga in 1827; Jane married Charles Hardie of Samoa in

95. Ross, *Women with a Mission*.

96. And again, Ross and Walls, "Mission," 185–87.

97. The (first) wives respectively of Rau, Anederea, Ruātoka, Henere, Adamu, and Piri. See Salisbury and Salisbury, "Manuscript XXXVIII," 2–4.

1834 or 1835; and Charlotte married James Sewell of Bangalore, India, in 1838. Combining their times in each field, the three sisters gave a hundred years to serving the LMS.[98]

Jocelyn Murray links the role of single sisters sent to help their widowed missionary brothers to the much wider fundamental, but still little studied, missionary involvement of single women more generally, highlighting another untapped field for fruitful missionary research.[99] But again, even in the global Anglophone scene, Anglican women are among the first to receive special attention. So there is still plenty of room for further evangelical analysis of the work of single women in the new era of missionary study opening before us.

A New Era for Evangelical Missional Evaluation in the Pacific

The end of World War II heralded a new beginning for missionary service in the Pacific. The coastal tribespeople of Papua New Guinea, the Solomon Islands, and other Pacific theaters of war had experienced previously unimagined disruption to their established ways of life. They watched as an apparently endless supply of material goods, mechanized equipment, weaponry, machinery, medicines, communications equipment, fuel, food, bedding, and vehicles on land, sea, and air which to the local people were of immense power and mysterious origin, were in several situations buried, or driven into the sea when the fighting moved back towards Japan.

98. See Sibree, *Register*, numbers 261, 332, and 366. In 1853, a fourth sister, Helen, married one of their brother George's employees in the family drapery business, Hitchcock and Rogers. This employee, George Williams, in 1844 had founded the first YMCA which met in the Hitchcock and Rogers employees' quarters. George Williams became a partner in the firm (and its owner on Hitchcock's death), and George Hitchcock became Williams's close friend, supporter, and mentor. Hitchcock also became a mentoring friend to Gordon Forlong, Scots evangelist and 1859 revivalist, who later worked extensively in New Zealand. Forlong's son, Houlton Forlong, served as a missionary trader on Tanna, Vanuatu, from 1894 until his untimely death there in 1908; Gordon Forlong's great-grandson, Howard Forlong, became a missionary educationalist in PNG, 1967–1980; and another of Gordon's great-granddaughters, Ruth (Mulholland), served in PNG, 1962–1984. See Hitchen, "Training Tamate," 11n51; Liddle, *Into the Heart*, 330, 390, 420; Binfield, *George Williams*. I am unsure of any spiritual significance in the fact that George and Helen Williams would also become the great-great-great-grandparents of one-time British Prime Minister, Boris Johnson! See Gimson, *Boris*.

99. Murray, "Role of Women," 66–90.

Highlanders, isolated from the theaters of war, saw aircraft of unknown purpose, and occasional patrols of soldiers sufficient to cause alarm and stir the imagination, moving in and out through their areas, but without substantial or intelligible explanation. The garbled reports filtering along jungle tracks raised questions and fuelled explanations with little basis in reality, only to be reinforced or rejected as more adequate versions were pieced together. Meanwhile, many Australian, New Zealand, and North American servicemen and women returned to their homelands with a new concern about the spiritual needs and future of those in whose countries they had served.

This soon led to a new wave of mainline church, and mainly evangelical Protestant missionary society representatives, coming into the Madang, Sepik, and Highland provinces of PNG in the 1950s, poised to enter other provinces as they were derestricted by the Australian Administration from the late 1940s and into the 1950s. The warm acceptance of Christianity in many of these areas, with significant mass movements of tribespeople adopting Christianity, called for a strong emphasis on literacy and education by virtually all this new wave of missionaries. By the mid-1960s the major church groups were developing their own secondary- and tertiary-level Bible and theological colleges: the Lutherans' Martin Luther Seminary at Lae; the United Church's Rarongo Theological College at Rabaul; the Evangelical Alliance's Christian Leaders' Training College at Banz; the Catholic's Bomana Theological College near Port Moresby; and likewise, the Seventh Day Adventist's Sonoma College. With several of these now delivering primary degree and master's level programs, together with the Pacific Theological College in Suva serving the wider Eastern Pacific, we have in the last decade or so seen the first graduates at master's level contributing Melanesian voices and perspectives to Pacific Studies.[100]

The Anthropology of Christianity

Changes in anthropological study since anthropology became a recognized academic subject in the late nineteenth century are a good test case for evaluating methodologies and social science approaches to academic study

100. As examples of recent research from CLTC students/staff, see Daimoi, "Exploratory Missiological Study"; Yandit, "Ownership and Support"; Mani, "Marital Violence"; Mombi, "Christ, Salvation, and Eschatology."

of Pacific peoples up to the present. As I have traced elsewhere,[101] much of the drive to study, gather, and publish information on other non-European societies which gathered momentum from the 1840s to 1860s, and provided much of the database for academic study of anthropology in the last four decades of the nineteenth century, came from Christian missionaries. Missionaries of that early period,

> . . . approached their interest in other cultures as part of their obedience to their biblical call to missionary work. Their training in Catechism and Scriptures had taught them to believe in God as the Lord of all races of humanity and as controller of history. As such, God used the religious beliefs of non-Christian peoples to prepare for the coming of the good news of Jesus Christ . . . these missionaries had been taught to look for evidences of the preparatory work of the Holy Spirit within the worldview of the "heathens". . . . This biblical "anthropology" required that they observe, note, and ponder the folkways of the people they served.[102]

Much nineteenth-century anthropology thus gave a proper place to Christianity, to missionary work, and to some extent, even to Jesus Christ himself. Through to around 1910, many missionaries published papers in the leading anthropological journals of those days.[103] But, we also show that, at the same time, from some of the earliest meetings of the [British] Anthropological Institute, the "Efforts of Missionaries among Savages" (as one 1865 Paper was entitled) came under "scurrilous but bitter attack."[104] Influential leaders in anthropological study like Edward Burnett Tylor and John Lubbock (Lord Avebury), by 1870 were espousing what they claimed was a "presupposition-less" ethnography—while failing to acknowledge their own dependence on "the philosophical presuppositions of thinkers such as Auguste Comte," the French philosopher.[105] From that point through the 1900s, secular views increasingly characterized the study of cultural anthropology, with few exceptions. In recent years we have seen further twists, calling for even more discernment.

101. See Hitchen, "Missiology and Anthropology," 455–78.

102. Hitchen, "Missiology and Anthropology, 462.

103. See the lists appended to Hitchen, "Missiology and Anthropology," 470–73.

104. Hitchen, "Missiology and Anthropology; see also *Anthropological Review*, 286.

105. Hitchen, "Missiology and Anthropology," 463; Tylor, "Preface"; Lubbock, *Origin of Civilisation*; and a Christian response at the time, from the 8th Duke of Argyll, George Douglas Campbell, in a series of articles in *Good Word* magazine and published in book form as Campbell, *Primeval Man*.

We are glad that Western anthropologists contributing to the discussion in this new stream of anthropology called "Anthropology of Christianity" are taking seriously the way many indigenous cultures today have integrated strong Christian commitments into their present-day community worldviews. These anthropologists recognize that you cannot study such cultures with integrity, unless you give attention to their Christian beliefs and behaviors. Thus, from many academic sources we have a new wave of careful ethnographic studies of indigenous cultures that are deeply Christian. For instance, from Melanesia, the area I know best, a good example is Joel Robbins's study of the Urapmin people of the Sandaun Province of PNG, *Becoming Sinners: Christianity and Moral Torment in a Papua New Guinea Society*.[106] In this study, Robbins describes and analyzes Christianity among the Urapmin in strictly Western anthropological terms and categories.[107] He particularly focuses on the Urapmin Christian concern about sin, and what he understands as the rituals used to handle it, presenting Christian ethics and practices as "rituals of redemption," or what Michel Foucault calls "technologies of the self."[108]

By relabelling Christian behavioral practices in these anthropological terms, instead of seeing them as thankful responses to the Triune God's loving actions bringing humans into a personal relationship with himself, Robbins is able to make very little reference to Jesus Christ (apart from his return as part of millennial thinking),[109] and to give no attention to the meaning of Christ's death and resurrection, or to other key aspects of the Christian gospel, like mercy, grace, and forgiveness. Although the book offers in-depth analysis of the awareness and response to sinfulness, it makes little, if any, reference to the moral and ethical centrality of love for others as evidence of experience of the forgiveness of sin. That key themes

106. Robbins, *Becoming Sinners*. For examples of other writings on Melanesia from an anthropology of Christianity perspective, see Barker, "Mission Station," 173–96; Burt, *Tradition and Christianity*; Douglas, "Appropriation of God," 57–92; MacDonald, "Christianity and Culture Change."

107. In his prologue, Robbins, *Becoming Sinners*, analyses the causes of lethargy in church and community life in, to him "abundantly clear," strictly Western socioeconomic terms (xxiv–xxvii), before, in the introduction, offering a methodology for understanding the situation in terms of anthropologist Marshall Strahlin's three models of cultural change: assimilation, transformation, and what Robbins calls adoption (6–11). Throughout the book, Robbins presents his material on the Urapmin church and people to fit these three models.

108. See particularly, Robbins, *Becoming Sinners*, 231–32.

109. See, for example, Robbins, *Becoming Sinners*, 343n12.

and a much fuller gospel understanding was known at Urapmin is certain when two of the main players in Robbin's story, Antalap and Diyos, are acknowledged as CLTC graduates (they were students in 1970–72).[110] Robbins shows no awareness of the content or emphases of Antalap and Diyos's CLTC study, although he refers to its foundational influence in their ministries. They were both informants for Robbins when he analyzed the revival patterns that have become central in the Urapmin church.[111] Thus, at least in the case of Robbins's Urapmin study, we have in the "Anthropology of Christianity" a reductionist and legalistic version of Christianity explained in Western anthropological terms, but missing any serious interaction with the PNG understanding and experience of redemption and new life offered by Jesus Christ, and represented in the biblical texts.[112]

Embracing a Holistic Cosmology

In search of a better basis for moving forward which will allow Pacific historians to more readily bring their contribution to the global quest for an adequate historiography, I return to the final point in my 1984 thesis methodology section where I referred to the way "the Christian scriptures also emphasise the influence of the 'powers' in the Christian world mission," and that in our methodology we sought "to do justice to . . . theological insights regarding the dignity of personality and community, and human relationships with non-personal powers."[113] In *Patterns of History*, Bebbington suggested that a fresh articulation of a full-orbed biblical "anthropology" could resolve the tensions between the positivist and idealist approaches to history writing.[114] That was the then major concern in Western historiography and addressed my concerns about respecting the dignity of human

110. Robbins, *Becoming Sinners*, 105–10, 115, 117–18, 126, 152 (for Antalap), 125–30, 340–41nn2–6 (for Diyos). Other CLTC graduates are also mentioned in passing: Antalap's brother Pais (118); Josi Bungsep (128); and Semis (Yemis) (152).

111. Robbins, *Becoming Sinners*, 132: "One new kind of knowledge the pastors could draw on to formulate and authorize their interpretations of revival was that which they gained from reading the Bible and textbooks about the Holy Spirit they had used at school." Note the Tok Pisin and English versions of the book written by CLTC staff, *Yu Ken Save Long Wok Bilong Holi Spirit.*

112. This, I suggest, is a present-day example of what Paul refers to as a philosophy based on human traditions, rather than on Christ (Col 2:8). See chapter 8 above.

113. Hitchen, "Training Tamate," 176.

114. Bebbington, *Patterns in History*, esp. 139–43, 159–61.

personality and community. But today the challenge is to bridge the gap between the Western and Pacific perceptions of "human relationships with non-personal powers."[115]

Referring to the second quite new course our Laidlaw College Māori Rūnanga developed for the graduate diploma program, I explained above that it focused on wairuatanga/spirituality and specifically addressed the need for a holistic worldview approach to all learning, including theology and history, and which embraces the spiritual and material in an integrated cosmological framework. Western rationalism leaves no place for serious consideration of the realm of spirit powers influencing human activity, or communicating through dreams, experience of sorcery and witchcraft, or spirit possession, let alone angelic presence, protection, or guidance. All these are bracketed out as unacceptable source data for historical investigation. But they are essential realities in Polynesian and Melanesian daily experience, and create an artificial sense of reality if they cannot be discussed according to the ruling protocols of academic study. But, just as Bebbington showed a more fully expressed biblical understanding of humanity offered a bridge to bring together with mutual respect the valid insights of both positivist and idealist, I am suggesting we need a better articulated biblically holistic cosmology, with appropriately developed epistemology and methodology built up from that holistic cosmology. Such a methodology could open the way for historians from other than Western backgrounds to contribute more wholeheartedly to the history enterprise. The new articulation will need to move from the cosmological worldview aspects to include the role of the Spirit and spirituality in the practical daily realities of Melanesian life. This will mean addressing desires for healthy births, productive crops, adequate family income, and attending to this-worldly concerns about sickness, broken interpersonal relations, fear of malevolent powers, job-finding, handling loss and failure, and finding joy and satisfaction at the daily family living level—what Papua New Guineans call *gutpela sindaun*.

In other words, it will mean heeding American anthropologist/missiologist, the late Paul Hiebert's warning that Western missionaries and Christian thinkers are prone to "the flaw of the excluded middle."[116] Hiebert reminded us that Westerners are strong on doctrines and discussion on human origins and eschatological issues, but are not so strong on

115. Hitchen, "Training Tamate," 176.

116. Hiebert, "Flaw," 189–201.

how our gospel relates to the "middle": the practical pressures of daily life just enumerated. Theologically we are strong on creation, on redemption's past and future applications, and on the Christian's future hope, but not so sure about the implications of the ascension, and present reign, and current work of Christ at the right hand of God. Such a new, full orbed, biblically robust cosmology that takes account of the "middle" seems to be essential in the face of the historical reductionism which currently threatens to dominate Western approaches to Pacific history writing.

Conclusion

In a 1995 address to the American Society for Missiologists, Mark Noll noted the historiographic problems historians were then facing with differing opinions over what he described as the premodern or ideological, the modern or scientific, and the postmodern or deconstructive approaches to historical method. He then outlined the way missiologists might contribute their specific insights about working in multiple diverse cultural settings as a way forward for historiography. He concluded with these words:

> It is, I realize, a mind-defying task that I want to assign to missiologists. But because they are already leading the rest of us Christian historians geographically beyond outright preoccupations with Europe and North America, and because they have already begun to show the rest of us how the history of Christianity can encompass the most diverse of particular cultural expressions, I have a great hope that they may also show the way in historical method. That hope, of course, does not rest ultimately in them, but in the fact that they so intensely study, and study from so many cultural angles, allegiance to the one who for us and for our salvation came down and was incarnated, made man, suffered, and arose on the third day, ascended into heaven, and who comes to judge the living and the dead.[117]

I am not quite so sure about missiologists' competence for the task Noll assigns, but I dare to believe that the *kairos* we face in contemporary historiography offers a missional challenge to Christian historians, anthropologists, and missiologists to work together towards a Christ-honoring resolution of the current tensions in the reductionist, deconstructive milieu of the social science sector, since both history and cultural anthropology

117. Noll, "Challenges," 62.

are integrally linked with our Christian faith. Perhaps this interchange may in some small way contribute towards grasping the challenge in the *kairos*.

Section 4

Contextualization in Context

Chapter 14

Clarifying and Confirming Convictions

Theological education has been my life's ministry. The years have brought memorable moments and periods with significant decision points. Many created precious family or personal memories stored in the mind and only recalled for an old man's reminiscing. But some led to written contributions dealing with the pressing issues of the day, while others were shaped with colleagues into policy statements for the colleges at which I served. This chapter explains the background and records a few of these moments, in roughly chronological order. As they fade into the passing times and seasons they are only brought into the light again to highlight ways my convictions were shaped, and to help clarify possible ways forward today, by remembering the factors and reasoning which took us down certain paths in our past. We did not get it right every time. But insights from those hours might be instructive for ongoing comparison and wisdom-building. At the very least, to record what I thought I was doing at the time may help present-day and future critics to understand a little more of the context of the times—and perhaps make their critiques more gentle!

Readers will appreciate that many other people were involved in the following instances, and I am indebted as always to their contributions, but as the responsible person I own my accountability and no other persons or colleges should be implicated in my views recorded here.

Involvement in Interdenominational Service: 1965

An early decision came into focus in my wife Ann's and my first few months at the Christian Leaders' Training College (CLTC) of Papua New Guinea from January 1965, the new college's first year of teaching. I had been appointed as the first Bible teacher under Rev. Gil MacArthur, the principal. CLTC was commencing as the English language, higher-level, interdenominational, Bible college serving all the evangelical missions and churches at work in the post-World War II surge of mission in PNG.[1] I had been appointed with the normal arrangements for the college to pay a monthly salary. But, as soon as we arrived at the college we were contacted by our fellow Christian Brethren missionaries who had been sent out from our group of home churches and worked under the internationally recognized mission name of Christian Missions in Many Lands. They made a clear proposal:

> Join us as Brethren "commended missionaries." We want you to be listed like us on the New Zealand Brethren missionary lists as fellow team members seconded to this interdenominational Bible teaching ministry at CLTC. That will show clearly that we Brethren missionaries have committed to share in developing CLTC, and that we will send our students to CLTC for Bible training. We regard you as an integral part of our work here in PNG, and want you to be known as part of our team. There is only one requirement. You cannot receive a monthly salary from the College. You will have to serve without any guaranteed salary, just trusting the Lord to provide your needs in answer to your prayer and faith, as all Brethren missionaries do.

Five years earlier I had joined the Brethren Church on conscientious grounds because of my evangelical convictions. I then had quite a tussle to be called to consider CLTC, to serve all the evangelical churches in PNG, not just the Brethren churches. A careful study of the beginnings of the Brethren movement had convinced me it would be inconsistent not to serve all other evangelicals, since the Brethren movement had come into being in part to welcome as fellow members of the body of Christ all who believed in Jesus Christ, without requiring them first to also become a member of a particular denomination. So, I was already clear that serving at CLTC did

1. For a survey of the development of the CLTC curriculum, see Hitchen, "Evangelicals Equipping," 110–36. For the CLTC history, see Price, *Live in Tents*; and Yandit, "Ownership and Support."

not contradict any basic Brethren beliefs. But I had simply assumed we would have to adopt the college's support system, and therefore could not be listed on the New Zealand Brethren lists, because at that time those lists only included missionaries serving Brethren churches. I had never thought our fellow missionaries would want us to identify so fully with them in the CLTC work, but was excited about the possibility. Ann and I replied that we were keen to make this change and started with proposals to the CLTC Governing Committee—then made up primarily of members of the Board of the Melbourne Bible Institute who had sponsored CLTC—and with our home church. The CLTC Committee were surprisingly keen to have another group sharing our support load and ceased the salary forthwith. Our home church gladly confirmed their official "commendation" of us to the work at CLTC.

But the directors of the New Zealand Missionary Funds organization in New Zealand, who authorized the names on the New Zealand Brethren prayer lists, could see problems. Particularly, the problem that at that time all who were included on the New Zealand prayer lists were also listed automatically on the "Echoes of Service" lists put out by the British Christian Brethren organization based in England. They would have to agree to list someone working in an interdenominational institution. But such Echoes of Service endorsement was not forthcoming. Echoes advised our missionaries in PNG that if the Hitchens went onto a New Zealand prayer list while working at an interdenominational college, then all New Zealand missionaries would be removed from the Echoes of Service lists in Britain. That would almost certainly cut off the limited, but important, support that New Zealand missionaries in PNG received from Britain. It seemed that would be the end of it. But, to our surprise, our fellow Brethren missionaries in PNG told New Zealand Missionary Funds they would rather be taken off the British lists than exclude the Hitchens from their New Zealand team list. And that is what happened.

From 1965 we enjoyed twenty years of support from New Zealand Christian Brethren churches for all our time in Papua New Guinea and on study leave in Britain. But it was at the cost of New Zealanders being removed from the British lists. We have continued to enjoy working and serving with these same churches since being back in New Zealand from 1985 to 2021, while also closely involved with the Bible College of New Zealand/Laidlaw College. We also gladly received a welcome at the Echoes of Service headquarters when on study leave in Britain from 1979 to 1984, and have been stimulated by attendance at International Brethren Training Network conferences in the 2000s, where several of the essays in this volume were first presented. We kept records of monies received for support all those years in PNG, and testify that we received within NZ$20 each year of the amount we would have received had we been on the CLTC salary—never more, and never less. We are glad our God is both bigger, and more dependable than any support system we may humanly devise, and in our experience he is happy to work through a range of such systems.

After ten years lecturing across a range of biblical subjects and coordinating CLTC's various programs as academic dean, in late 1974 I was appointed principal of the college. In the next five years we sought to ensure our senior teaching staff had opportunity to upgrade their academic qualifications with overseas study opportunities. I had all but given up on any hope of having such an opportunity myself, until, quite unexpectedly the college's auditor, Heaton Drake, came into my office one day and announced, "John, I want you to know there are fees and fares available for you to do postgraduate study wherever you think would be best, anywhere in the world." Thus, as I explain in another chapter in this volume,[2] the door opened for our family to go to the University of Aberdeen in Scotland, to study under Andrew Walls, leading British missiologist, eventually completing a PhD in religious studies.[3]

Doctoral Study with Other Involvements: 1979–1984

Our years at the University of Aberdeen, 1979–1984, were a thoroughly satisfying academic journey. I enrolled initially in the MTh program, until by writing a major paper on Dreams in Melanesia,[4] I demonstrated competence to qualify as a PhD candidate. As well as researching and writing my doctoral thesis itself, I appreciated sharing with and encouraging fellow overseas students in their research. As students we organized a regular Religious Studies Department seminar to update on our research progress and hear visiting speakers. I particularly enjoyed working with my supervisor, Andrew F. Walls, and encouraging him to make readily accessible more of his wealth of knowledge. Academically, it was a very formative experience.

2. See below in chapter 17.

3. Hitchen, "Training Tamate," available at the Pacific Manuscripts Bureau (PMB) MS 1351.

4. Eventually published as Hitchen, "Dreams in Traditional Thought."

As a family we became involved in the local Aberdeen Christian Brethren churches, at Assembly Hall till its closure, then at Hebron Chapel. Preaching opportunities, leading a Bible class for teenagers, and a "Teach the Word" course, run as a six-month weekly mini-Bible school for eighteen keen young people, were highlights. Stimulating church involvement kept the purpose of the academic work in focus.

But, unexpected and often demanding opportunities opened at our front door. The university arranged accommodation for us as a postgrad family. But not till we were well settled in Aberdeen did we realize that this arrangement was only for our first year. From then on we were at the mercy of the Aberdeen City Council, who managed the city's rental housing labelled from grades A to G. Legally they were only required to offer G-level housing until clients built up time-based merit points to qualify for a higher level house. Thus, we lived for nearly four years in G-level council housing. The Powis community comprised of nearly five hundred houses built at the end of the Depression as an identifiable separate community, and was known throughout the city as one of the poor and unsafe areas. The week we moved into this community, a flier dropped through our front door letterbox. Its contents influenced our remaining time in Aberdeen. It was the *Family Newsletter* put out and distributed by welfare workers in the community, offering a number of community initiatives. As time progressed, my wife Ann and I became involved in a number of these initiatives, and in so doing became involved in the life and lives of the Powis community.

After two years in the area, Andrew Walls talked us into bringing a report to the Ecumenical and Overseas Missions Committee of the "Kirk"—the Church of Scotland—in whose sphere of influence the Powis Community and its spiritual needs fell. The final section of our report follows, in which we reflect on our experience. It will allow you to judge whether or not we decided aright as we struggled with the question: How fully should theology students become involved in such a community while also doing postgraduate study?

Reflections on the Church's Mission and a Scottish Urban Subculture[5]

We have not been instrumental in establishing a new church in the area and so we are in no position to say, "Do this; it works!" We can only share some of our ongoing concerns.

How Can the Church Reach Such an Area?

In the current situation the church is noticeable only by its absence. Yet, in our experience, the people are neither antagonistic nor cynical towards the Christian message. If anything, they simply ignore it. Our experience would suggest a first step in rectifying this would be for some convinced Christians to move into the area with a view to identifying with it and becoming part of it. Having once passed the "probationary" tests and gained the first level of local acceptance then you would quickly find many opportunities for developing contacts. We have found the following opportunities all round us:

- visiting to encourage at times of bereavement
- sick visiting—both in the homes and when folk are in hospital
- crisis situations: cooking a meal where a family had a fire in their flat
- offering "open home" for youngsters and teenagers to spend an evening, or simply to pop in for a chat
- accepting some responsibility in existing community activities, for example, the children's clubs.

Further steps could no doubt develop into things like a Sunday school in the community center; a home Bible study group with interested adults or teenagers; and perhaps even a church service in the community center where informal dress and a lively liturgy (or program) suited to the interest of those attending would need quickly to be adopted.

We are frankly skeptical about approaches which focus on taking people out of the area for them to be evangelized. Although any Sunday

5. This section constitutes a lightly edited final major section of a paper presented to the Church of Scotland Ecumenical and Overseas Missions Committee, June 1982. Further details of the make-up of the Powis community, our involvements in the community, and its impact on us as a family may be read in the report.

school or church service may well need people from "outwith" the community helping, we would see it as essential to have some who belong within and are known as residents to form the core of any such work.

Implications for Our Attitude to "Ministry" and Mission

The ideal persons to initiate such a local Christian witness would be mature, working-class Christians who both love Christ and know how to speak of him and for him. If our church structures currently suggest only "ministers" should spearhead such a work then we need to revise our thinking in line with the emphasis of Eph 4:11–13, where those with specialist gifts are seen not so much as those who do the service, but as those who "service" ordinary Christians for this kind of service in such a community (John Stott's *One People* [Falcon Books] expands on these terms and concepts).

If our "gospel" assumes a person must move out of such a socioeconomic area to become or to live as consistent Christians, then I suggest we are guilty of the Galatian heresy and have added to the gospel expectations or requirements which not only do not belong to, but in fact deny, the essence of the good news of Christ. Notwithstanding the normal results of a changed value system and lifestyle when a person does turn to Christ, we must not let that confuse us about the need to distinguish between the good news and its possible economic fruits when deciding our evangelistic approach.

Implications for Theological Education

Since our missionary experience has centered on theological education, we are especially concerned about what this experience is saying about patterns of preparation for the "ministry."

In this situation we have been very conscious of the way our own missionary experience enabled us to understand and do what little we have done in the community. One wonders, therefore, whether the post-Christian situation in such areas in British cities does not indicate the need for the inclusion of "missionary" subjects in the regular training for the home ministry. In our experience here in this subculture, we have consciously been drawing upon training in aspects of our previous missionary training such as: "language learning"; cross-cultural communication; contextualization; and appreciation of alternative worldviews. I suggest the time is overdue for such matters to become a regular part of training for home ministry.

But the concern goes deeper than that. On first arriving in Aberdeen, to assist in my own postgraduate studies, I sat in on some undergraduate classes in the Divinity Faculty, alongside a class of mostly ministerial candidates for the Kirk. I was greatly excited and stimulated by the solid biblical exegesis which I found related directly to so many of the practical areas of ministry I had just left in Papua New Guinea. But I was deeply concerned to find the undergraduates in the class frankly and openly expressing plain boredom with the same, to me exciting, content. I began asking again the question we have struggled with in our theological education course structures in Papua New Guinea: Can you understand theology apart from practical involvement in pastoral and evangelistic ministry? Isn't practical responsibility for ministry essential *while* the exegesis and theology is being taught so that its meaning in life becomes evident? I was reminded of the way we have had to integrate weekly assignments in preaching, Sunday school teaching, religious education in schools, open-air services, and so forth, *into* our theology courses to make them vital—and to make the outreach spiritually effective. I thought, too, of the six-month pastoral internships now built into all our courses before the final year and graduation.

When I joined those reflections with the situation we are now living in, the exciting potential is obvious. Here in our community I have been describing—which is barely eight hundred yards from the university Divinity Faculty—there are daily opportunities to become involved in people problems, that is, truly theological problems! Could the university Lodgings Office not seek an arrangement whereby they have the use of one or two flats in this community which they can allocate for mature divinity students to live in (instead of in the artificial world of student dormitories), with specific responsibilities to become part of the local community—not just to establish a student enclave there. There are several patterns by which a situation could be integrated into the theological student's overall training.

Closely related to this is the concept of "missionary work" we are consciously and unconsciously inculcating through our theological education programs. What I have been describing in our Powis community is nothing less than a clear missionary opportunity on the doorstep of the Scottish churches which could be a most important factor in renewing and correcting the whole present attitude to mission.

In short, I find myself asking whether what to us as "incomers" appear to be the presuppositions of present patterns of theological education in Scotland do not need drastic revision. It seems to me we are assuming in present structures: that Scotland is a Christian nation; that to be Scottish means to have an accountability to the Kirk; and that, therefore, the basic role of the minister is to service the church machine. In the light of substantial subcultures which are distinctly non-Christian—such as the one we have described—surely the present situation demands distinctly missionary presuppositions to be built into our training for ministry programs and policies.

Perhaps, therefore, the Overseas Committee of the church has a prophetic role to play at this time to bring about such changes.

The Cost of the Enrichment from Our Experience

In conclusion, it is only fair to admit that it has not been easy at times to be involved as a family even in the imperfect way described.

- The local dialect and distinctive vocabulary have been hard to learn (and sometimes to accept).
- The common attitude and atmosphere haven't always been as "pure" as we may have liked for our eleven-year-old daughter. But this time has forced us to develop an ongoing dialogue with her about ethical values and attitudes which has brought us closely together as a family.
- Emotionally and physically it has been very demanding—especially on my wife—to have the open-door policy virtually all the time. Again, our daughter has at times felt deprived of parental attention—but that too has become a challenge to growth for all of us.
- Even materially we find we have to keep rethinking our attitudes to our own standards of clothing, eating, and the occasional "spoiling" of our goods cheerfully.
- I need not mention that I have had to accept that such involvement is a proper and necessary part of my study leave—for the tension between research and helping local people is very real at times—and no doubt my research timetable, if not program, has suffered at times.

But, finally, we have found the experience to be deeply enriching:

- It has corrected our misinformed views about those who live in such areas.
- It has given us rich friendships with youngsters and adults.
- It has shown us afresh the centrality of a "people concern" in Christ's life and ministry.
- It has revealed important weaknesses and challenged us to essential growth in our own family.
- It has confirmed to us the relevance of the good news of Christ for our neighbors in the community.
- It has humbled us to see how readily we have tended to assume certain material standards and "suburban" attitudes have the endorsement of Scripture when in fact Scriptures specifically warn against such.
- It has clarified important issues for our own theological education ministries back in Papua New Guinea.

And only God knows whether it has given anything of eternal value to the community itself!

Subsequently

Subsequent to the above paper being written, I completed my PhD, it was successfully examined, and we returned to New Zealand in the final months of 1984, expecting to have a brief furlough before returning to CLTC and our work in PNG. But the medical doctors in New Zealand had other ideas; they felt my wife needed to remain in New Zealand for medical reasons. I found this difficult to accept as the whole purpose of my thesis had been to equip me better for our PNG service. My home church in Christchurch offered me a position as a teaching elder, and I took up adjunct lecturing opportunities with the Christchurch Branch of the Bible College of New Zealand, until in late 1987 I was appointed Dean of the Christchurch Branch of Bible College. I had struggled with depression in those first years back in New Zealand, until some Māori friends helped me see how my thesis work could serve Māori Christians in the issues they were working through at that time. This was a major factor in our call to the National Principalship of the Bible College of New Zealand at the end of 1989.

Academic Freedom and Faith: 1990s

The decade of the 1990s was a challenging and exciting time as the advent of the New Zealand Qualifications Authority opened the door for the Bible College of New Zealand (BCNZ) to register and gain government accreditation for our courses at diploma, degree, and eventually, master's levels, and to take the first steps towards diversification into equipping students for qualifications in education and counselling.

As BCNZ applied for and gained New Zealand Qualifications Authority recognition and accreditation for its programs we found ourselves being challenged to explain and defend how the staff of an evangelical tertiary level theological college could uphold academic freedom (the recognized standard for a degree-granting institution), and at the same time be true to the college's doctrinal commitments.[6]

I do not offer my early drafts of our responses as if they are the last word on such issues; they are not. Such statements need to be updated regularly, particularly as nuances of word-meanings, and fresh practical concerns come into or go out of fashion. My thoughts as presented here were debated, edited, and reworked into policies of BCNZ before presentation to the relevant authorities. These suggest a rationale by which a college may uphold its doctrinal position within evangelical Protestantism, and at the same time encourage its teaching staff to express their academic freedom. We can summarize the position as "upholding responsible academic freedom."

Academic Freedom and the Use of a Statement of Faith[7]

The Function and Use of a Statement of Faith in a Faith-Based Bible College

The college's academic teaching staff and board members indicate that they subscribe to the college's statement of faith on their appointment. Teaching staff are required by our constitution to advise the board through the

6. This issue arose in various guises as BCNZ made program proposals to NZQA Assessment Panels in the 1990s; and again as CLTC worked toward government accreditation in PNG in the early 2000s.

7. What follows in this section is a BCNZ faculty discussion paper circulated in the mid-1990s, lightly edited.

national principal if they change their theological position and can no longer wholeheartedly endorse the statement.

The college's statement of faith defines the theological aspects of the special character of the college. It declares the theological context within which the college undertakes its overall task of equipping men and women for Christian ministry. It forms part of the understanding between the college and the churches it serves—its stakeholders—regarding the focus, values, and ethos of its programs. The statement declares openly where the college stands regarding key historic doctrines of the Christian church and indicates the theological presuppositions and spiritual ethos faculty bring to the task. A statement of faith of a Bible college fills a similar role to the confessional standards of the denominations served by other theological colleges in our nation.

Our statement of faith is not a narrow sectarian statement, but reflects the mainstream of historic evangelical Protestantism. It leaves open a range of doctrinal issues about which earnest Christians differ. The statement gives positive declarations of the truths we hold in common. It does not delineate required limitations to those beliefs. Nor does it list what its adherents are required *not* to believe. The breadth of the statement's acceptability is reflected in the breadth of denominational representation of the staff and student body of the college.

To guard against misunderstanding we place on record the following ways in which the statement of faith is *not* used in our college:

- The statement is not used to define or limit the topics presented to students in their study courses.
- We do not restrict input to students only to the views of thinkers who endorse such a statement of faith. Students have access, through the instruction of their lecturers, in library resources and from visiting speakers, to fair presentations of alternative views.
- Students are not required to endorse the statement of faith either before admission or as a condition of graduation.
- The statement of faith is not used to limit the areas of research open to teaching staff, as explained below.
- The college council is open to periodic updating of the wording of the statement of faith to more clearly reflect the doctrinal commitments we uphold as a scholarly learning community.

If the college has historically used its statement of faith in any of the ways refuted in the above, then we indicate that this is no longer the practice of the college.

Faith Statements and Academic Freedom of Teaching Staff

The nature, function, and usage of our statement of faith are not seen as incompatible with the college's commitments to open academic research nor as inimical to the academic integrity of its staff.

The College's Commitment to Being an Open Scholarly Learning Community

We reaffirm that as a degree and postgraduate teaching and award granting college, our college is committed to developing a learning community that respects and encourages open scholarship. We are committed to the ongoing quest for a better grasp of truth available in our universe and as revealed in the word of God.

Academic teaching staff are committed to the New Zealand Qualifications Authority's definitions of degree programs which are to be ". . . taught mainly by people engaged in research; and emphasise general principles and basic knowledge as the basis for self-directed work and learning (s254, The Education Act, 1989)," and which provide ". . . a systematic and coherent introduction to the knowledge, ideas, principles, concepts, chief research methods and problem-solving techniques of a recognised major subject . . ."

Likewise, we are committed, at postgraduate level, to programs which enable students ". . . to demonstrate mastery of theoretically sophisticated subject matter; to evaluate critically the findings and discussions in the literature; to research, analyse, and argue from evidence; to apply knowledge to new situations; and to engage in rigorous intellectual analysis, criticism and problem-solving."[8]

Our college gives continuing emphasis to the research activities of its teaching staff. Our academic staff's personal indication of their acceptance of the statement of faith does not restrict their openness in research, and the

8. The quotations in these paragraphs are from the NZQA definitions as in *The New Zealand Register of Quality Assured Qualifications*, June 2001.

college does not use its statement of faith to restrict such research. Rather, the college accepts responsibility to require teaching staff to be involved in ". . . activities which foster the spirit of enquiry, the concern for ideas and their application, the confidence to investigate and solve problems, and the recognition of the advancing nature of knowledge and practice." We seek to ensure that key issues and concerns being raised outside our constituency are brought to bear on our research and teaching.

Our theological stance, and the experience of our constituency lying behind it, also bring a responsibility to present the insights of our particular heritage to the wider academic world. Our theological position, recognizing the living God as the source of all truth, requires us to be open to interact with other schools of thought as both learners and interpreters on behalf of our constituency. We are concerned not only to discover and state the truth as we understand it, but also to listen to, interact with, and learn from other positions.

We recognize that a statement of faith could be used either openly or more subtly to engender a sense of research limitation amongst academic teaching staff. If we have done that in the past, then we indicate that is not our current intention or current practice.

Our Understanding of Academic Freedom Is Rooted in Our Understanding of God

There is no necessary link between holding a declared theological or philosophical position and restriction of academic freedom. Indeed, we maintain that the concept of total academic neutrality, especially in the human sciences, is an epistemological fallacy. Arguably, open-minded research is fostered more by consciously acknowledging one's preunderstandings than by the pretence that such preunderstandings do not exist.

The issue is not that teaching staff are committed to theological presuppositions, but to what kind of presuppositions are they committed? Do the presuppositions require or restrict academic freedom? In our case our presuppositions involve a commitment to the God who is truth; who entrusts both the resources of our cosmos and our intellectual ability to humans as a stewardship to be handled responsibly for his glory and the good of humanity, and the whole creation.[9] Both God himself and the

9. I expand on this claim in the later paper, Hitchen, "Confirming the Christian Scholar."

riches of his created universe are always greater and more profound than our highest thoughts or best description of them. Hence, our obligation to seek ever clearer understanding of truth and to cultivate open academic freedom amongst us as teaching staff.

If we, as a college, were to restrict the areas of permissible enquiry in God's world we would be dishonoring the extent of his lordship as we uphold it in our statement of faith. Rather than limiting academic freedom, we see this statement as placing the basis for academic freedom on the highest possible theological plane as it makes us accountable to God in our research. To remove the requirement to indicate endorsement of the statement of faith would be to put our commitment to academic integrity, and freedom, onto a lower and less academically rigorous basis. For us, the proof of academic freedom is not inherent in the signing or not signing of a statement of faith, but in the honesty, rigor, and openness with which we pursue our study and research before our Lord Jesus Christ who is himself the truth.

We welcome, and have in place, processes to assist and evaluate performance to ensure we measure up objectively to standards of academic integrity fit for serving God who calls us to discover and walk in an ever-growing knowledge of the truth.

Counselling within an Evangelical Bible College

This next section addresses whether and how to offer a counselling program in a Bible college. How far a Bible college should move into social science areas has always been contentious. Similar arguments apply to both equipping Bible college students as teachers for government or Christian schools, and to training for counselling through a Bible college. At BCNZ/Laidlaw we addressed counselling first, hence the focus of the paper below, written in 1998 when we were debating commencing a Bachelor of Counselling program following four years of interaction with Christian counselling professionals, and after an earlier unsuccessful application for accreditation for a master's level program.

Philosophical Basis for the Program[10]

This counselling program is being provided from within the Christian heritage and tradition. Thus its undergirding philosophy seeks authenticity and validity both theologically and biblically as well as psychologically and as a social science educational program.

The Christian church has a long history of involvement in serving the in-depth, holistic, mental, emotional, and spiritual well-being of humans. With the development of modern psychology and psychotherapy in the late nineteenth and twentieth centuries, the churches have, for a comparatively brief period within their long history, retreated from the forefront of intellectual debate, methodological innovation, and constructive service in the mental and emotional health fields. But the time is right for a recapturing of aspects of that heritage and for new patterns of relationship between the Christian heritage of the "cure of souls," as the task was classically termed, and the wealth of insight and growing experience of the social sciences. This counselling degree program is one example of this new rapprochement being called for from both the social science and the theological perspectives.[11] This does not mean this program is reactionary in either its philosophy or its methodology. We are committed to developing new patterns of respect for, and dependence upon, the best insights of the social sciences along with a critical reappraisal and updating of the wealth of still valid insights from the church's experience in understanding and serving humanity.

We note, therefore, the way we are using language about God. In essence God is suprahuman. Thus our human minds and language are inadequate to grasp or explain that essence fully. However, as creatures created in the image of God, and on the basis of God's self-revelation, we have confidence that human experience and language are adequate for a valid and sufficient grasp of God's being and purposes for humanity within the universe. While always more than merely human, God is never less than fully personal. We particularly note that God transcends gender distinctions. Both male and female are necessary to display the image of deity in human form. Thus human language about God, while inevitable, valid, and adequate, is always incomplete and figurative. This also means that in this

10. What follows below was written to present an in-house rationale for moving ahead with counselling programs at BCNZ, and to stimulate further faculty discussion in 1998, lightly edited.

11. See, e.g., Oden, "Recovering Pastoral Care"; Menninger, *Whatever Became of Sin?*

document when referring to God we have chosen to follow the common protocol of using masculine pronouns in a generic, gender-transcending sense.

The Sovereignty of God

We commence from a commitment to the reality of God's active rule in his universe. The living God, Father, Son, and Holy Spirit, sovereignly controls our universe. God is knowable because of his self-revelation in creation, history, and the special revelation of the Scriptures. God has declared himself as having good purposes for humanity both in the creation of our universe and in his provision for our salvation.

This primary commitment to the sovereignty of God is not a restrictive but liberating and guaranteeing foundation for the pursuit of knowledge and truth. The concept of a primary religious basis for knowledge can be, and often has been, construed as a means of restricting academic freedom, of narrowing the bounds of research and investigation, and of rejecting some lines of human enquiry without due investigation. However, none of these are necessary concomitants of a commitment to the sovereignty of the living God. It depends on the nature of the God to whom we give allegiance. The self-revelation of the God of the Christian and Hebrew Scriptures includes insights which encourage and demand the most open and persistent pursuit of all truth.

All Truth Is God's Truth

All truth, including psychological and theological truth, derives ultimately from God and is to be used for God's glory and human welfare. As creatures created in God's image, humans have both the capacity and responsibility to explore, understand, and appropriately utilize our whole world for the glory of the Creator. The pursuit of truth is understood as discovering the handiwork of God. Moreover, Jesus Christ is presented in the Gospels as the embodiment in human form of otherwise only partially appreciated aspects of universal truth. His identification with humanity, and his representative and redemptive work on our behalf were also necessary to disclose vital aspects of truth about universal meaning and purpose. Our quest for and presentation of wisdom and understanding will therefore have an added Christocentric dimension.

We are also responsible to grasp and properly utilize the global resources of knowledge and understanding for the good of our fellows. We are interdependent creatures and all truth should serve the welfare of humanity—whether discovered in the physical, social, moral, psychological, or any other sphere.

Moreover, universal truth needs to be earthed and expressed in particular contexts. While drawing on the wealth of humanity's cumulative experience in history and the traditions of the church, we need to relate the eternal verities to the fresh and distinctive issues and problems confronting humanity in our fast-changing modern world. Both from the "book" of nature and the human sciences, and from the "book" of special revelation in the Scriptures, we expect to discover fresh light relating to the contemporary predicament. God's multifaceted truth is always contextualized in particular cultures, social settings, and times. Our task in this program is to freshly relate and express its abiding and dynamic reality within our own diverse context.

The Autonomy and Interdependence of Different Fields of Enquiry

Given the diverse nature of knowledge as derived from God, each field of enquiry has its proper place and dignity. Both theological and social science study, for instance, are necessary and each is to be given its due authority. Methods of investigation, interrelationships of different parts within each field, and procedures for interpretation and explanation may well differ between fields as each adapts to the particular character of its data. The integrity and autonomy of differing areas of learning are to be respected and appreciated for the insights and complementary benefits each can offer. We eschew academic or intellectual reductionism when it restricts the way in which we approach the diversity of our real universe.

At the same time, again since all truth is God's truth, we respect the interrelatedness of all knowledge as part of a single universe. We must discover and uphold the relationships between different fields of enquiry so that each may enrich the other. We must listen and respond to the hard questions each asks of the other. We look for a theologically informed approach to psychology and a psychologically informed approach to theology.

Our commitment to the ultimate unity of all knowledge also requires us to work for a growing integration across the fields of learning. While aware of the range of ways in which "integration" can be, and has been, understood,[12] one of our concerns in establishing this program is to find useful ways of integrating theology and psychology in the field of counselling.

Self-Critical and Evaluative Enquiry

This program recognizes the need for a theological grasp, and hermeneutical methods, adequate to evaluate the presuppositional bases of psychological theories and praxis, and to articulate biblically faithful underpinnings for the methodologies and approaches utilized within the proposed program. We are concerned that no one approach to, or school of thought regarding, psychology and/or counselling can be uncritically adopted as the basis for the program. Any and all approaches must be open to the scrutiny of biblical presuppositions and teachings. Therefore, we shall not rely on the assumptions of any one school of psychological thought as a pragmatic basis for the program. Conscious of the Christian critique of the major schools of thought, we see a place for responsible eclecticism in approach and methodology.[13]

To balance this emphasis, however, we also recognize that it is impossible to teach a social science discipline without some precommitments in regard to the philosophical and methodological approach developed within the program. Thus our starting point in developing this program has given an emphasis to the integrative methodological philosophies current in present-day counselling. We would expect to self-consciously submit these approaches to the kind of self-critical and evaluative enquiry outlined in the previous paragraph.

Such an evaluative, self-critical approach also means we shall work for psychological authenticity in the theological presuppositions guiding the program. The formulation of biblical teaching and theology can all too easily be understood and applied with inadequate respect for valid psychological theory and practice. We expect the psychological insights and methods taught in the course to inform, challenge, and enrich the biblical/theological grasp of the students. The whole program should reflect the need to maintain a self-critical awareness of presuppositions (both theological

12. See Garwood, "Perspectives on Personhood."

13. Jones and Butman, *Modern Psychotherapies*, 226–53.

and psychological) and to keep working for an increasing integration of the philosophical framework for the program.[14]

Particular Features of a Christian Approach

A number of features will characterize our approach to counselling. The following are some of the more important foundational features.

View of Humanity

Our understanding of humanity is crucial in the social sciences generally and in the field of counselling particularly. Our program will aim to endorse at every level the significance of humans: created in the image of God; created to be free and responsible, but now marred and defaced by sinful human choice and often inexplicable evil and suffering; and yet still of unique dignity and accountable before God.

The program will seek to maintain the tension between the facts that God's good purposes are not yet fulfilled, that human nature is "incomplete," and the human predicament is disintegrative/ fractured/dysfunctional—and yet the goal and possibility remains of renewal, wholeness, and fulfillment.

Our understanding of humanity created in the image of God gives particular attention to the role of humans within the created order as fellow creatures and as stewards before God to relate to and responsibly manage the resources of the integrated ecosystems of our planet under the active lordship of Jesus Christ.

We also give full weight to the social nature of humans and to our interdependence as relational beings who find fulfillment in healthy communal relationships.

The program will stimulate an awareness and understanding of the central biblical teachings about human nature which inform a Christian approach to psychology and counselling. Emphasis will be placed upon evaluating psychological methods in the light of current research on human nature. We shall explore aspects of counselling in which the implications of biblical teachings need to be applied more adequately—such as in our

14. See Garwood, "Perspectives on Personhood," for useful guidelines for this task.

definitions of abnormality and maturity.[15] We see the breadth and depth of biblical understandings of humanity as focal points for one emphasis for ongoing research within our program and for positive contributions to the study of counselling within the social sciences at large.

Understanding of Wholeness

Our understanding of the goals of counselling will be consistent with the revelation of mature humanity demonstrated in the life, ministry, and death of our Lord Jesus Christ. He who "grew in wisdom and stature, and in favor with God and people," and yet who died in conscious dependence upon God, though misunderstood and in excruciating pain, offers a pattern of human perfection which can significantly enrich many contemporary models.

The atoning focus of the ministry of Christ, culminating in his redemptive work through death and resurrection, and made accessible through his personal presence in the ministry of the Holy Spirit, offers specific understandings and resources for dealing with central aspects of human experience. Christ speaks effectively into areas such as guilt and forgiveness, shame and honor, self-acceptance, human purpose and destiny, interpersonal relationships, attitudes to cosmic powers and the occult, personal significance before God, and hope in the face of grief—to highlight a few.

A Christian understanding of the distinction between physical and psychological "wholeness," on the one hand, and "holiness" on the other, will be thought through and upheld in the program and its related praxis. We shall seek to ensure that a preoccupation with attention to self-acceptance and self-affirmation, central as these must always be, does not obscure the way in which self-denial, discipline, and altruistic motivation are also integral to a biblical understanding of "wholeness." The Christian understanding of maturity gives dignity and meaning to difficulties and weakness and does not necessarily exalt their removal as of prime importance. Mutual acceptance, submission, restraint, and personal discipline, though unpopular in some modern circles, are highly regarded in the Scriptures, as are the courage, faith, and strength which resist servile exploitation and take a stand for justice and for God in compromising situations.

15. Garwood, "Perspectives on Personhood."

Likewise, the place of suffering in an adequate definition of "wholeness" is vital. A new understanding of suffering is an integral part of the apostolic presentation of the gospel—even though we may not have realized this from the caricatures often presented today in triumphalistic and "prosperity" teachings amongst some Christians. Our program aims for a biblical balance in these areas so includes a "theology of suffering."

Again, both the intrapersonal and interpersonal aspects of wholeness will receive due attention. The Christian understanding of humans as social creatures created for community with each other and with God must serve as an antidote to the individualistic and even narcissistic tendencies of some approaches to counselling.

Understanding of the Roles, Resources, and Processes Involved in Remedial Counselling

Our programs will respect, evaluate, and appropriately incorporate the proven processes, roles, resources, and skills of contemporary counselling praxis. We receive such as potential gifts from God for the welfare of his creatures and to be utilized for his glory. The program will equip the student to access, evaluate, and keep up-to-date professionally with developments in the fields related to counselling. The course will draw on and critically appropriate theoretical and practical insights from the spectrum of both Christian and other proven contemporary approaches to counselling, testing all for their biblical and psychological validity. The program will foster respect for and appropriate use of any approach which serves the client's wholeness and welfare before God.

The program will also respect and incorporate appropriately the "means of grace" provided by God through his active presence in the person of the Holy Spirit, through the empowering available in the example and indwelling of Jesus Christ, through the effective operation of his word upon the mind, heart, and conscience of his creatures, through the efficacy of prayer and sacraments, and through other supportive structures and "gifts" God provides in and through agencies such as the family and God's people, the church.

In the use of all such means or methodologies we shall demonstrate a full and proper respect for the personal integrity, freedom, and responsibility of the persons involved. We shall eschew manipulative, authoritarian, or otherwise coercive methods which may dehumanize the person. Honesty, integrity, upright ethical principles, trustworthiness, and respect for personal rights and susceptibilities will pervade any and all methodologies proposed.

We recognize that comparatively little serious theoretical or clinical insight has been contributed to the modern study and discussion of counselling from a distinctively evangelical perspective. The program will therefore encourage reflection and writing from such a perspective.

The program also recognizes the need for effective working relations both with academics working in the field of counselling in New Zealand and internationally, and with practitioners dealing with the range of modern counselling needs in our community and region. It will foster an awareness of the varieties of serious literature impinging on the field and the activities of the related professional societies and agencies involved in the counselling contexts of our nation.

Respect for Cultural Diversity

Biblical presuppositions require a respect for peoples of all cultures as equally significant before God. The Christian gospel is good news precisely because it breaks through cultural exclusivism and embraces and responds equally to the heart cries of peoples of all cultures and situations in life. Our college is committed to upholding the principles of the Treaty of Waitangi in all aspects of its ministry. The counselling program, like all its other teaching programs, will be subject to the scrutiny and encouragement of the Māori runanga of the college so as to develop healthy bicultural practices and sensitivities in all staff and students.

The college also has growing links with the other Polynesian and migrant Asian communities in our nation. We are committed to the kind of multicultural learning environment and experience which enables peoples of all cultures to feel at home and to contribute to, as well as receive from, the program as genuine partners.

The college and its Counselling Program Committee are responsible to uphold this undergirding philosophy and its inherent ethos in the administration and provision of this program.

In Closing

The learning situations chosen in this chapter are not comprehensive. I have not referred to anything from the seven years when the majority of my time was spent at our Christian Brethren Pathways College of Bible and Mission, from 2000 to 2007. Nor do I draw directly from my very satisfying board service with DeepSight Trust (the gospel and cultures group Harold W. Turner established on his return to New Zealand in 1990). Again, only the final chapter of the book comes from the thirty years on the Board of the New Zealand Education Development Foundation, which became Maxim Institute, upholding societal values in New Zealand. Insights and concerns developed while working with those groups are reflected in the other essays throughout this book.

Chapter 15

Pastoral Work and the Character of the Triune God

One area of Christian service where practitioners actively contextualize their faith, whether they realize it or not, is in the multifaceted task of pastoral care for one another. In each time of pressure, trial, hurt, shame, or surprise, joy, extra excitement, or even just in the humdrum routines of living and loving in present-day society, we are all applying or squelching our relationship with Jesus—which is the essence of contextualization. In this chapter, therefore, we shall explore some of the biblical foundations that show the importance, set the extent and parameters, or define the links between our lifestyle, actions, and pastoral work.[1] We are not using terms like "pastoral ministry" or "pastoral care" as is sometimes done, in a technical sense, to distinguish purely spiritual help from what is called "pastoral counselling," which treats people on a more psychologically informed way as whole people.[2] Rather we are using "pastoral ministry" or "pastoral care" as the most general terms to cover the whole work of "shepherding," caring for, or building up members of the church. What we mean will become clear as we proceed to paint broad strokes and deal with major concepts rather than to attempt narrow, specific definitions. People who offer pastoral care are known by different labels in different church traditions and contexts, whether pastor, minister, elder, carer, or simply as

1. This study draws on a paper presented at the Christian Brethren Research Fellowship New Zealand Annual Conference, Waikanae, New Zealand, May 1988, entitled "A Biblical Charter for Pastoral Care."

2. As does K. Heasman, cited in Barker, "Models of Pastoral Care," 231.

friend. To include all such people, we shall use the term caregiver regularly, but may at times simply say "pastor," using the word in this general sense.

Knowing our Triune God, Father, Son, and Holy Spirit, in the way he reveals himself in the Scriptures immediately brings implications for us as pastoral caregivers and how we understand and approach those we serve. Thus, thinking about fundamental concepts is vital. Too often we approach pastoral care merely from the point of view of technique; as if it is just a program or procedure we emulate or reproduce in the particular situations we face. But for effective pastoral care, we need to know why we are using a particular approach. We need to assess our methodology against fundamental realities. Adequate Christian pastoral care only grows from a Trinitarian basis. If our basis is anything other than God himself, Father, Son and Spirit, we soon lose our way.

Here, then, are some basic, care-grounding insights from the Scriptures. Each of the biblical foundations, or models, we explore teaches or implies something about God; something about our role, position, or relationships as we offer pastoral care; and something about those to whom we offer this care.

God as Father and Pastoral Caregivers as Hosts—Eph 3:14–15 (RSV); Luke 11:1; John 4:23–24

Pastoral care begins in the Father-heart of God. His essential nature as love is the source of our life, of our human image, of our social and communal potential, of our very identity as persons. In these aspects of our being as humans you will recognize many of the key issues in pastoral care. Many pastoral issues grow from the root of inappropriate understanding of God as our Father and that as such he is love. In pastoral contexts today, we are often told to avoid speaking of God as Father. This title for God is suspect because many people's images of fathers are thoroughly inadequate. Rather than avoid this fundamental description of God, the need is to redefine it. So, when speaking of God as Father, we mean:

i. God the Father is the one who yearns for a people of his own (Gen 17:7; Exod 19:4–6; Titus 2:14; 1 Pet 2:9–10).

Each of us who has reached maturity knows something of this parental yearning: the yearning for persons who are distinctly related to you and who reflect your life and personality. God yearns for a people to know him, who love him, who relate in a particular way to him as their personal God.

ii. God as Father brings us to new birth into his family as his children on the most personal and intimate of terms (John 1:12–13; Rom 8:16–17; Gal 4:4–7).

We have been adopted with the full rights of children and heirs within the family circle of the living God. The family name, language, business, and concerns become ours on a daily basis.

iii. God as Father yearns to protect, to bring fulfillment, to bring satisfaction to his people (Ps 103:13–14).

He feels our limitations; he knows our frailty. He wants to build us up, and to develop us to our full potential.

iv. God as Father also yearns to commune with, to trust, to relate to his children and to do so in a self-giving, committed, steadfastly loving relationship.

v. God as Father accepts responsibility for and provides the source of stable, dependable interaction with his people.

vi. God as Father fulfills and defines all that is best in true parental relationships.

It is not that God is like a father, as if some human patterns set the model for God's behavior. No, God is himself the true Father. All that is upright, honorable, and worthy in human parental actions derives ultimately from God's prototypical fatherhood (Eph 3:14–15).

Now because this is what God is like, this is the source out of which pastoral care grows. God's fatherhood provides the standard for pastoral care. Since God is this kind of Father, we as humans can find our true selves in him as our Father, and we as pastors can offer:

- *Acceptance*. We "belong" in him. He understands and welcomes us, appreciates and relates to us as a friend—just as we are. A favorite hymn by Bishop Handley Moule, captures this reality:

> Come, not to find, but make this troubled heart,
> A dwelling worthy of Thee as Thou art . . .[3]

3. *Keswick Hymn Book*, no. 29, v. 5.

- *Status*. As Father, God offers us a particular relationship with himself, a relationship of dignity, a relationship of status as his children. Our human worth and identity derive ultimately from our creation in God's image, confirmed in our redemption as his children (Gal 4:4–6).
- *Relationship*. This relationship with God the Father also confers on us a relationship with others. Christians, of all people, know the importance of being "brothers" and "sisters," of having family obligations, of being open and frank, being able to say it as it is to those to whom we are related in a blood-bought partnership. Knowing each other, accepting each other, enjoying mutual responsibilities and privileges, then, flow out of these facts that God is our Father; we are part of his family and we are related to each other as his children.
- *Roots*. Knowing God as Father offers us roots. Family speaks of home, a place where we belong, where we expect the father to know us, to direct us, to encourage us, and to care for us. At home we know we are welcome; we are trusted. In God is the place where we can come and go securely. So much of our pastoral care is trying to help people find that sort of place, a place from which they can venture out with confidence and to which they can return for acceptance, reassurance, and renewal.

All of these fundamental aspects of human well-being ultimately go back to the fact that the Lord, our God is Father, and he invites ordinary people like us to become his family. Any pattern of pastoral care that does not give due attention to God our Father as the source of human wholeness is likely to be defective. Perhaps, above all, pastors are family builders, inviting each actual and potential family member to enter more fully into their rights and heritage as children of God.

God as Our Refuge and Pastoral Caregivers as Reassurers—Pss 18:1–2, 31–32; 31:2–3, 19–20; 32:7; 46:1–2; 57:1; 59:1, 9–10, 16–17; 62:1–2, 5–8; 71:2–3, 7; 73:28; 91:2–4, 9–13; 141:8; 144:1–2

God is also our refuge, reminding us our human context is marked by the reality of evil and that we are caught up in conflict. Psalm 46:1–2 sets the scene: "God is our refuge and strength, an ever-present help in trouble. Therefore we will not fear, though the earth give way and the mountains fall into the heart of the sea." These are distinctly pastoral statements. An ever-present help in trouble is what pastoral care is all about. Freedom from fear becomes reality when God is our refuge. Or, again, in Ps 62:1–2, 5–7:

> "My soul finds rest in God alone, my salvation comes from him. He alone is my rock and my salvation; he is my fortress, I shall never be shaken. . . . Find rest O my soul in God alone; my hope alone comes from him. He alone is my rock and my salvation; he is my fortress, I shall not be shaken. My salvation and my honor depend on God; he is my mighty rock, my refuge."

Comparing this with what we have just said about God as Father, it is clear the human image has been distorted; something has gone wrong.

Here humans are in danger, evil is abroad, the family love is no longer the center, but conflict is around and engulfs the human. From the outside, the idea of a refuge suggests that there are storms abroad. Or, more often in the Palestinian image, we are in a dry barren wilderness and need protection from the fierce effects of the sun. We are under attack and enemies lurk nearby. Like all humans, we know we need help.

Or, as the references from Psalms also imply, fears are arising from within, there is a sense of depletion, exhaustion; perhaps a result of foolish unpreparedness, or perhaps simply the very human experience of downright failure and the vulnerability that comes with it. But refuge implies all of these pastoral ideas and it reminds us that the source of pastoral help in these situations is God himself.

We all need protection, rescue, shelter, and safety; we need security and reassurance. The realities of our human predicament are implied very clearly in this model. Our sin, our danger, our desperate need are answered by him, our God, as the only adequate strength, the only dependable, steadfast foundation to whom we can turn. Being humbly confident in a rock-like God is the basis on which we move forward to help others aware of those storms and conflicts around them.

The synonyms—rock, refuge, fortress—bring together the physical environmental, the legal fugitive, and the military metaphors, each with its own emphasis on danger, fear, loneliness, vulnerability, and helplessness. They can also imply victimization, exploitation, and unfair treatment. So, all of these common pastoral situations point us to the presence of the understanding, available, strong, secure, dependable Lord almighty, the compassionate Lord Jesus Christ, and the gently powerful Holy Spirit, our advocate. This Triune God is the only sufficient basis for confidence in pastoral crises and pressures.

God as Maker and Pastoral Caregivers as Accountable—Ps 95:6; 1 Cor 3:18—4:5

Knowing God is our maker and owner brings two effects: we humans are accountable; and we are responsible managers of our God-given resources.

The loss of awareness of God as creator, owner, and ruler of the universe is one of the most serious roots of pastoral needs today. One of the spin-offs of the science versus Scripture arguments and the general assumption of the validity of secular, godless, explanations of the origin of our species is widespread uncertainty about whether there is one final controlling being to whom we are accountable. Loss of that certainty has had tragic effects on attitudes to ourselves, to morality, and to choice and decision-making right across human experience. We need to recapture firmly, and to base our pastoral care, again, on the assured knowledge that there is an owner, a ruler, a creator of this universe, and he has declared himself and given instructions to those he has made and created.

Guilt, shame, blame, and forgiveness can all stem directly from this sense of accountability, or the lack of it. Again, it is interesting that in the Psalms, for instance Ps 95:6, we see this reality set in a pastoral context: "Come let us bow down in worship, let us kneel before the Lord our Maker; for He is our God and we are the people of his pasture, the flock under his care."

Since God is our Maker, it is possible to have this shepherding, caring relationship with him. On the one hand, because he is the owner of the world, we are accountable to him as our judge for the way we use all he has made and owns. Moreover, this accountability is fundamental when helping people to accept their responsibility as humans.

But God as owner of his whole creation also means he has made humans as responsible managers of his universe. We are stewards, to use the biblical term. He trusts us to master, to understand, to domesticate, to utilize, to conserve, but never to exploit, abuse, or waste, our material resources, our social resources, our psychological and our spiritual resources, as indicated in the "cultural mandate" in Genesis (Gen 1:26–30; 2:15–24).

Grappling with this God-given role of being responsible managers lies behind abuse problems which are at the heart of so much pastoral care.

The suffering and hardships stemming from the greed of others is a major factor as we try to help those who have been exploited by people's mismanagement. Failure to be responsible stewards lies behind so many of the problems of material and physical want. The sad destruction of body and mind through drug abuse can be another aspect of this mismanagement and failure to understand that God as owner has entrusted to us responsible management within this earth.

But human accountability is also an issue in another aspect of pastoral care, which is perhaps even harder to grapple with. Because God has made us responsible managers of the *whole* of his universe, in the pastoral task he has committed to us all the resources within the created universe. We are accountable to use all of them well, not just the spiritual ones (1 Cor 3:18—4:2).

That is difficult because it is so much more comfortable to be a reductionist, it is so much easier to say there are only spiritual problems, even when there are obviously medical, psychological, social, and material aspects of the problem we like to gloss over in our eagerness to treat the "real" issue, the spiritual thing. But that is irresponsible management. We are failing to appreciate what God has entrusted to us. God has given us a world that has within it medicinal qualities and he has given us the minds to understand those things. He has given us a heritage of medical experience which he expects us to receive as another gift to use for the pastoral task.

Likewise, our world is rich in social, psychological, and interpersonal resources, and we live at a point in time when we have a wealth of insight into how humans both benefit and suffer through good and evil application of these interpersonal capabilities. As pastoral carers we are irresponsible if we do not reap the benefits of those sociological and psychological lessons and principles. Not to utilize them in our counselling and guidance of others is to disregard part of the provision our creator has made for his creatures.

Paul makes this point in 1 Cor 3–4 when advising the Corinthians how to address the issues of immaturity and disunity. After introducing metaphors explaining how to properly perceive the leaders within the church—as household servants, as work colleagues in agricultural laboring, and as house builders under the master builder—Paul warns about the world's wisdom which God rejects (1 Cor 3:18–23). He warns particularly against worldly wisdom's tendency to preference favorite teachers, and disregard others, causing party factions. This, Paul says, is a blatant failure to use all of God's gifts for building up the church. God gives all the different perspectives and resources of an Apollos, Peter, and Paul: their different theological perspectives; different cultural backgrounds; different oratorical skills and intellectual capacities. God expects the church not to pick and choose between them, but to embrace and utilize the full range of their contributions.

But Paul goes much further than that. God has not only given differently gifted pastoral workers. Paul continues: "All things are yours, whether Paul or Apollos or Peter, or the world, or life or death, or the present or the future—all are yours" (1 Cor 3:22–23) for building up the church. The lessons of life and death—the psychological and medical lessons; the insights of the present or future—and all the historical and social knowledge accumulated over the years—the full range of secular study and knowledge—are all potential material for strengthening and building up the body of Christ. We dishonor the owner of our universe and what he has called us to be, if we do not use the medical, psychological, and social services which are there for us. True, we have to bring them back under his lordship and his ownership as we use them—"all are yours and you are Christ's and Christ is God's" (1 Cor 3:23)—but we must not reduce our task as if it does not involve those other aspects.

Little wonder then, that Paul goes straight on to say, "This then is how you ought to regard us (church leaders): as resource custodians and responsible managers of the entrusted riches of God" (1 Cor 4:1–2).[4] Pastoral caregivers are accountable custodians of the full breadth of God-given resources available as we faithfully fulfill our management task until the final assessment Paul speaks about in 4:5, when each such caregiver "will receive their praise from God."

God as Redeemer and Pastoral Caregivers as Evangelists

For adequate pastoral involvement we need not only a theological center but a christological, indeed a Trinitarian, center. We have stressed these creational and theological aspects of pastoral care first because traditionally, as evangelicals, we may have overemphasized the christological and redemptive dimensions of our faith to the detriment of other aspects, but we

4. For elaboration of this point see, Hitchen, "Confirming the Christian Scholar," 276–87.

must never underestimate the importance of these salvation-redemption realities.

The great Old Testament emphasis on the Lord as savior and redeemer (2 Sam 22:1–3; Isa 43:3, 11; 45:21–22; 49:26; 60:16; 63:8–9) is gathered up in the New Testament and applied in its fullness to Jesus, the one who saves. Christ is our redeemer and this is the foundation of so much of our pastoral work. Our self-worth, personal identity, and self-acceptance, all stem from our dependence on a saving redeemer. Christ's estimation of our worth sent Jesus to the cross, and that gives us true worth. His acceptance of us, through giving his blood to deal with the fundamental wrongs of sin and shame within us, allows us to accept ourselves. Christ Jesus bestows his identity on us as part of his body, as part of his bride. He gives us a name. He gives us a position. He gives us a dignity. These realities arising from his work on the cross give us the foundation on which we can move forward to offer hope and good news to those we counsel. Being in his body, being his bride, gives us purpose, and makes us partners with him. Our salvation in Christ gives us a proper pride and joy as fully developed humans. All would be impossible apart from the redemptive aspect of Christ's work.

By implication, then, the pastoral task includes evangelism and incorporating new believers into the church. This aspect of pastoral ministry has never been forgotten in our circle of churches; sometimes we have assumed it is the only pastoral task to the detriment of other aspects. Yet, we need to sustain the emphasis as addressing the deepest human needs.

The Lord as Shepherd and Pastoral Caregivers as Shepherds—Ps 23; John 10; 1 Pet 5:1–5

The Lord is our shepherd and we are his sheep; this is the classical, biblical model of pastoral care, but this is only one biblical model. Much of our pastoral care has suffered from thinking that shepherding is all that is involved and ignoring some of the aspects just mentioned. But, again, we can never neglect the shepherding metaphor in understanding pastoral care. Neil Summerton, in his handbook on the elder as pastor, *The Noble Task*, gives a good lead:

> The essence of the pastoral task can be understood in the metaphors of the Shepherd and shepherding. From this we are to understand that the pastoral care of God's people entails protecting them, feeding them, healing them, rescuing them, restoring them

> and carrying them spiritually. The whole being done with loving care and gentleness even when exercising the legitimate authority inherent in the Elder's right to rule the flock.
>
> The task can be grasped succinctly from Scripture as the precise opposite of Ezekiel's devastating condemnation of the spiritual leaders of his day and which can apply to today's congregational leaders too.[5]

Summerton quotes Ezek 34:2–5, which we shall focus on to discuss the shepherding pattern:

> Should not shepherds feed the sheep? You eat the fat, you clothe yourselves with the wool, you slaughter the fatlings but you do not feed the sheep. The weak you have not strengthened, the sick you have not healed, the crippled you have not bound up, the strayed you have not brought back, the lost you have not sought. And with force and with harshness you have ruled them so they were scattered because there was no shepherd.

These are seminal ideas, seed thoughts that can bear a rich harvest. We shall also draw on Derek Tidball's comments in his book, *Skilful Shepherds*.[6] Ezekiel describes our role in pastoral work; explains the requirements of those who do this work; identifies the concerns we should have as we go about it; suggests some curriculum areas for training such pastoral workers; and suggests for further growth, needs for those already involved. Nine aspects of the shepherding pastoral task may be discerned in Ezek 34:2–5.

Shepherding means *never exploiting the flock* (Ezek 34:2–3): "You've grown fat, you've taken their wool, their meat and you've not cared for them," is the fundamental accusation. The true pastor recognizes the rights and needs of those he or she is pastoring. We will be careful to respect the vulnerability of the person seeking help. We will also be sensitive to the productivity, the potential, and the rights that person has to enjoy for themselves, recognizing those capacities are not the pastor's to commandeer or control. In other words, we start by warning against becoming involved in pastoral work for the sake of our own psychological needs, or the sense of power, or of fulfillment we find when others are dependent on us in a pastoral relationship.

5. Summerton, *Noble Task*, 46–47.
6. Tidball, *Skilful Shepherds*, 45–47.

Being realistic, we do have needs which are met when we do pastoral work, but we need to take care that this is not our primary motivation. Our primary concern is ever about the welfare, the integrity, fulfillment, and needs of those we are serving.

Shepherding means to *feed the flock* (Ezek 34:2–3; Acts 20:28; John 21:15; 1 Pet 5). All the New Testament shepherding references emphasize the feeding aspect of the pastoral task. This assumes certain things: that the pastor/elder understands how people grow spiritually; that the pastor/elder understands the spiritual "dietary" needs of those who need to keep growing; that pastoral carers understand the "digestive procedures"—how people actually take spiritual truth and receive sustenance from it, that is, the processes by which the word heard or read is put into action; and, that the shepherd especially knows the qualities of the different parts of the pasture and when particular sheep need various kinds of grass to feed on.

Knowing where to find the diverse kinds of "food" in each different part of the Scriptures, and then preparing and effectively presenting the right Bible teaching to meet the needs of our group of believers, is the essence of the Christian pastoral task. Feeding the flock depends on Bible teaching. But it goes further than that.

Shepherding means *strengthening the weak* (Ezek 34:4). At this point Ezekiel becomes more specific about a range of special needs within the flock. The first mentioned is "the weak." This category is self-explanatory and is closely related to the next.

Shepherding means *healing the sick* (Ezek 34:4). How much do we actually know about the causes and the development of spiritual disease? Can we identify the spiritual disease carriers in our congregation? Are we aware of the patterns by which spiritual diseases spread? What happens once a disease takes root, and how does it spread? We wouldn't go to a doctor who is ignorant about such physiological and eating matters, and yet we often show less skill at recognizing what happens with spiritual maladies. Recent pandemics should remind us there is always more to learn about treatment procedures, or knowing which medicine, spiritually speaking, applies to newly occurring diseases.

Shepherding means *supporting and protecting the crippled and lame* (Ezek 34:4). This implies we will understand the effects of personal handicaps on those seeking pastoral care. We will know, or quickly learn, what sort of support to give: Do they need a sling, or a plaster? What pattern of support: How much, how strong, for how long? When should that support be reduced and how quickly? When should it be removed? Should it be removed altogether, or does this sheep need long-term support and special dietary additives? The skill of helping the disabled in the spiritual sense may again suggest areas for ongoing learning and further training if we are to be effective pastors.

The rest of our Ezekiel passage gives four more word pictures, images, or creative ideas for developing our shepherding task: *reclaiming the strays*—bringing home backsliders, Ezek 34:4; *finding the lost*—evangelistic work, Ezek 34:4; *avoiding harshness*—perhaps the primary occupational hazard for male pastors, Ezek 34:4; and *consolidating unity* within the flock—preventing division, Ezek 34:5.

Ezekiel's list suggests pastoral carers become skilled at identifying pastoral priorities. This is the church's distinctive task, which other social services cannot do. And as hinted above, this analysis provides a useful outline for developing training programs in pastoral care.

These various aspects of shepherding also show the mix of skills we need in a pastoral team. We need people who are good at helping the lame as well as others who are good at seeking the lost and reclaiming those who have gone astray. We will always need more than just the one who can teach and feed. But I am obviously not a farmer; I speak about shepherding from a "townie's" point of view. We need the farmers to explain what else is implied in these metaphors.

The Lord as Guide and Pastoral Caregivers as Accompanying Guides—Ps 23:2b–3; 25:4–5, 8–9; 32:8–9; 78:72; Acts 3:15; 5:31; Heb 2:10; 12:2

Some seminal ideas for understanding the pastoral task center around the roles of Christ Jesus and the Holy Spirit indwelling Christians as our guide, and our experience as pilgrims on our earthly discipleship pathway. Again, we often forget that the Lord leads, guides, directs, gives instruction, and is available continually for companionship as we receive and act upon his instructions. Psalm 23 links the Lord's leading and guiding role closely with that of shepherding. Moreover, as the Lord leads through the deepest valleys of life he does so as our closest friend. The "he leads me" of Ps 23:2 becomes "You are with me" in the darkness of v. 4.

The New Testament sharpens another aspect of the Lord's leading and guiding role. He is named the "chief leader" or "trailblazing pioneer" in Acts and Hebrews. In this role he defeats even death to give assurance not only along the pilgrim pathway, but even into the unknown beyond. The need to find our way in the confusing pathways of life, and even more important, the loss of understanding our human experience as pilgrimage, has created some of our distinctly Western pastoral problems. Our society lives as if we belong only on this earth. The degree to which we have established ourselves in this life, is held up as the real test of success. Our achievements and assets give our sense of belonging. Our earthly securities are supposed to give meaning to cope with the pressures of daily living. Much pastoral work has to address that lie and to replace it with the biblical understanding that we are in fact on a much greater pilgrimage. We are people who are part of a search. We are people who are moving forward, not just wanting to settle down and be established, but people who are on the move with a purpose and future to discover. Ultimately, we are looking for a city that has foundations of another kind, a heavenly city in a new heaven and new earth.

Hebrews 11 was right, and pastorally right, when the author held up before us as models for our faith— models to copy in daily experience— those who grasped the fact that they lived by faith as only sojourners in this world. If we can recapture that insight, it will help sort out many pastoral problems about time priorities and utilizing resources. Knowing we are pilgrims gives a sense of direction, confirming who we are, and ordering priorities, and therefore is an essential key for solving pastoral concerns. The pastoral challenge is to walk with our fellow believers in such a way as to guide their footsteps and give the necessary companionship to keep on track all the way.

God as Commissioner and Pastoral Caregivers as Equippers—Matt 28:16–20; John 20:21; Acts 1:8; Eph 2:10; 1 Pet 4:10–11

Perhaps the most significant theological advance of the twentieth century in the Western church has been the recovery of the truth that God is missionary in his basic essence. The generally accepted early twentieth-century view saw mission as only the responsibility of enthusiasts who served as willing volunteers through groups of such enthusiasts—the missionary societies. But this view changed radically by mid-century to the realization that mission is indeed the heart and essence of the nature of the whole church. "The church exists by mission as fire exists by burning," as Emil

Brunner put it in the 1930s.[7] But that perception was to change again by the 1970s to a realization that God is on the mission, and he invites the church to join him in his mission. So the work of mission is widely recognized today as the *missio Dei*—the mission of God.[8] God is recognized as missional in his essential nature. As love, he constantly reaches out beyond himself in the kind of self-giving generosity that came to fullness in the *agapē* love expressed at Calvary.

Since the mission is God's, his missionary nature is seen in two closely related ongoing activities. He calls people to himself to share with him and to become partners in his purposes and work. And he sends people, commissioning them to responsibly fulfill their allocated roles within his mission. The God who worked originally as creator, who has always continued working as sustainer and provider, who culminated his work of re-creation at the cross, works still by calling and sending his people to join him in fulfilling his purposes till the end of the ages. So the dual aspects of heeding a "calling" and obeying the "sending"—vocation and mission—summarize the Christian walk very well.

In the light of this recovery of the fact that God is a missional worker, pastors have an essential responsibility in sounding out his call to work, and in facilitating the sending of their congregation members.

The Holy Spirit as Teacher and Pastoral Caregivers as Disciplers

The distinctive mark of the current age—the age of the church—is that every member has direct access to the teacher himself. As the climax of his teaching while on earth, Jesus explained that he and the Father would come to be with believers continually (John 14:19–21). In introducing this promise of his abiding in believers, Jesus had just explained two things: he would not leave us like orphans but would come to be with us (John 14:18); and, as the verses before that explain, the Father would give the Holy Spirit as the advocate and Spirit of truth to dwell in believers constantly (John 14:15–17). This is how Jesus fulfills his promise to live with us. He lives in us through the indwelling Spirit. So, a few verses later, Jesus explains further that the Holy Spirit sent by the Father will remind and continue to teach believers of all the words of Jesus (John 14:26; 15:25–26). Thus,

7. Brunner, *Word and the World*, 108.

8. See, for example, Wright, *Mission of God*.

believers have the "anointing" of the Spirit to give us direct access to truth (1 John 2:27–28).

To fulfill the Lord's own promises in John 14:15–18 and 16:8–15, then, the Holy Spirit teaches Christ and his word. The Holy Spirit guides believers into truth. The Holy Spirit is the "Reminder" and "Explainer" of the Triune God for the church. The Spirit is the source of the apostolic message and he is its authority (1 Cor 2:10–15). He fulfills a special warning role (1 Tim 4:1). He is the source of illumination and growth into fullness of understanding of the whole intention of God for his people (Eph 1:17–23).

Most, if not all, of the metaphors explored above explaining God's nature carry an implication that God is our teacher. The true Father instructs his children; the ultimate guide teaches the way to go; the creator/resource provider teaches and commands what to do and how to use his provisions; the savior/redeemer says, "I am the way, the truth, and the life," and repudiates error as he claims there is only one way to the Father; and the shepherd teaches his sheep to know his voice and to feed at his hand.

The Spirit fulfills this teaching role within the Trinity, and is closely associated with the calling/sending, or missional, nature of God as well. Indeed the same metaphors also carry missional implications: the Father yearns to embrace others within the family; the shepherd has "other sheep who are not of this sheep pen" (John 10:16); the savior says, "There is no other way under heaven given amongst humans . . ." God is essentially missional in his very nature. So the Holy Spirit is only being true to the divine nature when mission concern is so close to the heart of the work of teaching. What is more, the same calling, teaching, and sending emphases were also the focus of Jesus's earthly ministry, so we should expect the Holy Spirit to have similar emphases (Matt 9:36—10:42).

Turning to the role of caregivers in this teaching ministry, the focus here is on regular, systematic instruction in the word of God, coupled with a lifestyle demonstrating the teaching in well-applied practice. While rooted in the renewal of the mind of each believer, both teaching and wisdom in the Scriptures lead to transformed behavior, habits, values, attitudes, and relationships. Without these lifestyle changes it is not biblical teaching or wisdom. While all elders are to be apt to teach (1Tim 3:2; Titus 1:9), some have a special teaching gift and are expected to "work at preaching and teaching," and to be honored and remunerated accordingly (Eph 4:11; 1 Tim 5:17; Gal 6:6).

The New Testament assumes that when Christian teachers use their gifts properly, they will multiply their gifting, not grasp this function to themselves alone. The New Testament charges each of the following groups with "teaching" responsibility in the local church:

i. Pastor–teachers and elders

Ephesians 4:11–12 refers to some with a specific spiritual endowment to teach the word. The New Testament expects the churches in a given geographical area to utilize, and where necessary, support such spiritual "gifts" in their work (e.g., Rom 12:6–7; 1 Cor 12:7–8, 28; Gal 6:6). These specially gifted persons are to "equip the saints for the work of the ministry" (Eph 4:11–12), and to keep teaching central in these leadership roles (1 Tim 3:2; 5:17; 1 Pet 5:1–5). The teacher is to "service" other Christians so they will all become active in fulfilling their God-given gifts or contributions to church and society.

But the New Testament references to teachers do not stop there. When those with particular teaching gifts are working properly, then all the following groups are given responsibility to share in aspects of the overall teaching task.

ii. Parents

In Eph 6:4 and Col 3:20 the father is responsible for bringing up children in the "instruction of the Lord."

iii. Older women

Titus 2:3–5 commands the older women to teach what is good so as to train the younger women in Christian marriage and homecraft, and in developing family lifestyles which bring credit to the word of God. Individualistic nuclear families in the West have dissolved the extended family patterns assumed in these verses. Thus we must find new settings within the church "family" to recapture this essential aspect of cross-generational learning today.

iv. Young people

Timothy and Titus are the classic examples of younger people who are commanded to stir up their teaching gifts and not allow their comparative youthfulness to preclude them from teaching in the local church (1 Tim

4:6–16; 2 Tim 2:22–26; 4:1–5; Titus 1:5; 2:15; 3:8). The role of such workers in training others for ministry is especially noted (Titus 2:1–3, 6).

v. "Those . . . who are spiritual"

Galatians 6:1–2 does not leave the responsibility for restorative pastoral teaching and burden bearing to elders or pastors alone. All who feel a spiritual concern for those who have stumbled in their Christian walk share the responsibility for leading others on in their obedience to Christ Jesus (1 Thess 5:14).

vi. "One another"

Colossians 3:16 puts a teaching responsibility on all Christians. Warning, encouraging, and stimulating to praise and worship are the concern of every Christian who allows the word to dwell within him or her. First Thessalonians 4:18 and 5:11–14 speak of comforting, encouraging, and building up as "one another" responsibilities. Paul is confident the Christians in Rome were "able to instruct one another" (Rom 15:14), for this is the normal pattern for a New Testament church (see 1 Pet 4:10).

As we cultivate this New Testament expectation that gifted Bible teachers in all these categories will fulfill their caregiving responsibilities, there will be no shortage of available personnel. The problem is not lack of gift, but of mobilizing those available, with every believer realizing they have a part in building up the fellowship. The Holy Spirit shows no cultural favoritism when giving teaching gifts to the church (Acts 6:1–7). International ministry teams gained hands-on experience alongside Paul, as the different ethnic regions represented in the team indicate in Acts 20:1–5.

The Scriptures highlight that teaching caregivers are to reflect the mind and attitude of their Lord as they teach others. In fact, certain attitudes of the pastor-teacher are essential for effective teaching. In Paul's autobiographical passages (e.g., 1 Thess 2:7–8; Acts 20:18–20; Col 1:29) he often quite incidentally refers to his own attitudes as exemplars for those of us who follow in his pastoral teaching footsteps. Together these attitudes make quite a list: gentle; cared with much love; willingly gave our lives as well as the gospel; with great humility; with tears; amid opposition; holding back nothing that might be helpful; proclaiming the whole will of God; combining extreme personal effort; and depending on Christ's enabling, both inspiration and perspiration!

In Jesus's culminating action and instruction for his future church leaders in John 13, the summary is, "You call me 'Teacher' and 'Lord,' and rightly so, for that is what I am. Now that I, your Lord and Teacher, have washed your feet, you also should wash one another's feet. I have set you an example that you should do as I have done for you . . . Now that you know these things, you will be blessed if you do them" (John 13:13–15, 17). This passage is foundational for teaching in caregiving. Setting an example in humble, thankless service is the unchanging essence of Christ's pattern of teaching authority and leadership.

This is the heart of the incarnation and atonement, and therefore also shows the essential mindset required in caregivers who teach (Phil 2:1–11). But, as for Christ, so for us today, effective teaching comes only with the price of costly, other-centered, self-denying suffering, shared with Christ who dwells within us through the Holy Spirit. Hence, Paul's constant call to imitate him. He commends those who set worthy examples for others (e.g., Phil 3:17; 4:9; 1 Cor 4:16; 10:31—11:1; 1 Thess 1:4–8; 2:6b–12). This is a very high standard, but it shows the significance of teaching which produces Christlike living and churches.

Conclusion

Our list of characteristics of God that inform pastoral care is not exhaustive or complete. We could add others—God our sanctifying Spirit, or God our wooing lover, for instance. But those chosen form a firm foundation for pastoral care in our churches. Healthy pastoral care and ministry spring from and are sustained by our knowledge of God. A narrow or truncated view of God will inevitably lead to narrow and partial pastoral care. Moreover, each of the marks of the nature of God we have highlighted, brings a corresponding indication of key aspects of the role of pastoral carers:

- God is our father and pastoral caregivers are hosts welcoming others into the family circle.
- God is our refuge and pastoral caregivers are comforting reassurers.
- God is our maker/owner and pastoral caregivers are responsible resource managers.
- God is our savior/redeemer and pastoral caregivers are evangelists.

- God is our shepherd and pastoral caregivers are shepherds under the great shepherd.
- God is our guide, companion, and trailblazer, and pastoral caregivers are accompanying guides.
- God is our mission commissioner and pastors are commissioning equippers.
- God, through his Holy Spirit, is our teacher and pastoral caregivers inform and form disciples.

This set of relationships lifts pastoral care from a mere routine, or even just professional task. Pastoral care is a God-given calling whereby we honor and serve God, and ensure the healthy development of his people and their communities. The personal characteristics of God himself, Father, Son and Holy Spirit, set the standard and pattern for the goals and methods of this people-focused service.

Chapter 16

Suffering and Death

A Contextualizing Test

A RECURRING TEST OF how well the good news has been contextualized in any society shows when local believers face suffering and death as a Christian community. This chapter brings together three pieces from personal experience. The first was written as an editorial column in the Bible College of New Zealand (now Laidlaw College) magazine, *Reaper* (later *Reality*), at a time when our college family struggled together with the death of one of our best-loved lecturers who had finally succumbed after a very long struggle with increasing muscular incapacity. The second section records outcomes of several months working with a local church in New Zealand, when arguments about suffering and faith were dividing the community and they had to build a new basis on which to move ahead again. The final piece goes back earlier to when my wife Ann and I lost our own son, and resorting to poetry helped us to handle the grief. One of the severest areas for proving faith is how we cope with suffering and death—probably the ultimate contextualization test.

Life's Meaning in Focus: Life through the Lens of Death[1]

The title was too hot for British sensitivities. Three times, the American writer, Joseph Bayly, had to bury one of his sons. When his moving account

1. The material in this section, lightly edited, first appeared as my "Editorial." Used with the permission of Laidlaw College Inc. (see bibliography for further details).

of the lessons he learned was published in Britain the title was changed. *The View from the Hearse* became *The Last Thing We Talk About*.[2] Both titles deserve thought. As we grasp for meaning in our modern society the final taboo forbids talking too much about death. Yet when facing death, the purpose of life comes into distinct focus. Life's meaning is uniquely focused when you watch a loved one being carried away in a hearse.

In our first nine years back in New Zealand after missionary service I shared in the funerals of three elderly aunts, my sixteen-year-old nephew, a respected colleague, my pastoral mentor, and my own mother. In the last nine months the wife of one of our faculty has lost her only brother and both parents. This week I learned that a second of our colleagues from Christian Leaders' Training College in Papua New Guinea is grappling with terminal illness.

But I cannot be silent. We need to talk about death. Our Christian view of death transforms our view of life. The apostle Paul's understanding of life shows when he is sharing his attitude to death. Facing imminent trial and the real possibility of death, Paul's spontaneous claim is: "To me to live is Christ and to die is gain" (Phil 1:21).

When we, too, face the shock, the pain, the questions, and the awful numbing grief of death we do well to review our understanding of life and death. Paul uses powerful imagery to instruct us.

Death Is Work Done and Race Won

For Paul, life is a productive task. An acquittal at his trial would mean more "fruitful labor." But one day this work would be completed and ready for the ultimate assessment. He aimed for his life's product to please the judge. "Not in vain," and "well done," would more than amply compensate for the energy and commitment he poured into the production process (Phil 1:21; 2:16; 2 Tim 4:7). Paul often linked this "life as productivity" attitude to an athletics image. He struggled continually to hit the finish tape with honor (Phil 3:12–15). He feared disqualification or a wasted race (1 Cor 9:24–27). We can sense his adrenalin pumping as he rounds the final bend (2 Tim 4:7).

This is a helpful insight on life's meaning for today. Our lifespan is not a meaningless rat race but a purposeful, significant task. We have a

2. Bayly, *Last Thing*.

distinctive personal contribution to make. We have a goal and prize for which to run. We no longer need merely to wander, drift, or "career" around.

This perspective makes death the completing of the task. It is the crowning achievement, the end of the effort. Death becomes true rest and fulfilment. Or, in terms of the race, death is crossing the finishing line. The marshal takes our hand and ushers us to our place before the great dais to await the final medal presentations.

For those of us left behind, death often means unfinished business. We have extra burdens to pick up without our loved one's help. We are left with the unanswered questions, with no more access to our loved one's advice. The very fruitfulness and true success of their work makes the completion of it harder to handle. We are deprived of a great coach, manager, instructor, or colleague. And we should express this awful sense of loss.

But we can only be thankful that our colleague has won the ultimate transfer. We can only endorse the selector's choice for promotion to the higher league. Even the wisdom of death's timing makes better sense if life is our opportunity to accomplish something worthwhile and death completes that task. The race controller, after all, best knows the kind and length of course to set to ensure we each display our full capabilities (Heb 12:1).

Death as a Departure

Two days before our colleague Gordon Mackie died, he sent me a message: "Tell John I'm straining at the hawsers." He was excited about Paul's further metaphor for death as "departure" (Phil 1:23; 2 Tim 4:6). We had discussed two aspects of the original meaning of this word. J. A. Motyer put it well: ". . . Paul, the old 'tent-maker' (Acts 18:3), resorts to the language of his trade . . . death for the Christian is the end of what was at best a transitory thing, a camp-life, in which he travelled, without permanent resting place and without sure foundation."[3] The "departure" of death is like pulling the tent pegs, striking camp, and heading home for the "house not made with hands, eternal in the heavens" (2 Cor 5:1). Gordon had spoken of how the Mackies had returned home early from a recent washed-out camping holiday. How much better to be back to real comforts, with no more living out of suitcases! Death is the final homecoming.

We had spent more time discussing Motyer's other suggestion, ". . . that this 'departing' is a 'weighing of the anchor,' a 'setting sail.'" Gordon

3. Motyer, *Message of Philippians*, 88.

had reread Bishop Moule describing Paul's use of "departure" as, ". . . that delightful moment when the friendly flood heaves beneath the freed keel, and the prow is set straight and finally towards the shore of home, and the Pilot stands on board, at length 'seen face to face' and lo, as He takes the helm, 'immediately the ship is at the land whither they go' (John 6:21)."[4]

This metaphor for death presupposes that life is a pilgrimage towards home. Having lived as foreigners and strangers in alien territory, at last we can put aside the foreign language, strange currency, and different culture, and embark on the final journey home. Earth's values, ambitions, and pleasures are always cramping for those whose citizenship is in heaven. We can enjoy them for a time, as on a camping trip, but eternity demands another kind of permanence and homelife. Foreign ports are the right place to do essential business and ambassadorial duty. But our king never expects us to become overstayers or to lose our true passport and identity during the sojourn. His kingdom has an appeal and fascination no foreign city can match.

Little wonder then, that that seasoned loyalist, Gordon Mackie, was straining at the hawsers eager to launch out on the journey home at the end of his foreign posting. For the Christian, death is loosing the moorings, launching out, setting sail across the new ocean. Death is not an end this time, but a new beginning. Death releases us for the great adventure. We are outward and homeward bound at last! All the uncertainties and dangers lie behind. All the certainties and safeties lie ahead in the presence of Christ. Alfred, Lord Tennyson expresses it pointedly with only slightly different imagery:

> Sunset and evening star,
> And one clear call for me!
> And may there be no moaning of the bar,
> When I put out to sea,
> But such a tide as moving seems asleep,
> Too full for sound or foam,
> When that which drew from out the boundless deep
> Turns home again.
>
> Twilight and evening bell,
> And after that the dark!
> And may there be no sadness of farewell
> When I embark:

4. Moule, *Second Letter*, 140.

> For though from out our bourne of time and place
> The flood may bear me far,
> I hope to see my Pilot face to face
> When I have crost the bar.[5]

But, again, for us who are left behind, departures are painful. Separations hurt. There is no return from this trip. This farewell leaves loneliness and yearning. We seldom find it easy to accept the departure and let a loved one go. Only the certainty that we, too, are booked for that same journey eases the pain of the interim separation. The richer and more varied our foreign assignments, the more we also come to appreciate the importance and priority of promotion to "home" service.

Death as an Offering Outpoured

In his third image for death, Paul sees himself being poured out as a drink offering over a sacrifice on the temple altar (Phil 2:17; 2 Tim 4:6). F. F. Bruce explains, ". . . When a sacrifice such as a burnt offering . . .was presented in the temple at Jerusalem, a drink-offering or libation of wine or olive oil might be poured over or beside it. This was added last and completed the sacrifice. 'If my life's blood is to be poured out,' says Paul, 'let it be poured out as a libation on the sacrifice that your faith offers to God . . .'"[6] For Paul death is "the willing yielding up of his life to God." The setting is worship. The worshipper senses the awesome attractiveness of the living God. Conscious of personal unworthiness, but overwhelmed that the holy God graciously accepts and smiles on such a needy creature, the worshipper cries, "Take my life and let it be, consecrated, Lord, to Thee."

This picture understands life as responsive service for God. To live is to relate gratefully to God in the realm of human experience. Trusting God becomes a daily celebration of adoration and thanks, a sacrifice or offering which pleases God. Paul describes the Philippians' faith as such a "living" sacrifice (Phil 2:17; cf. Rom 12:1). But then, in the company of such dedication, Paul sees his own death as the topping added to complete the Philippians' offering. His death becomes the "gravy" poured over the Philippians' service, making it even more acceptable to God.

5. See Tennyson, "Crossing the Bar." Note, "bourne" is dialect for a small stream (cf. Scottish "burn").

6. Bruce, *Philippians*, 64.

Like Abraham, David, and Mary before him, Paul knows some things are too precious to keep; they can only be wasted gloriously for God. Isaac cannot be held in Abraham's fatherly, yearning grasp. He must be surrendered to God's higher claim (Gen 22). David's brave warriors break through enemy lines and come back with a flagon of water from the well of his birthplace. To David, the water is too precious to selfishly gulp. He must pour it out as an offering to God (2 Sam 23). Mary's hoarded perfume is all she has to prepare her master lovingly for his coming death. So, again, her treasure cannot be reserved for some later occasion. She must pour it out in simple, total devotion—and bear the scorn of her economically minded fellow disciples. In the same way, as Paul faces death, he can only say, "Already my life is being poured out on the altar" (2 Tim 4:6, NEB). Only true worshippers understand such extravagance. Only those who have tasted the extravagance of Calvary's "wasted" life can understand the logic of this view of life and death.

Now, as then, when a life is poured out thus, the aroma of its beauty lingers long. But the loss is no less real. Lives so beautiful to God are sorely missed by those they served on earth. We dare not question the value nor the pleasure such an offering brings to the one for whom it is given. But "He who did not spare his own Son, but gave him up for us all—how will he not also, along with him, graciously give us all things" (Rom 8:32)?

Here, then, we find the measure of life. The view from the hearse calls for self-evaluation. Just how productive is our life's work? What lifestyle typifies our pilgrimage? How much pleasure is our service bringing to our Lord? These very practical questions about life echo back from the open grave as we watch a loved one die. These perspectives on death can transform the experience of bereavement. They do not remove the hurt, but infuse it with significance. They do not make us clam up in silence before the grim reality of this last enemy. They free us to face death squarely and see beyond the pain, grief, and separation to a fresh definition of life. And, in the light of that vision, to "press on towards the goal to win the prize for which God has called us heavenward in Christ Jesus" (Phil 3:14).

Towards a Biblical Perspective on Sickness and Suffering

One important aspect of contextualizing the gospel into the minds and behavioral patterns of Christians in our own society means we must help each other accept as our own these New Testament perspectives on life seen through the lens of death, as we make our own personal response to death, hardships, and suffering as they break into our own lives. Each culture has a history of emphasizing some of these teachings more than others. Our pastoral task is to work for the biblical balance in holding these different strands together as we live with suffering in our human world with all its imperfections.

The following strands of biblical teaching bring together a Christian understanding of suffering and sickness:

i. A new perspective on suffering is an inherent aspect of the Christian gospel.

Romans 5:1–5 lists the benefits of "being justified by faith." Along with peace with God, access into grace, and joyful hope, comes "knowing that suffering is productive." Suffering produces character through the love of God and work of the Spirit. This is good news indeed in our day and age. This radical reevaluation of suffering is a key distinctive of the apostolic gospel. Philippians 1:30 confirms this by including suffering along with faith as gifts God entrusts to all Christians. Romans 8:28–39 makes a similar emphasis. This new understanding of suffering is based on the full and perfect work of Christ for our salvation. This gospel perspective offers a focal point from which we address all that follows.

ii. By coming to earth Jesus demonstrated his kingly rule and lordship over all evil and every power that opposes and oppresses humans and his continuing availability to meet us in our physical needs.

Jesus's public ministry brought together healing, preaching, and teaching. These together express Jesus's compassion and love for people and point as signs to his deity and to the arrival of the kingdom in a new way in Christ. His death, resurrection, and present exaltation to God's right hand are the proof and assurance of his ultimate victory over all evil. Therefore in this age between the inauguration of Christ's kingly rule in his first coming and the full unveiling of his kingship at his return, we can turn confidently to Christ in any and all sickness and suffering, knowing that in his unchanging wisdom, love, and gracious sovereignty he will respond as our helper, healer, and great physician, as he knows what is best for us. He is free to choose whether and when to display his authority and power through miraculous interventions, through other means of healing, or by demonstrating the sufficiency of his grace to accept and endure the suffering for his glory. His compassion demonstrated in his earthly life, and culminating in his death at Calvary, also assures us that in times of sickness and suffering our Lord Jesus Christ draws intimately close to guide us through every valley of deep darkness by his personal presence, protection, and provision (Ps 23:3–4). Thus, Christ is our active source of hope, healing, comfort, and strength in times of physical need.

iii. Sickness, decay, and death are given realities of our fallen world—until Christ returns.

We live in and work out our salvation in a world tainted by sin, sickness, decay, and physical death. All Christians are subject to these realities as much as other human beings, until the great consummation and renewal of the earth at Christ's return (Rom 8:18–27). Then he will wipe away every tear, and death, mourning, crying, and pain will be no more (Rev 21:4). In this interim age we should not expect to be able to relate particular examples of sickness, decay, or death to specific identifiable sins, since the effects of sin are all-pervasive, not limited to a specific process or single pattern of influence.

iv. This continuing presence of sickness and suffering is a continuing "problem" in the Scriptures.

From Job's unexplained sufferings, through the psalmist's "My God, My God, Why?" (Ps 22), or "Why are you downcast, O my soul?" (Pss 42–43), on to the Lord's own "loud cries and tears" (Heb 5:7), there is an aspect of suffering that remains a mystery for the person of faith. There is no slick or easy answer to the question, "Why does an Almighty God who is love, allow the righteous and innocent to suffer?" We ought to be ever humble about how much we are able to explain of God's ways in the face of suffering.

v. Christ Jesus has, by his acceptance of the awful pain and suffering of his rejection, trial, and physical death as our savior given us a powerful example of suffering to fulfill God's purposes for good.

We have also been called to follow in his steps and to know fellowship with him in his suffering (1 Pet 2:20–23; Heb 12:3–13). His understanding, support, and upholding grace are part of the transforming encouragement we can know through suffering, as the apostle Paul demonstrated so clearly (2 Cor 12:7–10).

vi. The New Testament lists a wide range of sufferings that Christians can expect as they live for Christ.

When Paul lists his sufferings in 2 Cor 11:23—12:10 he groups these together: the pressures of hard work; imprisonment, beatings, floggings, and stoning for Christ's sake; constant travel and its associated dangers, from shipwrecks to bandits; sleepless nights from work pressure; hunger, thirst, and lack of adequate clothing; misunderstandings and attack from people of different cultures; the personal and emotional costs of identifying with church development problems; and the "thorn in the flesh" that confirmed his "weakness." He describes his own illness on one occasion in similar terms in Gal 4:13–15. He sums up all such problems under terms like weaknesses, insults, hardships, persecutions, and difficulties (2 Cor 12:10). Or, in 2 Cor 6:4–10 he lumps together terms like endurance, hardships, distresses, beatings, imprisonments, hard work, dishonor, sorrows, poverty, and others as part of the common experience of "everyone who wants to live a godly life in Christ Jesus" (as Paul says of persecutions in 2 Tim 3:12).

The Bible lists many possible reasons for, or causes of sickness, or experiences of darkness and/or anguish of soul. Among others, these include:

- as judgment for abuse of the sacrament of communion (1 Cor 11:29–30)
- to allow the work of God to be displayed for God's glory (John 9:2–3; 11:4; 12:27)
- to discipline us as God's children (Heb 12:7–12)
- as part of a Satanic contest against God, God's judgment on pride and presumption (Job 1:6–12)
- as part of the pathway of faith and reverent obedience towards God (Isa 50:10–11)
- as one factor in guiding to a particular place of service, as for Paul going to Galatia for missionary work (Gal 4:13–15).

Pastoral responses to each of these different situations will vary according to the nature of the suffering. We shall gently encourage each other to search our hearts and to be open to our Lord Jesus speaking words of loving warning or rebuke or calling us to learn of him in other ways through such situations. They all need to be faced realistically and accepted as potential means of growth in grace rather than too quickly assuming the sufferer should be delivered from them. They all call for Christian sympathy, support, and pastoral encouragement from fellow Christians, all the while discerning the appropriate continuing pastoral assistance needed. In support of that guidance, a number of biblical strands may be identified:

i. While in Jesus's day sickness was commonly attributed to sin, Jesus was cautious about that connection (Luke 13:1–5; John 5:14; 9:2–3).

He denied that those who suffered tragic deaths were necessarily more guilty than others, and warned the healed lame man that the consequences of continuing in sin may be worse than physical sickness. Jesus did not accept that the blindness of the man in John 9 was caused by his own or his parents' sin; it was rather an occasion for the glory of God to be demonstrated.

ii. Christians may become ill as part of the normal cost of their service for Christ.

We have already referred to Paul. Epaphroditus and Timothy are further New Testament examples (Phil 2:25–30; 1 Tim 5:23).

iii. Christians are expected to take commonsense preventive steps to overcome illness.

In the Old Testament, God's promises of physical protection and healing were linked with practical dietary and hygiene regulations; so too, Christians are warned not to allow anything to control their bodies—ruling out addictive habits (1 Cor 6:12)—and to take medication for recurrent health problems (1 Tim 5:23).

iv. We also see the medical profession and medical sciences as good gifts from God.

These are to be welcomed and used for the glory of God wherever they can offer help, healing, or alleviation of suffering. We reject any suggestion that turning to medical services is a lack of faith in God. He expects us to use wisely all his gifts with thanksgiving (1 Tim 4:4; 1 Cor 3:21–23).

v. The Christian community is expected to pray for people facing physical danger or suffering (Phil 1:19).

Suffering is an occasion for the church to demonstrate its love and solidarity and in faith to ask God for healing, as well as trustingly accepting God's will as right and best in each specific situation.

vi. Christians are encouraged to ask the church elders to pray for them in their sickness (Jas 5:17).

The initiative in asking for such prayer lies with the sick person, being confident that our church and its leaders want to stand with, support, and pray earnestly for any member who is ill. As a community, self-examination and humble confession of sin should accompany such prayer.

vii. Christians can face physical death with calm confidence and peace, knowing it is the transition into the presence of Christ (Phil 1:21–22).

By his own death and resurrection Christ has conquered the devil who once held the power of death, and used the fear of death to dominate us (Heb 2:14–15). Forgiveness of sin has removed the sting from death for the Christian (1 Cor 15:55–56). Jesus alone now controls the issues and timing of death (Rev 1:18). Thus, in the New Testament Christians can regard death as "striking our tent and going home" (Phil 1:23; 2 Cor 5:1), or as completing our mission and receiving our reward (2 Tim 4:6–8). We still sorrow at times of death, and we still regard death as a real enemy, so pastoral comfort and encouragement are vital at such a time. But our sorrow is mixed with hope, and we do not sorrow as others do (1 Thess 5:13, 18).

Biblical Teaching on the Concept of Intergenerational Sin

As a local church we express concern about the way some sections of the wider Christian church are teaching about what some call "intergenerational sin." In this regard we seek to hold together the following biblical teachings:

i. The Old Testament stresses the interrelationship and corporate nature of our fellowship with God.

This is so that our personal actions and practices have corporate effects on others—for good or for evil. We accept that our attitudes and actions can and do influence the habits and behavioral patterns of our children, friends, and communities. We therefore seek to model Christ-honoring lifestyles and behavior and to walk humbly and responsibly before one another.

ii. The Old Testament stresses the personal responsibility and accountability of children of each generation for their own actions before God.

Ezekiel 18, particularly, and the promised new covenant, as in Jer 31:29–34, more generally, indicate that in our day whatever hereditary effects a previous generation's lifestyle may leave, no one is judged or held accountable for the sins of a previous generation. Each person in their own generation must give account for their own actions before God. In the New Testament, Gal 6:7–8 stresses that a person is responsible for what they themselves sow in their own lives; we are not held accountable before God for any other person's, nor our own forefathers' sins.

iii. In Christ we are by God's grace regenerated, or made new creatures so that all our past is fully dealt with in the atonement of Christ.

While we may need help to appropriate and apply that perfect work of Christ to particular aspects of our previous lifestyle or background, we do not accept that the residual effects of other people's sins will blight a person's Christian experience unless they can specifically name and ask forgiveness for the sins, iniquities, or trespasses of their family's previous generations. We teach that God himself has laid on Christ the sins of us all and that his death and saving work is sufficient to fully and freely forgive, redeem, restore, and renew every humble believer through simple faith in Christ Jesus.

iv. Where a person may struggle with aspects of their inherited family background our church is willing to offer pastoral support in applying the finished work of Christ to their own situation, and in seeking appropriate counselling or other support where such is indicated.

We recognize that in such cases there may be a mix of spiritual, psychological, social, or physiological factors calling for different kinds and levels of support. We shall be careful to refer people for professional assistance in these areas and shall beware of offering simplistic solutions in complex situations. In addressing any spiritual aspects we shall be careful not to make the person dependent on any person, system, or procedures other than their own straightforward confession, faith, and active reliance on the life and work of Christ made real to them through the Holy Spirit.

Guidelines for Pastoral Approaches to Suffering or Sickness

We desire our church to be known for an approach to pastoral care characterized by the following:

i. We accept and respect each person as they are in whatever their suffering, sickness, hurt, or need.

Therefore our first concern is to support, care for, and encourage the person to discover God's presence, loving care, and adequacy in their situation.

ii. We respect the dignity and importance of each person taking responsibility for their personal and spiritual well-being before God.

As servants of Christ we see our prime responsibility as supporting, strengthening, and building up the individual so they may themselves move on to maturity in Christ Jesus. We shall respect the fact that Christ gently leads us personally along often different pathways as we face up to and accept the reality and implications of an illness or suffering, and that there may be a variety of causative factors in any particular situation. We shall therefore beware of trite or simplistic approaches.

iii. We shall also guard against developing dependency relationships or using any procedures that may pressurize or manipulate people when seeking pastoral care in our church.

As Jesus respected the will and desires of those who came to him for help, so we will respect each person's right to decide how to move forward in their journey.

iv. We shall cultivate a spiritually safe environment where people know their confidences are respected and where they can trust the integrity and intentions of our pastoral workers.

Particularly when helping people to face correction or personal challenges we shall ensure this arises from careful and loving presentation of biblical teaching with a view to gentle restoration and burden-sharing, not from judgmental or critical attitudes. We shall respect the Holy Spirit's role in bringing a person to conviction and repentance and not assume we can quickly understand or evaluate the motivation or desires of another.

v. We shall require our pastoral workers to prepare and adhere to a personal code of conduct, and to review its content and achievement with the elders in regular performance reviews.

A Personal Response

To all of us, suffering, sickness, or even death become a personal challenge both to our own faith and discipleship, as well as to how our communities of believers accept and grapple with these darker parts of our Christian pathway. For us as a couple, after being told that medically we should not expect to be able to give birth, my wife Ann did become pregnant. But the joy, hope, and wonder quickly turned to grief, when our firstborn child lived only seven hours, despite excellent gynaecological help being on hand. I found expressing our sadness and sorrow in a poem helped me to work through the grief. I offer that poem as a possible encouragement to others.

Too Precious To Keep—Given Gloriously[7]

Oh Lord our God, we bow in prayer,
This way You've led is hard to bear:
Our precious child, so briefly given
You've taken to Your home in heaven.

You know, Oh Lord, how we have sighed
And longed and planned—and often cried—
That we might have a child—our own—
To make our house a real home.

You know how once, yes twice, it seemed
We soon would taste of what we dreamed,
But once, yes twice, the surgeon's knife
Said, "No, you cannot have that life."

Yet through those trials so deep we found
Your love, Your grace, so full abound;
To bind us close and teach us sing
The richer tunes shared sorrows bring.

7. Hitchen and Hitchen, "Too Precious."

And then, so unexpectedly,
The news that we would parents be!
What seemed too hard our God had done:
In Your good time You gave our son!

But oh, how brief this joy of ours—
Our little boy lived seven hours.
And then You chose to take him home
Our precious son, our first, our own.

We want to, but we cannot, see
What good in this could ever be?
Conflicting thoughts—our dazed minds reel—
We don't know what to think, or feel.

We know that Your mysterious will,
Should not be questioned—and yet still
We find it hard, although we try,
Not to keep asking, asking, "Why?"

* * *

"Some things, My child, too precious be
For you to hold and keep for Me;
Too precious, too, to use, enjoy;
Too precious for your own employ.

"Some things, though won laboriously
Must be poured out—yes gloriously
Returned to Me, though great the cost:
To yield them thus they're never lost.

"My child, today, come walk with Me
And scan the sacred history
For others in this path have trod—
Their precious gifts poured out for God.

"This was the lesson Abel learned:
For firstling of his flock he yearned
To have and hold—but he must yield
His first, his best, to Me, his Shield.

"My child, see Abram give his son,
His only, longed for, cherished one—
As reason failed, His God he'd trust:
His God provides—obey he must.

"And watch as to the hunted King
A drink, from Bethl'hem, soldiers bring.
Dare David drink? Himself suffice?
Nay, pour it out—a sacrifice."

* * *

Again we bow at Jesus' feet,
See Mary bring her perfume sweet,
What purpose? Keep? Use? Help the poor?
Nay, waste it, and her Lord adore.

Yes, thus the sacred pages tell
How these did learn this lesson well
That they, if they would richly live,
Their precious things to Me must give.

Why this child—the one You gave—
So quickly come to death—the grave?
Our hopes, our plans have crashed—despair—
Why is it Lord? Do You not care?

"Our God not care?" Forbid the thought,
Be gone such doubts, bow down, be taught:
A "careless" God can never be
For God, our God, knew Calvary.

And so we come, oh Lord, to learn
Your lessons. Yes, for these we yearn.
Beneath the Cross we bow today
What is it, Lord, You have to say?

* * *

"My children, I have asked of you
To follow in this pathway, too.
But look you up—do not despair
For I with you this path do share

"This way so dark with mystery
It is the path of Calvary.
It was the same that awful day
My Son, My Best, I gave away.

"I understand, I know the pain:
My only Precious One was slain.
But since His death brought victory
Your precious one is now with Me.

"And thus, My children, please believe
That as I gave, and now receive
Again your child, he brings to Me
An echo sweet of Calvary.

"Just as the wastage of Christ's grave
New life did bring—the world did save:
They cannot lose who give their best
And cling to Me—though hard the test.

"And so, My children, dare to trust,
Despite the ache, your lives now thrust
More fully on My Shepherd care:
Rest on My peace, cast out your fear!"

* * *

Yes Calvary—this is the key
The Cross gives light to mystery—
Oh God You care, for You, too, gave
Your only Son to death, the grave.

Yes, Lord, You understand—we rest
Believing that Your way is best,
And if, from Calv'ry You can bring
Such riches to the sorrowing . . .

Then You still have Your ancient skill
To fully work Your loving will.
And as our precious gift You take
All glory gain for Your name's sake.

Chapter 17

Christians in Business?

EVANGELICAL MISSIONS, WHILE EVANGELIZING and establishing locally rooted churches, often did not give adequate attention to applying their theology to business, or work. They seldom enabled church members to develop sustainable economic ventures. Thus, evangelical faith communities often have not been well equipped for transitioning into the globalized and interdependent economic world of today. There were many reasons for this. Missionaries themselves often kept away from business or trading activities, as these were seen as a distraction from their higher calling. But missionaries were necessarily involved in purchasing, trading, and importing, to sustain their lifestyles. Thus, their examples and teaching on economic matters were sometimes confusing, if not contradictory to local people. Their teaching said business, and the love of money, were temptations, turning us away from our more important relationships with God. But a good proportion of missionary time and effort was devoted to acquiring the basics needed for living, and clearly depended on access to finance and economic know-how. The missionaries' own attitudes to work and business had often been "caught" rather than "taught" from their own Protestant Christian upbringing and surrounding lifestyles. Missionaries usually valued and assumed this "Protestant work ethic" was right for Christians, but seldom taught about business or work as a necessary aspect of basic Christian discipleship for their converts. As missionaries, trusting Christ as Savior and Lord was the highest priority, and there was a real concern not to encourage any idea that our "work" makes us acceptable before God. Faith and work were often contrasted, so that the value of manual or business work was either downplayed, or ignored, when teaching about Christian living. When our friend, Ossie Fountain, in 1966 looked at whether business programs helped or hindered church life in our Christian Missions in Many Lands (CMML)[1] work in Papua New Guinea (PNG), he concluded, "if a mission station places too great an emphasis on economic activities, it does not truly reflect what Christ intended the gospel to be."[2] That reflected the view of most CMML missionaries at the time.

In the first generation of the church in PNG after World War II, that was not too great a problem, at first. The newly arrived evangelical missions worked primarily in rural or village localities, where subsistence farming provided a basic lifestyle, although tropical diseases and malnutrition were endemic in many areas. Converts continued their subsistence living, with little need for economic change. But that situation has disappeared. Even the most remote villages today are surrounded by, and are usually involved in, commercial mining, forestry, fishing, agricultural and/or oil exploration ventures, which are part of global economic systems. Traditional subsistence lifestyles have radically changed, and economic questions are now of primary social, communal, ethical, and spiritual importance. The church is still a major, if not the major, agency for guiding change in many such settings, so inadequate teaching on economic and financial matters is now a serious concern, and a priority challenge.[3]

Although the lack of a strong theological understanding of the value of work and business is widespread, my purpose in this chapter is to address the topic with particular attention to the PNG context and cultures. While the foundations and principles proposed herein are particular to that context, I believe they continue to have a wider application.

The Other Side: Church and Mission Business Ventures

Despite the lack of attention to economic and financial matters on the part of the church, there is another side to the story of mission and economic

1. The official name under which Christian Brethren missionary work was registered with the PNG Government when it began working in PNG in 1952. Present-day Christian Brethren churches in PNG were established through the work of CMML missionaries.

2. Fountain, "Religion and Economy," 58.

3. The original version of this chapter was presented to the Christian Brethren Churches' Business Summit, Wewak, PNG, February 2014, and published as Hitchen, "Theology of Business." Used here with the permission of the Melanesian Association of Theological Schools (see bibliography for further details).

development in PNG. Alongside the gap in teaching, missionaries initiated several business activities. These were not always successful or sustained. They were always well meaning, and intended to benefit the mission work as well as local people. We can trace such efforts in PNG back to the work of the London Missionary Society (LMS) at both the eastern end of Papua, particularly on the island of Kwato, and in the Papuan Gulf in the early 1900s. As an example of what were called "industrial missions" in the Papuan Gulf, the LMS missionary, F. W. Walker, established Papuan Industries Ltd. This company took over coconut plantations, with copra production as the foundation of the business. Unable to raise enough money to make the business sustainable, despite some initial promise, the venture did not last.[4] At the eastern end of Papua, Walker's LMS colleague and friend, Charles Abel, made similar attempts, both at plantation work and at various kinds of vocational training and business during the last decade of the nineteenth and the first two decades of the twentieth centuries. Again, the success was only partial, and uneven. Abel tried again after World War I on the island of Kwato. The Kwato Extension Association gave training in vocational skills to support the desired business ventures. But, again, inadequate capital meant only partial business success.[5] The Kwato Mission, which grew from this initiative, however, has made long-term contributions to the training of tradespeople who have found employment across the whole of PNG, right up to the present.

Later in the twentieth century, the Lutheran Mission commenced a range of businesses, notably Lutmis Shipping, trading around the coastal ports of PNG; and Namasu (Native Marketing and Supply), the mission-initiated chain of locally owned cooperative trade stores. Namasu was heralded in the late 1960s as "New Guinea's largest indigenous-owned company."[6] Namasu provided the backbone of the post-World War II trade store and coffee marketing supply lines, which developed as the highway network extended from the coast into the highlands of PNG.

A number of Evangelical Alliance-related churches and missions developed similar business projects, such as Menduli, the United Church Southern Highlands business arm, and Pasuwe (Papuan Supply and Welfare) of the Unevangelized Fields Mission (UFM, Asia Pacific Christian

4. Smith, "Market in Mission," 75–100; Walker, *Papuan Industries*; Weymouth, "Gogodala Society," 64–89; Austin, *Technical Training*, 50–103.

5. Smith, "Market in Mission," 83–95; Wetherell, *Charles Abel*.

6. Fairbairn et al., *Namasu*.

Mission, now Pioneers) and Evangelical Church of Papua. Ross Weymouth explains:

> [Pasuwe] was established in 1969 by the UFM out of the existing mission-supply and trade-store operations, as a non-profit organisation. Prior to this, the mission had run a trade store on each of the mission stations. [Pasuwe's] main aims were: "to provide for the Papua New Guineans' Christian training, medical and educational facilities, general welfare services, and training in professional, commercial, and industrial skills."[7]

The patterns of development, and the flourishing and decline of these business programs deserve careful study, to inform present and future possibilities for business development. How these mission/church initiatives related to, and were influenced by, the transitions in the nation's retail industry generally might also be instructive. The transition of retail business from the hands of the long-established Pacific trading companies (such as Burns Philp, Colyer Watson, and Steamships), through the period of increasing migrant Chinese ownership, to the diversification of small, PNG-owned businesses today, could also clarify trends and highlight significant factors.

The contribution of the economic support programs of the Christian Leaders' Training College (CLTC) to the dairy, cattle, and poultry industries in PNG is another example. But the CLTC support story needs to be more fully described and analyzed.[8] CLTC's focus on producing income to meet part of the theological education costs for the college's students is a distinctive factor in its commercial involvement. CLTC has also modelled a pattern of locally generated support for Christian ministries to successive generations of students studying on its Banz campus. CLTC also gave birth to the short-lived Alliance Training Association (ATA), with programs in trucking, sawmilling, and timber products. Again, ATA offers significant lessons and warnings in its different attempts to build viable diversified business with limited, and ultimately inadequate, capital resources. ATA has, however, made an ongoing contribution, since some of its trade trainees are still running successful transport businesses.[9]

7. Weymouth, "Gogodala Society," 263, citing *Light and Life* (October 1973), 4.

8. Descriptions are given in Yandit, "Ownership and Support"; Hitchen, "Christian Leaders' Training."

9. For the ATA and its key personnel, see Price, *Live in Tents*, 136–43, 251–57, 286–87, 316–17. Within particular missions and churches, such as CMML and Christian

These historic aspects—the gap in missionary teaching about work or business, and the range of only partially successful ventures into mission or church-based business—deserve further evaluation to guide present and future church-related economic ventures. While the contextual focus of this chapter is primarily PNG, the foundations explored below are also relevant to other contexts for Christian mission and vocation.

Biblical Foundations

Key areas of biblical teaching provide a foundation for encouraging church members to take a lead in the economic development of their societies. We make an important assumption, that to chart a pathway through the present-day business challenges will require a transformation of worldview presuppositions. We will need to clarify, and either endorse or transform, traditional primal religious beliefs influencing the transition into the present-day world of business, commerce, and global economic interdependence. Alternative Western secular approaches do not offer the necessary integrated, holistic worldview. We need an approach that retains the benefits of traditional perspectives, and gives proper attention to spiritual needs and realities. An integrated biblical foundation will also enable informed choices about the motives, aims, and purposes of any business or commercial ventures. Not having such an accompanying integrative worldview may have contributed to some failed PNG business attempts in recent decades. We start with the record of God's self-revelation at creation.

God as Worker

The first pages of the Bible present God as the creator, making things, shaping, forming, designing, ordering, and evaluating his work (Gen 1). One particular Old Testament role of the Holy Spirit was to give human craftspeople the knowledge, abilities, and skills to create, fashion, and design buildings, utensils, garments, and ornaments for the tabernacle, in which

Brethren Churches, several local ventures also await analysis of their strengths and weaknesses, and why they declined and closed. Both expatriate and local perspectives on projects like BMB (Bia Mogo Bulene, The Helper) at Koroba, the World Vision agriculture projects, or Paradise Furniture at Lae, would be helpful for forward planning. There could also be value in comparing those short-lived ventures with the longer-term success of Christian Books Melanesia in its retail and publishing business.

his people would meet with God (Exod 31:1–11). Such craftsmanship is vital for business enterprises. When God became human, in Jesus of Nazareth, he sanctified and gave particular dignity to manual labor. Jesus was born into a worker's family, grew up as a carpenter's son, and followed his father's trade (Mark 6:3). So, as a basic reason, we are involved in business as one way to be like our maker God, who himself is a creative worker.

Intrinsic Value in God's Creation

The works of God's creating hand have worth and value to God their maker. We value and respect the dignity of the created world, because it expresses the mind and will of God. Creatures and the creation are not to be worshipped, but neither are they to be abused or exploited. Nor are they to be feared, since they are not, in themselves, gods or spirit powers. Rather, they have their own proper place in the ecology of the universe. Each species "according to their kind" has inherent powers of reproduction and intuition to live and flourish. Moreover, as we shall develop further later, creation and other creatures are good gifts from God. God entrusts them to us, as humans, to care for and responsibly manage. All the creatures and resources of the universe are essential parts of the environment, within which we know and serve God. The resources of the universe are vast, not limited. They are abundant, given for us to explore, discover, and use wisely (Gen 1:28—2:24).

Many primal societies have believed there is only a limited amount of good in the world. They say we can only gain access to this good when we carefully follow the tribal laws (*lo*) and rituals the ancestor spirits gave us. Moreover, if one tribal group has more than another, it is said they have used some spiritual power to steal what should be equally available to every tribe. But, while there are limits to the non-renewable resources on the earth (like oil and gas), humans have only discovered, and are only using, a small proportion of the riches God has provided for all humanity to enjoy in the physical world around us. PNG has never been short of good resources in its environment. This wealth of potential resources provides incentive to constructively utilize them through business ventures.

These two beliefs—that God is a creative worker, and has provided a rich abundance of good resources to discover and enjoy—differ significantly from traditional Melanesian primal religious thinking. They also differ from the assumptions of secular Western worldviews. They give a fresh understanding of the nature of material things and their place in the cosmological order. The Bible tells us God has given us this abundance of developmental potential, so that we can become productive workers like him, with a sound basis for business ventures.

Humans as Creative Workers

Our basic human identity, and our value as persons, come from being made in the image of God. Humans reflect and represent our maker God within his creation. Thus, as part of that image-bearing reality, we are workers by nature. We have inherent abilities to think, plan, and design. Like our God, we are able to make, form, and shape things from and with the raw materials and active forces of the physical world. Humans are business-capable creatures in a universe inviting good exploratory business.

Humans as Responsible Managers and Trustees

Human beings have been given by God a unique responsibility for God's creation. God expects us to work with, and to look after the physical creation. God gives, or entrusts, his creatures, and all the potential of the creation, to humans to guard, protect, and "keep," or conserve. This is not a licence to exploit, or dominate and use to excess, the resources of our planet. Rather, we are to make good use of it, to develop it, and to wisely make it productive, as a trust from God, for the good of our fellow creatures and for the good of future generations. The Bible explains that, as humans, we will give an account to God about the way we have fulfilled this responsibility for the resources God entrusts to us. This is explained in the first commands God gave to the first human beings (Gen 1:28–30; 2:15, 19–20). These instructions are called the "cultural mandate" for humanity. Our human purpose is to bring the material and cultural world under ordered control, to organize and regulate it, and to name, care for, sustain, and make it productive.

Business and the Cultural Mandate

This cultural mandate in the first two chapters of Genesis speaks about our human responsibility for the created world, and its creatures: "Be fruitful, increase (multiply) . . . fill the earth . . . subdue it . . . work it, take care of it . . . name them." Let us consider what these commands involve.

Be fruitful, multiply, fill the earth means we are to live to the full, as people developing all our human capacities for thinking, speaking, and communicating. We are to develop our capacity for learning, and all kinds of knowledge, for art, music, drama, and imagination. We are to flourish and discover all we are able to do, personally, and as societies. We are to enjoy the full range of our competencies. Multiplying also means reproducing: to explore all the possibilities of parenting, of family life, of extended family, clan, tribe, and community life. This involves social organization, political activities, leadership structures, intergroup relationships, and international affairs. Being fruitful, then, means not sitting and doing nothing, but studying, exploring, experimenting, evaluating, and improving our world. It means growing, and fully developing all these areas of human life.

Subduing the earth, working and caring for it, and naming the creatures involves the whole human enterprise of exploration, discovery, manufacture, and invention. Our God-given human responsibility includes all of both the theoretical and practical realms of science, technology, ecology, geography, physics, zoology, biology, agriculture, horticulture, economics, business, commerce, and so on. For humans to do what these commands require, we need to organize ways of sustaining our lives together. We need to produce and share the materials and products necessary to thrive and flourish in our different communities. Once different peoples have settled in different areas, with different access to the range of resources needed for humans to flourish, we have to develop some means of trading with each other. In this way we can access the materials we need to sustain life, and to develop further. Therefore, trading, marketing, and businesses are an essential part in humans fulfilling this original cultural mandate.

Many different patterns of business and trading have been developed in different cultures. For example, we might think of a gift- and relationship-based *wantok* business, as against a commodity- and capital-based market business.[10] We are not suggesting that any particular one is right and the others wrong; they are just different, and both work well in different cultural contexts and business situations. When God created humans in his image, he created us with the ability to develop distinct cultures, with varying approaches to every aspect of life. Thus, a group considering setting up

10. In illustration, see the content and diagrams in Curry and Koczberski, "Relational Economics," 377–92. Their article investigates oil palm farming on New Britain, PNG.

a business needs to work out which kind of cultural approach will best meet the needs and opportunities of the business they are considering.

Guidelines from the Commandments

If we compare a Christian business to a well-constructed house, then we now consider the strong walls that are built on the "foundations" we have laid in the previous section. Strong "walls" are vital to enclose the business safely and protect it from collapse or failure. We find these "safe walls" for a "business house" in the biblical commandments, and these, too, apply to businesses in any cultural setting.

The Ten Commandments are pointers to the good life for God's people. Commandments are never sufficient to bring us into the good life God planned for us; we must have faith in Christ for that. But the commandments were given to point the way to Christ and to prepare the way for the fullness of life, which is available only in Jesus Christ (John 10:10). Some of the commandments are like signposts, marking the way, not only to the good life, but also to good business practice.

The Fourth Commandment: Work, Refreshment, Worship

The fourth commandment (Exod 20:8–11; Deut 5:12–15) lays a strong foundation for good business practice. Here is the secret to a productive, good life. Businesses can only succeed if both employers and workers give a full week of reliable work each week; this is what Exod 20:9 requires. Consistent, regular work from the whole team is the first essential for a good business. Before this commandment says anything about times for rest, it says: "Six days you shall labor and do all your work." Having a day for rest only makes sense when we work for the rest of the week. The Bible takes for granted that a commitment to a well-ordered work life is the proper, normal thing for us to do. In 2 Thess 3:10–12, Paul is quite clear: "We gave you this rule: Anyone who is unwilling to work shall not eat. We hear that some among you are idle and disruptive. They are not busy, they are busybodies. Such people we command and urge in the Lord Jesus Christ to settle down and earn the bread they eat." So, the first clue this commandment gives, in pointing towards a successful business, is the expectation that staff will be on time, do a full day's work, every day, each week. This is a real challenge to employees and employers alike, both in Western cultures and in Melanesian culture. But, if there is a "secret" to business success, this is where it starts.

The same commandment also stresses that good businesses give proper, regular times of rest and refreshment for their staff. Proper rest means time for spiritual renewal and worship, as well as physical refreshment. The Sabbath pattern of one day's rest in seven recognizes the basic needs of our human bodies, minds, and spirits. We cannot keep giving out in fruitful work without time to pause, and be restored as whole people. This command to keep one day in seven free from work is not a harsh law, imposing a heavy duty on us. Jesus clarified this when he said, "The Sabbath was made for people, not people for the Sabbath" (Mark 2:27). The rhythm of regular work and rest is a gift from God for our human fulfillment. God himself followed this pattern in creation (Exod 20:11). The wise business manager knows the workers are happier and more productive when businesses follow this rhythm. The chief thing about this command is keeping this well-ordered pattern of regular work and rest, not the particular day on which the rest is taken. Good businesses, then, care about the whole person of the workers, and do not exploit, or take advantage of them. A Christian business will provide both definite expected work times and working hours, as well as rest times and holidays. When employers fulfill their duty in regard to giving proper rest times, then we can expect the workers to fulfill their part and work consistently for the agreed times.

The Eighth Commandment: Ownership and Value

The eighth commandment is the command, "Do not steal" (Exod 20:15; Deut 5:19). This also has an important application in the business world. All the materials, products, and equipment we use in a business have been designed and produced through someone else's ideas, time, labor, and, usually, expense. The work materials also now belong to someone else, or to the business, who have spent time, effort, and expense to procure them. What we make with our ideas, our skills, our abilities, and our resources is special in God's eyes. We are producing things to serve and honor him. Therefore, the products we make have special value to God, and before others. This is why our personal and communal possessions are to be protected, respected, and looked after. This command requires us to respect the value of other people's efforts, and of their ownership of property. Theft and stealing do not respect another person's rights to own what they have properly made, or earned, or purchased. We should reimburse those who have used their effort, time, and expense to make the goods available. This is still true when the goods are owned by, or on behalf of, a group to which we belong. Every community has its own rules for granting permission for members to use the group's possessions. Not gaining that permission in the proper way is stealing. So is wasting materials, willfully destroying property, borrowing equipment without intending to return it, and wrongly recording quantities used on a job. These are all forms of theft, which destroy trust between workers and management. Theft like this can easily cause financial difficulties for the company. Ephesians 4:28 warns that the Christian way is not to steal, but to work, so we can earn sufficient to be able to help others in need.

The command not to steal also calls for fair wages and adequate working conditions. Employers can steal from their employees if they do not provide proper conditions for work. Passages like Eph 6:5–9 and Col 3:22—4:1 stress these principles. "Masters" were to properly care for their "slaves." In biblical times, the "master" filled the role of an "employer" in modern society, and (in a limited sense) "slaves" can be compared to "employees." The command not to steal protects both our right to own personal property, and for our work to be properly valued. Reliable business requires a workplace where there is no stealing.

The Ninth Commandment: Words and Promises

Lying, telling only half the truth, exaggerating, and making promises you never intend to fulfill are examples of the "false witness" condemned by the ninth commandment (Exod 20:16; Deut 5:20). Using deceitful words to entice someone to do what you want, spreading rumors or false stories about others, or signing papers you know are incorrect: all these are also forbidden by this command for a Christian business. Ephesians 4:15 and 25 are wise guidelines for business practice: "speak the truth in love," "each of you must put off falsehood, and speak truthfully to your neighbor, for we are all one body." Dishonesty destroys trust. But trust is the necessary foundation for all business transactions. Businesses are like "bodies," we often call them "corporate bodies." So, as Eph 4:25 says, if you cannot rely on the promise a member of the body gives, then everyone gets hurt. This warning about false witness also includes what we say in our bookkeeping and financial accounts. False figures are just as wrong as false words, and equally destructive in business. Jesus's advice is best: "All you need to say is simply 'Yes,' or 'No'; anything beyond this comes from the evil one" (Matt 5:37). Nothing is more important in business than to be able to trust the word and promise of those with whom you work and deal.

The Tenth Commandment: Ownership and Desire

Like the eighth commandment against stealing, the tenth commandment (Exod 20:17; Deut 5:21) against coveting the possessions of others, protects the proper value of what belongs to us, or what we produce through our work. Each of the behaviors warned against, has a present-day equivalent in business: "Do not covet your neighbor's wife," reminds us that seeking sexual favors has no place in business. "House or land" (Deut 5:21) included the living place and business place in Bible times when most business operated from the home. Land was the business resource, which could be made profitable. So, we should not try to deceitfully gain for ourselves the business assets which rightfully belong to someone else. The "male or female slaves" were the workforce of Bible times. So, here is a warning against enticing to your business someone in whom their present employer has invested training, trust, and responsibility. This is a particular problem for businesses in PNG today. There are only a few well-educated, experienced businesspeople. So, we should properly negotiate with owners of the business a person works for, not just pull them away by offering better pay. Doing this spoils business plans, and steals the previous hard work and trust others have invested in their workers. In Bible times, "the ox or donkey" were the "tools" or "equipment" needed to make the person's business productive. So, again, enviously using underhanded ways to get another business's equipment or specialist tools or knowledge is forbidden. These listed persons or things we may not covet are only examples. The command ends, "Do not covet . . . anything that belongs to your neighbor." Open honesty is essential in all business dealings; there is no place for selfish greed, deceit, or trickery.

We could go on to show how all ten of the commandments have valuable business lessons, but these four are especially important to protect good business. We do well to ponder where and how they need to be worked out in our own business attitudes and behavior.

Essential Concepts and Commitments

As well as these foundational teachings and "safe-wall" protective instructions, the Scriptures explain key concepts and attitudes, which are like the ceiling and roof of the "business house," completing its framework, and tying it together for good business.

Responsible Manager or Steward

The Bible describes Christian workers as stewards, or responsible managers. Responsible managers are accountable to God for how they fulfill the trust God has shown by giving all the earth's resources to develop for his glory, and for human good. Joseph is a good biblical example of a responsible manager or steward (Gen 39–50). Joseph showed how to be a God-honoring leader in the worlds of government and business, as well as in leading God's people. Joseph demonstrated reliability, trustworthiness, open integrity, compassion, and faithful accountability. These are the marks of a good manager. Jesus's parable of the talents (Matt 25:14–30; Luke 19:12–27) builds on those ideas. We are each trusted with a measure of competence, ability, and resources to develop productively. Jesus again stresses the accountable responsibility which such a trust brings. Paul adds to this in 1 Cor 4:1–5 by saying faithfulness, and knowing who our true judge is, are central in this responsible-manager concept.

Thinking of business as responsible management also reminds us that we receive these gifts of resources, abilities, opportunities, and accountability, as members of communities: our families, tribes, and wider societies. While we have a personal responsibility to fulfill the trust God puts in each of us, God also expects us to fulfill our management roles as partners in his family and body. Again, our relationships with *wantoks* and our wider communities are also vital, as we exercise care for creation, and responsibly serve each other and God with all our gifts and abilities. Christian businesses recognize they have a social responsibility for the welfare of the community, and not just a responsibility to make profit for the individuals in the business. A Christian business, therefore, gives special attention in its purpose statement to identify the social benefits it seeks to meet. The business will set out how it aims to improve the health, education, and communal well-being of its society. The New Testament teaching that we are all members of the body of Christ, each with our own contribution to make, and each needing the contribution of all others, can be applied to the "body corporate" of the business world, too.

Business as Vocation or Calling

Christians understand work as a vocation—a calling—in which we personally fulfill the will of God. This gives added incentive to the quality, standards, and motives for our work. At times in Christian history, people have thought that only those who are serving the church as ministers, pastors, or full-time workers are doing God's work. But, at the time of the Reformation, that was seen to be wrong. The Reformers rediscovered the biblical teaching that God calls—or gives a vocation to—every believer. He calls us all to follow Christ, and he calls us all to serve him in our daily lives, through our regular occupations. This sense of work as a "vocation" (from the Latin word for "calling") gives our daily occupations dignity and proper respect. As Paul reminded the Colossian Christians, "whatever you do, whether in word or deed, do it all in the name of the Lord Jesus. . . . Whatever you do, work at it with all your heart, as working for the Lord, not for human masters, since you know that you will receive an inheritance from the Lord as a reward. It is the Lord Christ you are serving" (Col 3:17, 23–24). For many of us, that means we are called to serve God in business.

This is good news for many Christians not just in Melanesia. We, too, have often had the wrong idea that only work in the church, or for the church, is God's work. Sometimes we were told that we should not make money in ordinary work, we should show our love for God by serving him in Christian church work. God does call some people to do this. But he calls many more to serve him in various workplaces as our lives and work habits serve our workmates. We need to rediscover the dignity and honor of serving Christ in the workplace.

Work as Service and Worship

The cultural mandate was part of God's gift to all humans as part of God's work as creator. The mandate gives all humans opportunities and responsibilities. But those who know God, not only as creator but also as savior, have extra reasons for wanting to serve God through all we do, including our business lives. Ephesians 2:8–10 explains that God, by his undeserved grace, has saved us, so that we can become committed to good work. When we have received his free salvation, which cost us nothing but cost our Lord Jesus his life on the cross, God remakes us for his original purpose: that we can do his will, and do good in our world. So, we are responsible to work, because we are human beings made in God's image. That is true of all humans, everywhere. But, when we know we are also new creatures, remade by the love and kindness of God, then our work becomes doubly important. For Christians, giving our best in developing a high-quality business, or doing our best to make the business, of which we are part, become a better business, are ways we can say thank you to God for his gift of new life and salvation. I once heard Robert Laidlaw, the well-known Christian businessman, after whom Laidlaw College (where I work in New Zealand) is named, say, in a sermon on Christians in business: "When I look down the newspaper lists of jobs available, why don't I see on every job advertisement the words, 'Christian preferred . . . Christian preferred'? If we really appreciate what Christ has done for us at Calvary, then we Christians should be the most committed, hard-working employees in the country. So, every sensible boss would want to employ Christians! Why isn't that happening?"[11]

Business Guidance and the Bible

As we seek to serve God in our daily business, we need to take care how we use the Bible to guide our business life. The Scriptures often give more than one perspective on the same question. We have to learn to hold these different perspectives together, and in balance. As just one example, there is always a tension between two aspects of the management or stewardship responsibility we have just mentioned. On the one hand, as we noted, we are responsible to serve, care for, and sustain our *wantoks*, communities, and nation. Indeed, we have a duty to support our fellow humans, wherever they are in need, right around the world. One key purpose and goal of business is to fulfill this social responsibility. So, we will share business profits with our extended families, as soon as we can, to help meet their many needs, like health and education costs. But, on the other hand, we are also directly accountable to God not to neglect, or abuse, or waste the potential in the resources he entrusts to us. As creative humans, made in God's image, God expects us to find the potential in our land, our minerals, our store of cultural knowledge, and our intellectual abilities. We need to create and

11. For a biography of Robert Laidlaw and especially his business principles, and leadership at the New Zealand Bible Training Institute, see Hunter, *Robert Laidlaw*.

develop new materials and articles, using the potential we have discovered in God's gifts. But, to do this, we need to keep some capital for this research, and to develop new products. If we give away all our income as soon as we earn it to meet our social responsibilities, we will never have the funds to develop new products, or to improve the business, to ensure it grows and lasts. Unless we reinvest enough money into developing the business, we will not be able to ensure it has a secure future. So, we must put enough of the profits back into developing the business to make sure the business becomes strong and secure.

Finding the balance between these two aspects of serving God in our business is not easy. The parable of the "talents" in Matt 25:14–30 emphasizes this aspect of developing the full potential of what God has entrusted to us. The parable also implies we should plan well for longer-term results in the way we use our resources. Stimulating a long-term view of business processes, by not just adopting a "get rich quick" way of thinking, is part of the challenge facing business processes in PNG.

Making Money

As well as the clarifying concepts above for moving into business as a Christian, we also add that earning money through honest, upright hard work is not wrong, and we are not giving in to temptation when we work hard for proper wages or profit. The Bible does not teach that money is evil; rather, according to 1 Tim 6:10, "the *love* of money is the root of all kinds of evil." If we only desire more and more money, then we will fall into temptation (1 Tim 6:9); but when we go into business and work well for a good wage and a fair profit, if our motives and desires are to please God, and to help our own communities, then that is the way to bring glory to God. Money, itself, is neither good nor bad. It is what we want it for, and the way we use it, that make money either good or bad. The Christian way is to see earning money as part of our service and worship to God.

Character Attributes for Business

We now need to address some key emphases arising from all we have said so far. To run a successful business, we not only need business knowledge, skills, and technical ability. Even more important are the following character patterns, attitudes, and habits. These are the characteristics that anyone entering our "business house" should see displayed in every part of our business.

Trust and Trustworthiness

To participate productively in the global business world today, we must be able to trust our staff, our business clients, our accounting staff, and the various other officials or agents with whom we work in the business. The necessary foundation is not there for a business to work well, without openness, mutual respect, and knowing we can trust the word and promises of all whom we serve or depend on. But, if we are to trust others, then they must find us worthy of their trust, too. Trust works both ways; we expect it in others, and we must prove trustworthy in every way ourselves. This two-sided character quality of trusting and being trustworthy is basic for good business.

Honesty and Integrity

Speaking and doing the truth at all times is the next mark of a successful businessperson. Honesty is always the best policy in the business world, where "you can be sure your sins will find you out." Honesty when problems or difficulties arise, with the governing board, with staff, customers, suppliers, and also ourselves, gives strength to any business. We join this quality with integrity: the attitude which means we are consistently open and transparent. This means never accepting a bribe, or twisting the facts to manipulate others for our own advantage; never using deceitful measures, or untrue reporting to turn decisions in our own favor. Keeping our motives pure, and "walking in the light" is sound biblical advice in business practice (Phil 1:9–10; 1 John 1:5–7). Integrity calls us not to cover up the truth, and not to hide, or hide from, problems that need attention. There are times when an employer needs to "not let his left hand know what his right hand is doing" (Matt 6:3), when, for instance, you are at the early stages of a project, and you need more information, or need to do more testing before making your plans or product known. But that does not mean being deceitful or twisting the truth. The wrongdoing of Ananias and Sapphira was their lack of integrity, not their decision to only give a part of their income to the apostles (Acts 5:1–11). They were always free to do that, as Peter said. But they were lying to God the Holy Spirit when they tried to make the church think they had given all the proceeds of their property sale to the church. God judged them for this deceit and lack of integrity. Having integrity, and being trustworthy, go closely together in business dealings.

Dependability and Accountability

Being dependable is also linked with trustworthiness. Both managers and workers need to be able to depend, or count on, each other. An unreliable member of staff can spoil teamwork and affect the whole business. Arriving at work on time, being there for the full time expected, carrying out a job to the end, keeping your word, and fulfilling your commitments, are habits other workers respect, and that employers really appreciate. No one needs special qualifications to show these characteristics. Accountability adds to dependability the extra quality of taking responsibility for the quality of our work, and reporting it properly. Blaming others for things we have not done properly spoils relationships among staff. We demonstrate our accountability by keeping good records of the operation of our part of the business, and reporting regularly to those above us in the business structure. It is very difficult to evaluate where a business can be improved if responsible people at each level do not accept these accountability duties. Recordkeeping and reports provide the data we need to plan well for growth, and to correct problem areas in any business. Dependability and accountability are essential habits in business and in working life generally.

Justice and Fairness

Treating employees fairly, and consistently treating all staff with the same respect and personal or emotional support, should set Christian businesses apart as good places of employment. This means, of course, fair pay and no inappropriate pressure on staff to do overtime. To be just and fair, managers will need to know their staff personally, so as to help them in their times of family or personal needs. Favoring one person, or group of persons over others, or changing the way company policy is applied to different groups, soon undermines morale and confidence in the staff team. But open fairness without favoritism creates loyalty and a willingness to "go the extra mile" when necessary for the business. Good businesses have clear pathways for staff to express a concern, or make a complaint about the way the business is running, and wise managers attend promptly to any such concerns.

Compassion and Kindness

Justice and fairness are not enough on their own when they are administered coldly and without much feeling for the people involved. So Christian businesses seek also to blend compassion, empathy, and kindness into their operations. Words of appreciation and encouragement, both when things are done well and when the task is hard and demanding, and thoughtfulness in the way new requests or changes are introduced to the workers, are simple ways to show compassion among the workers. Most workers like to see the senior managers walking around among them and talking personally with them. Our Lord Jesus himself is our model in these aspects of interpersonal relationships with staff and customers in a business.

There are no magical secrets which can automatically guarantee success in any business. But where a united team of management and workers aim for these qualities of personal character, attitudes, and habits, they foster a good working environment—a strong "business house."

Worldview Summary

We can say these teachings seek to introduce a number of fundamentally new attitudes at the worldview level. We can bring them together, using ideas developed by the late Harold W. Turner, whose studies on primal societies are still of vital significance. He suggested, in an article presented to a South American seminar on religion and global poverty in 1985, that there are five basic movements needed in a primal society's worldview if it is going to participate successfully in the global economies of today.[12] Each of his five points deals with one of the major areas of human understanding which a worldview seeks to explain.

Cosmology

Traditional primal thinking believes in the cosmos, or whole universe, as a closed, fixed, and unchangeable system which is too sacred to work on or develop. That view needs to change towards seeing the cosmos as open, full of potential for development, and natural, not sacred. Thus, we can study, explore, and creatively improve the material world and its parts. The world is not "necessary," or fixed and unchangeable, but "contingent," or able to

12. Turner, "Relationship," 84–110.

be changed by the decisions of humans making choices about how to work with the resources and materials in the physical world. We can use human powers either for the ongoing good of the planet, or we can exploit and spoil our environment.

Epistemology

We also need to change the way we think humans gain access to proper understanding and power to make changes and improvements in our world. This does not come through magical beliefs and religious rituals, nor through incantations and repeating fixed practices to influence the spirit powers.[13] Rather, the way to properly understand the reality of our whole universe is to use the lessons of science and technology to learn about the physical world; and to understand and relate to the spiritual world by following faith and obedience to God's revelation in the Scriptures.

Eschatology

To understand time, the traditions and myths which have come from the ancestors are not enough on their own. We need to add a clear grasp of the progress of history, and a sense of meaning and movement towards a final goal, as an essential context for our human story.

Sociology

The primal worldview understands society as made up of a single, closed, and sacred set of relationships in extended families, clans, and tribes, with fixed cultures, and with each tribe thinking they were inherently better than others.[14] Instead, we need to understand society as open to change, with many different patterns of belief and relationships, and as secular, not too special or sacred to change. So, new social relationships with people

13. Don McGregor explained and illustrated that this was the way Papua New Guineans traditionally thought in his important paper, "New Guinea Basic Assumptions," the revised form of a paper presented at the CMML Annual Brethren Missionary Conference, August 1966, Anguganak, PNG. See Assumption 3 (4–11).

14. McGregor, "New Guinea Basic Assumptions," 2–3, explains this point as the first Assumption.

from other clans, tribes, religions, and cultures are both possible and to be accepted.

Ethics and Morality

Our understanding must no longer think that evil is just something outside us, coming from spirit beings, or from the environment.[15] Rather, we should understand evil as also present in us internally as human beings. Our own choices and desires are often the source of evil, selfishness, greed, and deceit. Moreover, we do not become evil, or unclean, or polluted, because we did not observe some laws and rituals in the right way. Rather, evil is a moral reality, which comes from our wrong choices and actions as responsible humans.

Changes in these five areas of thinking take time. But they are important if we want to grasp how business works in the global world of today. The biblical teachings we have set out above form the basis for changes at this worldview level of understanding.

Conclusion

These basic biblical teachings lay the worldview level foundations for Christian involvement in business, commerce, and industry. These Christian values and assumptions have deeply and richly informed and shaped Western culture, and global economic thinking over the past four hundred years. But attempts to retain the fruit of the Christian gospel, without any commitment to their roots in that gospel, is one of the biggest concerns in the Western world today. We need to keep both the roots and the fruit alive, in fostering new business ventures in PNG and elsewhere.

Let me conclude with a personal story. In 1978, a Christian businessman friend of ours, Heaton Drake, from Nelson, New Zealand, was at CLTC in PNG. He was auditing the college books before the annual College Council meetings. As we talked, he surprised me by saying, "John, I love making money." When he saw the shock on my face, as I wondered what he meant, he smiled and went on, "I love making money, so that I can give it away, and help others in God's service." We went on to talk about the need

15. Again, this belief is illustrated by his explanation of Assumption 3 in McGregor, "New Guinea Basic Assumptions," 5–9.

for money to help God's work in PNG. Later that same visit, Heaton offered fees and fares for me to go to the other side of the world, to Aberdeen University in Scotland, to study the history of Christian mission in the Pacific, and to complete PhD study. Our family's whole service for Christ from that time was changed and enriched through Heaton's generosity. Even when Heaton was tragically killed in a work accident two years later, he had made arrangements so that the fees and fares my family and I needed to complete the PhD were still available. We owe a huge debt of thanks to this man who "loved making money" for the right reasons. He also provided the money to start the Bia Mogo Bulene business venture at Koroba, Hela Province.

Our prayer for Papua New Guinea, as for wherever the gospel is proclaimed, is that Christian businesspeople will manage their businesses well, so that, like Heaton Drake, they, too, can serve God faithfully through making money and using it well for God's glory.

Chapter 18

Christians and Politics

ATTITUDES TO POLITICAL INVOLVEMENT are changing amongst Christians in the South Pacific as we settle into the twenty-first century. The exuberance and high hopes of newly gained independence in several previous colonies have settled as the realities of responsible statehood press home. The first few decades of the new Mixed Member Proportional electoral system in New Zealand saw the rise, and then disappearance, of a number of overtly "Christian" parties. The long-delayed recognition of the rights of Australian Aboriginals, and then the defeat of the "Yes" vote in the 2023 referendum have shown the ambiguity and uncertainties inherent in contemporary Australian politics. The participation of Christians in political action throughout this time may be linked with the recovery of the centrality of the kingdom of God in the teaching of Jesus. But the ongoing role of Christians in the political directions of South Pacific nations is much harder to predict. Whether the moment of opportunity has been irretrievably lost and discouragement and disillusionment will set in, or whether more recent setbacks will lead to lessons learned and a more effective and better informed Christian involvement, has yet to be determined.

One thing is sure, Christians in our region need to think much more deeply about the political task. The political environment and opportunities surrounding recent elections raised practical questions for serious Christians: why vote; how best to uphold Christian principles, by supporting Christian candidates in major parties, by supporting Christian parties, or by lobbying all the parties; how to use the voting systems of our various nations; whether to insist on supporting our local *wantoks* or whether we can work together with wider groups of like-minded candidates for better influence. These and other practical questions need answers. But the recent election experiences have shown that Christians do not have a consistent framework of biblical and theological understanding within which to apply those answers. For some the political arena is still seen as part of the "world" they are to shun. For others it is a stage to commandeer for a public evangelistic testimony to the nation. Others appear to regard politics as the scene in which to work as reactionaries to bring in a Christian theocracy in which legislated morality will overcome all the woes of modern society—assuming political coercion can change the human heart. Others, who see political involvement as a human responsibility they share with all their fellow citizens, are at odds about the way to develop economic, educational, or welfare policies. As one commentator noted before the 1996 elections, when listing "themes missing almost entirely from theological thinking" in New Zealand, "we need a theology and philosophy of the political realm."[1]

This chapter offers a few starting points for developing such a theology of politics by suggesting answers to the foundational question: *Why be involved in the political system at all?*[2]

Because God Is Already Involved

God the Father instituted and oversees the political realm as much as every other part of creation. His nature and his role as the active ruler of our universe provide the basic reasons for our political involvement. We must be involved in the political issues of our day because we share the life of the living God who is himself just, and who seeks justice among humans.

God the Father "executes justice for the oppressed"; "[he] gives food to the hungry." "The Lord sets the prisoners free; the Lord opens the eyes of

1. Turner, "Recent Orthodoxy," 44.

2. This paper has grown from material prepared for the Papua New Guinean scene in the late 1970s, and papers written to stimulate social involvement in New Zealand in 1987 and 1995. It was hastily brought together as a working document to be abridged and popularized by the Evangelical Fellowship of New Zealand before the 1996 elections, and republished by the Australian Evangelical Alliance. A version was submitted at Vision New Zealand's request for inclusion in their 1997 Congress volume; see Hitchen, "Involved in Politics," 174–96, 205–7. It is now revised with the insights of more recent elections behind us. The material in the Vision New Zealand volume is used here with the permission of Vision Network, now the New Zealand Christian Network (see bibliography for further details).

the blind. The Lord lifts up those who are bowed down"; "the Lord watches over the sojourners, he upholds the widow and the fatherless" (Ps 146:7–9). God the Father expects his children to be involved in political action like this because he is so involved.

God the Son, during his earthly life, did not hesitate to challenge the national political leaders of his day. His running battle with the oppressive views of the Pharisees and Sadducees is well known. It's no surprise that Peter, after living in Jesus's shadow for so long, writes in one paragraph, "For the Lord's sake accept the authority of every institution, whether of the emperor as supreme or of governors . . . Fear God, honor the emperor." Then, in the very next paragraph Peter goes on to say, ". . . to this you have been called, because Christ also suffered for you leaving you an example that you should follow in his steps" (1 Pet 2:13–14, 17, 21). As the central theme of his earthly teaching ministry, Jesus announced he had come to inaugurate the "reign of God" (Mark 1:14–15; Luke 17:20–21). Although his kingdom is not "of" this world (John 19:36), it is not less than this world. His kingly rule embraces and influences every realm of human life, politics included. He is indeed, "Lord of all." Our political task involves demonstrating to our modern world with all its political forces what it means to represent the one whose lordship embraces all the powers at work in the universe.

The Holy Spirit is into upholding righteousness in the world. There is a direct parallel between the work of the Spirit in the world as outlined in John 16:7–8, and the work of governments as set out in Rom 13. The Holy Spirit is God's power at work convicting the world of sin and righteousness and judgment. God delegates to governments power to approve what is good, and to judge the wrong. When the Spirit is leading us, then, we will do what he is doing in the world: caring about right, wrong, and justice in society. That means being involved in politics, sensitively, discerningly, co-operating in the Spirit's ongoing task: "It is therefore the Spirit who gives his people a tender social conscience, and impels them to immerse themselves in humanitarian relief, development and the search for justice."[3]

Our concern about politics is rooted in the character of our God, Father, Son, and Holy Spirit. Since he cares about truth, honesty, justice, and equity, so must we.

As Christians we understand that all power belongs ultimately to God. Political power is but one delegated area of authority in a universe ordered by our living, active God. Like the psalmist, the Christian can say, "More

3. "Evangelism and Social Responsibility."

than once I have heard God say that power belongs to him" (Ps 62:11). Our understanding of God determines our understanding of the government. The living God is the God of power and the God of order. These two facts undergird the Christian understanding of government, and are at the base of our obligation to be politically involved.

The true God is the "only Ruler, the King of Kings and Lord of Lords" (1 Tim 6:15). The risen Son of God makes as his final claim before his ascension, "I have been given all authority in heaven and on earth" (Matt 28:18). Therefore, all other power, lordship, or authority comes from and depends upon God.

The true God is also a God of order. From the very creation of the universe he has worked to bring order out of chaos. He distributes and controls his power in an orderly way. He is the God of "law" who puts things in their proper relationship and expects that "law" and order be maintained.

The New Testament offers a wide range of words to describe the powers controlling and operating in our world: for example, spiritual powers (thrones); lords (dominions); rulers (principalities); authorities; spiritual rulers; cosmic powers of this dark age; ruling spirits of the universe (elemental spirits of the universe); or angelic rulers and powers (see Col 1:16; 2:10; Eph 2:2; 3:10; 6:12; Rom 8:38–39).

The biblical writers saw the power of the state as one of these many kinds of powers, along with various other secondary authorities with delegated powers, such as families (Eph 3:15; 5:23). The Christian good news is that in heaven "Christ rules there above all heavenly rulers, authorities, powers and lords; he has a title superior to all titles of authority in this world and in the next. God put all things under Christ's feet and gave him to the Church as supreme Lord over all things" (Eph 1:21–22; cf. Col 2:10; 1 Pet 3:22). Christ controls and rules over all these kinds of power both by his work as their creator (Col 1:16) and by his work as redeemer (Col 1:20). In his death Christ overcame the powers which had rebelled against God. They are already subject to him even though their final overthrow will not be complete until Jesus consummates his kingdom in all its fullness at his return (Col 2:15; 1 Cor 15:23–28).

This confidence that Christ is in control of even the evil governing authorities enabled the early Christians to accept persecution and even martyrdom. Nothing could separate them from the victorious love of God they enjoyed in Christ (Rom 8:37–39). We need to recapture this same confidence as we face fresh opportunities for being part of the processes of government in our own society. We start from this reality: since God is so deeply into politics, we can be sure he expects us, as his people on earth, to be similarly involved.

Because Jesus Requires It

Jesus was often surrounded by active members of the political parties of his day, particularly in the incident recorded in Mark 12:13–17. The Pharisees, with their strong nationalistic fervor and general dislike of the Roman overlordship, on this occasion joined forces with some Herodians—collaborators who depended on the Roman presence to keep the Herods in power. Luke notes that the scribes and chief priests, who were mostly Sadducees, were also behind this interrogation of Jesus. The chief priests administered daily political power under the watchful eye of their Roman rulers. So Jesus is facing a strange coalition of normally antagonistic political groups. Their introductory comments smack of common political cant: "Teacher, we know you are right in what you say and teach . . ." But Jesus is not taken in by their crafty question, "Is it lawful for us to pay taxes to the emperor or not?" They expected to catch him out whichever way he answered. They could either accuse him to the Roman powers as a rebel, or condemn him before the people as a traitor to the Jewish nation. But Jesus acted deftly in this political environment. He recognized and showed up their hypocrisy. They only caught themselves in their own trap. Jesus's answer was unanswerable. They couldn't use it against him in any way.

Jesus's response to this question sets out the basic answer to all such questions about our duty to government: *Give back to the emperor what rightly belongs to him and give to God what rightly belongs to him.* For Jesus, the Christian has a duty both to government and to God. We are to repay what we owe the government for the services it provides. But at the same time we are to honor God as our true King and true Lord.

Jesus was not teaching that political responsibility and our duty to God are two distinct areas of duty to keep separate from each other. One part of our life does not belong to God and a different part belong to the government. Nor was Jesus simply saying that obeying the state is one small part of our greater duty to obey God. That may be true but that is not the point Jesus was making. Rather, for Jesus, obeying God and fulfilling political responsibilities are two interrelated duties which we must always hold together. These two are woven together in every part of our lives. We are to fulfill our obligations to the government in such a way that at the same time we also continue to obey God.

Christ's response to this question about the tax money indicates three Christian political duties. We need to hold all three together and in balance:

- Discern clearly what our duty is to God and what our duty is to government in each practical situation we face. Make responsible decisions about where the government's rights begin and end, and about what obeying God means in each particular setting.
- Give back to each what is their proper due: to God what belongs to him and to the government what is its due.
- Remind the government of the limits of its power and refuse to go beyond those limits. Like the prophets of old, we remind the government its powers are not totalitarian. God alone can demand the worship of his creatures.

Jesus demonstrated the impact of these basic attitudes to governing authorities during his own trial. He respected their authority as God-given. The amazing thing about the trial of Jesus is the quiet respect Jesus showed towards those who condemned him. He quickly stopped the disciples when they attacked those who came to arrest him (Matt 26:50–52). He quietly and clearly referred to the injustice of what they were doing; but as he did so he also showed clear respect for these rulers and their positions (Matt 26:55; John 18:19–23). John 19:11 explains the reasons for this respect: "You have authority over me only because it was given you by God." Like David before him (1 Sam 24:6), Jesus saw the rulers of his day as people with a responsibility under God for what they were doing. This respect for the rulers as persons accountable to God led to the second part of Christ's attitude.

Jesus meekly submitted to the unjust condemnation of the political leaders of his day. At each point—from the arrest in Gethsemane; before the Jewish Council; before Pilate; before Herod; and in the hands of the soldiers—Jesus submitted without fighting back. As Peter summed it up, "He committed no sin, and no one ever heard a lie come from his lips. When he was insulted, he did not answer back with an insult; when he suffered, he did not threaten but placed his hopes in God the righteous Judge" (1 Pet 2:22–23, GNT).

But this was not weakness. Christ was not afraid of those to whom he submitted. Christ was in control of each situation. In the garden, the soldiers are afraid, not Jesus (John 18:3–8). When being questioned, Christ controls the direction of the conversations and chooses whether he will answer or not. Pilate is afraid of him and of the implications of condemning him (Matt 23:4, 13–25). Christ is in full control of himself and of his own power and refuses to use it against these ruling authorities. He is indeed giving himself up to death (cf., John 10:17–18). His understanding of what is happening gives this humble submission.

Jesus realized that higher powers were at work over and through these human rulers. Jesus understood the situation in a way which enabled him to accept and submit to the injustice and the shame of the situation without hitting back. His prayer from the cross sums this up clearly, "Forgive them Father! They don't know what they are doing" (Luke 23:24, GNT).

This different understanding of the situation centered on Jesus's belief that both satanic forces and the will and power of God were at work in and through these decisions and actions of the rulers of his day. As he prepared for this confrontation in Jerusalem, Jesus said, "Now is the time for this world to be judged; now the ruler of this world will be overthrown" (John 12:31, GNB). As he went to his trial, he knew the evil one was both active in the workings of the trial and was on trial himself. Jesus recognized evil powers at work through these government authorities: "I was with you in the Temple every day, and you did not try to arrest me. But this is your hour to act, when the power of darkness rules" (Luke 22:53, GNT).

Jesus also knew that his father God was fully in control of all that was happening. He turned to his Father for strength and help. His submission to the earthly rulers is the direct result of his earlier submission to his father's will (Mark 14:32–42). At each point Jesus knows the declared will of God as set out in the Scriptures is really controlling the events (Matt 26:54, 56, and elsewhere).

In their early preaching the apostles were quick to point out that neither the rulers themselves nor the people as a whole understood this deeper involvement of the will of God and the forces of evil in the events of the cross (see Acts 3:17). In fact, Paul is so bold as to imply that even the evil spirit powers themselves did not understand the deeper significance of what they were doing (1 Cor 2:8).

In summary, then, Jesus's relationship to the ruling authorities at his death was marked by these three attitudes: respect for their authority as God-given; meekness despite their injustice; and recognition that spiritual forces were working in and through these government actions.

Translating these principles into our political situation not only means we should pay our taxes. We live in a political situation where each citizen has both the right and duty to vote responsibly at elections. Christ's basic command to render to government its dues will, for us, include our duty to vote. Not to exercise this right will, for Christians, be as irresponsible as refusing to pay taxes. Moreover, in our democratic systems of government in the South Pacific today, the whole political process depends on citizens accepting their democratic responsibilities. Each citizen shares the duty to ensure good government. Christ's command requires us to fulfill this duty. This surely means being active in the whole political process. In our democratic systems each citizen has the opportunity to influence the kind and content of legislation our parliamentarians enact. We are free to lobby our members of parliament. It is our responsibility to clearly convey our opinions about the kind of laws and society we desire. Grasping this right to lobby and influence legislation is one way of "giving to government its due." Likewise, creating and supporting political parties are fundamental rights of citizens in a democratic system. So we have a further Christian duty to ensure the right kind of parties and potential members of parliament are contesting the elections. We could perhaps have been excused for being cynical about our influence under previous patterns of colonial rule, or even the old "first past the post" electoral system. But the newer systems, like MMP in New Zealand, have brought both new opportunities and new responsibilities. In a fresh way each citizen has the duty to determine the mix and composition of parliament. Our political duty has been significantly extended. Just as we are to pay our taxes, so we need to grasp these significant new political duties with both hands.

Godward Duty

Jesus's basic teachings take us further. Seeing the difference between what belongs to the government and what belongs to God is foundational in New Testament teaching about the Christian attitude to the state. Christians always seem to have had problems with this. We all too easily lose our powers of discernment in the heady atmosphere of politics. We need parliamentarians, and political parties, who are strong on astute discernment. Other New Testament examples of the way the church worked out Christ's teachings can help us here.

1 Corinthians 6:1–8

At Corinth Christians were taking each other to the local government courts to sort out their differences and arguments. The apostle Paul says shame on the Christians for going to a non-Christian court to sort out their problems. Paul was not teaching, as Oscar Cullman suggests, that, "everywhere the Christian can dispense with the State without threatening its existence, he should do so."[4] Rather, the Christians had confused their responsibilities in this situation. They were not judging correctly what belongs to God and what belongs to government. The government was not responsible for social order in the church. Social order and discipline in the church belong to the head of the church, Jesus Christ. Christians should turn first to him to solve their disagreements. Some civil legal wrongs may need to be taken to a government civil court. But matters between Christians should be dealt with first within the church. We are wrong to take what belongs to Christ and expect the government to sort it out.

Acts 19:21–41

The Ephesian local government officer reminded the rioting citizenry very clearly about proper government responsibility. The Ephesians had wrongly taken into their own hands what belonged in the power of the properly constituted legal authorities. Reminding the crowd of the right place to handle law and order problems protected the early Christians at that time. Upholding the rule of law and expecting fellow citizens to respect government procedures and authority is still fundamental for Christians today.

Romans 12:17—13:14

The problem here was the issue of "payback" or retribution for wrong done. Christians are never to take revenge into their own hands, for only God can give proper retribution (Rom 12:19). But in the very next verses (13:1–4) God delegates this work of "bearing the sword" or "carrying out God's wrath" to the government. Again, we are required to judge properly about who has the responsibility for the political task of retribution and then to give that responsibility to the proper authority. Don't confuse things by

4. Cullman, *State*, 61.

retaining in our own hands what God has put in the government's hands. The government is God's servant entrusted to fulfill this particular work.

Acts 4:19–20; 5:29

When Peter and John are taken before the council the issue is clear for them. Human courts do not have jurisdiction to decide whether or not we should proclaim God's word. God himself has given clear commands about this and therefore we must obey him. The government has no control over when, where, or how God's gospel is to be shared with others. We are accountable directly to God to obey his commands to preach regardless of what the government says. Reminding government authorities of the limits of their power is part of our Christian duty.

Acts 18:12–17

Here, too, the Roman governor of Greece is commended because he knew and upheld the limits of governmental authority. The Roman government had no right or concern to enter into judgments on religious questions. Paul was working out the principle we see in the words of our Lord.

Each of these examples warns us not to be politically naive. We need politicians who are not merely power hungry, but who respect the limits of proper political power. Ability to discern is one of the prime requirements for a politician. Reminding government of the limits to its authority is still a Christian duty. Speaking to New Zealand businesspeople in 1995 on trends in politics today, Paul Johnson concluded with these words:

> The best way to ensure that we get the politics we want and need is to make certain that politics as such impinge only on a limited part of our lives. For public policy to be right, we must work to preserve the strength, integrity, and extent of the private sphere. Whoever is in office . . . we must make sure the individual citizen remains in power over his or her life, and that the great majority of the key decisions which affect it are taken according to his or her own interests and conscience. . . . For what the great majority of people want today, and have probably always wanted, is for politics to be kept in their place, and for government to be efficient, honest, practical—and tame.[5]

5. Johnson, *Paul Johnson*, 62.

These examples suggest some distinctly Christian questions to ask of parties and potential candidates today. How well can they discern the beginning and end of political responsibility? Where do they draw the line between religious freedom and loyalty to government policy? Do they treat Christian citizens, schools, welfare agencies, and other community services—yes, even Bible colleges—on the same basis as they treat other comparable persons or agencies? Do all taxpayers have comparable access and rights to the government dollar, or are religious groups precluded regardless of the quality of their services? What is the member's, or party's, policy on minority groups? Do all have the same opportunities and protections, even when they are challenging the current policies of the party? The biblical emphases would give these often neglected issues an important place in party policy.

Shared Humanity

The next reason "why" we should be salt and light in the political arena is because we follow the example of him who came "not to be served, but to serve . . ." (Mark 10:45). We have accepted our God-given duty to "do good to all" (Gal 6:10).

We should be involved in politics as Christians primarily because we share common human responsibilities along with all our fellow citizens. Christians should not be in politics because we want to be over against other citizens, but because we want to be more responsible citizens. Our political duties are basically the same as those of every other citizen. Our Christian obligations may, and do, heighten and confirm these duties, but they do not make our duties radically different. To put it another way. Our duty politically arises primarily from our common humanity, as men and women created in the image of God, rather than from the fact of our salvation in Christ. Certainly, our salvation has alerted us to the importance of this involvement, but it is our common duty as humans and citizens that is the basis for our political service.

Good government, and valid political and societal concerns, all derive ultimately from God. But he gives his gifts without partiality. Christians do not have a monopoly on political common sense; other people have sound moral judgment. Many well-meaning people are involved politically because they have valid insights into the needs of our community. Christians in politics will be quick to recognize and acknowledge the validity and insights of others, and to work with them for the common good.

Christians in politics will seek to bridge the differences between different sections of the community. While there are issues against which we must take a stand, a merely combative mentality will ensure Christians are marginalized in the political arena. We need to become known for what we are for, rather than for what we are against. Several key New Testament passages dealing with societal and political involvement stress "peacemaking" rather than a belligerent approach for followers of the Prince of Peace. The "salt and light" passage immediately follows blessings upon the meek, the merciful, and those who make peace (Matt 5:1–16). The commands to submit to government authorities are preceded by strong pleas to "Do what is right in the eyes of everybody. If it is possible, as far as it depends on you, live at peace with everyone. Do not take revenge . . ." (Rom 12:14—13:7). Or, in Peter's teachings, ". . . by doing good you should silence the ignorant talk of foolish people . . . live as servants of God. Show proper respect for everyone . . ." (1 Pet 2:13–23).

Just as our Lord "went about doing good" in every sphere of his life (Acts 10:38), so as ordinary citizens we, too, will seek to do good for the welfare of society as well as for Christ's glory.

Basic Virtues

God has declared in his word fundamental values and virtues which are good for humanity as a whole. We also see a widespread recognition that these values are fitting for our society. Many have imbibed the commonsense virtues and values of the Ten Commandments and the social teachings of Christ as of fundamental importance for societal well-being. Thoughtful men and women across a wide spectrum of our community, regardless of their religious affiliations or the lack of them, still accept the importance of these basic moral guidelines for society as a whole.

As Christians, we can account for this widespread agreement about basic morals on three grounds.[6] First, on the grounds of *an inborn awareness of right and wrong*. Romans 2:14–15 speaks of people without any access to God's written word showing, "that what the law requires is written on their hearts." This basic knowledge of good and evil, or conscience, is

6. For discussion of these issues, and the whole of this section, see Triton, *Whose World?*, 80–103.

part of human nature, or of God's image in humans. The moral sense which goes with this can be understood as part of humanity's residual awareness of the original image of God in humankind. Theologians of earlier generations made much of this "original law of obedience given to man" which, they claimed, "was a law, not only to the first man, but to the whole human race."[7] Thus Richard Watson, the Wesleyan theologian and influential missionary spokesperson writing in the 1820s about non-Christian nations across the globe could say: ". . . even the Heathen have always been under a moral government. The laws of God have never been quite obliterated, though their practice has ever been below their knowledge . . ."[8]

We, too, can recognize and respect this widespread awareness of basic moral values as evidence that "In the Word was life and the life was the light of men. The light shines in the darkness, and the darkness has not overcome it" (John 1:4–5). Or again, we can recognize this awareness as part of the general work of the Holy Spirit in the world convincing all peoples of righteousness and restraining evil (John 16:8–10; 2 Thess 2:6–7).

Secondly, there is an inbuilt awareness of *the reasonableness of God's moral principles for humankind.* A wide spectrum of thinking men and women endorse the creation ordinances and their moral value because they make common sense. Practical human insight, observation of the way societies tick, and certainly the lessons of history show that healthy moral standards are good for any society. For instance, we can readily show the importance of speaking and writing the truth as basic for communal trust and business confidence. Ephesians 4:25 hints at just such a natural communal reasonableness as the motive for honesty in speech: "Let every one speak the truth with his neighbour, for we are members one of another."[9]

Paul appeals to the thinking person's awareness of the "unnaturalness" of homosexual relations as part of his evidence that godless societies had rejected an adequate basis for their moral behavior (Rom 1:26–28). When warning of the danger of prostitution, Paul appeals both to the original intention of sexual union and the "natural" argument that the sexually immoral person is threatening the well-being of his or her own personality (1 Cor 6:16–18). Thoughtful people today with an awareness of the part fear,

7. Watson, *Theological Institutes*, 1:491.

8. Watson, *Theological Institutes*, 1:54. For a discussion of the way such ideas were basic to missionary thinking in the nineteenth century, see Hitchen, "Training Tamate," 350–63.

9. Cf. Triton, *Whose World?*, 2–83.

shame, unresolved guilt, and lack of self-respect due to sexual immorality play in contributing to emotional instability and inability to communicate in marriage, will endorse Paul's argument. We don't need the threat of AIDS to confirm the basic sense of the biblical moral values.

This basic rationality or common sense reflected in the creation ordinances and Ten Commandments wins the respect of a wide range of morally responsible thinkers today.

Thirdly, there is *an acceptance of the worth of the ethical teaching of Jesus Christ.* Despite the general rejection of the theological and spiritual roots from which Christ's ethics grow, there is still an interest in retaining the fruits of his teaching. Once a society has been exposed to the teaching of Christ—as Western society has over a long period of time—it can never wholly forget the challenge and the appeal of his teachings: "Love your neighbour as yourself"; "Do unto others as you would have them do to you"; "Turn the other cheek"; and other popular, though partial, distillations of Christ-centered behavior, still win acclaim in our community. We all suffer a gap between our ideal and our actual when it comes to standards, and many in our society will still pay lip service to the validity of Christian standards as the most worthy ideal.

So, recognizing these three factors—an inborn awareness of right and wrong; the reasonableness of God's moral principles; and the continuing attraction of Jesus as an ethical teacher—we will respect and build on the widespread community awareness of the appropriateness of basic Christian moral virtues. This should spur us on to political involvement and to speak up on moral issues.

This reason also suggests some aspects of "how" to be involved on moral issues. We do not need to keep telling everyone who expresses a right moral judgment, "There you are, you have an inborn moral awareness of God's original commands given to the first human pair." Many of our hearers would not be impressed. But, in talking about our concerns about morality, we should appeal to that awareness, that sense of conscience, in our friends. We should appeal to their sense of what is "reasonable," "sensible," and "fitting" in regard to truth, honesty, moral uprightness, marital fidelity, and so forth. Let us build on the common ground. And by all means, appeal to a broader respect for the standards and example of Jesus.

Rights and Responsibilities of All Humanity

We agree with J. N. D. Anderson's dictum that Christians "must accord to others that liberty of conscience which they claim for themselves."[10] In calling for a proper community respect for moral standards we will keep people at the center of our political concern. Where minorities—even minorities that we find hard to identify with—are discriminated against, we will, like Christ, take our stand with them against their oppressors. Our distinctly Christian ethic has taught us that all the parties in social relationships have both rights and responsibilities (see Col 3:18—4:1). In taking our stand on public issues, then, we will see our duty both to stand up for the underprivileged and the underdog, and at the same time to call on them to "acknowledge the duty which accompanies every right."[11]

Priority of Public Opinion over Legislation

Our final reason for seeking to be salt and light in our community arises from lessons from biblical history. Legislation is inadequate to give moral guidance to society. The frailty of human nature and the fickle changes of public opinion hinder the effectiveness of legislation. We know that the "Power of the Prophet,"[12] although seldom respected and often opposed, is of more lasting value than the might of the sword or the legislation of the state. Thus, we recognize the importance of influencing public opinion on moral questions. Where the law no longer reflects public opinion the law lapses.

As comparatively insignificant minor prophets we know that the good news we gossip to our neighbor about right living before Christ Jesus contains the dynamic to transform both individuals and, through them, communities. Thus, we recognize our Christian responsibility to lobby politicians and other opinion formers to ensure they understand a well-presented Christian position on the issues before parliament. Hence also, our concern to ensure humble, discerning, and widely respected Christians are elected to parliament. We want their presence and words to continue

10. Anderson, *Into the World*, 48.

11. Per the motto of the YMCA Y's Men's Clubs.

12. To borrow a phrase from the essay by Jeffries, *Beyond Neutrality*, a penetrating application of this point in the area of educational theory.

to inform, to challenge, and to guide opinion by contributing positively to public moral awareness and good political sense.

We confess that too often we have said too little, and that too late, so that we have only ourselves to blame if Christians are regarded as reactionary traditionalists rather than astute moral leaders.

Towards a Political Platform

The Scriptures give us a set of fundamental reasons for fulfilling our political responsibilities in a constructive, positive way. We have a view of God, his world, and our human significance which we know is true for, and applies to, all men and women. We want to share these views for the common good of our society. We do not want to be in politics just so that we can oppose what we see as the wrong views of others, nor merely to fight for the religious rights of Christians.

We believe the Maker's instructions for human welfare apply universally. As the creator of humankind, our God has declared what is best for his creatures. We seek to uphold these insights in our political involvement, and can summarize their importance in statements such as these:

- Our God is the living lord of the whole creation. This is his world first and foremost. He has not abdicated his sovereign rule. We do not believe that the enemy is the true ruler of our world.
- Women and men are all created in the image of God with the spiritual capacity to know God and the moral capacity to know right from wrong as part of the expression of their nature as human beings. Though damaged by the fall, this "image of God" has not been obliterated and still constitutes our common nature as humans.
- God has entrusted this planet to us as humans as a trust to be enjoyed and managed for the glory of God and for the good of our fellow creatures of both this and future generations.
- God has structured and ordered our world so that moral principles are recognized by human conscience as it is informed by God's testimony to himself, even apart from the special revelation of Scripture. The lessons of creation, the light of "natural law," and conscience are available to all humans even without a commitment to knowing the Scriptures. The eternal Word has not left himself without witness in

any society. The Holy Spirit, likewise, is doing his restraining, convicting work amongst all humankind, not only amongst Christians.

- God sends his gifts and mercies upon all humans, whether they acknowledge him or not. Moreover, he gives and respects their personal right to choose whether or not to respond to him. He does not withhold his gifts of life, understanding, intelligence, moral judgment, interpersonal concern, and the like from people just because they refuse to own him as lord.
- God controls and rules history. The migratory movements of peoples, their ethnic heritage, and their social and political experiences are all known and superintended by our lord God. He appoints times and seasons politically as well as in nature. Thus we need to come to grips with present realities like the modern pluralistic society. It is inappropriate to simply wish or work for its reversal or to hope for a reactionary return to the monolithic realities of Christendom. Simply to fight against pluralistic society may be to fight against the ongoing purposes of God, if he is offering this political and intellectual environment as an opportunity for a new kind of societal experience.
- All truth is God's truth, wherever it is found. All valid insights into human life and behavior are part of the God-given resources we are to utilize for the glory of God and the good of all our fellow human beings, as 1 Cor 3:18–23 suggests.
- All humans carry in their persons the biases, stains, and effects of their inherent sinfulness. We are not gullible, nor naive about the lust for power, the self-serving motives, and the potential for deceit, corruption, and dishonesty in the corridors of power. Thus, we recognize the importance of a prophetic upholding of public virtues and standards of righteousness in a nation, ever mindful of the need for personal integrity and transparent moral purity on the part of would-be politicians.
- We particularly note the global applicability of the Ten Commandments as a firm basis for political involvement.

Further, in terms of political involvement, the Ten Commandments suggest eight key principles to keep to the fore:

- respect for worship and for the public use of God's name

- respect for human life, and its wholesome sustenance and preservation
- respect for parents and constructive family life
- respect for human sexuality and its fulfillment in healthy marriage
- respect for work and for the products of human creativity
- provision for replenishing recreation, leisure, and adequate weekly rest
- respect for truth in speech and communication
- guarding against the social cancers of theft and greed.

We do not expect all our fellow citizens to recognize these basic moral responsibilities as part of their maker's revelation for their welfare. But we believe, nevertheless, the values enshrined in these ordinances are fundamental to wholesome community life. This puts us under obligation to work for the widest possible recognition of these basic values—in short, to be involved in politics!

Conclusion

We offer these comments as a basis for shaping our approach to the political task. We have not presented a pragmatic list of expectations or practical obligations as "the Christian" approach in present-day politics. In fact, as we conclude, we need to sound a number of warnings.

While we can expect to come to agreement on basic principles about political involvement, such as those we have outlined above, we should expect different Christians to choose a range of culturally appropriate ways of working out these principles.

Only a few of us are likely to be called into a full-time career in politics. Even amongst these we need to beware of assuming that the "right" thing is for them to express their calling through membership in an overtly Christian party. There is good reason for some to work for the respect and support of existing mainline parties, while others may see advantages in working for a party based explicitly on Christian principles.

This need to respect alternative Christian views on any political issue is of prime importance in small nations like New Zealand or our Pacific neighbours. The media, and other political groups, can all too easily marginalize Christian views if they are inadequately or inappropriately presented, or if Christians can be shown to be at loggerheads amongst themselves on an issue. This highlights the importance of clear thinking as to whether or not any grouping of Christians should overtly use "Christian" in the title of their political party or lobby group. We need always to be careful about claiming that we represent "the" Christian position on a political issue. Richard Neuhaus, in a significant article on the topic, quotes Reinhold Niebuhr's warnings that "we must never declare our politics to be 'Christian politics,' thereby implicitly excommunicating those Christians who disagree with us."[13] Peter Mackenzie, writing in the run up to the 1996 New Zealand elections, quoted C. S. Lewis's similar warnings on the dangers of claiming to be, or of being thought of as, "the" Christian party.[14] Neuhaus says pointedly,

> Christians engaged in politics will bring personal integrity and devotion to the common good. But that does not make their engagement "Christian politics." It is still just politics. A Christian engineer who builds a really good bridge has not built a "Christian bridge." The merit of the project depends upon qualities pertinent to the "bridginess" of the thing, although we may believe that these qualities are well served by the Christian conviction and integrity of the builder.[15]

Christlike humility will surely characterize any Christian involvement in politics, so one-eyed dogmatism and/or proud triumphalist approaches will therefore be excluded for the Christian. To quote Neuhaus again, "Christians are called to walk not the road to political victory but the way of the cross."[16]

We need to be careful, too, not to assume that putting effort into fostering a Christianly based party is the only way to be involved in our political scene today. Creating public awareness of Christian viewpoints on a wider front may be just as significant. We need a range of lobby groups speaking into the full range of political issues in such a way that all political parties will take note of their opinions. Some of us may see such opinion forming as more strategic than working for a single political party. Likewise, some of us may see local school or local body politics, rather than national party politics, as the sphere in which our personal political efforts should have their major focus.

13. Neuhaus, "Christian Politics," 72–74, cited by Turner, in "Editorial," 4.

14. Mackenzie, "Christian Party," 12–14.

15. Neuhaus, "Christian Politics."

16. Neuhaus, "Christian Politics."

In summary, then, the way we work out the obligations we have outlined above will need to be sensitive, flexible, and diverse. But the theological principles we have set out as reasons for our involvement will also inform whatever practical approach we may choose.

We cannot ignore our political duties as Christians. We will recognize both the potential and the limitations of all our political effort. As citizens of a higher world we will not be deceived by the allure and dangers of merely earthly political power. Nor will we hesitate to exercise such power humbly and responsibly before Christ if we are entrusted with it. As servants of the coming king we will be alert to the weaknesses of all politics this side of the eternal kingdom—especially those championed by our own friends and fellow believers. But with our eyes wide open to our own as well as other people's political shortcomings, we shall still work for the kind of quiet, peaceable, godly, dignified, and truth-honoring society for which we are obliged to pray (1 Tim 2:1–4). As those entrusted with the pastoral care of our fellow citizens, we will particularly look for ways to bring pastoral encouragement to all who are called into politics. We know that those who serve through politics share all our own frailty and spiritual need and that as our national leaders they stand in special need of our prayer. This prayer duty reminds us that we will be called to give an account of our personal political involvement on that last day—when in the fullness of Christ's kingdom we shall also discover firsthand what politics were always meant to be.

Chapter 19

Towards a Theology of Social and Cultural Change

God calls Christians to become involved in promoting social justice and transformative change in their societies today. This paper explores the New Testament vision of God's long-term intention for societies and communities under the kingly rule and lordship of Christ. We focus on scriptural metaphors relating to ways God calls us. Thus, we offer it as a concluding chapter, bringing together and reinforcing the themes of this book.[1]

Discussing theological truth involves explaining things about God which by their very nature require ideas and concepts human minds are incapable of grasping fully. Serious study of God always encounters this gap between human experience and intellectual capacity, and the transcendent reality of the nature and purposes of God that we are trying to understand and express. Thus, as mere humans, we have no option but to use metaphors to make sense in any discussion of God. As Craig Ott explains, "At its most basic level a metaphor is a means of transferring characteristics from the familiar to the unfamiliar by way of analogy or likeness. . . . Through use of metaphor one seeks to enhance understanding or gain insight that would be otherwise difficult using more literal language."[2] Moreover, because metaphors illuminate universally comparable human experiences

1. An earlier version of this material was presented as a paper to the Maxim Institute, see Hitchen, "Reform The World?"

2. Ott, "Power," 360. This article is a useful introduction to the wealth of recent discussion of metaphors in theological and missional discussion.

and situations, they are also effective means of communicating biblical truth cross-culturally. Hence, we take for granted that through the imagery of scriptural metaphors, by their very nature as metaphors, God speaks to us afresh in our own cultural settings. Biblical metaphors refer to artefacts, events, experiences, or relationships sufficiently common to human experience worldwide, that the metaphors' purpose and meaning can be reliably communicated across time and cultural gaps into present-day situations, provided we take care to understand the original historical and cultural setting as fully as possible.[3]

We focus first on the transforming vision of the kingdom of God in the New Testament, then consider our Christian responsibility for social involvement and influence, through the lens of God's call and call-related metaphors. We explore both the general call of God to personal holiness and its consequences, and selected particular vocational callings to different roles in society. The conclusion briefly relates the discussion to the process of contextualization.

The Transforming Vision

Matthew's carefully constructed introductory chapters authenticate Jesus as the anointed Messiah of Israel—initially on the basis of his genealogy, his Holy-Spirit initiated unique birth, his star-guided homage from learned foreigners, and his family's prophecy-fulfilling refugee experience in Egypt. The authentication continues with John the Baptiser's preparation, and Jesus's own baptism, divine attestation, and guidance by the Holy Spirit through testing. On this foundation Matthew focuses the rest of his gospel on the kingdom of God. The good news of Christ's radically different kingly rule is central to his whole teaching, proclaiming, and healing ministry, as Matthew's repeated summaries confirm (4:17, 23; 9:35; 11:1). Little wonder, then, that Matthew sets out a clear vision of what this kingly rule of Jesus is like in his first extended discourse in chapters 5–7. Later chapters of Matthew will explain and confirm the emphases of this "Sermon on the Mount." But here in chapters 5–7, Jesus delineates the scope and core of his society-transforming vision of life in the kingdom of God.[4]

3. For discussion of aspects of such cultural factors in our hermeneutical methods, see chapter 12 above, and Hitchen, "Clarifying the Contribution," 91–120.

4. For the purposes of this paper, it is not appropriate to discuss the various ways both the Sermon on the Mount, particularly, or the concept of the kingdom of God, generally,

Throughout this explanation of the expected lifestyle of citizens of the new kingdom, we note the call is not merely to personal change but to societal transformation. Wherever Christ's kingly rule is established it is expressed in new patterns of communal living. We can but highlight the central themes in these chapters.

Character Profile of Kingdom Citizens

Jesus directly challenges the complacent pride, self-confidence, exploitation of power, never-satisfied greed, coldheartedness, benighted pleasure in impurity, divisiveness, and popularity and comfort-seeking values of his, and every, age. He knows societies can only be impacted by those who experience an inner change of character and value system. Citizens of his kingdom find deep delight and real satisfaction—what the text calls "blessing" in Matt 5:3–12:

- facing up to their own spiritual impoverishment
- finding renewed strength through the sorrows of hardship and loss
- humbly controlling their strength in confrontational relationships
- yearning for upright relationships and justice
- offering generous kindness to the undeserving
- pursuing the purity that opens our eyes to God himself
- mediating reconciliation in our broken world
- accepting the cost of taking a public stand for justice
- maintaining integrity when wrongly accused.

These beatitudes are far from a list of other-worldly benedictions for a passive recluse. They are, but they are not simply, the essential characteristics of those who accept the kingly rule of Christ in their lives. But also, in Matthew's Gospel they are the motivating, empowering, character foundations for those who care about the messy world in which we live. Discovering and realizing this, for Jesus, is real joy. Matthew simply records the requirements as Jesus pronounced them. The New Testament writers

have been explained in biblical studies or New Testament theology. For introduction to such, see commentaries and other works, such as Ladd, *Crucial Questions*; Beasley-Murray, *Jesus and the Kingdom*; Marshall, *Kingdom Come*. For a brief earlier introduction of mine, see Hitchen, "Evangelical Understanding," 5–10.

John and Paul will explain the impossibility of adopting such foundational qualities apart from the redemption-securing death and resurrection of Jesus and the new birth and inward enabling of the Holy Spirit. But Matthew's listed qualities are foundational for impacting any society. Transformation begins in our own experience of character renewal, changed values, and new goals implied in these "blessings." Nothing less will do.

Impacting Roles of Kingdom Citizens

To confirm his purpose in renewing the character of those who live under his reign, Jesus explains his followers' twin roles in public life (Matt 5: 13–16). Notice the global scope of these two roles—they are earth- and world-impacting. In the costly context of standing up for justice and facing misunderstanding or false accusation on Jesus's behalf, the roles are clear.

First, kingdom citizens are as *salt*, to bring relish to life and counteract corruption where bland, superficial, existence passes for real life, and where evil holds sway and has become accepted and entrenched. Since salt must penetrate the food to have any influence, the metaphor implies Christ's followers are to be immersed in the real affairs of their society: not to be some exclusive, separatist club living in isolation, but communally connected participants in the planning, decision-making, and standard setting of their time. Those who own Christ's rule over their lives bring out the unrealized tastiness, relish, and satisfaction latent within their communities. Christ followers radiate a wholesome preservative influence by being available and involved.

Kingdom citizens are also openly and publicly as *light*, to show up and dispel the shadowy, tawdry, and sinister encircling darkness of our day, and enlighten our worlds by dependable, God-glorifying commitment to the good. Light not only overcomes darkness; it also shows new ways, attracting and guiding towards more productive paths, and encouraging and protecting as we move forward. Working for good in a darkness-preferring environment may bring scornful criticism as "do-gooders." But those who prove the will of God in the real world know that it is truly satisfying and fulfilling only because it is also consistently good (Rom 12:2). There is no shame in being like Jesus, who "went about doing good," rather than just going about (Acts 10:38).

These two metaphors both stress the kingdom vision for societal involvement. The dual roles are not expressed as imperatives we are expected to strive for, but as simple facts of what we are when Christ is our king. Bringing added flavor to our environment and attracting others out of dark situations are inherent, essential aspects of following the kingly rule of Christ in our own culture and society. For most Christians this means vocational involvement. The challenge to bring out the enjoyable potential in and to protect against the tendency to downgrade the value of our professions and workplaces is central to Christ's understanding of the kingdom of God. He places us as attractive, brightening influences to reveal the good inherent in our fields of responsibility, research, and daily routine. The rest of the sermon highlights the wide-ranging and abiding issues confronting those entrusted with these salt and light roles.

Societal Standards and the Kingly Rule of Christ

Jesus sets out the basic sanctities that undergird every healthy society and clarifies our motives and responsibility for each as kingdom citizens:

The sanctity of life, dignity of human worth and the priority of interpersonal relationships mean that working for respect, reconciliation, and enhanced personal relationships will replace anger, hatred, and murder. Moreover, kingdom citizens work to restore broken interpersonal relationships as essential preparation for properly prioritized worship (Matt 5:21–26).

The sanctity of sex and family life where Christ is king requires a radically distinctive, biblical, understanding of the nature and purpose of sexual morality and marital integrity and of stable families as foundational for any healthy society. This also challenges Christ followers to equip one another with inner discipline and resources to maintain pure and wholesome thought-lives and social relationships (Matt 5:27–32).

The sanctity of human speech and thought require simplicity, honesty, and sincerity in interpersonal communication, as the essential basis for conducting all societal business (Matt 5:33–37). A foundation of trust in the public square grows from and depends on personal and professional integrity and honesty. Without such trustworthiness in speech, the marketplaces, business and financial transactions, law courts, research centers, and classrooms of a nation quickly become unreliable and vulnerable to manipulation and exploitation.

Generous unselfishness instead of self-serving retaliation is essential for societal wellbeing (Matt 5:38–42). The culture of litigation, demanding of rights, and grasping after material possessions which predominates in our present-day societies, contrasts sharply with Christ's example calling kingdom citizens to demanding and often costly service for others (1 Pet 2:21–24).

Self-denying, Christlike love is still the distinctively Christian contribution to a society's wellbeing (Matt 5:43–45). Christ's kind of love is not restricted to the in-group, is not motivated by potential recompense, and transcends the common social and class barriers. But it requires a heavenly Father's life for his children to attain it (Matt 5:48).

Godly personal piety in generous, disciplined lifestyles and prayer are essential to fuel and sustain kingdom citizens who are upholding these transformational societal standards (Matt 6:1–18).

Goals and Values of Kingdom Citizens

Jesus continues on to address four areas controlling our societal value systems and points to new basic assumptions to guide the vision for his kingly rule as his subjects influence their society:

- ensuring eternal realities inform our value systems and define our treasures and delights (Matt 6:19–21)
- keeping every aspect of our lives open to the light of God's scrutiny (Matt 6:22–23)
- choosing, not whether to obey a higher authority, but which one, as materialism is a poor, empty, and deceitful alternative to a living, submissive friendship with the loving Lord of the universe (Matt 6:24)
- pursuing the personal reality of God's rule and justice in human relationships as the only right goal for kingdom citizens; selfish materialism, again, is a poor alternative (Matt 6:25–34).

Relational Commitments for Kingdom Citizens

As well as the foundational sanctities of Matt 5, other relational issues and matters regarding the ultimate meaning of life guide a kingdom lifestyle. Jesus moves freely between personal and communal matters in this section, with no rigid line between the public and private aspects of faith:

- Deal honestly with our own faults as we look for the best in others (Matt 7:1–5).
- Spiritual realities are too sacred to flaunt before those with no spiritual appreciation (Matt 7:6).
- Pray earnestly and persistently to achieve good in our societies, since God is the active heavenly Father involved in every aspect of his children's lives (Matt 7:7–11).
- Do to others as you want them to do to you; the golden rule for interpersonal relationships orders life under Christ's kingly rule, as it effectively encapsulates the whole Judaeo-Christian ethical heritage (Matt 7:12).
- The road to life under Christ's direction is not normally popular but requires kingdom citizens, as responsible humans, to discern between truth and error and good and evil as they identify and assess the practical outcomes of moral choices (Matt 7:13–20).
- Eternal acceptance by our heavenly Father is only guaranteed by doing God's will through obeying his revealed word, not by claims to spectacular spiritual power, nor unapplied, unheeded knowledge (Matt 7:21–27).

The salt and light roles require citizens of Christ's kingdom to grasp and apply these fundamental worldview commitments, values, and communal "sanctities" through their personal lifestyles and professional and vocational involvements. These are the virtues kingdom citizens promote across every aspect of their own culture. They focus the will of God for Christ's followers to contribute to the welfare of their society.

The rest of Matthew's Gospel expands and clarifies these various kingdom themes through Jesus's teaching, preaching, and actions. Especially, Jesus's own death and resurrection are shown as the essential outcome of him consistently doing what he had taught. But more than that, the events of the cross and the open grave culminate the developing vision and inaugurate this carefully prepared for kingdom of God in human history.

The Kingdom Vision Refocused

The crucifixion, resurrection, and ascension of Jesus the Christ and his consequent sending of the Holy Spirit at Pentecost fulfilled the preparation and inaugurated a new phase of the kingdom of God in and through those who believed in Jesus as their Messiah and Savior (Acts 1–2). This unexpected manner of fulfilling the long expected Messianic hope of the Jewish nation, also further clarified the vision of the kingdom of God (Eph 1:1–23).

Refocusing the Kingdom on Jesus

As we have explained elsewhere:

> In this present age the Kingdom is not about restoring international supremacy to Israel, Acts 1:6. Instead it centres on witnessing to the kingly reign of Jesus Christ, and calling people of every culture to trust in him, Acts 1:8. The apostles were not ready for mission until they grasped this fundamental reorientation of expectation. As David Bosch succinctly puts it: "The good news of the reign of God is Jesus Christ, incarnated, crucified and risen, and what he accomplished. We too often separate what these verses combine, the message of the Kingdom and witness to the living Jesus here and now.[5]

We see this refocusing of the kingdom message onto Jesus himself, developing in the earliest preaching of Peter in Acts 2–5. "Peter skilfully enriched the use of concepts common in the Gospels when he spoke of Jesus as fulfiller of prophecy, a prophet like Moses, fulfiller of the covenant, and seed of Abraham in [Acts] 3:21–26; or rejected stone, now capstone in [Acts] 4:11."[6] Peter applies to Jesus a range of titles and metaphors from the Hebrew Scriptures, or introduces new ones, which further reorient the kingdom vision onto the person and work of Jesus: "Jesus is the 'God-Accredited man,' [Acts] 2:22; he is 'Lord' and 'Christ,' 2:36; 3:18; he is the Spirit-giver, 2:17–21, 33; to him belong Isaiah's favorite titles, 'Holy and Righteous Servant,' 3:14; 4:27, 30; Jesus bears the powerful name, 3:6, 16; 4:10, 12, 30; and he is the new pioneer or author of life, 3:15; 5:31."[7] This first stage of contextualizing the message for Jews shows increasingly, as Acts 1:8 had intimated, the focus shifts in emphasis from announcing the vision of the inaugurated kingdom, to preaching the gospel of Jesus as Savior and Lord.

5. Hitchen, "Missional, Multi-Ethnic Church," 64, citing Bosch, *Transforming Mission*, 116.

6. Hitchen, "Missional Multi-Ethnic Church," 66.

7. Hitchen, "Missional Multi-Ethnic Church, 66.

The Cosmos Redeemed

When we turn to the apostle Paul's writings, we find fresh concepts, explanatory language, and metaphors used as the gospel comes to peoples of other cultures—the gentiles, or "uncircumcised," as the Jews called them. Ephesians 1 is a good example. Paul calls "God's set apart people" who are "faithful in Christ Jesus" to praise God for the manifold "blessings"[8] of having embraced the vision expanded in three dimensions under Christ as head.

First, the vision is expanded in time—fulfilled now but not yet—as it is revealed that the blessings had begun with God's choosing of the believers "before the foundation of the cosmos." The blessings were made a present reality, experienced through the lavish gift of God's grace received when believers heard and received the gospel's "word of truth"; and the blessings are guaranteed by the indwelling of the Holy Spirit to extend beyond "when the times reach their fulfilment," onward to a share in "the riches of [God's] glorious inheritance in his people" in future eternity (Eph 1:4, 10, 13–14, 18).

Secondly, the vision is expanded to show Christ is head over every sphere of cosmic life. This long planned, already commenced, but not yet consummated experience of the blessings is described repeatedly through Eph 1 as being "in Christ," dependent on glorious riches of freely given grace, consisting of redemption and forgiveness of sin, and all "for the praise of God's glory."

Moreover, the vision is categorized in Eph 1:9–11 by a number of related terms including the "mystery of [God's] will"; "[God's] good pleasure he purposed in Christ"; "a strategic plan for the fullness of time"; and "the plan of him who works out everything in conformity with the purpose of his will." All these descriptions of the depth of God's intention combine to emphasize the ultimate goal of this Christ-centered vision, which is "to head up all things, in heaven and on earth, under Christ as head" (Eph 1:10). No longer just a national salvation for one cultural group, the Jews, the "all things" means Christ is to be Lord over every realm: political, economic, philosophical, scientific, technological, social, psychological, religious, artistic, imaginative, relational, and any other imaginable earthly realm. But there is more—Christ is also to be over the heavenly realms of

8. Paul uses the more common Greek, *eulogia*, rather than *makarios* used by Jesus in Matthew's Gospel, to refer to "blessings" Christ bestows on Christians.

humanly unseen spiritual and cosmological authorities, powers, and regulative forces of whatever kind operating in our cosmos. All of the spheres are included within the scope of Christ Jesus's kingly intentions, purposes, and reign.

This time-expanded, well-planned vision is also extended geographically and culturally to embrace peoples of all cultures who believe the gospel. Seeing God's purposes as narrowly confined to one favored nation is firmly put aside. The comprehensive vision now includes all peoples as well as every realm of creation. Our Lord Jesus Christ expects this transforming vision to be proclaimed, translated into the language and thought-forms, and applied to the worldview assumptions of every culture, as peoples of that culture respond to him as their "Christ," or promised king and Lord over their culture.[9] By implication, therefore, when a culture has moved away from an earlier commitment to these kingdom values and no longer accepts nor upholds the principles and sanctities inherent in the gospel's society-transforming vision, then Christians have a fresh responsibility to reevangelize and to once more reshape the worldview foundations of their society for Christ.

This is precisely the situation, distinct in Christian history, facing us in our post-Christian Western societies today. In a new way, cultures that were once deeply influenced by Christian values and have come to reject them, are being presented another opportunity for a renewed application of the gospel's societal vision in fresh ways adapted to the now vastly different ruling worldviews of those cultures.[10]

This, then, is the refocused vision of the kingly rule of Christ into which God speaks his call, with wide-ranging implications, to direct Christ's followers for the fulfilling of this vision within their own cultural location.

Believers and Sociocultural Transformation

But where do we start? Paul's letter to the Ephesians goes on to present a fully developed vision of God's purpose with an emphasis on Christ's

9. On the significance of this translatability and application of the gospel across cultural boundaries, see the writings of Lamin Sanneh, Andrew F. Walls, and Lesslie Newbigin, variously cited in this volume.

10. See Turner, "Gospel's Mission." An edited version of the original was presented as the Canon William Orange Memorial Lecture for 1992 and reedited for publication in 1993; then reprinted in *New Zealand Made* in 1994.

redemption as the basis of hope for all peoples. The letter's message centers around repeated references to God's choice and call, that is, his specific intentions for Christ's followers. All believers are chosen or called to be holy and fully acceptable before him (Eph 1:4). The apostle also prays they may have opened hearts and minds to know and embrace God's call to the hope-filled vision achieved by Christ's ministry (Eph 1:18; 4:4). These calls lead to a further call to "live a life worthy of the calling you have received" (Eph 4:1). In Ephesians God's basic call to be his set apart people becomes the incentive for grasping and working out the vision of being Christian citizens within our different societies. With this concept of "being called" beckoning us forward, we turn now to the seminal metaphors suggesting ways to pursue effectively the vision for societies transformed to fulfill God's pleasure and purpose in our time and location.

The living God takes the initiative for transforming human societies. The motivating and enabling dynamic comes from his prior actions and direct intervention in the lives of his followers. His speaking and calling assures us of his presence and active purposes as the bedrock on which transformative involvement in society is built. By taking the first step towards transformative action by means of calling, God has chosen a distinctly human and personal basis for societal change, as we should expect when the essence of God's nature is love. Being called involves reciprocal social relationships which are applicable worldwide by people of every culture. By initiating transformative action through a call, God has ensured that responsive relationships, rather than merely technological means or non-personal forces, are most basic for the changes God desires. God's call to those who have come under the kingly rule of Christ by faith in his saving gospel is a double call. It is both a general call to all believers to fellowship with him and to become like him, and it is also a call to follow him out into action in the world where he has placed us. Thus we can refer to both a general call to all believers and the specific calls, or callings, to particular kinds of service with Christ for each believer.

People in the World

The general call to all believers is a call to come to Christ and learn of him. But, far from being merely a comforting and comfortable call to enjoying his love and care, which it is, it is also a call to be formed and equipped for serving him in society.

Jesus's first direct encounter with those who were to become his disciples sets the pattern: "Come, follow me," Jesus said, "and I will make you fish for people" (Mark 1:17). Or again, in the follow-up meeting: "Jesus went up on a mountainside and called to him those he wanted, and they came to him. He appointed twelve that they might be with him and that he might send them out . . ." (Mark 3:13–14). This was a call to be distinct, or set apart for Christ and devoted to him in a special way, summed up biblically as "called to be holy," or in its older form, "called to be saints" (Rom 1:7). Articulated clearly at the time of the exodus (Exod 19: 4–6), God has always greatly desired to have a people as his own "treasured possession," a "holy nation." The prophets echoed the yearning (e.g., Hos 2:23), and in the New Testament Peter repeats it to Christ's followers: "But you are a chosen people, a royal priesthood, a holy nation, God's special possession that you may declare the praises of him who called you out of darkness into his wonderful light. Once you were not a people, but now you are the people of God: once you had not received mercy, but now you have received mercy" (1 Pet 2:9–10).

Paul reminds Titus, Christ "gave himself for us to redeem us from all wickedness and to purify for himself a people that are his very own, eager to do what is good" (Titus 2:14). Jesus confides his great desire as he speaks intimately with his Father: "My prayer is not that you take them out of the world, but that you protect them from the evil one. They are not of the world, even as I am not of it. Sanctify them by the truth: your word is truth. As you sent me into the world, I have sent them into the world. For them I sanctify myself that they may be truly sanctified" (John 17:15–19). The importance of this call to set apart purity—being sanctified or holy—and devotion to Christ is the basis for any effective influence in our societies today. John summed up the outcome of this call to be holy in his first letter: "As he is, so are we in the world," or as the TNIV puts it: "In this world we are like Jesus" (1 John 4:17b).

Time dedicated to communing with Jesus, to hear and grasp his alternative teachings to equip and nourish our minds and discipline and to strengthen our hearts and wills, is clearly essential as the first step towards transformative influence in our communities. Given the ubiquity, subtlety, persistence, and power of present-day technology and media to present and inculcate their secular views, attitudes, and motives, making time for transforming and discipling our minds and wills requires determined effort and conscious priority choices. Romans 12:1–2, Eph 4:22–24, 1 Tim

4:11–16, and 1 Pet 1:13, 4:7, and 5:8 are a few of the reminders that it is only by disciplined cultivation of alternative Christlike motives, values, and critical reflection on our behavior—consciously developing "the mind of Christ"—that we can build up the strength of character necessary for courageous influence in our society. Paul's prayers (Phil 1:9–11; Col 1:9–12) and James's explanation of the "wisdom from above" (Jas 3:13–18) list the attitudes, interpersonal character traits, and spiritual resources needed for cultivating social justice with integrity and without hypocrisy. But such character growth means heeding Jesus's ongoing call to be with him for the fellowship that ensures dedicated intake of biblical principles and perspectives, for cultivating higher desires, and replenishing our mental resources and insights.

The first purpose of God's call to believers, then, is that we become like Christ as a distinct people for him within our own communities. This implies fulfilling the consequent roles within our society which characterize all followers of Christ.

Metaphors of the Holy

As we "learn of him," transformation of character and lifestyle shape us as a particular kind of people. The biblical writers use a range of seminal metaphors to show the potential influence Jesus expects to flow from our union and communion with him.

Salt and Light to Glorify God (Matt 5:14–16)

In a context describing the distinctive character traits which qualify those who would impact their own societies, and who know the opposition that can arouse (Matt 5: 3–12), Jesus declares that those who have responded to his call are in the world as salt and light. We note the balance between these two roles. Salt is widely dispersed and works largely unnoticed by being fully involved in direct contact with the substance it is influencing (which is perhaps echoed interpretively in Jesus's later prayer for his disciples that the Father not take them out of the world, but keep them from evil as they are involved in the world [John 17:15–19]). Jesus also emphasizes the importance of ensuring the ongoing quality of the salt (Matt 5:13). For the second metaphor, Jesus emphasizes the publicly visible, in evidence, on display, nature of light. Christians have tended to embrace one or the other of these metaphors as their stance towards the culture they are to enrich and enlighten, whereas our Lord challenges us to fulfill the dual roles.

Friends of Christ, Bearing Fruit (John 15:15–16)

The productive fruit-bearing metaphor recurs at key points in the New Testament to describe the impact of Christ's followers in their societies. John's Gospel likens the essential mutual indwelling relationship between Christ and his followers to being branches abiding continually in the vine that provides and sustains their life. Moreover, the purpose and result of this communion with Christ is an ongoing mutual friendship, producing Christlike character and action. Paul identifies this mutual indwelling as the Holy Spirit's work, and the resulting inward transformation and interpersonal social relationships as the "fruit of the Spirit." Galatians 5:19–26, Phil 1:9–11, and James 3:13–18 describe lifestyles characterized by wisdom, discernment, integrity, and single-minded commitment, demonstrating increasing love and reconciliation in the surrounding society, as the fruit or harvest of justice or righteousness. Believers then, by definition, are fruit-bearing agents in their societies. Jesus's words addressing all the disciples at the Last Supper as his chosen friends (John 15:16) indicate literally that he has "placed" his friends in situations where they are to bear lasting fruit.[11] Again, this "placing" is most likely to be in our daily work or vocational settings.

Witnesses through the Empowering of the Holy Spirit (Acts 1:8; Eph 4:17—5:18)

As Jesus's public ministry drew towards its close, Jesus warned his disciples that soon they would be called before civil councils, religious leaders, and the political authorities of the day to give evidence about what they had seen and knew personally concerning him (Mark 13:9–11). Jesus's final post-resurrection message to the disciples summed up their role on his behalf as being his "witnesses" (Acts 1:8). As the Acts account unfolds, events confirmed that the Holy Spirit enabled and endorsed their testimony as they were called upon to give it. Many followers of Christ today have narrowed

11. The AV translation (1611) of the word "placed" as "ordained," or in more recent English versions as "appointed," suggest a sacerdotal nuance where the original carries no such overtones.

the concept to assume that "witnessing" to Jesus is giving a simplified explanation of the way of salvation in one-on-one conversations, and inviting non-Christians to make a decision to follow Christ, as if "witnessing" is a particular method of personal evangelism. While it may involve that, witnessing is basically giving evidence about what we have experienced personally of the Lord Jesus. For the first generation of Christians this meant giving clear, factual testimony about the life, work, and especially the death and resurrection of Jesus (e.g., Acts 2:32; 3:15; 5:32; 10:9–11).

In the later New Testament writings this original focus on testimony about the life and work of Jesus is broadened, as Peter puts it, into a readiness to "in your hearts revere Christ as Lord," which means, as the verse goes on to explain, and the whole of 1 Peter elaborates: "Always be prepared to give an answer to everyone who asks you to give the reason for the hope that you have. But do this with gentleness and respect, keeping a clear conscience, so that those who speak maliciously against your good behavior in Christ, may be ashamed of their slander" (1 Pet 3:15–16). Witnessing now included "good behavior in Christ" for relating to non-Christians. The apostle Paul likewise saw the quality of our lifestyles as the way to witness to Jesus. He challenges believers to "no longer live [or, more literally, walk] as unbelievers do," nor as in their "former way of life," but to put off the old lifestyle, and "live in the way of love," "live as children of light," "live not as unwise, as wise" (Eph 4:17, 22; 5:2, 8, 15). Or more succinctly, "live lives worthy of the Lord" (Col 1:10). Or again, changing the imagery, particularly when speaking of public leadership, be "above reproach," "blameless," "worthy of respect" (1 Tim 3:2, 4, 8, 11; 4:12; Phil 1:9–10).

The role of witness, then, involves sharing our experience of Christ with others, by living a lifestyle that honestly demonstrates what we know of, and how we are relating to Jesus Christ. Such lives of integrity that reflect well on Christ, form an essential foundation for any effective, transformative, Christian influence in the wider society.

Humble Servants of Others in Love (Gal 5:1, 13–16; Mark 10:42–45; 1 Pet 2:16–17)

Metaphors have particular emotive and psychological significance when the reality to which they refer is being lived out around you on a daily basis. So, metaphors relating to slavery and freedom carried special impact for first-century followers of Christ. As the centuries have passed, Christians and their societies have used various perceptions and names to describe the spiritual and mental enslavement experiences of their communities. But for each generation, release from spiritual captivities and freedom from evil, dominating spiritual forces have been vital existential realities when people have encountered the living Lord Jesus Christ by grace through faith. Their resulting transformation of lifestyles and worldview have been major factors in their subsequent influence for social justice in their communities. Galatians 5:1 declares explicitly what the letter's earlier references to rescue and redemption (Gal 1:4; 3:14; 4:4) had implied, that Christ liberates his followers from the bondage and domination of spiritual powers which had previously enslaved them. In those early verses of Galatians, bondage to religious ritual requirements, particularly those imposed by the religious system of Judaism, was the slavery the Galatian believers needed to avoid. The antidote was for believers to stand firmly in the freedom of faith, hope, and love applied appropriately in their own culture (Gal 5:5–6).

Paul, writing to the Galatians, applies the redemptive metaphor in 5:13–25 to the root of the problem in the more general human experience of slavery to our own self-centered heart, mind, and will, which Paul calls our "sinful nature." This release from the cramping restrictions of our own selfishness is only possible as the Holy Spirit sets us free from the "works of the sinful nature" on the basis of Christ's redeeming death, and as the Holy Spirit produces his Christ-centered fruit within us as we "walk" or live in the Spirit (Gal 5:16–25). Thus, and only thus, are we free "not to indulge the sinful nature," but "rather to serve one another humbly in love" (Gal 5:13). Here, then, we find the motivating and enabling source of that other-centered freedom, exemplified so clearly by Christ himself (Mark 10:42–45), which is the proven basis for Christian social justice and influence in any society.

Salt, light, being friends, productive fruit-bearing, being witnesses, and being free from self to serve others, are the simple but powerful metaphors which describe both the character and the characteristic roles by which those who respond to Christ's call are equipped to be sent out for transformative influence in their societies. These metaphors describe those who are heeding the apostle Peter's challenge: "just as he who called you is holy, so be holy in all you do" (1 Pet 1:15).

Vocational Calls

While the roles we have just described are fundamental, they are not the full methodology by which Christian influence permeates and infiltrates a nation for its good. God's method is people in other senses as well; he also calls each believer to a missional stance with particular tasks under Christ's kingly rule. Christ Jesus allocates specific tasks within his strategic plan, and equips each of us for them by the gifts he supplies through the Holy Spirit as we work out our particular calling or "vocation." In other words, the general call for all believers to be set-apart, distinctive people, is further expressed and implemented through specific callings in the sense of "vocations" or calls for each Christian to do a particular kind of work.

We see specific New Testament examples in Paul sharing in the general call for all believers to be Christ's set apart "holy" people (Rom 1:7), but also having his own specific call to be a "sent one" or missionary/apostle to other cultures (Rom 1:1). Or, within the general missionary/apostle grouping, Peter is recognized as being entrusted with a particular responsibility for Jews while Paul carries a similar but specific trust for those of other cultures (Gal 2:7–9). The principle that "to each one the manifestation of the Spirit is given for the common good," or that "we have different gifts according to the grace given to each of us," is set out clearly in such well-known lists as those contained in Eph 4:8–12, Rom 12:3–8, and in 1 Cor 3:5–9 and 12:7–31. The principle is well illustrated in action in Paul's brief pen-pictures scattered through his letters, of his co-laborers like Timothy and Epaphroditus (Phil 2:19–30), or Stephanas (1 Cor 16:15–18), or those in the greetings lists (e.g., in Rom 16).

These particular callings are described in various ways and based on gifts of grace which the Holy Spirit endows to enliven natural abilities and enhance spiritual readiness for the particular roles entrusted to each believer. First Corinthians 12:4–6 uses three different terms describing these personal callings: "spiritual gifts," "ministries," or "kinds of service," and "ways of working." Or, in Gal 2:9 and 2 Tim 1:14, as a "deposit" or "trust" received. Personal callings are not restricted to "church-related" service, but include secular vocations.

The Scriptures give a diverse range of metaphors to describe ways in which these callings operate in varying situations. These are not specific rules or instructions, but dynamic, pregnant word pictures describing roles and responsibilities to apply in local contexts. We can group these together in various ways:[12]

- metaphors explaining the gospel itself: "receiving eternal life," "beginning a journey with Jesus," "entering the kingdom," and "being saved"
- metaphors explaining the significance of Christ's death, including word groups like: "redemption/ransom," "reconciliation/peacemaking," "righteousness/justification," "priest/sacrifice," "conflict/defeat/victory/soldiering," "new birth/life/adoption/family of God." Each explains particular perspectives on our human predicament, the breadth of the love of God at work in Christ's death, and calls for our human response of repentance and faith
- metaphors describing distinctive features of the gospel such as: "grace and truth," "love, faith, and hope," and "intimate experience of the triune God"
- metaphors elaborating a particular aspect of service for Christ: for example, household servants, agricultural laborers, construction workers, resource custodians, responsible managers, fools for Christ, and responsible parents (the seven metaphors occurring in 1 Cor 3–4).[13]

We could explore the way each of these terms, explanations, or features carries implications to be worked out personally and communally in our vocational callings. But we focus on the way one cluster of related metaphors presents our vocational calling to orient Christians for societal transformation.

The sample metaphor we have selected is: *our Christian calling as exiles entrusted with the ambassadorial task of reconciliation*. The apostle Peter identifies those who have received the general call to be holy as "exiles" (1 Pet 1:1), "foreigners" (1:17), or as both "foreigners and exiles" (2:11). These metaphors, stemming, as we have noted, from Christ's prayer that his Father God not take believers out of this world but keep them from the evil within it, are elaborated also by Paul declaring that as believers, wherever we may be residing as citizens of some nation or state, our true citizenship is in heaven (Phil 3:20). The author of Hebrews develops the metaphor

12. See Hitchen, "Gospel for Today," 29–44; reprinted as "Gospel for New Zealanders," 7–24.

13. The original version of this chapter included discussion of these seven leadership metaphors. See also Hitchen, "Confirming the Christian Scholar," 276–87.

from Abraham's example of living by faith in tents in the promised land, "as a stranger in a foreign country . . . looking forward to the city with foundations, whose architect and builder is God" (Heb 11:9–10). Hebrews shows this was characteristic of all the Old Testament heroes of faith who: "did not receive the things promised, they only saw them from a distance, admitting they were foreigners and strangers on earth. People who say such things show that they are looking for a country of their own. . . . they were longing for a better country—a heavenly one. Therefore, God is not ashamed to be called their God, for he has promised a city for them" (Heb 11:13–16).

The people of God in Old Testament times were already familiar with this exile–foreigner–stranger metaphor. Their own exile experience had etched deeply into their national DNA the temporary nature of their present earthly dwelling place; the costs and hardships of living under an alternate dominant culture; the temptations to compromise values, morals, and lifestyles for acceptance and recognition from the opinion formers and leaders of the foreign power; and the yearnings for their own true home. They also knew from prophets like Jeremiah the importance of "seeking the welfare of the city" to which they had been exiled (Jer 29:7), and knew well the example of Joseph in Egypt and Daniel and his friends in Babylon showing how to influence the alien society as an exile. The New Testament authors needed only to make the metaphorical allusion in exile terms for their scripturally literate hearers to draw out the implications.

Let us make two further links with this exile–foreigner–stranger metaphor. The New Testament describes Christian discipleship as "commencing a journey with Jesus."[14] As followers of Jesus of Nazareth we should expect to be taking steps which lead steadily to new values and worldview challenges and tensions differing from the ruling powers of our day. Not being "of this world," but commissioned to be "in it," involves willingness to be different in the way we "walk" in this world, as we have already noted in discussing the witness metaphor. But let us also highlight the theological atonement metaphor which links closely with the exile–foreigner–stranger metaphor and sets our stance towards our secular and increasingly anti-Christian dominant culture.

Paul brings a distinctly New Testament emphasis to the rich Old Testament exile metaphor when he likens Christians to foreign ambassadors (2 Cor 5:11—6:2). Knowing whose kingdom we truly belong to, Christians are not carried away simply as slaves into the alien worldview-dominated

14. Hitchen, "Gospel for Today," 32.

state of exile. Rather, "with our feet fitted with the readiness that comes from the gospel of peace" (Eph 6:15), we go to our "foreign" placement with humble confidence, and with the dignity and honor of ambassadors of the King of Kings. Appointed to uphold the concerns and honor of our King Jesus, we have a positive role to fill in the land of exile. Paul explains this in 2 Corinthians as the diplomacy demanding "ministry of reconciliation," carrying with us the "message of reconciliation." Or, to pick up the term Jesus had used and James also explained, we go as peacemakers (Matt 5:9; Jas 3:18). This means we cultivate all the respect and understanding, and do the serious study, research, contact making, and relationship building needed, to effectively represent and communicate the concerns, expectations, and desires of our commissioning king. The ambassadorial role is not merely defensive, protecting the rights, possessions, and intentions of our King, but proactively opening doors, establishing friendships and footholds, clarifying misunderstandings, and presenting honest, appropriate information about the values, importance, and priorities of our King and his message.

Moreover, since the ministry and its message focus on reconciliation, in our vocational location we will be alert to places where employee relationships are broken or at risk; situations where division or divisiveness are rife; where fear, blame, abuse, or misunderstanding have brought shame and hurt; or where entrenched viewpoints are damaging or hindering the productivity of the workplace; and we will seek both to humbly work for reconciliation and to demonstrate the King's message of reconciliation at work by the way we address such situations. As we have explained elsewhere:

> In this [reconciliation/peace-making metaphor's] explanation of the Gospel Jesus Christ acts as mediator. He steps into the breach to represent God to humans and humans to God. As the fully representative human Jesus understands, empathises and offers the ultimate advocacy based on experience. . . . Sin is shown as alienation, as loss of face, as shame, as letting down a faithful lover, as breaking our vows of loyalty and as retreat instead of open-faced confidence to approach our eternal lover, the awesomely holy God.

The reconciler's voluntary, vicarious death makes the needed peace. Christ offers the relationship-renewing power of forgiveness. The sweep of the reconciliation is all-embracing. Each believer now has peace with God. But Christ's mediatorial death also has inherent power to dismantle every man-made wall of separation. At last a basis has been laid for reconciliation at the societal and racial level. The radically new basis of receiving the proffered peace, by faith alone, removes any grounds for favoritism, for partiality, or for pride of clan or class. There is at last a genuine "level playing field" at the foot of the cross, answering a deeply rooted aspect of the post-colonial Kiwi psyche. The acceptance and integrity of purpose this reconciliation instils is pregnant with renewing and re-motivating strength for the bruised and crushed of our society. The scriptures even depict the peace achieved as the means of pacification of rebellious spirit powers in the heavenly realm.[15]

As ambassadors bearing this restorative message, then, we see our daily vocations as charged with challenge and opportunity. We work certainly in enemy territory, but with this missional understanding of our ordinary employment we are on the lookout for the points of relationship breakdown, and, not priggishly or self-righteously, but as respectful, sensitive ambassadors, we seek ways to bring peace and uphold the dignity of our peacemaking King. This, we suggest, is a significant pathway towards social justice in our fragmented, increasingly divided society.

Time and space preclude working through the other seminal metaphors explaining the death of Christ to identify comparable ways in which their descriptive explanations lead on to fresh conceptions of our vocations.

Conclusion

As we face the challenge to bring Christian influence for justice and wholesome transformation in our needy societies, we have outlined the New Testament vision as introduced by our Lord and elaborated after Calvary and Pentecost by the apostles. We found a hope-filled vision of Christ's kingly rule and an all-embracing gospel expectation of renewed peoples being brought to unity and fullness under Christ Jesus as head. To implement this transformative, Christ-centered vision, we focused on the way God actively calls followers to Christ Jesus, to become like him so he can send them out to reform their worlds for social justice. We outlined features of this general call to all believers to be holy, set apart people conformed increasingly to Christ's character, actively fulfilling the roles consequent on having met Jesus. We then explored examples of particular vocational calls and their explanatory metaphors, through which transformed people take steps towards the influence, reforms, and transformation needed in today's

15. Hitchen, "Gospel for Today," 34.

societies. God's method for fulfilling the vision of Christ's cosmic rule is for transformed people, shaped and motivated in line with these biblical metaphors, step by step transforming our vocational placement for Christ's honor and the good of our fellow citizens.

To conclude, we need now to prayerfully consider which of these metaphors speaks most relevantly as a living call for us, at this time, in the specific location in which the Lord has placed us. Which of the metaphors is scratching where it itches in our particular areas of influence? In clarifying which metaphor is conveying the most relevant call to us, we can also expect to clarify the group(s), or segment(s) of our society the call conveyed through this metaphor is fitted for best. With that clarified the task begins.

The diversity of callings and range of complementary metaphors presented in Scripture indicate that societal influence and change for justice is normally progressive. As one kind of service or call addresses and satisfies one set of needs, it also prepares for further needs to be addressed in their turn. As changes in the societal or group culture take place, local Christian leaders need to reassess, or listen for fresh calls and metaphors to address the newly emerging needs.

This process of finding the right metaphor or calling to meet immediate needs, then sensitively adjusting or changing the roles and descriptive metaphors to meet the changing needs or stages of development of the group membership and/or the surrounding culture, is what we refer to as "contextualization" in mission studies. Contextualization progressively relates the most meaningful biblical metaphors, themes, and callings to the progressively changing needs of a local culture, or society. It starts with finding the most relevant metaphor or calling and applying it in the local context, and then progressively broadening the range of metaphors understood and applied, so the community reaches ongoing maturity and fruitfulness in their pursuit of righteousness and justice.[16]

This final chapter has sought to indicate the way the contextualization process works for social justice in our societies, by showing the imaginative, informative, and formative potential available when we hear God's call to us, and heed the wealth of biblical metaphors elaborating these calls.

16. We have explained this process more fully in Hitchen, "Culture and the Bible," 30–52.

Appendix A

Hymns by John Hitchen

(Relating to Biblical Text Explored in Chapters 1, 5–8)

A Living Sacrifice
(Romans 12:1–5)

1. What shall I bring to You my God?
My life, my all, I give:
So many mercies You have shown
For You I now must live.

Chorus:
Jesus my Lord, I give myself
All that I am to You.
My life and mind to be transformed
Each day Your will to do.

2. My body, set apart and clean,
A pleasing offering:
This is the only worship true
A grateful heart can bring.

3. No more to copy this world's ways,
But, changed, renewed in mind
To prove Your will is perfect; and
Acceptable and kind.

4. To see myself as You now see—
No more puffed up with pride,
To work within Your church, and use
Each gift You have supplied

5. Our global debt we must repay
For those who've still not heard
Christ yearns that all will choose his way
As we make known his Word.

JMH, 11/1974
Tune: Kevin Taylor, or Vox Dilecti

I Died with Jesus
(Galatians 2:20; 6:11–18)

1. I died with Jesus when He died for me;
Self has been conquered, nailed upon the tree;
Buried and risen, united with Him;
He gives the vict'ry over law and sin.

2. No longer I, but Christ is living now,
Sharing His fullness within me each hour,
Thinking and speaking all yielded to Him;
Christ indwells now as Master and as King.

3. Moment by moment by faith now to live,
For He so loved me Himself he did give;
Crucified with Him filled by His own power;
Trusting Him daily, I walk with Him now.

4. Bearing His marks, and by your burdens bent,
Till Christ be formed in you, I now am sent;
Bearing your birth pangs, hard tho' be the cost,
Dead to the world, His cross my only boast.

JMH, 14/5/1974 and 16/11/1996
Tune: Ellers

Calvary—Viewed from Galatians
(Galatians 2–5)

Allured, deceived, imprison'd,
our evil age within,
Christ gave himself, 'tis written,
to rescue us from sin:
Obeying thus his Father,
fulfilling thus His will,
Raised up from death, our Savior,
Christ offers freedom still.

This Gospel truth invites us,
whate'er our culture be,
To stand upright, forgiven,
by faith in Christ set free.
Keeping laws won't justify,
in Christ we put our trust,
His work for us sufficient,
rely on him we must.

Though self and pride condemn us,
his death redeems, restores.
No matter place or status,
united in Christ's cause.
Rescued, justified, redeem'd,
explained in many ways,
Christ's death for us at Calv'ry,
the love of God displays.

With humble hearts and eager,
we bow before the Cross.
New values and new lifestyle,
replacing this world's dross.
Raised now from death, our Savior,
Lord, rule our lives today,
Your grace, Your love, Your Spirit,
enough to guide our way.

JMH, 19/4/2019

Come Gracious Spirit
(Ephesians 5:15–21)

1. "Take care, My child, just how you walk, Be wise in all your way;
Grasp firmly your entrusted time
To know My will each day.
For all around this age prefers
The foolish and the wrong;
My proven wisdom holds no place
Within mod' culture's song."

2. But where, within our frantic world
Can well-planned wisdom grow?
How can we order mind and time,
Your will, O Lord, to know?
"Yield to My Holy Spirit now,
Be filled afresh with Him,
Until His life, His mind, His will,
Refresh you deep within."

3. Then come Most Gracious Spirit, come,
Flood through our lives, Restore
Your rule, Your sacred, gentle love
More richly than before.
Come, teach us, Spirit, how to speak,
In psalm and song and hymn;
Relating each to other, as
Deep joy and thanks o'erbrim.

4. Accepting one another marks
The measure we've achieved;
For yielding each to other shows
The fullness we've received.
O Lord, this will and wisdom, may
You now on us bestow
Till our relationships display
Your fullness here below.

JMH, 13/3/1996

Growing in Christ
(Colossians 1:1–11)

1. Our Lord desires that we should grow
As we receive His Word,
By love and faith and hope to show
Our thankful hearts are stirred.
2. Christ longs that we His truth will take,
No matter what our race,
'Till it bears fruit and for His sake
We share this news of grace.

3. Through faithful servants Christ works still,
Who teach and serve in love,
Glad as the Spirit makes their work
Exalt their Lord above.

4. Our Lord still looks for further growth,
That knowing all His will,
We may walk worthy of our God
His pleasure to fulfill.

5. God gives His own dynamic power
To patiently endure,
For when our weakness we confess,
His mighty strength is sure.

6. To God who makes us fit for heaven
Our thanks now let us show;
With sin forgiven and lives redeemed
In Christ, now let us grow.

JMH, 9/1972
Tune: Martyrdom

Knowing Christ
(Colossians 1:15–23)

1. In Christ our God is seen,
The unseen God draws near:
He owns and rules our world;
Our Maker, He is here:
He is our source; He is our goal,
In all the worlds He has control.

2. Christ is the Lord of all—
Of earth and space and time—
Of pow'rs both great and small
And subtle and sublime.
He is the first; He is the last,
All forms of life His hand holds fast.

3. Christ is the Church's Head,
He is our life and breath;
In all things He must lead,
For He has conquered death:
He must direct; He must hold sway
In all we think and do and say.

4. This Christ is truly God:
In Him God's fullness dwells:
And by His cross and blood
Our peace with God He spells:
He reconciles; He brings us near:
Through Christ with God we freely share.

5. So let us then hold fast
Our faith in Christ alone,
Still trusting 'till the last
In all that Christ has done:
No other God; No other Name:
In all the world our Lord proclaim.

JMH, 11/1972
Tune: Darwall

Living in Christ's Fullness
(Colossians 2:6—3:4)

1. As you received Christ Jesus
In Him now live and walk;
For many would deceive you
With clever sounding talk;
But words of men and spirits
Full life can never bring,
For all is vain and useless
Apart from Christ our King.
2. In Christ we find all fullness
For He is God indeed;
Our Head—He is Almighty—
He answers ev'ry need.
In Him our "self" is conquer'd,
In Him we are made new;
By faith we share His dying
And resurrection too.

3. Our trespass is forgiven,
Our judgment set aside,
Our enemies are vanquish'd,
For Christ our Lord has died:
So man-made regulations
For us have lost their power:
Instead of heeding visions
We grow in Christ each hour.

4. Since we have died in Jesus
To passing things of earth,
Our minds are set on values
Which have eternal worth;
Risen with Christ already,
In Him we are made whole;
Each word and thought and action
We yield to His control.

JMH, 9/1972
Tune: Aurelia

Christ's Life in Us
(Colossians 3:5–21)

1. Life in Christ brings new demands
To abide in His commands;
Put to death those selfish ways
Which destroy a life of praise;
Sins of flesh, desire, and word—
Put them off, since Christ is Lord.

2. Putting on His nature new,
Showing Christ in all we do:
Leaving pride of clan and place,
Seeing Christ in ev'ry face;
We are known as His elect,
So His image now reflect.

3. In the things we think and do,
Putting on Christlikeness too:
Sympathetic, kind, and meek,
Offering the other cheek
When there's cause to rant and rave
Just forgive, as Christ forgave.

4. Let His love and peace control
Heart and mind and all our soul;
Let the Word of Christ indwell,
Teach and warn with songs as well;
Giving thanks by word and deed,
Living Christ, this is our creed.

5. Most of all within our home
May the love of Christ be shown;
Man and wife in Christ unite,
Sharing full and deep delight,
That our homes and hearts may be
Ruled by Christ con-tin-ual-ly.

JMH, 9/1972
Tune: Toplady

Christ's Life in Action
(Colossians 3:22—4:17)

1. All those who let Christ Jesus
Invade their mind and heart,
Soon find a transformation
Of life in ev'ry part;
Their work style He soon changes
Till what was toil and grind,
Becomes a daily service
For Christ and all mankind.

2. He teaches us when praying
To keep on constantly;
Not growing tired or weary
But asking, thankfully,
That He may open for us
A door to speak His Word,
Until the heav'nly secret
Is clear to all who've heard.

3. So let us then walk wisely
Before all those outside,
Rememb'ring each is precious
To Him who came and died.
Let speech be always gracious,
And wholesome, like good salt:
As we buy up each moment
So others can't find fault.

4. Fullness of life in Jesus
Means Christ in us each day;
'Till home and work and witness
The love of Christ display:
This is the Christian pattern,
There is no other way
To stand mature in Jesus
And do His will today.

JMH, 7/1975
Tune: Stand Up For Jesus

Good Servants of Christ
(1 Timothy 4:6–16)

1. Our churches need good servants
Who know and love their Lord,
Who feed on God's true teaching
Of faith from his own Word.
Who guard against false stories,
And guard all that they tell
So others they are teaching
May know and love Christ well.

2. They keep themselves in training,
That they may godly be;
For godliness is worth it—
Now and eternally.
They set a good example,
Though they still young may be
By word and deed love showing
And faith and purity.

3. They spend time at their reading,
And at their preaching, too;
They use each gift the Spirit
Gives them his work to do;
By hard work and by practice
They progress every day—
They watch their walk and teaching
That all may find Christ's way.

JMH, 27/6/1975
Tune: Aurelia

Appendix B

Writings by John M. Hitchen

Hitchen, John M. *Bible Teaching in the Local Church.* Palmerston North: Gospel Publishing House Society and Christian Brethren Research Fellowship (NZ), 1969.

———. "Bible Teaching in Local Churches." *The Harvester* (September–November 1982).

———. "A Biblical Charter for Pastoral Care." Paper presented at the Christian Brethren Research Fellowship New Zealand Annual Conference, Waikanae, New Zealand, May 1988.

———. "The Christian Leaders' Training College of PNG—A Case Study of a Christian Contribution to Economic Development and to Theological Change at Worldview and Social Imaginary Levels for Sustainable Development in Melanesia." Paper presented at "Woven Together" Conference on Christianity and Development in the Pacific, Victoria University, June 2016.

———. "The Church's Role in Mission Today: An Overview of Mission Themes in the Acts of the Apostles." Paper presented at the Annual Meeting of Wycliffe Bible Translators, NZ Branch, Auckland, March 29, 2003.

———. "Clarifying the Contribution of Culture to our Methodology for Contextual Theology: Three Guiding Principles." In *Theological Formation for Christian Missions: A Festschrift for Ian Walter Payne*, edited by Roji Thomas George and Aruthukal Varughese John, 91–120. Bangalore: SAIACS Press, 2019.

———. *Commentary on Romans.* Translated to Bengali by John Garwood. Chandpur: Christian Literature Centre, 1990.

———. "Confirming the Christian Scholar and Theological Educator's Identity through New Testament Metaphor." *Evangelical Review of Theology* 35 (2011) 276–87.

———. "Cross-Cultural Communication of the Gospel." In *God at Work in New Guinea*, edited by K. W. Liddle, 25–37. Palmerston North: Gospel Publishing House Society, 1969.

———. "Culture and the Bible—The Question of Contextualization." *Melanesian Journal of Theology* 8, no. 2 (1992) 30–52.

———. "Culture and the Bible—The Question of Contextualization." Presented at the South Pacific Association of Bible Colleges Biennial Conference, Adelaide, July 1–5, 1991.

———. "Dreams in Traditional Thought and in the Encounter with Christianity in Melanesia." *Melanesian Journal of Theology* 27, no. 2 (2011) 5–53.

———. "Editorial." *The Reaper* 75, no. 3 (1993) 4–5.

———. "The Eighth Duke of Argyll and the Formation of a Missionary Worldview." *Bulletin of the Scottish Institute of Missionary Studies* 8–9 (1992–1993) 9–28.
———. "An Evangelical Understanding of the Kingdom of God." *Christian Brethren Research Fellowship Journal* 112 (February 1988) 5–10.
———. "Evangelicals Equipping Melanesian Men and Women: An Interpretation of the Training Ministries of the Christian Leaders' Training College of Papua New Guinea, 1965–2010." In *Gospel, Truth and Interpretation: Evangelical Identity in Aotearoa New Zealand*, edited by Tim Meadowcroft and Myk Habets, 110–36. Auckland: Archer, 2011.
———. *Evangelism and Mission: What Is the Gospel?* Auckland: Impetus, 1996.
———. "Evangelism and Mission: What Is the Gospel?" *Scottish Bulletin of Evangelical Theology* 19 (2001) 4–30.
———. "Fresh Insights from Diverse Margins of Mission History? Anthony Norris Groves as a Test Case." In *The Brethren and Mission: Essays in Honour of Timothy C. F. Stunt*, edited by Neil T. R. Dickson and T. J. Marinello, 49–75. Glasgow: Brethren Archivists and Historians Network, 2016.
———. "Furloughs and Catechisms: Formative Strands in New Zealand Evangelicalism." In *Gospel, Truth and Interpretation: Evangelical Identity in Aotearoa New Zealand*, edited by Tim Meadowcroft and Myk Habets, 20–48. Auckland: Archer, 2011.
———. "George Douglas Campbell, Eighth Duke of Argyll." In *Scottish Dictionary of Theology and Church History*, edited by Nigel M. de S. Cameron, 128. Edinburgh: T.&T. Clark, 1993.
———. "The Gospel for New Zealanders." Reprinted in *New Zealand Made*, edited by J. Crawshaw and Alan Vink, 7–24. Wellington: Signposts, 1994.
———. "The Gospel for Today's New Zealanders." In *The Vision New Zealand Congress*, edited by Bruce Patrick, 29–44. Auckland, Vision New Zealand, 1993.
———. "The Holy Spirit and His Gifts," "How Do We Use Spiritual Gifts?," and "Test the Spirits," and three Songs about the Holy Spirit. In *The Holy Spirit and the Church*, Staff of the Christian Leaders' Training College. Wewak: Christian Books Melanesia, 1976, 13–19, 24–31, 49–56.
———. *I Want to Follow Christ*. Wewak: Christian Books Melanesia, 1972. Translated by Ces Parish, *Mi Laik Bihainim Krais*.
———. *I Want to Meet God*. Wewak: Christian Books Melanesia, 1972. Translated by K. W. Liddle, *Mi Laik Go long God*.
———. "Involved in Politics—Why?" In *The Vision New Zealand Congress 1997*, edited by Bruce Patrick, 174–96. Auckland: Vision New Zealand, 1997.
———. "J. G. Paton." In *Scottish Dictionary of Theology and Church History*, edited by Nigel M. de S. Cameron, 648. Edinburgh: T.&T. Clark, 1993.
———. "J. Oswald Sanders: An Antipodean Hero?" *Stimulus* 21, no. 1 (2014) 40–43.
———. "James Chalmers." In *Scottish Dictionary of Theology and Church History*, edited by Nigel M. de S. Cameron, 158. Edinburgh: T.&T. Clark, 1993.
———. "Joseph Angus." In *Scottish Dictionary of Theology and Church History*, edited by Nigel M. de S. Cameron, 17. Edinburgh: T.&T. Clark, 1993.
———. *"Leading Like Christ": Bible Studies on the Kind of Leaders We Need Today*. Wewak: Christian Books Melanesia, 1981. Tok Pisin translation, 1982: *Lida olsem Krais: Kristen lida em i wanem kain man?*
———. "Mission to Primal Religious Groups in a Postmodern Context." In *Mission and Postmodernities*, edited by Rolv Olsen, 139–71. Oxford: Regnum, 2011.

———. "The Missional, Multi-Ethnic Nature of the Church." In *New Vision New Zealand: Volume III, 2008*, edited by Bruce Patrick, 63–78. Auckland: Vision Network, 2008.
———. "Missionary Work in a Changing World." In *God at Work in New Guinea*, edited by K. W. Liddle, 84–89. Palmerston North: Gospel Publishing House Society, 1969.
———. *Only Faith Brings Freedom: Paul's Letter to the Galatians*. Christchurch: Syndoulos, 1986.
———. "Our Approach to Bible Teaching in Church Building." *Missiology* 8 (1980) 211–21.
———. "To Reform The World?" Colloquium on the Gospel and Socio-Cultural Change, Laidlaw College, Auckland, August 2019.
———. "Relations between Missiology and Anthropology Then and Now: Insights from the Contribution to Ethnography and Anthropology by Nineteenth Century Missionaries in the South Pacific." *Missiology* 30 (2002) 455–78.
———."Response: Contextualization Stages, Boomerang Challenges and Transitions." In *Living in the Family of Jesus: Critical Contextualization in Melanesia and Beyond*, edited by William Kenny Longgar and Tim Meadowcroft, 406–19. Auckland: Archer, 2016.
———."Response: Contextualization Stages, Boomerang Challenges and Transitions." In *Point Series* 40, 376–88. Goroka: Melanesian Institute, 2016.
———. "Sex and National Leadership: Where Have All the Josephs Gone?" *Reality* 4 (August–September 1994) 3, 55.
———. "Some Biblical Patterns of Ministerial Training and Their Relevance for Melanesia Today." *Point* 1 (1976) 85–121.
———. "Steps to the Field." In *God at Work in New Guinea*, edited by K. W. Liddle, 90–93. Palmerston North: Gospel Publishing House Society, 1969.
———. "Theological Education and Formation in Mission: An Evangelical Response." In *Edinburgh 2010: Mission Today and Tomorrow*, edited by Kirsteen Kim and Andrew Anderson, 240–48. Oxford: Regnum, 2011.
———. "Theological Roots of a Nineteenth Century Missionary Worldview." *Stimulus* 7, no. 2 (1999) 40–47.
———. "Theological Scholars' Self-Perceptions and Their Contribution to the Unity and Maturity of the Pacific Churches." *Melanesian Journal of Theology* 28, no. 1 (2012) 9–25.
———. "Towards a Biblical Agenda for Addressing Cultural Issues—Part 1." *Reality* 2, no. 8 (1995) 22–26.
———. "Towards a Biblical Agenda for Addressing Cultural Issues—Part 2." *Reality* 2, no. 9 (1995) 25–27.
———. "Towards a Theology of Business for Christians in a Primal Religious Society in a Globalising World." *Melanesian Journal of Theology* 30 no. 2 (2014) 74–104.
———. "Training Leaders for Melanesian Churches." In *God at Work in New Guinea*, edited by K. W. Liddle, 49–58. Palmerston North: Gospel Publishing House Society, 1969.
———. "'Training Tamate.' The Formation of the Nineteenth Century Missionary Worldview: The Case of James Chalmers of New Guinea." PhD diss., University of Aberdeen, 1984.
———. "Understanding the Church and Training from which the Cook Islander Missionaries brought the Christian Message to Papua New Guinea in the 1870s." *Journal of Pacific History* 57 (2022) 148–85.

———. "W. G. Lawes." In *Scottish Dictionary of Theology and Church History*, edited by Nigel M. de S. Cameron, 473. Edinburgh: T.&T. Clark, 1993.

———. "What Is Our Gospel?" In *New Vision New Zealand*, edited by Bruce Patrick, 146–57. Auckland: Vision New Zealand, 1993.

———. "What It Means to Be an Evangelical Today, An Antipodean Perspective: Part One, Mapping Our Movement." *Evangelical Quarterly* 76 (2004) 47–64.

———. "What It Means to Be an Evangelical Today, An Antipodean Perspective: Part Two, Confirming Our Core and Engaging Our Changed Context." *Evangelical Quarterly* 76 (2004) 99–115.

———. "When Different Teachings Divide the Jesus Family: Reading First Timothy in Context." In *Living in the Family of Jesus: Critical Contextualization in Melanesia and Beyond*, edited by William Kenny Longgar and Tim Meadowcroft, 173–93. Auckland: Archer, 2016.

———. "When Different Teachings Divide the Jesus Family: Reading First Timothy in Context." In *Living in the Family of Jesus: Critical Contextualization in Melanesia and Beyond*, edited by William Kenny Longgar and Tim Meadowcroft, 157–176. Point Series 40. Goroka: Melanesian Institute, 2016.

———. *The Work of the Church*. Wewak: Christian Books Melanesia, 1980.

Hitchen, John, Kenneth Fleck, and Elizabeth Ann Smythe. "Hermeneutics of Self as a Research Approach." In *International Journal of Qualitative Methods* 10 (2010) 14–29.

Hitchen, John, and Ann Hitchen. "Too Precious To Keep—Given Gloriously." Christian Leaders' Training College, Banz, Papua New Guinea, July 1969.

Hitchen, John, and Barry R. Mason. *One Hundred and Fifty Years of the Mason Family in NZ 1837–1987*. 2nd ed. Christchurch: Syndoulos, 1987.

Hitchen, John, and Edward Sands. *"Towards a Quality Framework": A Paper Responding to the New Zealand Qualifications Authority's "Consultation Package" for Implementing the National Post-Secondary Education Framework*. Auckland: Impetus, 1992.

Hitchen, John, and Geoffrey Smith. "Papua New Guinea." *The Church in Asia*, edited by Donald E. Hoke, 500–22. Chicago: Moody, 1975.

Bibliography

Abrahamsen, Valerie A. *Women and Worship at Philippi: Diana/Artemis and Other Cults in the Early Christian Era*. Portland, ME: Astarte Shell, 1995.

Ahdar, Rex. "Indigenous Spiritual Concerns and the Secular State: Some New Zealand Developments." *Oxford Journal of Legal Studies* 23 (2003) 611–37.

Anderson, Gerald H. "A Moratorium on Missionaries?" *Christian Century* 91, no. 2 (1974) 43–45.

Anderson, J. N. D. *Into the World: The Need and Limits of Christian Involvement*. London: Falcon, 1968.

Anthropological Review and Journal of the Anthropological Society of London 3 (1865).

Arnold, Clinton E. "Ephesus." In *Dictionary of Paul and His Letters*, edited by Gerald F. Hawthorne and Ralph P. Martin, 251–52. Downers Grove, IL: InterVarsity, 1993.

Austin, Tony. *Technical Training and Development in Papua 1894–1941*. Pacific Research Monograph 1. Canberra: ANU Press, 1978.

Barclay, Glen. *A History of the Pacific from the Stone Age to the Present Day*. London: Sidgwick and Jackson, 1978.

Barker, John. "Mission Station and Village: Religious Practice and Representations in Maisin Society." In *Christianity in Oceania: Ethnographic Perspectives*, edited by John Barker, 173–96. Lanham: University Press of America, 1990.

Barker, Montagu. "Models of Pastoral Care: Medical, Psychological and Biblical." In *Behavioural Sciences: A Christian Perspective*, edited by Malcolm A. Jeeves, 230–45. Leicester: Inter-Varsity, 1984.

Baron de Miklouhu Maclay and Rev. J Chalmers to Rt. Hon. Lord Derby, 1 June 1883. *British Parliamentary Papers* 1884 c3863, 5–6.

Barth, Karl. *Church Dogmatics: The Doctrine of Reconciliation, Part 1* (IV/1). Translated by Geoffrey W. Bromiley. Edinburgh: T.&T. Clark, 1958.

———. *God Here and Now*. London: Routledge and Kegan Paul, 1964.

Bauckham, Richard. *Bible and Mission: Christian Witness in a Postmodern World*. Carlisle: Paternoster, 2003.

Bayly, Joseph. *The Last Thing We Talk About: Help and Hope for Those Who Grieve*. Elgin, IL: David C. Cook, 1992.

Beach, Richard. *A Teachers' Introduction to Reader-Response Theories*. Urbana, IL: National Council of Teachers of English, 1993.

Beaglehole, J. C. "Some Philosophies of History." *Historical Studies, Australia and New Zealand* 2, no. 6 (1942) 95–113.

Beales, Derek. *History and Biography: An Inaugural Lecture*. Cambridge: Cambridge University Press, 1981.

Beasley-Murray, G. R. *Jesus and the Kingdom of God*. Grand Rapids: Eerdmans, 1986.

Bebbington, David. *Patterns in History*. Leicester: Inter-Varsity, 1979.

Bediako, Kwame. "The Holy Spirit, the Christian Gospel and Religious Change: The African Evidence for a Christian Theology of Religious Pluralism." In *Essays in Religious Studies for Andrew Walls*, edited by James Thrower, 44–56. Aberdeen: Department of Religious Studies, University of Aberdeen, 1986.

Berg, Johannes van den. *Constrained by Jesus' Love: An Inquiry into the Motives of the Missionary Awakening in Great Britain in the Period between 1698 and 1815*. Kampen: J. H. Kok, N.V., 1956.

Bevans, Stephen B. *Models of Contextual Theology*. Rev. ed. Maryknoll, NY: Orbis, 2002.

Binfield, Clyde. *George Williams and the Y. M. C. A: A Study in Victorian Social Attitudes*. London: Heinemann, 1973.

Boer, Harry R. *Pentecost and Missions*. London: Lutterworth, 1961.

Bosch, David. *Transforming Mission: Paradigm Shifts in Theology of Mission*. Maryknoll, NY: Orbis, 1991.

Bromiley, Geoffrey William. *Christian Ministry*. Grand Rapids: Eerdmans, 1959.

Bruce, F. F. *The Epistle to the Galatians: A Commentary on the Greek Text*. Exeter: Paternoster, 1982.

———. *The Epistles to the Colossians, to Philemon, and to the Ephesians*. New College International Commentary on the New Testament. Grand Rapids: Eerdmans, 1984.

———. *New Testament History*. London: Nelson, 1969.

———. *Philippians: A Good News Bible Commentary*. Glasgow: Pickering & Inglis, 1983.

Brunner, Emil. *The Word and the World*. London: SCM, 1931.

Burt, Ben. *Tradition and Christianity: The Colonial Transformation of a Solomon Islands Society*. Langhorne, PA: Harwood Academic, 1994.

Butterfield, Herbert. *Christianity and History*. London: Fontana, 1949.

———. "God in History." In *God, History and Historians: An Anthology of Modern Christian Views of History*, edited by C. T. McIntire, 192–204. New York: Oxford University Press, 1977.

———. *History and Human Relations*. London: Collins, 1951.

Cameron, Averil, and Amelie Kuhrt. *Images of Women in Antiquity*. London: Routledge, 1993.

Campbell, George Douglas, 8th Duke of Argyll. *Primeval Man: An Examination of Some Recent Speculations Contained in a Paper by Sir John Lubbock upon "The Early Condition of Mankind," and in a Lecture by Archbishop Whateley on the "Origin of Civilization."* London: 1869.

Campbell, Ian. *Thomas Carlyle*. London: Longmans for the British Council, 1978.

Carlyle, Thomas. *On Heroes, Hero-Worship and the Heroic in History: Six Lectures Reported with Emendations and Addition*. 4th ed. London: Chapman and Hall, 1852.

Carson, Donald A. ed. *Biblical Interpretation and the Church: The Problem of Contextualization*. Nashville: Thomas Nelson, 1985.

Carson, Herbert M. *The Epistles of Paul to the Colossians and Philemon*. Tyndale New Testament Commentaries. Leicester: Inter-Varsity, 1960.

Chalmers, James. *Adventures in New Guinea*. London: Religious Tract Society, 1886.

———. "New Guinea—Past, Present and Future." *Proceedings of the Royal Colonial Institute* 18 (1886–1887) 103–7.

———. "New Guinea: A Trading Voyage (Continued)." *Brisbane Courier* 3 (January 1884) 5b.

———. "Our Own Correspondent." *Brisbane Courier*, October 13, 1883.

———. "The Pretended Land Sale in New Guinea." *Brisbane Courier*, October 20, 1883.

Chalmers, James, and William Wyatt Gill. *Work and Adventure in New Guinea:1877–1885*. London: Religious Tract Society, 1885.

Chidester, David. "Credo Mutwa, Zulu Shaman: The Invention and Appropriation of Indigenous Authenticity in African Folk Religion." In *Religion, Politics and Identity in a Changing South Africa*, edited by David Chidester et al., 69–88. Religion and Society in Transition 6. Munster: Waxmann, 2004.

Christian, Jayakumar. *God of the Empty-Handed: Poverty, Power and the Kingdom of God*. Monrovia: MARC, 1999.

CLTC Staff. *Yu Ken Save Long Wok Bilong Holi Spirit*. Port Moresby: Christian Books Melanesia, 1976.

Coe, Shoki. "Contextualizing Theology." In *Mission Trends No. 3: Third World Theologies*, edited by Gerald H. Anderson and Thomas F. Stransky, 19–24. Grand Rapids: Eerdmans, 1976.

Cohen, A. P. *The Symbolic Construction of Community*. London: Tavistock, 1985.

Conn, Harvie M. "Contextual Theologies: The Problem of Agendas." *Westminster Theological Journal* 52 (1990) 51–63.

Costas, Orlando. "Evangelical Theology in the Two Thirds World." *TSF Bulletin* 9 (1985) 7–13.

Cullman, Oscar. *The State in the New Testament*. New York: Scribners, 1956.

Curry, George N., and Gina Koczberski. "Relational Economics, Social Embeddedness, and Valuing Labour in Agrarian Change: An Example from the Developing World." *Geographical Research* 50 (2012) 377–92.

Daimoi, Joshua Kurung. "An Exploratory Missiological Study of Melanesian Ancestral Heritage from an Indigenous Evangelical Perspective." PhD diss., University of Sydney, 2004.

———. "A Melanesian Theology of Christ as Leader: Reading Hebrews 1." In *Living in the Family of Jesus*, edited by William Kenny Longgar and Tim Meadowcroft, 117–26. Auckland: Archer, 2016.

Davidson, J. W. "The New Zealand Scholar: A Note on J. C. Beaglehole, 1901–1971." *Journal of Pacific History* 7 (1972) 151–54.

———. "Problems of Pacific History." *Journal of Pacific History* 1 (1966) 5–21.

Dollar, Harold E. *A Biblical-Missiological Exploration of the Cross-Cultural Dimensions in Luke-Acts*. San Francisco: Mellen Research University Press, 1993.

Donnell, Phillip John. "Where the World Is Welcome: Towards an Ecclesiology for the Multiethnic Church in Aotearoa/New Zealand." 2 vols. MTh diss., Melbourne College of Divinity, 2000.

Douglas, Bronwen. "Power, Discourse and the Appropriation of God: Christianity and Subversion in a Melanesian Context." *History and Anthropology* 9 (1995) 57–92.

Douglas, J. D., ed. *Let the Earth Hear His Voice*. Waco, TX: Word, 1974.

Duff, Alan. *Once Were Warriors*. Auckland: Tandem, 1990.

Dundon, Alison. "DNA, Israel and the Ancestors—Substantiating Connections through Christianity in Papua New Guinea." *Asia Pacific Journal of Anthropology* 12 (2011) 29–43.

Dye, T. Wayne. *The Bible Translation Strategy: An Analysis of Its Spiritual Impact*. Dallas: Wycliffe Bible Translators, 1985.

Encyclopaedia Brittanica. "John Robinson." *Encyclopaedia Brittanica Online*. https://www.britannica.com/biography/John-Robinson-English-minister.

Engen, Charles van. *Mission on the Way: Issues in Mission Theology*. Grand Rapids: Baker, 1996.

Engen, Charles van, et al., eds. *The Good News of the Kingdom: Mission Theology for the Third Millennium*. Maryknoll, NY: Orbis, 1993.

"Evangelism and Social Responsibility: An Evangelical Commitment." *Lausanne Occasional Papers* 21. https://lausanne.org/occasional-paper/lop-21.

Fairbairn, I. J., et al. *Namasu: New Guinea's Largest Indigenous-Owned Company*. New Guinea Research Bulletin 28. Canberra: ANU Press, 1969.

Fergie, Robert Digby. "A Study of Church/Government Relations in Papua New Guinea: With Particular Reference to the Evangelical Alliance of the South Pacific Islands and Its Involvement in the Government's Youth Movement Program during the 1980s." DTh diss., Australian College of Theology, 2000.

Ferguson, William. *Carlyle as Historian*. Occasional Paper 2. Edinburgh: The Carlyle Society, 1966.

Fife, Wayne. "Creating the Moral Body: Missionaries and the Technology of Power in Early Papua New Guinea." *Ethnology* 40 (2001) 251–69.

Flemming, Dean. *Contextualization in the New Testament: Patterns for Theology and Mission*. Leicester: Apollos, 2005.

Flett, John G. *The Witness of God: The Trinity,* Missio Dei, *Karl Barth, and the Nature of Christian Community*. Grand Rapids: Eerdmans, 2010.

Forman, Charles W. "Finding Our Own Voice: The Reinterpreting of Christianity by Oceanian Theologians." *International Bulletin of Mission Research* 29, no. 3 (2005) 115–22.

———. "The South Pacific Style in the Christian Ministry." *Missiology* 2 (1974) 421–35.

———. "The Study of Pacific Islands Christianity: Achievements, Resources, Needs." *International Bulletin of Mission Research* 18, no. 3 (1994) 103–12.

Fountain, O. C. "Religion and Economy in Mission Station-Village Relationships." *Practical Anthropology* 13, no. 2 (1966) 49–58.

Garrett, John. Review of *The Island Churches of the South Pacific: Emergence in the Twentieth Century*, by Charles W. Forman. *International Bulletin of Missionary Research* 7 (1983) 78.

Garwood, John. "Perspectives on Personhood: An Examination of Attempts to Integrate Theological and Psychological Explanations." ThD diss., Australian College of Theology, 1995.

Gimson, Andrew. *Boris: The Adventures of Boris Johnson*. London: Simon & Schuster, 2012.

Goldsmith, Martin. "Contextualization of Theology." *Themelios* 9, no. 1 (1983) 18–23.

Gray, Joe D. "A History of Rarotonga 1800–1883." PhD diss., University of Otago, 1975.

Green, Michael. *Called to Service: Ministers and Ministry in the Church*. London: Hodder and Stoughton, 1964.

———. *Evangelism in the Early Church*. London: Hodder and Stoughton, 1970.

———. *I Believe in the Holy Spirit*. Rev. ed. London: Hodder and Stoughton, 1985.

———. *The Second Epistle of Peter and the General Epistle of Jude: An Introduction and Commentary*. Tyndale New Testament Commentaries. London: Tyndale, 1968.

Grenz, Stanley. *A Primer on Postmodernism*. Grand Rapids: Eerdmans, 1996.
Groves, Anthony Norris. "Christian Devotedness." *Project Gutenberg*, January 15, 2008. https://www.gutenberg.org/cache/epub/24293/pg24293.txt.
Guder, Darrell L. "God's Mission Is Good News." In *The Continuing Conversion of the Church*, 28–48. Grand Rapids: Eerdmans, 2000.
Gunson, W. Niel. *Messengers of Grace: Evangelical Missionaries in the South Seas, 1797–1860*. Melbourne: Oxford University Press, 1978.
———. "Victorian Christianity in the South Seas: A Survey." *Journal of Religious History* 8 (1974–1975) 183–97.
Hanson, Allan. "The Making of the Māori: Culture Invention and Its Logic." *American Anthropologist* 91 (1989) 890–902.
Harrison, Simon. "Cultural Boundaries." *Anthropology Today* 15, no. 5 (1999) 10.
Harvey, David. *The Condition of Postmodernity: An Inquiry into the Origins of Cultural Change*. Oxford: Blackwell, 1990.
Hesselgrave, David. J. "Contextualization of Theology." In *Evangelical Dictionary of Theology*, edited by W. A. Elwood, 294–95. Grand Rapids: Baker, 1984.
Hesselgrave, David J., and Edward Rommen. *Contextualization: Meanings, Methods, and Models*. Leicester: Apollos, 1989.
Hiebert, Paul G. *Anthropological Insights for Missionaries*. Grand Rapids: Baker, 1985.
———. *Anthropological Reflections on Missiological Issues*. Grand Rapids: Baker, 1994.
———. "The Category *Christian* in the Mission Task." In *Anthropological Reflections on Missiological Issues*, 107–36. Grand Rapids: Baker, 1994.
———. "Critical Contextualization." In *Anthropological Reflections on Missiological Issues*, 75–92. Grand Rapids: Baker, 1994.
———. "Critical Contextualization." *International Bulletin of Missionary Research* 11, no. 3 (1987) 104–12.
———. "Flaw of the Excluded Middle." In *Anthropological Reflections on Missiological Issues*, 189–201. Grand Rapids: Baker, 1994.
———. "Syncretism and Social Paradigms." In *Contextualization and Syncretism: Navigating Cultural Currents*, edited by Gailyn van Rheenen, 31–46. Pasadena: William Carey Library, 2006.
Hilliard, David L. *God's Gentlemen: A History of the Melanesian Mission, 1849–1942*. St. Lucia: University of Queensland Press, 1978.
Hitchen, John M. *Bible Teaching in the Local Church*. Palmerston North: Gospel Publishing House Society and Christian Brethren Research Fellowship (NZ), 1969.
———. "Bible Teaching in Local Churches." *The Harvester* (September–November 1982).
———. "A Biblical Charter for Pastoral Care." Paper presented at the Christian Brethren Research Fellowship New Zealand Annual Conference, Waikanae, New Zealand, May 1988.
———. "The Christian Leaders' Training College of PNG—A Case Study of a Christian Contribution to Economic Development and to Theological Change at Worldview and Social Imaginary Levels for Sustainable Development in Melanesia." Paper presented at "Woven Together" Conference on Christianity and Development in the Pacific, Victoria University, June 2016.
———. "The Church's Role in Mission Today: An Overview of Mission Themes in the Acts of the Apostles." Paper presented at the Annual Meeting of Wycliffe Bible Translators, NZ Branch, Auckland, March 29, 2003.

———. "Clarifying the Contribution of Culture to our Methodology for Contextual Theology: Three Guiding Principles." In *Theological Formation for Christian Missions: A Festschrift for Ian Walter Payne*, edited by Roji Thomas George and Aruthukal Varughese John, 91–120. Bangalore: SAIACS Press, 2019.
———. *Commentary on Romans*. Translated to Bengali by John Garwood. Chandpur: Christian Literature Centre, 1990.
———. "Confirming the Christian Scholar and Theological Educator's Identity through New Testament Metaphor." *Evangelical Review of Theology* 35 (2011) 276–87.
———. "Cross-Cultural Communication of the Gospel." In *God at Work in New Guinea*, edited by K. W. Liddle, 25–37. Palmerston North: Gospel Publishing House Society, 1969.
———. "Culture and the Bible—The Question of Contextualization." *Melanesian Journal of Theology* 8, no. 2 (1992) 30–52.
———. "Culture and the Bible—The Question of Contextualization." Presented at the South Pacific Association of Bible Colleges Biennial Conference, Adelaide, July 1991.
———. "Dreams in Traditional Thought and in the Encounter with Christianity in Melanesia." *Melanesian Journal of Theology* 27, no. 2 (2011) 5–53.
———. "Editorial." *The Reaper* 75, no. 3 (1993) 4–5.
———. "The Eighth Duke of Argyll and the Formation of a Missionary Worldview." *Bulletin of the Scottish Institute of Missionary Studies* 8–9 (1992–1993) 9–28.
———. "An Evangelical Understanding of the Kingdom of God." *Christian Brethren Research Fellowship Journal* 112 (February 1988) 5–10.
———. "Evangelicals Equipping Melanesian Men and Women: An Interpretation of the Training Ministries of the Christian Leaders' Training College of Papua New Guinea, 1965–2010." In *Gospel, Truth and Interpretation: Evangelical Identity in Aotearoa New Zealand*, edited by Tim Meadowcroft and Myk Habets, 110–36. Auckland: Archer, 2011.
———. *Evangelism and Mission: What Is the Gospel?* Auckland: Impetus, 1996.
———. "Evangelism and Mission: What Is the Gospel?" *Scottish Bulletin of Evangelical Theology* 19 (2001) 4–30.
———. "Fresh Insights from Diverse Margins of Mission History? Anthony Norris Groves as a Test Case." In *The Brethren and Mission: Essays in Honour of Timothy C. F. Stunt*, edited by Neil T. R. Dickson and T. J. Marinello, 49–75. Glasgow: Brethren Archivists and Historians Network, 2016.
———. "Furloughs and Catechisms: Formative Strands in New Zealand Evangelicalism." In *Gospel, Truth and Interpretation: Evangelical Identity in Aotearoa New Zealand*, edited by Tim Meadowcroft and Myk Habets, 20–48. Auckland: Archer, 2011.
———. "George Douglas Campbell, Eighth Duke of Argyll." In *Scottish Dictionary of Theology and Church History*, edited by Nigel M. de S. Cameron, 128. Edinburgh: T.&T. Clark, 1993.
———. "The Gospel for New Zealanders." Reprinted in *New Zealand Made*, edited by J. Crawshaw and Alan Vink, 7–24. Wellington: Signposts, 1994.
———. "The Gospel for Today's New Zealanders." In *The Vision New Zealand Congress*, edited by Bruce Patrick, 29–44. Auckland, Vision New Zealand, 1993.
———. "The Holy Spirit and His Gifts," "How Do We Use Spiritual Gifts?," and "Test the Spirits," and three Songs about the Holy Spirit. In *The Holy Spirit and the Church*, Staff of the Christian Leaders' Training College, 13–19, 24–31, 49–56. Wewak: Christian Books Melanesia, 1976.

———. *I Want to Follow Christ*. Wewak: Christian Books Melanesia, 1972. Translated by Ces Parish, *Mi Laik Bihainim Krais.*

———. *I Want to Meet God*. Wewak: Christian Books Melanesia, 1972. Translated by K. W. Liddle, *Mi Laik Go long God.*

———. "Involved in Politics—Why?" In *The Vision New Zealand Congress 1997*, edited by Bruce Patrick, 174–96. Auckland: Vision New Zealand, 1997.

———. "J. G. Paton." In *Scottish Dictionary of Theology and Church History*, edited by Nigel M. de S. Cameron, 648. Edinburgh: T.&T. Clark, 1993.

———. "J. Oswald Sanders: An Antipodean Hero?" *Stimulus* 21, no. 1 (2014) 40–43.

———. "James Chalmers." In *Scottish Dictionary of Theology and Church History*, edited by Nigel M. de S. Cameron, 158. Edinburgh: T.&T. Clark, 1993.

———. "Joseph Angus." In *Scottish Dictionary of Theology and Church History*, edited by Nigel M. de S. Cameron, 17. Edinburgh: T.&T. Clark, 1993.

———. *"Leading Like Christ": Bible Studies on the Kind of Leaders We Need Today.* Wewak: Christian Books Melanesia, 1981. Tok Pisin translation, 1982, *Lida olsem Krais: Kristen lida em i wanem kain man?*

———. "Mission to Primal Religious Groups in a Postmodern Context." In *Mission and Postmodernities*, edited by Rolv Olsen, 139–71. Oxford: Regnum, 2011.

———. "The Missional, Multi-Ethnic Nature of the Church." In *New Vision New Zealand: Volume III, 2008*, edited by Bruce Patrick, 63–78. Auckland: Vision Network, 2008.

———. "Missionary Work in a Changing World." In *God at Work in New Guinea*, edited by K. W. Liddle, 84–89. Palmerston North: Gospel Publishing House Society, 1969.

———. *Only Faith Brings Freedom: Paul's Letter to the Galatians.* Christchurch: Syndoulos, 1986.

———. "Our Approach to Bible Teaching in Church Building." *Missiology* 8 (1980) 211–21.

———. "To Reform The World?" Colloquium on the Gospel and Socio-Cultural Change, Laidlaw College, Auckland, August 2019.

———. "Relations between Missiology and Anthropology Then and Now: Insights from the Contribution to Ethnography and Anthropology by Nineteenth Century Missionaries in the South Pacific." *Missiology* 30 (2002) 455–78.

———."Response: Contextualization Stages, Boomerang Challenges and Transitions." In *Living in the Family of Jesus: Critical Contextualization in Melanesia and Beyond*, edited by William Kenny Longgar and Tim Meadowcroft, 406–19. Auckland: Archer, 2016.

———."Response: Contextualization Stages, Boomerang Challenges and Transitions." In *Living in the Family of Jesus: Critical Contextualization in Melanesia and Beyond*, edited by William Kenny Longgar and Tim Meadowcroft, 376–88. Point Series 40. Goroka: Melanesian Institute, 2016.

———. "Sex and National Leadership: Where Have All the Josephs Gone?" *Reality* 4 (August–September 1994) 3, 55.

———. "Some Biblical Patterns of Ministerial Training and Their Relevance for Melanesia Today." *Point* 1 (1976) 85–121.

———. "Steps to the Field." In *God at Work in New Guinea*, edited by K. W. Liddle, 90–93. Palmerston North: Gospel Publishing House Society, 1969.

———. "Theological Education and Formation in Mission: An Evangelical Response." In *Edinburgh 2010: Mission Today and Tomorrow*, edited by Kirsteen Kim and Andrew Anderson, 240–48. Oxford: Regnum, 2011.

———. "Theological Roots of a Nineteenth Century Missionary Worldview." *Stimulus* 7, no. 2 (1999) 40–47.

———. "Theological Scholars' Self-Perceptions and Their Contribution to the Unity and Maturity of the Pacific Churches." *Melanesian Journal of Theology* 28, no. 1 (2012) 9–25.

———. "Towards a Biblical Agenda for Addressing Cultural Issues—Part 1." *Reality* 2, no. 8 (1995) 22–26.

———. "Towards a Biblical Agenda for Addressing Cultural Issues—Part 2." *Reality* 2, no. 9 (1995) 25–27.

———. "Towards a Theology of Business for Christians in a Primal Religious Society in a Globalising World." *Melanesian Journal of Theology* 30 no. 2 (2014) 74–104.

———. "Training Leaders for Melanesian Churches." In *God at Work in New Guinea*, edited by K. W. Liddle, 49–58. Palmerston North: Gospel Publishing House Society, 1969.

———. "'Training Tamate.' The Formation of the Nineteenth Century Missionary Worldview: The Case of James Chalmers of New Guinea." PhD diss., University of Aberdeen, 1984.

———. "Understanding the Church and Training from which the Cook Islander Missionaries brought the Christian Message to Papua New Guinea in the 1870s." *Journal of Pacific History* 57 (2022) 148–85.

———. "W. G. Lawes." In *Scottish Dictionary of Theology and Church History*, edited by Nigel M. de S. Cameron, 473. Edinburgh: T.&T. Clark, 1993.

———. "What Is Our Gospel?" In *New Vision New Zealand*, edited by Bruce Patrick, 146–57. Auckland: Vision New Zealand, 1993.

———. "What It Means to Be an Evangelical Today, An Antipodean Perspective: Part One, Mapping Our Movement." *Evangelical Quarterly* 76 (2004) 47–64.

———. "What It Means to Be an Evangelical Today, An Antipodean Perspective: Part Two, Confirming Our Core and Engaging Our Changed Context." *Evangelical Quarterly* 76 (2004) 99–115.

———. "When Different Teachings Divide the Jesus Family: Reading First Timothy in Context." In *Living in the Family of Jesus: Critical Contextualization in Melanesia and Beyond*, edited by William Kenny Longgar and Tim Meadowcroft, 173–93. Auckland: Archer, 2016.

———. "When Different Teachings Divide the Jesus Family: Reading First Timothy in Context." In *Living in the Family of Jesus: Critical Contextualization in Melanesia and Beyond*, edited by William Kenny Longgar and Tim Meadowcroft, 157–76. Point Series 40. Goroka: Melanesian Institute, 2016.

———. *The Work of the Church*. Wewak: Christian Books Melanesia, 1980.

Hitchen, John, Kenneth Fleck, and Elizabeth Ann Smythe. "Hermeneutics of Self as a Research Approach." In *International Journal of Qualitative Methods* 10 (2010) 14–29.

Hitchen, John, and Ann Hitchen. "Too Precious To Keep—Given Gloriously." Christian Leaders' Training College, Banz, Papua New Guinea, July 1969.

Hitchen, John, and Barry R. Mason. *One Hundred and Fifty Years of the Mason Family in NZ 1837–1987*. 2nd ed. Christchurch: Syndoulos, 1987.

Hitchen, John, and Edward Sands. *"Towards a Quality Framework": A Paper Responding to the New Zealand Qualifications Authority's "Consultation Package" for Implementing the National Post-Secondary Education Framework*. Auckland: Impetus, 1992.

Hitchen, John, and Geoffrey Smith. "Papua New Guinea." In *The Church in Asia*, edited by Donald E. Hoke, 500–22. Chicago: Moody, 1975.

Holmes, Stephen R. "Trinitarian Missiology: Towards a Theology of God as Missionary." *International Journal of Systematic Theology* 8 (2006) 72–90.

Howard, David. *Student Power in World Evangelism*. Downers Grove, IL: InterVarsity, 1979.

Hsu, Francis L. K. "Passage to Understanding." In *The Making of Psychological Anthropology*, edited by George D. Spindler, 142–73. Berkeley: University of California Press, 1978.

———. *Rugged Individualism: Essays in Psychological Anthropology*. Knoxville: University of Tennessee Press, 1983.

Hunter, Ian. *Robert Laidlaw: Man for Our Time*. Auckland: Castle, 1999.

Huyssens, A. "Mapping the Postmodern." *New German Critique* 33 (1984) 5–52.

Ihimaera, Witi. *The Whale Rider*. Auckland: Heinneman, 1987.

Jacobs, Donald R. "Contextualization in Mission." In *Toward the Twenty-First Century in Christian Mission: Essays in Honor of Gerald H. Anderson*, edited by James M. Phillips and Robert T. Coote, 235–44. Grand Rapids: Eerdmans, 1993.

Jeffries, M. C. V. *Beyond Neutrality*. Manchester: Pitmans, 1953.

Jenkins, Philip. *The Next Christendom: The Coming of Global Christianity*. Oxford: Oxford University Press, 2002.

Johnson, Paul. *Paul Johnson in New Zealand*. Wellington: New Zealand Business Roundtable, 1995.

Jones, Stanton L., and Richard E. Butman. *Modern Psychotherapies*. Downers Grove, IL: InterVarsity, 1991.

Keown, Michelle. *Postcolonial Pacific Writing: Representations of the Body*. London: Routledge, 2004.

Kirk, J. Andrew. *What Is Mission? Theological Explorations*. London: Darton, Longman & Todd, 1999.

Knight, G. W., III. *The Faithful Sayings in the Pastoral Letters*. Kampen: J. H. Kok, 1968.

Kolig, Erich. "From a 'Madonna in a Condom' to 'Claiming the Airwaves': The Māori Cultural Renaissance and Biculturalism in New Zealand." In *Shifting Images of Identity in the Pacific*, edited by Toon van Meijl and Jelle Miedema, 135–58. Leiden: KITLV, 2004.

———. "Legitimising Belief: Identity Politics, Utility, Strategies of Concealment, and Rationalisation in Australian Aboriginal Religion." *Australian Journal of Anthropology* 14 (2003) 209–28.

Kowal, Emma. *Trapped in the Gap: Doing Good in Indigenous Australia*. New York: Berghahn, 2015.

Kraft, Charles. *Anthropology for Christian Witness*. Maryknoll, NY: Orbis, 1996.

———. *Christianity and Culture: A Study in Dynamic Biblical Theologizing in Cross-Cultural Perspective*. Maryknoll, NY: Orbis, 1979.

Kraft, Charles, ed. *Appropriate Christianity*. Pasadena, CA: William Carey Library, 2005.

Ladd, George Eldon. *Crucial Questions about the Kingdom of God*. Grand Rapids: Eerdmans, 1953.

Langmore, Diane. *Tamate—A King: James Chalmers in New Guinea 1877–1901*. Melbourne: Melbourne University Press, 1974.

Latukefu, Sione. "Conclusion: Retrospect and Prospect." In *Mission, Church and Sect in Oceania*, edited by James A. Boutilier et al., 457–65. Association for Social

Anthropology in Oceania Monograph 6. Ann Arbor: University of Michigan Press, 1978.

Lausanne Movement. "The Lausanne Covenant." *Lausanne Covenant*, 1974. https://lausanne.org/content/covenant/lausanne-covenant.

———. *The Willowbank Report: Consultation on Gospel and Culture*. Lausanne: Lausanne Committee for World Evangelization, 1978.

———. "The Willowbank Report: The Gospel and Culture." Lausanne Committee for World Evangelization Occasional Paper 2. Wheaton, IL: Lausanne Committee for World Evangelization, 1978.

Lawrence, Peter. *Road Bilong Cargo*. Melbourne: Melbourne University Press, 1964.

Liddle, Kay W. *Into the Heart of Papua New Guinea: A Pioneering Mission Adventure*. Book One. Auckland: Kay Liddle Trust, 2012.

Linnekin, Jocelyn. "Contending Approaches." In *The Cambridge History of the Pacific Islands*, edited by Donald Denoon et al., 3–36. Cambridge: Cambridge University Press, 1997.

Lubbock, John. *The Origin of Civilisation and the Primitive Condition of Man: Mental and Social Condition of Savages*. 2nd ed. London: Longmans, Green, 1870.

Lyotard, Jean Francois. *The Postmodern Condition*. Minneapolis: University of Minnesota Press, 1984.

MacDonald, Fraser. "Christianity and Culture Change among the Oksapmin of Papua New Guinea." PhD diss., Australian National University, 2013.

Mackenzie, Peter. "Should There Be a Christian Party?" *Reality* 15 (June–July 1996)12–14.

Maddock, Kenneth. "Revival, Renaissance and the Meaning of Modern Constructions in Australia." In *Politics of Indigeneity in the South Pacific: Recent Problems of Identity in the Pacific*, edited by Erich Kolig and Hermann Muckler, 25–46. Munster: Lit Verlag, 2002.

Maier, Harry O. "A Sly Civility: Colossians and Empire." *Journal for the Study of the New Testament* 27 (2005) 323–49.

Malina, Bruce. *The New Testament World: Insights from Cultural Anthropology*. 3rd ed. Louisville: Westminster John Knox, 2001.

Mani, Maxon. "Marital Violence in Papua New Guinea: A Theological Critique and Response." PhD diss., University of Otago, 2018.

———. "A Theological and Missiological Response to the *Wantok* System in Melanesia." In *Living in the Family of Jesus: Critical Contextualization in Melanesia and Beyond*, edited by William Kenny Longgar and Tim Meadowcroft, 57–78. Auckland: Archer, 2016.

Marshall, Chris. *Kingdom Come: The Kingdom of God in the Teaching of Jesus*. Auckland: Impetus, 1990.

Marshall, I. Howard. *Acts*. Tyndale New Testament Commentaries. Leicester: Inter-Varsity, 1980.

———. *Beyond the Bible: Moving from Scripture to Theology*. Grand Rapids: Baker Academic, 2004.

———. *A Critical and Exegetical Commentary on the Pastoral Epistles*. International Critical Commentary. Edinburgh: T.&T. Clark, 1999.

———. "Culture and the New Testament." Paper presented at the Willowbank Consultation, Bermuda, 1978. In *Down to Earth: Studies in Christianity and Culture: The Papers of the Lausanne Consultation on Gospel and Culture*, edited by John Stott and Robert T. Coote. London: Hodder and Stoughton, 1980.

McGregor, Don. "New Guinea Basic Assumptions." Paper presented at the CMML Annual Brethren Missionary Conference, Anguganak, August 1966.

Meadowcroft, Tim. "Introduction." In *Living in the Family of Jesus: Critical Contextualization in Melanesia and Beyond*, edited by William Kenny Longgar and Tim Meadowcroft, 17–25. Auckland: Archer, 2016.

Menninger, Karl. *Whatever Became of Sin?* New York: Hawthorn, 1972.

Miller, G. "Romans." In *International Standard Bible Encyclopedia*, edited by Geoffrey W. Bromiley, 4:22–23. Rev. ed. 4 vols. Grand Rapids: Eerdmans, 1982.

Mombi, George. "Christ, Salvation and Eschatology from Colossians: Developing a Response to Melanesian Concept of *Gutpela Sindaun*." PhD diss., University of Otago, 2019.

———. "Jesus Our Wapiken: Seeking a Model of Holiness among the Abelam People." In *Living in the Family of Jesus*, edited by William K. Longgar and Tim Meadowcroft, 79–99. Auckland: Archer, 2016.

Moreau, A. Scott. *Contextualization in World Missions: Mapping and Assessing Evangelical Models*. Grand Rapids: Kregel Academic, 2012.

———. "Evangelical Models of Contextualization." In *Local Theology for the Global Church: Principles for an Evangelical Approach to Contextualization*, edited by Matthew Cook et al., 165–93. Pasadena, CA: William Carey Library, 2010.

Moreau, A. Scott, et al., eds. *Introducing World Missions: A Biblical, Historical and Practical Survey*. Grand Rapids: Baker Academic, 2004.

Motyer, J. A. *The Message of Philippians: Jesus Our Joy*. Bible Speaks Today. Leicester: Inter-Varsity, 1984.

Moule, H. C. G. *The Second Letter to Timothy*. Devotional Commentary Series. London: Religious Tract Society, 1906.

Murray, Andrew. *The Key to the Missionary Problem*. London: James Nisbet, 1901.

Murray, Jocelyn. "The Role of Women in the Church Missionary Society, 1799–1917." In *The Church Mission Society and World Christianity, 1799–1999*, edited by Brian Stanley and Kevin Ward, 66–90. London: Routledge, 2019.

Myers, Bryant L. *Walking with the Poor: Principles and Practices of Transformational Development*. Maryknoll, NY: Orbis, 1999.

Narakobi, Bernard. "Christianity and Melanesian Cosmos: The Broken Pearls and a Newborn Shell." In *The Gospel Is Not Western: Black Theologies from the Southwest Pacific*, edited by Garry W. Trompf, 32–37. Maryknoll, NY: Orbis, 1987.

Neuhaus, Richard John. "Against Christian Politics." *First Things* 63 (May 1996) 72–74.

Newbigin, Lesslie. *The Gospel in a Pluralist Society*. London: SPCK, 1989.

———. *The Open Secret*. Rev. ed. Grand Rapids: Eerdmans, 1995.

Nicholls, Bruce J. "Towards a Theology of Gospel and Culture." In *Down to Earth: Studies in Christianity and Culture: The Papers of the Lausanne Consultation on Gospel and Culture*, edited by John Stott and Robert T. Coote, 49–62. London: Hodder & Stoughton, 1980.

Niles, Daniel T. *That They May Have Life*. New York: Harper, 1951.

Noll, Mark. "The Challenges of Contemporary Church History, the Dilemmas of Modern History and Missiology to the Rescue." *Missiology* 24 (1996) 47–64.

Oden, Thomas. "Recovering Pastoral Care's Lost Identity." In *The Church and Pastoral Care*, edited by LeRoy Aden and J. H. Ellens, 17–30. Waco: Baker, 1988.

Ott, Craig. "The Power of Biblical Metaphors for the Contextualized Communication of the Gospel." *Missiology* 42 (2014) 357–74.

Packer, James I. *Knowing God*. London: Hodder & Stoughton, 1973.

Padilla, C. René. *The Contextualization of the Gospel: A Learning in Dialogue Experience with C. Rene Padilla*. Abington: Partnership in Mission, n.d.

———. "The Interpreted Word: Reflections on Contextual Hermeneutics." *Themelios* 7, no. 1 (1981) 18–23.

Paton, David M., ed. *The Ministry of the Spirit: Selected Writings of Roland Allen*. London: World Dominion, 1960.

Patrick, Bruce, ed. *New Vision New Zealand*. Auckland: Vision New Zealand, 1993.

Payne, Michael W. "Mission and Global Ethnic Violence." *Transformation* 19 (2002) 206–16.

Phillips, James M., and Robert T. Coote, eds. *Toward the Twenty-First Century in Christian Mission: Essays in Honor of Gerald H. Anderson*. Grand Rapids: Eerdmans, 1993.

Piggin, F. Stuart. "The Social Background, Motivation and Training of British Protestant Missionaries to India, 1798–1858." PhD diss., University of London, King's College, 1974.

Potter, Sarah Caroline. "The Social Origins and Recruitment of English Protestant Missionaries in the Nineteenth Century." PhD diss., University of London, 1974.

Price, David J. *Live in Tents, Build Only Altars: Gilbert Macarthur, His Story*. Vermont South: MST, 2019.

Reynolds, Henry Robert. "A Charge." *The Christian World Pulpit*, June 4, 1890.

———. *Lamps of the Temple and Other Addresses to Young Men*. London: Religious Tract Society, 1895.

———. "A Study in Heno-Christianity." *The Expositor*, 5th Series, 2 (1895) 321–41.

Rheenen, Gailyn van, ed. *Contextualization and Syncretism: Navigating Cultural Currents*. Evangelical Missiology 13. Pasadena, CA: William Carey Library, 2006.

———. "Syncretism and Contextualization: The Church on a Journey Defining Itself." In *Contextualization and Syncretism: Navigating Cultural Currents*, edited by Gailyn van Rheenen, 1–30. Pasadena: William Carey Library, 2006.

Richardson, Don. *Peace Child*. Glendale: Regal, 1974.

Robbins, Joel. *Becoming Sinners: Christianity and Moral Torment in a Papua New Guinea Society*. Berkeley: University of California Press, 2004.

Robert, Dana. "Shifting Southward: Global Christianity since 1945." *International Bulletin of Missionary Research* 24 (2000) 50–58.

Ross, Cathy. *Women with a Mission: Rediscovering Missionary Wives in Early New Zealand*. Auckland: Penguin, 2006.

Ross, Cathy, and Andrew F. Walls, ed. *Mission in the 21st Century: Exploring the Five Marks of Global Mission*. London: Darton, Longman, & Todd, 2008.

Roxborogh, John. "Loyalty to Christ, Contextualization, and Religious Syncretism." In *Living in the Family of Jesus: Critical Contextualization in Melanesia and Beyond*, edited by William Kenny Longgar and Tim Meadowcroft, 345–58. Auckland: Archer, 2016.

Salisbury, Kevin, and Mary Salisbury. "Manuscript XXXVIII, Rau's Report on the Work of the Cook Islands *'Orometua* in Papua, 18 June 1872–14 June 1877." *Journal of Pacific History* 57 (2022) 2–4.

Sanneh, Lamin. *Translating the Message: The Missionary Impact on Culture*. American Society of Missiology 13. Maryknoll, NY: Orbis, 1990.

Schwarz, Brian, ed. *An Introduction to Melanesian Religions: A Handbook for Church Workers*, Book Two, Point 6. Goroka: Melanesian Institute, 1986.

———. *An Introduction to Ministry in Melanesia: A Handbook for Church Workers*, Book Three, Point 7. Goroka: Melanesian Institute, 1986.

Shaw, R. Daniel. "The Wantok System: Local Principles and Expatriate Perspectives." *Catalyst* 11, no. 3 (1981) 190–203.

Sibree, James. *Register of London Missionary Society Missionaries*. London: London Missionary Society, 1923.

Smith, Geoffrey, and John Hitchen. "Papua New Guinea." In *The Church in Asia*, edited by Donald E. Hoke, 501–21. Chicago: Moody, 1975.

Smith, James K. A. *Desiring the Kingdom: Worship Worldview and Cultural Formation*. Grand Rapids: Baker Academic, 2009.

Smith, Linda Tuhiwai. *Decolonizing Methodologies: Research and Indigenous Peoples*. Dunedin: University of Otago Press, 1999.

Smith, Russell. "The Place of the Market in Mission." MTh diss., Laidlaw Graduate School, 2010.

Sprague, Joey, and Mary K. Zimmerman. "Overcoming Dualisms: A Feminist Agenda for Sociological Methodology." In *Approaches to Qualitative Research: A Reader on Theory and Practice*, edited by Sharlene Nagy Hesse-Biber and Patricia Leavy, 39–61. New York: Oxford University Press, 2004.

Stendahl, Krister. "The Apostle Paul and the Introspective Conscience of the West." In *Paul among Jews and* Gentiles, 78–96. Philadelphia: Fortress, 1976.

———. *Paul among Jews and Gentiles*. Philadelphia: Fortress, 1976.

Stott, John R. W. *The Lausanne Covenant: An Exposition and Commentary*. Lausanne Occasional Papers 3. Wheaton, IL: Lausanne Committee for World Evangelization, 1975.

Strelan, John G. *Search for Salvation: Studies in the History and Theology of Cargo Cults*. Adelaide: Lutheran, 1977.

Summerton, Neil. *A Noble Task: Eldership and Ministry in the Local Church*. Exeter: Paternoster, 1987.

Tennyson, Alfred. "Crossing the Bar." https://www.poetryfoundation.org/poems/45321/crossing-the-bar.

Thiselton, Anthony C. *The Two Horizons: New Testament Hermeneutics and Philosophical Description*. Exeter: Paternoster, 1980.

Tidball, Derek. *Skilful Shepherds: An Introduction to Pastoral Theology*. Grand Rapids: Ministry Resources Library, 1986.

Tienou, Tite. "Christian Theology in an Era of World Christianity." In *Globalizing Theology: Belief and Practice in an Era of World Christianity*, edited by Craig Ott and Harold A. Netland, 37–51. Nottingham: Apollos, 2007.

———. "Forming Indigenous Theologies." In *Toward the Twenty-First Century in Christian Mission: Essays in Honor of Gerald H. Anderson*, edited by James M. Phillips and Robert T. Coote, 245–52. Grand Rapids: Eerdmans, 1993.

Timmer, Jaap. "Straightening the Path from the Ends of the Earth: The Deep Sea Canoe Movement in Solomon Islands." In *Flows of Faith: Religious Reach and Community in Asia and the Pacific*, edited by L. Manderson et al., 201–14. New York: Springer, 2012.

Tippett, Alan R. "Conversion as a Dynamic Process in Christian Mission." *Missiology* 5 (1977) 203–21.

———. "Parallaxis in Missiology: To Use or Abuse." *Studies in Third World Societies* 25 (1983) 91–151.

Towner, Philip H. *The Letters to Timothy and Titus*. New International Commentary on the New Testament. Grand Rapids: Eerdmans, 2006.

Triton, A. N. *Whose World?* London: Inter-Varsity, 1970.

Trompf, Garry W. *Melanesian Religion*. Cambridge: Cambridge University Press, 1991.

———. *Payback: The Logic of Retribution in Melanesian Religions*. Cambridge: Cambridge University Press, 1994.

Turner, Harold W. "Editorial." *New Slant* 12 (October 1996) 4.

———. *Frames of Mind: A Public Philosophy for Religion and Cultures*. Auckland: DeepSight Trust, 2001.

———. "Gospel's Mission to Culture in New Zealand." *Journeyings* 5, no. 1 (1991) 3–17.

———. "The Gospel's Mission to Culture in New Zealand." *Latimer* 112 (1993) 23–36.

———. "The Gospel's Mission to Culture in New Zealand." In *New Zealand Made: Perspectives on Mission in Aotearoa*, edited by J. Crawshaw and W. Kirkland, 91–105. Wellington: Signpost Communications, 1994.

———. "New Religious Movements in Primal Societies." In *A New Handbook of Living Religions*, edited by John R. Hinnells, 581–93. London: Penguin, 1997.

———. "Recent Orthodoxy in New Zealand." In *Considering Orthodoxy: Foundations for Faith Today*, edited by Paul Trebilco, 31–45. Orewa: ColCom, 1995.

———. "The Relationship between Development and New Religious Movements in the Primal Societies of the Third World." In *God and Global Justice: Religion and Poverty in an Unequal World*, edited by Frederick Ferre and Rita Mataragnon, 84–110. New York: Paragon House, 1985.

———. *Roots of Science: An Investigative Journey through the World's Religions*. Auckland: DeepSight Trust, 1998.

———. "Three Levels of Mission in New Zealand." In *New Vision New Zealand*, edited by Bruce Patrick, 61–68. Auckland: Vision New Zealand, 1993.

———. "The Way Forward in the Religious Study of African Primal Religions. Paper presented at African Studies Centre Seminar, Leiden, December 1979.

Tylor, E. B. "Preface" to George Turner, *Samoa, a Hundred Years Ago and Long Before, Together with Notes on the Cults and Customs of Twenty-Three Other Islands in the Pacific*. London: Macmillan, 1884.

Vanhoozer, Kevin J. "'One Rule to Rule Them All?' Theological Method in an Era of World Christianity." In *Globalizing Theology: Belief and Practice in an Era of World Christianity*, edited by Craig Ott and Harold A. Netland, 85–126. Nottingham: Apollos, 2007.

Walker, F. W. *The Papuan Industries Ltd., Its Progress and Aims*. London: London Missionary Society, 1908.

Walls, Andrew F. "Commission One and the Church's Transforming Century." In *Edinburgh 2010: Mission Then and Now*, edited by David A. Kerr and Kenneth R. Ross, 27–40. Oxford: Regnum, 2009.

———. "Converts or Proselytes? The Crisis over Conversion in the Early Church." *International Bulletin of Missionary Research* 28 (2004) 1–6.

———. *The Cross-Cultural Process in Christian History: Studies in the Transmission and Appropriation of Faith*. Maryknoll, NY: Orbis, 2002.

———. *Crossing Cultural Frontiers: Studies in the History of World Christianity*. Maryknoll, NY: Orbis, 2017.

———. "Culture and Coherence in Christian History." *Evangelical Review of Theology* 9 (1985) 214–25.

———. "Ephesian Moment." In *The Cross-Cultural Process in Christian History: Studies in the Transmission and Appropriation of Faith*, 72–81. Maryknoll, NY: Orbis, 2002.

———. "The Gospel as Prisoner and Liberator of Culture." *Faith and Thought* 108 (1981) 39–52.

———. "A History of the Expansion of Christianity Reconsidered: Assessing Christian Progress and Decline." In *The Cross-Cultural Process in Christian History: Studies in the Transmission and Appropriation of* Faith, 18–26. MaryKnoll, NY: Orbis, 2002.

———. "In Quest of the Father of Mission Studies." *International Bulletin of Missionary Research* 22 (1999) 98–105.

———. "Mission and Migration: The Diaspora Factor in Christian History." *Journal of African Christian Thought* 5, no. 2 (2002) 3–11.

———. *The Missionary Movement in Christian History: Studies in the Transmission of Faith.* Maryknoll, NY: Orbis, 1996.

———. "Old Athens and New Jerusalem: Some Signposts for Christian Scholarship in the Early History of Mission Studies." *International Bulletin of Missionary Research* 21 (1997) 147–53.

———. "The Translation Principle in Christian History." In *The Missionary Movement in Christian History: Studies in the Transmission of the Faith*, 24–44. Maryknoll, NY: Orbis, 1996.

Warren, M.A.C. *The Missionary Movement from Britain in Modern History*. London: SCM, 1965.

———. *Social History and Christian Mission*. London: SCM, 1967.

Watson, Richard. *Theological Institutes*. 3rd ed. 2 vols. London: John Mason, 1829.

Webster, Steven. "Postmodernist Theory and the Sublimation of Māori Culture." *Oceania* 63 (1993) 222–39.

Wetherell, David. *Charles Abel and the Kwato Mission of Papua New Guinea, 1891–1975*. Melbourne: Melbourne University Press, 1996.

———. *Reluctant Mission: The Anglican Church in Papua New Guinea, 1891–1942*. St. Lucia: University of Queensland Press, 1977.

Weymouth, Ross M. "The Gogodala Society in Papua New Guinea and the Unevangelized Fields Mission, 1890–1977." PhD diss., Flinders University, 1978.

Whiteman, Darrell L. *Melanesians and Missionaries: An Ethnohistorical Study of Socio Religious Change in the Southwest Pacific*. Pasadena, CA: William Carey Library, 1982.

Whiteman, Darrell L., ed. *An Introduction to Melanesian Cultures: A Handbook for Church Workers*, Book One, Point 5. Goroka: Melanesian Institute, 1984.

Wieland, George. *The Significance of Salvation: A Study of the Salvation Language of the Pastoral Epistles*. Paternoster Biblical Monographs. Milton Keynes: Paternoster, 2006.

Winter, Bruce W. *Roman Wives, Roman Widows: The Appearance of New Women and the Pauline Communities*. Grand Rapids: Eerdmans, 2003.

Witherington, Ben, III. *The Acts of the Apostles: A Socio-Rhetorical Commentary*. Grand Rapids: Eerdmans, 1998.

World Missionary Conference. *Report of Commission IV: The Missionary Message in Relation to Non-Christian Religions*. Edinburgh: Oliphant, Anderson, and Ferrier, 1910.

Wright, Christopher J. H. "The Christian and Other Religions: The Biblical Evidence." *Themelios* 9, no. 2 (1984) 4–15.

———. *The Mission of God: Unlocking the Bible's Grand Narrative*. Downers Grove, IL: Inter-Varsity, 2006.

Wright, N. T. "Poetry and Theology in Colossians 1:15–20." *New Testament Studies* 36 (1990) 444–68.

Yandit, Kirine. "Ownership and Support of Theological Education Institutions in Papua New Guinea: The Case of the Christian Leaders' Training College of PNG Inc." DMin diss., Australian College of Theology, 2017.

Author Index

Scripture Index

Genesis

Exodus

Psalms

Isaiah

Jeremiah

Ezekiel

Hosea

Micah

Habakkuk

Haggai

Zechariah

Matthew

Mark

Luke

John

Romans

1 Corinthians

Ephesians

Philippians

Colossians

1 Thessalonians

2 Thessalonians

1 Timothy

2 Timothy

Titus

Hebrews

James

1 Peter

2 Peter

1 John

Revelation

www.ingramcontent.com/pod-product-compliance
Lightning Source LLC
LaVergne TN
LVHW020516100826
845148LV00010B/1249